To John Ta
for Rolling Thunder
Bill Bell

Leave No Man Behind

Bill Bell and the Search for American POW/MIAs from the Vietnam War

Garnett "Bill" Bell
with George J. Veith

Best wishes! 5/29/04
Jay Veith

Goblin Fern Press
Madison, Wisconsin
www.goblinfernpress.com

A portion of the proceeds from the sale of this book will be donated to Rolling Thunder, http://www.rollingthunder1.com/index.htm; The National League of Families of American Prisoners and Missing in Southeast Asia, http://www.pow-miafamilies.org/; and the National Alliance Of Families For the Return of America's Missing Servicemen, http://www.nationalalliance.org/.

Published by Goblin Fern Press, Inc., Madison, WI, 1-888-670-BOOK (2665)

www.goblinfernpress.com

To order additional copies, contact your local bookstore or the publisher. Quantity discounts available.

ISBN 0-9647663-4-5

Book design and typography by Crocker Design Company

Index by Willard & Associates

Publisher's Cataloging-In-Publication Data
(Prepared by The Donohue Group, Inc.)

Bell, Garnett, 1943-
Leave no man behind / Garnett "Bill" Bell with George J. Veith.

p. : ill. ; cm.
ISBN: 0-9647663-4-5
Includes bibliographical references and index.

1. Bell, Garnett, 1943- 2. Vietnamese Conflict, 1961-1975--Missing in action--United States. 3. Vietnamese Conflict, 1961-1975--Prisoners and prisons. 4. Prisoners of war--United States. 5. Prisoners of war--Vietnam. 6. Vietnam--Foreign relations—United States. 7. United States—Foreign relations--Vietnam. I. Veith, George J., 1957- II. Title.

DS559.4 .B45 2004
959.704/37

Printed in the United States of America
First edition
10 9 8 7 6 5 4 3 2 1

Cover photos: Ha Bac NVN, 1991. Bill Bell and SFC James Williams of CILHI with local officials in Ha Bac, Vietnam during field investigation. (Inset) Nick Rowe and Dan Pitzer in VC captivity in a Mekong Delta "tiger cage" in an undated photo.

This book is dedicated to our children

Andrea, Scott, and Elisabeth Bell,

and

Analiese, Austin, Allegra, and Aida Veith—

may they never know war.

And to our wives,

Nam-Xuan Bell and Gina Katherine Veith,

for their infinite patience as we completed this project.

And to

Nova and Michael Bell—

may they rest in eternal peace.

Contents

Introduction

George J. Veith

MANY PEOPLE HAVE ASKED ME over the years why I became involved with the POW/MIA issue. I wanted to help the families was my answer, which was true then and remains true today. Anyone who spends even one hour with a family would have a hard time not wanting to help. Not only is their pain still palpable, the sheer frustration of not knowing what happened to their father, son, brother, or husband, and worse, being so powerless to solve the mystery, resonates a particular helplessness that any listener would want to comfort. Still, after many meetings and long hours spent studying and researching the issue, it dawned on me that there was another, more subtle, reason that drove me beyond mere outrage at what had happened to many American families. It is the sense of meeting a national commitment, an awareness of honoring those who came before us and who sacrificed everything.

That sense of national honor is personified in Garnett "Bill" Bell, a man who, as the U.S. government's top POW/MIA field investigator in Southeast Asia for many years, doggedly pursued the answers to the fate of over twenty-five hundred Americans missing from the Vietnam War. It was his ability to articulate precisely why this quest was so important that compelled me to continue to seek answers. That is why we wrote this book—to help the American people truly grasp the evolution of the POW/MIA issue, and to show whom the real culprits are—the cold-hearted rulers of Hanoi. During Bell's career some three hundred and fifty Americans were recovered and identified; this detailed account of the many trials and tribulations encountered attempting to identify those missing men, as well as the events that ultimately caused him to seek retirement and abandon his official involvement in this noble effort, will help the American people understand the history of the issue, the possible fate of some MIAs, and why this matter continues unresolved.

I first met Bill Bell at the annual National League of POW/MIA Families meeting in July 1994. I was just beginning to work on what later became my first book, *Code Name Bright Light: The Untold Story of U.S. POW Rescue Efforts During the Vietnam War.* I had called him shortly after he had retired and moved back to Arkansas from Thailand. After I introduced myself and asked to interview him at the meeting, he graciously accepted and then rather unexpectedly told me to "come on down to Ft. Smith" and stay a few days with him. Surprised by his spontaneous gesture, I politely declined due to work reasons, but inside I was stunned at his desire to help a complete stranger, which was light years from the suspicious activists I had met as I first tried to learn the issue.

Our talk that day eventually grew into a close friendship and working relationship. In speaking with Bell, over time I developed a fascination with the nuances of a subject on the surface so simple yet so breathtakingly complex. For me, learning the full history of the POW/MIA issue (which in Bell's view—beyond the moral component—was a matter of national security), was akin to peering behind the curtain, like Dorothy in the Wizard of Oz, and discovering unseen powers at work.

Over the years the issue devolved into three camps: a small group of families and activists hardened by frustration and convinced that successive administrations were covering up a horrendous crime—the abandonment of hundreds of American prisoners to the Communists; a larger group of families less suspicious of the accounting effort but desperately wanting an answer, and a bureaucracy often trying to do the right thing, but hamstrung by national policies ill suited to a democratic society's demands for results. Despite the best intentions, however, often it appeared that some in the bureaucracy sought to control the issue for their own personal agenda, responding in a knee-jerk fashion to the slightest whiff of criticism, some of it justified, some not. At the other end of the spectrum, for a few other Americans, the issue became their Holy Grail, and as with most fanatics, reason and truth played no part in their worldview, only embellished tales and the spun fantasies of con men. The attention of the American public, unable to follow the intricacies, ebbed and flowed like the tide. As time passed or each new hot revelation was explained away, the nation slowly developed "compassion-fatigue" and turned away from the anguish.

Bell is in the middle, seeing neither some vast conspiracy to abandon hundreds of American soldiers nor understanding why the truth could be so difficult to accept, that most likely some Americans were kept prisoner by the North

Vietnamese after the war, or that they could rapidly account for many missing Americans if they made the political decision to do so.

No doubt this book will rankle some current and former government POW/MIA bureaucrats, along with many activists. Both groups want the public to see the issue from their perspective, and they manipulate the data to achieve that context. Much of the still on-going debate revolves around the "live-prisoner" issue. To be clear, there is little doubt that most men died in their incident or shortly thereafter. For about half the missing men, witnesses saw the deaths, and battlefield emergencies prevented their compatriots from recovering their remains. Nevertheless, for many others major questions linger, and when placed within the framework of the well-known Communist Vietnamese efforts to exploit American POWs for diplomatic concessions, or their remains and personal effects for financial rewards, these questions become deeply disturbing. "Only Hanoi knows," claimed the bumper sticker from years ago, a phrase more apt than the vast majority of Americans comprehended then or today.

What is most difficult for the newcomer reading this book and listening to the various commentators to understand is that much of the intelligence on the missing men is not black or white, but multiple shades of gray, which in combination with a seemingly implacable foe who controlled the old battlefields and who was determined to use this leverage to extract concessions from its imperialist enemy, created questions seemingly impervious to American efforts to answer. This "grayness" enables certain people to slant their analysis on the POW/MIA perspective a particular way, claiming selected facts reveal the truth, which of course, is the truth as they want you to see it. Plus, a cottage industry peculiar to Southeast Asia of bone hunters seeking rewards and working in a culture where embroidered hearsay is far more prevalent than a Westernized version of truthfulness, have led to years of wild tales and dead-ends. This book is designed to help the American public see through the smoke and mirrors, to understand precisely what occurred and understand the mis-steps that were made.

This chronicle details the many events surrounding the career of Bill Bell, from his time as a young infantryman going to war in 1965 to his retirement in 1993. It is his memoirs, not an in-depth examination of the POW/MIA issue from a policy level. While the book recounts most of the major actions and organizational changes that influenced the U.S. government's handling of the issue, it is written solely from his perspective as a witness to these historical proceedings. His account is designed to amplify the record, to provide one insider's account, to the extent memory and documentation are able, so that future generations may know and understand his role in the monumental task of recovering our soldiers and civilians who went missing from the conflagration known as the Vietnam War. Without a doubt, many other people served with distinction and honor. Their omission reflects not any overarching role by Bell, but are simply far too numerous to mention.

One might reasonably ask, then, who is Bill Bell and why is he significant? What makes his voice unique, his experiences fascinating, his knowledge vital, and his analysis of the issue and the Vietnamese Communist plans so critical? The answer is simply this: for all the people who have worked or toiled in the U.S. government's efforts to account for the nation's missing men in Southeast Asia, Bill Bell is the only government official who has been directly involved in every aspect of the complex issue at each stage of the events that unfolded over the years. Only someone with Bell's dogged perseverance and his encyclopedic knowledge of the Vietnamese Communists, combined with his fluency in the various regional languages, could hope to penetrate the system the Communists had created to essentially milk a humanitarian effort for revenue to support themselves. Patience and persistence, traits more often associated with the Asian mentality than the go-getting Americans, along with Sun Tzu's famous dictum to know one's enemy, allowed Bill Bell the opportunity to get close to the heart of the mystery. In particular, Bell's candor and unflinching honesty won him an extraordinary trust among the families, a rarity for a government official working in the issue. While the family organizations counted upon Bell to protect their interests, as a government official in a politically sensitive position, it was a trait that did not always endear him to his superiors.

Perhaps to give the reader a sense of the families' anguish, to comprehend what would propel a man like Bell to sacrifice so much in an almost Don Quixote-esque pursuit of the truth, let me provide what was for me an epiphany into the families' sorrow. On the day I was to meet Bell at the hotel where the National League of Families was holding their annual get-together, I dropped off my bags in my room. Realizing I left my notebook in my car in the basement-parking garage, I rode the elevator back down to retrieve it. On the way back up, the car stopped at the Lobby. As the door opened, an elderly couple tried to enter. Seeing they were straining to move a large suitcase, I offered to assist them, which the lady quietly accepted. They walked inside, each taking a spot on opposite sides of me. As the door closed on the three of us, I spotted a badge on the woman's jacket. Not clearly reading the text, I asked her "What brings you here?" The woman said nothing. She looked away from me, her gaze drifting down to the floor. In a soft voice from the other side of the car, her husband's voice answered:

"Our son."

As I turned to look at him, it was then I could clearly read the badge on his shirt—"National League of POW/MIA Families." I could hear the strain in his voice, an emotion that clipped off further words, as if he wanted to say something more, but was unable to explain to a complete stranger thirty years of anguish over a missing child, to make me understand why they kept coming to a POW/MIA Family meeting, desperate for answers, when surely there was no hope of their son being alive. Nothing more was said. The car went up five more floors and they got off. I felt foolish for asking such a seemingly innocent question; I wish I could have said something, anything, but like them, I, too, was helpless. I saw them at subsequent meetings, but I never spoke to them again. I doubt they would even remember me, but I never forgot them.

Bill Bell tried desperately, as hard as any man can over a period of many years, to find the answer to what happened to the son of those grieving parents, and the sons and brothers and husbands of many other American families. From his days as a young infantryman on covert missions into enemy areas in the Central Highlands, to receiving the American POWs as part of "Operation Homecoming," to assisting with the evacuation of the U.S. Embassy in Saigon until the morning of April 30, 1975, one of the last Americans to get into a waiting helicopter as the North Vietnamese Army tanks rolled into the defeated city, to slogging his way for almost a decade visiting forlorn, malaria-ridden camps to interview hapless refugees, to his return as the first U.S. government representative assigned to Vietnam as Chief of the U.S. POW/MIA office, to his televised testimony in front of the Senate Select Committee on POW/MIA Affairs where Bell told Congress, as the government's top POW/MIA expert, that he believed the Communists had held men prisoner after the formal release, Bell saw it all.

In human terms, however, despite his incredible experiences, for him it was not without cost. He learned first-hand the pain of those families, in a way none of us ever want to experience, when he lost his own wife and son in the crash of an American plane evacuating Vietnamese orphans and American dependents on April 4, 1975. No doubt his personality unconsciously reflects the struggles and suffering of over twenty-five years of dealing with a cunning and ruthless enemy, who, despite today's fashionable rhetoric about healing the past, remain committed to monopolizing Vietnam's political power. Still, despite his loss and the almost insurmountable difficulties of trying to get answers from a foe determined not to provide them, Bell persevered, not only for the POW/MIA families, but also for America. In a sense, it was for all our families, but the cost of persistence is high, and Bill Bell has paid a full measure.

This is his story.

Chapter One

From Texas to Tet

I SUPPOSE IT'S A CLICHÉ to begin your memoirs with "I grew up poor in a small town," but that's the truth. I was born in Greenville, Texas in April 1943 and I came from a family of cotton farmers. Looking back at it now, I suppose it was a good builder of character, but while the broad expanses of fertile black land throughout eastern Texas were ideal for the cultivation of "King Cotton," falling prices resulted in a rather dismal economic situation for most of my childhood.

To add tragedy to my lowly economic status, when I was a small boy my father was killed by a train while processing the family's cotton at a mill near our home. About the only memory I have of him is that of a neighbor coming to the front door while holding out a pail and telling my mother that it contained the only recoverable remains of her husband. Despite her devastating loss, my mother was able to recover and find happiness again when she married a former Navy Seabee who had served in the Pacific during World War II.

As a child in Greenville, I spent much of my time as a frequent patron of the local movie theaters. I especially loved the stirring war films starring World War II hero Audie Murphy. He was from nearby Farmersville, and the slight, soft-spoken Texan soon became my idol. After watching many of his movies, it's not surprising that I soon discovered a yearning inside me, as is true for many boys growing up poor in the South, to also become a soldier. My own personal dream was to be a paratrooper, and since Greenville at that time was the home of the

101st Airborne Division Association, I wanted to be just like them.

Perhaps soldiering was also in my blood, since my grandfather was a World War I veteran. He later became the Commander of the Veterans of Foreign Wars (VFW) post in Marshall, a small town east of to Greenville. My grandmother was also head of the Ladies Auxiliary, and so my stepfather frequently took me to the VFW meeting hall to visit them and the vets. I often played in an old tank parked outside. Sitting in the commander's hatch, I pretended to be a tank-gunner fighting Hitler's Panzer forces, or beating back waves of Communist Chinese and North Korean troops pouring across the 38th parallel into South Korea.

So, at the tender age of fifteen I found myself standing in front of an Army recruiter's desk. One look and they turned me down. Not dissuaded, I returned at age sixteen only to be told that I would have to wait another seemingly endless year before I could be legally inducted. Finally, as I was about to turn seventeen, I convinced my parents that military life would afford me the best possible future, so on my birthday they took me to Shreveport, Louisiana, where I finally managed to enlist. Unbeknownst to me, it wasn't all handshakes and signing paperwork. Induction included humiliating physical examinations of some rather tender body cavities, along with countless tests. Finally it was all over and I was accepted. Someone appointed me "Group Leader," which meant I was placed in nominal charge of a band of ten raw recruits herded onto a bus bound for the airport.

As with most young men when they leave home for the first time, my emotions churned inside me as the plane lifted off. The first glimmer of daybreak reflected off the silver wing of the DC-3 aircraft as it maneuvered its way up through an early morning Louisiana fog into a clear blue southern sky. I choked back nausea, embarrassed by an uneasy stomach caused by my first plane ride. Peering out the window I saw cypress studded Caddo Lake in the distance. Memories of childhood fishing expeditions on the dark green water draped in ghostly "Spanish Beard" moss caused tears to well in my already reddened eyes. I searched vainly for the familiar flat bottom boat of Henry, a well-known local black man who knew the intricate lake better than anyone alive. In years past Henry had taught me the art of fishing, and I wondered whether I would ever again have an opportunity to fish with him.

Despite my original uneasiness, I quickly adapted to Army life. After an uneventful period of basic infantry training at Fort Jackson, South Carolina, I was sent on a very uncomfortable Greyhound bus headed for Fort Campbell, Kentucky, home of the Army's elite 101st Airborne Division. I was elated to finally fulfill my boyhood dream of becoming a paratrooper, and like me, the group of khaki-clad privates who had volunteered for airborne training were animated by the possibility of new adventures. We were energized also by the fact that if we could successfully complete jump training, our meager monthly salaries of $78.10 would soon be supplemented by an additional $55.00 per month of hazardous duty pay. As the cumbersome bus lumbered through the main gate of the post I saw olive green parachutes begin to unfurl in the air beneath the gray bellies of C-119 aircraft flying in trail formation. I watched intently as the parachutes drifted gently behind the slow-moving airplanes, colorfully and accurately nicknamed "flying boxcars."

I found the training at Fort Campbell invigorating. At seventeen, I could run for miles without breaking a sweat. The thirty-four foot jump tower and suspended harness rigs used for simulated airborne training at the school were far less challenging than the makeshift rope and cable swings on the creek back home. The physical training was harsh by most standards, but for me it was easier than stacking seventy-five pound bales of Bermuda grass hay in a barn loft from daylight to dark. Exiting an aircraft in flight, however, was a different matter altogether. This was unlike anything many of the young trainees had ever experienced before, and some who had previously performed well in the course failed when the time came to apply their training. Faced with making an actual jump at an altitude of 1,250 feet, some were too terrified to leap out into oblivion and place their lives in the hands of anonymous parachute riggers.

I managed to overcome my own initial fears of jumping out of a "perfectly good airplane," and shortly after completing my training as a paratrooper, my unit and I loaded onto a Navy C-118 aircraft bound for Goose Bay, Labrador for my first experience involving international tensions in what turned out to be a life filled with them. After a refueling stop in the Azores Islands the plane touched down at Wheelus Field near Tripoli, Libya. We then switched to huge C-124 "Globemasters." The operation took place in Turkey, the drop zone right on the border of the Soviet Union. While I landed safely on the drop zone, I saw several men killed or badly injured by malfunctioning and entangled parachutes. Once the Globemasters had passed over the drop zone, we rolled up our chutes and linked up with Turkish forces on the ground. We then made a demanding foot march across northern Turkey, followed by a jarring train ride to the border of Greece.

Young and curious, some of the men asked our squad leader, Staff Sergeant Hubert R. Smith, the only Airborne-Ranger in the platoon, the purpose of the operation. A native North Carolinian from tobacco country, Smith could be found anytime during his waking hours with a non-filter cigarette dangling from his lips. Although Smith was respected for his stamina and military skills, normally his grasp of international events was somewhat lacking. Apparently, however, Smith was up to date for this mission. According to him, the Soviets had shot down an American U-2 aircraft flown by Captain Gary Powers. The unfortunate aviator had been captured and was being tried in Moscow as a spy despite the considerable objections of the U.S. government. The 101st Airborne was conducting the parachute operation in close proximity to the Soviet border to "fly the flag," thereby demonstrating to the Soviets that the United States was serious in its demand for the pilot's release. This incident was my first exposure to the complexities of the POW/MIA issue, and I found it hard to believe that one pilot could be the source of so much activity and concern. Nonetheless, it would stay in my mind as my first lesson in Great Power diplomacy. The U-2 pilot remained a prisoner of the Soviets until February 10, 1962, when he was exchanged for a Soviet Military Intelligence Colonel.

The rest of my tour at Fort Campbell with the 101st was uneventful, with two exceptions. The first incident occurred just prior to the controversial "Bay of Pigs" operation in Cuba. My fellow paratroopers and I were loaded onto C-119s and flown to Hurlburt Field in Florida. After machetes and mosquito nets were issued, Cuban mercenaries from an organization called "Alpha-66" were attached to our units to act as guides once we had been parachuted into Cuban territory. Obviously, we never had the opportunity to find out how proficient the Alpha-66 personnel were, as the mission was aborted at the last minute. Fidel Castro's forces captured hundreds of POWs, and I later heard that the U.S. government was compelled to pay ransom in the form of heavy equipment to Cuba's Communist regime to secure their release. To me, the idea of payment for the return of prisoners seemed strange. I had always believed that at the end of hostilities all POWs were unconditionally released to go home. I would someday learn how naïve I was.

The second incident happened when my unit, the 327th Airborne Battle Group, was deployed to Oxford, Mississippi, where James Meredith was attempting to enroll as the first black student to attend the University of Mississippi. The 327th was selected for the mission due to the unit's previous experience during a similar deployment in 1957 to Central High School in Little Rock, Arkansas. At the University, a riot by students and local residents led to several police vehicles being overturned and burned in the streets. As a result, I was assigned to guard the main gate of the campus with the mission of searching each vehicle entering the area for weapons or contraband. Despite my Texas heritage and obvious accent, one time when I leaned down to ask the elderly female driver of a shiny new Cadillac to open the hood and trunk of her car, I was pointedly told to "take your hand from my car Yankee!"

While stationed at Fort Campbell my family underwent another tragedy when my brother-in-law was killed in a head-on car crash in Marshall. My sister, my only sibling, was eight months pregnant at the time and the incident devastated her. As with the sudden death of my father, my mother was deeply affected by the loss of her son-in-law, but she quickly regained her composure by concentrating on her grandchild, who would eventually become a medical technician in the Air Force. My sister went into a predictable state of deep depression, but eventually she too relied on her inner strength to pull herself back to normalcy. Eventually, she became a judge in East Texas.

Having missed any real combat during my three-year tour, I decided to leave the 101st and search for new adventure. After being placed in reserve military status I was employed by Southern Air Inc., a small airline piloted almost exclusively by former or reserve military personnel. The airline specialized in delivering men and cargo to small airfields, primarily those co-located with military installations throughout the southern United States. For longer hauls to Asia, the airline relied on cargo transfer points for links to special charter aircraft owned by Continental Airlines.

I liked the job at first, but it didn't take long for me to surmise that my position of "Aircraft Operations Agent" was little more than a glorified title for "Loadmaster," and I found the job increasingly monotonous. During my time with the airline, however, I began to meet former Army friends who were returning from assignments in the faraway nations of Vietnam and Laos.

I knew virtually nothing of the two countries. I had first heard of Laos in 1962 when I learned through the grapevine that Army Special Forces had deployed training teams into Laos on a project called "White Star." The mention of Vietnam also meant very little to me, and I wasn't even sure where Vietnam was. I recalled the word "Saigon" mentioned in a conversation between James Mason and Kirk Douglas on board the Nautilus in the movie "20,000 Leagues Under the Sea," but like most Americans I had no idea where the city was located. Notwithstanding my limited knowledge of Asian geography, the stories told by my returning comrades led me to the conclusion that some type of major military action in Indochina was on the horizon. I soon reenlisted, and I quickly received orders for the 25th Infantry Division based in Hawaii.

Shortly after my arrival in Honolulu, I found myself back in infantryman mode carrying a rifle and a field pack. Our initial training consisted of treks up and down the Waianae Mountain Range. The steep slopes were even more challenging than the cornfields and pine forests of Kentucky and South Carolina, but of greater concern were the swarms of bloodthirsty mosquitoes that haunted us anytime we ventured into the low laying areas normally planted in sugar cane.

The 25th Division, called the "Tropic Lightning," was the strategic ready reserve for the Pacific theatre and therefore trained mainly to fight in the jungle environment of Asia. The Division created a Jungle Warfare Indoctrination Center to provide realistic instruction for its soldiers, including a critical block of training in Survival, Evasion, Resistance and Escape (SERE). The SERE course was badly needed, as several hundred members of the 25th had already been deployed to Vietnam as door gunners on "Huey" helicopters in what was called the "Shotgun Program." From the beginning to the end of the war, the "Huey" was the workhorse of the U.S. military. These men received training on firing the M-60 machine gun to prepare them for ninety-day temporary duty assignments with aviation units throughout Vietnam. Veteran "Shotgun" volunteers were constantly rotating back to the Division from Vietnam as new groups of gunners went out to replace them. The returning soldiers had plenty of war stories to tell about combat in Vietnam, which caused considerable excitement within the Division. As the intensity of the fighting in Vietnam continued to build I became concerned that it would all be over before I could get there. I believed the quickest way to see action was by volunteering for the "Shotgun" missions, and I headed to the Orderly Room with that thought in mind.

My Company Commander, however, disagreed. He already had other plans in mind for my future development. I was going to Vietnamese language training. For a poor farm boy from East Texas, I could not have found myself in a stranger situation, nor could I have known this was the first step down a path I could never have imagined.

Clutching a textbook tightly to her chest, my eagle-eyed Vietnamese teacher[1] peered over her horn rim glasses at the struggling students still remaining in the class. "Repeat after me!" she demanded, while pursing her lips to form the next line of dialogue: *Toi la nguoi linh My, lang nay co Viet Cong khong?* (I am an American soldier, are there any Viet Cong in this village?) One-by-one the seven remaining young soldiers of the 25th Division tried their best to pronounce the strange sounding words. All were concerned by the possibility of being sent back to their units at Schofield Barracks with the shame of having failed to complete the language course. Only the seven of us had persevered to this final phase of the course. The others had failed miserably, ultimately surrendering to the fact that most Americans simply could not grasp the difficult Vietnamese language with its tonal cadences and inflections.

Equally demanding was another course I had to take as part of my new training. The Foreign Orientation Course was taught at the Division Language School by South Vietnamese officers of the Army of the Republic of Vietnam (ARVN) on temporary duty assignments to Hawaii. A part of this course included training on Communist weapons and booby traps, as well as unconventional warfare tactics. The reason for the language and country orientation course stemmed from the World War II experience of the Division's Commanding General, then Major General Frederick C. Weyand. Having served as an Intelligence Officer in the Pacific Theater, General Weyand realized the importance of knowing one's enemy. His goal was to have at least one infantryman in each Division rifle company trained in the language of one of the five countries to which we would most likely be deployed (Vietnam, Thailand, Korea, Indonesia, Philippines).

Glancing out the window, I squirmed in my hard, wooden chair, constantly shifting my legs to stimulate circulation. Long harboring disdain for foreign language study, I had been conscripted into the course based on my high score on a language aptitude test. Though a temporary student in language school, I still saw myself as an infantryman assigned to Alpha Company, 1st Battalion/35th Infantry Regiment. Regardless of my lack of interest in foreign languages, I was determined to succeed in learning Vietnamese and I had done well in the course. The language test was right, and I discovered within me a natural ability to pick up the words and nuances of the unfamiliar language. Still, like all young men away from home in a boring classroom, my mind often drifted back to my youth.

This was the fall of 1965, and having been raised in a rural area, I loved this season when the warm rays of the daytime sun followed clear chilly nights, announcing the arrival of Indian summer. This was a time of the year when most of the demanding farm work had been completed, or as we said back home in Texas, "laid by." I vividly remembered the fall foliage of crimson blackgum and orange sweetgum leaves splashed across a dark green background of tall Texas pines. In 1965 I had been away from home for five years, and the continually lush vegetation of Hawaii just could not replace the sights and smells of my native soil. Except for the familiar poinsettia, the tropical surroundings engendered an eerie feeling of being in a strange foreign land.

My daydreaming was interrupted when a young Army Captain paid an unexpected visit to the spartan classroom. After briefly entering the room both the Captain and my teacher moved outside. As the two gazed intently through the glass at the top of the door, I gained the impression I was a topic of the conversation. As the eyes of the Captain met mine, I experienced an uneasy feeling in my gut. The look on the Captain's face revealed an element of interest, almost concern, and I wondered to myself whether this was a death notification for another of my family members. But it was not the case, and shortly after his arrival the young officer smiled to the instructor and departed the area. I felt embarrassed by my initial speculation, but at the same time I felt relieved not to be the subject of the visit after all.

Or so I thought. When class was dismissed at the end of the day, the teacher reminded the students of their nightly responsibility for memorizing the dialogue to be presented orally the following morning. As I stood to leave, she asked me to remain behind after class. "Huan," the teacher said, using my classroom Vietnamese name, "I think you might be leaving the class prior to graduation." Stunned by the sudden disclosure, I stammered to ask why. According to Mrs. Miller, the Captain who visited the class was the Intelligence Officer for the 1/35th. The Captain had come to get her opinion as to which student already possessed the ability to speak and understand Vietnamese without having completed the course. Staring down at the floor, my teacher sheepishly told me that she had given the Captain my name. She also told me the Captain wanted to see me in his office ASAP. She ended the conversation by handing me a small piece of paper containing a telephone number and the abbreviation "S-2." As instructed, I called the number and informed the person answering the phone that I was to report to the S-2, the Battalion's staff section for Intelligence. Without hesitation the voice asked me for my location and told me to wait for a vehicle, which would pick me up shortly.

When I walked through the door of the S-2 office, the first thing I noticed were stacks of wooden crates with large green and white "Confidential" stickers taped on them. Glancing into a box with the lid off, I noticed that the crates contained topographic maps, and the sheet on top read "Dak To." The Captain who visited the language class that same day introduced himself as John Fielding, the S-2 for the 1/35th Infantry Battalion. Captain Fielding got straight to the point. He told me that due to heavy casualties recently suffered by the 1st Cavalry Division in Vietnam's Ia Drang Valley, the Commander of U.S. forces in Vietnam, General William C. Westmoreland, had requested that a brigade of the 25th Division be dispatched from Hawaii to supplement his forces. After arrival in Vietnam, the brigade would be placed under the operational control of the 1st Cavalry. Captain Fielding informed me that the unit filling the request would be the 3rd Brigade, of which the 1/35th was a part. Due to my language skills, I had been transferred to the S-2 shop, and I would be leaving shortly on the Brigade's advance party. The Captain also reminded me that this information was classified and could not be shared with anyone outside the office. Leaving the office both excited and scared, I went back to Alpha Company to gather my gear.

I had finally achieved my goal of going to Vietnam. We were headed for a city called Pleiku, which was located in the area of South Vietnam called the Central Highlands. The province, also called Pleiku, was bordered on the north by Kontum province and on the south by Darlac province. The area only had two seasons: the rainy season from May until November, and the dry season from December to April. Average rainfall measured from seventy-five inches in Pleiku up to 125 inches in the bordering province of Kontum. When I arrived in December 1965 as a young Private First Class, the rainy season was just ending. The C-130 Hercules aircraft carrying me broke through the low hanging clouds and headed toward Pleiku airfield. I saw a large, tree-rimmed lake surrounded by outlying rice fields. The name of this lake, located near my soon-to-be base camp, was "Bien Ho," literally "Sea Lake." Bien Ho was said to be one of the largest natural lakes in Vietnam, created by rainfall in a crater left after a volcanic eruption. In addition to being the most prominent terrain feature in the general area, the lake served as a source of water for bathing and washing clothes, as well as a local Rest and Recuperation site for members of the 1st Cavalry and the 25th Infantry. It was at this lake that I met some former buddies from the 101st Airborne who had been transferred to the 1st Cavalry. I asked them about other Army friends from the past, which only brought disheartening responses. Many old comrades had recently been killed-in-action (KIA) in the deadly Ia Drang battles.

After unloading at Pleiku airfield the advance party began digging fighting positions on a hill a few kilometers from Bien Ho Lake. The first Vietnamese people I observed were members of an ARVN Ranger unit and a smaller unit of the Strategic Technical Directorate (STD) located near the airfield. The STD was a strategic reconnaissance element assigned directly to the ARVN Joint General Staff. The STD engaged in intelligence gathering behind enemy lines and other classified operations. Women and children dependents of the ARVN troops were quartered near Bien Ho Lake in a family housing area consisting of makeshift wooden and thatched huts and lean-tos constructed of canvas and tin.

A few days after my arrival in Pleiku I was placed on temporary duty with the brigade's Military Police Detachment in order to arrange liaison with the Government of Vietnam (GVN) National Police. I was excited about this assignment. I would be taking several trips into the local town, and I wanted to quickly compare what I had learned in school with reality. I was eager to speak the language, taste the food, and generally see the sights in this strange land I had heard so much about.

Fortunately, I found the atmosphere of Pleiku City like a scene right out of my Vietnamese teacher's language class. I was amazed by how easy it was for me to communicate with the local residents. Speaking was one thing, however, eating Vietnamese food was another. In testing the local cuisine I had my first rude exposure to Vietnamese condiments. During my language training and country orientation I had been warned of the pungent Vietnamese fish sauce and everyday staple called *nuoc mam*. But even after being cautioned in advance, I was instantly repelled by the powerful odor of the strange elixir. Straight from the bottle it wasn't bad, but when poured into a hot frying pan the thick brown liquid quickly vaporized into a gut wrenching cloud of nauseous gas. Not quite as powerful as tear gas, but close in my opinion. Equally distressing were the flies. I was accustomed to Texas flies that frantically flew away at the swipe of a hand. But Vietnamese flies were more tenacious and they would actually cling tightly to a flailing hand only to quickly return to the food after the hand again became stationary. The flies were so bad that the street food stands provided small round screens to place over the dishes while customers were eating.

In Pleiku I also had my first taste of another Vietnamese specialty, a small bottle of beer called "Beer 33," or as the Vietnamese called it, *ba muoi ba*. Another less potent brand was called *Bia Larue,* or *Bia Lon* (big beer) by the locals. It was in a larger bottle and went for about half the price. I heard from the local vendors that both beers were brewed in a French owned and operated brewery in Saigon. "Beer 33" had a bad reputation among Americans. The rumor mill claimed one ingredient of the beer was formaldehyde. I quickly learned, however, that the "Beer 33" bottles had paper labels affixed with glue, and due to the high heat and humidity, the labels slid down the bottles exposing the foul smelling glue right next to the nostrils of the consumer. The smell of the glue resulted in nausea, which was blamed on formaldehyde in the beer. I solved this problem by sticking to the larger, cheaper Bia Larue that had a permanently embossed label.

Outside the city, aside from a few Vietnamese, ethnic minority hill tribes called *Thuong* (Highlander), by the Vietnamese and "Montagnard" by the French and Americans, mainly inhabited the Pleiku area. Most of the hill people in the Pleiku region were members of the Jarai tribe. Actually the original name for Pleiku province was "Gia Lai," derived from the tribal name of Jarai. The Jarai people were a hardy lot and slightly bigger than the average Vietnamese. I observed a scattering of mixed-breed children, called Metis, in small Montagnard villages throughout the area. I also noticed that the faces of many of the Montagnards had been permanently scarred by smallpox. It was an obvious indication of the tribe's previous close association with the French forces fighting against the Communists during the First Indochina War that ended in 1954.

For most Americans, the language and the food were difficult enough to overcome, but the cultural differences, even between the Vietnamese and the Montagnards, were overwhelming. For instance, the first time I went to Bien Ho Lake to bathe I was stunned to see bare-breasted Montagnard females filing into the water. Seemingly unconcerned by the American stares and presence, the women proceeded to wade around in chest-deep water groping for mussels near the shore. Many of the females would have been considered beautiful by any culture's standards, but a local tribal custom of breaking off the front teeth at puberty had left them with a somewhat unsightly appearance. In researching this practice I heard two rationales. One story was that the teeth were broken off to make the girls more attractive. The second version was that the tribal leaders broke off the teeth to make the girls less attractive to other tribes periodically conducting raids and abducting female captives. These polar opposites summed up the country perfectly.

Once the rest of the unit arrived, and after a short period of acclimatization, battalion-sized elements of the 3rd Brigade began planning for operations that would take us into the tri-border area, a location where the borders of Vietnam, Laos and Cambodia converge. The first area of operations was the Mang Giang Pass on Highway 19, the scene of one of France's bloodiest defeats during its Indochina War. The charred hulls of vehicles from the French Mobile Group 100 were still visible in the grass along the road. They served as silent reminders of the savage and sudden Communist ambush. At the foot of the pass small thatched huts of lowland Vietnamese hugged both sides of the highway, convenient for trading rice and other produce with both passers-by as well as Montagnard hill tribesmen inhabiting the high ground above.

Our unit's initial mission was to cut the lines of communication used by North Vietnamese People's Army of Vietnam (PAVN) units infiltrating along the Ho Chi Minh Trail. One of the first missions assigned to the battalion called for our Reconnaissance (Recon) Platoon to conduct a sweep in the area of the remote Montagnard village of Ban Dung. The Recon platoon was a small element designed to scout in front of the main body of the battalion and gather intelligence on enemy movements and positions. Captain Fielding and myself from the S-2 section were assigned to assist the Recon Platoon. We flew by helicopter to a landing zone (LZ) near the village. At the time of the 3rd Brigade's arrival, the only aviation unit in the area was a helicopter outfit located at Camp Holloway just outside Pleiku. When I entered Camp Holloway for the first time I saw a sign on the side of a small Quonset hut that read "Freddy D. Dodson Memorial Library." Freddy Dodson was one of my former high school classmates in Texas, and sadly was one of seven Americans killed during an enemy attack in February 1964 on the camp.

After landing, both Captain Fielding and I walked into the village to meet with the local Chief. Our first mission also would be my first exposure to combat, as we were unaware that enemy forces were close by. As we walked into the village, both of us passed within ten meters of a well-concealed PAVN squad busy digging out weapons buried inside hand-hewn wooden caskets in the village cemetery. No doubt hoping to remain unnoticed, the enemy held their fire as we passed by.

As Fielding and I stood in the village looking for the Chief, the Recon Platoon Leader, First Lieutenant Gene Familetti, led his platoon up the trail from the LZ into the village. Suddenly, a burst of automatic weapons fire raked across his buttocks. That would be Lieutenant Familetti's first and last mission in Vietnam. Captain Fielding and I hit the ground. The remainder of the platoon began to move through the dense underbrush toward the village. Squad leaders yelled for their men to deploy and "get on line," the traditional Fort Benning infantry style tactical formation. The first man to come into the enemy's view was a former airborne trooper, Sergeant Benjamin Spears. When Spears emerged from the brush he took an AK-47 round through the forehead and toppled forward to the ground, the blood spurting from his forehead. Captain Fielding grabbed the radio I carried and called for an A-1E "Skyraider" on station out of Pleiku to deliver an air strike on the enemy position. Minutes later a 500-pound bomb detonated close to the centermost grave. Steaming shrapnel rained down throughout the village as the A-1E returned in a wide arc to follow up with a napalm strike. As the large egg-like pod impacted the ground the jelly-liquid ignited, quickly burning away all the underbrush in the cemetery and exposing the enemy to effective fire from the platoon.

As the fighting continued, a headcount determined that one rifleman had become separated from the platoon during the initial movement from the landing zone to the village. He was soon located, but he had wandered close to the enemy positions and was now pinned down. One of the squad leaders, Staff Sergeant Wilbert Wilkerson, braved the enemy fire and crawled across an open field to within a few yards of the PAVN position. Platoon members stared in awe as he retrieved the young soldier and guided him back to safety. Fielding and I then joined the Recon platoon in an assault on the smoldering area, firing into the open positions, killing the last few survivors of the air strike. As I moved across the positions I saw Spear's upturned helmet filled with blood. Wooden-handled Chinese Communist hand grenades burned and spewed as we swept the area. An exploding 7.62mm round somehow found its way into the eye of one infantryman wearing glasses held tightly to his face by a rubberband. He screamed in pain as he dug for the burning round. As we began policing up the weapons from the dead enemy troops, I was exposed for the first time to the pungent smell of burning human flesh. The stench was so strong and awful that it remains seared in my memory, a smell unimaginable to those who have never experienced it. Although I gagged on the horrible odor and the sight of the burned flesh, secretly, I was glad I had done my job without panicking. As a result of this first action, Staff Sergeant Wilkerson was awarded the Bronze Star for his courage under fire, while the main base camp of the brigade at Pleiku was named "Camp Spears" in honor of the squad leader killed at Ban Dung.

After the action at Ban Dung, I remained assigned to the S-2 shop as an interpreter, assisting the Recon platoon and other units on operations to recover enemy weapon and ammunition caches throughout the provinces of Darlac, Pleiku, and in Kontum, where the cloud-shrouded peaks rose over seven thousand feet. While I was mainly involved in recon and intelligence gathering, I still managed to get caught up in some heavy fighting. One day in mid-March 1966, the PAVN had fired a bunch of mortar rounds at the battalion's landing zone. The next morning, 3rd Platoon of Alpha Company was sent to search for the culprits. They followed the Ea Wy stream and eventually found the launch site. The 3rd Platoon continued patrolling along the stream when the point man discovered a piece of communications wire lying on the ground. Following the wire, the Platoon waded across a streambed and discovered where the wire ended. It was affixed to a field telephone at an enemy observation post, and it had led the Platoon right into the perimeter of a company of well-entrenched PAVN. Discovering the Americans in their midst, the enemy opened fire from close range. Another former airborne trooper, Staff Sergeant William R. Holbrook, took the first round into the side of his head, killing him instantly. The ensuing firefight was intense and resulted in heavy casualties on both sides. Several other platoon members were killed in the initial burst of enemy fire. A fifty-year old medic named "Doc" Johnson made several trips across the streambed under intense fire to drag wounded men back to safety. Johnson was later awarded the Bronze Star for his efforts.

Badly outnumbered, the Platoon was forced to call for help. Rapidly appearing overhead, the helicopters transporting the battalion reinforcements circled around to land at a nearby landing zone. While slowing to make their descent, the helicopters received a heavy volume of fire. As the lead chopper began to land, a round to the face immediately killed the Major piloting the craft. The copilot, a young Warrant Officer, sat frozen, hovering about ten feet off the ground while the aircraft was systematically shredded by automatic weapons fire. Seeing what was happening to his fellow soldiers in the chopper, one young squad leader, a Sergeant named Eddy Porter, stood up and completely exposed himself to enemy fire. Only moments earlier Porter had watched several of his closest friends being killed. Now sobbing violently, unable to control his anguish, Porter's feelings had suddenly metamorphosed into rage. Oblivious to his own safety, he ran forward, jamming an M-26 fragmentation grenade into the firing slot of a well-constructed bunker, killing the occupants. Part of his hand was blown off by enemy small arms fire in the process. Porter's one-man charge set off a chain reaction as frenzied platoon members surged forward, assaulting the fortified enemy positions while screaming at the top of their lungs. PAVN troops routed from their bunkers were methodically shot or beaten to death in savage hand-to-hand combat. Seeing the carnage sweeping toward them, several occupants of a command bunker located at the enemy's rear fled their position and hurled themselves headlong into a thick stand of bamboo, disappearing from view in a matter of seconds.

I had come in on the second lift when much of the battle was over. Still, the bloodshed from such a small battle seemed immense to me. I saw men crying over dead friends or weeping from the revulsion of having killed men in hand-to-hand combat. Even as the horrific sounds of battle gradually diminished, moans vented from the contorted mouths of both the wounded and the unscathed. I thought the nightmare was over, but several members of the platoon soon began dragging the bloodied PAVN bodies into a clearing and stacked them into piles. Collecting bottles of mosquito repellent from the surviving members of the unit, they squeezed the thick liquid onto the piles and ignited the funeral pyre with C-ration matches. With many of the American leaders dead, none of the sobbing men raised any objections. I knew what they were doing wasn't right, but when I looked into their eyes somehow it just didn't seem wrong. Hearing the thud of Hueys in the distance, I turned and walked toward the LZ, sickened again by the already too familiar smell of burning human flesh. For his gallantry in action, Sergeant Porter was awarded the Silver Star.

While I walked away from that battle, I did not escape the escalating combat action. In mid-April 1966, shortly after Alpha Company's battle, I was wounded in the leg by an enemy booby trap on a hot landing zone near Dak To in Kontum province. Several other men were also wounded during the helicopter insertion, and we were all evacuated to the 2nd Surgical Hospital of the 1st Cavalry located next to Hong Kong Mountain in An Khe. After surgery I was placed on a cot in a Quonset hut next to the Medevac chopper pad. During my recovery, I watched as helicopters brought in wounded troops around the clock. It was a gruesome sight to see the green canvas litters, dripping blood, being carried from the helipad into the nearby operating room. Once the wounded had been unloaded, medics used water hoses to wash blood from the litters before leaning them against the metal building to dry in the sun. Although I dreaded the fungus, leeches and mosquitoes in the field, the hospital was a morbid place and I became anxious to return to my unit.

Fortunately for me, the battalion changed commanders in April 1966, which brought into my life someone who eventually became my mentor. Lieutenant

Colonel Robert C. Kingston now commanded the 1/35th. His previous assignment in Vietnam had been as an advisor to a Vietnamese Ranger Battalion. Kingston, a Special Forces officer, had trained in England with the Special Air Service (SAS). His willingness to cooperate closely with Special Forces units would be a key factor in the future success of the battalion. I would work for Kingston several more times in the future, and he would help my career a great deal.

Kingston was an incredible officer. In May 1966 a major battle occurred when the battalion was deployed around a landing zone designated "Ten Alfa" in the Chu Pah area of Pleiku province. Shortly thereafter, a section of the battalion's perimeter manned by Alpha Company was overrun by elements of the 66th North Vietnamese Regiment. I heard from buddies in my old company that while the troops hugged the ground and fired their weapons to repel the assault, Captain Anthony Bizantz walked calmly through the area killing charging PAVN with his .45 caliber pistol. After the firing subsided, the bodies of 175 enemy dead troops were counted around the entire position.

As the rainy season descended on the Central Highlands I was given new duties, one that would send me further down a path that would last almost thirty years. Due to my Vietnamese language capability and growing familiarity with Viet Cong tactics, before Captain Fielding left the S-2 shop he gave me a vital mission: take charge of the Montagnard scouts and PAVN ralliers being used by the battalion.

When we first arrived in South Vietnam, our tactics were straight out of the Ft. Benning manual: get on line and move through the brush until we encountered the enemy. After taking casualties from booby traps and snipers, we learned this style didn't work in the jungle of South Vietnam, and we gradually began to develop other techniques. By late January 1966, Kingston began experimenting with using some of the captured enemy soldiers to scout ahead and point out booby traps or areas where the enemy was hiding. The experience gained from employing the PAVN to scout the areas in advance of American units was critical. What was even more important was how they helped us change tactics. By putting them on point, they helped us uncover caches and avoid booby traps, and they showed us how to maneuver in the jungle, how the PAVN worked, and how we could beat them.

We also used local Montagnards as scouts. When we entered Montagnard areas, we needed to communicate with the local people to gather intelligence on enemy movements. Out in the more remote areas, few Montagnards spoke Vietnamese, let alone English. Captain Fielding sent me to the Montagnard Training Center at Pleiku to find "Yards" who spoke Vietnamese and the local dialect of whatever area we were operating in. Then the Montagnards, most from the Jarai tribe, and I would join the Recon platoon and scout in advance of the battalion. As operations pulled us further south into the Ban Me Thuot area, I also recruited members of the Rhade tribe, called the E-de by the Vietnamese, who were able to communicate with the other ethnic hill tribes of Darlac province. While many Montagnards worked for us, many others in the remote areas were indifferent to either side and simply wanted to be left alone. They knew that eventually we would move out of the area and the Viet Cong would move back in. In fact, most Americans don't realize that many Yards also worked for the Communists as porters and guides. For example, in the tri-border area most of the porters carrying supplies for the Communists by foot or by bicycle were conscripted Montagnards.

Still, the Montagnard scouts we used were incredibly loyal and hard working. An added plus of operations with the Montagnards was the variety of food they had or could find. It seemed as though they could always locate some type of wild vegetable that went well with C-rations, no easy feat for anyone who ever has had the pleasure of dining on cold C-rations. Displaying another culinary trick, the Yards always dug good, deep fighting positions before nightfall, and the following morning they were always quick to check them to see what had fallen in during the night. More often than not, one or more large paddy rats could be found at the bottom of the holes. The rats were skinned and gutted and then rotated on a bamboo stick over an open fire until done. After feasting on this newfound delicacy, I decided that the Central Highlands paddy rats tasted exactly like the fox squirrels back home in East Texas. Another benefit from working with the Yards was their ability to come up with a jar of the locally produced rice wine called *ruou can*. Several gallons of rice and water were put in a clay urn covered by banana leaves for at least a period of one month. While the concoction fermented, the tribesmen added small amounts of water to the mix to keep it from dehydrating. When ready, the slightly sweet-tasting brew was sipped through a long straw passed from drinker to drinker sitting in a circle. Since the battalion only received one can of hot beer and soda per man on rare occasions, the rice wine was considered a solid contribution to morale by the Montagnards.

After I learned the basics of two dialects of Montagnard from the trainees at the Training Center, my first opportunity to put the language to use was on a patrol into a village near Pleiku. It also was the scene of one of the most bizarre incidents I ever witnessed. As I entered the village, I first approached an elderly Montagnard man who was squatting down in the center of the village. When I asked the man *khoa buon nao pah* (Where is the chief?), the man indicated that he was the village chief. I then noticed that he was using a foot long flat piece of bamboo inserted into his rectum as a probe to remove chunks of hardened feces from his anus. Ignoring me, the man kept digging for several minutes before being satisfied that his constipation problem had been resolved. I later learned from trainees at the center that due to the hilly terrain, the Montagnards did not eat the regular rice harvested from flat inundated terraced fields like the lowland Vietnamese. Instead, they ate glutinous "sticky" rice that could be cultivated on hillsides with very little water. The rice was said to be nutritious, but the downside was that unless considerable leafy vegetables were eaten in conjunction with the rice to provide lubrication, chronic, painful constipation was a certainty.

As helpful as the Montagnards were, it was our employment of the captured PAVN soldiers that helped save dozens of American lives. The scouts were selected from a group of PAVN prisoners of war captured by either the 3rd Brigade or by Special Forces "A" Teams scattered strategically along the borders of Laos and Cambodia. In addition to the POWs, many PAVN decided to "rally" or defect to the side of the Government of Vietnam (the South Vietnamese called this program *Chieu Hoi,* "Open Arms"), bringing their weapons and vital information about enemy supply caches and trails with them. Both the captured and rallied enemy soldiers proved to be a gold mine of intelligence. Because of the proximity to the Ho Chi Minh Trail, the ralliers lead us to many enemy weapons that were still new and packed in greasy Cosmoline preservative. Much of the ammunition we recovered was hidden in waterproof lead containers and buried in muddy streambeds, making it extremely difficult for us to detect during our sweeps. Without the help of the defecting PAVN soldiers, our various missions would most likely have yielded sparse results.

But, we were skirting the regulations by using the enemy in this manner. In September 1965, the U.S. and South Vietnamese had signed an agreement that stipulated that PAVN soldiers captured by American forces were to be turned over to the ARVN for processing into POWs. Afterwards, we could then go down to the Chieu Hoi center to recruit them. Instead, because they were saving so many American lives, we would often keep them for several weeks before turning them in.

During the first few weeks of working with the ralliers and scouts I quickly learned from them how to detect and interpret the secret markings and trail signs used by Communist forces to guide their troops, including cuts on trees and piles of rocks placed by trails. For example, three machete marks cut into a tree on the right-hand side of a well-traveled trail meant that a newly infiltrating unit must proceed three hundred more meters before turning right onto another hidden trail. Infiltration trails were generally oriented north to south and so were easy to spot. I also learned to look for signs indicating the location of enemy base camps. One sure-fire indicator was the placement of bamboo fish traps in streams near the camps. One fish caught in the trap, along with some jungle vegetables, rice from the Yards, and occasionally a can of meat from China, could easily feed several enemy soldiers.

In addition to trail markings, I learned where to look for hidden caches. One of the best places to find concealed caches was inside huge clumps of bamboo trees. The Communists had considerable skill in hollowing out areas inside the bases of large bamboo growths, creating natural storage vaults that were not only safe from the elements, but also virtually invisible to the naked eye. I also found documents hidden by the clever PAVN in hollowed out bamboo poles used for rafters in houses.

I also learned from the PAVN ralliers extensive jungle crafts most Americans were never taught. I learned how they were able to rapidly abandon bivouac sites by hanging gear on quick-release hooks made from wood, and I studied how to carve these hooks from tree branches. The PAVN also used a technique for keeping rain out of their hammocks that was so efficient I wondered why I didn't think of it myself. They solved the water-entry problem by tying their hammocks with the cords on each end rising upward to poles, and then from the poles the cord was routed down to a tree trunk. In that manner the rain flowed down the tree to the ground, rather than down the tree and into the hammock. The amount of rain on the small poles placed between the trees and the hammocks was negligible, thus keeping the hammocks dry. The thin black nylon PAVN hammocks were much better than our cotton ones. They weighed about one pound, dried fast, and didn't mildew.

Although we definitely appreciated the assistance provided by the PAVN ralliers in locating enemy base camps and caches, I felt that I could not completely trust those who had recently been captured. It was impossible to predict if they might suddenly grab a weapon or hand grenade and turn on us, so I had to use caution at all times in dealing with them. During nighttime operations, whenever I wanted to grab a few hours sleep I always gave my bayonet and hand grenades to another American. As another precaution, I placed my web gear with ammunition magazines beneath my head. I then tied their hands with a nylon poncho cord looped around my belt several times. If they tried to escape or gain a weapon during the night their movements would awaken me.

Coupled with my newly acquired Jarai and Rhade language abilities, the PAVN ralliers gave me the proficiency to safely guide American units through enemy territory in search of Communist base camps and supply caches. While I loved my new job, I found it physically and emotionally challenging. I spent most of my time with the fast moving Recon Platoon, the usual point element for an always-on-the-move battalion. However, because of my language skills and successful work with the PAVN defectors and Montagnard scouts, whenever the Recon platoon returned to base camp or was given a temporary guard-a-bridge assignment as a rest break, I was moved to help another line unit. This kept me constantly in the field, and during the first six months of scouting I lost almost fifty pounds.

While I had become successful at locating small hidden enemy caches, my first big find was during early March 1966 in the village of Mewal twenty kilometers outside of Ban Me Thuot, the provincial capital of Darlac. The Brigade's Intelligence Section had received information from the local CIA field office in Ban Me Thuot that the harvest from the nearby Mewal Coffee Plantation might be lost due to the presence of Communist guerrillas. The small hamlet of Mewal was located adjacent to a possible Communist haven, and the sympathies of its inhabitants were unknown. The Italian owners of the plantation, a family named Santilli, whom I would meet again years later, requested security from the Americans so that pro-GVN Montagnards residing near the plantation could harvest the coffee crop. Without the harvest, the local economy would suffer, so my battalion was tasked to provide security for the area.

Acting on a tip from an informant, Captain Fielding sent me, accompanied by several members of the Recon Platoon for security, to excavate an earthen bank near the plantation. After recovering several rifles wrapped in grease cloth, we entered Mewal Village and linked up with the remainder of Recon Platoon. I then asked the locals if they knew the whereabouts of the Viet Cong. After being told by sullen villagers that there was no VC in the village, the members of the platoon conducted a systematic search of the area. We found nothing. Satisfied, the platoon prepared to return to base camp. But something was bothering me, and I was unconvinced by the villager's protestations. I decided to try one more time. Acting on a hunch I began using a long metal welding rod to probe beneath the ashes of a cooking fire in the kitchen of one home. The metal rod slid easily into the ground about one meter before striking a solid object. The solid object proved to be a sheet of metal placed over a bundle of rifles and shotguns, most of which were of American manufacture. We repeated the same procedure in each house and ultimately enough weapons were recovered to fill two three-quarter ton trucks.

While the men from the Recon platoon continued digging up the arms caches, I started scouting to the rear of Mewal Village. On a small trail leading out of the village, I encountered three men walking toward it. My first impulse was that they were Communist guerrillas, and I had better fire first before they did. The man walking in front of the trio appeared to be the eldest, and I pegged him as the leader of the group. As the man's eyes met mine he must have discerned something that told him he should immediately run for his life. When he turned and started to flee, the other two quickly followed. I raised my rifle and started to fire, but since they were not armed, and I wasn't positive they were Communists, I lowered my rifle and stood watching as the three men disappeared into the jungle.

After collecting the weapons, I decided to screen the village for possible covert Communist cadre. After gaining the cooperation of a Communist agent who resided in the village, I used a tarp from a military trailer to make a confidential reviewing stand. After cutting a small hole in the tarp, I suspended it around four large tent poles creating a small compartment about the size of a telephone booth. Standing inside and peering out the hole the cooperative cadre was able to identify other covert agents without his identity being compromised. This tactic definitely facilitated cooperation from prisoners and suspects

One of the most valuable scouts I ever had was a courier of the PAVN Commo-Liaison system. Commo-liaison stations are rest stops along a trail. On the Ho

Chi Minh Trail, they were small way stations located one day's walk apart, and were placed between the bigger and more permanent *Binh Tram,* or "Military Stations." Couriers carried messages or acted as guides for other units moving between the rest stops. This courier was captured after being hit in his buttocks by shrapnel from an M-79 round while hiding in a tree. Treated by a medic attached to the Recon platoon, the young courier was grateful for the medical attention and decided to remain with us. He quickly began to locate booby traps and carefully concealed enemy positions. Having worked in the area as a courier for almost a year, the wounded PAVN knew the trail systems well and our operations proceeded smoothly. One such operation enabled troops of Alpha Company to catch several field grade Communist officers by surprise, killing them with no American casualties. But the courier's wounds became infected, and I decided to take him for treatment at the Brigade. When the surgeon on duty discovered he was being rousted out of bed in the middle of the night to treat a PAVN Private, he went into a tirade, refusing to provide medical treatment to the courier. I was unmoved by the surgeon's disdain, and I related how the enemy soldier had been responsible for saving American lives. I finally had to threaten to go to the Commanding General if necessary in order to obtain proper treatment for the man. The surgeon finally relented, and the courier was back in the field the following day.

It all went for nothing, however. Soon afterwards he began to exhibit symptoms of malaria, an often-fatal illness. Increasingly delirious and feverish, he soon lost touch with reality. I immediately requested a medical evacuation helicopter, but heavy rain and low cloud cover delayed the flight for two more days. By the time I was able to put the courier on a Huey for transport back to the rear the man had already lapsed into a coma. I later learned that he died a few days after arriving at base camp. I felt terrible, as he had helped us immensely.

Another of the most effective scouts I employed was a PAVN Supply Sergeant captured shortly after infiltrating into Darlac province from the Ho Chi Minh Trail. I initially declined to use the seasoned enemy because he was evasive during my questioning and yielded very little information. Several days after his capture, however, the enemy POW was taken to a Special Forces camp for "debriefing." When the man returned to the battalion he apologized to me for having deceived me and immediately began to cooperate. When I asked him to explain the sudden turnaround, he described how he had just been interrogated with a hand-cranked telephone attached to his testicles. He said he had tried to hold out as long as possible, but had lost his bowels and finally gave in due to the pain. The sergeant said he didn't feel too badly about cooperating because he had been trained to resist for only the initial period of capture to ensure that his unit had ample time to withdraw into a sanctuary. Once he was certain his unit had escaped he was willing to cooperate. I put him on point and in the ensuing weeks he guided the Recon Platoon to several important caches. During the time that the Supply Sergeant scouted for the platoon we didn't lose one man to enemy fire or booby traps.

Shortly after setting up an ambush at one site pointed out by the PAVN Supply Sergeant as being a well-used Commo-Liaison trail, three Communist soldiers approached our location. Due to the rain the three were carrying their weapons slung over their shoulders with the barrels down. An alert rifleman quickly placed automatic weapons fire on the three, instantly killing the first PAVN and wounding the other two. The wounded men managed to disappear, but in their flight they left clearly visible blood trails. A member of the Recon platoon accompanied me to search for the two North Vietnamese, but we were unable to locate them in the dense brush. In order to prevent compromise of our ambush location I decided to move the body off to the side of the trail. I had the soldier's feet, and a member of the Recon platoon whose name I never knew had his arms. As we began to drag the body into the brush the same rifleman who had killed the PAVN opened fire on our location, spraying the area with automatic weapons fire. The man helping me move the body immediately went down on the ground as I shouted "cease-fire!" In examining the American I could only see a small black dot on his side with no exit wound. A helicopter arrived on the scene to evacuate him and I never saw him again, but I heard the following day that he didn't survive.

As we were preparing to leave the ambush site one of the platoon's squad leaders, a redneck Sergeant from the hills of Arkansas, dragged the enemy's body back onto the trail. Using a mess-kit spoon the Sergeant dug a round hole in the ground and placed an M-26 fragmentation grenade inside with the handle up. He then placed the dead man's head down with his forehead on the handle and removed the pin. The Sergeant reasoned that when the next unit of PAVN passed by on the trail they would turn the man over to identify him and be killed in the process. The Sergeant, who didn't seem to have any qualms about booby-trapping bodies, proudly displayed several ears suspended from a bootlace worn around his neck.

Incidents like this one, combined with the dangerous missions looking for enemy base camps, took a tremendous toll on me. By the fall of 1966 and at the end of my tour with the 1/35th, I had grown increasingly depressed by the daily routine of mangled bodies, death and destruction. But it was not only the horror of combat that had consumed me, the living conditions were appalling as well. We wore our uniforms until they rotted from our bodies. Only then were new ones choppered in. Even more dreaded than the fungus and "jungle rot" that grew between our toes, under our arms and even in sinus cavities, were the leeches that constantly stuck to us. Under such awful conditions, my soon-to-be-completed tour of duty in Vietnam had almost convinced me to finish my remaining time in a garrison job and then leave the service. I had come a long way from the naïve young man looking to test his mettle in combat. Plus, although I had enjoyed many opportunities to learn the language and culture of the country, it become obvious to me how little the other men knew about Vietnam, other than it was a war they were trying to survive. Once I observed a machine gun squad setting up a position to fire into a small hamlet displaying a large banner reading "Viet Nam Cong Hoa." When I asked why the men intended to fire in the hamlet, the Squad Leader, a young man from Alabama, advised me that he was certain the hamlet was enemy because he had seen the banner saying "The Cong Will Win." The man's face turned crimson when I informed him the "Viet Nam Cong Hoa" actually meant "Republic of Vietnam."

Shortly before my departure, however, Lieutenant Colonel Kingston called me in to speak with him. Kingston reviewed the battalion's operations conducted during the previous year while underscoring the contributions I had made to the success of the unit. It was the first time a commander had taken the time to express his appreciation to me for a job well done, especially on a one-on-one basis. Kingston's briefing that day considerably raised my morale and I decided to request orders for assignment back on "jump status" with an airborne unit.

My first tour in Vietnam ended in October 1966, and my new orders directed me to return to the 101st Airborne Division at Fort Campbell, Kentucky, where I was assigned to Company "C" 2/506th Battalion, the famous "Currahees." Still, even while in the States, Vietnam would not release me from its grip. While undergoing training in the field I became ill with chills, fever and general aches and pain. A visit to a combat medic resulted in the typical infantry unit medical advice of "take two aspirins and come back in a few days if you don't feel better." My First Sergeant, Henry Cardenas, a Korean War veteran, accused me of trying to avoid field duty by pretending to be ill. Angered by the critical remarks, I stuck it out for almost a month until my fever reached 106 degrees and I became delirious, finally slipping into unconsciousness. After being taken to a military hospital, the initial diagnosis was Spinal Meningitis, but after more careful scrutiny it was determined that I was the first soldier at Fort Campbell to be admitted to the hospital for malaria contracted during the Vietnam War. I could not help but think of the courier who had died from malaria, and how close to death I had come because of the same disease.

Back in the States, my personal life also took a turn for the better. In June 1967, I married Nova Lynne Orange of nearby Old Hickory, Tennessee. Nova had a three-year-old son named Michael from a previous marriage. I grew to deeply love the little boy and I eventually adopted him. We rented a house in New Providence, a small town near the base inhabited primarily by soldiers of the 101st and their dependents. Shortly after we were married, the Division Intelligence Officer (G-2), Lieutenant Colonel "Chargin' Charlie" Beckwith, contacted me. Like Kingston, Beckwith was another Special Forces officer trained by the British SAS. He had returned to the Division after serving as commander of a classified unit called "Project Delta" in South Vietnam's Central Highlands. Apparently Beckwith had received advance word that the entire Division would soon be deployed to Vietnam, and due to the absence of Vietnamese linguists within the Division he requested I be assigned to the 101st Military Intelligence Detachment (MID) under his direction.

After a short tour again as an infantryman, I was back to Intelligence. The 101st MID was assigned to the Division's main staff element for Intelligence, the G-2 shop, and was comprised of about thirty men who specialized in Imagery, Order of Battle (OB), Counter-Intelligence, and interrogations. After signing in at the new unit I received orders for intelligence training at Fort Holabird, Maryland, followed by advanced Vietnamese training at the Defense Language Institute Southern Command located at Fort Bliss, Texas. Shortly after completing this training I received new orders for reassignment to Vietnam, and Nova and Michael moved to live with her parents.

I arrived back in Vietnam in November 1967 for my second tour, ready to take on the Communists again, but now as a young Staff Sergeant. The 101st Airborne Division, which already had one brigade deployed in Vietnam since 1965, moved from Fort Campbell to a base camp adjacent to Bien Hoa Air Base. The large American military base was located in the Republic of Vietnam's III Corps, and the airplanes at Bien Hoa served as the main air support for III Corps, a military region that included the capital city, Saigon.

Bien Hoa proper was a relatively small city situated on the east bank of the Dong Nai River. Although Bien Hoa province contained numerous French-style rubber plantations, much of the land in the northern portion of the province, a region called "War Zone D," remained covered in triple canopy jungle. This verdant foliage provided excellent concealment and staging areas for PAVN units recently infiltrated from North Vietnam. Because of the area's strategic importance and its close proximity to Saigon, General William C. Westmoreland elected to deploy both the 101st Airborne Division and the 173rd Airborne Brigade into the zone.

Shortly after arrival in Bien Hoa, Beckwith called all personnel involved in reconnaissance and intelligence to a meeting near the Division Tactical Operations Center. After everyone was assembled in a "GP" (General Purpose) medium tent, and "standing to" for Beckwith's arrival, he exploded through the tent flaps. Beckwith didn't care for long meetings, and being an old Ranger, he rarely used the term "intelligence." His aversion for administrative terminology aside, he quickly delivered his prepared remarks: "Boys, I need some mutha fukin' POWs and documents! Get your asses out there and get them!" Beckwith went on to emphasize that his view of intelligence work boiled down to "we can't kill them if we can't find them." After a few moments of shaking hands and reminiscing with some old timers, he disappeared back through the dusty flaps.

After Beckwith's brief pep rally all intelligence-gathering units within the Division shifted into high gear. Patrolling activities increased steadily due to Beckwith's belief that a small, well-trained patrol was better than aerial imagery and informant reports disseminated by intelligence analysts sitting in the rear working in air-conditioned vans. Plus, on-the-ground reconnaissance had for years been emphasized throughout the Division. Beckwith had an especially high degree of confidence in personnel trained at the Division Recondo School.

The increased patrolling quickly began to yield results, and soon valuable captured documents arrived on Beckwith's desk. One good example of these enemy documents was taken from the body of a PAVN artillery Major that was killed north of Bien Hoa Air Base. The Major's document pouch included an overlay for a nighttime fire mission by 122mm rockets scheduled to be launched that night onto the air base. If successful, such an attack would be devastating. In analyzing the document, I plotted the range and reversed the azimuths on the overlay. After I gave the results to Beckwith, he quickly scheduled a strike by fighter-bombers from Bien Hoa. The result was several secondary explosions at the firing position across the river and no night rocket attack.

Another valuable captured document, classified by the Viet Cong as *Toi Mat* (Ultra Secret) listed the code designations for all key locations and terrain features throughout the division's area of operations. As soon as I saw that the document was typed on "onionskin" to facilitate swallowing if the courier was captured, I knew it was something very important. Beckwith told me to take the document down to the 265th Army Security Agency unit, which was the element responsible for monitoring Viet Cong radio traffic in the Division's area. The Signals Intelligence (SIGINT) specialists at the 265th were excited about the document. With the high degree of VC security, they were having difficulty cracking the enemy codes. Whereas before they were only able to estimate locations mentioned in intercepted traffic, the document allowed them to pinpoint with accuracy just when and where the VC would be at a given time. Unfortunately, however, a scant few days after the document was seized an overzealous Public Affairs Officer in the Division Headquarters (HQ) decided to publish the document's capture in the Division's Daily Bulletin. The Military Intelligence Detachment Executive Officer conducted a cursory investigation but no particular person was held responsible. Beckwith, however, was livid. After he chewed considerable ass it was agreed that any future references to intelligence and security matters would be cleared through his shop prior to publication in any local media.

During that same time frame, some troops from the Division's Aviation Company brought in a female suspect they described as "acting suspicious." One of the Americans saw her walking on the flight line where the helicopters were parked, and he believed the lady was measuring distance on the tarmac with her paces. The lady was known to be a "hootch maid," a woman who cleaned the living quarters for some of the Aviation Company men. An examination of her labor documentation revealed that she was a bonafide worker inside the base. She also was carrying a scrap of paper. As I looked closer at the grease-smeared paper, it riveted my attention, and I realized the men were right. The paper was actually a sketch of the flight line, complete with measurements in meters.

One of the soldiers from the aviation unit also turned in a leather glove he found next to a helicopter. Inside the glove was a hand grenade with the pin pulled. The troop believed the same lady had placed it on the flight line. The lady at first maintained that she had "found" the paper on the ground and knew nothing about the grenade, but a short stint on the polygraph proved she was lying. She ultimately revealed that she decided to "secretly follow the revolution" many years prior to her arrest. She said her first husband "regrouped" to North Vietnam with the Communists when the country was partitioned in 1954, and since that time she had married two South Vietnamese officers. They, along with many members of their units, had been killed as a result of Viet Cong (VC) ambushes planned from the information she had passed. In other words, the meek little old hootch maid literally was a black widow. When asked how she managed to get such free access to the flight line, she admitted that per the instructions of her handler, she had gradually established a sexual relationship with a senior American officer. This degree of intimacy had allowed her to virtually come and go as she pleased. After being briefed on the incident Beckwith handled the matter quietly, and I was never informed as to the action taken. Knowing Beckwith, however, I feel certain the dancer paid the fiddler in the end.

As the Vietnamese Lunar New Year holiday called "Tet" approached, which was the major celebration in Vietnam, the Intelligence Detachment received reports of an impending attack in the Division area, but the details were sketchy at best. On January 3,1968, another important document was captured during an ambush in Tan Uyen district. The district, code named U-1 by the Communists, was located north of Bien Hoa. The document was found on the body of Major Ut Hiep, the Commander of the Dong Nai Battalion, which was the battalion operating as a dedicated reconnaissance and security element of the Central Office for South Vietnam (COSVN), code named "R." COSVN was the southern arm of the Political Bureau in Hanoi, and maintained political and military control over the area of South Vietnam from Cam Ranh Bay down to the southern tip of Vietnam, the Ca Mau peninsula. The PAVN called this area the B-2 Front. According to the document, Major Hiep was returning from a meeting at COSVN Headquarters where he had been given the mission of conducting a point reconnaissance at "B H Air Base" and "Binh My Village," during the period 7 to 14 January 1968. Major Hiep had been ordered to report to COSVN immediately after completing his mission. Although the document was handwritten in Vietnamese and difficult to read, my interpretation of its contents indicated that COSVN was planning a major attack in the area. Considering the locations, I believed mortars would probably be positioned in Binh My village, just north of the flight line. Attacking the flight line would prevent tactical aircraft at Bien Hoa, the most important weapon in the American arsenal, from departing the airfield in support of American and ARVN units in III Corps.

I recorded my opinion for Beckwith in the form of a "Spot Report." I didn't hear anything further on the document for over two weeks until I was informed by the Order of Battle shop in the Division G-2 that experts of the Combined Documents Exploitation Center (CDEC) in Saigon disagreed with my opinion. Acting on instructions from Beckwith, I went down to Saigon and talked to the CDEC experts, who were quite adamant regarding their analysis that the document was not associated with Bien Hoa Air Base. American intelligence personnel at the Document Center deferred to their leading expert, a Vietnamese civilian official assigned to the center. I found him to be an arrogant little guy who thought he knew everything. We argued but could not reach agreement on the meaning of the document, and I returned to Bien Hoa angry and frustrated. A few days later, the Division's Order of Battle Officer and the G-2 Sergeant came to our Detachment to discuss the document. I went over it with them assisted by the appropriate maps and charts, but ultimately they departed noncommittal, saying it was Beckwith's call.

In late January, shortly prior to the looming Tet holiday, Beckwith called me over to the G-2. He said his people were receiving reports of enemy troop movements in the area and he wanted to know what I thought about the opinion of the Saigon experts. I told Beckwith that as far as I was concerned, *san bay B H* and *xa Binh My,* as contained in the document, referred to Bien Hoa Air Base and nearby Binh My village. I added that the village was in mortar range of the runway and flight line, and that I considered it unusual that enemy cadre from the area would be called back to COSVN headquarters after a recon effort. Beckwith replied that he only knew two kinds of troops, "piss cutters and strap hangers." Looking stern and peering intently into my face, Beckwith said he believed I was a "piss cutter" and a good Vietnamese linguist. Although Beckwith professed to have confidence in me, he nonetheless cautioned me not to "put his ass out on a limb."

Two days before Tet, Beckwith summoned me again. He wanted to send me to Binh Duong Province, northwest of Bien Hoa, to interrogate a Communist defector. I loaded onto a chopper and landed at Phuoc Vinh that same afternoon. The defector proved to be a young troop, sick with malaria and very weak. He said he was a local who had just joined the VC, and he didn't know anything about his unit. But I had become so conversant in the Vietnamese language that I was able to detect variations in accents. To me the manner in which the defector substituted his Ns for Ls in the northern dialect told me he was lying about being a local, and that based on his accent he was most likely a PAVN regular from the area between Thai Binh and Haiphong. I didn't even believe he was a genuine defector, but rather a straggler who was so sick he decided to "rally" for "three hots and a cot," plus free medicine. After talking to him at length, I was able to confirm my suspicions that he was a Main Force soldier, rather than a VC guerrilla, and that his unit was moving at such a fast clip he was simply unable to maintain the pace.

Later that same day I went back up in the chopper with the defector and eventually found the trail on which the young PAVN had been moving south. As we were flying along, I observed other Communist troops running south along the same trail, which was just north of the Song Be River. As soon as they realized they had been spotted, the PAVN troops left the trail, kneeled down and flipped woven rattan camouflage racks over their heads, making them virtually invisible to the naked eye. When I reported the sightings to Beckwith, he seemed excited by the fact that regular PAVN troops were in his area of operation and moving toward Bien Hoa at a fast rate of march.

With most of the Division's tactical units in Binh Duong and Phuoc Long provinces, the perimeter at Bien Hoa Air Base was stretched thin and Beckwith seemed to be in the typical quandary of an Intelligence Officer. If he recommended pulling troops in from outlying positions, those locations might be attacked. If he didn't, and the base was struck, he could be blamed for not properly identifying the gathered intelligence and thus failing to warn the unit of a pending attack. Ultimately my analysis of the captured document containing the COSVN reconnaissance mission, and my report on the PAVN troops moving at a fast pace convinced Beckwith that I was right, and that Bien Hoa Air Base was in serious danger of being overrun. Just prior to Tet, Beckwith made what was perhaps one of the most important decisions during the "Tet" offensive by convincing the Division Commander, Major General Olinto Barsanti, to move a battalion of the 326th Engineers from Phuoc Vinh down to the air base perimeter. This proved to be a prudent, last minute adjustment.

On the eve of Tet, as everyone prepared for the festivities, a delegation of young Vietnamese females visited the ARVN guard post just off the end of the Bien Hoa runway. In appreciation for the guards dedicated service throughout 1967, they were presented with traditional Tet gifts of liquor and candy. The beautiful young sirens sang songs and wished the grateful guards a happy New Year. The guards' holiday was short-lived, however. Soon after consuming the liquor, the entire guard force fell unconscious on the floor of their critical post. At about the same time, lead elements of the crack 274th and 275th PAVN Regiments were emerging from the shadows of War Zone "D." Following the railroad tracks west, they were headed toward a major Allied nerve center: Bien Hoa Air Base, the ARVN III Corps Headquarters compound, Camp Frenzel Jones of the 199th Light Infantry Brigade, and the primary Military Assistance Command Vietnam (MACV) logistical base in Vietnam, Long Binh. If Bien Hoa was captured, then tactical air support in the III Corps area would have been cut just as major enemy units were assaulting Saigon and the surrounding area.

Although the one Brigade of the Division already in country had been engaged in violent engagements with Communist forces for several years, this was to be the first large-scale battle for the remaining two brigades of the 101st. During the so-called acclimatization period, the paratroopers had hung out in tin roofed "hootches" used as makeshift clubs, chugging down hot Carling Black Label and Hamms beer. As they waited to attack the enemy, in typical G.I. fashion they mocked each other while boasting about who was going to be alive at the end, and who was going to kill the most Cong. The morale was as high as I had ever seen it in the 101st, or for that matter any other American unit in Vietnam, and the men of the 101st were all proud to be "Screaming Eagles." The bragging, the fistfights, and the airborne songs ringing out through the night may have been perceived by nearby support troops as arrogance. But just like the spontaneous yelling and foot stomping that preceded going out the door of an aircraft in flight, this was simply another method of relieving tension and fear. At the same time, there was a real desire to "close with and kill, destroy, or capture the enemy, or repel his assault by fire." That's what they had trained for, and that's why they were there. Like their brothers at Bastogne before them they wanted their "rendezvous with destiny." They were about to get it.

Sometime around 0300 hours on January 31, 1968, with the indigenous guard force incapacitated, Viet Cong sappers wearing only undershirts and wire-cutters suspended around their necks on nylon laces began to infiltrate the minefield at the end of the runway. As the sappers probed for mines, one lone soldier of the 101st manning an M-60 machine-gun saw something moving and began to fire. The firing was steady for a few minutes when someone yelled out to "shut that crazy sonofabitch up!" He didn't, and his actions alerted the rest of the base perimeter guard. Moments later, the situation became hectic when the entire perimeter opened up, reminiscent of a stateside live fire demonstration for visiting Soviet Generals. The alert M-60 machine-gunner who fired first that night probably saved many lives. I never learned his identity, but I promised myself that if I ever met him someday I would make sure to shake that crazy sonofabitch's hand.

Although the main attack on Bien Hoa was blunted, PAVN troops continued deadly automatic weapons fire throughout the first day of Tet. During the ensuing sweep around the perimeter, the firing was so intense that an Army Specialist 7, who worked as the secretary for the Commanding General, was killed when he took a round in the neck while typing at his desk in the General's office. The bodies of the PAVN troops, as well as the wounded, were scattered in the brush and tall grass around the perimeter. Some of the enemy dead were apparently "Special Action" unit personnel, commando's who worked in urban areas. Inside their packs I found South Vietnamese Air Force uniforms starched and pressed. Although the Special Action personnel managed to penetrate the airbase they were quickly attacked and either killed or repelled by hard-fighting members of the Air Security Police assigned to the air base. Had the Special Action personnel been able to reach the actual flight line, this tactic of pretending to be South Vietnamese Air Force personnel would have created considerable confusion between the American and South Vietnamese assigned there, even after first light.

When the smoke cleared at the air base perimeter, 115 Viet Cong and PAVN bodies were piled in the wire. The following day, the bodies were covered with lime and buried with a Caterpillar bulldozer in one common grave at the end of the runway. Throughout the Tet attack, most of the Communists in the forefront were local natives of the area who regrouped to the north in 1954 and later reinfiltrated into the south. Prior to the Tet general offensive, many of these cadre were placed in frontal or guide positions due to their familiarity with the local terrain. In later years I came to the conclusion that the main purpose of the Tet offensive was to enable the Communists to enter into negotiations with the U.S. side from a position of strength and to prove the legitimacy of the National Liberation Front. Others have speculated that the northern party hard-liners took advantage of the offensive to rid their ranks of southern nationalists who might otherwise have been prone to cause political plurality problems in a postwar government.

As it was, over five hundred PAVN were killed and forty more captured in the Bien Hoa-Long Binh area. Among those not included in this figure for captured were the sum total of patients from the Bien Hoa Mental Hospital caught up in the counteroffensive. As a result of this mix-up many of the captured PAVN pretended to be insane, while many of the insane pretended to be PAVN. The situation was so confusing that in order to separate fact from fiction I borrowed an ARVN Sergeant from the attached 9th ARVN MID. I dressed him in a typical Communist uniform complete with canvas map pouch. With great fanfare I escorted him into the POW compound. By the following day the new "PAVN POW" was able to ascertain that most of the captured PAVN had provided not only inaccurate information, but also completely false backgrounds. One senior cadre, who had claimed to be a junior enlisted man, reprimanded the ARVN Sergeant for not destroying his maps prior to capture. All the captured personnel had to be reinterrogated and correction copy reports issued. Years later, the ensuing ordeal in handling this unusual group served as a reminder to me of the complexities encountered in dealing with some of the rehearsed and orchestrated witnesses "introduced" by the Vietnamese Government during postwar MIA cases investigations.

The 101st moved north to act as a blocking force against North Vietnamese units who might attempt to reinforce the Communist forces entrenched in the northern city of Hue. Soon after, the 101st began to operate in the A-Shau valley, one of the most important supply areas for the PAVN in South Vietnam. When the heaviest Tet attacks were over, the intensity of the fighting had apparently rekindled a smoldering fire in Beckwith, and he cleaned out his desk in the G-2 shop and departed for a new assignment in Hue. Beckwith eventually took command of one of my former units from the 101st working in the bloody A-Shau Valley. Out of respect and admiration for Beckwith, the Division's best recon expert, Roger "Hog" Brown, decided to follow him into the unforgiving A-Shau. I later met Brown after he was reassigned to the Ranger Department at Fort Benning, Georgia. Smiling, Brown told me that his dedication to Beckwith had gotten him only two things: "a sucking chest wound and a Silver Star, and in that order."

While in the Hue-A Shau area I worked closely with Vietnamese Intelligence Specialists from the 9th ARVN MID. It is my recollection that this arrangement was unique in that it was the only instance during the Vietnam War in which Vietnamese personnel were formally assigned to an American unit and under the command of an American officer. The experimental unit stayed busy in the months after the Tet offensive processing numerous important prisoners and documents. One such document was a notebook removed from the body of a noodle vendor in Hue. The notebook contained very accurate, specific details concerning the daily activities of a significant number of high-ranking South Vietnamese military and civilian officials in the Hue area. Special Action forces of the Communist side marked many of those officials for assassination, and the remains of several were uncovered in mass graves containing more than five thousand bodies. Many of the Vietnamese had been buried alive with their hands and feet bound with wire.

After Beckwith left for the A-Shau, I was paired off with Captain Dennis Marasco, a crusty, cigar-chewing Counterintelligence Special Agent from Bloomfield, New Jersey. While working in the Hue-Phu Bai area, Marasco insisted on eating in Command Mess facilities, which were normally reserved for Colonels and above. Since both of us wore no rank insignia except for a "US" on each collar, nothing was ever said about the visits, but being a twenty-four year old Staff Sergeant I felt a little nervous. Marasco and I worked the Quang Tri-Hue area for a few months before Marasco transferred to Special Forces. The security compromises that led to the mass execution of innocent civilians by Communist death squads in Hue had a strong impact on Marasco, and he became deeply suspicious of all Vietnamese, especially GVN intelligence personnel. Marasco would later be charged as the alleged "trigger man" in the famous "Green Beret" murder case involving the death of a Vietnamese double agent who was reportedly executed off the coast of Nha Trang.[2]

On several occasions I had to work with some national level intelligence personnel based in Saigon, who filled me in on some of their activities. I soon became fascinated by the prospect of working in a higher-level intelligence outfit. They recommended I visit their hearquarters for an interview. Lured by the prospect of an assignment in plain-clothes, with credentials authorizing me to carry a concealed weapon, have my own Honda motorcycle, and live in hotels while traveling throughout the country, I found the opportunity too interesting to pass up. I traveled down to the 525th MI Group Headquarters in Saigon and had a successful interview. I was about to enter a whole new world.

Chapter Two

Communism 101

AFTER THE INTERVIEW, in May 1968 I transferred to the 525th Military Intelligence Group. While each Division had an organic intelligence unit, the 525th was the Army's main theatre-level intelligence unit in Vietnam. When I arrived at Group headquarters, it was decided that given my prior experience with Communist prisoners, I would be best suited as an interrogator. I was told to report to Captain William Frank at the Combined Military Interrogation Center (CMIC).

The Center was one of several jointly manned Vietnamese-American intelligence operations created to gather and analyze enemy intentions and capabilities. CMIC's particular function was to interrogate and exploit captured enemy soldiers for military intelligence. The other two were the Combined Document Exploitation Center (CDEC), which translated captured documents, and the Combined Intelligence Center, Vietnam, which did Order of Battle studies and terrain analysis, among other responsibilities. Order of Battle intelligence is the effort to identify enemy units, their locations, strengths, command personalities and missions. The combined Centers had been formed in 1965 and were the brainchild of the former head of MACV Intelligence, Major General Joseph D. McChristian, who sought to streamline and integrate the intelligence process between the American and the South Vietnamese militaries. The Centers had succeeded admirably in delivering valuable intelligence to the Allied forces.

Frank was an attorney who specialized in the Law of Land Warfare and International Law and who had recently worked for a prominent Manhattan law firm. A seemingly odd selection for a collection team chief, but I was immediately impressed by Frank's attitude toward the exploitation of human sources. Although he was in full agreement with the intelligence doctrine that stated, "obtain the maximum amount of usable information in the shortest time possible," Frank nonetheless realized that more subtle techniques were needed to extract important information from hardened Asian revolutionaries. Patience and developing rapport were absolutely essential if one was to properly debrief high-ranking Vietnamese Communists. Even then, one could never be sure if they were telling you everything. The defectors often were cagey about certain facts, and it was always necessary to realize that no matter how cooperative they might seem, they still concealed information from the interrogator.

After guiding me on an orientation tour of the CMIC, Frank assigned me as a liaison to the two other interrogation Centers, the National Interrogation Center and the National Chieu Hoi Center. Intelligence officers of the Government of Vietnam's Central Intelligence Office (CIO) and the American Central Intelligence Agency (CIA) jointly staffed the National Interrogation Center (NIC), located in downtown Saigon at #3 Bach Dang Street.[1] The CIO was the GVN counterpart to the CIA. Most Americans involved in Vietnam never knew about the top-secret NIC facility until after the war, when two former CIA employees, Frank Snepp and Orin Deforrest, separately published books that discussed the grilling of Communist prisoners at the National Interrogation Center. Ironically, despite being a location where thousands of Communist prisoners were interrogated, after the GVN's collapse, the mission of the NIC did not change. Under the Communists the Center was renamed the "Criminal Investigation Interrogation Center," and the street was changed to "Ton Duc Thang" in honor of Vietnam's ailing President, who had replaced Ho Chi Minh in the ceremonial post after Ho's death. Surprisingly, President Thang turned out to be the father-in-law of South Vietnam's chief economic advisor, Harvard-educated Nguyen Xuan Oanh.

The National Chieu Hoi Center, located in the Thi Nghe area of Saigon, was home or point of contact for several hundred former high-ranking Communists who had decided to abandon the revolution and side with the South Vietnamese government. Even though the Chieu Hoi Center was in an insecure area and was a principal target of the post-Tet attacks in the late spring and summer of 1968, as CMIC liaison I visited this site frequently to work with these sources. While the serious defeats suffered by Communist forces during and after Tet reinforced the accommodating attitude of many who had crossed-over to the GVN, I did everything I could to establish trust and credibility with all the defectors. I made it a point to respond as truthfully as I could to their questions, instead of manipulating them in the more traditional intelligence method. Further, with some help from my friends in the supply system, on several occasions I was able to obtain excess rations for the men. I also gave them other needed items such as toiletries, cigarettes, and batteries that I purchased from the huge military Post Exchange in downtown Saigon.

My technique soon paid off, and they appeared to genuinely appreciate my efforts, not only for the gifts but also for the unexpected kindness. On various occasions senior Communist officers who did not speak English would engage me in political discussions concerning the potential fate of South Vietnam's government. Having defected, they were naturally concerned about the future of the Thieu administration and the possibility of retribution by their former comrades if the GVN fell. In one such chat during October 1968 with former PAVN Regimental Commander Colonel Phan Mau, he asked me about the ongoing Paris Peace negotiations and what would be the future U.S. commitment to the defense of South Vietnam. I'm sure he wasn't the only one who was apprehensive, and he probably had been nominated as a spokesperson for the rest. I answered his question frankly by telling him I believed all U.S. forces would be withdrawn from Vietnam within four years. He seemed to accept my remarks stoically. What I didn't realize was that the South Vietnamese Commander of the Chieu Hoi Center was listening in on the conversation. He immediately complained to the Vietnamese Commander of the CMIC, Colonel Lam Van Nghia, that I was "undermining the confidence of the defectors in the viability of the GVN."

When the resultant shock wave crashed down on Captain Frank, I was called in for counseling. Although Frank found the incident humorous, he cautioned me to be more diplomatic in expressing my opinions. He told me that in defending me before the American CMIC Commander, Lieutenant Colonel Santiago Acosta, Frank reminded him that my straightforward manner in dealing with the defectors had gained me a solid reputation among that population. As evidence, he pointed out that much important information previously withheld by the defectors since crossing over or being captured had been revealed recently only to me. Frank noted that this vital intelligence, which had led to the discovery of several major weapons caches and secret Communist facilities, had undoubtedly saved many American lives. Acosta agreed and the matter was dropped, at least on the American side.

Frank was referring to an incident that had happened the previous month. I was working with a PAVN defector who had provided another debriefer some information, but little of actual use. Frank asked me to work with him and we slowly developed a connection. During one conversation, he suddenly turned to me and whispered that he could help me if I could help him. In exchange for a sum of money, he would tell me where his unit had stored their weapons and ammo. I agreed, and he immediately led a local unit out to the site, where several tons of weapons and ammunition were found. It was the biggest weapons cache I ever helped uncover. We gave him several hundred dollars for his assistance, which was a large sum of money for a Vietnamese, enough for him to build his own house.

After the lecture, I was allowed to continue my work at the National Chieu Hoi Center, but I followed Frank's advice and became more discreet. At the CMIC and National Interrogation Centers, however, I soon noticed that while conducting new interrogations with former Communist cadre, GVN intelligence personnel, including Colonel Nghia, would frequently linger just outside the door of my interrogation room in order to monitor my conversations. Since the rooms were already equipped for surreptitious audio surveillance, I understood what they were trying to signal me. Their overt form of eavesdropping indicated continued South Vietnamese concern over my honesty with the Communist cadre without appearing to violate my professional stature by actually coming into the room. It was typical Vietnamese behavior: understated yet sent with a clear signal to those who could comprehend its true underlying meaning. It is a mind-set difficult for Westerners to grasp, one that underlined the differences in perception between the Vietnamese and the more straightforward Americans.

Such understanding had not come easy to me. The cultural gap between the Vietnamese and Americans, and even more surprising to an outsider, between the Communists and the Nationalists (as the non-Communist South Vietnamese called themselves), was a difficult chasm to bridge. For example, I was astonished by the uniqueness of the civilian and military patois developed by the Communists after three decades of clandestine operations and guerrilla warfare. Equally amazing was the fact that the average South Vietnamese was completely ignorant of this modern vernacular of his own language. To assist other interrogators in debriefing Communist personnel, and with the permission of my bosses, I worked day and night for weeks with the defectors in a time-consuming project that resulted in the compilation of a "Viet Cong/North Vietnamese Army (VC/NVA) Terminology Guide." This publication included four volumes of atypical vocabulary routinely used by Communist organizations in their operations and communications. Having already completed two Vietnamese language courses that included instruction on both northern and southern dialects, I believed that teaching this type of jargon would have been extremely helpful had it been added to the normal curriculum at the military language schools. But it wasn't, and I could only surmise that the terminology was excluded for political reasons.

This trend continued for years into the future, as young graduates from these courses arrived in Vietnam during the 1990's ill-prepared to conduct important POW/MIA case investigations. Moreover, after spending considerable time in the sparsely populated areas of the highlands, I became one of only a very small number of Westerners able to master the unique cadence of the "Hue" dialect. My combined knowledge of Communist terminology and adoption of the rare Central Vietnam dialect would ultimately prove to be a source of both admiration and amusement for postwar Vietnamese officials assigned to work with me.

By talking with the defectors, my familiarity with Communist tactics and organizations continued to rapidly grow. After having worked closely in 1966 with the enemy enlisted soldiers who had rallied to our side and with whom I had operated in dangerous conditions in the jungle, I had gained some insight on how the average PAVN soldier lived and fought. Now I spent countless hours at the three Centers delving into the minds of higher-ranking and more seasoned Communist officials. There were times when I would spend up to eight hours each day for several days with the same cadre, probing deeply into all aspects of Communist Vietnamese structure and thought processes. I was engaged mainly in various intelligence taskings, but sometimes I lingered well into the night, inquiring about their views of different events in the war. My incessant curiosity enabled me to gain deep insight into their secret world, a viewpoint few Americans ever heard except through the harsh and distorted Communist propaganda rhetoric.

Although many of the defectors claimed to have abandoned the North Vietnamese side due to their disillusionment with Communism, I had serious doubts regarding their true rationale. In fact, I found that a prime-motivating factor for the defectors had been the sudden shift from guerrilla warfare to conventional tactics, resulting in the large-scale Tet offensive. Most of the men staying at the Chieu Hoi Center were in agreement that the change in tactics was made too suddenly, resulting in the unnecessary slaughter of thousands of their fellow Communist Party members. The loss of non-party members didn't seem to be an issue, as Vietnamese Communist doctrine regarded the people as an important resource to be consumed in fighting the enemy. It was even acceptable to exploit women and children if their deaths would promote the goals of the party.

Few if any defectors at the Chieu Hoi Center had anything critical to say about the Communist Party. The Party was organized like a secret brotherhood not altogether different from the Mafia, with its own system of justice and exclusive jurisdiction over Party members. In their eyes, the Party was the catalyst to achieve independence and protect the land and the people from invaders, since in their paranoia they believed all foreigners harbored ill intentions toward Vietnam, especially the Chinese. The Army and the Security organs were the instruments the Party used to achieve the goals of protecting the nation and the people. To the Communist cadre, the people were like children, and only the Party's infallible leadership could instill the necessary discipline and guidance to protect and direct them. Furthermore, while the government provided day-to-day management of state affairs, it was essential that the Party (through a select few) remain absolute in controlling the nation and the people. Therefore, the Party managed all aspects of life. In dealing with the POW/MIA issue, this was the central tenet in comprehending their actions and motivations.

While the northerners were extremely proud of having wrested their independence from the French after extended periods of disunity and foreign domination, it was the Vietnamese experience with the long centuries of Chinese occupation that truly shaped their perception of dealing with the outside world. The Vietnamese noted that China would always be next door. As they often stated to me: "Whatever happens in China will eventually happen in Vietnam." After centuries of negotiating with the Chinese from a position of vulnerability, the Vietnamese ultimately become skilled, tough negotiators, as U.S. representatives participating in the Paris Peace talks would come to realize. To the Vietnamese time was meaningless and patience was an important virtue. Their undeclared mantra was that any compromise made during negotiations resulted from weakness and that there was no such thing as mutual benefit from concessions. For the many foreign officials throughout the world who dealt with them, the Vietnamese gradually gained a perhaps well-deserved reputation as "cunning and sly."

If their negotiation style was drawn out and pedantic, most Americans had even less conception of the Vietnamese method of warfare. If your vision of the Communists is one of rice farmers by day and rag-tag guerrillas by night planting booby traps and pungi sticks along jungle trails, then your impression is far from complete. The PAVN had a superior logistics system and a well-organized Army. But it was their attitudes toward political warfare that stood out. While most Americans probably recognized that there was a tremendous political aspect to the war, political in the sense that public relations and image played a critical role in shaping how the war was fought, we never seemed to grasp how significant it was. Americans tend to dismiss propaganda as hackneyed attempts at persuasion, easily recognized for what it is. But allow me to attempt to distill one essence of the role of politics in their style of warfare, the crucial task of what is known as proselytizing.

There are three main types of proselytizing: Civilian, Military, and Enemy, with many minor variations such as Religious, Chinese, and Intellectuals. Proselytizing cadre, men and women whose sole and direct undertaking was to approach and then educate specific groups or types of people to the Party's viewpoint, were engaged in a substantial and unrelenting effort to target and influence these various strata or classes of society. In essence, their purpose was behavior modification on a grand scale: the reality was to sway the few and gain a passive acceptance by the many. Further, not only were specialized cadre called upon to perform this mission, each military unit was to engage in this type of image building, all in an effort to create an adjustment in the thought patterns of the audience, regardless of how tiny.

Civilian proselytizing was aimed at convincing the Vietnamese population to support the Communists, either directly through guerrilla warfare or partially with food, shelter, or intelligence. In many ways civilian proselytizing was the most important type, because as the Communists wrote, "the revolution pertains to the people," and without the support of some part of the South Vietnamese populace, the Communists would have withered quickly. There were as many types of this propaganda as the mind could dream up. Armed teams, for instance, would enter villages at night and provide staged plays. The main theme of the rollicking revolutionary dramas was resistance to the invading Americans and overthrow of their Vietnamese "puppets," the blood traitors who had sold out the Fatherland and its freedom to the American imperialists, the ones who now wanted to continue what the French had started.

Military Proselytizing was directed at the South Vietnamese military and its governing apparatus. It sought to use human emotions and frailties to undermine ARVN morale. The fear of war and death, the repeated articulation of an eventual North Vietnamese victory, playing on the racial aspects of working for foreigners, no sentiment was left untouched or unexamined in the attempts to convince ARVN soldiers to desert, or at least refuse to fight very hard. ARVN dependents were an especially inviting target for the military proselytizers. Massive crusades were undertaken to convince the wives and family members of the ARVN soldiers to contact their relatives and request they stop fighting, return home and surrender to the inevitable. It was a brilliantly orchestrated symphony: a campaign of penetration agents into the ARVN ranks who provided intelligence and who relentlessly sought to lower morale, of leaflets and gossip spread in the villages, and of radio broadcasts and bullhorn messengers near the front lines. If it appeared ludicrous and laughable to the more cynical and sophisticated American leadership, its total impact, both conscious and unconscious, on the morale of the war-weary and poorly educated, mostly illiterate South Vietnamese peasants, let alone on the American public or the more nebulous entity known as "world opinion," has never been truly appreciated. This was an effort organizationally controlled and directed by all Party elements, which provides a glimmer of its true importance to the Communists in the conduct of the war.

Enemy proselytizers aimed at foreigners, and hence they controlled American POWs. It was essentially the same as military proselytizing, with several important differences. Enemy proselytizers were political officers assigned to military units who reported through their own channels to the General Political Department (GPD)[2] of the PAVN High Command, while military proselytizers reported directly through separate Communist Party channels. Enemy proselytizing cadre were essentially a combination of intelligence collector and propaganda artist. So were the Military proselytizers, but with more clout. Military proselytizers worked closely with the Intelligence and Public Security services of the Party so that when persuasion did not work they could turn to the next weapon in the propagandist's arsenal, terror tactics. When the efforts at influence were futile, the appeals to Vietnamese nationalism had failed, the whisper campaigns had proven fruitless, or simply when a particular individual had accumulated too many "blood debts to the people," terror was used, terror in the form of assassinations of GVN officials, or bombs in the cities, or any number of means to cow those who stood against the Communist tide. It is easy to see any particular piece of this orchestra, but few Americans have realized its magnitude or cumulative effect on almost all facets of our interaction with the Communists, how the political aspects dominate their thinking, and in turn, their designs on the POW/MIA issue.

During the time I worked at the Chieu Hoi Center I met some very interesting former Communists, who taught me much of this. Colonel Phan Mau whom I mentioned previously was one such individual. In the earlier stages of the war he commanded a Battalion, and eventually he was promoted to Regimental Commander. His Battalion had captured an American named James McLean in 1965 when it overran a camp in Phuoc Long province. McLean never returned home and he eventually became a well-known discrepancy case, but at the time I was only vaguely aware of this information. Mau never mentioned McLean by name but he did tell me that in his opinion one of the best methods to use in capturing American troops was to arrange for them to develop relations with Vietnamese females working for the Communist side. According to Mau, once the soldier became intimate with the woman he could be plied with liquor and easily captured during an illicit rendezvous. Even those investigating the POW/MIA issue have rarely understood this technique.

Mau was an intelligent man who had worked his way up the ranks. But after he saw the senseless slaughter of his men during the Tet offensive, he decided to rally. Mau provided me with tremendous insights into the Communists, but there was no doubt he was a prima donna. He wanted a monthly stipend for cooperating, a Honda motorcycle and a Zenith "Transoceanic" radio. To me, it was a useful exchange for the education I received in Communist military and political structures. Since he was a native of Nha Trang, I took him out occasionally for dinners of the famous Nha Trang lobster at the "Viet-My" restaurant in Saigon. It was rumored that the spraying of Agent Orange by the U.S. Air Force in the Central Highlands was the main reason Nha Trang lobsters were some of the world's biggest. Once sprayed with the powerful chemical, leaves from the trees fell into the streams and rivers to be carried out to sea. Floating down to the ocean with the leaves were all types of insects. All the lobsters needed to do for food was to wait at the mouths of the waterways. I can only imagine how much of the powerful carcinogenic chemical I ingested from the food and from drinking the water in the streams of the Central Highlands.

Besides Mau, I was fortunate to have unlimited access to many other cadre on a wide range of subjects. On several occasions I worked with the Phoenix Project and the highly secret Studies and Operations Group (SOG) to interrogate captured enemy cadre and soldiers. One major mission was determining how the Communists had achieved such a degree of surprise in launching the 1968 Tet offensive. MACV intelligence tasked us to examine routine enemy actions taken prior to major offensives, hoping that the survey results would serve as a base line for indications of future Communist attacks. I spent a significant amount of time interrogating personnel involved in the decision making process from near the top to the very bottom of the Communist infrastructure. I worked diligently on this assignment with many cadre, especially with Senior Colonel Tam Ha,[3] the highest-ranking cadre I ever interrogated. The insights I gained from this and many other similar projects served me tremendously in the years ahead.

For instance, another subject assigned to me was Scientific/Medical. I was periodically called to act as an interpreter for meetings of the Joint Herbicide Review (Agent Orange) Committee. Representatives from the GVN, the American Embassy in Saigon, and the Chemical Operations Division of MACV Intelligence held these meetings to discuss recommendations for areas to be sprayed, as well as for the number of sorties to be flown. Although the regions proposed by the American side were selected based on the need to deny cover to Communist forces, I gained the impression that the GVN side had another agenda. It appeared that the South Vietnamese officials were proposing areas for defoliation in which they had a personal economic interest, such as land clearing for the harvesting of timber or agricultural production.

As part of my Scientific/Medical duties, I was also occasionally tasked to conduct interrogations of doctors and other Communist medical personnel at the National Interrogation Center. This was a field for which I was understandably lacking in knowledge, so extensive research on my part was required prior to each session. Although I was never reluctant to undertake such assigned tasks, I was constantly puzzled by the persistent American requests for information on aspects of biological warfare. Judging from the content of the questions, the U.S. Intelligence Community was far more interested in learning the effects of biological warfare on Communist forces than the ability of the Communists to employ such weapons on American units. Many of these questions involved the level of bubonic plague and malaria in the Communist units, and the use of rodents or parasites as vectors. There were also a surprising number of questions concerning the effects of chemicals on Communist forces. While I'm not suggesting that U.S. forces ever used such weapons, I believe that the efforts by the Chinese Communists during the Korean War to smear United Nation (UN) forces with such crimes probably sparked an effort by American Intelligence to uncover any such information in case these charges were resurrected. Forewarned is forearmed as the saying goes.

Aside from my Scientific/Medical acquisition tasks, I was also focused on Third Country Order of Battle intelligence regarding Vietnamese Communist forces operating in Laos and Cambodia. My responsibilities included tracking the different methods of Communist infiltration and logistics into South Vietnam. One of the strangest interrogations I conducted in this area was with a PAVN truck driver who was captured inside Cambodia near the COSVN headquarters. Due to security controls the driver had not been permitted to examine his cargo, but he was certain that he was hauling a load of dishes for high-ranking officials because he had seen pictures of glasses on the exterior of the containers as they were being loaded. I submitted my report through normal channels, but my gut told me there was something wrong with a "shipment of dishes" down the Ho Chi Minh trail. Several months later, I had my answer. As I waited in line at the Army Post Office, I saw glasses printed on the sides of shipping boxes denoting "Fragile." At that point I realized that the PAVN driver was most likely transporting sensitive equipment rather than dishes.

Many interrogations like this produced confusing intelligence, or sources would get many things right and some points wrong, and vice versa. It is simply the nature of the beast, and individuals not trained in the skill of interrogation don't realize how hard it is to produce useable intelligence from any person, let alone someone from a different culture who speaks another language. Sources ranged from the outright deceptive, to the sullen and uncooperative, to individuals that were trying their best to help, or at least tell their new master what they thought he wanted to hear. The general lack of education among the enemy population, the staggering cultural differences and many other issues could often impede the gathering of constructive intelligence. Further, the heavy compartmentalization of information in the Communist system also served to obstruct this goal. The incident with the PAVN truck driver was just one of many lessons I learned, not only about interrogations, but about understanding seemingly inconsistent pieces of information.

I was also assigned to a mobile "Go Team" specially tailored for rapid-response missions throughout Indochina, including captured Lao or Cambodians. These teams were designed to quickly exploit recently captured high-ranking cadre or other important sources of information. Normally reserved only for Communist cadre with the rank of Major or above, this category also included sources involved in intelligence duties or those with special knowledge of signal communications or codes. Sometimes the POWs weren't Vietnamese, so we had to bring along French-speaking Vietnamese who would translate from English into French and then back again to tell us what the source said. This system did not work very well, and I vowed that I would never get caught in this situation again. It was on these "Go Team" missions that I received my first introduction to the POW/MIA issue, which began almost twenty-five years of work on the recovery of American prisoners and missing in action. Not only did I gain new information on specific cases, the sessions served to make me particularly aware of enemy tactics designed for Americans such as the luring strategy described by Colonel Mau.

Finally, my second tour in Vietnam was over and I left in November 1968. I had spent all of it engaged in exploitation of enemy POWs or those who had rallied to our side. I had also worked closely with hundreds of captured enemy documents. The constant demands for Intelligence placed us all under a great strain, but as a learning experience it was without peer. I had survived and had helped to blunt a major Communist offensive. Now it was time to head home. Having requested an assignment on "jump status," I was assigned to the 6th Special Forces Group at Fort Bragg, North Carolina. This was my first assignment to the Special Forces and the legendary Green Berets, and for an infantryman, it was a tremendous honor. Although I had already completed jump school and jumpmaster training, since I had not made any parachute jumps while assigned to the 525th MI Group, I was required to complete a refresher course in basic airborne subjects prior to receiving any other training.

Although I appreciated all the training I received while at Fort Bragg, I especially relished the education in unconventional warfare, demolitions and psychological operations. Although I believed the training on the more mundane topics might someday save my life, the Psychological Operations instruction was actually more interesting because it enabled me to compare what I learned in an American school with what I had gleaned from the Communist cadre at the three interrogation Centers in Saigon. The priceless insights I gained into their mindset through the months of interrogation and study were a wonderful foil for my American textbooks. While I soon came to the conclusion that the methods utilized by both sides for the development of propaganda themes for selected audiences and influence groups were not that far apart, the difference was that the Communists truly believed in propaganda's significance and the critical role it could play in shaping the battlefield, while the Americans, as is our national culture, only paid lip service to it.

While I continued to ruminate about these issues, I had few opportunities to apply them. Eventually I was transferred from the 6th Special Forces Group to the Joint Unconventional Task Force Alpha, which was located in an area of the JFK Special Warfare Center known as the "Birdcage." Although the majority of my time was spent in training for specialized missions, I did remain involved in the POW/MIA issue when I worked to plan scenarios for prisoner and hostage rescues. Our initial dry run mission was scheduled for the Roosevelt Roads area of eastern Puerto Rico, and I was told this was one of the first missions of its kind by the American military. In this remote naval reservation the plan called for the rescue of "hostages" from an "American Embassy" compound. The exercise involved not only Special Forces personnel from Fort Bragg, but Air Commandos from Hurlburt Field in Florida and Navy SEALs as well. The SEALs participating in the exercise were launched from a naval training facility at Vieques Island, just off the coast of Puerto Rico. The hypothetical rescue conducted by the elite units of several different services uncovered one very important lesson. Inter-service coordination, particularly in rescue operations requiring split-second timing, was an extremely complex undertaking. I was told lessons learned from this initial experiment would be remembered in planning actual rescues in the months to come. Considering the disaster that befell the Americans in the desert of Iran, apparently those early lessons were lost.

After the practice exercise concluded, I went for a "Rest and Recuperation" stint in the Virgin Islands on board an aging C-47 piloted by the Task Force Chief of Staff, Brigadier General Harry C. "Heinie" Aderholt. I immediately liked Aderholt because of his many years of special operations experience, along with his gung-ho personality. He was a legend in the Special Operations field, and consequently he had been picked in 1966 to be the first commander of MACV's Joint Personnel Recovery Center, the military's POW rescue office in Vietnam. Eventually Aderholt would hold the distinction of being the last Commander of U.S. forces in Thailand. I would coordinate closely with Aderholt in postwar years after he returned to Thailand to conduct private MIA recovery efforts, some of which were successful in finding remains.

Although I was assigned as an intelligence specialist, I spent months in the field undergoing training exercises and practice missions. We honed our military skills for any eventuality, including both jungle and desert warfare, by participating in training missions in remote areas of North Carolina and Utah. I learned a great deal about character from the tough men I worked with in Special Forces. Most of the officers were former enlisted men and quite a bit older than the officers in regular line units. The majority of the enlisted men were senior noncommissioned officers with many years of experience in several different military occupational specialties. In addition to regular duties involving weapons, demolition and intelligence, some were capable of digging water wells, operating heavy equipment, constructing buildings, or performing surgery. The Special Forces personnel were entirely pragmatic and they hated anything considered "Mickey Mouse." If it wasn't mission essential, they didn't carry it; if a tactic wasn't likely to succeed, they didn't use it. Sitting around a fire while telling jokes and drinking beer, the jovial Special Forces men reminded me of fun-loving construction crews or field workers back home. But at the same time I realized that if the mission called for it, they could immediately transform themselves into calculating killers. Deceivingly docile in appearance and demeanor, it is difficult to describe these men, but the movies "Wild Bunch" or the "Magnificent Seven" bring them to mind.

Having completed two tours in Vietnam already, I felt a certain sense of *déjà vu* during the arduous reconnaissance missions of the Buck Mountain radio station in the Uwharrie National Forest, because they were somewhat similar to previous treks in the Central Highlands of Vietnam. Upon completion of the rigorous field exercises, we were served delicious food furnished by the local citizenry at Community Centers across rural North Carolina. The home-style meals brought to mind the previous treks to Montagnard villages in Vietnam. There, instead of fried chicken and potato salad, the team members had been induced to drink the fresh blood of sacrificial white chickens followed by rice wine sucked from earthen jars through hollow reeds. If it doesn't sound very appealing, you would be right, but to refuse was a major insult.

One fortunate aspect of being assigned to Special Forces was the relatively large budget available for training. One military school I had always wanted to attend was the Army's Ranger Course. The Rangers were the regular Army's top reconnaissance forces, and the right to wear the coveted "Ranger Tab" required surviving one of the most difficult schools in the Army. I found that few members of my unit at Fort Bragg were interested in Ranger training and that most held the opinion that they "didn't need to be taught how to be miserable." But Special Forces always had several slots available for Ranger school, so I took and passed the Physical Training test. However, my colleagues who declined attendance proved to be right, because Ranger school was a gut-wrenching nine-week course with no shortage of misery from day one until the end of the classes. We lived on one C-ration meal a day and only an average of two hours sleep per night while undergoing extremely intense training and physical exertion. Many of the soldiers at the school were preparing to go to Vietnam, and they would need all the insights the demanding instructors could provide them. While I graduated at the top of my class in several military schools, I was happy simply to finish the Ranger course. I consider it one of the high points in my career when I graduated from Ranger School at Eglin Air Base, Florida, because at one time the Florida Ranger Camp was commanded by my former boss, Colonel Charlie Beckwith, while the Air Base Commander, Brigadier General Heinie Aderholt, pinned on my Ranger tab.

The holiday season during the winter of 1969 was a truly joyous occasion for my family. Our daughter, Andrea Christine, was born Christmas Eve night. However, Andrea was only two months old when my request for language training was finally approved. I had previously requested training in the Thai language, and I quickly received orders for reassignment to the Defense Language Institute West Coast Branch located in Monterey, California. The course was hard, as the Thai language is quite different from Vietnamese, especially the method of writing. During the French colonial period the Vietnamese language had been romanized by a Jesuit priest, Alexander de Rhoades. Thai, however, was based on ancient Hindu Sanskrit known as "Pali." Although difficult to learn, I had already established good study habits and was accustomed to the regimen of memorizing dialogue. After a considerable amount of hard work and dedication, I received a 97.8 academic average for the course. I wrote a lengthy term paper entirely in Thai on the Thai system of government, which earned me the prestigious "Commandant's Award," the highest award possible at the Defense Language Institute. Although the Lao language was not taught at the Defense Language Institute, I was interested in this language as well. I remembered the frustrating episodes from the "Go Teams" when we had to use French-speaking Vietnamese to translate for us with the captured Lao and Cambodians, and so I decided also to learn Lao. But the Language Institute didn't teach Lao. Only the State Department did, so I ordered the books from State. Since the Thai and Lao were related languages, and since I had already ordered the Lao language books, I was able to convince my instructors to allow me to study Lao as a secondary language during the last few months of the twelve-month Thai course. At the end of the year, I could speak Thai and Lao, plus several different dialects of Vietnamese and Montagnard and a smattering of French.

After the completion of the course in February 1971, I had planned on a subsequent assignment back to Southeast Asia. However, due to the withdrawal of U.S. troops from the area in conjunction with the "Vietnamization" program, I was assigned instead to the 50th Military Intelligence Detachment (MID) at Schofield Barracks in Hawaii, my old stomping ground. Indochina specialists primarily manned the 50th MID in a sort of military holding pattern, while waiting for the outcome of the Paris Peace negotiations. Since all realized they were subject to deployment back into Vietnam at any time, there was a genuine effort by everyone to stay current on the situation.

The men who manned the 50th MID were some of the best Vietnamese linguists in the Army. One man, Chief Warrant Officer (CWO) William G. Hutchinson, had served in Vietnam as early as 1955. One of the military's most experienced Intelligence Specialists, "Hutch" continued to work in Vietnam as late as 1999 as a member of the Defense Intelligence Agency's (DIA) "Stony Beach" team conducting interviews with Vietnamese on American POW/MIAs. Another Vietnamese linguist, CWO Charles McDonald, had been awarded the Distinguished Service Cross in September 1966. As a Sergeant with the 101st Airborne, MacDonald had led his platoon on a POW camp raid in VC infested Phu Yen Province. Rounding out the "Vietnamese Mafia" in the MID was CWO Robert Destatte, another fluent Vietnamese linguist who had served with the 173rd Airborne Brigade in Vietnam.

Since the war was far from over, and with the POW/MIA issue looming ever larger in the Vietnam imbroglio, the importance of preparing U.S. military personnel en route to Vietnam for possible capture by Communist forces was stressed by the command. A POW training program had been in existence in prior years, but it displayed little initiative. The preponderance of the curriculum consisted of harassment and depravation, and not on overcoming the psychological aspects of captivity. Thus, the training was perceived as unrealistic and a waste of time. Since Vietnamese Communist doctrine called for the exploitation of POWs through heavy emphasis on reeducation, pressure for anti-war statements, and then possible recruitment, the 50th MID was tasked to make the training more effective. Using our fevered imaginations, we created a hypothetical Communist country in Hawaii, and the resultant "People's Republic of Falconia" was established at the Jungle Warfare Indoctrination Center. It was a chance to put some of what I had learned to the test.

As part of the scenario to make the training as realistic as possible, the MID instructors fashioned a Communist POW camp with fabricated uniforms complete with Communist rank insignia and headgear. We obtained Communist propaganda leaflets, posters, and flags from the Combined Documents Exploitation Center in Saigon to display throughout the fictional POW compound. To add realism, Mr. Destatte wrote to the People's Republic of China and requested Chinese Communist publications. Shortly after the glossy periodicals began to arrive at the unit mailroom of the 50th MID, Destatte found he was under investigation for maintaining contacts with a foreign country considered hostile to the United States. Although the other members of the training team found this state of affairs humorous and kidded him about it, Destatte was obviously less amused by the situation than we were.

To facilitate indoctrination, I obtained verbatim transcripts from the Foreign Broadcast Information Service (a U.S. office that monitors and translates foreign media) of Radio Hanoi. After taking the transcripts to a professional Navy broadcaster for recording, he made several propaganda speeches using all the typical Communist terminology. The tapes were then played over a loudspeaker system in the camp. To increase the loneliness and despair of the POWs, I recruited my wife Nova to record a "letters from home" segment with accompanying sobs and moans. The broadcasts were very effective and most who heard them and became POWs later agreed that they were as good as anything Hanoi Hannah produced.

The program was available to Army personnel as well as Navy and Marine Corps aviators from the Hawaii area. In their critiques the majority of aviators truly appreciated the training because they had very little knowledge of the Communist exploitation efforts. They indicated that the program instilled confidence in them by making them aware of what they were up against if captured. Most of the Army ground troops, however, reluctantly participated because they viewed the possibility of being captured in much the same way they considered protection from venereal disease: "it always happens to the other guy."

Therefore, the MID Commander wanted to conduct serious training to grab the troops' attention, but at the same time he was hindered by the prohibition against excessive force. To solve this problem I took several new rookies from the MID and had them "assigned" to the troop units scheduled for training a few days before the units were to report at the Jungle Center. As the camp's "Indoctrination Officer," I began my lectures by eliciting the cooperation of the new "replacements." After they appeared to be recalcitrant I followed up with feigned physical attacks on them. Since I had already rehearsed these movements with the men in advance and they wore padded liners beneath their fatigues, the sessions were frightening but safe. After I coerced cooperation from them, I turned my attention to the regular trainees. Even though the trainees had already been counseled by their commanders not to provide any information or cooperate with the "enemy," it was not unusual to see many of them begin to immediately collaborate after the feigned capitulation of my foils.

Many of the units undergoing training had been told in advance to stick together and work as a team. In order to demonstrate how easily confidence in the leadership can be broken, the instructors delivered several full boxes of rations to a compound housing the officers and NCOs while at the same time delivering similar empty boxes to the enlisted men. The officers and sergeants assumed the enlisted men were being fed, while the enlisted men assumed their leaders would save them some of the food they received. It didn't take long for morale to drop in this situation. Another ruse was to invite the officers in one at a time for an "off the record" critique. Playboy magazines, hot coffee and pastries were placed on a table in the waiting room. While the officers gazed at the magazines and gorged themselves a hidden camera photographed the scene. Then we held an indoctrination session the following morning to emphasize to the enlisted men the futility of not cooperating. As I harangued the hungry soldiers, they stood in formation beneath a large bulletin board on which the photos of the pastry-eating officers were posted.

As the peace negotiations dragged on in Paris, support for the Vietnam war ebbed to its lowest level. It was not a good time to go anywhere in a military uniform. Soon the entire 25th Infantry Division relocated back to Hawaii. After the signing of the Paris Peace Agreements in January 1973 everyone seemed content to "give peace a chance." For the most part I had forgotten about Vietnam and continued sharpening my Thai language skills in preparation for a tour in that country. To further increase my knowledge of Asia, I also attended Chaminade University full time at night and on weekends for three years. Despite a heavy class schedule, I was still required to perform my regular intelligence duties within my unit. It was an incredibly stressful time for me; between doing my regular duties, going to the field and various temporary duty trips, I had to concentrate on the complex area-related courses such as Asian Philosophy, Religion, and Political Science. Eventually, I strained my eyesight so badly that before long I literally began to see yellow. Only after a Doctor's intervention did I relax enough to regain my normal eyesight. Despite my separation from Vietnam, I continued to make an earnest effort to fathom Asian Communist thought patterns in preparation for future assignments to other countries. In conjunction with my studies at Chaminade I also took full advantage of the Language Laboratory at the East-West Center in Honolulu, focusing again on Thai, Lao and Vietnamese. In 1973, I graduated with a Bachelor's Degree.

In late January 1973 my attention was abruptly returned to Vietnam when I received a call from my old boss and fellow Chaminade graduate, Colonel Charlie Beckwith, who was now the J-3 (Operations Officer) at the Pacific Command. After determining that I still maintained proficiency in the Vietnamese language, Beckwith informed me that I would be returning to Vietnam immediately to assist with "Operation Homecoming," the special program established to support the repatriation of American POWs from Southeast Asia. The Pacific Command had been tasked to provide an interpreter and Beckwith had chosen me.

In early February I flew to Clark Airbase in the Philippines to join Air Force Colonel James R. Dennett, the Chief of the U.S. Delegation to Hanoi. I also had my first meeting with Dr. Roger Shields, the Deputy Assistant Secretary of Defense for POW/MIA Affairs. For the next few months I worked as an Interpreter-Translator for both Shields and Dennett as the Communist authorities released almost six hundred American POWs. The POWs were released in increments scheduled to correspond with the withdrawal of U.S. military forces from Vietnam, with the last group of POWs to be released on March 29, 1973 simultaneously with the final departure of U.S. troops.

When the North Vietnamese began releasing the American POWs in Hanoi, I was tapped to go as an interpreter with the American officials. This was one of the true honors of my career. On my first mission to North Vietnam in February 1973 the aircraft landed at Gia Lam, an aging French-era airfield located across the Red River from Hanoi. As the aircraft approached for landing I could see empty Surface-To-Air missile pads deployed on top of dikes constructed along the Red River, as well as rain swollen streams and rice paddies around the area. I thought about how U.S. pilots had been restricted from bombing the dikes due to humanitarian concerns, while the deceitful North Vietnamese took advantage of the situation by using the dikes as solid firing positions from which to down American planes. I also recalled the huge outcry from various anti-war types about how the Air Force was deliberating bombing the dikes, which in fact they had been ordered to avoid. A crime against humanity they shouted, while never mentioning how the North Vietnamese had used the dikes as launch platforms. Now, at the last minute, the North Vietnamese had removed the missiles to prevent the international news media from disclosing their treachery. I also observed that what at first appeared to be houses of local residents were actually anti-aircraft firing positions. In a crafty disguise the North Vietnamese had removed one half of each thatched roof and draped blue plastic sheeting over the guns.

Although I expected to see some destruction from the Christmas bombing campaign, the sight of the still smoldering ruins of the Gia Lam railroad yard two months removed from the air assault astounded me. Contorted locomotives and freight cars were strewn haphazardly throughout the huge compound. Blackened steel rails twisted like pretzels protruded from the pockmarked ground. Local residents walking by the facility actually maintained gaits more akin to a stagger while staring out endlessly into space, giving me a sobering indication as to the severity of the final bombing attacks. Based on the way the people on the street acted, I considered it a possibility that at the time the bombing was halted the North Vietnamese were on the verge of capitulation.

To ensure that the release was conducted in an orderly fashion, both sides agreed that as the men were turned over to U.S. authorities, their names would be called off from a list provided by either the Democratic Republic of Vietnam (DRV, or North Vietnam), or the Provisional Revolutionary Government (PRG, or Viet Cong). The Communists were continuing to maintain the fiction of a separate and indigenous movement in the South. Depending on where they were captured, a POW belonged to either group.

During their years of incarceration, the American POWs had given nicknames to the various Communist cadre who had served as their interrogators and guards. The returning POWs identified the Communist cadre who called off the names of the prisoners over a public address system at Gia Lam Airport as "Rabbit." The POWs described Rabbit as a sadistic zealot known for his brutal treatment of the prisoners. While the freed POWs provided us the nicknames they had given the prison cadre, few knew any real names. I would later learn that Rabbit was actually Nguyen Minh Y. In later years, he would be promoted to Colonel, and became Chief of the Civilian Proselytizing Department of the People's Army of Vietnam. Another prison cadre who served as my counterpart interpreter for the North Vietnamese delegation during the operation was First Lieutenant Nguyen Van Ngoc. The American POWs held in the North knew him as the "soft soap fairy." While the "Rabbit" had earned his nickname for some prominent teeth and not his character, Ngoc had tried the opposite, gentler approach with the Americans and hence had earned the sobriquet. I considered the possibility that Nguyen Van Ngoc and Nguyen Minh Y were using a "good cop-bad cop" routine on the American prisoners.

Trying to completely identify Communist cadre involved with the handling of American POWs, both in the South and in the main prisons of the North, was difficult due to Vietnamese security measures. A strange combination of Buddhist self-reserve and Communist paranoia combined to make normal biographical data the hardest information to uncover in Vietnam. Most Communists assumed an alias or a cover name, called *bi danh* (secret name) in Vietnamese, to protect their identities. When one joined the Party, they changed their given name to a Party name. Then their Party name was concealed behind their cover name. For instance, during the release in Hanoi of the American personnel captured in the South, the primary interlocutor was Colonel Bui Van Thanh. In 1993, while working in Can Tho, a city in the Mekong Delta region of South Vietnam, I met Thanh again. At the time I had the impression that Thanh was a face from the past but I was unable to recall him. One evening after dinner, and after having consumed a large amount of rice whiskey, Thanh disclosed the fact that he was actually Senior Colonel Bui Thanh Ngon, Chief of the Enemy Proselytizing Department of the South Vietnam Liberation Armed Forces (the Communist name for the Viet Cong forces) during the war. I was not surprised to learn that during the repatriation operation Thanh had used a cover name. In the South, even the Communist military units used secret codes to identify themselves.

The importance of this came years later as the United States tried to determine whom on the Vietnamese side would possess important POW/MIA knowledge. If they had fully cooperated, we wouldn't have had to attempt to divine who were the various prison cadre, but the Vietnamese weren't interested in assisting us. For example, throughout the POW release I noticed an inconspicuous PAVN Major observing the proceedings from a vantage point to the rear of the signing table. I had no idea who the man was, but some eighteen years later I would learn he was Pham Duc Dai, now a Colonel and a key member of the POW/MIA Archives Research Program. In 1992 he would provide information on missing American personnel associated with what would become known as the "Discrepancy Case List" to members of the Senate Select Committee on POW/MIA Affairs. More importantly, Dai was instrumental in turning over thousands of documents and photographs on American POW/MIAs collected by the PAVN Central Military Museum, of which Dai was the head.[4]

Although I was assigned to the Homecoming Project primarily due to my Vietnamese language capability, the Communist Pathet Lao inadvertently involved me in their orchestrated release of American POWs. The command element of the Homecoming Project had planned to utilize the Lao skills of a young U.S. Army Special Forces Captain assigned to a unit on Okinawa. I met with the Captain several times but did not have an opportunity to gauge his language skills. I did have some reservations, however, because the Captain had only recently developed his abilities at a local Education Center in Okinawa. I knew that such courses were vastly inferior to the structured language training organized by the Defense Language Institute. I did inquire as to whether the young Captain contemplated any problems when called upon to go to Hanoi, but he indicated that he did not anticipate any difficulties.

In a surprise announcement, on March 28, 1973 the Homecoming Command suddenly informed us that the Pathet Lao would be releasing its American POWs in Hanoi the following day. That same evening I heard a knock on my door. Apparently, at the last minute the young Captain had qualms about his newly acquired ability to interpret the proceedings. Considerably embarrassed, he admitted to me that his language skills were not adequate to go on this sensitive mission. He added that he had been led to believe that a release of American POWs by the Pathet Lao was highly unlikely and that was why he had decided to remain at Clark, rather than return to his unit in Okinawa. Sheepishly, the

Captain told me that since there was no time for sending a replacement from the U.S., the Command element would only release him from the assignment if he could find a Lao speaker there in the Philippines. The young Captain was greatly relieved when I agreed to take his place on what would prove to be one of the most novel trips of my career.

When I arrived at the flight line the following morning I found no one else waiting to board the aircraft bound for Hanoi. While trying to locate the other passengers on the manifest, I soon learned that I was the only passenger scheduled for the flight. Apparently the Pathet Lao had agreed to meet with a maximum of two U.S. officials. The second individual was Lieutenant Colonel Lawrence Robson, who was then assigned to the Four Party Joint Military Commission in Saigon. Lieutenant Colonel Robson was to fly directly to Hanoi where we would meet. I boarded the empty aircraft and as luck would have it, I arrived in Hanoi several hours prior to link-up. Having attended numerous briefings about the dangers of falling into Communist hands, I backed up to a wall in the airport and remained vigilant throughout the morning. Being all alone in the enemy capital caused my imagination to run wild, and I thought that everyone who approached me was an international terrorist or perhaps a spy. After what seemed to be an endless wait, I was greatly relieved when Robson entered the old-fashioned terminal.

Since almost six hundred men were MIA in Laos, practically everyone involved in Operation Homecoming anticipated a large number of live POWs would be released from that country. This belief was largely based on wartime statements made by the Pathet Lao spokesman in Vientiane, Soth Pethrasy (who was allowed to maintain an office in the city), about holding men, and the known capture near Sam Neua, the Pathet Lao wartime capital, of aviators Charles Shelton and David Hrdlicka. The situation quickly became tense, however, when the Pathet Lao informed the U.S. side that during this sole repatriation of Americans by the Pathet Lao, only nine American POWs would be returned. These men, currently held captive in Hanoi, had either been captured by Vietnamese forces in Laos or had been turned over to them by the Pathet Lao. No American POWs were coming directly from the Pathet Lao. It quickly became obvious the Lao were there grudgingly, having been forced by their Vietnamese counterparts. The Lao instead hoped for direct negotiations and recognition by the U.S. They also appeared disinclined to release the nine POWs. After some discussions, they relented, but the Pathet Lao insisted that Lieutenant Colonel Robson sign a document acknowledging receipt of "the U.S. POWs captured in Laos during the war," with no indication as to the actual number. Robson was unsure of what he should do, so I recommended that the documents be amended to reflect the actual number nine. Robson agreed and to the chagrin of the Pathet Lao, I quickly made pen and ink changes to both the English and Lao language versions of the papers.

After signing the document, Robson passed them back to the Pathet Lao side with a request for an explanation as to the small number of men being released. The Pathet Lao representative avoided answering the question by saying, "the fighting in Laos has not yet ended," and "the situation in Laos is different from that of Vietnam." While brooding over the changes made to the documents, the Pathet Lao representative informed us that he was not authorized to accept any changes. Seemingly disconcerted, the senior Lao officer called for a recess as his delegation proceeded to follow him from the meeting room to a communications shack at the end of the terminal. At the same time, the waiting American POWs were being held nearby, unaware of the events swirling around them. It was quite possible the Lao would renege on releasing "their" American POWs. Thankfully, however, after a short break the Lao delegation returned to the table and agreed to sign the documents and release the nine Americans to U.S. control. One additional POW, a Canadian, was set free at the same time but in a separate ceremony.

After the release by the Pathet Lao the operation continued smoothly, and eventually all the men were safely transported from Vietnam to Clark Airbase. There were some other tense moments, however, such as the next day when the Vietnamese cadre in charge at the pick-up point indicated that some of the men might want to remain in Vietnam rather than return home. Specifically mentioned was Bobby Joe Keese, a civilian pilot who hijacked an aircraft chartered in Thailand and forced the pilot to land inside North Vietnam. According to the cadre, Keese was having second thoughts about returning to the States. However, upon reflection, he got on the plane.

Keese was a very unstable man. He ultimately served time in American prisons for several different crimes, including posing as a federal official in two schemes to bilk a company in a purchasing scam, theft of an airplane, and for conspiracy in the death of a U.S. Consul in Hermosillo, Mexico. In August 1998 Keese was released from prison after a sentence for kidnapping and ransom. Several months later in January 1999, Keese was arrested again for stealing another airplane. Although Keese had the rings, Rolex watch, and the driver's license of the dead pilot with Keese's picture glued on it, and the man's credit cards in his possession when arrested, the body of the pilot was never found.

I could only assume that other than Keese, the reference to possible stay-behinds pertained to members of the so-called "Peace Group." The Peace Group was comprised of approximately ten junior enlisted men that were captured in South Vietnam and later moved to the outskirts of Hanoi prior to Operation Homecoming. This group cooperated with the enemy in providing information and in making propaganda broadcasts aimed at lowering the morale of American troops.

There was one last odd note before the release of American POWs was completed, one that has always troubled me for its implications about other unreleased Americans. On March 29, 1973 the final day of the release of the American POWs in the North, in Saigon the senior Communist officer participating in the implementation of the cease-fire in the South, Major General Tran Van Tra, approached the Chief of the U.S. Delegation, Major General Woodward. Tra informed Woodward of one additional POW in South Vietnam who had not been released in early February with the other Americans still held in the South. The last POW was Army Captain Robert White, who was captured when his OV-1C "Bird Dog" was downed by enemy fire on November 15, 1969. According to Tra, difficulties in communication had prevented the repatriation of this American officer in Tra Vinh province in South Vietnam's Mekong Delta region.

Tra related to Woodward that if given the means to travel to Hanoi for a few days, he would arrange for the repatriation of the last POW. Tra also hinted to Woodward that he might "stop by Laos," thus raising the possibility that he might use his good offices in convincing the Pathet Lao to release additional U.S. personnel detained in that country. Woodward quickly arranged for a C-130 aircraft to fly Tra to Hanoi, where he arrived on the morning of March 30. Although Tra kept part of the bargain by arranging the release of Captain White on April 1, 1973, when the C-130 arrived at Gia Lam Airport in Hanoi three days later, Tra was nowhere to be seen. One of Tra's staff officers did arrive at the airport to inform the C-130 crew that Tra would not be returning to Saigon. When the C-130 arrived back at Tan Son Nhut with no passengers on board, hope for the release of more POWs from Laos were quickly replaced by frustration and disgust. Everyone involved saw Tra's maneuver as another deceptive ploy by the Communists, in this case, a trick to remove the senior Communist cadre participating in the implementation of the peace process in the South from what was to ultimately become the scene of fierce combat. For those who suspected the Communists would again go back on their word and violate the cease-fire, Tra's devious departure provided convincing evidence of continuing duplicity on the part of Hanoi. It was a standard Communist Vietnamese military tactic, wherein the Commander always personally conducts his own reconnaissance prior to launching the attack on an objective. Having completed his reconnaissance, Tra eventually returned to COSVN headquarters on the Vietnam-Cambodia border to plan for the final attack. Further, Tra's statement that the Communists had not known White was still a prisoner was a sheer lie in my opinion, and the question as to whether other American POWs were still being held in South Vietnam or in Laos as bargaining chips was an obvious one.

After Operation Homecoming was over I returned to the 50th MID. No sooner had I landed than Colonel Beckwith contacted me again. Beckwith said he had just spoken with my old battalion commander, now Brigadier General Robert C. Kingston, who had been chosen as the Commander of the newly formed Joint Casualty Resolution Center (JCRC) at Nakhon Phanom (NKP), Thailand. During the Vietnam War the air base at Nakhon Phanom had served as the main location for Search and Rescue and Special Operations missions into Laos. The new JCRC organization was a joint service unit designed to replace the wartime Joint Personnel Recovery Center. According to Beckwith, Kingston was mobilizing teams to go back into postwar Vietnam and search for MIAs, and he had requested me by name to go on these missions.

I soon found myself at Bangkok's Don Muang Airport boarding a sweltering aircraft headed for NKP. When I arrived at NKP, located on the western bank of the Mekong River separating Laos from Thailand, I found that many former comrades from the JFK Center were already training there. Since the ceasefire agreement prohibited the introduction of armed units back into the territory of Vietnam, Kingston began difficult negotiations with the Government of Vietnam, as well as the American Embassy in Saigon, to permit our teams to carry shotguns for protection against "wild animals." In reality this was a legitimate concern, because large carnivores, most notably man-eating tigers, inhabited Vietnam. After considerable haggling, both the South Vietnamese and the embassy conceded to Kingston's request. To maintain proficiency with the new weapons, a skeet range previously used by Air Force Security Police was modified for the MIA search teams. Other training consisted primarily of physical exercise, emergency medical training, and repelling from helicopters. The search teams were finally organized into "Field Team Alpha" for operations in Vietnam, commanded by Colonel Beckwith, and "Field Team Bravo" for operations in Laos and Cambodia commanded by Lieutenant Colonel Sully Fontaine. I was assigned to Colonel Beckwith's team working for Major Chester Garret, who had attended Jump School with me in 1960.

Operations in Vietnam began with the field teams being guided to crash sites in the Central Highlands by Montagnards. Initially the teams met with considerable success. However, in other areas serious problems were encountered. Seeking approval for search operations from the upper echelons of both the U.S. and South Vietnamese governments quickly became a cumbersome process. The problem was further compounded by the requirement to fully inform all delegations of the Four Party Joint Military Team (FPJMT), tasked with the responsibility of implementing Article 8(b) of the Paris Agreements pertaining to the accounting for POWs and MIAs.

The FPJMT had replaced the Four Party Joint Commission at the end of the first sixty days following the signing of the Peace Accords, and was comprised of delegations representing the United States, the Republic of Vietnam, the Democratic Republic of Vietnam and the Provisional Revolutionary Government. Article 8(b) formed the basis for recovery efforts of all four parties to the conflict. According to the wording of Article 8(b): "The parties shall help each other to get information about those military personnel and foreign civilians of the parties missing in action, to determine the location and take care of the graves of the dead so as to facilitate the exhumation and repatriation of the remains, and to take such other measures as may be required to get information about those still considered missing in action." The Communists had different plans, however.

Aside from coordinating the U.S. field efforts, I traveled to Hanoi to assist in the repatriation of the remains of those Americans who had died in captivity in North Vietnam. During one trip in May 1973, North Vietnamese officials escorted me to a small cemetery located south of Hanoi. The Vietnamese called this walled compound "Van Dien." Shrouded in sea pine trees, it served as the municipal cemetery for the city of Hanoi. According to Vietnamese tradition, when a death occurred the body was buried in order for the natural decomposition process to occur. After the process was completed, the remains were exhumed and prepared in a limewater solution as a preservative. The remains were then returned to the native village of the decedent for final burial. The contagious disease section of the Ministry of Health normally required a waiting period of three years before remains could be exhumed. In the countryside, however, this requirement was often lowered to one year.

I was also taken to a larger cemetery called "Ba Huyen" located near the town of Bac Giang in Ha Bac province north of Hanoi. The Ba Huyen cemetery was for French soldiers. The PAVN Graves Management Agency of the Military Justice Department administered the cemetery. The French government paid handsomely for maintenance of this large burial ground containing some 40,000 graves of French military personnel. I was not sure if our visits were for accounting purposes or for psychological effect. The task of recovering and identifying over twenty-five hundred men was already mind boggling, but the feeling in the pit of my stomach as I walked through thousands of French graves at Ba Huyen served as a reminder of the awesome responsibility I and others involved in the accounting effort faced. It was obvious that many of the French servicemen were casualties of the famed Foreign Legion, since the array of headstones included Christian crosses, Stars of David, and the Muslim crescent and star. All were painted ghostly white from powdered lime mixed with water.

Both the Ba Huyen and Van Dien cemeteries contained the remains of American POWs who died while being held prisoner in North Vietnam. Although the remains of most of the Americans were interred at Ba Huyen, some graves were also observed at Van Dien. Based on the names inscribed on the headstones at Van Dien, at least one man buried there was a Thai national named "Thong Dy." According to the Vietnamese officials, the American POWs had been first interred at Van Dien and later disinterred and moved to Ba Huyen. At some point during the disinterment the remains of the Thai national had been confused with the remains of an American. The officials never did clarify the matter but they did maintain that the mistake was resolved prior to repatriation of the remains.

During my first trip to Van Dien I observed a rotund Asian man in a small masonry building near the entrance to the cemetery. The white-clad individual was leaning over human skeletal remains laid out on a concrete slab at the center of the building. I later observed the same man at Gia Lam Airfield where American remains were normally examined prior to being placed on board U.S. Air Force aircraft. Six years later this same individual would defect and become known to the world as "The Mortician." This Vietnamese official of ethnic Chinese origin became our first source who had actually been involved in processing remains. For years the Vietnamese had denied they were storing the remains of dead Americans, but the Mortician provided us first hand evidence that in fact the Vietnamese had exhumed and stored the remains of several hundred American dead, men whose fates often were unknown to the U.S. government and consequently to their families. Eventually, the weight of the Mortician's testimony before the U.S. Congress concerning Vietnam's manipulation of the POW/MIA issue, combined with the discovery of chemical preservatives on the skeletons of American MIAs unilaterally turned over by the Vietnamese, forced them to recant.

Despite this inconvertible proof, the Vietnamese would only grudgingly admit they had been warehousing remains and personal effects of the deceased. Hanoi had pledged in early April 1973 to "scrupulously" implement Article 8(b) of the Paris Agreement, and the North Vietnamese Delegation to the FPJMT informed the U.S. side that a campaign had been launched throughout North Vietnam to gain information about missing U.S. personnel. From the outset of negotiations, however, not only had the Communists claimed to hold absolutely no American remains, they professed to be offended by suggestions to the contrary.

The visits to Ba Huyen and Van Dien cemeteries to inspect American graves laid the groundwork for the first major repatriation of U.S. remains to American soil. In February 1974 DRV representatives informed us that based on Saigon's release of some political prisoners, Hanoi would return the twenty-three remains in March, which they did.

To facilitate coordination and to prepare for anticipated future large-scale operations throughout Vietnam, the JCRC established two Liaison Offices. One was called the "Hanoi Liaison Office," while the second carried the title "Saigon Liaison Office." Since I had already been working in North Vietnam with the Operation Homecoming Repatriation Team, I was assigned to the "Hanoi Liaison Office." Because Communist claims of cooperation in resolving the important issue were only feigned, the DRV stalled the establishment of the Hanoi Liaison Office. Kingston, however, was determined to take full advantage of what was most likely a temporary lull in the fighting, and he decided to place both Liaison Offices in the Special Operations Division of the Defense Attaché Office (DAO) in Saigon. These offices served as the focal point for all Joint Casualty Resolution Center field operations in Vietnam. A similar Liaison Office was established in the American Embassy in Vientiane, Laos.

In conducting field investigations in the South, the JCRC meticulously followed the procedures involved in obtaining permission and informing all parties concerned. As a further courtesy and to show "good faith" to the Communist delegations that the operations were strictly of a humanitarian nature, we invited them to accompany the search teams into the field. We also asked the South Vietnamese to participate.

Although the GVN delegation routinely accepted the invitations from the Joint Casualty center, neither the DRV nor PRG ever gave a positive response. In fact, these delegations rarely rendered any response at all. In the interim the search teams continued to arrive from Thailand to participate in field operations throughout South Vietnam. Recovery efforts were also planned for American aircraft losses out at sea. As a qualified diver, I participated in one operation off the coast of Central Vietnam. The operation involved a 120-foot "Seatender" vessel pulling a six-foot long "sonar fish" in an overlapping grid pattern that afforded full coverage of the ocean floor. Although we were able to locate some aircraft wreckage and take it aboard, we didn't discover any human remains during the four month long operation. Due to the lack of significant results and the cost involved the project was abandoned.

Unilateral ground recovery efforts proceeded smoothly with twenty-five crashes and site investigations conducted. However, progress came to an abrupt halt on December 15, 1973, when a routine operation in a populated area south of the capital in Gia Dinh province quickly deteriorated into a bloody ambush. After obtaining the necessary approvals and informing the Communist side, an unarmed JCRC team boarded clearly marked helicopters for the trip from Saigon. Shortly after arrival in the area, the team began to receive intense automatic weapons fire from what appeared to be prepared positions. As a result, two men were killed and several more seriously wounded. One of the men killed was an American Captain named Richard Rees. The second man was a Vietnamese member of the support element.

The vicious slaughter of the team members resulted in the cancellation of all unilateral American search efforts in Vietnam. In order to drive home the U.S. outrage at the vile conduct of the Communist side, the Chief of the U.S. Delegation to the FPJMT, Colonel William Tombaugh, quickly called a meeting of all four parties to the conflict. After all delegations were assembled at the regular meeting table, Tombaugh erupted into a fiery speech clearly designed to mortify even the most shameless Communist cadre. To add further emphasis Tombaugh tossed the American's fatigue shirt, still covered in blood, onto the center of the negotiation table. Tombaugh's presentation was so genuine that it had an obvious effect even on the hardened Communist cadre. However, Tombaugh had the snake by the tail instead of the head. The Communists rejected the U.S. protests, and the murder of Captain Rees was left unsolved. Like the French before them, the Americans were dealing with an adversary void of compassion but replete with perseverance in realizing its goal of placing the entire country under Communist rule.

After the American recovery operations were suspended, the JCRC continued to supervise and assist indigenous Vietnamese efforts. With the removal of the Americans, however, it quickly became obvious that our potential for success was severely diminished. With a growing lull in the activities, I requested and received a curtailment of my tour. When I returned to the 50th MID I quickly submitted a request for reassignment to Thailand, but the Military Intelligence branch had other plans. I received orders for a tour as an instructor to the U.S. Army Intelligence Center and School at Fort Huachuca, Arizona. After working as an instructor for several months I was selected for Advanced Intelligence Training at the same school.

Shortly after completing my training, in mid-summer 1974 I was contacted by the MI Branch concerning future assignments. In an odd twist of fate, according to the personnel specialists, the FPJMT sorely needed a qualified linguist to complete its mission. I was told that due to the diplomatic nature of the assignment, only volunteers would be accepted and that each member of the team must be nominated by the appropriate service chief.

At that point I had grown weary of being involved with Vietnam. The years had taken their toll on me physically and mentally. The combat, the night missions into enemy controlled areas, the interrogations and the postwar psychological games of the Communists had worn me down. After I left I paid little attention to anything in the newspapers or on television if it was associated with Vietnam. I wasn't alone. Throughout the military services there existed a feeling that America's war in Indochina was a lost cause and the word was "if you value your career, forget about Vietnam." But the uncertainty surrounding the fate of so many of my comrades continued to haunt me, and I finally decided to at least listen to what the people in the personnel shop had to say. When I called MI Branch the assignment specialist explained to me that the new job would be that of Chief Interpreter-Translator for the U.S. Delegation, FPJMT in Saigon. The specialist stressed the importance of the new position and how critical it would be in conducting negotiations with the Communists to account for over twenty-five hundred Americans still missing in Southeast Asia.

I was noncommittal and promised that I would give the new assignment serious consideration. One thing that bothered me was that only volunteers would be accepted. I had undergone rigorous and dangerous training in the past where the same "volunteers only" rule applied. Another consideration was the Thai/Lao language aspect. Becoming proficient in the new languages had required a full year of hard work, and it would be difficult for me to take an assignment where the tedious language training I underwent would most likely be wasted.

When I returned home to discuss the potential new assignment with Nova, I could see that she was deeply concerned by the thought of my returning to a war zone, as well as the prospect of having the family separated for at least another long year. At the same time, however, Nova realized that there was no assignment more important than that of accounting for more than twenty-five hundred Americans who were missing or otherwise unaccounted for. After debating the pros and cons of the new job late into the night, we both agreed that I should accept the new assignment.

After the hard decision was made I began to plan for the move back to Vietnam, while Nova began preparing to return to Old Hickory, Tennessee. At first Nova thought it would be best if she took our two children, Michael and Andrea, back home to live with their grandparents during the time I was overseas. But through research with the military wives network and general post gossip, Nova learned that after the cease-fire a significant number of American wives had moved to Vietnam to be with their spouses. She learned that most of the American wives had found employment in administrative positions in the American Embassy and Defense Attaché Office, and that schooling was available for children. Surely there would be room for three more dependents.

I was not convinced by her pleas. I recalled that Communists from all previous wars had a horrible record of respecting peace agreements, and I was wary about the presence of my family in the country. But since I had already spent so much time in Vietnam away from them, and several people assigned to the FPJMT already had their families in Saigon, I finally concluded that the cease-fire agreement had been implemented, and if it was violated, President Nixon had pledged that America would retaliate swiftly in response. I could never imagine how wrong I was or what a mistake I was making.

Chapter Three

The Wolf at the Door

I RETURNED TO SAIGON in August 1974. By any standards I had become a senior NCO, an old hand both in the Army and Vietnam. This was my third or fourth tour, depending on how you counted, but stepping off the plane, the oppressive heat hitting me like a punch in the face, no matter how hard I had previously tried to forget Vietnam, I felt like I had never left. The swirling rumors on the latest corruption scandals or what the Communists might do next were almost as bad as the climate. Saigon was always ground zero for the perverse notion of Rumor Control, known locally as "Radio Catinat," named for the street that ran past the Continental Palace Hotel, the frequent home of many news correspondents and journalists reporting on the Vietnam War.[1] Only the Vietnamese could turn the most innocuous coincidence into a wild conspiracy. Vietnamese political culture was permanently rooted in factionalism and intrigue, a survival mechanism inherited from centuries of foreign oppression, from, as one noted Western scholar would later write, "having always lived in an armed camp."

Driving around the city, I soon realized Saigon had undergone some interesting changes in the eight months I had been gone, not all for the better. Saigon in 1974 was a peculiar mix of aging French architecture, innumerable street vendors, and shantytowns bustling with swarming Vietnamese, many poor, some rich, but all hustling to survive. Saigon's charms tantalized at first, but closer inspection soon revealed her flaws. She was called the "Pearl of the Orient," but her streets were home to wounded veterans, beggars, prostitutes, and the ubiquitous police. Surprisingly, despite the American troop withdrawal, the place had become even more Americanized. Many Vietnamese had traveled to the States for training on military equipment or to receive education in civilian management. They had brought back American cultural themes like steak houses and rock bands, over-running the former colonial ambience with a cornucopia of American tastes. One Vietnamese girl singer in the Crazy Dog band sounded exactly like Janis Joplin. If you could have heard her singing "Me and Bobby McGee," you would have sworn Janis had faked her death and was living in Saigon.

A psychic frenzy seemed to possess the local citizens, pervading everything they did. I believe that subconsciously the people knew the Communists would strike again. That feeling was especially true among the older generation, which had heard the same promises from the French that the Americans now placated them with. Still, for those Americans who lived and worked there, Saigon exerted a bizarre charm, an almost magical allure that insidiously wormed its way into your heart, its name synonymous with an erotic combination of Eastern pleasures, sudden death, and the strangely mystifying. The Vietnamese people were the same way, and without admitting it, most Americans who lived and worked there had come to love these small, tough people, whose fate now so heavily depended on the proverbial "kindness of strangers."

When my family arrived in Saigon I was fortunate to find a small house to rent. It was owned by a Vietnamese landlord in a compound located at the rear of the newly constructed People's Hospital near Tan Son Nhut Airbase. The compound was inhabited entirely by refugees who fled from North Vietnam in 1954 when the Geneva Accords divided the country. I was worried about how Nova, a country girl from Tennessee, would adapt to her new surroundings. Luckily, through some miracle of spiritual fortitude, my family quickly became accustomed to living in the strange, exotic city that was Saigon. Nova also enrolled in the Far East Division of the University of Maryland, while both Mike and Andrea attended the International School of Saigon.

The only remaining American military institution was the Defense Attaché Office (DAO). The Paris Peace Treaty authorized the office a maximum of fifty military personnel, but it had well over one thousand American civilians doing construction, aircraft maintenance, and many other tasks. However, the American military secretly augmented the fifty through a variety of methods, deceiving no one in the process. Many men, for instance, were assigned on "temporary duty." Although the old one-year tour was still in vogue, by regulation, personnel could only be assigned on temporary duty for 179 days. They would then sign out, leave for Bangkok for one day, and then return for another 179 days. Other men were "sheep-dipped," a procedure whereby military personnel were discharged and then rehired as civilians. At the end of their time they would return to their military duties with no loss of time in service or rank. Other military men fully retired and became civilian employees.

After getting my family situated, I rapidly assumed my duties as the Chief Interpreter for the U.S. side during the continuing difficult negotiations between the four delegations of the Four Party Joint Military Talks. In addition to interpreting for the discussions, I supervised a team of Vietnamese translators involved in processing the seemingly endless flow of official documents, as well as handling the non-stop protests between the four sides. As expected, the presumably four-sided discussions degenerated to bilateral ones, with the U.S. and Government of Vietnam delegations on one side and the DRV and PRG on the other. My job also involved being a conduit between the GVN and the Communists, a sort of unofficial messenger between the still bitter foes.

My liaison visits to the three Vietnamese delegations were conducted at Tan Son Nhut Airbase. The South Vietnamese members were quartered in buildings formerly serving as offices for the American 7th Air Force, while the two Communist delegations occupied a small, heavily guarded locale called "Camp Davis," well inside the perimeter of the airfield. In an ironic twist of fate, this site once housed elements of the highly classified Army Security Agency, which was responsible for the clandestine monitoring of GVN, Communist, and Third Country signal communications. Camp Davis was named for a member of the unit who had been one of the first Americans killed in the war, Specialist Five James Davis, who died in December 1961.

After the withdrawal of American forces from the base in late March 1973, support services such as water and electricity were disorganized and barely functioning. Always suspicious of GVN motives, the two Communist delegations constantly accused the South Vietnamese of deliberately interfering with their utilities. GVN officials just as adamantly denied the "baseless" Communist charges. Eventually, under pressure from the American Embassy, the South Vietnamese got the facilities at Tan Son Nhut up and running.

In addition to supplying the Communists with their billets and other supplies, the GVN also provided them communications to the International Control Commission and with access to Saigon telephone circuits. Although the GVN eventually repaired all the services, the Communists continued to publicly castigate the South Vietnamese on a variety of issues. Despite the constant haranguing, the GVN did not prevent the PRG from holding weekly press conferences, even though the Communists took advantage of such opportunities to call for the overthrow of the South Vietnamese government.

The GVN was trying to cooperate with the United States on other levels as well. In order to entice an increasingly unfriendly Congress toward further military and economic assistance for their faltering republic, the South Vietnamese leaders quickly and gladly conceded to requests by large American oil companies for off-shore exploration. Both American and South Vietnamese spokesmen heralded the event. The media followed suit and the temporary illusion of an oil bonanza was created. But in reality, behind closed doors senior engineers from Mobil Oil were painting a rather bleak picture regarding production levels and the long-term viability of the project due to the relatively high paraffin content of the oil, which was reportedly slightly over 40 percent.

While the Communists made paranoia seem normal, the GVN security services were equally suspicious, perhaps justifiably so, and thus kept an extremely close eye on the Communist personnel. This vigilance extended to surveillance of all visitors in and out of Camp Davis, including maintenance people working on the utilities. As a part of my in-processing at the Defense Attaché Office, I was required to obtain different badges and passes from both American and GVN security for entry to various facilities throughout the Saigon area. At the beginning of my assignment I was required to show a special *passe-partout* badge before I could enter the sensitive part of the airbase, especially the Camp Davis section. Since my duties required me to travel extensively throughout Tan Son Nhut on a daily basis, soon both the GVN and Communist security personnel began to view me as an innocuous passerby. This chameleon status would ultimately enable me to help rescue a significant number of people during the last hectic days of the final offensive before the airfield came under fire.

While the Four Party discussions centered on the POW/MIA issue for both sides, it didn't take long to conclude that a significant degree of animosity still remained. While the U.S. and GVN viewed the deliberations as a serious forum for efforts to account for the missing, the Communist side used the talks as a thinly veiled delaying tactic. Their forces sorely needed time to recover from the massive losses they suffered during the 1972 Easter Offensive, and perhaps more importantly, time to make new preparations for a full-scale invasion of the South. After the war, one American author and former CIA Vietnam analyst, Frank Snepp, would call this interlude a "decent interval."

While the Communists used the talks to stall, they did have one legitimate concern. During the negotiations at Camp Davis, whenever the U.S. and GVN negotiators pressed for an accounting, the Communist side continually raised the issue of their "civilian" prisoners who were still held by the GVN. The GVN countered that the number of South Vietnamese prisoners freed was absurdly low, and accused the Communists of still holding thousands of ARVN and civilian prisoners. Yet, when pressed by the American side about any remaining Communist prisoners, the GVN delegation avoided the matter. In side conversations with members of the GVN Central Intelligence Office, however, I learned that the "civilian" category of prisoners mainly included captured personnel from the Communist Intelligence and Security services. According to the South Vietnamese officers, President Nguyen Van Thieu had refused to release several hundred such personnel even though the GVN side claimed to have completely complied with the provisions of the Paris agreements stipulating the return of all prisoners captured during the war. They were adamant that release of these highly trained people was both dangerous and foolhardy, and that the hard-core Communists would simply return to the jungle to continue the war.

While I didn't sympathize, I at least understood the GVN position. For example, the wife of the Saigon-Gia Dinh Political Commissar, Major General Tran Bach Dang, was exchanged in a POW swap during 1968. In 1975 she was arrested again while trying to infiltrate Saigon just prior to the GVN collapse. Another important POW never released was the Chief of Public Security for southern Vietnam, Nguyen Cong Tai. He had been captured in Ben Tre in late 1970 and he was considered by the South Vietnamese to be the highest-ranking Communist prisoner ever captured in South Vietnam.[2] In addition to Tai, in April 1975 more than two hundred other "special category" prisoners languished in cells in Saigon and on Con Son Island, home to the infamous "Tiger cages." I surmised that if the Communist side was looking for a reason to withhold American POWs, they had no better excuse than this one. But if true, they never directly linked American POWs to their own remaining prisoners, so it became impossible to know for certain.

Throughout the American involvement in Vietnam there had obviously never been a safe, dependable means of transportation from South to North Vietnam. In fact both GVN and DRV law prohibited such travel. Under the terms of the treaty, however, liaison flights between Hanoi and Saigon were initiated so that Communist personnel involved in the negotiations or monitoring of the cease-fire could travel back to their capital. However, this raised enormous security concerns for the South Vietnamese. One reason for the alarm was the duplicity exhibited by the Communist side at the end of the war with the French. Similar "Joint Teams" and "Commissions" were formed but ultimately the Communist side used the missions to infiltrate intelligence personnel, or they hid weapons in graves that they were allegedly inspecting for humanitarian purposes. Many of the weapons eventually used to kill Americans were hidden in such secret caches at the time of the withdrawal of French military forces. After the Communists were caught, all liaison missions and regular civil transport between North and South Vietnam were terminated, forcing Communist intelligence operatives and key command personnel to travel a circuitous route through Laos and Cambodia or on boats across the South China Sea.

As a part of my normal duties, I routinely participated in weekly Four Party liaison flights between Saigon and Hanoi. In addition to members of the Four Party talks, a typical passenger manifest also included members from the Communist delegations of the International Commission for Control and Supervision (ICCS), which wags in Saigon claimed stood for "I Can't Control Shit." Basically, the mission of the Commission was to monitor implementation of the cease-fire. In the beginning stages of the Commission the member nations included Canada, Indonesia, Poland and Hungary. Since the cease-fire was basically a sham and fighting was still occurring throughout the countryside, the Canadians withdrew from the Commission and were replaced by Iran.

Not surprisingly, according to our information the Polish and Hungarian delegations of the ICCS were saturated with intelligence operatives. American delegation members were regularly debriefed concerning the activities and contacts of the Communist personnel. Vietnamese agents from President Nguyen Van Thieu's personal security force, as well as the Central Intelligence Office were frequently added to the list of GVN official passengers going on the flights. I found this situation humorous: an American Air Force aircraft scheduled to transport "administrative" personnel on what was supposed to be a humanitarian mission was in essence a planeload of spies trying to recruit each other. Both the CIA and American military intelligence also actively attempted to recruit members from the two Communist delegations. Methods included the compromise of targeted members by utilizing Vietnamese female agents trained by American handlers. These covert operations continued until the final days.

Apparently the Communist side realized some degree of success in recruiting Americans. During 1991, personnel from the Army's Foreign Counterintelligence Activity at Fort Meade interviewed me concerning an American supposedly recruited. Based on the line of questioning I reached the conclusion that it was an Army Warrant Officer and linguist assigned to Saigon after the cease-fire. According to the investigators, the individual was suspected of passing classified documents to Communist ICCS members. At least some of the documents were lists of American POWs the U.S. believed were captured alive but never returned by the Communists.

At times during my duties as Liaison Officer I felt considerable pressure from the spy situation. Another contributing factor in making the flights stressful was our own security measures. Since those of us placed in charge of the liaison flights were temporarily out of contact with our government and were in a Communist country considered hostile toward the United States, we were required to sign a document prior to each flight indicating we would be held personally responsible for any incidents. The American members jokingly called this document the "sign your life away" form. Each time an aircraft touched down at Tan Son Nhut after a mission in the North the person who signed the form felt a big sense of relief.

As had been the case in their dealings with the French, the Communists sought to exploit the American-sponsored post cease-fire liaison flights as much as possible. Although by agreement the costs of such flights were to be borne equally by the four parties of the Joint Team, the Communist side never paid their share, despite repeated protests by the U.S. Embassy in Saigon and the White House. To add insult to injury they also used the flights for movement of key participants involved in implementing the cease-fire from the South back to Hanoi. As I mentioned earlier, in one instance I believe the Communists purposely held back an American POW, Robert White, until after the completion of Operation Homecoming, so that Tran Van Tra could have an excuse to leave Saigon and return to Hanoi.

Even though the atmosphere on the flights to Hanoi was edgy, I enjoyed the missions to North Vietnam, as they provided a welcome change of scenery from the stifling Saigon heat. While the mood was tense, especially between the GVN and the DRV/PRG, the animosity was muted compared to the constant bickering and recriminations of the Four Party discussions. Although the liaison flights to Hanoi were a break from the routine and a respite from the wearying negotiations, and despite the tension of the "sign your life away" form, at times humorous incidents occurred. On one flight a member of the JCRC Liaison Office, Staff Sergeant Edward Davis, began drinking vodka given to him by one of the Poles returning from a holiday in Hanoi. Davis, a young Special Forces veteran with several combat tours under his belt, harbored a great deal of fondness for the Vietnamese people. Although unsympathetic to the Communist cause, Davis did admire the tenacity and perseverance of the Communist light infantry troops. After several drinks of the powerful Polish lubricant, Davis decided to personally mediate the war. Grabbing both a Viet Cong and a North Vietnamese representative by their collars, Davis physically pulled them across the aircraft to hold a spontaneous trilateral talk with a South Vietnamese officer. Able to speak Vietnamese, Davis demanded to know why the cease-fire continued to be violated. Equal in his condemnation of both sides he wanted to know why Vietnamese were still killing Vietnamese, and why each was unable to forgive and forget.

Although Davis did prompt a lively discussion on the subject of ending the war, and while all three factions of the Vietnamese appeared to sincerely appreciate his non-diplomatic approach to international problem solving, his efforts failed when he and the Polish officer passed out. After the C-130 arrived back in Saigon, both Staff Sergeant Davis and the Pole had to be carried from the aircraft on stretchers. Not surprisingly, that was Davis' last trip to North Vietnam. When I next met Davis shortly after the fall of Saigon he was assigned to a Military Police unit at the Indochina Refugee Reception Center in Fort Chaffee, Arkansas. Davis did a marvelous job at Chaffee and later retired from the Army as a Master Sergeant.

Like all things between the three Vietnamese factions, nothing simple lasted long. Another liaison flight resulted in a literally hot confrontation between the parties. It was considered normal for the security conscious POW/MIA section of the PRG delegation to closely guard their official documents, which were hand-carried by courier from Hanoi to Saigon. The members usually carted such correspondence in standard Russian or Chinese issue leather pouches. During one particular flight a pouch placed directly beneath a PRG officer sitting in the aluminum framed folding passenger seat on the Air Force C-130 aircraft exploded and burst into flames. The fire quickly spread along the nylon webbing of the seats causing thick, caustic smoke to fill the aircraft. At first no one could determine the cause of the fire. Once the source of the fire was identified, efforts by the crew to douse the flames were misread as attempts to take possession of the important pouch, which almost caused a fight on the airplane. A subsequent investigation revealed that the fire had been started when the aircraft encountered turbulence, causing the aircraft to rise and fall sharply. Unknown to everyone else, the pouch was equipped with an incendiary device designed to burn the contents if the pouch was disturbed or opened prior to being disarmed by the courier. Since the pouch had been placed directly beneath the buttocks of the PRG officer, the weight of his body suddenly being forced down by the turbulence on the locking mechanism was enough to set off the device. As a result, seven people on board suffered burns. After the initial round of panic subsided the next thought of both the Americans and GVN personnel was that the Communists had jeopardized the lives of all on the aircraft in the interests of their own internal security.

When the plane landed, the exploding pouch incident caused GVN security officials at Tan Son Nhut Air Base to immediately challenge the legality of the "privileges and immunities" clause of the Paris Agreements reserved for the four parties of the Joint Team. As the GVN security men began to scrutinize the cargo brought on the airplane from Hanoi by the Communist delegations, obstinate members of the DRV and PRG delegations refused to disembark from the aircraft, clutching their leather document pouches tightly to their chests. From a diplomatic standpoint, the U.S. Government retained sovereign control over the military aircraft and its contents, not the South Vietnamese, even though the aircraft had landed at a facility owned by the GVN. The discerning Communist officials called upon me to protect their interests while at the same time GVN security officers asserted they were correct in identifying and removing explosive devices endangering all parties involved. The volatile situation forced me into the role of a referee between the quarreling Vietnamese delegations.

On that particular flight there was a considerable number of food rations. The Communist delegations had frequently complained about the quality of the provisions they were able to purchase on the local economy in Saigon. The U.S. side came to the conclusion that the Communists were fearful of being poisoned by the South Vietnamese. To belay those fears we agreed that if the GVN delegation had no objections, the U.S. would allow foodstuffs to be transported as cargo on the return flight from Hanoi. The GVN security officials realized that forceful seizure of the hand-carried document pouches would lead to a bloody confrontation, so they turned their attention to the collective food cargo shipment instead. To make their point the officials ransacked the food containers, spilling most of the contents onto the tarmac. After everything but the individual pouches had been inspected the irate GVN security personnel left the aircraft to wait for instructions from their government before continuing the search.

Shortly after the departure of the GVN agents, I learned from my command that the American Ambassador was in a meeting with senior GVN officials and word would soon be passed to me concerning the "privileges and immunities" issue. A few minutes stretched into hours, and long after the GVN security personnel returned to their air-conditioned offices the Communist members of the Joint Team and I sat inside the sweltering aircraft staring at each other. Late that same evening I received word that the immunity from search and seizure would be respected and the tense situation was diffused. No one from the U.S. side ever learned what was in the pouch that the Communists considered so critical that they would risk so many lives, including their own. The incident only served to heighten anxieties in the formerly placid atmosphere of the liaison flights.

During the meetings held at Tan Son Nhut, the U.S. side continued to press hard for an accounting, especially for extremely compelling cases where the missing men were known to be alive at the time of their loss incidents. In August 1973 the U.S. side began providing dossiers containing information on various missing men. Some of the files passed to the Communists even contained actual photographs of the men alive in the custody of Communist forces. During the life of the FPJMT, we passed over one hundred separate cases to the North Vietnamese. Although the Communists readily accepted all the files passed to them and often requested even more information, the U.S. requests for feedback were ignored. Even the most optimistic American officials participating in the talks began to feel angry and frustrated by the lack of response.

In marked contrast to the duplicity demonstrated by the Communists delegations, the GVN provided superb cooperation. They assisted in the excavation of twelve crash sites, and the search and exhumation of nineteen positively identified U.S. servicemen. The announced policy of the GVN was based on the three principles of legality, sense of responsibility and humanitarianism. They published a proclamation that stated:

> *On the principle of legality, GVN always respects and pledges to implement Article 8(b) of the Paris Agreement and Articles 8(d) and (e) of the Joint Communiqué, GVN never accepts linking Article 8(b) with the other provisions or imposing conditions of a* sine qua non *nature.*
>
> *On the principle of sense of responsibility, GVN constantly affirms its sacred responsibility not only toward GVN and US allied comrades in arms who, so that South Vietnam can remain free and independent, were either killed or missing in action, but also toward all the personnel of the concerned parties (i.e., DRV and PRG) who have been killed or missing in action in GVN territory.*
>
> *On the principle of humanitarianism, with regard to the dead people, GVN does not discriminate friend or foe, even though while they were alive, they*

> *fought in the hostile ranks. GVN considers that 'death is the final act,' therefore, regarding those who are dead, it is only one act, humanitarian act. This humanitarianism is embodied in the following tasks: burial, care of graves, and return of remains when so requested by the other side.*

As is well known today, the end of South Vietnam began in December 1974, when PAVN forces attacked the capital of Phuoc Long province. There was considerable anxiety among both Americans and Vietnamese in Saigon about the offensive as the ARVN defenders in the province capital were gradually defeated. The PAVN sensed the weakened state of the South Vietnamese military from the deep cutbacks in U.S. military aid, and began to move, having strongly reinforced their units in the two years since the Paris Accords. Most observers, both casual and trained, knew that this capture of the first provincial headquarters since the cease-fire would be seen as a test by the PAVN. Not only was the viability of the American trained and equipped but thinly stretched ARVN military forces in question, so was the political will of the American leadership. President Richard Nixon had obtained President Nguyen Van Thieu's acceptance of the Paris Agreements by guaranteeing American military action in the event of a major Communist offensive. But he was no longer in office, and the question now was how would the new American President, Gerald Ford, and the Congress and American people for that matter, react.

Although a stream of dignitaries, including a Congressional delegation, poured in and out of Saigon during the spring of 1975, it became increasingly apparent that the only utility of the brief "fact finding missions" was to demonstrate the dreaded moral and political support normally afforded a low priority ally of a major power. As predicted by most observers, the lack of any firm American response to the Communist victory in Phuoc Long on January 6, 1975, was not only immediately devastating to GVN morale, it served as a pivotal signal to Hanoi's strategists. After more than ten years of fighting and 58,000 dead and missing, America had finally had enough.

Many including myself knew that the successful attack on Phuoc Long was important. A sense of unease gripped South Vietnam. But I had no idea of just how alarming it was to American planners until I was advised that my boss, who had returned to the States on leave for the Christmas holidays, would not be returning to Vietnam. In fact, most if not all official American personnel who were out of the country at that time were informed that their tours were being curtailed and that they would receive new orders for assignments elsewhere. As a result, the head of the U.S. Delegation, Colonel John H. Madison, Jr., notified me that henceforth I would be the new Chief of the Liaison Division.

After the initial test at Phuoc Long, Hanoi's Politburo judiciously instituted its own version of a "decent interval." This consisted of a two month time period in which Hanoi's forces prepared for a new Dry Season offensive, this time centered on the southern part of the Central Highlands. With infantry, armor and artillery forces hidden along the Ho Chi Minh Trail west of Ban Me Thuot, the PAVN began to conduct reconnaissance and resupply missions in anticipation of what was to be the final and decisive campaign.

Just as the fighting was about to erupt again, I became possibly the last American service member to reenlist while stationed in the Republic of Vietnam. In February I signed on for another six years of service, which meant that my military identification card had expired, so I had to go to the DAO Security Section to apply for a new card. While waiting in line I chatted with a clean cut, energetic young man who identified himself as Jim Lewis. Later I would learn that rather than being an Army Captain as Lewis claimed, he was actually an officer of the CIA's paramilitary arm. Lewis' mission during the final Communist offensive called for him to join an ARVN Forward Command post at Phan Rang, a city along the coast near Cam Ranh Bay that the ARVN were attempting to maintain as a blocking position on Route 1. On April 16, 1975, Lewis himself became one of the last American POWs captured during the Vietnam War. Communist forces, after overrunning the Thanh Son Airfield near Phan Rang, seized both Lewis and two South Vietnamese generals commanding the Forward Headquarters, Army Lieutenant General Nguyen Vinh Nghi and Air Force Brigadier General Pham Ngoc Sang. Although Lewis was tortured in a North Vietnamese prison, he was released in December 1975 with the other Americans swept up at the end. Unfortunately, his luck ran out when he was killed in the bombing attack on the American Embassy in Lebanon in April 1983. After I retired, I met frequently with Lieutenant General Nghi, who resettled in Fort Smith, Arkansas after being released from a Communist prison camp in 1987.

As February slowly slipped by, the main question was not when a Communist attack would come, but from where. As I look back on it now, I wish I had been much more forceful in presenting some information I had received about the Central Highlands. That is, however, part of the conundrum of intelligence work. Finding a critical piece of intelligence is one thing, but getting higher echelons to accept it in the face of their preconceived notions or policy decisions is another. In February 1975 my old friends the Santilli family from the Mewal coffee plantation in the Ban Me Thuot area had just arrived in Saigon and had stopped to visit me. I had first met them in early 1966 when I served with the 25th Infantry Division in Darlac Province and we had provided security for them to harvest the coffee crop. The uncovering of the arms caches in the village had also greatly reduced the influence of the local Viet Cong, at least for a while. The head of the family was a former paratrooper of the French Foreign Legion who remained in Darlac Province with his Rhade Montagnard wife and Rhade/Italian children after French forces departed Vietnam in 1954. When the family arrived in Saigon I invited them to lunch at the "Golden Deer at Bay" Restaurant in Thu Duc on the outskirts of Saigon.

While chatting over our food I learned that one member of the family had just returned to Vietnam from Italy. He complained of the massive red tape he was encountering in dealing with GVN bureaucrats as he attempted to sell the family plantation, as well as their commercial properties in downtown Saigon, which included the Royal Hotel. Once the properties were sold, the entire family would depart for Italy with no plans to return to Vietnam. Realizing the attachment Santilli held for his plantation, I was astonished by this revelation. I then began to make subtle probes to learn the reasons behind this interesting development.

After some hesitation, the Santilli family explained that the rural Montagnards with whom they had enjoyed a long-standing relationship had recently come to them out of concern for the family's safety. According to the tribesmen, North Vietnamese forces were massing along the Cambodian border due west of Ban Me Thuot. The Montagnards believed a major attack in the area was imminent. The Rhade described how they observed PAVN soldiers who appeared to be logging timber, but after closer scrutiny they were able to determine that the large trees were being sawed only half way through. To anyone with military training, this was an indicator that preparations were being made for armor to traverse the area.

All things considered, the Santilli family came to the conclusion it was time to dispose of everything they owned and leave the country. Since I wasn't permitted to collect human intelligence, I invited some of my former colleagues from the spy community to attend a luncheon to hear this recent information on this remote but strategically important region of the country. This group included William O'Brien, a close friend of mine who was assigned as a Polygraph Examiner in Detachment "K" of the 500th MI Group temporarily assigned to DAO. After hearing their story and discussing the ramifications of the account provided by the Santilli family, O'Brien returned to Saigon and submitted a report through his channel. There was no response to it.

In order to evaluate the accuracy of the report on the impending attack, I arranged to meet with some key intelligence personnel of the South Vietnamese Central Intelligence Organization. The group arriving at my home one evening included Colonel Lam Van Nghia, the former Vietnamese CMIC commander and now the Deputy Commander of the Capital Police, and Lieutenant Colonel Nguyen Van Long of the National Police Special Branch.[3] Despite the incident in 1968 with the PAVN Colonel, Nghia and I held each other's professional opinion in high regard. Also attending was Major Chac, the Director of the Combined Documents Exploitation Center, and also a former alumnus of the CMIC. Those attending from the American side included Captain Andrew Gembara, a former Special Forces officer transferred to intelligence duties after the loss of an eye in combat.[4]

As the conversation turned from Vietnamese food and Saigon nightlife to the situation in the field, it became apparent that none of the GVN officials present had been informed of the Santilli family account. On the contrary, it seemed that the officials had recently focused their attention away from the Central Highlands toward the Mekong Delta region. When the other Americans and I disagreed with this contention and offered the Ban Me Thuot-Pleiku areas as being the most likely target for the next PAVN attacks, the GVN officials found the idea amusing and implausible. After dancing and drinking away the evening, the cheerful group departed unconvinced. I pledged to renew erstwhile ties with future visits to the offices of my old friends, unaware at the time that I would not be able to keep my promise. I would never again meet the unfortunate Major Chac, and I would only fleetingly meet with both Colonel Nghia and Lieutenant Colonel Long as I placed them on departing aircraft during the final hectic hours of the evacuation.

During the waning days of February it felt as though an eerie fog-like calm was slowly settling over Saigon. The peace was finally broken on March 10 when Communist armor and infantry units attacked Ban Me Thuot. Caught off guard, the startled ARVN fought back hard but were badly outnumbered. The NVA soon overran the town, although one ARVN battalion at a local airfield fought off a series of attacks for over a week.

After the capture of Ban Me Thuot by North Vietnamese forces it became obvious that a full-scale enemy offensive was underway. In a surprising move President Nguyen Van Thieu gave the order for his military forces to withdraw from the Central Highlands. The departure began on March 16. Poorly planned and executed, the retreating ARVNs attempted to withdraw down a little used and badly maintained mountain road called Route 7B. The PAVN forces mauled them, crushing within days most of the effective ARVN forces in the crucial Central Highlands. In I Corps, by the end of March blitzing PAVN forces occupied both Hue and Danang. It became evident that the GVN's existence was tenuous. The collapse of the two northern military regions of Vietnam resulted in a mass exodus of refugees headed toward Saigon by air, land and sea.

Unsure as to the number of American citizens being evacuated south by sea, and concerned by reports of rioting ARVN soldiers aboard ships carrying refugees from I Corps, Colonel John Madison decided to detach me and another Vietnamese speaker, Gunnery Sergeant Ernest L. Pace, to assist in refugee control. A hard-drinking, fun-loving Marine from Chattanooga, Tennessee, Pace was not at all apprehensive about leaving the safety of Tan Son Nhut to take on this formidable task. The mission was almost cancelled after it was determined that the DAO possessed no means of waterborne transport for traveling down the Saigon River to Vung Tau where the ships were scheduled to arrive. But I was determined to carry out the assigned mission, so I contacted Art Gallagher, a neighbor and civilian employee of the DAO's Army Division who owned a personal pleasure boat. Gallagher was proud of his 16-foot fiberglass boat equipped with an eighty-five horsepower motor, and therefore was hesitant to risk losing it to Communist fire from the riverbanks. But after some convincing the former Army NCO volunteered to become the third member of our crew.

Armed with only pistols and Motorola radios for communications, our hardy trio spent the next two days going up and down the Saigon River inspecting ships packed with refugees. After surveying the situation on the ships a report was relayed back to the American Embassy Evacuation Command Post. The ships were then guided to the designated off loading point so that the refugees could to be moved by ground transportation. Although in later days Gallagher would be forced to abandon his prized boat to Communist forces, I was able to successfully lobby with the DAO to ensure that he received a letter of commendation for his efforts.

With the Central Highlands collapse, DAO and Embassy staffers began to reassess the situation at hand, and began planning for the evacuation of American dependents and female employees from South Vietnam. Since the Embassy believed such an evacuation would signal American abandonment of the GVN, a decision was made to disguise the movement by placing the employees and dependents on aircraft publicly described as evacuating Vietnamese orphans from orphanages throughout the Saigon area. On April 2, 1975, the U.S. Agency for International Development dubbed the plan "Operation Babylift."

"Operation Babylift" actually served two purposes. First, it allowed for massive C-5A aircraft to bring in much needed supplies and equipment to the faltering ARVN military forces under the guise of a humanitarian mission. Second, by claiming that the American female employees and dependent wives were boarding on the returning flights as "escorts" for the orphans, it concealed the fact that an evacuation of any American personnel was underway.

Shortly after the operation was approved I was called into the office of the Deputy Commander of our delegation, Lieutenant Colonel Conrad Wilson. He asked about the current status of my wife and children. I informed Wilson that my family was already ticketed on a Pan Am flight the following week. As added insurance, I had also made reservations on Air France. Wilson mentioned how fortunate that all my family members were American citizens with valid passports. Without explaining fully, Wilson hinted that in the near future there would be other personnel requiring evacuation, and that they did not have the American citizenship or passports necessary to board official U.S. Government aircraft. Wilson suggested that I consider moving up the departure date for my family. As added incentive, he informed me that Air Force C-5A aircraft would be departing on a regular basis for Clark Air Base in the Philippines; such flights would be free of charge for dependents of assigned official personnel.

I considered the seemingly generous offer of assistance but in the end declined because I felt uneasy about my family being loaded like cargo on aircraft with little or no safety features or passenger comforts. Unbeknownst to me, the matter had already been decided in advance. Wilson quickly lost his composure. Raising his voice, Wilson informed me that I would have my family on the next departing C-5A and that this was not a suggestion, it was an order. Shortly thereafter I was handed movement orders for my family for a flight scheduled to depart on April 4, 1975.

On the afternoon of April 3, I went to the Bachelors Officers Quarters #1 located on the perimeter of Tan Son Nhut. I had resided at this wartime mini-apartment complex during previous tours. The complex was conveniently located near the base and had a dining hall that served American food. Since my family was now departing and the situation up-country was rapidly deteriorating, I thought it would be wise to move back into quarters nearer the evacuation point. After completing the necessary paperwork I followed a Vietnamese clerk from the reception desk down a corridor near the swimming pool to inspect a room. Pausing at the swimming pool bar I noticed a cheerful group of U.S. Air Force personnel tossing down drinks while frolicking in the pool with a group of Vietnamese females clad in scanty bikinis. One crewmember and a female were fervently engaged in underwater sex.

According to the billeting clerk, the Americans were crewmembers from a C-5A that had arrived that same day and the females were "girls from the street" who frequented the Bachelor Officers Quarters to obtain money from the American guests. I noticed that one of the females was a light complexioned, attractive Eurasian girl named Collette Emberger. Rumor was that her father had been a member of the French Foreign Legion captured by the Viet Cong during the 1950s. I would later learn that after being indoctrinated, the father was proselytized by the Communists to conduct terrorist operations, including assassinations of both French and GVN officials. I also learned that Collette herself worked secretly for the Communists and that she was involved in assisting American defectors. Collette had also served as a guide and interpreter for MIA family members traveling to Vietnam for private negotiations with Viet Cong officials to secure the release of their loved ones, or their remains.[5] I didn't recognize any of the Air Force personnel partying in the pool, but I would never forget the pilot, a man whose face I would see again on the front page of the "Stars and Stripes."

I returned home to inform Nova that the family had been ordered to board the C-5A, rather than a commercial aircraft. She accepted this order as just another sacrifice required of a military wife. Nova and I then hurriedly packed a few personal items in preparation for the trip. On the morning of April 4 I drove my family to the DAO compound located adjacent to Tan Son Nhut Air Base where Nova and our two children were placed in a movement group being processed for departure. After bidding my family farewell I returned to my hectic duties at the DAO. Later that same morning while driving through the compound I spotted my family at a small bookstore next to the Post Exchange. When I stopped to chat with them Nova informed me that the processing was almost completed and that she had brought the children to the bookstore to buy comic books to read on the plane. I noticed that our son Michael was holding one of his favorite comics, Donald Duck. Assigned as escort for the parting group was Captain George Petrie, a Special Forces Officer with the JCRC and who had been one of the Son Tay raiders.[6] Petrie told me that everything was going well; I felt a sense of relief knowing that an officer of his caliber was involved in the hastily organized operation.

That same afternoon I was tasked to coordinate requests for records on MIAs as well as some administrative matters, such as creating the manifest for the next liaison flight to Hanoi with the DRV/PRG delegations at Camp Davis. I left the DAO compound in a vehicle driven by my local hire employee, Mr. Tran Van Nga. On the way over Nga talked about the weather and about how foolish it was for the U.S. Government to paint all their official vehicles a heat absorbent black color. Nga also subtly broached the subject of a noticeable increase in the number of American dependents departing the country. Nga wondered aloud whether there would be a major attack on Saigon and what the outcome would be. He was also curious about what his life would be like if he had the opportunity to resettle in America. Realizing that Nga was a polygamist, I reminded him that in America the law dictated only one wife. This caused Nga to be somewhat perplexed throughout the rest of the trip. I smoothed over the fact that there was an increase in the number of evacuating dependents by relying on the standard American line in use at the time: "we can fight the Communists much more effectively if the women and children are out of the way."

Entry into the Communist compound at Camp Davis began with the usual routine of being served gut searing acidic tea and strong filter-less cigarettes from North Vietnam. Although first time guests were generally unable to consume these robust products over which the northerners exhibited considerable pride, my time in the North with Operation Homecoming made me an old hand. I anticipated some initial queries because during a visit to the camp only a few days earlier I used my Special Access badge to admit an unauthorized visitor into the compound. I knew that the Communists would be curious about exactly who the man was. Although interested, the Communist officials were unconcerned because I had done this once before. On the previous occasion I had snuck in a cadet from the U.S. Military Academy at West Point. The young lad was the son of Colonel Harry Summers, the Chief of the U.S. Delegation's Negotiations Division and future editor of *Vietnam Magazine*.

The Communist officials always seemed to enjoy any opportunity to explain the righteousness of their cause to anyone who would listen, but this most recent unofficial visitor was quite different. Rather than a recent arrival from the U.S. with no Vietnam experience, this man spoke the Vietnamese language with the northern dialect and demonstrated considerable knowledge of the country. When asked what position the man held, I jokingly told my counterparts that he was a member of the U.S. House of Representatives. This revelation sent one of the liaison cadre scurrying off to inform his superiors of the important visitor. Actually the new visitor was my old friend from the 50th MID days, Robert Destatte, who had arrived in Vietnam on a temporary assignment from Detachment K of the 500th MI Group. When he explained to me that although he had been involved with Vietnam for many years and had ample opportunities to meet with POWs and defectors, he never had a chance to sit down and talk at length with Communist officials. When he asked to meet with the Communists, I simply could not refuse to arrange a meeting.

One of the Communist representatives with whom I dealt with frequently, Mr. Le Van Long, wore the PAVN uniform and claimed to be a member of the DRV Delegation. However, when I first met him in Hanoi during the release of American POWs he had been assigned to the PRG Delegation. Curious, I inquired concerning Long's change of uniforms, governments and delegations but he was evasive and never gave a straight answer. Given Long's ambiguity, it was obvious that the Viet Cong never existed in South Vietnam. The entire scenario concerning the National Liberation Front and the Provisional Revolutionary Government were nothing more than strategic deception designed to deceive world opinion, especially the anti-war faction in the States.

It was difficult to judge the backgrounds of many of the cadre from the DRV and PRG delegations based at Camp Davis, let alone those directly associated with the POW/MIA issue. Some were known to have had previous involvement with American POWs. For example, the Deputy Chief of the DRV Delegation, Lieutenant Colonel Nguyen Thuc Dai, was a former cadre of the Military Proselytizing Office of the Headquarters, South Vietnam Liberation Armed Forces. At least three other officials at Camp Davis, Lieutenant Pham Teo, Lieutenant Tran Trong Khanh, and Captain Tran Hao would cross paths with me again while working on the POW/MIA in the years to come. In fact during the 1980's all three would find themselves traveling to Hawaii on official U.S. Government orders with me as their escort. Of the three, Pham Teo would eventually become a key player in the POW/MIA issue. In the years ahead I would also learn that the chief spokesman for the Communist side, Colonel Vo Dong Giang, was not really a Colonel at all, but rather a high-ranking member of the Communist leadership in Hanoi whose real name was Pham Ba.

Many of the officers in the GVN Delegation to the Four Party talks had equally murky backgrounds. I was aware that at least some of the members were secretly assigned to the CIO. The Chief of the GVN Delegation, Colonel Duong Hieu Nghia, was an armor officer who seldom associated with members of the U.S. side. According to old timers in the DAO, as a young ARVN Lieutenant, Nghia had participated in the assassination of President Ngo Dinh Diem and his brother Ngo Dinh Nhu in the back of an armored personnel carrier. Nghia was known in the South Vietnamese army as the "coup" expert, the guy you went to if you were planning a takeover. A junior member of the GVN Delegation, Captain Nguyen Van Muoi, was said to be the nephew of the Chief of the PRG Delegation, Lieutenant Vo Tho Son. Although I had no firsthand knowledge of such contacts, Captain Muoi reportedly served as a separate and undisclosed channel of communications between the GVN and the PRG.

After the usual greetings, Long opined to me in his antiquated English that my recent feat of bringing a Congressman into Camp Davis must have been "a feather in my cap." Needing to stay credible, I sheepishly admitted to Long that Destatte wasn't really a member of Congress. Long seemed to be satisfied and the meeting turned to the more important aspects of accounting for the missing and the impending liaison flight to Hanoi. But this time things were different. When I received the passenger manifest from the Communist side I immediately noticed that it contained some of the most senior personnel from both the DRV and PRG Delegations. I noticed another deviation from the norm when none of the Poles or Hungarians from the ICCS appeared on the return flight manifest from Hanoi to Saigon. I thought it odd that so many senior members of the Communist delegations of the FPJMT wanted out, while at the same time none of the Communist delegations of the ICCS were interested in coming in.

I mentioned none of this to Long. The drive from Camp Davis back to the DAO was torrid and I perspired profusely. Shimmering heat waves rising from the concrete and asphalt created an almost surrealistic foreground for the huge, rusting metal hangers scattered across the broad expanses of the airbase. As the vehicle rounded the Base Operations building I noticed a towering column of dense black smoke rising east of the main runway. The first thing that came to my mind was that an aircraft had crashed. Knowing that my family was scheduled to depart that very afternoon, my pipe-smoking Vietnamese driver Mr. Tran Van Nga told me not to worry, that he was sure the fire was caused by airbase personnel burning a pile of old tires he had seen recently near the airbase perimeter. Relieved by the information from the normally judicious Mr. Nga but still unsure, I decided to call my wife at Clark Airbase in the Philippines that evening to see how the trip had gone.

Shortly after the vehicle passed the security checkpoint and entered the DAO compound I saw a throng of people suddenly pour from the building onto the asphalt parking area. One of them was my friend and neighbor O'Brien. When asked what was going on, O'Brien gave me a troubled stare and told me he would be right back. Puzzled by the strange reply I tried to ask for more details, but O'Brien suddenly turned and ran to board the last departing vehicle. I stood there flabbergasted, watching as the entire DAO vehicle fleet disappeared at high speed in the direction of the Air America flight line. Alarmed, I entered the FPJMT Operations Section and sought out Air Force Master Sergeant David T. Boggs. I knew Boggs was on radio watch, and he would know what was happening. When I found him, I asked why there was a flurry of activity in the compound. When Boggs saw me, his face contorted and he suddenly appeared to be on the verge of tears. He started toward me, then abruptly wavered, his voice straining as he spoke the words "the C-5A is down, it's bad, real bad."

Stunned, I moved closer to the radio in the operations section. Suddenly the squelch was broken by a cracking voice reporting how the aircraft had impacted in a muddy rice field. The same voice said survivors would be flown by helicopter from the crash site to both the ARVN Republic Hospital and the Seventh Day Adventist Hospital near the front gate of Tan Son Nhut airbase. In a trance I slowly turned toward Boggs. My tongue seemed locked in my mouth, and I could barely murmur, "This just can't be happening... I can't lose my family like this."

Staggering to the door I began an aimless walk through the corridors of the huge building called "Pentagon East." My entire life began to flow through my mind; I saw myself from the time I was a small child and continuing on through the harrowing experiences I had encountered in Vietnam, seeing how all my choices had brought me to this terrible moment. The surrealistic fantasy included scenes of combat with mangled bodies lying about, the heat of napalm and the smell of burning human flesh. My mind envisioned horrible pictures of my children's skin curling in the intense fire of the airplane crash. And like the men I had seen slip slowly into death during my infantry days, I began to cry out for help. In the same manner as those dying men, rather than calling on friends, or relatives, or on Old Glory, I instinctively called out to God. I begged for my family's safety and cried out for the lives of my children.

When I came out of my shock I found myself walking around the DAO compound asking people returning from the crash site if they had seen my family. Everyone I met replied in the negative. Those who knew me closely expressed their sympathy, adding that there was little chance that any of my family survived the crash. The aircraft had impacted on its belly and the dependent wives and children had been located in the cargo hold where there were few, if any, survivors.

Unconvinced that my family was gone, I entered the building and began walking the halls searching for anyone who could help take me to the crash site. One of the first people I met was Captain Stuart A. Herrington, one of the FPJMT members. Like others I had queried earlier, Herrington told me that he had not seen any member of my family at the site. Herrington also told me that it was useless to try to go out to the crash because all survivors had already been taken to the hospital. Herrington added that the bodies of the deceased would be flown to the mortuary of the Central Identification Laboratory in Thailand.

Darkness was approaching and acting on impulse I went to find a four-wheel drive vehicle for the trip to where the aircraft had gone down, an area called Go Vap. When I arrived in the parking area I met a group of Special Forces personnel assigned to the JCRC. The group was just returning from the Seventh Day Adventist Hospital where they had assisted in unloading the survivors and bodies of those killed in the crash. When I inquired about my family the men avoided eye contact and explained that since they were recent arrivals in country they simply had not been able to recognize anyone involved in the crash.

However, one of the men, a medic on temporary duty assignment to the DAO, pulled me off to the side. The man was Sergeant Steede, a red haired young man who had been to my home several times during his stint. Steede's courage and ability in a recent incident had impressed me, and I had written him up for an award citation. The award was for bravery Steede exhibited when he left the safety of his compound to rescue an American civilian wounded by small arms fire from a Vietnamese man who had gone berserk due to the deteriorating situation.

Steede told me that only Vietnamese survivors were being taken to the ARVN hospital, and so I should concentrate my search on the Seventh Day Adventist Hospital. Steede said he could not be certain, but he believed he had seen one of my children in the emergency room of the same hospital. He recalled that about one month prior to the crash Nova had brought the two children into the DAO Medical Clinic for immunizations, a boy and a girl. He said it was difficult to be certain due to the muddy conditions of the survivors, but he believed it was my daughter whom he had seen being brought in from the C-5A.

Encouraged by the promising news, I rushed to the hospital. Shortly after my arrival there I again met O'Brien, who was now accompanied by his wife, Yen. After hearing the report on my daughter, the O'Brien's told me to look for her while they both looked for my wife and son. A few minutes later I found my daughter, Andrea, lying on a military litter in a corridor off the emergency room. I felt an uncontrollable wave of relief crash through me, and tears rolled down my face. When I kneeled down beside her all she said was "Dad, the airplane crashed and I hurt my back." Even though finding my daughter alive was one of the happiest moments in my life, I was already dreading the inevitable questions I knew she would be asking about her mother and brother.

It seemed like hours before I finally encountered the O'Brien's in another area of the hospital. The couple reported that they had not had any success in finding Nova and Michael. After we returned to the Emergency Room a nurse walked up and asked if anyone there was related to Andrea Bell. I quickly indicated yes and the lady explained that she believed hospital personnel had located Andrea's mother. The nurse then guided me to the Intensive Care Unit where I was asked to identify a female survivor. Looking down at a tag tied to the woman's hospital gown I clearly saw the name "Bell," printed there. In looking at her face I saw the resemblance that I so wanted desperately to see. I told the nurse I was sure that the lady was Nova. Unconvinced, the nurse asked me to consider the head bandages and injuries to the face before making the identification. I refused to entertain the possibility I had mistakenly identified the woman and insisted she was my wife. I firmly told the nurse that the only thing I needed to do now was find my son. At that point the O'Brien's, who were huddled in a side conversation, turned and told me, point blank, that they were certain that the unconscious woman was not my wife. Their compassion for me was expressed on their faces, so I turned and stared at the woman again for a few moments. Reluctantly, I was forced to agree. I had to accept that my beloved wife and son were probably dead.

After being treated and X-rayed Andrea was moved by hospital staff to a ward. A Vietnamese official from the Presidential Palace arrived and paced up and down surveying the casualties being brought in from the ER. After conferring briefly with hospital staff he walked over to Andrea's bed and nervously expressed his sympathy for the tragic incident. The official then placed a small stuffed animal on the bed and quickly departed. A card pinned to the animal read, "presented by the wife of the President of the Republic of Vietnam."

The doctor informed me that Andrea had suffered burns to part of her body and several compressed vertebrae in her back. Another potential problem, which would be difficult to evaluate, was the lack of oxygen after the aircraft depressurized. According to the doctor, after the rear door separated from the aircraft several passengers located in the cargo hold died in their seats due to a lack of oxygen. Since Andrea was also in the cargo hold and without oxygen for an estimated five to six minutes, it was possible she had suffered brain injuries. Unfortunately, the doctor's prediction proved true, and Andrea would suffer emotional problems far into the future.

Although I had been tasked many times during my career to inform young servicemen in my unit concerning the deaths of their loved ones, I dreaded making the phone calls to apprise my mother, as well as Nova's parents, of the deaths of their daughter and Michael. I was especially apprehensive about telling my mother. I knew the past traumas she had endured due to the unexpected deaths of her husband and son-in-law would make this even harder to take. The two late hour telephone calls I made that night were emotional to say the least.

While residing in Saigon our family had been blessed with the employment of a Vietnamese maid known as Chi Tu (sister number four). Although the woman was uneducated and toothless, she had a great deal of common sense and a wonderful heart. Perhaps more important, Chi Tu had a genuine affection for Andrea, and I was thankful for her assistance in caring for my daughter during the trying post-accident period during which Chi Tu and I took turns spelling each other at the hospital.

During the times I was away from the hospital I scurried about trying to find personal items to facilitate Nova's identification. I was told that all bodies taken to the lab were being examined and I would be notified if my wife was identified. Since the lab had only requested personal items used by Nova for comparison of fingerprints, I assumed that a tentative identification of Michael had already been made. I also reasoned that since there were few Caucasian children on board the aircraft at the time of the crash, Michael's blonde hair and other physical features would simplify the identification process. On the other hand, since the passenger manifest included a number of adult Caucasian females, including Mrs. Barbara J. Kavulia, a secretary for the U.S. Delegation's Negotiations Division, an identification of Nova's body would be far more complicated. After searching my home I was only able to locate a toothpaste tube and hairbrush that belonged to Nova. The Central Identification Laboratory provided absolutely no feedback, and I had no way of knowing whether or not the personal items I supplied were helpful.

Further hindering the identification process, just prior to her departure I had purchased a gold "four seasons" bracelet and two rings for Nova as gifts. Sometime between the time that the aircraft crashed and when her body was recovered, looters amputated Nova's arm and several fingers in order to remove the jewelry. The lab eventually requested that I attempt to locate Nova's birth certificate to see if it contained a footprint. All the family's documentation, however, had been packed in luggage that was strapped to the back door that blew off the aircraft over the South China Sea. In the end I had to call Nova's parents in the U.S. and ask them to send a copy of her birth certificate to the lab in Thailand.

On April 8 I sat on a stool next to Andrea's hospital bed and continued my faltering attempts to explain how her mother and brother had gone to be with God. Suddenly a loud boom resonated through the hospital, followed closely by the sounds of automatic weapons fire. Surprised, I went to look out a window of the hospital to see if an attack was underway. I knew that Communist attacks on densely populated areas were rare, but after surviving both the "Tet" Offensive at Bien Hoa and the May 1968 "Tet II" offensive on Saigon, I also knew that such attacks were entirely possible. Not seeing hordes of PAVN pouring over the walls of the compound, I returned to Andrea's bedside.

Apparently prompted by the sound of the exploding bomb Andrea suddenly shouted, "a purse suitcase blew up, just like the one on the plane!" When asked for an explanation, Andrea said that the C-5A crashed because a piece of luggage that looked like a large purse exploded. She said the sound of the detonation was like the one she had just heard. She also told me that after the explosion she was not able to see anything because the aircraft quickly filled with smoke. Sobbing, she said that prior to the explosion she and Michael had been seated on either side of Nova and holding her hands. But after the blast a lady brought a Vietnamese baby over to Nova and asked her to hold it. Andrea recalled that in order to hold the infant Nova had to let go of her hand, and that was how the three became separated when the plane crashed.

That afternoon I returned to the DAO and reported Andrea's account of the incident to Lieutenant Colonel Wilson. Wilson indicated he would discuss this with someone in Air Force channels and re-contact me with feedback. Later, Wilson informed me that apparently Andrea had been mistaken concerning the explosion. He said that Air Force officials responsible for investigating the incident were aware of the cause of the crash, but that they were not permitted to discuss it. He told me that more information would be forthcoming after his return to the States.

Also that same afternoon I learned that the explosion I heard while at the hospital was actually made by two 500-pound bombs. According to the DAO Intelligence Section, a Vietnamese Air Force First Lieutenant named Nguyen Thanh Trung defected to the Communists along with his F-5E aircraft and launched a bombing attack on the Presidential Palace in Saigon. Fortunately for President Nguyen Van Thieu, however, the bombs missed their intended target. In the days ahead my attention would again be focused on Trung. Rather than President Thieu, I would be the target of a bombing attack.

The attack on the Presidential Palace caused me to consider changing my plans for Andrea's evacuation. I had hoped that during the period of Andrea's recovery the bodies of both my wife and son would be tentatively identified, and all family members would be accounted for prior to my return to America. But the attack by the former Vietnamese Air Force officer in an American supplied aircraft convinced me that it was time to get Andrea out of the country now. The doctor, however, believed it was too soon for Andrea to be moved due to her spinal injuries. Adding to my dilemma, Andrea was terrified at the thought of getting on another aircraft, C-5A or otherwise. Eventually the doctor reluctantly agreed.

I soon managed to get Andrea on an Air Force C-141 bound for Clark Air Base in the Philippines. It was not a medical evacuation aircraft, but fortunately there were few passengers on the plane and Andrea did have room to lie down on a webbed nylon seat suspended from the wall of the aircraft. Aware of Andrea's fear of flying, I told her that I had examined the aircraft carefully, and that the C-141 was the safest aircraft in the world. This reassurance seemed to calm her and she remained in good spirits throughout the trip. This had been a difficult task because even I felt a knot tighten in my stomach as I lined up to board the aircraft. Once at Clark Air Base Andrea and I changed to a commercial flight en route to San Francisco. After placing Andrea in the care of her grandparents I discussed the fates of their daughter and grandson with them. They understood when I made the decision to board a return flight for Saigon.

People often ask me why I returned to Saigon after the death of my wife and son, as my daughter obviously needed care and attention. It was a difficult decision, with many emotions pulling at me. The remains of Nova and Michael were not yet identified, and I wanted to assist in that process. But I also knew that this was a critical juncture in the war. History was being made, and I wanted to witness it unfold. Ultimately, it was my sense of duty to my friends, to the South Vietnamese, and to my country that made me want to return. Duty is that implicit obligation that separates those who serve in the military from the civilian world, the sense of a moral responsibility to my unit and everyone with whom I served. With my language skills and contacts, I believed I could still make a solid contribution to help the South Vietnamese survive the fire that was coming. Even though I knew I could have used Andrea's injuries to forego returning, I wouldn't have thought very highly of myself if I had. I knew she would be in good hands with her grandparents, so that made it easier.

In San Francisco I ended up on the return leg of the same Pan Am flight I had arrived on. After landing at Manila the Pan Am flight was placed on hold due to the deteriorating situation in Saigon. Airline personnel informed the passengers that all commercial flights into Vietnam were being cancelled but a final decision as to the exact timing of the cancellation had not been made. After an all day wait in the terminal an announcement was made informing passengers that the flight would soon depart for Tan Son Nhut. I later learned that the flight I returned on to Vietnam was the last commercial flight approved for departure to Saigon prior to the Communist takeover.

The end game was about to begin.

Chapter Four

Out of the Maelstrom

I REPORTED BACK TO THE FPJMT on April 17, 1975. The next day I was informed that a tentative identification had been made for Michael but that efforts for Nova were still ongoing. In the ensuing days I received an enormous number of personal visits, calls and letters from friends and relatives around the world. One quarter from which I did not expect condolences was the Communist delegations at Camp Davis. I was startled, however, when during my next visit several of my Communist counterparts gathered in a ceremony the Vietnamese call *chia buon,* or sharing grief, to express their sympathy for the death of my family members. Although they were our mortal enemies, they nevertheless appeared sincere, and it was a moving moment for me. I can only describe this scene as something that clearly underscored the futility of war, but which also drove home the point that on an individual basis perhaps even Communists are human, if collectively inhumane.

While we continued to surreptitiously remove American citizens, shortly after I returned to Saigon we started adding Vietnamese nationals to the list of evacuees. Most of the Vietnamese placed on departing aircraft were women and children who were immediate family members of officials whom the American Embassy had classified as "high risk." This group included many locals who were employed by the U.S. government in sensitive intelligence and security positions, such as the Special Branch Police or Central Intelligence Organization.

At the same time, the FPJMT delegation also began receiving numerous telephone calls and messages through official channels requesting assistance in evacuating relatives and loved ones from Vietnam to the States. The calls originated from a broad spectrum: the White House, heads of government agencies, military installations where active duty veterans who previously served in Vietnam had been reassigned, and from private citizens who formerly had a close involvement with the GVN. Although most of these demands concerned Vietnamese who would have been considered legitimate evacuees, suddenly however, it seemed that every old girlfriend and hootch maid needed to be evacuated immediately. In order to respond to these requests, Colonel Madison called a meeting of his American personnel. After cautioning everyone present on the need for secrecy, he gave a verbal order to begin the clandestine evacuation of Vietnamese nationals on U.S. aircraft dedicated to the DAO.

Colonel Madison would not have made such a decision without approval from someone above him. But faced with the deteriorating situation, and aware that U.S. Ambassador to South Vietnam Graham Martin was dead-set against an overt evacuation, Madison risked his career and bypassed both the head of the DAO, Major General Homer D. Smith, and the American Embassy for approval. He sent a back channel message to Dr. Roger Shields, the Deputy Assistant Secretary of Defense. He convinced Shields that if we didn't evacuate the Vietnamese working for America, a potential bloodbath could ensue when the PAVN entered the city. Shields agreed, and it was his courageous decision that eventually saved many lives.

Madison relied on his two main Vietnamese linguists, Pace and me, for this mission. Beginning on April 20, Madison's clandestine plan initially used a panel truck "borrowed" from the command mess facility. The truck was normally used to haul meat, so holes were bored in the floor of the truck to allow air inside for ventilation. Vietnamese employees of the American FPJMT Delegation and their immediate family members were considered the top priority for the covert evacuation. Employees were directed to gather at strategic points that could be easily accessed by the delivery truck. Once the evacuees had gathered, we used the vehicle day and night for several days to ferry the employees into Tan Son Nhut. After our local national employees and their families had been evacuated, we began to concentrate our efforts on family members of the South Vietnamese Delegation, as well as a small number of official ARVN delegates who would serve as escorts.

Soon however, security at the airbase began to tighten and bringing in the small numbers of remaining evacuees scattered throughout the Saigon area posed a real problem. During the initial stage of the evacuation an order from President Nguyen Van Thieu prohibited the transport of any adult males who were capable of aiding in a last-ditch effort to defend the capital from the final Communist onslaught. This policy began crumbling after President Nguyen

Van Thieu resigned from office on April 21. Thieu's departure on April 25, and the increased Communist military pressure, also convinced senior military and civilian GVN officials to re-think their future in a Communist-dominated society. Soon we were being asked to grant many exemptions to the "no military age males" policy.

Pace and I knew that the only way to get people into Tan Son Nhut was to smuggle them in by vehicle, but we quickly discovered that the panel truck was simply too cumbersome for the narrow side streets and back alleys of the city, so we decided to use a smaller vehicle. At the same time we realized that the locally hired Vietnamese drivers were subject to being stopped and searched by the guards on the gates at the air base. Since the guards had been instructed to prevent entry by ordinary Vietnamese citizens we decided to use an FPJMT vehicle, a large black Ford LTD, to smuggle people onto the airbase. Pace would act as the driver and I would be the passenger. The delegation's Administrative NCO, Master Sergeant William B. Herron, helped coordinate the list of evacuees and the locations for pick-up throughout Saigon.

As the names and addresses of evacuees were passed to us, we began making shuttle runs to points all over the city. People were hidden in the trunk and floorboard of the vehicle on each trip to the airfield. On one such expedition we packed a group of seven women and children, who somehow managed to stifle any feelings of claustrophobia, into the trunk of the large military sedan. Each time the vehicle driven by Pace approached Tan Son Nhut's main gate, the guards only saw me sitting in the rear seat of the vehicle. Consequently, they merrily waved us through. Once inside the base the passengers would be off-loaded near the flight line where they were quickly transferred to a waiting C-141 aircraft. Pace and I would continue transporting evacuees in this manner until almost the last day, when the Communist shelling of Tan Son Nhut forced its closure.

Prior to initiation of our secret evacuation plan, Communist officials at Camp Davis had attempted their version of a similar strategy: the furtive removal of their key cadre. I had noticed earlier that the Communists appeared to be withdrawing all key personnel by gradually adding their names to the weekly Hanoi liaison flights. I was the first member of the U.S. delegation to detect this maneuver, and I immediately informed Colonel Madison. I reasoned that the transfer of key cadre from Saigon to Hanoi by the Communist delegations was an indicator that an all-out attack on Saigon was imminent. Yet if we could manage to keep the remaining important cadre in Saigon, the Communists might hesitate in attacking, fearing the loss of their own people. I recommended that Madison find a method to delay the flights.

Some other members of the American side had not yet gained an appreciation for the gravity of the situation, and they objected to any attempt to restrict the liaison flights, thus temporarily undermining my attempt to halt the flow of principal cadre from Camp Davis. Captain Stuart Herrington was unconvinced that the senior members of the Communist delegations were planning on leaving the FPJMT for Hanoi. But Madison had considerable experience in dealing with Communist strategy and he also respected my opinion. After closely examining the manifests he came to the same conclusion I did; the DRV and PRG delegations were taking advantage of the liaison flights in order to extract their principal cadre. Not only had the most recent manifests included a number of key Communist personnel who had already returned to Hanoi, the list for the next flight contained the names of the remaining top three Communist cadres assigned to the cease-fire mission in the South.

This created a dilemma for Madison because he did not want to provide grist for the ever-ready Communist propaganda mill. If he cancelled any future flights the Communist side would publicly attack the U.S. by claiming that we were violating the provisions of the Paris agreements by restricting the free movement of the DRV and PRG delegations. On the other hand, if Madison allowed the Communist side to remove all of its key personnel from Saigon, the North Vietnamese planners would have no qualms about concentrating rocket and artillery barrages on the base, which was obviously critical to our overall evacuation efforts.

Contemplating the creation of a de facto "hostage" situation, I reminded Madison that I had seen situations in the past where Communist units had been willing to accept horrific casualties. But these casualties were comprised primarily of young farm kids who had never joined the Party and whose families had little or no political clout back home. I surmised, however, that although the Politburo would not be reluctant to sacrifice large numbers of its field troops, it would most likely hesitate about inadvertently killing senior party members. Undoubtedly, a second Politburo concern was what the U.S. reaction would be to a final assault on the capital.

After pondering the ramifications, Madison accepted my recommendation and passed it up the chain, where it was approved. Now we had to develop some method of holding them on the base. We solved our predicament by creating a ruse. Madison, acting on instructions from the American Ambassador, accepted the DRV and PRG manifests without question while secretly arranging for the departing aircraft to develop "mechanical difficulties." Shortly after takeoff on April 18, 1975, the C-130 aircraft veered in a circle around the sprawling air base and touched back down. As the aircraft mechanics dutifully examined the plane, members of the Communist delegations on the tarmac launched into a bitter tirade, complaining of American deception regarding the regularly scheduled flight. The senior American officer at the scene, Lieutenant Colonel Wilson, directed me to inform the two Communist delegations "you have insulted the U.S. side." Later that week during a subsequent trip I made to Camp Davis, haughty members of the DRV delegation imperiously chided me concerning the "mechanical difficulties." Full of themselves and sensing their eminent victory, they loudly reminded me that Americans should remember that because of its involvement in Vietnam, the United States was no longer the world's strongest superpower. Normally, I gave the Communists a lively response to their lectures, but this time I was so caught off guard by the arrogant comment that I was speechless.

With the liaison flights temporarily suspended I refocused my attention on screening classified documents in the Liaison Division for destruction or evacuation. Although most of the documents would be moved to the DAO alternate command element in Hawaii, a significant number would have to be burned. As I sat at my desk scanning through mounds of files, I could not help but feel apprehensive about the plastic explosives and wiring strung along the walls inside my office, placed there by Captain George Petrie's JCRC team. I kept trying to reassure myself that the explosive team was comprised of professional Special Forces personnel, and it was unlikely that anything could go wrong. But the hectic manner in which the task was done considerably raised my anxiety level.

During that same time frame I noticed an ARVN Lieutenant Colonel standing silently outside the DAO's Liaison Division. I had seen the same officer inside the DAO several times in the past accompanied by Douglas Bergner, an agent of the 500th MI Group's Detachment K in Bangkok. Bergner's current "assignment" was as the American military representative to Binh Dinh province. According to Bergner, the ARVN Lieutenant Colonel was Pham Xuan Huy, the G-2 of the ARVN 22nd Division and the Secretary of the Phoenix Project Committee in Binh Dinh where Bergner had been working for the past several years. Bergner's unit rated Lieutenant Colonel Huy as one of the most professional intelligence officers in the South Vietnamese military, and at one point had funded him for advanced training at a facility in Okinawa. Bergner also related how Lieutenant Colonel Huy had used his own money to place a memorial to a U.S. pilot who had been killed while supporting ARVN troops on Hong Kong Mountain near An Khe. Not knowing Huy's circumstances and sensing that he was in need of help, I was on the verge of offering him assistance. Since I was already in the process of evacuating many Vietnamese personnel, I felt that one more family would not make much difference. But I hesitated and ultimately decided against it. While I was aware that the Liaison Division was responsible for intelligence, including US/ARVN bilateral operations, I erroneously assumed that the Liaison Division would arrange the evacuation of Huy and his family. I had no idea that his American counterparts would forget Huy, neither did I realize that I was in effect abandoning my future father-in-law.[1]

In the midst of all the confusion a man visited me who called himself "Bill Jackson." Jackson was assigned as a Liaison Officer to the ARVN Joint General Staff. Since Jackson never provided any details concerning his duties, I suspected that he was using a cover name and that he actually worked for the CIA, a fact later confirmed by Frank Snepp in his book. At Jackson's request I had recently completed a translation of the book *Battle of Binh Long* (an account of the 1972 offensive in that province, mainly the battle for An Loc) from Vietnamese to English. Jackson was impressed by my command of Vietnamese and later returned to the DAO to request my assistance in identifying and recruiting "stay-behind" agents from the available pool of DAO local hire employees.

The U.S. intelligence community was no doubt aware that it was on the verge of losing all its assets in Vietnam, and Jackson was probably tasked to make sure that the CIA had the ability to monitor activities inside Vietnam after the withdrawal. I recalled that the CIA had organized a similar plan in North Vietnam at the time of the French withdrawal and the closure of the American Consulate in Hanoi. I surmised that Jackson was not the only CIA operative working on the project, and I wondered if the recruited "stay-behind" agents would be as quickly compromised and arrested as their predecessors in North Vietnam only two decades before.

I was curious but never did learn if Jackson knew of similar "stay-behind" operations already being undertaken by the Department of Defense. Since human intelligence operations are compartmentalized I did not raise the issue with him. I knew the DOD was working on this mission since several Vietnamese colleagues had recently approached me for advice. After my transfer from intelligence duties to the POW/MIA accounting mission, many of my former GVN counterparts had likewise received similar transfers. Some worked the POW/MIA issue, but others found themselves in Intelligence Unit 101 of the ARVN, while others ended up in Intelligence Unit 701 of the RVN Navy, or the Military Security Service.[2] They were programmed to deliberately miss the evacuation, and they were being issued gold, dollars, and communications equipment to conduct post withdrawal spy operations. Not realizing the urgency of the situation at the time of their recruitment, they were now justifiably concerned about what might happen to them if their roles were discovered after the American withdrawal. Realizing they had little chance for success, but knowing our critical need for intelligence in a country with little future American presence, I could only assure them that they would not be forgotten, while secretly hoping I was not signing their death warrants.

During the same time as the late night visits from the nervous Vietnamese intelligence personnel, I went to Tan Son Nhut to pick up an old friend, William Loveless, aka the "Budget and Fiscal Officer" for the 500th MI Group in Bangkok. That was his official title, one I teased him about since he was carrying the money to fund the ARVN intelligence units and the "stay-behind" operations.

Loveless was a flamboyant, adventure-loving character. At the time of the American withdrawal from Vietnam in March 1973, he volunteered for an undercover assignment in Saigon to ferret out American military deserters who had remained behind. Hanging out in an area of Saigon known as "100 P Alley," Loveless posed as a deserter to infiltrate this community. While he was successful in penetrating this group, during an altercation with a deserter Loveless accidentally dropped his badge and credentials, which identified him as a Counterintelligence Agent. As word of his deception spread the hunter quickly became the hunted, and he narrowly escaped with his life. When Loveless arrived on an unmarked C-47, and knowing his current occupation, combined with the sudden appearance of my nervous Vietnamese friends, I assumed he was involved in this new adventure and was associated with at least some of the Vietnamese intelligence personnel recruited for the stay-behind operation.

As for Jackson's covert endeavor, I agreed to assist him, but there were few Vietnamese takers, since almost everyone was preparing to flee. One of my most experienced translators, Mr. Nguyen Cong Phu, who had fled North Vietnam for the South in 1954, wanted to remain and work in the new program. Phu rationalized that since he had worked for the Foreign Broadcast Information Service prior to his current employment with the FPJMT, he had nothing to fear. Only those who had been involved in any intelligence and security related duties, Phu assumed, would have anything to dread from the Communists. When I reached in a drawer and produced a line and block chart showing that the Foreign Broadcast Information Service was an official U.S. Government agency controlled and funded by the CIA, Phu's face suddenly turned ashen. Normally sluggish in his endeavors, Phu quickly shifted into high gear and headed home to pack. As for those who decided to remain, although I passed the names to Jackson as requested, I had strong suspicions as to why they were willing to pass up the opportunity to escape.

While I never knew exactly what happened to all the stay-behinds, I understand that the 500th MI Group in Thailand received radio communications from some of the agents for several days after the Communist takeover. Soon after, however, all communications ceased. Other 500th MI stay-behinds were captured on the coast near the city of Vung Tau. The Communist intelligence services held trials for the captured agents, but I never knew precisely what happened to them. I also never knew whether we received any useful intelligence, but given what had occurred in North Vietnam in 1954, I doubt it.

Jackson also was in a quandary as to what counsel he should give to the senior ARVN generals he was advising. I agreed with him that it was only a matter of time before the country fell. When Jackson said he needed to find some way to buy time, I internally debated the possible options that could force the PAVN to refrain from attacking Saigon. Like many others, I came to the conclusion that only the direct application of American bombing attacks could stabilize the situation, or the threat of an amphibious attack against North Vietnam. Realizing either American option was unlikely, I suggested that he arrange for the South Vietnamese Joint General Staff to plan a company-size airborne operation in the North. I mentioned

Nghe An province. Once a specific target had been identified, I would then visit Camp Davis. After several slugs of rice wine I would let the information slip, along with some amplifying details indicating that the small scale airborne operation was only an advance reconnaissance mission for a full scale invasion of North Vietnam in Nghe An. I reasoned that such an impending threat might cause Communist strategists to redeploy PAVN forces back to the North, or at the very least give them more incentive to seriously negotiate for a peaceful settlement. Jackson didn't appear to have much confidence in my impromptu plan, but that was all I could come up with on the spur of the moment.

On April 23, Madison informed me that I would have to abandon my thus far successful rescue efforts in lieu of a more critical mission. In a hurriedly called session Madison informed me that the resignation of President Thieu on April 21 had increased the possibility of a political settlement and I would participate in a last ditch effort to negotiate with the Communist side. This hastily organized mission would only include two Americans, the Chief of the Negotiations Division, Colonel Harry Summers, and myself. According to the plan, both Summers and I were to keep the information "close-hold" and be ready to depart on what would be publicized as a routine liaison flight scheduled to depart for Hanoi early on April 25.

It was a skillful maneuver by the Politburo. By asking for the Americans to visit Hanoi to discuss a possible negotiated end to the fighting, they accomplished several objectives. First, the flight was the death knell for our efforts to keep the senior Communist cadre at Camp Davis. Since the Tan Son Nhut flights were the only reliable direct air transport into North Vietnam from Saigon, almost all the remaining senior Communist cadre were on the flight. Second, by bringing the cadre back, the Politburo would receive the latest intelligence on the conditions in Saigon and the ARVN plans for the defense of Saigon. We knew the DRV/PRG delegations had agents in the city, and by allowing the Communist cadre to return, we removed for the PAVN generals the final roadblock to an assault. By also appearing to acquiesce to the many requests for a negotiated settlement, they placated world opinion and stymied any potential U.S. efforts to re-intervene militarily. It was a textbook maneuver from their old tactic of "talking while fighting." They knew, given our domestic situation, that the anti-war crowd would vociferously condemn the U.S. government for any military action undertaken simultaneously with efforts to find a peaceful solution. Worse, the anti-war faction was not unfamiliar with this Communist tactic, and I always had the sense that many of the hard-core left approved of it, hoping to quickly bring about the defeat of South Vietnam. We soon learned, however, that these weren't the only reasons to ask for the flight to Hanoi.

The war was fast approaching Saigon as North Vietnamese units pressed forward. Beginning on April 9 at a small provincial city called Xuan Loc about forty miles northeast of Saigon, the troops of the ARVN 18th Division, led by Brigadier General Le Minh Dao, made a courageous stand and suffered high casualties in beating off six attacks in five days by elements of three PAVN divisions, the 6th, 7th, and 341st. Although the beleaguered ARVN defenders at Xuan Loc put up tremendous resistance, PAVN units set up a strong roadblock between the city and Saigon at the junction of National Routes 1 and 20, effectively isolating Xuan Loc. On the morning of April 20, the 18th Division was ordered to retreat. Years later during interview trips to refugee camps in Southeast Asia, I learned that South Vietnamese Air Force C-130s dropped two 15,000 pound "daisy cutters" and one CBU-55 (an oxygen depleting bomb, called a Fuel-Air-Explosive), attempting to stem the PAVN advance. The former PAVN soldiers who had been present near Xuan Loc described their own casualties from the bombs as "bodies turned to ash."

Despite the tough struggle at Xuan Loc, the PAVN advance was relentless. The members of the DRV and PRG delegations could barely hide their excitement as reports of Communist victories continued to filter in. I began to notice that the normally poker-faced Communist delegates were in the process of undergoing a transition from their usual quiet, somber mood to a more insolent demeanor, with a collective bearing bordering on arrogance. To make matters worse, this irritating behavioral change was coupled with a major concern for our safety on this flight. The PAVN had deployed shoulder-fired heat-seeking anti-aircraft missiles to the Saigon area. We could only hope that the PAVN anti-aircraft gunners had been thoroughly briefed on our departure.

Fortunately, we made it safely into the air. Once the C-130 Hercules was airborne the Communist members wasted no time in engaging their American counterparts in a one-sided dialogue. The collective theme, established on cue from the senior representative of the DRV delegation, Colonel Nguyen Tu, was obviously oriented toward lessening the impact of "a loss of face" by the Americans in losing the war. I found this ironic since I had attended numerous classes emphasizing the dire consequences of causing an Asian to "lose face." Now the situation had reversed. I found comments such as "you Americans should not feel so badly, you did everything you could" even more loathsome than the standard comments extolling the virtues of Socialism.

These exchanges prompted what later became one of the most widely quoted remarks of the war. In an attempt to deflate the growing air of presumptuousness, Summers reminded Tu quite pointedly that the American military had never lost a major battle during the war. Colonel Tu seemed to ponder that statement briefly before rendering his now famous reply: "Yes, this is correct, but it is also irrelevant." Prior to ending the conversation, a somewhat defiant Summers reminded Tu that in Vietnam, American policy makers had tried their best to ensure that the war was fought as humanely as possible. He added that in any future military action undertaken by the United States, the opponent would meet such force the likes of which had never been witnessed. Although Tu seemed somewhat bewildered by this statement, he nonetheless appeared to accept Summers' remarks as unfeigned.

When the aircraft landed at Gia Lam Airfield in Hanoi, central government cadre quickly appeared on the flight line. The senior man present informed Summers and I that we would be meeting at the Thong Nhat Hotel. Since the term *thong nhat* in Vietnamese translates to "reunification," and NVA units were surrounding Saigon, I could easily see the symbolism afforded to the selection of the meeting site. I wasn't surprised as I had been accustomed since 1968 to the subtleties employed by the Communists throughout all phases of negotiation. Almost everything they said or did had some signal or hidden meaning. It was essentially a second language whereby one communicates with his adversary without ever having spoken directly to him.

The ride into the city took our group across the bomb-scarred Long Bien Bridge, called the Paul Dumier by its French builders. The bridge had been a constant target during the war, and the Vietnamese had expended considerable resources in its defense, seeing it as a commentary on their defiance of the massive American military machine. The bridge had survived the onslaught, but not without some serious damage, much like the rest of North Vietnam.

Vehicles concentrated at the head of the bridge waited for soldiers to inform drivers as to which side of the bridge to enter. For a short period of time vehicles entering the city would proceed onto the right lane of the bridge, and then the traffic pattern would be switched so the next increment of vehicles would enter onto the left side. Vehicles departing from Hanoi were similarly alternated in the opposite direction. I learned from our accompanying officials that the reason for the lane change was the instability of the bridge's piers due to the bombing. According to the cadre, the constant switching of the flow of traffic between the in-bound and out-bound lanes balanced the stress on the weakened bridge, preventing total collapse.

While crossing the huge span a Communist cadre related a humorous story about the Long Bien Bridge. A famous French architect, Paul Dumier, had designed the bridge during the colonial period. A French teacher of Vietnamese students at the French Lycee in Hanoi decided to include this topic in a test for his students. When he asked one student, "Who built the bridge over the Red River," the lad said he didn't know. The teacher informed him that he would receive an "F" for his grade. When the teacher directed the same question to a second student, who also did not know the answer, the young man mumbled under his breath *du me,* which in Vietnamese means "mother f---!" The delighted French teacher loudly exclaimed "Dumier! That's correct!"

Downtown Hanoi was a dismal place with swarms of women and children dressed in rags riding rusting Chinese bicycles. Considering the massive number of North Vietnamese troops currently flowing down the Ho Chi Minh Trail into

South Vietnam, I could understand why the only men observed on the street were either elderly or infirm, many of them without arms or legs. Almost every business establishment in the city had been converted into a machine shop for manufacturing weapons or some type of military equipment. The shrill pitch of the grinding metal was deafening and I found it difficult to converse with the man in the seat next to me. I figured that since we had designated Hanoi off-limits for bombing attacks, the North Vietnamese had moved their major weapons plants into the city where they could operate in safety. The PAVN had also used Catholic churches as warehouses for the storage of ammunition and grain, a maneuver that struck me as sacrilegious and unsportsmanlike at the same time. The only foreigners seen were Caucasians dressed in gray work uniforms. These Soviet and East Bloc "civilian technicians" scurried about between the machine works in unmarked trucks and vans.

Lunch was uneventful, but prior to the meal I found myself seated with the members of the GVN delegation in the small lobby of the Metropole hotel. We had been taken there instead of the Thong Nhat hotel. Conspicuously located nearby, a delegation of PRG officials just in from Paris loudly rehashed the results of a recent meeting apparently held to hammer out the details of an imminent election of a new government of "national reconciliation and concord." It was as if a *fait accompli* had already taken place in Paris, and regardless of GVN desires, a new government was already on the verge of being formed in South Vietnam. The group of southern "Viet Cong" exchanged comments about how the voting process would take place in the South and what percentages of territory they believed the PRG already controlled. Likely mindful of recent French efforts to negotiate separately with the Communists for a peaceful settlement of the war, the senior GVN delegate, Lieutenant Colonel Dinh Cong Chat, seemed concerned by the exchange, but at the same time reluctant to become involved. The orchestrated dialogue was complemented by a display of large sacks of rice strategically placed around the lobby. The sacks were adorned with bold labels written in Vietnamese indicating, "rice donated by the people of China." The rice sacks were obviously designed to demonstrate the unwavering support by the People's Republic of China during Hanoi's final offensive.

After lunch, we were informed that our meeting had been cancelled. One of the DRV officials said we needed to return to the airplane, so we loaded onto a bus to go back to the C-130. Summers and I were crestfallen, while the GVN delegates were stoic, almost resigned to their fates. Based on discussions with the Embassy political section both Summers and I had anticipated important deliberations with the North Vietnamese representatives during the trip. There was no shortage of rumors around Saigon to the effect that President Thieu's resignation would remove the last remaining obstacle to the formation of a coalition government between the GVN and the PRG. The hope was that the establishment of this new government would forestall a predicted bloodbath should Communist forces seize power by military means. Now it appeared that even that slim hope had been crushed.

The atmosphere at Gia Lam Airport prior to boarding the return flight to Saigon that afternoon was even more tense than the morning session at Tan Son Nhut. Scanning the surrounding area I experienced a sense of both melancholy and curiosity as I watched jubilant Soviet advisers loading communications equipment onto Yakovlev 40 jet aircraft. Normally concerned with concealing their presence in Vietnam, the heretofore-nocturnal Soviets were now out in the open for all to see. One by one the small, sleek aircraft taxied onto the runway and rapidly ascended before turning south toward a besieged Republic of Vietnam, a place that I had come to love and hate at the same time. I surmised that the aircraft were bound for Danang, which had fallen on March 29. I wondered to myself how the Vietnamese people would react when they realized that aircraft of the USSR were quickly replacing the recently departed American-made planes.

While waiting to board the aircraft I surveyed the passengers to confirm my suspicion that Colonel Tu would not appear for the return trip. As soon as the aircraft leveled off and passengers could move about the cabin, Major Huyen, now the senior member of the DRV Delegation, approached the anxious Americans for what in essence would be the last key exchange between the two sides prior to the Communist victory. After some small talk about the weather a relaxed Huyen abruptly changed his demeanor in order to demonstrate the appropriate degree of rigidity normally required by a junior Communist official when tasked to deliver remarks prepared in advance by the Politburo. Huyen began by saying that there would be no more negotiations between the DRV and the United States. He did, however, have three points to be relayed to the White House:

1. The United States has three days in which to dismantle and remove from Vietnam the entire Defense Attaché Office.
2. The American Delegation to the FPJMT should remain in Vietnam and continue its work on the POW/MIA issue.
3. The American Embassy shall be allowed to work out its future with the new government in Saigon.

Having performed his chore Huyen returned to his side of the aircraft and slumped down for a nap, indicating he had nothing more to say and didn't wish to discuss the message any further. This was typical Communist behavior; they would always stiffen up when delivering prepared remarks composed by the Politburo. After the delivery, they returned to their normal self. Now the episode in Hanoi and the call for negotiations were clear, and my earlier suspicions confirmed. Hanoi had seen through our deception regarding the plane and had reacted to persistent American requests for negotiations by asking for an American team to come to North Vietnam. The Communists knew that the only way to Hanoi was via the Liaison flight. The whole affair was designed for Colonel Tu and the others to get back, and then for us to receive the final Politburo demands, and then for Summers to provide them to the U.S. government. It was a brilliant riposte, one they knew we could not turn down.

Since Huyen had provided no details concerning what he called a "new government," both Summers and I were unsure as to exactly what the next move by the Communists would be. After some thought, we both agreed that at least the U.S. delegation now knew where it stood, and there would be at least three more days remaining in which to continue the evacuation of the DAO. Based on the information from Huyen that we should remain in Vietnam to continue our work on the POW/MIA issue, I produced a notepad and began the difficult task of planning for continued operations after the closure of the Attaché office. Summers decided to recommend to Colonel Madison that the delegation expropriate the DAO mess compound to use for both office space and living quarters. Since the DAO offices had provided the bulk of administrative and logistical support, this seemed like a logical choice, as the compound was equipped with a dining room and house trailers that served as sleeping quarters.

After compiling my list of equipment for support of future POW/MIA accounting operations, I decided to relax for the remaining flight time back to Saigon. I borrowed some recent issues of the "Stars and Stripes" newspaper from one of the C-130 crewmembers. On the front page of the first paper I pulled from the stack my eyes locked on the face of the C-5A pilot I had seen in the swimming pool at the Bachelor Office Quarters #1 with the Vietnamese prostitutes on April 3. The photo accompanied an article relating how the pilot had exhibited considerable heroism in maneuvering the crippled aircraft back to Saigon. Another article provided a journalist's account of the scene at the crash site and described how the pages of a Donald Duck comic book lying next to the wreckage "flipped in the breeze." As I read the paper, a wave of emotion struck me. I felt the knot in my stomach again and I guessed I was developing a fear of flying. I recalled the flash of anger I felt at seeing the Russians slapping each other on the back, so confident in their approaching victory. As I watched them I felt my skin crawl, which was soon replaced by feelings of guilt for South Vietnam as it went down the proverbial tubes. But most of all I felt my stomach turn cold inside as I read the words that the pilot of the C-5A was a hero. He and most of his crew had survived, while my wife and son were dead. He would have been more of a hero if I hadn't seen him carousing at the swimming pool bar the night before the plane crash. But I told myself, perhaps he did act heroically in wrestling a badly damaged aircraft back over land. I spent most of the remaining flight staring into space and debating these conflicting emotions.

Upon our return to Saigon, we reported Major Huyen's remarks through the Embassy's political officer to Ambassador Graham Martin. Other intelligence channels also debriefed us on the state of affairs in Hanoi, and as trained observers, we rendered our reports on road and rail conditions and other matters in the north. Huyen's statement eventually became known as the "conditions for the evacuation of Saigon." Several days later I heard that the Ambassador optimistically viewed Huyen's remarks as renewed hope for possible negotiations to reach a political solution, as well as confirmation of Dr. Henry Kissinger's view that the North Vietnamese were willing to permit a gradual withdrawal of the American presence. Martin knew that President Thieu would be departing Vietnam that same evening, thus removing the last major obstacle to a negotiated settlement.

I disagreed with the Ambassador's analysis. Based on the language used by Major Huyen, I believed that he was in fact relaying what the North Vietnamese considered to be their final terms for a "political solution" to the conflict. In the case of the FPJMT Huyen had used the word "should," which implied that although the North Vietnamese preferred that the U.S. delegation stay and work on the POW/MIA issue, they were leaving the decision up to the American government. In the case of the American Embassy he used the terms "will be allowed," implying that regardless of the political makeup of any new government in Saigon, the North Vietnamese had no objections to the presence of an American Embassy. But as the Americans would unfortunately soon learn, by his usage of the term "must," Huyen was unambiguous concerning the requirement for complete removal of the DAO within a three-day period.

The following day Pace and I continued our clandestine delivery of evacuees from sites throughout the capital into the airfield. As the cumbersome black military sedan sped by the Air America hangar toward the main flight line, pillars of smoke rose from the outskirts of Saigon, a clear sign that NVA artillery units were displacing forward. With each passing day the frequency of the long-range fire gradually increased. As Pace and I continued our missions, the anxiety caused by the looming possibility of an attack on the base seemed to overshadow the more immediate danger posed by the still distant 130mm artillery units.

Although we had planned to terminate the shuttle runs as soon as possible, the list of people to be evacuated continued to swell. As I loaded Vietnamese women and children into the sedan I was amazed at the number of U.S. civilian and military officials with "close" Vietnamese ties. Cohabitation with foreign nationals was strictly prohibited, and in order to prevent the loss of sensitive security clearances, many of the officials, including members of the U.S. delegation, had lived two lives, and in some cases with two wives. What was most astonishing was the fact that some of the senior personnel, who had insisted on disciplinary action for lower ranking men who became too closely involved with Vietnamese women, were equally guilty of the same violations.

Many of these shuttle trips were fraught with danger. We would often drive to poor neighborhoods on the outskirts of Saigon looking for what were described as close female friends but who in reality were probably prostitutes. In these insecure areas, we faced threats not only from possible ambushes by city based guerrillas or PAVN sapper and recon units that had infiltrated Saigon, but also from roving bands of ARVN deserters. We also considered the remaining South Vietnamese military forces as potential threats, as we never knew what they would do. Several Americans had already been shot at by some ARVNs, who believed the United States was abandoning them. Despite the hazards, we managed to handle every situation calmly, although our main problem was to get high-ranking officers and their families out without destroying the South Vietnamese command structure. We also needed to maintain the illusion that we weren't abandoning them, just assisting the South Vietnamese in fighting the Communists. For example, after the bombing of the Presidential Palace, the DAO discussed with the South Vietnamese command staff how to prioritize the evacuation. It was decided first to remove the families of the remaining F-5 and A-37 pilots, since if they turned against the Saigon government while in mid-air carrying a bomb load, they could do significant damage. It worked, and no more Air Force pilots defected to the Communist side, but it was all a high-wire act, one I believe we performed well.

On April 26 I received an urgent call from First Lieutenant Do Van Thuan, Director of the Airborne Training School. I liked Thuan a great deal; he was a straightforward, outstanding soldier who spoke good English with a distinct British accent, which coming from a Vietnamese was at times surreal. Thuan requested assistance in evacuating the wife and children of the ARVN Airborne Commander, Brigadier General Le Quang Luong. Since both Thuan and General Luong had signed off on my Vietnamese jump wings, I promised to help. I advised Thuan that I would stop by that same afternoon to talk to Brigadier General Luong about his family.

Before my departure, Colonel Madison called me into his office to relay a request from the Chief of the Army Division of the DAO. The request called for me to go to Camp Davis and ask the Communist delegations for a copy of Mao Tse Tung's book on guerrilla warfare. I immediately became very uneasy because of the obvious implications, but at the same time I was compelled to carry out my instructions.

As expected, the book request at Camp Davis caused a furor among the Communists. Not unexpectedly, they perceived the request as a veiled threat that the U.S. intended to begin guerrilla warfare in Vietnam after they took over the country. I emphasized that I was only doing my job, but that didn't seem to assuage the Communists. Noticing an unusual degree of tension in the air, I sensed that the men in Camp Davis were not only worried about how the GVN leadership might react to their presence during the imminent offensive, they were also uncertain about the actions of their own forces during the impending attack. If the PAVN tried to take the base and the ARVN made a stand, Camp

Davis would be caught right in the middle of the crossfire. Exiting the compound gate I could see both PRG and DRV personnel busily digging bunkers next to their Quonset hut living quarters.

Continuing on to the Headquarters of the ARVN Airborne Command, I waited as a guard called for First Lieutenant Thuan to admit me through the heavily fortified gate. Thuan escorted me into the Commander's office where a tired and discouraged Brigadier General Luong sat holding a bottle of Hennessy cognac. Luong was a decorated combat veteran, having fought in some of the toughest battles of the war, including An Loc and Quang Tri in 1972. Staring at me through bloodshot eyes Luong asked me what the Americans were planning to do. Unable to provide a good answer I could only tell Luong that the sole plan I was aware of called for the total evacuation of the DAO, and with the exception of the FPJMT, all United States military personnel. When I asked Luong what the GVN had in mind he shook his head slowly, saying that he wished there were some last minute action he could take, but he was afraid that it was already too late.

Suddenly I thought of the option I had suggested earlier to Jackson. I mentioned to Luong that since he was the Airborne Commander, he might consider an airborne operation into the North. Luong said he had already researched that possibility but had come to the conclusion that it was far too complicated. I reminded Luong that the ARVNs had a number of American supplied C-130 aircraft capable of transporting heavy loads, and that Vietnamese paratroopers were small and light. Luong opined that the aircraft would probably be shot down en route to the objective. I advised him that I had just returned from Hanoi and it appeared that most, if not all of the missiles and air defense systems had already been moved south for the final offensive. I added that northern air defense crews were accustomed to seeing the C-130 aircraft of the FPJMT travel from Saigon to Hanoi on a weekly basis, and a C-130 packed with his troops would certainly be able to seize the international airport near Hanoi. Once the airfield was secured some of the remaining C-130s could land while others dropped their troops in a ring around Hanoi. If he could capture the capital city, along with the Politburo and Party Central Committee intact, Luong would have some impressive bargaining power.

The weary airborne general looked at me as if he could not tell whether I was serious or only joking. After pondering the idea for a moment he whispered that he just didn't think it would work. Seeing the cognac bottle was now empty, I set my glass back on the table and asked Luong to bring his family to the DAO the following day, ready to board an aircraft. An Airborne-Ranger myself, I was deeply affected by Luong's predicament. Walking out the door of his office I couldn't help but wonder what an American or Israeli Airborne general would do in a similar situation.

The following morning I entered Colonel Madison's office to find Deputy Secretary of Defense Eric Van Marbod lying on the Colonel's sofa. I had heard that Van Marbod was a laid back fellow and now I believed it. Looking at the ceiling Van Marbod described how one of his staff, Richard Armitage, was at that moment busy arranging the evacuation of the RVN Navy. According to Van Marbod's plan, not only would naval personnel and their families be evacuated, he had also instructed Armitage to take out as many ships as possible. I felt somewhat relieved, because I knew that at least some of those scheduled for pick-up by our vehicle would now be able to depart by sea. I knew that Armitage was a former Naval officer, and that regardless of the degree of peril he would never abandon his men or turn back. Ultimately the sea escape was very successful; I would have the pleasure of working with Armitage again during postwar refugee resettlement operations in Arkansas and on the POW/MIA issue after he became Assistant Secretary of Defense for International Security Affairs.

On the afternoon of April 28 I stopped by the headquarters element to see if there was any decision on the future status of our delegation. I was told that White House policy-makers were still deliberating the issue and that in the interim I should begin preparations to move the delegation into the Command Mess compound. Pace and I immediately began to prepare large signs in both English and Vietnamese that read "This Compound Has Been Reserved for the US Delegation FPJMT." When we arrived at the compound to post the signs, we encountered a group of local hire employees actively looting the dining facility. Surprised to learn that any American personnel were still interested in the dining hall, the collective attitude of the looters quickly changed when they read the caption on the signs. Reassured that many, if not all of them would continue to be employed, the group ceased its looting operation and began to put things back in order. As if to demonstrate renewed loyalty, an obese cook in a white apron sprang into action and seized a large box of meat being dragged out the door by an elderly lady.

While placing the sign over the main entry gate to the compound I observed five Vietnamese Air Force A-37 "Dragonfly" aircraft approaching the airbase from the north. At 1800 hours the aircraft circled Tan Son Nhut and then began to dive down toward the flight line. As the aircraft lifted back skyward a series of loud booms reverberated across the compound. One of the aircraft circled back and began another dive, this time straight for the command mess compound. I stood staring at the A-37 as it increased its speed downward, its wings wavering steadily from side to side. When I moved to the right it appeared that the aircraft followed my movement. When I moved to the left I felt the same sensation. Petrified, I became frozen in place as I watched the bomb load hurtle downward into an open area next to the compound. Following an earth-shaking explosion large rocks and chunks of dirt plummeted down onto the roofs of nearby trailer houses. Stunned by the resounding blast a drunken U.S. Army Colonel staggered from a nearby bunker waving a 45-caliber pistol in the direction of the high-flying aircraft, seemingly oblivious to the fact that the effective firing range of his weapon was only fifty yards. About that same time anti-aircraft fire erupted, causing the aircraft to suddenly break off their attack and depart to the north. Shortly thereafter two South Vietnamese Air Force F-5s made a belated and unsuccessful attempt to overtake the A-37s and shoot them down.[3]

Still rooted to my place, I slowly grasped that for the first time in my military career I had been the subject of an air attack. I was astounded by the degree of panic I experienced that day. I thought about how the U.S. and its allies had enjoyed unlimited air superiority since the beginning of the war, and how close air support was always on call during my days in the infantry. I had witnessed air attacks on PAVN troops on numerous occasions, but I simply did not have any appreciation for the inherent power and shock resulting from an aerial bombardment. As I pondered these emotions, I suddenly realized that the spartan PAVN light infantry, which had been fighting for many years under this constant threat, must have equally felt the same sense of helplessness I had just experienced. My already high regard for these tough soldiers increased dramatically.

Although we were not anxious to revive our shuttle runs, Pace and I began to receive more frantic calls that night from a number of colleagues in Bangkok who had recently evacuated. Most, if not all, of the callers had planned to evacuate common-law wives and girl friends early on, but the rapidly onrushing PAVN had short-circuited those plans.

Moved by the emotional pleas for help, Pace and I decided to proceed again with our two-man evacuation operation. However, at roughly 0400 hours on the morning of April 29, gunners in PAVN artillery units surrounding Saigon hammered the base with a massive barrage. The fire was deadly and accurate. At first they used a combination of rockets and the big guns, but after the first hours switched to rockets only. One rocket fired into the base hit our compound and killed two U.S. Marines on guard at the quarters of the Defense Attaché.

Besides the enemy salvos complicating our efforts, many of those scheduled for pick up were completely unprepared for departure. Some flatly refused to leave unless numerous family members were allowed to accompany them. Others simply could not make up their minds whether they wanted to go or not. Due to the time constraints, although many were successfully evacuated, those who paused too long in making what was likely the most important decision in their lives were left on the doorstep. Pace and I spent the entire night transporting women and children who exhibited mixed emotions, some thrilled by the possibility of escape, and others apprehensive as to what their new life in America might bring. All were terrified by the ride as the vehicle careened around eerily glowing mounds of tangled wreckage left by both vehicles and aircraft caught out in the open by the deluge of PAVN ordnance. By daybreak both Pace and I were physically and mentally exhausted. In order to return to the DAO compound Pace steered the banged up sedan on a circuitous route along taxiways and service roads pock-marked with craters from bombs, rockets and artillery.

Not long after our final trip, Major General Homer Smith began a survey of the airbase. His assessment was grim and he passed his opinion to the Ambassador. He reported that in the interests of safety, operations involving fixed-wing aircraft should now be terminated. Ambassador Martin, suspicious, almost paranoid of any assessment other than his own, arrived on the scene for a first hand look. While still optimistic that the ARVN military forces could hold, airfield conditions were so bad that he was forced to cancel the evacuation using airplanes, and instead use helicopters only.

Later that morning, the U.S. delegation protested to both the DRV and PRG concerning the attacks: "The U.S. Delegation strongly protests the threats to our safety by your wanton shelling and calls upon you to immediately guarantee our safety as required by the agreements on privileges and immunities." The response from the PRG Delegation was "even I don't know why." The response from the DRV was "we are in the same boat."

Back at the office of Colonel Madison the remaining FPJMT members gathered for a final briefing. The group had now dwindled to a six-man team comprised of Madison, Summers, Herrington, Herron, Pace and me. Everyone complained of hunger, and the few cans of C-rations found in a rucksack pulled from a closet weren't enough to go around. Colonel Madison called upon his favorite "jacks-of-all-trades" to use their initiative in finding food, so Pace and I headed for the DAO snack bar on the ground floor. Similar to the scene encountered at the command mess compound, local snack bar employees were hastily sacking the last remaining food. I grabbed packages of bologna, some boiled eggs and several cans of beer. Pace was only able to find some slightly stale bread.

As the exhausted men wolfed down the meager provisions, Madison announced that the group would shortly leave the DAO for the Embassy in downtown Saigon. Madison explained that although the DAO would be evacuated completely, our six remaining members would stay and continue our mission. Instructed to take care of any last minute details and to secure all weapons and equipment, the group scurried about the maze of corridors of the almost uninhabited DAO. There was no time to lose. More than two hundred thousand North Vietnamese soldiers were poised less than an hour's drive from the Embassy, held back only by a rapidly disintegrating South Vietnamese military.

Not knowing what the situation would be like after the evacuation or whether the U.S. delegation would stay, I was concerned about how American officials would be able to survive in the event of a Communist takeover. Realizing that there would be no American banking facilities in Saigon after the DAO was abandoned, I hurried to the Finance Office on the first floor. Fortunately one of the Finance Officers, a lady named Ann, had remained behind. I exchanged my travelers checks for more easily convertible American currency. While waiting to complete the transaction I peered out the window to watch Marine guards hastily burning large stacks of U.S. dollars removed from the massive vault. Although all of the currency was ordered destroyed prior to the evacuation of Saigon, one stack containing $10,000 would somehow find its way to the Citizens Bank and Trust located outside the main gate of the Indochinese Refugee Reception Center at Fort Chaffee, Arkansas. An investigation of the incident resulted in a dead end with no leads as to who deposited the money some thousands of miles from where it was supposedly burned. As far as I know, the identity of the person depositing the money was never learned.

When Madison gave the order to secure weapons and depart for the Embassy, due to restrictions contained in the provisions of the cease-fire agreement, no regular issue firearms were available. The group began to gather an odd assortment of personal weapons normally stored in living quarters, which included AK-47s, Swedish Ks and several less exotic American made rifles and pistols. Since many of the personal weapons were chrome plated war trophies removed from walls, when we returned the six-member team looked more like an armed band of desperados than an official U.S. delegation.

The group's four-vehicle convoy then departed the base and proceeded quickly down Cong Ly Street in the direction of the Embassy. Frightened residents clogged the roads. GVN police were still directing traffic, while others roamed the streets, halting and searching local vehicles headed toward Tan Son Nhut. It was hard to determine whether the spot-checks were based on orders from higher authorities genuinely concerned with security, or simply an independent means of extracting last minute bribes from those hoping to reach the airfield in time for the evacuation. Seemingly dumbfounded to see anyone going in the opposite direction away from the evacuation point, the armed officials gave the strange looking U.S. convoy a wide berth. Nevertheless, the artillery fire raining down on Tan Son Nhut and the chaotic swarms of terrified people rushing from downtown toward the base caused everyone to be nervous during the drive.

As we pulled up to the main gate of the American Embassy, throngs of panic-stricken people attempting to escape the final North Vietnamese offensive were already beginning to gather around the walls. It was a nightmarish scene of begging, crying people, with a group of Marines and Embassy staff guarding the main entrance. They periodically pushed back the first tier of the crowd in order to admit American citizens and their dependents through the heavy steel gate. Marine security guard personnel perched along the top of the walls were busily retrieving agile Vietnamese climbers. Impatient mothers handed up wailing babies to the Marine guards, begging them to take their beloved children away from their native land. Some were waving documents while wealthy merchants with no official connections to the Embassy or DAO stuffed thick wads of U.S. currency through the gate in an attempt to purchase last minute American compassion. Others, some clutching animals or carrying luggage and fearful of being left behind to face the Communist wrath, pressed forward, pleading for a space on the evacuating helicopters.

Once safely inside the Embassy, our group reported to Mr. James B. Devine, the Chief of the Political/Military Section. We expected to be staying behind to form the POW/MIA section of the FPMJT, but the group was told that there had been a change in plans. The President had made the decision to evacuate every American in the country. Normally, I would have been very disappointed, but after having been up for three days at that point I was just a robot, too tired to feel anything.

Devine asked us to help in organizing the evacuation, which would be accomplished by helicopter. The first step was to survey the compound in anticipation of the Marine helicopters that would be arriving soon from carriers in the South China Sea. A large Tamarind tree at the edge of the parking area, which was chosen to serve as the main landing pad, posed a dangerous obstacle to rotary wing aircraft. Major James H. Kean, the commander of the Embassy's Marine Security Guard Battalion, asked to fell the tree. His request was denied. It seemed that Ambassador had not only grown especially fond of the giant tree, (it had been planted at the time the Embassy was constructed), but he feared cutting it down would "scare the locals." Oblivious to nostalgia and protocol, Kean located a chain saw and barked an order to a young Marine who quickly proceeded with clearing the landing zone. Up to that point, many of the American personnel inside the Embassy appeared uncertain as to whether an evacuation would even occur. But the high-pitched roar of the chain saw and the sight of the huge tree crashing down in the middle of the compound brought home the gravity of the situation. Suddenly the evacuation was real.

I was ordered to determine the best place to coordinate the evacuation. I decided to go to the roof to look around. As I was stepping out of the elevator next to the office of the Ambassador, I collided with ARVN Lieutenant General Tran Van Don. I recognized Don right away, since he had recently become the Deputy Prime Minister and Minister of Defense in President Thieu's short-lived "fighting" cabinet. Accompanied by his family, Don appeared to be handling the situation well, and he managed a weak smile as he backed up against the wall and allowed me to pass. Apparently maintaining his stature as a leading South Vietnamese official, I noticed that Don was dressed in a dark business suit and tie for his helicopter ride. After rendering the traditional Vietnamese greeting to Lieutenant General Don, I passed by the Ambassador's office. It was crowded with last minute visitors and Embassy staff frantically pleading with their besieged boss for instructions. I continued to the sixth floor and then took the stairs up to the open roof.

The roof afforded an excellent view of the Embassy grounds. As I stood and surveyed the surrounding area, beneath me I saw scenes that are seared into my memory. Surging crowds of Vietnamese clutching meager belongings were banging on the gates, while inside the compound employees and dependents dragged large trunks and assorted pieces of expensive luggage along the sidewalk from the chancery building to the landing pad. Contributing to the bizarre panorama were American women in ankle length evening dresses and high-heeled shoes stumbling forward beneath the weight of precious cultural treasures, no doubt painstakingly collected during exotic foreign tours. In the distance I could see long bursts of automatic fire pouring from a C-119K airplane, a more recent version of what the Americans had called "Puff the Magic Dragon." Further away, artillery rounds impacted in clouds of dust, while nearby an occasional explosion shook the building as grenades were used to destroy important equipment. On the roof just below the concrete landing pad a lone Marine methodically crammed plastic bags filled with documents and typewriter ribbons into an incinerator belching caustic smoke. My eyes soon began burning from the flying ash, so I moved and began quickly checking the rooftop for guy wires and debris before descending the stairs. After considering the size and density of the concrete slab poured on the roof, I concluded that only the smaller Hueys could safely land on top of the chancery.

At about 1400 hours Colonel Madison was placed in overall charge of the Embassy evacuation. Although the parking lot had been cleared for the Marine helicopters en route, guy wires supporting an antenna tower on the roof of a nearby building obstructed the flyaway at the head of the landing zone. Madison knew the importance of communications, but being an infantry officer with considerable combat experience in Vietnam he also knew that a chopper downed on such a small LZ would close it to future lifts. Against the protest of Embassy officials Madison dispatched a Marine to climb the tower and cut the wires.

To better organize the swelling crowd the Marine guards opened a rear gate to allow people into a sub-compound of the Embassy that had served as a recreational area for the Combined Recreation Association (CRA). This was a club designed to provide rest and relaxation for all official members of the U.S. Mission and their guests. The physical layout included an impressive dining room with a bar and a fairly large swimming pool. To comply with security a twelve-foot high chain link fence surrounded the CRA. The design was ideal for controlling the mixed horde of Americans, Vietnamese and citizens of third countries anxious to board the helicopters and flee to safety. While thankful for the useful configuration, at that point I didn't care whether the design came as a result of advance thinking by some prudent Security Officer, or just plain luck.

Outside the embassy wall, the Vietnamese banging on the main gate were becoming frantic. Some even resorted to cunning to get inside. I watched as one Vietnamese woman and a very drunk American appeared at the gate. The woman was very meek and clung to the arm of the American, who shouted at the Marine guards to let him in. Seeing that he was a U.S. citizen, the Marines opened a path for the American, who insisted on bringing along the woman. Once the pair was safely inside and lined up in the CRA area to board the helicopters, the woman's demeanor abruptly changed. She began cursing at the still drunk American to get away from her, calling him a bastard. Eventually the man stumbled off, and the woman went to the other side of the pool. Both made the evacuation, but not together.

I also watched about ten Vietnamese nationals come to side gates and show ID cards to the guards, who immediately let them in. They were carrying weapons and small General Electric "Slimline PocketMate" radios, a miniature radio that could transmit up to fifty kilometers on line of sight. These radios had labels that pealed off so you couldn't determine the country of origin. The radios were equipped with earphones for surveillance and an external antenna to increase the range. As the radios were collected, the CIA communication personnel on the fourth floor started smashing them with hammers. Soon the floor of the commo shack was littered with the shattered remnants of the radios.

The first helicopters to arrive at the Embassy weren't there to pick up passengers; to the contrary they discharged people onto the roof. This group consisted of U.S. government employees and high-ranking Vietnamese officials who had been instructed to rendezvous with the pale gray Air America Hueys at locations throughout the Saigon area. Watching the Hueys hover and then quickly depart, it was obvious that the pilots were professionals with many years of experience. I hoped that the Marine pilots on the outbound leg would be equally skilled.

Although the Air America helicopters actually dropped off passengers from local rendezvous points and left empty, people crowded into the CRA compound interpreted their arrival and departure as evidence the Embassy was already being evacuated and that they were being abandoned. A sense of mounting fear seemed to sweep through the crowd as people began to press forward against the wire fence. Although Ambassador Martin was present, it soon became obvious that the Deputy Chief of Mission, Mr. Wolfgang J. Lehmann, was actually in charge within the Embassy. In conferring with Mr. Lehmann concerning the crowd of people already gathered inside the compound, our band of six hardy men received his assurance that everyone currently inside the compound would be evacuated and that no one would be abandoned. To alleviate the mounting panic, a few of us entered the CRA area and passed this information directly to the people gathered there. The crowd was told that the evacuation would proceed in three increments: first the American citizens and dependents; second, third country nationals; and lastly, Vietnamese employees and other eligible evacuees. As a further guarantee of sincerity, the six of us pledged to remain in the Embassy until all other evacuees had departed.

The first people to be evacuated by helicopter were members of the Embassy staff, including personnel from the United States Information Service and the United States Agency for International Development. This initial stage of the evacuation was conducted from the roof of the chancery with Air America helicopters. When the second stage began and the first Marine CH-53 began its descent into the compound, dust and debris left over from the end of the current dry season formed a dense haze of stinging projectiles. With the ensuing sorties the dust would gradually diminish, but the mass of frantic people continued to increase. Like mother eagles guarding their young, a pair of Navy F-4s streaked in a broad arc around the Embassy. The air cap would continue to provide cover until the last lift of the evacuation.[4]

As the other team members and I began moving people from the CRA area into the parking lot turned Landing Zone, it became obvious that the helicopters could not handle the heavy loads. Repeatedly the huge CH-53s would attempt to lift off only to settle back down again while team members removed some of the passengers and luggage. Some of those crowded into the CRA compound came to the gate straining under the weight of unbelievably heavy pieces of luggage. A secretary from the Republic of Korea Embassy fought fiercely with Captain Herrington to prevent her suitcase from being taken from her tight grasp. When it became obvious that the lady was not willing to listen to reason, she was physically carried onto a helicopter, minus her luggage. Feeling the weight of the suitcase I could only assume that it was filled with gold. When I dropped it into the swimming pool it sank immediately to the bottom. By this time, the pool reeked of urine, the bottom littered with weapons confiscated by the Marine guards.

The movement of people from the CRA area proceeded so smoothly that we divided into two teams in order to simultaneously evacuate people from both the parking area and the roof above. During the boarding of groups of Vietnamese I saw Marine Master Sergeant Juan Valdez[5] pull one passenger wearing the uniform of the Special Branch Police from the ramp of the aircraft. I immediately recognized the man as Colonel Lam Van Nghia, the former CMIC Commander, currently the Deputy Commander of the Capital Police Command. I wasn't sure how Nghia had managed entry into the compound, but having worked with him in the past, I knew that in addition to his public duties, Nghia had other covert missions and secret contacts with American intelligence. I surmised that someone from the CIA had brought him in through a seldom-used private entrance that connected the Ambassador's residence with the main compound.

Looking dejected, Nghia moved to stand by the chain link fence. When I questioned Valdez concerning the reason for his actions he indicated that the South Vietnamese government had issued an order to the effect that no military or police personnel would be evacuated. In checking with Nghia, however, I learned that after President Thieu left the country on April 25 it became unclear as to who would be allowed to evacuate. Pointing to a Police Lieutenant Colonel standing on the roof of a building overlooking the CRA compound, Nghia told me that the officer was his second in command. Nghia added that he had personally arranged for exterior security of the Embassy until the evacuation was completed.

Aware of his background and satisfied that he had done his duty, I quickly came to the conclusion it was time for Nghia to go. Picking Nghia up by the seat of his pants, I dumped him inside the already raised ramp just as the helicopter lifted off. Moments later, having witnessed the incident, Summers walked over to me and asked me if I was aware of whom that was. I replied "How about the Chief of the Political Intelligence Department?" Surprised, Summers nodded in the affirmative but he never did say how he came to know about Nghia's true position. Summers did agree that if Nghia missed the evacuation and fell into the hands of Communist interrogators he would not survive the ordeal, and he had no objections to his departure. Since other Vietnamese personnel assigned to intelligence duties were joining the evacuation, I scanned the compound to see if the civilian translator from the Combined Document Translation Center, the man who in 1968 had declared invalid the important document warning of the Tet offensive, had made it. He was nowhere to be seen, and I wondered whether the man even tried to make the evacuation at all, or if he was now leading PAVN intelligence personnel on a guided tour of the CDEC compound.

The final evacuation of the DAO compound at Tan Son Nhut began just before midnight. The diversion of aircraft from the Embassy to the DAO for the last lift resulted in a lull in air activity at the Embassy causing rumors to spread through the crowd that the evacuation was being discontinued. This led to mounting panic in the CRA compound, and tension was climbing to the point where people were in danger of being trampled to death by pressure at the gate. The situation was beyond the control of the Marine guards, who began to resort to force.

In order to calm the people's fears we entered the compound, making ourselves hostage to the crowd, demonstrating by our actions that no one would be abandoned. The few Vietnamese-speaking members of our small group walked through the crowd making personal guarantees that everyone would be taken. Using bullhorns, we separated the crowd into two sections using the swimming pool as a divider. As soon as the crowd saw that the American team members were willing to share their predicament, the evacuees were willing to follow our instructions. They complied and organized themselves into two separate columns of family groups. Alternating between columns, we led the groups onto the roof of the firehouse overlooking the LZ and into a small parking lot in front of the mailroom. As the evacuees filed from the CRA compound into the compound proper we determined that some twelve hundred people remained to be evacuated.

At approximately 0030 hours the lift resumed with six consecutive sorties flown by CH-53 helicopters. During the time that the larger helicopters extracted evacuees from the lower LZ, smaller CH-46s continued to lift people from the roof of the chancery building. Due to the darkness crewmembers on the helicopters ignited flares beneath the aircraft to aid the pilot during descent. This caused burning debris to fall on those of us guiding the choppers onto the pad.

Just as one CH-53 lifted off a frail old man stumbled forward onto the LZ. Only a few minutes earlier I had noticed that the man was acting erratic, clearly on the verge of panic. As the old man approached the LZ, Major Kean grabbed him by his collar and began punching him in the face with his fists. Yelling as loud as I could from the roof of the fire station, I attempted to intercede but could not be heard over the roar of the helicopters. Removing a round from my 38-caliber revolver I threw it, striking Kean in the back. When Kean looked around over his shoulder I gestured with my hands for him to cease his actions and he immediately released the old man. The elderly gentleman identified himself as a retired Master Sergeant of the ARVN Airborne. He was distraught because his family members, including his grandchildren, had been included in a previous lift. He had tried vainly to rejoin his family but the Marine guards had pushed him back inside the gate, effectively separating him from his loved ones. I apologized to the old trooper for the humiliating treatment he had received, and I promised him he would be on the next lift.

At 0400 hours we were informed that future lifts of evacuees would be made only by the CH-53s. This meant that the people who had been guided up the stairs to the roof would have to be brought back down to the lower LZ. At that point approximately three thousand people had been successfully evacuated from both the upper and lower LZs, leaving some four hundred and twenty people waiting patiently on the ground by the lower pad. This group included the Embassy fire department employees. Madison had asked them to stay until the final lift in case of a fire or other emergency during the operation, promising them he would get them out on the last lifts. Since their families had been moved out early, they agreed to remain, trusting Madison would keep his promise. The remaining group of evacuees consisted of a German Priest, several Vietnamese Catholic nuns, some official staff members from the Korean Embassy, including the Defense Attaché, plus local Embassy employees and their dependents. All of these people had voluntarily abandoned their luggage in order to reduce the weight load. Considering the number of people, we estimated that six more CH-53s would be needed to complete the evacuation. Our experience indicated that it took three minutes to load and lift one group, so we estimated that the time required to complete the operation was approximately twenty minutes.

When Madison informed Lehmann of the requirements for completing the evacuation, he was told that there would be no more lifts made by CH-53. Unfazed by the unexpected response Madison replied that we were not going anywhere until all those presently marshaled inside the compound were evacuated. Unexpectedly acquiescing to Madison's demand, the DCM assured him that the six necessary choppers would be called in. Shortly thereafter, the Ambassador's Special Assistant, Mr. Brunson McKinley, reiterated this promise. Just then, Ambassador Martin suddenly appeared at the ground floor of the chancery carrying his pet poodle. Wandering in a lurching gait Martin located Deputy Lehmann. Both men sauntered slowly around the interior of the compound for a firsthand look at the situation, followed by a heavily armed Marine bodyguard dressed in civilian clothing. Less than an hour later, with no notification to Colonel Madison, Ambassador Martin and his staff departed from the roof of the chancery.

After the Ambassador left the Embassy, Madison went to get an estimated time of arrival for the last lift. Finding only Major Kean, Madison inquired when the next lift would appear. He was stunned when Kean informed him that the remaining sorties had been cancelled by order of the President. According to Kean, there would be no more lifts except for the remaining Marines and us. Armed with an order from the Commander-in-Chief, and seemingly oblivious to Madison's protest, Kean informed the Colonel that he could no longer risk the safety of his Marines, and that his entire contingent was preparing to depart the Embassy. Without a means of communication there was simply no way for Madison to challenge Kean's statement. In short, there was little he could do, save for passing the order for us to begin a slow withdrawal to the roof.

As I began making my way across the compound to the front door of the chancery I trembled with emotion. But after not sleeping for several days, I simply lacked the strength necessary to act on the rage I felt inside. When my gaze turned to the remaining group of evacuees sitting quietly in rows at the edge of the lower pad, my attention focused on the old ARVN Airborne Master Sergeant. Rather than the expected hatred, I saw a pair of eyes filled with trust. Not trust for just the men working on the evacuation, but for what they represented, America, the world's richest and most powerful nation. Millions of Vietnamese had sacrificed everything they had by placing their trust in America, and I was repulsed by the growing realization that they, like the old sergeant, were about to be abandoned. Mentally and physically exhausted from several days without sleep, I slumped against a wall for a moment. I thought about the thousands who had died, the blood spilled, the horribly wounded, all the terrors of war that had been visited on Vietnam and the Americans who had fought for her, all for nothing, gone in the instant we few stepped aboard the last helicopters. In its final form, this was not "peace with honor."

Sometime around 0530 hours Summers, Madison and Herron departed in a CH-46 from the roof of the chancery. Waiting for the next chopper I looked down from my lofty perch and watched as the Marine guards slowly backed themselves into the chancery, trying not to look obvious. It was only a matter of minutes until the next CH-46 throbbed its way onto the roof. When it arrived in a swirl of rotor wash, Pace, Herrington, and I climbed on board, thus completing the evacuation of the U.S. delegation. We were the last three official Americans to leave Vietnam, as the Marine guards were only stationed there on a temporary basis. However, I had lingered near the bottom of the ramp until the other two were on board, and then I made my way slowly up the ramp, the last one on the helicopter. In that instant I became the last American formally assigned to Vietnam to leave the country.

As the helicopter began its ascent over the city the sun was just beginning to rise and I could see faint streams of red and green tracers crossing its emerging silhouette. Fires burned in the distance and black smoke rose from the impact of artillery shells. A collective sense of guilt prevented the three of us sitting in the back of the cavernous chopper from making eye contact with each other. Feeling the cool wind on my face through the door of the chopper I gradually resigned myself to the fact that the war was finally over, but I remained tense until the helicopter gained altitude and became immune to ground fire. At that point I began to contemplate what it would feel like if a heat-seeking anti-aircraft missile suddenly slammed into the helicopter, and I also wondered if my newfound fear of flying would resurrect itself. But my exhaustion was so deep that I felt no fear, only curiosity.

We reached the American ships after a short ride. The rat-a-tat of gunfire, the rumble of shelling, the clamor of panicky residents had faded, replaced by the roar of the helicopter engines and the rushing wind. As we slowly passed over the South China Sea, I watched in amazement as Marines and Sailors below me rushed frantically around like ants pushing ARVN Hueys into the swirling water from the decks of crowded American ships. Once on board the USS *Okinawa* we learned from Lieutenant Colonel Jim Bolton, the helicopter Squadron Commander, that he had no idea that only six more lifts were needed to complete the evacuation. To the contrary, Bolton and other flight commanders had been led to believe that they were dealing with a "bottomless pit." This created relentless pressure to end the operation and it was finally terminated, leaving some four hundred and twenty marshaled evacuees stranded at the American Embassy in Saigon.

Despite the chaos, the helicopters had evacuated several thousand American and South Vietnamese from the doomed city. Historians will undoubtedly long continue to debate the decisions that lead to our ill-fated involvement with Vietnam. In the end, the South Vietnamese, given their own many failings and defects, paid the price—their freedom and existence as a sovereign nation. The CIA analyst Frank Snepp later wrote that the last Agency message from the Embassy declared: "Let us hope we do not repeat history. This is Saigon station signing off." I can only pray that they were right.

Chapter Five

Gearing Back Up

THE VIETNAMESE WHO WERE FORTUNATE enough to reach the ships were immediately provided food and clothing, while Navy medical personnel quickly treated those requiring attention. Early in the afternoon of April 30, word began to spread throughout the flotilla that South Vietnam's new President, General Duong Van Minh, had announced the unconditional surrender of the RVN to the Communists. As reality overcame the South Vietnamese on board the USS *Okinawa,* some began weeping openly, especially the military personnel. Apparently a few had the impression that a counterattack would be launched from the U.S. 7th Fleet, and that they might be involved. The announcement of total surrender was devastating and their faces carried the haunted look seen on the terminally ill after being informed by their doctor that they have no chance for survival. Shortly after the capitulation was announced, American naval officers passed the word that South Vietnamese military rank and positions would no longer be recognized. The dazed officers, including Colonels and Generals who were graduates of the prestigious Dalat National Military Academy, began shedding their uniforms and placing them into rubbish cans. Their morale at a lifetime low, the officers gradually changed the manner in which they addressed each other, obviously conscious of their sudden loss of stature and authority. With one short announcement the once proud officers had been relegated to the caste of homeless and unemployed refugees. It seemed like callous treatment, but I guess there was no easy way to make the transition.

When I woke up on May 1, 1975, the ship was still anchored off the port of Vung Tau. The next morning the six of us were transferred by helicopter to the USS *Coral Sea*. This marked the first time that I had ever been on an aircraft carrier, and I was amazed by the size and complexity of the huge vessel. The ship's executive officer, Captain T.W. Durant, sensed that the members of our team had been under considerable strain and promptly guided us to the "Captain's In-port Cabin." The food was better than any five-star restaurant I had ever visited. We feasted on steak and lobster served by ethnic Filipinos who had been recruited to serve as stewards. I was told that this special dining room was normally used by the ship's Captain to receive high-ranking dignitaries at the various ports-of-call along the ship's route. However, the luxury was short lived; later that afternoon, I joined Colonel Madison and Colonel Summers for a jolting ride on a small C-2 aircraft bound for Cubi Point in the Philippines.

While strapped in and waiting for the catapult to sling the tiny aircraft from the *Coral Sea's* enormous deck, I chatted with a civilian aircraft technician seated next to me. The man identified himself as Mr. Lovelace, an employee of the aviation manufacturing giant Lockheed Aircraft Corporation. According to Lovelace, he had been summoned to the area from California due to the recent crash of the Lockheed C-5A at Saigon. Intrigued, I began to probe for answers regarding the cause of the accident that killed my wife and son. Lovelace was disturbed by the recent mishap, and expressed bitterness that the company's leadership had not heeded the advice of technicians like him. He pinpointed the problem as the locking mechanism on the aircraft's rear door, a long-known manufacturing defect. He said that the initial investigations should have forced a general recall of the model, but due to the cost involved, Lockheed upper level management had vetoed such an expensive resolution.

Lovelace went on to explain how sudden pressurization resulting from the rapid tactical ascent from Tan Son Nhut airbase, combined with the weight of the luggage stacked on the rear ramp, caused the door to tear from the fuselage, cutting the hydraulic control cables in the tail section. This left the pilot with no means of controlling the aircraft, save for increasing or decreasing the fuel to the engines, and using the ailerons for directional control. One crewmember was blown out the gaping hole in the rear of the aircraft, his body later recovered in shallow water off the coast of Vung Tau. The pilot attempted to return to the airfield, but as the plane neared the ground it lost its air volume and fell like a rock into a rice paddy on the east side of the Saigon River. The aircraft then bounced over the river and disintegrated in a marsh. Of the 382 people aboard, 206 were killed, most of them children. Considering the burns that Andrea suffered prior to the impact, I concluded that the wetness of the swamp ensured her survival. Unfortunately, the same rush of water that saved Andrea had resulted in many others being drowned inside the aircraft. I was deeply angered by the information that Lockheed had cut corners to save money, but realized there was little I could do. While I was relieved to learn that the cause of the crash was not a Communist missile, discovering that it was most likely a design flaw did nothing to salve my pain.

The team finally reassembled at Cubi Point Naval Air Station in the Philippines on May 3, 1975. After hot showers and cold San Miguel beer our six-member group boarded another helicopter for Clark Air Base near Angeles City. The following day we loaded onto a C-141 bound for the sprawling Air Force base at Utapao in southeastern Thailand. Upon landing and seeing the rows of menacing black B-52s parked on the flight line, the first thought that crossed my mind was: how could we have evacuated Saigon so haphazardly when we had so much power ready and waiting only scant minutes away? To add to our misery, local baggage handlers at the airbase stole most of the personal property items we managed to hand-carry out of Saigon. Nevertheless, our weary band was happy to finally arrive at the delegation's alternate Command Post in Samae San.

Shortly afterwards, I contacted the Army's Central Identification Laboratory, Thailand. During the "Vietnamization" phase of the war and concurrent withdrawal of U.S. forces, the Thailand lab had gradually taken over the responsibility of the Central Identification Laboratory in Saigon. The huge Saigon Mortuary located at Tan Son Nhut had also been transferred to Thailand. Due to the condition of Nova and Michael's bodies, it took several visits to the morgue before I was able to make positive identifications. I then began preparations for the funeral back in Tennessee.

In addition to identifying the bodies of my family, I spent the first part of May working with the other team members to compile an After Action report on the final days and to close out the records of the FPJMT. Our team was temporarily diverted from this administrative mission when Khmer Rouge troops illegally seized the merchant vessel Mayaguez in international waters off the coast of Cambodia. The subsequent rescue attempt proved to be a disaster, and American casualties were unusually high. At the beginning of the operation twenty-one Air Security Police being transported from Nakhon Phanom Air Base in northeastern Thailand to Utapao on the southern coast were killed in a helicopter crash while en route to the scene. An investigation into the incident revealed that the Air Force technician responsible for maintenance had failed to place a cotter pin in a bolt holding the main rotor assembly. The vibration of the aircraft caused one of the most critical pieces of the helicopter, known as the "Jesus nut," to come loose, leading to the loss of the main rotor. When the main rotor comes off the helicopter in midair, your only hope is to pray to Jesus. It was later determined that the mechanic was addicted to drugs, which caused his dereliction of duty. I would later learn through refugee interviews that as many as three Marines were left behind alive on the island.[1]

In the meantime I received orders reassigning me to my previous duty position in Arizona as an instructor in the Department of Exploitation and Counterintelligence, U.S. Army Intelligence Center and School. Faced with the task of organizing a double funeral for Nova and Michael, and with Andrea still recovering from her injuries, I was not enthused by the prospect of returning to the remote desert area. Fortunately, I soon received a call from General Kingston, who offered his assistance. With the General's help, I was able to have my orders changed. When I called Personnel I learned that I was being assigned instead to Detachment F (Collection) of the U.S. Army Intelligence Agency and that my new duty station would be Fort Chaffee, Arkansas. Although I had never been to the post and knew nothing about it, I was reassured to learn that Fort Chaffee, located near the town of Fort Smith, was conveniently situated between the homes of both my parents in East Texas and my in-laws in Tennessee.

I departed Samae San around May 20 and returned to America to pick up Andrea and finalize last minute funeral details. We buried Nova and Michael in the early hours of May 30 in a ceremony that strained my soul. The sky was drizzling, the ground muddy from the intermittent rain. The casket was closed, but Nova's father actually looked inside the coffin prior to the service, probably to gain a final visual image that would allow him some form of closure. Shortly after the memorial service was completed, I loaded my few remaining possessions into a U-haul trailer pulled by my step-dad's car, and Andrea and I departed for Fort Chaffee. When we arrived that same afternoon, I was surprised to learn that within the previous few days the post had been converted to an "Indochinese Refugee Reception Center." Driving from the main gate to the Personnel Office I felt like I was back in Saigon. Crowds of Vietnamese were gathered throughout the cantonment area to receive an issue of clothing and bedding. In the distance young Vietnamese boys played soccer on a parade field while old ladies with beetlenut-stained teeth gawked from the steps of wooden two-storied World War II-era barracks.

Seeing the Vietnamese milling about brought back all the emotions I felt in the terrible last days in Saigon. I could physically feel the heat and sense the fear again, a swirl of images and sounds churning in my heart and mind. I knew I had to somehow discard those feelings, otherwise they would haunt my dreams and fill my waking hours. Instinctively I reminded myself that my daughter looked to me to repair our lives; dwelling on what I could not change would only leave our scars raw and unhealed. Looking at the now destitute Vietnamese, I resolved that I would be strong for my daughter, and that we would face the future together. Just as important, perhaps by staying busy while helping the refugees, we could find a source of contentment and solace for ourselves.

At the post Administration Office, I was directed to report to the Fort Smith Resident Agency, Defense Investigative Service. Upon arrival I met with the Special Agent in Charge, Mr. James White. After in-processing, I was taken to a building next door that had been divided into interrogation rooms. There I was happily reunited with my friend and neighbor from Saigon, William O'Brien. As O'Brien began to fill me in on the mission, I could hear another familiar voice over the walls of the hastily constructed plywood room dividers. The voice was that of another Polygraph Examiner, Mr. Steve Diduch, who had also worked for Detachment K in Bangkok, and who had conducted examinations in the Saigon DAO. Diduch would later find employment as an examiner for the Department of Energy's Nuclear Branch.

As luck would have it I was able to find a vacant house near the O'Brien's in nearby Fort Smith. Andrea and I moved in that same evening. I was also pleasantly surprised to learn that Bill Hutchinson and his family, my old friends from the 50th MID in Hawaii, as well as Master Sergeant Ed Davis and his family, (despite his misguided attempt to negotiate an end to the war aboard the C-130 flight to Hanoi), were also residing just a few doors down from the O'Briens in the same apartment building. I quickly grew to enjoy Fort Smith and found it to be inhabited by friendly, caring people, the same type of folks I had known as a child in rural East Texas. The lady who rented the house to me lived next door, and she had a daughter the same age as Andrea. Realizing my plight, the kind lady offered her services as a baby sitter. In another stroke of good luck, our maid from Saigon, Chi Tu, miraculously ended up in Fort Chaffee as a refugee. She was thrilled to learn that Andrea was living near the camp, and she immediately asked for her old job back. After the necessary paperwork was completed, I became Chi Tu's official sponsor and she was considered resettled. After a few trips to the furniture and grocery stores, I was ready to go back to work. My fortune in finding so many old friends went a long way to helping Andrea and me recover from our ordeal.

My new job involved debriefing former high-ranking GVN officials regarding the potential of the Communist Vietnamese to wage war against their neighbors. In particular, we were concerned about the PAVN ability to employ their newly acquired American war-material to threaten Thailand. The overt portion of the project was designated as "Operation Doberman Dawn," and was publicly described as an "investigative effort of the Defense Intelligence Agency." At the same time, behind this intelligence operation lurked yet another clandestine venture associated with the "stay-behind" program initiated prior to the collapse of the Republic of Vietnam. To this day, that program remains highly classified.

Our routine operations were temporarily suspended when the team was directed to focus its efforts toward providing security for a visit to Fort Chaffee by then President Gerald Ford. In preparation for the President's arrival, the team worked closely with personnel from other federal agencies in screening records to identify potential threats among the refugee population. Once those considered a potential threat to the safety of the President were identified and located within the confines of the camp, the team recruited "favorably known" Vietnamese nationals for the purpose of surveillance. These personnel were previously employed by or associated with the various agencies of the U.S. government, and no derogatory information existed in the employee's file. U.S. or other Free World intelligence and law enforcement services had hosted many of them for training during the war, and we were able to take advantage of their prior education.

Although the team concentrated on possible threats from the refugee population, we never thought to look at ourselves. As it turned out, one American employee at Fort Chaffee would later enter the history books as an assassin. A mild-mannered civilian laborer who kept to himself most of the time, Mark David Chapman was later successful in his attempt to kill former Beatles singer John Lennon on August 24, 1981. To the best of my knowledge, Chapman's name was never mentioned in conjunction with President Ford's visit to Fort Chaffee.

After the President's departure, we returned to debriefing the key GVN bureaucrats. The heads of the various South Vietnamese government agencies were interviewed in detail concerning the number and types of weapons, armor, aircraft, and motorized vehicles, along with other types of equipment captured by the PAVN. Senior officials were asked to provide complete assessments of the potential for Communist forces to develop the highway, railroad, and banking systems, the harbors and ports, and the river transport capability. Information obtained during these sessions was surprisingly accurate, especially in evaluating North Vietnam's intentions toward Cambodia. Once the project was well under way, topics for the debriefings expanded to include the type of classified material left behind by South Vietnamese government agencies. Although orders had been carefully formulated to ensure the destruction of all classified material prior to the evacuation, the results of the debriefings indicated that with some rare exceptions, such plans generally were not carried out.

One reason for the failure was that the GVN considered making a stand by holding onto some coastal enclaves and the southern part of South Vietnam. American military officers had earlier in the war recommended this enclave strategy, whereby the ARVN would defend the main cities along the coastline and the more prosperous southern half of South Vietnam. Some South Vietnamese leaders also had hoped to fall back into the Mekong Delta and continue the fight from there, as they still had three relatively untouched divisions in the region. This being the case, the classified material was considered essential for planning and conducting future operations against an even stronger and more determined enemy. The South Vietnamese had other plans to continue fighting after we left, but none of them came to fruition. When General Minh surrendered, with the combination of evacuation or in some cases suicide of their leaders, most of the South Vietnamese military believed it was senseless to prolong the war.

Many agencies of the U.S. Government also failed to destroy much of their classified material because the decision to evacuate came far too late, and even then the very plan itself was a closely held secret. For example, the CDEC files (although the agency was now run by the South Vietnamese, they shared captured documents with U.S. intelligence), containing all the captured enemy documents were supposed to be burned, but instead I heard they were boxed up and sitting at Tan Son Nhut waiting to be sent out when they fell into Communist hands. Ambassador Martin held the view that any indication of a pending evacuation would cause panic among the South Vietnamese, and possibly create a backlash against the American community. He may have been partially right, as a few South Vietnamese fired on American convoys and evacuating helicopters.

Much worse than the liberation of the documents was the failure to destroy the agent lists. In addition to American unilateral intelligence operations, both the CIA and the DOD conducted bilateral operations with the GVN, as well as with agencies of countries still maintaining a presence in South Vietnam. As a result of the joint operations, shared plans and lists of agents fell into the hands of North Vietnam's Ministry of Public Security. Undoubtedly this contributed to the failure of the "stay-behind" operation. Other high-level officials of the Thieu Government described in detail how these and other important files were left in place, even including the "moon rock" presented by President Richard Nixon. Another official even requested support in excavating and removing a cache containing several tons of gold, which he claimed was abandoned by Imperial Japanese forces in the Dalat area at the close of World War II.

As I settled into my new assignment, unexpected changes happened again in my life. Chi Tu became engaged to a man in the camp. He was in the process of moving to New Orleans to open a restaurant, so naturally she moved there with him. I again met the ARVN officer I had seen inside the DAO building, Lieutenant Colonel Pham Xuan Huy. I was surprised to see Huy so quickly, and I inquired how he had escaped. He told me he and his family had managed to get on a boat named the *Truong Tin,* which fled from Saigon on the last day. It sailed for the Philippines and made it to safety. He quickly identified himself to U.S. officials at the refugee camp and they promptly moved him to the States, where he arrived at Ft. Chaffee in mid-May 1975.

I was happy that he made it out. Since he was the former G-2 of the ARVN 22nd Division, which had fought splendidly in March 1975 in Binh Dinh province, he was hired as an employee for our project. While working together, Lieutenant Colonel Huy and I became well acquainted and eventually the entire Pham family also befriended my daughter Andrea. After signing up for a sponsor in order to leave the camp, Huy learned that he faced enormous difficulty in finding an American family willing to take in a non-English speaking refugee family with nine children. Realizing that it was difficult for me to care for Andrea as a single parent while working full time, Huy suggested that I sponsor his two oldest daughters to resettle in Arkansas. Huy believed that with my sponsorship of his two daughters, he would be helping me with my situation while at the same time increasing his chances for resettlement.

I agreed to sponsor the two older daughters, Nam-Xuan and Nam-Huyen, but in July he was notified of an opportunity for resettlement in Tennessee. After the family learned that they would have adequate housing for all nine children, Huy and his wife decided that the family should be reunited and that Nam-Xuan and her sister Nam-Huyen would rejoin the family. In keeping with Vietnamese tradition where in the absence of the mother the eldest daughter takes charge of the household, Nam-Xuan had firmly grasped the reins at our house and word of her pending departure was a huge shock. Both Andrea and I had grown very fond of her, and we simply could not bear the thought of her leaving. In discussing the move with Nam-Xuan, it quickly became apparent that she also did not want to leave. However, although she was an adult and able to make her own decisions, the desires of her family were paramount to Nam-Xuan, and she felt obligated to seek their permission prior to making a decision about her future. When she asked, her father became concerned about the image projected by two unmarried people living in the same household with a small child. Huy offered the opinion that if Nam-Xuan wanted to stay then we should consider marriage. He then added that even if we were leaning toward marriage, due to the family's religious beliefs, certain important factors would need to be considered before he could offer his family's blessing.

This placed me in a somewhat awkward position. First, I was naturally apprehensive about the feelings of Nova's family regarding my re-marriage so soon after their daughter's death. Second, my own uncertainty as to whether or not I would remain in the military left my immediate future cloudy. At the same time, however, I realized that somehow I had acquired a great deal of affection for Nam-Xuan. I also felt in my heart that for Andrea's sake it was highly unlikely that I would ever meet anyone as loving and caring as Nam-Xuan who would be willing to take on the awesome responsibilities of being a step-mother to a child recently subjected to severe physical and emotional trauma. On this point I really couldn't tell whether I truly believed it, or whether I was merely rationalizing with myself, but I became convinced that considering the circumstances, if Nova were to select someone to care for Andrea in her absence, that person would be Nam-Xuan.

Equally important was whether Nam-Xuan really wanted to enter into marriage with me, or whether she was simply trying to help her family by ridding them of what she perceived to be as a burden. While Nam-Xuan understood the ramifications of marriage, I needed to be completely honest with her. In our discussions I could only tell her that I didn't want her to leave. While she understood that although we did not love each other, we nevertheless did have genuine feelings for each other. After giving it much thought, she finally concluded that the only way we could stay together was through marriage. To an American, such a union might seem odd, but she was in many ways symbolic of her culture: family-oriented, tradition bound, morally conservative, yet ever practical. Therefore, in accordance with the Vietnamese tradition called *le hoi,* if I wanted to marry her, I would have to begin the official process with an "asking ceremony," wherein the prospective groom meets with the parents of the potential bride to officially announce his intentions and request permission to marry their daughter.

Normally, a middleman highly regarded by both sides will represent the groom. But we couldn't meet this and other cultural requirements, so I represented myself. I had to set an appointment with her parents in Fort Chaffee barracks building 1201, which served as the family's temporary living quarters. When I went to see Colonel Huy and his wife and children, they had cleaned their spartan rooms and dressed the other kids in their best clothes. After I was formally seated, the kids were paraded in, said hello, and then left us alone. Huy and his wife and I then spent a few minutes discussing the weather, had tea and cookies, and engaged in other small talk. Finally, after the humidity began to noticeably increase in the plywood-walled room, I asked to marry Nam-Xuan.

They agreed to think it over. After the "asking ceremony," Huy and his wife began the process of seriously considering my proposal. Devout Buddhists, they consulted various astrological charts and discussed the matter with elders whose opinion they respected. The first step was to ascertain whether our zodiac signs were compatible. Since by their charts Nam-Xuan was a "chicken" and I was a "goat," they were convinced that there would be no astrological incompatibilities between us. Huy and his wife also noted that on the day of Nova and Michael's death, the Buddha spared not only the life of Andrea from the crash of the C-5A but also spared the life of Nam-Xuan, who managed to reach a ship in Nha Trang. Huy also found other signs which he considered auspicious, such as the fact that Nam-Xuan had arrived in Saigon on the day prior to Andrea's safe departure for the U.S., the fact that Nam-Xuan had escaped from Vietnam by boat on the same day that I was evacuated by helicopter, and the fact that Nam-Xuan had arrived at Fort Chaffee on the day of Nova and Michael's funeral. According to Huy, all these coincidences indicated that our marriage would mesh with our fate that had been predetermined by Buddha. Assuaged by the various signs and portents, the family's blessing was readily granted. We were married shortly thereafter on August 28, 1975. Perhaps the Buddha was right, as Nam-Xuan and I quickly grew to love each other. I could only hope Nova and Michael had also granted us their blessing.

My father-in-law's concern for astrological compatibility aside, in discussing the ordeal of the final Communist offensive in Vietnam with Nam-Xuan I eventually came to the conclusion that it was indeed virtually a miracle that had brought together two people from opposite sides of the globe. I had lost my wife and child and Nam-Xuan had lost her country. Prior to our meeting at Fort Chaffee the only common link between us was Douglas Bergner, who had no idea that I would ever even meet, much less marry the daughter of his counterpart in faraway Binh Dinh province. Like me, Nam-Xuan had also undergone considerable difficulty in surviving the Communists' final push southward. She described how she had been living a normal life in the An Khe area of Binh Dinh province when her father received intelligence indicating that an all-out offensive by Communist forces was imminent. Eventually, Nam-Xuan, her mother and her eight siblings arrived in Nha Trang in a military truck. The road south was littered with abandoned vehicles, and bands of ARVN soldiers roamed the highways. Shortly after arrival in Nha Trang they received two items in the "bad news" category. First they heard that Communist forces were rapidly closing on Nha Trang, and second, they were told that Communist forces had interdicted Highway 1 east of Saigon, near the town of Xuan Loc. The family was trapped in Nha Trang.

Faced with this dire situation, Nam-Xuan's mother decided to risk everything by entering the chaotic harbor area to take their chances competing with fleeing and panicky ARVN troops. Since the only escape to Saigon was by sea, Nam-Xuan's mother relied upon their driver for help in getting on board anything that would float. Fortunately the family was able to climb hand-over-hand onto a large cargo vessel bound for Saigon, and except for thirst and hunger, the three-day voyage was uneventful.

In Saigon the family remained at the home of a fairly influential relative who had served as the Director of the South Asia "Nam Do Ngan Hang" Bank. Although Colonel Huy was deployed south of the capital with remnants of the recently arrived 22nd ARVN Division, he managed to frequently visit the family in Saigon. On April 30, as the last U.S. helicopters were departing from the roof of the American Embassy, Huy realized that the end was near. He crammed his eleven-member family in an automobile left at the home by the former Bank Director and instructed his driver to head for the Saigon port. At the port the family heard the gut-wrenching final radio broadcast by newly appointed President Duong Van Minh calling for an unconditional surrender and complete cessation of hostilities by RVNAF personnel. At that point Huy felt that his duty as a military officer was over, and he guided his family through throngs of panic-stricken people to reach a ship that also belonged to the Bank Director. Huy tried to convince his driver, an ARVN NCO, to board the ship also, but the driver was so excited about taking possession of the car the family was leaving behind that he decided to risk it all by staying in Vietnam to become a private taxi driver under a Communist regime.

Heading down the Saigon River the ship transporting Huy's family was subjected to small arms fire several times but finally reached the open sea. Ultimately the ship docked at Subic Bay in the Philippines, and after a brief stay there the family was flown to Guam and then on to California where housing had been provided in a refugee camp located at Camp Pendleton. Due to crowded conditions at Camp Pendleton the family was rerouted to Fort Chaffee, Arkansas, where we met. Every year on the anniversary of the fall of Saigon, I look back at the seemingly endless number of twists and turns made by both Nam-Xuan and I over thousands of miles prior to our first eye-to-eye contact. Then, when I look at the two Amerasian offspring created as a result of our union, Elisabeth and Scott, I sense a comforting awareness that the hands of both God and Buddha were instrumental in bringing Nam-Xuan and I together in order for us to create such fine children.

As the interview program with the former GVN officials began to wind down, once again I became deeply involved in the search for our missing men. It seemed even in the States the POW/MIA issue was still with me. Despite the frustrating episodes in Saigon dealing with the uncompromising North Vietnamese, I was still personally committed to uncovering whatever information I could about American MIAs. At the time of the evacuation of Saigon over twenty-five hundred Americans were still unaccounted for. About half this number were acknowledged as dead at the time of their loss. The rest fell into various categories: from completely unknown to definitely captured but not returned. After the 1973 ceasefire, potential sources that lived in unsecured areas of Vietnam had been difficult to reach, but the establishment of the refugee camps in the States afforded a new opportunity to obtain information on missing American servicemen. I worked for the rest of 1975 debriefing the remaining Vietnamese refugees on POW/MIA and other matters. As we begin to canvass the refugees, my colleagues and I received one intriguing report from two American missionaries who were working in the coastal highlands at the time of the collapse and who moved to Ft. Chaffee to continue assisting the refugees. They mentioned one Caucasian seen by the missionaries in the Quang Ngai area, and also a different man in one of the lead tanks at the time victorious North Vietnamese troops entered the capital. Although the information was not correlated to any missing American servicemen, the information was placed in the so-called "Salt and Pepper" file for future analysis. The "Salt and Pepper" file contains a significant number of reports of two American servicemen, one Caucasian and one black, who reportedly cooperated with Communist forces in the area from Danang down through Quang Ngai during the later part of the war. As of this writing the "Salt and Pepper" reports have not been solved.

Due to the POW/MIA aspect and the sense of satisfaction realized from helping people help themselves, I enjoyed working with the refugees. By Christmas 1975, over 54,000 refugees in the Vietnamese Diaspora were processed through Fort Chaffee. Almost every American involved in the program expended extraordinary effort in finding homes for the displaced Vietnamese. All of us felt a great deal of compassion for these unfortunate people, and it was a pleasure working with them in the resettlement process. Hardworking and frugal, they quickly adapted to their austere surroundings. Initially, the old Army barracks with no electrical outlets did pose a problem, but by breaking light bulbs in the ceiling and attaching extension cords to the exposed filaments, the creative refugees were able to tap a source of electric power for operating newly acquired appliances. By using tin snips they were also able to manufacture makeshift cook stoves from metal five-gallon cans. As hot tea brewed and sewing machines hummed the efficient Vietnamese fashioned white dress shirts from bed sheets, as well as stylish business suits and topcoats from government issued gray colored blankets. Despite their efforts, adjusting to American life southern-style was often difficult for the Vietnamese, not only because of the language and culture, but also because of hostility and no small amount of racism. Many people in the area did not like the camp being used to house refugees from a country in which so many Americans had died.

After the Vietnamese left, I remained at the post awaiting a potential influx of new refugees. We were informed that a large ship loaded with refugees had arrived in the Philippines, and the hapless souls were headed our way. However, the United Nations High Commissioner for Refugees (UNHCR) decided to intern them in the Philippines. Afterwards, the Post Commander asked me to stay and assist him in running the base. For the next four years I remained at Fort Chaffee and assumed new duties as the post Admin NCO, basically helping to shut it down. My business degree from Chaminade University came in handy at this point, but as time went on I began to think about a new assignment.

Unfortunately, just as some of the local animosity toward the Vietnamese refugees was beginning to dissipate, the community was shocked by the news "The Cubans are coming to Chaffee." Shortly thereafter some 20,000 Cubans from the Mariel Boatlift began to enter the camp, and the atmosphere changed rapidly. Whereas during the Indochinese resettlement only wooden sawhorses placed around the refugee housing with signs saying "Do Not Cross This Line" were necessary to keep the people in, with the Cubans it was a totally opposite story. Escape incidents became so frequent that a three-echelon chain link fence topped with razor wire was constructed around the entire housing area. Federal Marshals with guard dogs were deployed inside the fence, but this did not prevent the Cuban refugees from escaping into the local community. The main item stolen from both local residences and U.S. Army facilities on the post were knives, any type of knife. Stabbings within the wire enclosure occurred around the clock, and medical personnel at the Post hospital emergency room struggled to handle the caseload. The local citizenry became so alarmed that armed vigilante patrols were formed in communities surrounding the camp. This resulted in several Cubans being killed by gunfire as the escapes continued.

Not long after the arrival of the Cuban refugees I received a call in early 1980 from the MI branch advising me of a potential new assignment to the

66th MI Group in Stuttgart, Germany, working on debriefing refugees from behind the Iron Curtain. All things considered I decided to throw in the towel on the POW/MIA issue and return to the Regular Army. About the only thing I knew about Germany was that it was cold, so I began to prepare accordingly. Shortly after buying cold weather wardrobes for the family, the tiresome chores of packing and out-processing began and the POW/MIA issue slipped slowly from my mind. But before the movers had the family's household goods loaded, I received another telephone call that would place me squarely back into the POW/MIA arena.

The call came from newly promoted Major George Petrie, the Executive Officer of the Joint Casualty Resolution Center, now located in Hawaii. After being created in late January 1973, the JCRC had remained at Nakhon Phanom, Thailand. In 1976, a new Thai Government demanded the removal of all U.S. forces from the country. Increasingly reluctant to be allied with a recently defeated America, and wary of the dual regional threat posed by an awakening China and a militant Vietnam, the Thai's asked the American military to leave. Only a small garrison dubbed the "Joint US Military Assistance Group Thailand," was allowed to remain in the kingdom. During the withdrawal the JCRC was relocated to Barbers Point Naval Air Station on the southwest shore of Oahu in Hawaii, where the unit shared a small building with the Naval Investigative Service. Three JCRC members were allowed to remain in Bangkok as a satellite Liaison Office.

The first thing Petrie wanted to know was whether or not Andrea was up to traveling long distances. Second, he inquired if I had retained fluency in Southeast Asian languages. After learning of my impending assignment to Stuttgart, Petrie outlined a possible new position for me in the JCRC designated "Chief of Operations." According to Petrie, if I took the job, one of my primary tasks would be supervising field operations and the repatriation of American remains from Vietnam. The other major task was the collection of POW/MIA related information from Indochinese refugees, who at that time were arriving in waves from Southeast Asia. Petrie explained how my area of responsibility would be centered on Manila, with refugee camps located in the Bataan peninsula of Morong province, the Puerta Princess area of Palawan Island adjacent to Vietnam, and the Jose Fabella camp on the outskirts of Manila.

While a number of refugees had fled the three Communist countries, the flood did not really begin until March 1978 when the Vietnamese began to impose restrictions on the ethnic Chinese living in the country. Soon the Vietnamese were forcing out the Chinese. Others quickly followed behind them. Camps were set up to house the homeless refugees, but the host countries did not exactly welcome them with open arms. It was quickly decided to move them to more permanent locations in Australia and the United States. While the U.S. government had created programs to interview the refugees during the late 1970s, the

JCRC leadership realized that an enormous cache of POW/MIA information could be uncovered with a properly structured interview program. Language and area specialists would be needed to accomplish this new mission, hence Petrie's call.

After agreeing to sleep on the possibility of returning to the JCRC, I did some serious soul searching. Nam-Xuan had given birth to our son Scott in April 1979, and now she was pregnant again. Moving the family to Hawaii would be difficult on her, Andrea, and Scott. Frankly, the POW/MIA issue was at its lowest point. Moreover, I was not certain that either side was ready to fully address it, as many formidable obstacles remained before a full accounting could be accomplished. All sides were locked into their respective positions. The families were angered at what they saw as the Carter Administration's pursuit of normalized government relations at their expense, DOD was trying to close the DIA organization responsible for investigating American POW/MIAs, the JCRC had been downgraded and scaled back, and the Vietnamese were their usual stubborn selves. In this seemingly intractable mess, what could I hope to accomplish?

For the next several days, I weighed the pros and cons of returning to the accounting process. As always, my greatest concerns were for the MIA families. Even under the Ford Administration, the families had felt increasingly marginalized. The National League of Families of POW/MIAs in Southeast Asia, a group of families whose men were either Prisoner of War or Missing in Action, had coalesced on May 28, 1970 to protest North Vietnamese wartime actions regarding American POW/MIAs. The organization had remained intact and was continuing to press for an accounting of the men still currently listed as MIA. Further, they had recently rejected the conclusions of a 1975-76 Congressional Committee headed by Representative Sonny Montgomery, which reported that the committee believed no Americans remained alive as POWs in Vietnam, although several members dissented. Although the Committee had visited Vietnam in an attempt to re-open POW/MIA discussions with the Vietnamese (the issue of live American POWs was high on their agenda), Rep. Montgomery accepted the Communist claim that absolutely no Americans were being held anywhere within the territory of Vietnam. However, at least three Americans and possibly more were currently alive and being held in Vietnam: former CIA employee Tucker Gougleman, who later died from torture while jailed in Saigon, Marine Private Robert Garwood, who had joined the Party after being captured in 1965: and CIA contract employee Mr. Arlo Gay, who was being held only a few kilometers from where Montgomery was seated at the time. When Jimmy Carter was elected President, he also sent a Presidential Commission, headed by Leonard Woodcock, to Hanoi in March 1977 to continue negotiations on postwar relations. Woodcock also asked about living Americans, and Prime Minister Pham Van Dong denied any were still in Vietnam. Although Gay had been released by this time, Garwood was still living nearby and no information was provided concerning the fate of Gougleman.

Despite the families' protests, the Carter Administration continued to work towards normalization of relations with the Socialist Republic of Vietnam (SRV), which was finally brought to a halt by the 1978 Vietnamese invasion of Cambodia and continuing Vietnamese demands for reparations. Various family members, many of whom belonged to the League, had also recently fought a series of legal battles with the Ford and Carter Administrations to prevent the automatic re-classification of men from MIA to Killed in Action (KIA). In the summer of 1973, the wife of one MIA had sued the Service Secretaries on the grounds that the procedures for making official reports of death or presumptive findings of death were unconstitutional. Their argument was that the U.S. statutes governing these matters violated the missing man's rights to due process, the procedures for making determinations were unfair, that the government had failed to diligently search for all information on the MIAs, and that as a result of these findings of death, the missing men were being deprived of their rights under Article 8(b) of the Paris Peace Accords.[2]

A three-judge panel found that the U.S. government had in fact violated the MIA's due process rights, and issued a restraining order on the Service Secretaries from making any more status changes. The services immediately suspended the process, except when requested by the next of kin. Some families wanted to move on with their lives, and without a declaration of death, they were unable to collect the serviceman's insurance benefit. The court mandated that the notification procedures for the families be revised, provided them "reasonable" access to the information upon which the status review would be made, and allowed them to present any evidence they considered relevant. However, it was a narrow victory, as it applied only to those still listed as "MIA," as the court would not allow the finding to be applied retroactively. The other points were dismissed. On April 22, 1974, following issuance of the judgment, each of the military departments published amended regulations or promulgated new ones in order to satisfy the minimum due process standards required by the decision.

Once again, the process started up, but in 1976 another group of families challenged the Government over the new presumptive finding of death process. They lost.[3] In August 1977, the Government announced that it would resume case reviews. Within months, another group of families, including most of the senior leadership of the League, sued President Carter and the Service Secretaries over the due process claims of notification and the viewing of important information in the case. On September 29, 1977, the Judge ruled against them, which was affirmed in a ruling by the Court of Appeals on March 10, 1978. The Court, trying to assuage the families, noted:

> *There is nothing that the government of a grateful people can ever do fully to compensate or comfort the next of kin of those who have given 'the last full measure of devotion,' and for whom there is no hope of return. But it is beyond*

> *dispute that the government now provides every opportunity for the discovery and consideration of any evidence militating against a determination of death. The government is acting generously and compassionately in sparing no pains to ascertain as conclusively as possible what has actually happened to those missing in action before reaching any determination adverse to their interests or those of their next of kin. The conclusion is inescapable that the measures taken by the government suffice to defeat any claim that the constitutional rights of the plaintiffs are being or may be violated.*[4]

Despite the warm sentiments, it seemed to many families as if their own government was rushing to declare the men dead without any persuasive evidence other than the passage of time. That wasn't the truth, but since there was some political pressure being exerted to finalize the issue, it appeared that way, and I had learned from the Communists that a half-truth spread in a field of willing believers is a difficult mind-set to change. A final blow came in December 1979 when the DIA began classifying the previously unclassified postwar live sighting reports being generated by the refugees. Ominously, the words "cover-up" and "abandonment" began appearing much more frequently.

The March 1979 release of Robert Garwood reminded everyone that men could still be alive. In many ways it wasn't a big surprise, and in fact some expected more to come out. As I considered the ramifications of the new job, I understood that it wasn't just bones we were after, men's lives might be at stake. At that time, many of us considered Garwood's delivery a possible signal from the Vietnamese, despite their consistent statements that they had freed all POWs in 1973. The Communists, however, continued to maintain that Garwood had crossed over and had requested to live in Vietnam after the war. Even if it was only bones we would ever find, many of the families wanted answers. However, despite my deep sympathies for them, I knew the families did not represent a monolithic bloc. Some accepted fate and turned their backs away from the prolonged drama and pain, while the behavior of a few bordered on martyrdom. Mostly they wanted the certainty, the essential truth of what happened, as well as could be determined. Fractured by the issue of live Americans, consumed by grief, some families became even more radicalized. In this emotional cauldron the Vietnamese took full advantage.

During the war, the Communists hoped the resultant frustration of the families, coinciding with clever propaganda ploys aimed at convincing the rest of American society (not to mention the world) that it was United States policy that was responsible for this intolerable situation, would in turn create anti-war pressure on the government. For the Communist planners, the uncertainty factor, when coordinated with a predictably consistent rejection of American demands for answers or access to the prisoners, was the perfect vehicle to attempt to affect Allied morale. By promoting a policy to the grunts on the ground that declared leniency for captives, the Communists hoped to sap the soldiers' will to fight. Why fight to the death when you can surrender and not be killed, or instead disappear forever into the maelstrom of Southeast Asia? After the war, denial became a ritual, a ceremonial refusal of knowledge for which we had no option short of resuming the conflict to force them to impart that information, which by treaty they had obligated themselves to supply and yet so sparingly provided. And since the nature of war creates ambiguity, generates its own mythology, eventually the families began to mistrust the government-furnished answers to their questions, which often amounted to "we don't know," or worse, "we can't tell you." In pain some families' wrath and aggravation turned inward, so that the U.S. government became the mortal enemy, not the hard-hearted rulers in Hanoi. From a distance, one had to grudgingly admire the simple yet profound cleverness of the Vietnamese proselytizing strategy: a fiendish virus of crushed hopes and destroyed faith let loose in American society that not even its makers could predict would be its ultimate manifestation.

The Vietnamese had continued their usual intransigence by blatantly linking POW/MIA results with various economic or political concessions from the U.S. At that point, the Communists had returned in various stages the remains of seventy-two Americans, but had tied their release to "positive" political developments or a visit by American delegations.[5] Furthermore, to relegate Vietnam to the dustbin of history, President Carter had granted general amnesty to those who evaded military service during the war and had instructed the U.S. Ambassador at the United Nations in September 1977 to abstain from voting against the proposed membership for Vietnam. It was a major mistake in my opinion, because it broke Hanoi free from international isolation and at the same time provided the political cover necessary to permit a Vietnamese invasion of a weakened and war-torn Cambodia.

Other than the live prisoner issue, the most important factor to consider in gauging Hanoi's intentions was the intelligence we had just recently received from the previously mentioned "Mortician," the man I had seen in 1973 in Hanoi. His real name was Tran Viet Loc, an ethnic Chinese who was a long-time employee of the Graves Management Agency of the General Political Department of the PAVN High Command. During the postwar purge of Chinese citizens, he managed to escape by boat and arrived in Hong Kong in 1979. The Communists threatened to assassinate him if he revealed to the West what he knew about the collection of American remains. He wasn't intimidated, and forcing out the Mortician was undoubtedly the biggest mistake the Vietnamese ever made in the POW/MIA issue. I shudder to think where we would have been without his priceless information. In November 1979, shortly after the Mortician was processed into a holding camp, an alert Defense Attaché in the American Consulate, Lieutenant Colonel Robert Jordan, became aware of the man's true status. Realizing the importance of debriefing the Mortician, Jordan gained a wealth of valuable information concerning the Communist Party's secret policies and procedures regarding America's fallen heroes.

When Jordan's report reached Washington, it set off a furor. In January 1980, Congressman Lester Wolff, then chairing the Subcommittee on Asian and Pacific Affairs, traveled to Hanoi to discuss the POW/MIA issue. He confronted the Vietnamese with the information we learned from the Mortician, but as usual, the Communist officials stonewalled the U.S. representatives, calling this intelligence a "Chinese fabrication." Even at this early date the Vietnamese had prepared what would be standard lines regarding the impossibility of finding remains: the terrain had changed too much, locating wreckage in isolated jungle would be very difficult, along with the amount of time that had elapsed.

After the delegation returned to the States, in April 1980 the Vietnamese issued a "White Paper" outlining the steps they claimed to have taken to support the search for missing American servicemen. It was a tortured compilation of quotes taken out of context interspersed with pure propaganda. Although Hanoi had again denied the fact they had stored the remains of any American servicemen, and had repeatedly promised that any such remains would be repatriated immediately after being discovered, Jordan's report proved this to be merely a ruse. The Mortician's testimony was a devastating blow to Hanoi's negotiators because it exposed them for what they were—inhumane merchants of human bones. All these years later, Americans need to understand that the Communist POW/MIA strategy was more than a simple clash of political philosophy or a Vietnamese negotiating tactic. It was a deliberate, calculated policy, designed to gain them economic and political concessions in return for answers about American POW/MIAs, and Americans need to remember that the ability to lie effectively to Westerners is considered an asset by the North Vietnamese. The other key point was that dual tendencies were usually hard at work—we always underestimated them, and they always overestimated us.

According to the Mortician, Hanoi had a lengthy tradition of manipulating the remains issue. Prior to his involvement with American remains, the Mortician had worked on French dead. I had observed firsthand the cemeteries containing thousands of French bodies in North Vietnam, and I knew that upon conclusion of the war against the French, the Vietnamese had quickly fashioned the POW/MIA issue into a valuable tool. Watching Hanoi's postwar efforts to manipulate the American government in a similar fashion, I came to the inescapable conclusion that the same strategy was already underway. From 1958 until his transfer in 1969 to begin processing American remains, the Mortician was responsible for French cadavers in cemeteries located throughout northern Vietnam. From 1969 until the war ended, the Mortician claimed he personally processed and cataloged close to four hundred American remains. The Mortician stated that at one point the remains were housed in a camp for U.S. prisoners in Hanoi called the "Citadel" by the Americans and "17 Ly Nam De Street" by the Vietnamese.

A detailed description of the storage area provided by the Mortician, including his mention of a black tar paper fence to conceal the remains from the POWs, was confirmed through analysis of aerial imagery.

Our forensic specialists also debriefed the Mortician. They were quickly convinced that he was reporting truthfully regarding his previous duties in Vietnam. The Mortician subsequently passed two polygraph exams with no deception indicated, although on the first one some discrepancies were noted, and the original CIA polygraph examiner balked enough that the DIA brought in a second one, who validated the Mortician's story. In addition to information on the American remains, the Mortician also provided a very vivid description of three Caucasians in the Hanoi area from 1974 until just prior to his escape in 1979. Although the Mortician voluntarily cooperated with a composite sketch artist from the Criminal Investigation Division of the Air Force Office of Special Investigations to compile drawings of the three men, none were identified at that time. During a subsequent encounter with Robert Garwood, the Mortician positively recognized him as being one of the three Caucasians in Hanoi.

In addition to these problems already besetting the issue, I also carefully studied the present grim state of American-Vietnamese relations and their impact on the POW/MIA issue. American-Vietnamese affairs were at their lowest point. The Vietnamese expulsion of the Chinese, the 1978 invasion of Cambodia, their increasingly close alliance with the Soviet Union, the retrenchment following the Mortician's devastating testimony, all served to place our contacts in a deep freeze. I concluded that given the current state of affairs, the first jobs Petrie mentioned, field operations and remains repatriation ceremonies, would be few and far between.

In spite of these imposing hurdles, I realized that with my language skills and background knowledge and previous experience interrogating Asian Communist cadre, I could be very productive doing what I had always done—collecting intelligence from the Communists. I quickly convinced myself that with so many American servicemen still unaccounted for in Southeast Asia, I simply could not turn my back on the issue or walk away from years of work. I had been involved with the topic on and off since 1968, when I began grilling captured or rallied Communist personnel at the old interrogation centers. In many ways I had never left the issue. The fact that a large number of MIA families were clamoring for a final answer and would continue to suffer if Hanoi gained the upper hand and delayed the accounting for America's missing for years into the future was in itself adequate motivation to re-enter the field. By re-joining the accounting process and doggedly pursuing answers from the large number of fleeing refugees who were no longer under Communist control, perhaps in some small way I could prevent Hanoi from succeeding in completely exploiting the issue and adding further pain to long-suffering American families. Still, even though I decided to accept the important JCRC job, I knew it would take a great deal of expertise and perseverance to achieve a full accounting in the shortest possible time. Seven years had passed since Operation Homecoming; the U.S. was still without any closure. Another important rationale for me was the death of my wife and son. I felt compelled to do everything I could to ensure that Nova and Michael had not died in vain. Having already gone through the difficult identification process for two loved ones of my own, it made me distinctly aware of the pain that waiting generates. I was reassured by the thought that in returning to the search for the missing men, I was doing precisely what Nova would have expected of me. In my heart I knew it was time to once again join the search.

So, in June 1980, I found myself on a plane headed for Hawaii. I was concerned about the U.S. government's commitment to the issue, and it turns out my suspicions were correct. When I reported for duty for my third JCRC tour, the American POW/MIA agencies had reached their nadir. Only a two-man office in the DIA, comprised of Charles Trowbridge and my old colleague Robert Destatte, remained actively engaged on the issue. However, Lieutenant General Eugene Tighe, head of DIA, was trying to shut them down. The JCRC offices were badly understaffed and poorly funded. Although Major Petrie had assured me I would have an overlap with the outgoing Chief of Operations, and that Petrie himself would personally brief me on my new responsibilities, when I walked through the front door of the Joint Casualty Resolution Center I found it almost deserted. The Commander, Lieutenant Colonel Steve Perry, was away on temporary duty and I learned that Major Petrie had retired only a few days beforehand to work for H. Ross Perot in Dallas. Unsure what to do, I put my gear in the Operations Section. Being the highest-ranking man present for duty I decided to use the desk in the front office normally occupied by Petrie, the Executive Officer. When an old friend called a few days later to inquire about the degree of challenge in my new job, he was surprised to learn that in a matter of only a few days I had become the acting Commander, acting Executive Officer, and Operations Chief of a joint service command. No small feat for only a Master Sergeant.

The cramped offices allotted to the JCRC held only a small team of Army and Air Force intelligence analysts who mulled over the few refugee reports collected by various agencies of the U.S. government, including local Defense Attachés, the JCRC Operations Section, and the JCRC Liaison Office located in the American Embassy in Bangkok. I later learned that between 1975 and 1978, only 126 refugee reports had been collected. The JCRC had put posters and booklets in the camps, and had tried to get the local agencies assisting the refugees to ask about POW/MIA information. The National League of Families had taken out advertisements in Vietnamese language newspapers in the U.S. and France asking for information. As a result, in 1979, the pace had quickened considerably, with over four hundred gathered. By 1980, that number was growing, and while some useful intelligence had been collected, the entire process was haphazard at best.

The chief enlisted man present at the Hawaii headquarters, Air Force Senior Master Sergeant Raymond Spock, greeted my arrival with skepticism. Observing the combat decorations on my uniform, Spock asked rhetorically "when you were with the JCRC before, you must have been on one of those field teams?" After I nodded in the affirmative, Spock continued his spontaneous interview by diplomatically questioning my ability to interview Indochinese refugees unassisted by an interpreter. It seemed he simply could not accept the fact that an infantryman and former JCRC field team member could be fluent in an Asian language. Actually, Spock's attitude came as no surprise to me, because many Americans with whom I had worked in the past experienced difficulty in communicating directly with interview subjects, especially Asians, even if they had undergone extensive language training.

Although Spock would undoubtedly carry his disdain for infantrymen to his grave, after my refugee interviews began to yield results he seemed to change his attitude somewhat regarding my ability to collect and record intelligence information. But the quality of my effort proved a two-edged sword in our working relationship, because Spock was also concerned about the quantity of reports being added to his workload. It seemed that he wanted enough information coming in to justify his section's existence, but not to the point that he would be required to change the current four-on, three-off work week in order to keep up with the increase. Later this became a moot point and Spock was forced to accept the inevitable when a change in command resulted in the entire organization being required to follow the normal military procedure of a five-day work week with most weekends free. Once the change was made and the analysts became accustomed to working full time, the animosity gradually diminished.

As part of my initial orientation plan, one of my first steps was to visit the JCRC's sister organization, the Central Identification Laboratory, Hawaii, more commonly known by its acronym, CILHI. I needed to reacquaint myself with the personnel and operations capabilities of the lab. The laboratory and its operations were part of an effort begun in the 1840s when the U.S. government instituted a concerted effort to recover and properly intern service members killed in war. It was not until the Civil War, however, that the government assumed the dual obligation of identifying and then burying the dead in registered graves.

The Spanish-American War sparked another major policy development. For the first time in our history, the remains of military servicemen buried in battlefield cemeteries on foreign soil were systematically disinterred and returned for permanent burial in the United States. With the outbreak of World War I, the U.S. government applied the lessons learned in Cuba and moved quickly to authorize the return from Europe of American remains. To meet this mission, a Graves Registration Service was introduced for the purpose of recovering and identifying American war dead. During World War II, Congress again recognized the importance of returning the remains of service members to their native soil, and delegated this responsibility to the Secretary of the Army. Several temporary Army identification laboratories were established for this purpose, and for the first time, trained physical anthropologists and anatomists were employed for the task.

The laboratories were dissolved in 1951 when their congressional charter expired. With the onset of hostilities on the Korean Peninsula, the U.S. reestablished a central identification unit in Kokura, Japan, to process United Nations war dead. Like its predecessors, this laboratory had only a temporary charter and in 1956, closed once more. Within a few years, however, when young Americans were again making the ultimate sacrifice in a far-away land, two U.S. Army mortuaries were created in South Vietnam to identify the deceased.

After the American withdrawal from South Vietnam and the subsequent closing of the mortuaries in 1972 and 1973, the Army established the Central Identification Laboratory, Thailand. In May 1976, the Central Identification Laboratory, Hawaii was established in Honolulu, Hawaii. With its reopening came an expanded mission: the retrieval and identification of all non-recovered U.S. service members from past wars. The laboratory's mission was to continue the search, recovery, and identification of American service members killed in Indochina. I was very familiar with the laboratory's work because of the many heart-wrenching visits I made there in the process of identifying my wife and son. The laboratory relocated back to American territory shortly after I confirmed the preliminary identifications and took custody of my loved ones' remains for burial back home in the U.S.

My next step involved reviewing the old files. In the summer of 1980 the unsolved cases still lingering in the JCRC files covered a very broad spectrum. Most situations in South Vietnam involved the typical ground combat losses involving soldiers and Marines whose bodies had been left on battlefields all across the country, while the fates of others were simply unknown. In such cases the locations or circumstances had been confused due to the heavy fighting. In many instances search operations to locate the missing infantrymen had been delayed due to continuing enemy fire. When a search was finally possible, neither the men nor their remains could be found. It was as if they had simply disappeared into the thick jungle.

The providence of many aviators was similarly mysterious, even though a relatively large number of aircraft had crashed in close proximity to enemy forces, especially in the North. In a few instances American eyewitnesses had personally observed enemy troops closing in on downed aviators after they reached the ground, men who never turned up on POW lists or came back at Homecoming. They remained missing-in-action. Once a man went missing-in-action, by regulation responsible commanders quickly convened boards of inquiry comprised of officers from the same or similar type units. Such boards routinely concluded that the men were missing-in-action, sometimes because the evidence was unclear, other times simply to continue pay and benefits for the man's family. Those men whose names appeared on lists provided by the Communists indicating that they were being held as "Prisoners-of-War," or whose photographs appeared in Communist news media, or whose voices were recognized in Communist radio broadcasts after their capture, continued to be carried as "MIA." If, however, no new information was developed on the missing men during a twelve month period following the end of the war, their status was changed to "Presumed Dead," or as it was known in the casualty resolution business, "Dead-F."

Some of the cases were extremely challenging. As I have mentioned previously, I believe that in a few situations American servicemen were lured to capture by the employment of Communist agents, primarily female. Far from home and lonely, the men were usually enticed by the promise of sex by the English-speaking female agents. If they resisted, in most instances the men were brutally stabbed or beaten to death and buried near the spot where they were killed. This method of capturing or killing young Americans was most often employed in the Danang-Chu Lai areas, and there were contemporary reports indicating that female agents were being trained in the English language to conduct such operations. Getting the Vietnamese to acknowledge these intelligence operations would undoubtedly prove impossible without detailed, on-the-scene investigations.

Considering the low priority afforded the POW/MIA issue by the Carter administration, and with the Vietnamese heavily occupied in war-torn Cambodia, I considered it likely that Hanoi would first consolidate its recent victory in Cambodia before reengaging its old American adversary. Until the Vietnamese government could discern how it could control increased cooperation on the POW/MIA issue with the American government, it would not permit genuine access by our investigators in the areas associated with last known detention sites and loss incidents. Access to Vietnamese files was even more of a dream. Everything seemed to be in a holding pattern. In essence, it was a critical time for gathering information in preparation for that future reengagement.

I realized that the most important contribution I could make to the overall effort was the collection of information from refugees who had knowledge of American casualties. In looking over individual case folders at the JCRC it was apparent that most of the files had become stagnant since the time of the individual's disappearance. There was very little subsequent information from any new sources. In other words, in most instances often-scant information provided by Americans was all the analysts had to go on. In many cases it was a solid first hand account by an American survivor of what happened, but often it was a hurriedly recorded description given in a dangerous and often chaotic situation. Some new information had been uncovered during the time the JCRC was able to send field teams into South Vietnam, or had been collected from

Vietnamese citizens who had decided to escape the new totalitarian government. But unfortunately, almost all of the reports collected from the fleeing refugees pertained to crash sites and gravesites. I knew that in order to solve the much more important live prisoner issue, additional information was needed, and collecting it wouldn't be easy. The refugees were scattered in camps over a wide area in the Pacific. As I had done in similar situations in the past, I tried to summon all possible energy and determination in order to make the most of every available moment. Even though I had uprooted my family recently, it was time for me to travel.

Within three weeks of my arrival in Hawaii, I was on a plane bound for Manila. As instructed by the JCRC commander, Lieutenant Colonel Steve Perry, when I arrived at Manila International Airport I took a taxi to the office of the Defense Attaché in the American Embassy where I was briefed on the in-country travel situation. This was an important stop, as the Republic of the Philippines had its own growing insurgency problem. Armed teams of the Communist-oriented New People's Army were just beginning small-scale operations. Lt. Col. Perry had been a Captain commanding a Special Forces "A" Team during the war, and he was well aware of the dangers inherent in travel to remote areas beset with guerrilla activity.

A second matter was the receipt of authorization to visit the camps. A prerequisite for entering the refugee camps were passes containing my photograph and the time of visit. Although the Philippine Government issued the passes through the American Embassy, the Philippine military and constabulary controlled all access to the sites and physically secured the camps. However, the officials who actually ran the camp were from the United Nations High Commissioner for Refugees. After the security briefing and pick-up of the passes, I then checked in with the Embassy's local Refugee Office where a JCRC map kit had been prepositioned for my use. Staff officers who had served in Vietnam in the former U.S. Agency for International Development primarily manned the refugee bureau.

Armed with the set of 1/50,000 scale Indochinese series maps and camp passes, I proceeded to a local car rental agency, LTD Limousine, which was located in the Quezon City area of Manila. Local American Embassy officials routinely utilized this particular rental agency, as did visiting officials from Washington with business in the refugee sites. LTD Limousine took its name from the small fleet of large 1972 Ford LTDs it rented to its customers. The owner of the car rental company, Mr. Le Van Phap, was a former ARVN Major who was serving in the GVN Embassy in Manila at the time of the collapse. When the other GVN officials departed the former South Vietnamese Embassy for resettlement in third countries, Phap decided to "acquire" the fleet of Ford LTDs the U.S. government had provided. Thinking ahead, Phap had also commandeered an adequate number of desks, chairs, filing cabinets and typewriters to start his new business.

The largest camp for Vietnamese refugees in the Philippines was located in a very secluded area on the Bataan peninsula in Morong province. The only way to reach the camp was by car along a difficult route through the countryside. The road to the camp followed the same tragic path taken by American and Filipino POWs captured by the Japanese Imperial Army in World War II. Traveling along the route of the infamous "Bataan Death March" gave me chills as I thought about the hundreds of men who had been bayoneted and beaten to death by the brutal Japanese soldiers.

The camp at Bataan was a sprawling facility with clusters of hastily constructed tin-roofed wooden barracks-type buildings scattered over several acres on a windy plateau overlooking the blue-black waters of the Pacific. On a deserted beach below the camp a huge but mostly abandoned nuclear power facility operated by the Westinghouse Corporation stared out at the sea. For many impoverished Filipinos the construction of this plant, costing billions of U.S. dollars that had been furnished as aid to the country, was a telling commentary on the regime of President Ferdinand Marcos. The plant never opened due to corruption by Marcos and his wealthy family, along with a growing antinuclear sentiment in the region. The fact that no local residents ever received any electric power from the problem-plagued worksite only added to the festering societal wound that the Communist insurgents hoped to exploit.

Another fear of the UNHCR officials and the Philippine government was that the Filipino people residing in the area of both the Westinghouse Plant and the Bataan refugee camp were so poor that they might become resentful of the life style enjoyed by the Vietnamese residing temporarily within their territory. Further compounding the Filipino government's anxieties was that the newly arrived Vietnamese might attempt to establish a base of support for not only the Communist New People's Army, but any potential Communist insurgents from Vietnam as well. As had been the case in selecting a site for the nuclear power plant, security was the most important matter. In the years ahead I would find that one of the most difficult aspects of collecting POW/MIA information was the host countries' choice of far-flung locations to detain the refugees.

According to the United Nations personnel, there were three viable solutions for Vietnamese "boat people" arriving in the Philippines: resettlement to a third country, voluntary repatriation, or local resettlement. The UNHCR policy sounded good, but with the unstable economy and the insurgency problem, the Philippine government did not consider local resettlement a viable alternative. I also learned that operational costs had been a primary consideration in selecting Bataan over Fort Chaffee, which is why the second influx of refugees had never arrived. Whereas it would have cost over $25.00 per day to maintain them in the U.S., in the Philippines this cost fell to approximately $1.60 per person. In looking at the situation throughout Southeast Asia at the time, where over 40,000 refugees were temporarily housed, this arrangement amounted to a considerable savings. While I could see the economic sense in this, it was very hard on the refugees.

Upon arrival at the Bataan camp, I was subjected to the usual scrutiny and long waiting period normally experienced by first-time visitors. But having been warned beforehand by members of the Embassy staff concerning the lack of hospitality routinely displayed by the Philippine guards at the camp, I followed their advice and waited for the proper opportunity to pass out several bottles of Johnny Walker scotch. The effect was immediate and I soon had unlimited access to the facility.

The consortium of agencies responsible for initial interview of the refugees and record set-up was called the Joint Volunteer Agency (JVA). Staffed primarily by young altruistic Americans, who seemed to prefer the rustic life style offered by working in isolated foreign areas, the JVA operated on a periodically renewable federal contract negotiated and funded by the State Department. Although salaries for the JVA volunteers were far below those of American officials performing similar work, they were in general highly dedicated and some appeared more qualified than their State Department supervisors. After only a brief period of working with the JVAs, I concluded that if I could increase their awareness of the POW/MIA accounting effort and also gain their cooperation (no easy trick since many had come from the anti-war side), they were capable of making a valuable contribution to the program. Contrary to the attitudes of their State Department colleagues, I found the JVAs to be short on attendance on the diplomatic cocktail circuit but long on patience and compassion.

The majority of refugees at Bataan Camp were in a "second asylum" status, having been moved there from "first asylum" camps located in other countries, such as Thailand and Hong Kong. During my initial visit to the Bataan Camp, I was not able to obtain a great deal of useable information, but I did lay the groundwork for future trips. After being apprised of the situation and the mission of the JCRC, the most important initial accomplishment was my success in convincing the JVAs to support the effort. Unlike many government officials and politicians who viewed the POW/MIA question as an irritating problem to be quickly resolved, I tried to convince the JVAs for what it truly was: a legitimate national issue with a compelling basis for an honest and fair resolution. Some of the volunteers whom I met were aware there were at least a small number of American servicemen still missing from the war, but most were astounded when they learned the true magnitude of the issue. Eventually I had great success with them, but some resented anything remotely connected to the military, regardless of our mission.

Another resource were the internally-formed Vietnamese Camp Committees, comprised entirely of refugees awaiting resettlement. They were anxious to assist in the humanitarian effort to account for the former allies of their beloved Republic of Vietnam. The Vietnamese seemed to be natural organizers, and each camp was carefully structured into subcommittees responsible for important tasks. These subcommittees included External Affairs, Security, Religious Affairs, Sanitation, Military Veterans, Food, Housing, and other tasks depending on the locations and camp populations. The organizational abilities of the Vietnamese refugees contributed greatly to my ability to be able to locate potential sources of information in a timely and efficient manner.

After permission from both the JVAs and the Camp Committees, I began to make loudspeaker announcements in the Vietnamese language calling upon anyone within the camp to come forward who had any information on Americans who were still being held prisoner or who had been killed-in-action. Although JCRC personnel had visited the camp in the past, my language ability proved to be a real asset. During future trips, I received a considerable amount of fresh information, including live-sighting reports from new sources. U.S. analysts ultimately correlated several of these reports to Robert Garwood. A number of other live-sighting reports were matched to American personnel who were held prisoner at one point but later released. Ominously, although a significant number of live-sighting reports collected from Bataan were provided by sources that appeared to be credible, they could not be correlated to any specific individual. I also received a large number of reports pinpointing the location of both crash and gravesites of American MIAs.

Another camp located in the city of Manila was the Jose Fabella Camp. This camp only housed refugees who were either awaiting air transportation from Manila International Airport to their country of resettlement, or who were transitioning between other camps. All refugees in the city camp had already been processed through either the Bataan Camp or a third camp on Palawan Island. Although I made it a point to visit the Jose Fabella camp on each trip, the small number of people and the paucity of the information I gained forced me to curtail my time there in order to devote a greater effort to more recent arrivals at the remote camps.

When I returned to Manila International Airport from Bataan, I boarded a small aircraft owned by Philippine Airlines for a trip to the third camp at Palawan Island. I found it more than a little ironic that I was traveling to a place to collect intelligence that could be possibly used to rescue U.S. POWs, when on this very island the Japanese had executed some 150 American prisoners during WWII.

As I crossed the ocean and approached the island I noticed that the only facility of significant size visible from the air was a huge maximum-security prison operated by the central government. As we approached the airport at Puerta Princessa, the main city on the island, the aircraft suddenly plunged downward and skimmed just above white-capped waves before landing on the tiny runway. The small airport enabled the Philippine Air Force to maintain at least a scant military presence in an area adjacent to the hotly contested Spratley and Paracel Island chains. Both China and to some extent Vietnam claim certain sections of the islands and nearby reefs. Whoever controlled the atolls could extend their military power into the South China Sea, and also claim the potentially huge untapped reservoirs of oil. As the small commercial airliner touched down, a U.S. manufactured F-8 "Crusader" jet-fighter plane prepared to taxi out for takeoff on a routine island patrol.

Hailing a three-wheeled pedicab, I traveled to the enormous and ornate Palawan Raffles Hotel located in a jungle clearing just outside the town, my quarters for my short stay. The hotel was elegantly constructed from marble and teakwood but there were few guests, creating the ghostly air of an abandoned castle. Stunned at the incongruity of such a low occupancy rate for this magnificent building surrounded by lush tropical splendor, I inquired among the hotel staff and learned that construction had been prompted by the recent discovery of oil just off the shore of Palawan Island. Although investors rushed from Manila to make their fortune in what was believed to be the Philippine's last frontier, the oil strike failed to materialize when the field provided only a trickle of oil from an isolated pocket.

The Palawan camp for Vietnamese refugees was located at one end of the airfield and next to the beach. Rimmed by graceful palm trees, the small simple cottages built to house the refugees had the appearance of a typical Asian fishing village. Upon entering the camp I noticed a petite grotto with a statue of the Virgin Mary placed at the rear of its overhang. The ingenious refugees had built the grotto by piling sand into a large mound over which they then poured concrete. Once the concrete had hardened over the mound the sand was dug by hand from beneath the structure, giving the appearance of a cave. The motif was completed with an adornment of seashells and colorful flowers.

Most of the refugees detained in the Palawan camp had begun their dangerous journey from South Vietnam's central coast along an area from Hue south to Nha Trang. A small number of them, however, had departed from Saigon by proceeding down the Saigon River to Vung Tau and then out to sea. The ocean currents and prevailing winds were oriented in a generally easterly direction away from the coastline from April until sometime around October. By relying on the seasonal drift and a great deal of luck, most of the refugees were able to steer their motorless fishing boats along the edge of the Paracel or Spratley Islands chains, where they eventually reached the Palawan Camp. Due to the poor condition of the small boats a significant number simply disappeared, never to be heard from again.

I soon discovered that even more horrifying than the treacherous sea journey was a modern day version of the seafarer's ancient enemy. I encountered some refugees who had departed South Vietnam en route to Malaysia or Indonesia but were raided at sea by vicious pirates. Knowing that the refugees would be escaping carrying everything of value they owned, especially jewelry, the normal tactic employed by the pirates was to strip search everyone on the boat and take all items of value. One elderly lady even described how the pirates used electrician's pliers to remove her gold teeth. Once all valuables had been collected some of the pirates wielding firearms would guard the men while the women and girls were moved to the pirate's boat and raped repeatedly for hours, sometimes days. The cut off point for females spared from the rape gangs was eleven years of age.

After the rapes subsided the pirates picked out a number of younger females to remain with them on their boat. Then the boat carrying the refugees was rammed so it would sink. The people who related the story to me were fortunate to have been rescued. Shortly after the pirates departed the vicinity, a merchant vessel sailing through the area from Singapore had found them adrift. Like the families of the American MIAs, the relatives of the young girls who were abducted by the pirates would try desperately to locate their loved ones for years into the future. At times their perseverance would pay off. A few of the girls were found enslaved in brothels in southern Thailand near the border of Malaysia.

Checking in at the camp headquarters building, I found the atmosphere much more relaxed than at Bataan. There was no requirement for signing in and no one asked for identification. I was escorted to the office of the Camp Commander, First Lieutenant Pagaduan. After accepting an invitation for lunch at the Tree House Restaurant near the airfield, I briefed the young lieutenant on my mission. Between bites of grilled prawns and rice I was surprised to notice that in several of the bamboo dining booths situated beneath the branches of a large tree were Vietnamese refugees from the nearby camp. Pagaduan explained that due to the camp's remote island location, security was not a problem and the refugees were allowed to come and go as they pleased. Pagaduan did not seem overly concerned about any potential criticism from his superiors of his leadership style in managing the camp. The camp's distant setting drastically curtailed the number of visitors from Manila.

Shortly after making my first loudspeaker announcement in Vietnamese, I was approached by two men. Both wanted to surrender themselves to U.S. authorities, which in this case happened to be me. During interviews both men confessed they were Communists who were attempting to emigrate to the U.S. without revealing their true political orientation. The two men explained that when they saw me arrive at the camp, and then begin making announcements in the Vietnamese language over the camp's loudspeaker, they had assumed that the visit was for security screening of personnel within the camp. Believing that they were on the verge of being discovered, they decided to voluntarily turn themselves in.

One of the men was a former ARVN Noncommissioned Officer who had defected to the Communists in June 1974. The second man was an officer of the North Vietnamese army who had entered Saigon at the time of the collapse in 1975. He married a South Vietnamese girl and later became disillusioned with

Communism, prompting his escape by boat to the Philippines. Both men were able to provide valuable information concerning American MIAs. The former NCO reported on the location of possible graves of American POWs who died while being held in a prison camp in Binh Dinh province. The former NVA officer provided information on two Navy pilots, Lieutenant David Hodges and Commander Richard Rich, who were shot down in separate incidents southwest of Hanoi during 1967. Cdr. Richard Rich's crash site recently has been the scene of much activity, including a visit to the dig by then Secretary of Defense William Cohen. Rich's remains have subsequently been identified.

After word passed through the camp that a U.S. official was present for interviews concerning American POW/MIAs, the recently arrived refugees began appearing at the camp headquarters with varying types of information. Some reported on Americans who died while being held in wartime prison camps. Others reported on incidents where POWs were observed in prison and still alive. Unfortunately they could only provide the last known location where they had observed the American at the time, since either the prisoner or the source of the report had since moved from the area. Reports were also received concerning men killed or captured when their aircraft was shot down by enemy fire. In most cases the dead were buried near the incident site, while those who survived were led away by the capturing forces.

More importantly, others commented that Communist officials went to considerable effort to find and document the bodies of American personnel. After the corpses were photographed, the burial location was recorded. In some cases where no cameras were available at the time of the incident, the Americans were buried, only to be exhumed and photographed by officials at a later date. This information confirmed our suspicions regarding Vietnamese policies regarding American remains. Not all stories revolved around POW/MIA, however, since some refugees reported on the deaths of servicemen due to robberies and muggings.

During my first few visits to the Palawan camp I received a number of intriguing reports on live Americans. A lady who had lived in the South prior to the Communist takeover but who had journeyed to northwestern Vietnam after the war ended provided a fascinating statement. The lady was married to a South Vietnamese military officer arrested in the South and later moved to the North when he was sentenced to "reeducation" in a labor/thought-reform camp in Hoang Lien Son province. The lady described in detail an arduous trip to visit her incarcerated husband that included travel on trains, busses, ferries and finally on foot. According to the lady, as she neared the camp where her husband was being held she encountered a small group of foreign prisoners working in a field. Having observed many American military personnel in South Vietnam during the war, the lady felt certain that the group she saw while en route to visit her husband were Americans.

After visiting with her husband in the camp and relating her observation to him, he confirmed to her that the men she saw were Americans held behind after the war ended. The Defense Intelligence Agency, however, did not believe her. Yet, neither the DIA nor the CIA nor any other organization involved in analyzing the report could come up with any credible evidence why the lady was being untruthful. In fact, at the time of my interview the lady already knew that she had been accepted for resettlement in the U.S., leaving her with no apparent motivation to lie about the sighting of the American POWs.[6] This report and others like it nagged at my conscience.

Much has been written about the validity of reports generated from refugees who have a vested interest in pleasing their American interlocutors. While a significant number of refugees were confident of resettlement opportunities in America and other free-world countries around the globe, there were many who held little hope of going anywhere. Literally the dregs of the earth, those who had escaped confinement in Vietnam on criminal charges, or those who were faced with starvation and decided to risk their lives at sea based solely on economic concerns, often felt compelled to fabricate some type of valuable information to use as a bargaining chip when being interviewed by officials in the camps.

Some of the stories told by desperate refugees were incredulous to the point of being comical. Such accounts were replete with drama, and often contained details indicating that large numbers of Americans with long beards and dragging chains were being used as slave labor to harvest peanuts and other crops. However, in most cases the amount of specific details related by such sources was far less than what one would expect of someone who had personally witnessed the claimed events and was relating a firsthand observation. While at least some unscrupulous attempts by refugees in such wretched situations could reasonably be anticipated, at times both analysts and policy-makers tended to devalue the reporting effort as a whole because of them. Although the stated policy was to judge each report based on its own merit, it always bothered me when reports of live-sightings proven to be fabrications were highly publicized, while similar reports judged "inconclusive" received little fanfare. Perhaps due to the political climate this was to be expected, because the standards for judging live-sighting reports as "confirmed" were inconceivably high. In reality, before any live-sighting report would be considered valid it would not only have to be confirmed by a second, independent report, it would also have to contain the name of the live American, and in some cases additional proof, such as identifiable photographs, fingerprints, or blood samples.

During the course of my interviews I also collected information for the U.S. intelligence community regarding the current situation inside Vietnam. With virtually no access inside the country, the State Department was especially interested in obtaining the latest information on political and military events.

Since State was involved in a postwar resettlement program whereby Vietnamese nationals closely associated with the old Saigon government would be accepted for immigration to America, I held numerous interviews with these people. I also used the time to gain insight into the prison system in Vietnam. Not only did such interviews mesh well with the effort to identify areas where U.S. personnel might still be under detention by Communist authorities, it resulted in a significant amount of information regarding the overall policies of Vietnam's Ministry of Public Security, periodically called the Ministry of Interior. In addition to other Communist organizations, this was the postwar organization most likely to be directly involved with American prisoners if any were still being held.

During one such interview I learned that shortly after the fall of Saigon, the former Chief of the RVN Delegation to the FPJMT, Colonel Duong Hieu Nghia, was arrested and held in a prison camp near Bien Hoa. Soon a high-ranking Communist cadre from Hanoi arrived at the camp in a black American-made sedan to visit Colonel Nghia. After further checking I discovered that the cadre was Minister Without Portfolio and Chairman of the Committee for Overseas Vietnamese, Mr. Vo Dong Giang. I knew that Vo Dong Giang's real name was Pham Ba and his trip to visit Nghia was significant, because not only had Giang served as a high ranking political cadre during the war, after the ceasefire he was the chief spokesman for the PRG delegation at Camp Davis until the very end. Since both Giang and Nghia had been assigned to implement Article 8(b) of the Paris Agreements relative to POWs and MIAs, I was certain that Giang's trip to the prison camp where Nghia was held was not a coincidence. I assumed Giang wanted to debrief Nghia for any information on American plans and personnel involved with POW/MIA accounting, and on the extent of our knowledge regarding Vietnamese policies. To reinforce my theory, Giang would later be assigned as the principle negotiator discussing the POW/MIA issue with U.S. officials in Hanoi in 1982.

Traveling around remote areas of the Philippines for a year interviewing refugees was arduous. The winding routes through rebel infested territory, the threat of assassination on the streets of crowded cities, the overall unsanitary conditions and the torrid heat all combined to make the mission difficult. But the large amount of valuable information collected made it all worthwhile. In reality, however, the degree of challenge posed by the Philippine interview trips would ultimately pale in comparison to other, even more desolate areas on the horizon. I had survived mainland Southeast Asia several times in the past, but I was about to be tested once again by that dangerous environment.

Chapter Six

Riding the POW/MIA Circuit

I CONTINUED MY INFORMATION GATHERING trips throughout the rest of 1980 and into 1981. During that time, Lieutenant Colonel Perry was transferred to become the Army Attaché in the American Embassy in Manila. Perry's replacement to head the JCRC was Lieutenant Colonel Joe Bob Harvey, a former Air Defense Artillery and Foreign Area officer who had served previous tours in both Vietnam and Thailand. Since the JCRC at the time was subordinate to the Commander-in-Chief Pacific (CINCPAC) Special Operations Section, and since Harvey did not have a Special Operations background, almost everyone involved in casualty resolution read his assignment to the unit as further indication the overall accounting effort was being downgraded.

While a good officer, Harvey lived in constant fear of being forced to resign from the Army as a result of being overweight. The military had embraced strict weight standards whose limits Harvey continually tested. As a result, the men of the JCRC dubbed Harvey "Boss Hog" from the TV show "Dukes of Hazzard." Since Harvey was a Texas native and exuded syrupy dialog with everyone he came in contact with, especially his superiors and the family members, I lobbied with my colleagues on behalf of the name "Billy Sol," after the well-known Texas con man "Billy Sol Estes." But due to an unfortunate lack of historical perspective on the part of the men, and an over-reliance on the merits of popular culture, the name "Boss Hog" eventually gained permanence.

Fortunately for me, in mid-summer 1981, a new job opened up, one that would enable me to canvass the entire refugee population. As a consequence of organizing an effective POW/MIA information collection program in the Philippines, I was offered an assignment to the JCRC Liaison Office in the American Embassy in Bangkok. At that time the JCRC headquarters in Hawaii was responsible for interviewing refugees in the Philippines, while the smaller three-member liaison team in Bangkok was responsible for conducting interviews in Malaysia, Indonesia, Hong Kong, Japan, Macao, and Thailand. Air Force Lieutenant Colonel Paul D. Mather directed the Liaison Office (LNO) in Thailand. His entire staff consisted of a civilian Casualty Resolution specialist named James E. Tully, and the JCRC's token Marine, Gunnery Sergeant William S. Whorton. Realizing that I was the only member of the organization able to speak Vietnamese, Thai, and Lao, and knowing that new sources for POW/MIA information were arriving daily at the camps, I was very excited about the new assignment and I decided to accept. I replaced Gunnery Sergeant Whorton when I arrived for duty at the Bangkok LNO in August 1981.

Once again, I had to uproot my family, which now included my new daughter Elisabeth, who was born on January 13, 1981. Scott, now two-years old, Andrea, and the baby made the long and tiring trip across the ocean guarded closely by Nam-Xuan. We were lucky to find a house in a compound for foreigners only four miles from the American Embassy. Even in those years Bangkok traffic was maddening, and I wasn't sure if I would ever become accustomed to the "dog-eat-dog" manner of driving in Bangkok. While the normal travel time to and from work was approximately forty-five minutes to an hour, during holiday periods or in times of heavy flooding, traffic would sometimes grind to a complete halt. Despite the relatively short travel distance, on one occasion it took me almost three hours to drive the four-mile route. Since the roads were impassable I often waded the four miles to work carrying my duty uniform and shoes in a plastic bag. In contrast to its neighbors, at the time of my transfer Thailand was enjoying a fairly strong economy. Streets in Bangkok and other cities that had once been intended for bicycle traffic and an occasional motorized vehicle quickly reached gridlock with an ever-increasing number of new cars and trucks purchased by newly affluent Thais. A joke around Bangkok was that in Thailand there were more cars than roads.

Fed by the conflict in neighboring Cambodia, the economy in the eastern part of the country was even stronger than in Bangkok. A large number of wealthy war profiteers resided in Aranyaphrathet, a rural town located at the border that served as the Thai gateway to Cambodia's capital, Phnom Penh. This group possessed the means to import expensive vehicles from both the U.S. and Europe. The resultant display of luxurious cars on the streets of the rustic town led to yet another humorous story. The gag was that the Thais in Bangkok would never have to worry about being invaded by the Vietnamese currently occupying Cambodia, because shortly after the offensive started the road from the border to Bangkok would be so choked with fleeing Mercedes Benzes the Vietnamese army could not pass.

Unfortunately for our family, we moved into our new home during the middle of the rainy season. Like most of Vietnam, Thailand has only two seasons: hot and wet, and hot and dry. At certain times the runoff caused by rains in the area north of Bangkok met with the incoming tide from the ocean south of the city, resulting in the entire metropolis being inundated, sometimes for as long as three weeks. During the heavy flooding we had to move everything on the lower floor of our home upstairs, including the refrigerator and other appliances. Another result of the overflow was that the area became plagued with venomous snakes. During one period of heavy flooding I found a King Cobra in the kitchen. He was about five feet long and nasty looking, but our little dog Jaws ran him out of the kitchen after I graciously opened the door and stood far back. Given that it was taboo to kill a snake in Thailand, a mind-set based on their religious beliefs, Jaws was the next best thing.

The LNO office turned out to be a tiny, crowded cubbyhole at one end of the Embassy's Defense Attaché Office. I knew what it was like to be in a military unit on a shoestring budget, but this was incredibly bad. Space was so tight there was barely room to maneuver between the three plywood desks crammed into the corners of the room. I wondered how the liaison office personnel had ever managed to get the desks into the room. Information processing consisted of one IBM Selectric typewriter with two typing balls and a few reams of paper borrowed from the DAO. The office did not even have one assigned vehicle, and office personnel relied on local taxis for transportation, paid for out of their own pocket.

In sizing up the situation, I recalled how during the early 1960s my infantry squad leader came around to collect money from the men to buy such necessities as light bulbs, mops and brooms. But I had arrived at the Liaison Office in the early 1980s after President Reagan had already made it obvious he intended to spend the Soviet Union into oblivion. Nevertheless, the effect of increased defense spending bent on winning the Cold War had not yet trickled down to the Liaison office, and the operation still suffered under the effects of the Carter administration's budget. Frankly, this wasn't just low priority, this was no priority.

While Tully and Whorton had done some interviewing of refugees in the various camps, their efforts had been primarily reactive rather than proactive, and no systematic program for collecting information had ever been established. Tully was a jovial worker but he was not trained for interrogations or intelligence gathering. Whorton was a decorated Marine veteran, but his interviewing skills had never been developed and his Vietnamese was barely understandable. Although Tully and Whorton had managed to collect some useful information they continued to make the same mistakes that I had seen throughout the war effort in Vietnam.

The basic problem was not being able to identify those few Sources with valuable information among a large number of candidates. Even in those cases where knowledgeable Sources were uncovered, for the most part the interviewers failed to unearth the amount of detail necessary to support investigators in the field. It was as if they were collecting data without ever considering that at some point in the future, someone would have to take that information and proceed to a remote location in Indochina and investigate on the ground the validity of the report. While it was well-known that Communist cadre used cover names to protect their identities and subterfuge to conceal organizations, there had hardly been any effort expended to obtain detailed descriptions of cadre or the disposition and composition of Communist units involved in the processing of American prisoners or remains.

To me, this was critical, because I knew that the DIA files contained hundreds of reports concerning missing or captured Americans that were never correlated to any specific individual. In December 1978, the League had forced the DIA to reproduce and release this enormous amount of information into a fifteen-volume set titled "Uncorrelated Information relating to Missing Americans in Southeast Asia." Granted, in many cases the Sources did not know enough details to permit correlation to a missing American, and a lot of it was pure bullshit generated during the war by scam artists, but others were quite detailed. While I lobbied constantly for a total reevaluation of these reports, the potential workload created by such an endeavor caused considerable consternation for both the JCRC and the DIA analysts. For them it was a non-starter.

I sensed that I had a great deal of work to do in order to increase the flow of useable information from the field back to both the JCRC Records and Analysis Division at headquarters, and to the DIA's Research and Analysis Branch. Plus, I had to accomplish this mission with little support from other U.S. agencies, since all American military forces, including supporting intelligence organizations, had been asked to leave Thailand. Therefore, DIA was left with no organic collection capability in the region, and the gathering of POW/MIA information quickly fell by the wayside. Additionally, by the end of 1976, the CIA had passed the responsibility for collecting POW/MIA data to the DOD, since the CIA had bigger fish to fry in Southeast Asia.

A few months after my arrival at the Bangkok Embassy a team of Foreign Area Officers arrived in Thailand for a temporary assignment with the DAO. Due to the lack of space the JCRC Liaison Office was "encouraged" to move downstairs to the second floor in an office formerly occupied by personnel of the Refugee Office. Although the new office did not have the prestige of being located in the DAO on the prestigious "Top Secret" uppermost floor, the location did consist of two separate rooms with slightly more floor space than the previous office.

After I began working the camps, and as the volume of information gathered from refugees began to increase, Mather found himself struggling to keep up with editing and typing the resultant reports. Like James Brown in the music world, Mather was "the hardest working man" in the POW/MIA business. With no photocopy machine in the JCRC, Mather had to climb the stairs repeatedly each day in order to copy the manually typed reports, which he then sent out by registered mail. When Tully and I came to work in the morning, Mather was already there. When we went home at night he was still there, either bent over the typewriter or talking on the telephone to the JCRC headquarters, or with journalists of both the U.S. and international media. Mather believed in keeping the media informed, and he held the opinion that "an ignorant media will write ignorant stories." Perhaps the only Air Force officer during the Vietnam War to graduate from the Army's Special Warfare Center Psychological Operations course, Mather was a natural in dealing with the press.

In addition to having a strong work ethic and excellent rapport with the press, Mather was a good supervisor who believed in taking care of his people and their families. Although at times he was somewhat parsimonious with U.S. Government funds, Mather always made sure his men were taken care of first before he even thought about taking care of himself. I believe his frugality had more to do with the manner in which Mather was raised on a family farm back in Iowa than any budgetary accountability. Unfortunately, people from private POW/MIA organizations, activists and some MIA family members drifting in and out of Bangkok over the years took plenty of cheap shots at Mather. Somehow they believed he was the main obstacle to bringing home their missing comrades or loved ones. Some even went out of their way to criticize him publicly in a bald attempt to have him fired. Mather occasionally received threatening comments from family members and mail addressed to him as "Scumbag." But to me, who saw his extraordinary hard work and daily effort, if there was ever an American official working on the POW/MIA issue who deserved the gratitude of the American people, especially the families of the MIAs, it was Paul Mather.[1]

Based on a briefing from Mather, I learned that the basic plan called for me to maintain what Mather called "circuit rider routes" throughout Southeast Asia. Initially I would be working in refugee camps on Thailand's eastern border with Laos and Cambodia. This route would be called the "border route." I would then begin another route, called the "southern route," to camps in Malaysia, Indonesia and Singapore. As the exodus of refugees from Vietnam gained momentum my route would later expand to include the "Hong Kong route," which was comprised of at least six camps located throughout Hong Kong, the New Territories and several nearby islands. The Hong Kong route also included Macao, which at that time was a colony of Portugal. Once I had a complete picture of the refugee camp system I initiated a route that would swing by every camp, including ones for ethnic minority hill tribesmen, jails for illegal emigrants and smugglers, as well as base camps of the Lao and Cambodian resistance forces, including the Khmer Rouge.

My first trip was to the camps along the Thai/Cambodian border. This new itinerary made the remote locations of the Philippines seem like the proverbial milk run. Royal Thai Army or paramilitary units assigned to various task forces organized specifically for the refugee problem guarded the routes into the camps. Once inside the camps, however, it was a virtual no man's land, with only untrained members of each camp's Refugee Committee to maintain law and order. I had endured combat in some arduous areas, but I was unprepared for the awful climate and the precarious locations of the camps. Aside from the dangers of military action, during the hot summer months the temperature was unbearable. In addition to the intolerable heat, camp conditions were made even more appalling during the summer when the entire Thai/Cambodia border was normally subjected to drought. At times water became so scarce that the refugees had violent confrontations over small amounts of the precious liquid. Food was so limited that the daily distribution of supplies often ended in riots. After the meals were cooked the refugees often fought over leftover portions of burned rice scraped from the bottoms of cooking pots.

Even more ghastly was the horrible stench wafting from open pits filled with raw excrement from diarrhea-plagued people. Beside dysentery, the constant infestation of snakes, mosquitoes, flies and parasites increased the likelihood of malaria, encephalitis, dengue fever, dysentery and a host of other incapacitating diseases. I had almost died from the malaria I contracted during my first tour in Vietnam's Central Highlands. To prevent a relapse, I now had to religiously take a dose of 100 milligrams of vibramycin (generic doxicycline) issued by the American Embassy Medical Section. When stomach problems occurred I increased the dosage to 200 milligrams of the powerful antibiotic. I continued to take the medication for twelve years and this left my intestines in terrible condition. Sometimes the only way I could bear the situation was to constantly remind myself that while I was able to return to Bangkok at the end of my trips, the hapless refugees were stranded in the desolate camps for prolonged periods, in some cases as long as ten years.

Although already fluent in Vietnamese, Thai, and Lao, interviewing the Cambodians posed a serious new problem for me, especially those people arriving from the remote jungle camps of the Khmer Rouge. Whereas people from eastern Cambodia were able to understand considerable Vietnamese, and Cambodians from the western part of the country were able to converse in Thai, the Khmer Rouge were for the most part from the inaccessible jungle highlands of northern Cambodia. Therefore, they were able to understand only the traditional Mon-Khmer rural dialect known by few Westerners.

To overcome this deficiency, I applied for and received additional funding from the JCRC headquarters to study Cambodian. Although the size of the small office made time a scarce commodity, I managed to get in several hours of language study each week. I hired a member of the Foreign Broadcast Information Service staff who worked in their headquarters in the Shell Building across the street from the American Embassy. He was employed as a contractor to translate radio broadcasts emanating from Cambodia on a daily basis. Luckily for me, the ethnic Cambodian translator was not only a bright young man but current on the latest Cambodian Communist terminology as well.

In a few short weeks of training, although I had not reached any degree of fluency in Cambodian, I felt confident that I could conduct and control preliminary screening interviews in the camps. After determining which refugees possessed information of interest, the next step would be to coordinate with the local JVA or Refugee Committee for an interpreter to support more thorough questioning, which would include sketches, drawings and other documentation.

Similar to the operation in the Philippines, I spent a considerable amount of time briefing the JVAs, as well as the Thai military forces involved in detaining and caring for the stateless refugees. I also worked closely with the various committees in every camp on the Thai/Cambodian border, including the Khmer Rouge who were located just inside the poorly defined boundary of Cambodia in the gem mining area near the village of Bo Rai. This area was fiercely contested for political and military considerations, but also for the mining and smuggling of some of the world's most valuable rubies and sapphires.

Rather than suffering on leaky boats drifting in the South China Sea or the Gulf of Thailand, land refugees depended almost entirely on their feet for salvation from the harsh Communist rule in both Vietnam and Cambodia. Unlike their brethren escaping by sea, pirates, sharks, typhoons, and drowning were not areas of prime concern for the land refugees. What sparked their nightmares were mines and the work gangs of the dreaded Khmer Rouge. The undetectable wooden and plastic Chinese-made land mines took a heavy toll. Every camp I worked in held an unbelievably high number of limbless people, many of them women and children. Considering the lack of medical treatment available to the unfortunate refugees, I harbored no doubts that for every limbless person I saw there were several more whose bodies lay rotting in the jungle. Many new arrivals had departed from their native villages months earlier but had been detained by the Khmer Rouge while attempting to cross Cambodia. As a result of having been used as forced labor, this particular group was comprised of emaciated individuals in extremely poor health. It appeared the only reason for their continuing survival was because they could no longer function in any productive capacity and it was simply not worth the effort to kill them.

In addition to the normal liaison with the JVAs working at interview sites near the camps, I established a good working relationship with the local CIA field station located at the border. The CIA station was primarily engaged in intelligence gathering and monitoring of the political and military situation in Cambodia. It also clandestinely supported the noncommunist Cambodian resistance forces against the Vietnamese-backed Cambodian Communist forces led by Hanoi-educated Pen Sovann. I also developed close ties with the Thai Border Police and Special Operations contingents operating in the area of the refugee camps. The CIA and the Thai Intelligence/Law Enforcement units proved to be a valuable source of leads. Likewise, when I encountered refugees with information of interest to the intelligence units, after conducting a preliminary interview, I passed the information on to the appropriate agency along with the identity and current location of the Sources.

The CIA Field Stations scattered throughout the remote areas of Thailand were like desert oases. Without exception they had electricity, running water pumped from drilled wells, and kitchen facilities staffed by indigenous cooks. The team houses also had air-conditioned sleeping quarters and secure, state-of-the-art communications. The basic layout of the stations reminded me of the camps built for Special Forces "A" Teams in Vietnam during the war. Some had animal cages teeming with exotic wildlife captured by Thai military and Border Police patrols. In the beginning of my new tour I rarely visited the CIA stations, but after I learned how austere the refugee camps were and their total lack of communications, I quickly changed my schedule.

Despite the incredible conditions, during the first few months of my arrival in Thailand, I worked hard and the Cambodian interview project quickly gained momentum. I began to produce a large number of reports from both Cambodian and Vietnamese land refugees arriving in the border camps scattered from Trat province on the South China Sea to the city of Surin, Thailand's "elephant capital," located on the southern rim of Northeast Thailand's Korat Plateau. Since most of the Vietnamese refugees walking across Cambodia were southerners, the majority of the MIA reports pertained to loss incidents in the Mekong Delta and the region of Vietnam located along the border of Cambodia to the West and Southwest of Saigon. However, because JCRC records contained only approximately eighty MIA cases in Cambodia, the number of reports paled in comparison to those associated with Vietnam. With the exception of the strategic incursion into Cambodia by U.S. forces in the spring of 1970 to hit COSVN and clean out the border sanctuaries, Americans were generally prohibited from crossing from Vietnam into neighboring Cambodia. As a result, the MIA list in Cambodia was comprised primarily of passengers and crews of aircraft shot down in support of the attack, or American and foreign journalists who were either killed or captured while trying to cover the operation. The Cambodia list also included a small number of Special Operations personnel who were lost during intelligence gathering missions, many of which were conducted in preparation for the 1970 incursion.

Much like in Laos, it was obvious that the Vietnamese held the bulk of the answers to the ultimate fates of Americans and others that were lost in Cambodia, since Vietnamese forces controlled the sanctuaries in eastern Cambodia where most of the Americans were lost. It was impossible, however, to tell precisely what the Khmer Rouge knew, since it was assumed that the genocidal regime had left little in the way of a paper trail. Eventually to our surprise, this turned out to be not true.

One unanticipated part of my new job was travel guide. Early in my tour I began accompanying a large number of visiting U.S. officials on trips to the area. Due to the ongoing fighting between the Vietnamese/Cambodian forces, the Communist Khmer Rouge forces headed by Pol Pot, and the two non-Communist forces of former Cambodian Prime Minister Son Sann and Prince Sihanouk, border security was a hot topic for official visitors to Thailand. While the non-Communist Cambodian military only sporadically engaged the Hanoi-advised army of Pen Sovann with small-scale guerrilla attacks from sanctuaries along the border, the Khmer Rouge troops were busy inflicting serious casualties on the combined Vietnamese/Cambodian alliance.

To American strategists, it almost seemed too good to be true: Communist Vietnamese and Communist Cambodians killing each other with weapons, equipment and munitions paid for by Moscow and Beijing. Considering the lack of any real incentive for the United States to initiate a process capable of bringing the fighting to an end, I surmised that it would be at least several years into the future before recovery operations inside Cambodia could begin. Yet, many members of the House of Representatives who visited the region on other matters took the opportunity to gain better insight into the POW/MIA issue. For example, Congressmen Ben Gilman (R, NY) and Charles Rangel (D, NY) showed genuine interest in POW/MIA matters. Although they had come to Thailand primarily to oversee efforts toward opium eradication and other programs to stop the flow of drugs from the Golden Triangle area, they were eager to hear the latest POW/MIA information. I made frequent trips throughout Thailand accompanying numerous Congressional delegations in the Defense Attaché Office's C-12 aircraft. During each excursion I took every opportunity to lobby for improvements in the accounting process.

Satisfied that the collection program in the Cambodian border camps was on track, I focused my attention next on the camps detaining Lao refugees located along the border between Thailand and the Lao People's Democratic Republic. When first Cambodia and subsequently Vietnam fell to the Communists in April 1975, a small number of Lao, mostly H'mong who had worked closely with the U.S., began entering northeastern Thailand. The CIA evacuated most of these personnel. As long as both the Royal Lao and the Communist Pathet Lao were content to share power, albeit as part of a confusing ad-hoc arrangement, there was little impetus for most of the citizenry to flee.

However, as Pathet Lao officials became more emboldened and finally usurped total power in the capital city of Vientiane in December 1975, people immediately began to vote with their feet. Most of those desiring to escape Communist rule were in a good position to do so, as the only thing separating them from freedom was the Mekong River. This huge river emanating from deep in central China served as a natural boundary between Thailand and Laos. During the dry season, the escaping Lao encountered little difficulty in crossing the river by small boat, by clinging to flotation devices such as empty fuel or water containers, or by simply swimming to the opposite bank. During periods of prolonged drought in some parts of northwestern Laos refugees were able to cross by simply walking around isolated pools of water in the almost dry riverbed.

The Thai Government was far more concerned with the security aspect of Vietnamese and Cambodians refugee operations than they were with the Lao. Unlike the Vietnamese and Cambodians, the Thai treated the Lao with some degree of compassion, and the Lao camps were loosely controlled. Not only had they been neighbors for centuries, they both originated from the Yunnan region of southern China. Given the similarity of language and customs, there is little doubt in my mind that if the Communist Pathet Lao leadership had not had such close ties to both Vietnam and China, the Thais most likely would have considered the Lao as distant relatives in dire circumstances arriving on a temporary visit.

There were two camps for minority hill tribes such as the H'mong. One was located at Chiang Kham in northern Chiang Rai province, and the other at Ban Vinai in Nan province. Many of the H'mong exiles were followers of two former officers of the Special Guerrilla Units formed to fight the Pathet Lao and their North Vietnamese advisers in northeastern and central Laos. The two well-known officers, Generals Vang Pao and Pak Kao Her, drifted in and out of the camps on a regular basis. While Vang Pao was based in the United States, Pak Kao Her maintained a residence in Thailand and frequently crossed the border into Laos.

Camps holding the ethnic Lao were scattered along the border. A significant number of illegal Lao emigrants resided at Mukdahan, just south of Nakhon Phanom. Many had formed themselves into a "Lao resistance force," and as such, they were not required by the Thai Government to reside within the confines of any particular camp. The Lao resistance forces were a hodge-podge group comprised of remnants of the Royal Lao Army supported by the Thai Special Operations Directorate.

While the H'mong kept up a degree of military pressure on the Pathet Lao, the impact of the fractured ethnic Lao resistance was insignificant. Backed by Vietnamese forces, the Pathet Lao were able to easily deal with them. Yet from their standpoint, the appearance of former CIA trained H'mong guerrillas and ethnic Lao resistance forces added to the Communists security concerns, which delayed gaining permission to begin recovery operations in Laos. Further, corrupt members of the ethnic Lao resistance began producing numerous bogus reports of live Americans along with fake remains, which consumed large amounts of analytical time in Washington. Eventually, U.S. government officials put a halt to this.

Since the JCRC Liaison Office did not have any vehicles, I had to rely on my own 1969 Toyota Corona 1900 compact for transportation on this route. The small, aging vehicle soon became a familiar sight to Thai Border Police assigned to the most remote areas of the country. It was probably an unusual spectacle for them when they observed a small civilian passenger car passing by in a convoy of military tanks and trucks. Some of the roads were in terrible repair and on one trip to the H'mong camp at Ban Vinai I had to buy a gallon of castor bean oil from a local farmer after my transmission cooling line ruptured while driving over the rough terrain. After forcing a piece of wood into the gaping hole and binding it with my belt, I completed my mission to the camp. I then limped slowly to the nearest town, adding more castor bean oil along the way, where I was finally able to have the line brazed by a welder. The following day I was back on the road to interview refugees in Nakhon Phanom.

In the summer of 1982, the JVAs working for the Refugee Office in Thailand added a section pertaining to missing Americans on their standard report for processing refugees entering the country. The revised questionnaire asked all refugees whether or not they possessed any knowledge of Americans currently or previously being held prisoner, or if they had any information on crash sites or grave sites associated with Americans. The response was encouraging and the number of POW/MIA leads began to climb. In turn, I worked feverishly to debrief every possible Source we collectively turned up. The increased reporting resulted in a steady grind of traveling the back roads of the country, with frequent stops at camps, border crossing points and village jails. Although the hours were long and the environment harsh, I was determined to collect every piece of information that might one day facilitate case investigations.

During my trips along the border it was not uncommon for me to be approached by refugees, members of the ethnic Lao Resistance forces, or smugglers who were interested in obtaining a reward from the U.S. government. Although U.S. policy prohibited payment of rewards for remains or information, I nevertheless tried, at times successfully, to convince the Laotian sources to hand over anything associated with missing Americans without payment. While some of the Sources professed to have information on personnel being held prisoner by Communist forces, most sought to sell human remains and items of personal effects scavenged from crash sites. Although the interviews designed to gain information on remains were considered important, greater emphasis was placed on obtaining intelligence concerning live Americans. I spent a considerable amount of time conducting detailed debriefings of anyone claiming to possess this type of data, regardless of whether or not they demanded a reward. Having been in the information gathering business for many years, I was keenly aware that any report, surfacing at any time, could be genuine. Therefore, I never flatly refused anyone who requested a reward, but rather treated each Source in a straightforward, businesslike manner, politely explaining the situation and offering to pass on any requests they made to U.S. authorities.

Complicating matters, a private foundry in northeastern Thailand involved in manufacturing metal cooking equipment, such as pots and pans, put out the word that it would pay good money to acquire metal from American aircraft downed in Laos. This commercial advertisement led to the scavenging of many of the more accessible crash sites in Laos. To prevent fraud and destruction of these sites, the U.S. government instituted a strict rule of "no rewards for information or remains" of missing Americans. I never broke this rule, but on one occasion I was working in the American Embassy when a guard at the main gate called to inform me that I had a visitor waiting in the unsecured area downstairs. I met the man and learned that he had just returned from visiting a crash site inside Laos. After I escorted him to an interview room inside the Embassy, the ethnic Lao produced a human femur and some personal effects from a bag he was carrying. He reported that he had recently recovered them from the wreckage of a U.S. aircraft. I recorded the man's information, obtained an address for future possible contact, and then thanked him on behalf of the U.S. Government for his efforts. Somewhat sheepishly the man explained that he had come a considerable distance to bring me the remains, artifacts and information from the downed aircraft. He asked me if I could give him enough money for transportation home and to buy food along the way. The man planned to travel from Bangkok back to northeast Thailand by regular passenger bus, and I knew the trip would take at least a day. When asked as to how much money he would need, the man replied five hundred Thai baht (approximately $25 at that time).

In similar cases I had usually been asked for larger sums or some type of support for the Lao resistance forces for use in fighting the Communists. In many cases the information and items received later proved to be bogus. But in this case I was able to quickly determine that the personal effects were genuine, and based on appearance I was fairly sure that the remains were American. Perhaps even more important I could tell by the way that the man recounted his story that he was sincere. I knew it was against policy to give money in exchange for information or remains, but against my better judgment I gave the man the requested money. In my mind I wondered how much time I had before I would be called in on the carpet by some Inspector General or before a Congressional Committee conducting a hearing. I felt somewhat relieved when the results of CILHI's forensic analysis confirmed that the remains were American. The aircraft turned out to be a U.S. Navy OP2E with a crew of nine men on a reconnaissance mission when it was shot down by enemy fire. The information provided by the Lao man resulted in an excavation at the crash site where remains and personal effects were collected and returned to the families of the crew.

Further complicating the reward situation, during the war, U.S. intelligence agencies, especially the CIA in Laos, had traditionally paid money to indigenous agents providing information. Another aggravating factor was the so-called "blood chits" carried by aircrews and some Special Operations personnel involved in high-risk operations deep in enemy territory. Escape flags, blood chits, and identification flags were all terms used somewhat interchangeably by veterans and collectors alike. Technically to truly be a "chit" there must be a pledge of reward for the safe conduct and return of the bearer. Generally these items were designed to provide rapid identification for a downed pilot and facilitate assistance from any local allies. Most featured a flag with a message printed in one or more native languages.

In addition to the blood chits, pilots in many instances were issued gold coins to be used as bargaining chips in the event their aircraft went down in enemy territory. Some pilots carried American currency as an extra insurance measure to prevent being handed over to the enemy. Other bargaining items included watches, rings and other jewelry. It was not unusual for local villagers to reach crash sites prior to the arrival of Communist military forces. The looters would usually find some item from the wreckage to convert to household use, or finding the pilot's remains, they would find the gold coins or other valuable articles. As a result, it quickly became common knowledge that American pilots, dead or alive, were a potential source of immediate wealth. This mind-set created serious problems for collectors of POW/MIA information because the scavenging villagers badly disturbed the crash sites, seeking any piece of bone or other identifiable material they could carry.

This oft-stated policy of non-payment by interviewers created a paradox for the American collectors. When confronted with this guiding principle, the impoverished refugees often could not accept my contention that such a policy was in effect because based on their own past experiences, they knew better. Worse, the personal knowledge of the refugees concerning blood chits extolling rewards and gold in the possession of the pilots led to an unfounded perception among the unsophisticated refugees. These simple people from rural farming communities throughout Indochina were used to corrupt bureaucrats, and so inevitably concluded that the American collectors were also corrupt, when in fact we were only following orders.

Another factor complicating the collection of valid information were the reward offers spread by POW/MIA activist groups. At one point eight congressmen, a former congressman and a former POW assembled for a press conference while displaying one million dollars in cash stacked on a table offered as a reward to anyone who could bring out a live American POW. After the photo was published in the media some members of the group came to Thailand to release gas-filled balloons containing the reward offer. After encountering difficulty obtaining the gas and fluctuating wind patterns, the activists finally resorted to floating the balloons down the Mekong River in the hope that they would drift across to the Lao shoreline and be picked up by local residents. The amount offered as a reward by the activists gradually grew to 2.4 million dollars. After the offers were publicized our telephone in the American Embassy began ringing constantly, mostly from people wanting information about the reward.

Rather than offer rewards some other activists actually took matters into their own hands and tried to conduct potentially dangerous rescue missions into Laos. The most well known member of this group was Lieutenant Colonel James "Bo" Gritz, a retired member of the U.S. Army Special Forces. I vaguely recalled having met Gritz at Fort Bragg, NC, in late 1969 while marshalling for a desert warfare training exercise conducted near the Army's nerve gas storage facility in Utah.

I knew Gritz had acquired official Communist documentation of the interrogation of an American POW (which he altered), and the Air Force class ring of another POW, Lance Sijan, who had died in a North Vietnamese prison. Gritz initially refused to turn over the ring to the man's family, but after U.S. government officials intervened on behalf of the family, he relented. A veteran of the Vietnam War, Gritz claimed to have intelligence concerning a number of American prisoners being held in the Xepone area in central Laos. After training the American team members in the U.S., Gritz traveled to northeast Thailand where he recruited additional members from the Lao resistance. The American Embassy in Bangkok, as well as the CIA Station in Udorn, closely monitored Gritz's movements while he was in the country, but no one could say with certainty whether the former Green Beret had actually deployed American citizen volunteers, including Gritz himself, across the river into Lao territory. Ironically, some of the Lao guerrillas recruited and trained by Gritz were former members of the CIA-sponsored team that had already crossed the border as part of an official U.S. sponsored covert operation in March 1981 to conduct the now famous reconnaissance of a camp suspected of holding American prisoners in the Gnomarrath area.

Much speculation has swirled around this attempt to determine if American POWs were in the camp. In early 1981, aerial photography and HUMINT had indicated the possible presence of American POWs in this Lao prison. A Thai Special Operations team was sent in to observe and take pictures. Upon their return they reported they did not see any Caucasians. Since the CIA operatives had surreptitiously placed electronic beepers in the equipment provided to the team members during the mission, there was no doubt that they had in fact reached the target. On May 13, 1981 a Washington Post article reported on an inconclusive U.S. reconnaissance operation "aimed at confirming the presence of live Americans in Laos." After the operation was leaked, any further missions were halted. Although the combined intelligence was some of the most promising developed on possible American POWs, later interviews with prisoners held in the jail indicated no Americans were kept there.

In February 1983, media publicity of another alleged Gritz mission into Laos caused two major problems. First, the Lao were already deeply suspicious that the U.S. government was covertly supporting the Resistance, and reports of his foray caused an eleven month suspension of negotiations to excavate the first postwar crash site. Second, while I had been able to move freely throughout the northeastern part of Thailand in the past, for some time after his incursion I was routinely stopped and asked to produce identification. Aside from that, the Lao refugees read Gritz's temporary presence in the northeast as a sign U.S. military forces had returned to the area. As a result of this erroneous perception, I began to receive numerous requests for arms, ammunition and funding to support Resistance operations.

Other private American POW hunters included two retired Air Force officers, Colonel Jack Bailey and Lieutenant Colonel Al Shinkle. Bailey and Shinkle both claimed to have "agent nets" actively collecting information for their operations. Bailey and some of his colleagues purchased a large cargo ship (which had once been used to rescue fleeing refugees out at sea), which they docked at the southern Thai port of Songkhla on the Gulf of Thailand. Although Bailey sent out appeals for donations, especially from Vietnamese refugees in the U.S. who had relatives escaping by boat, the rusting ship never raised anchor. Nevertheless, this didn't prevent him from sending out his pitiful handwritten pleas for money describing how difficult it was for him to write while being tossed about by the waves. Bailey was finally unmasked when he became involved in a scheme involving phony photographs said to depict an actual live MIA. In a fit of anger upon being exposed Bailey punched a journalist in the face and then disappeared into oblivion. Shinkle continued to operate on a shoestring budget and seemed to be a cut above Bailey on the privateer totem pole. Shinkle was fairly well organized with computer equipment, and he relied on at least some training he had received as an Intelligence Officer during the war years in managing his collection efforts.

As the tempo of my circuit routes increased, my collection duties were gradually expanded to include camps holding refugees in other countries that the LNO had responsibility for. On the "southern route" I flew from Bangkok to the capital city of Malaysia, Kuala Lumpur, where I boarded a small propeller aircraft bound for Kuala Trenganu on Malaysia's eastern coast. Upon arrival at the sleepy fishing town I transferred to a United Nations chartered cargo boat for a wave-pounding ride to the tiny island of Pulau Bidong located about twelve miles off shore. Although the trip lasted only a few hours, the smell generated by the crowded cabin jammed with vomiting passengers, mixed with the pungent smell of clove cigarettes the Muslim crewmembers smoked incessantly, made it seem as though the voyage lasted several days.

I prepared in advance for the arduous trip (which included considerable climbing from boat to boat at the pier), by packing everything I needed in a carry bag with a shoulder strap. When the boat arrived at Pulau Bidong, the Muslim security force performed a careful search of each passenger's luggage. In addition to the items normally restricted in other parts of the world, prohibited contraband included cameras, communications devices and any beverages containing alcohol. Knowing I would be on the island for three days, I circumvented the beverage problem by filling an empty 12-ounce Pepto Bismal bottle with Jack Daniels prior to departing Bangkok.

After coordination with the JVA and the Refugee Committee I began my usual routine of making loudspeaker announcements in Vietnamese. Once the interviews were under way it didn't take long for word to spread through the camp that an American official was present on the island. Although a significant number of refugees arriving at the interview site possessed information of POW/MIA interest, the vast majority of the people crowding into the area wanted help in getting off the island. In contrast to other island camps I had worked in, no one here seemed content. The Malaysian officials were tense due to the large number of foreigners arriving at a steady pace in their country. The Vietnamese hated the island due to its filthy, crowded conditions. American officials, who periodically came to the island, such as Immigration and Naturalization officers from the INS Office in the American Embassy in Singapore, complained bitterly about camp conditions. I soon came to understand firsthand that the complaints were entirely justified.

Malaysian government officials on the island appeared to be disconnected from the daily camp routine. A solid corps of Muslims, the swarthy officials viewed the hapless refugees as brethren of the resented but economically influential community of overseas Chinese already present for several generations on the Malay Peninsula. Unlike the Chinese, who were tolerated out of political and economic necessity, the Vietnamese were viewed as a temporary inconvenience requiring close monitoring lest they too eventually pose a long-term threat to national security. The only segment of the refugee population afforded any genuine sympathy from the Malaysians was the ethnic Cham Cambodians. In addition to being devout Muslims, the dark-skinned Chams from the marshy deltas of southern Vietnam and Cambodia shared an age-old language and religion which seemed to form a cultural bridge linking modern day Malays to their historic past. Considering the language and culture, in informal social conversations with Malaysian officials they seemed willing to privately acquiesce to a kinship with the Cambodian Chams, albeit reluctantly. But they were, nevertheless, quite dogmatic in refuting even the slightest chance of a past link to the Buddhist or Hindu Cambodians.

The first night on the island I decided to make my bed on the plywood picnic bench that served as my interview table during the day. The counter was the only dry and relatively level sleeping spot I could find, and I considered myself fortunate to have it. But sleep would prove to be a mirage. As the sun disappeared into the South China Sea, huge blue sewer rats suddenly appeared everywhere. I had seen plenty of field and barn rats when I was a kid on the farm, and I had seen fairly large paddy rats in Vietnam during the war, but I had never seen or smelled anything like the blue sewer rats on Pulau Bidong Island. It proved impossible to get rid of them, and each time I managed to doze off the fidgety movement of the big rats would awaken me. When the sun began to appear on the horizon I was exhausted but nevertheless happy to see the rats shrink back from the rays of light gradually penetrating the darkness beneath the crowded coconut palms.

During my second day on the island I recruited members of the Refugee Committee to act as my representatives with the mission of recording the names and camp addresses of anyone who claimed to have POW/MIA information. In addition to billboards prominently displayed in the camp, the agents were instructed to provide hand-held flyers to any new arrivals that managed to reach the small, desolate island. They were also instructed to pass the lists of names of potential new Sources to American JVAs working in the camp in order for the information to be forwarded to me by diplomatic pouch via the American Embassy in Singapore. Some of the informants turned out to be very efficient, while others did not. It took me months and several trips to Malaysia to recruit and train a dependable collection net.

After the first night's disaster, I thought I located a new and hopefully more peaceful locale. Once again, I was sadly mistaken. I spent the second night in a shed made from plywood and tin measuring about twenty feet long by twenty feet wide. The shed was subdivided into small rooms with hand-cranked glass jalousie windows. Unfortunately, the windows did not have any screens and due to the metal roof the temperature inside the hut soared to 110 degrees along with very high humidity. However, every time I cranked open a window to allow fresh air inside, some of the more enterprising rats would slither forward into the hut. I would then kill the rats and place the carcass in a far corner as a warning to their rodent brethren, but they seemed oblivious to the growing mound of corpses. And, as the pile grew, the stench from the carcasses became incredible, making tear gas seem like a pleasant potpourri. However, I soon learned the temporary storage of the dead rats inside was unavoidable. If I opened the door to throw the bodies outside, more rats would take advantage of the breach and rush inside. To add to my dream vacation, the wooden bunks in the hut were so filthy and infested with both lice and fleas that I began a tormented dance of slapping and itching all night. Needless to say, I spent another sleepless night. When the third night finally arrived I was so exhausted I fell into the wooden bunk and left the windows closed all night, oblivious to the sweltering heat and pesky critters.

From Pulau Bidong Island I traveled by boat back to Kuala Trenganu where I boarded a small twin-prop plane to Kuala Lumpur. Upon arrival at the airport I took a taxi to the local Refugee Office of the American Embassy. I was happy to learn that my point-of-contact in Kuala Lumpur was Douglas K. Ramsey, a former Vietnam War POW. Ramsey was a State Department Foreign Service Officer who was captured by Communist forces while driving a truck a few kilometers northwest of Saigon on January 17, 1966. After being held in a number of temporary jungle camps inside South Vietnam, Ramsey was moved to the main American POW camp located near the COSVN's wartime headquarters in Kratie province in Cambodia. Fortunate to have survived the horrible camp conditions, Ramsey was released during Operation Homecoming in February 1973. With his personal background in both the POW/MIA issue and Vietnamese affairs in general, along with great fluency in the language, Ramsey proved to be a staunch ally in the quest for information on the fate of Americans held prisoner or missing at the close of the war.

During late December 1979, one of the senior cadre of Ramsey's former POW camp in Vietnam suddenly appeared as a refugee in Malaysia. The defecting Communist official, Major Nguyen Van Tuoi, who had worked for many years in COSVN's Enemy Proselytizing Department, (which controlled American POWs in the South), and who later transferred to Public Security, was debriefed several times. At first he claimed that he had learned from a high-ranking friend in early 1979 that the Vietnamese were still holding American POWs and that the Communists had gathered between three hundred and four hundred sets of American remains, mainly from the North, but the recovery operations in the South were a shambles. When asked how, after repeated denials, Vietnam could release these prisoners and not lose face, Tuoi stated that Westerners never understood the Communist way of thinking. Tuoi claimed that these prisoners had been held back for future insurance in case the U.S. decided to attack Vietnam, and because Vietnam always expects to have to bargain and negotiate in dealing with outsiders. As for saving face, the Communists always leave themselves an opening. To them, "whether or not the excuse is believed is of little significance because the offering of the excuse is more important than its plausibility."[2] Tuoi did remember Ramsey clearly, as well as several other American POWs held in the camp where he had been assigned. In particular, Tuoi had worked closely with a well-known American deserter, McKinley Nolan.

But when it came to pinpointing the locations of burial sites of those who died in captivity, Tuoi blamed the American B-52 bombing attacks as the foremost obstacles to his providing assistance in locating American graves. In further interviews Tuoi also claimed that the interpreter during the first interview had misunderstood him about the live POWs, but that his high-ranking friend, who was now the head of the entire Enemy Proselytizing Department, had provided him the remains figure.

Major Tuoi also revealed that during the war years his sister had married a U.S. Army officer assigned to MACV Headquarters in Saigon. This information was startling to me, mainly for the counterintelligence aspect of the situation. Tuoi's plan was to be resettled from the Malaysian refugee camp to Belgium where his American brother-in-law was now assigned to the Supreme Headquarters of the Allied Powers Europe. While I never interviewed Tuoi, I never fully understood why Tuoi defected, and it seemed strange to me that a cadre of his level would leave so suddenly. I recalled how during the war the Communists would send in fake ralliers to infiltrate the Chieu Hoi centers. I can imagine they used the same method in order to monitor the refugee population.

It was also determined that while a member of the Public Security Bureau, Tuoi had worked with Ms. Tran Le Linh, a female cadre who had served as an interpreter for interrogations conducted by the highly secretive COSVN Public Security Section. Linh, who had held the rank of Senior Captain in the Public Security Bureau, was involved with a number of American and other foreign prisoners who were executed after interrogation. When the war ended Linh worked in the Ho Chi Minh City (formerly Saigon) Public Security Office for several years before being accepted by Australia for permanent resettlement in that country. Years later she was interviewed, claimed she knew little about American POWs, and then promptly cut the interview short.

I always had deep suspicions about the COSVN Public Security POW camp, which was different than the main military POW camp for Americans that was run by the Enemy Proselytizing section. Prisoners like civilians Henry Wallis and Gustav Hertz disappeared into that camp and never came out. During the war, we actually recovered a document on another captive, Specialist Four Edward Reilly, who while on an operation with the 1st Division had stumbled into the Security camp and was captured.[3] Several months later, some mysterious people attempted to contact his wife in the United States trying to get her to engage in anti-war activity. My intuition told me that the Communists were using that camp for something besides a simple detention facility. Years later I tried to prove my theory but ultimately the camp's true function remains unknown.

From Kuala Lumpur I again boarded a commercial aircraft to Singapore where I checked in at the local Refugee Office of the American Embassy for an update on camp conditions and the in-country travel situation in Indonesia. After obtaining a visa to enter Indonesia and the necessary camp visitation passes, I proceeded to the only site for refugees in Singapore, a small transit camp called "Hawkins Road." The Hawkins Road camp was located in the northern part of the island, not far from the causeway linking Singapore to Johore on the Malay Peninsula. The camp was created to detain refugees who were rescued at sea by ships headed from international ports to Singapore. Some of these refugees were accepted for resettlement by the countries where the ships were based, while others entered regular refugee processing channels to second asylum camps in Indonesia or the Philippines.

The refugee population at Hawkins Road appeared to be in better physical condition than at any camp I'd previously visited. The refugees also seemed well educated and better organized than most, causing me to speculate that some of the rescues may not have been as spontaneous as I had been led to believe. The escape routes and timetables mentioned by the refugees during their detailed debriefings pointed toward some type of organization with both international connections and an effective communication network. As a result of the thorough planning by the refugees prior to and during the escape process, and the involvement of the international shipping community, with the lone noted exception of commercial air travel, the Hawkins Road/Singapore escape route was probably the fastest and safest method of getting out of postwar Vietnam. Whether the ocean going vessels were rescuing the refugees in return for money, or if they were genuine humanitarian efforts aimed at saving the lives of the escaping Vietnamese, was never determined. Considering human nature, however, I speculated that it was a combination of both, but I never did get to the bottom of the organization. A relatively large portion of the POW/MIA reports received at Hawkins Road came from former RVN military officers and civil servants who had recently been released from prison camps by the Communists.

After conducting my interviews in Singapore I hailed a cab to the city's crowded inter-island public ferry pier where I embarked on a commercial ferry bound for Tan Jung Pinang Island, Indonesia. After arriving I transferred to a large cabin cruiser operated by the United Nations High Commissioner for Refugees, which would take me on the final leg of the trip. The sea voyage terminated at a huge camp for boat refugees called "Galang" located on Pulau Galang Island, about thirty-five miles south of Singapore. The Galang camp was the largest of the four camps on the southern route and it contained approximately 16,000 refugees.

Once again the conditions on the ferry were quite crowded, and the cabin was filled by thick, blue smoke from countless clove cigarettes. As a part of the fare, the boat crew handed out Styrofoam containers of curry mixed with dried fish and rice. The smell of the cloves mixed with the sharp odor of curry gave the voyage a certain Persian or Arabian air. Although the meals were probably sanitary, they contained numerous strains of bacteria unfamiliar to most expatriates. The uninformed immediately plunged into the food with reckless abandon, unaware that many of them would not sleep that night due to constant diarrhea and stomach cramps.

On arrival at Galang, I received a briefing on the layout of the camp from the local JVA rep. After a quick tour of the facility the JVA rep offered me temporary living quarters in a austere but adequately furnished hut occupied by several JVA volunteers. I was pleased to learn that the hut came complete with cots, a Ping-Pong table and a kitchen. Upon entering the hut I noticed an Indonesian houseboy, doubling as a cook, was in the process of preparing an evening meal from vegetables grown in the camp by the refugees. After a hearty dinner I found an empty cot and was quickly lulled to sleep by the cascading tympani of a Caribbean-style rhythm played by large rats jumping around on upturned pots and pans in the kitchen.

The following morning, after making the usual loudspeaker announcements and conducting refugee interviews, I visited the leaders of the various refugee committees and associations scattered throughout the sprawling camp. The associations included Buddhists, Catholics, Protestants, veterans, and the so-called "Security Committee," comprised of former RVN police and intelligence officials, predominately from the Central Intelligence Office.

Throughout my visit to Galang, refugees within the camp complained bitterly of corruption on the part of the Indonesian officials responsible for camp administration. According to the refugees, they were being constantly coerced into paying bribes for food, or in some cases to be allowed to meet with visiting American and other foreign officials for resettlement interviews. I found the Indonesian military and police officials in charge of camp security unmotivated, uneducated, untrained, and unimpressive. These officials sauntered slowly about the confines of the camp like predatory reptiles on a rocky island outcropping with an abundant supply of smaller, weaker prey in their captive food chain.

Although the initial response to loudspeaker appeals for POW/MIA information was limited, the leadership of the various groups pledged to canvass each housing area of the camp in preparation for my next visit. The assistance provided by the committees and associations would prove to be invaluable, and the number of reports pertaining to both missing and dead American personnel received at Galang began to increase steadily. Such reports would eventually lead to a surprising number of correlations to actual wartime loss incidents occurring in areas that had been under wartime Communist control, such as the U-Minh forest of Vietnam's Mekong Delta. The reports described POW camps where Americans were hidden from the view of aerial observers in bamboo cages deep inside the thick mangrove forests constantly inundated with brackish water from the canals and tributaries flowing south from the Mekong River throughout the delta region.

During late February/early March 1982 I was ordered to make an unexpected trip to Beijing, China. The Chinese had refused to allow us to interview any refugees who had fled to their country, although they stated they would be willing to let us send questionnaires. The most important Vietnamese who ever fled to China was Politburo member Hoang Van Hoan, who defected in 1979 after he lost an internal battle with Vietnamese Party Secretary Le Duan. While the Chinese claimed they had passed our requests for information to him, Hoan replied through them that he knew nothing about American POW/MIAs, an interesting denial given his former status. The purpose of my expedition was to interview a group of Vietnamese men and women who had escaped in September 1981 by helicopter from Vietnam. One member of the group was described as an officer of Vietnam's Public Security Bureau who reportedly was seeking to defect to the West. Given his position, we hoped that the man might possess POW/MIA information.

After some initial coordination with the local CIA station and the DAO it was decided that I would conduct my interviews of the Vietnamese defectors in an office of the Defense Attaché located in the chancery building of the Embassy. Prior to beginning the interviews, personnel from the Navy Seabees who had received specialized "Defense Against Sound Equipment" training conducted a sweep of the office looking for "bugs." Once the site was declared "clear," I informed my CIA escort that I was ready to begin. Shortly before the arrival of the first interview subject, the CIA officer informed me that his office had just received a message from Headquarters authorizing the conduct of a "hostile" interrogation. Since I had not yet had an opportunity to evaluate the subjects, I politely informed him that I planned to first conduct preliminary interviews on selected members of the defector group prior to making any decision as to the methods I would use during the formal interrogations. The CIA officer seemed perturbed, but he accepted my recommendation.

Next he informed me that throughout the course of the interviews, I would be working with cadre from the Chinese Public Security Bureau. With no knowledge of the Chinese language, I became apprehensive about being able to effectively communicate with the Security Bureau cadre. When I mentioned my concerns, the CIA contact told me that many of the Public Security cadre were conversant in English. When the first armed cadre arrived at the American Embassy escorting the initial interview subject I was relieved when the man addressed me in fluent Vietnamese using the northern dialect. When I responded to the cadre in the same Vietnamese dialect, the man didn't seem the least bit surprised by the exchange. I suspected the officer was an Indochina specialist of the Chinese. Although I had expected rather token Chinese cooperation, over the course of the next several days I gained the impression that the Security cadre were not only professionally polite, they were genuinely trying to be helpful. They also seemed friendly with the local CIA personnel. As I attempted to understand the apparent recent thaw in relations between the Intelligence and Security services of the two sides, I recalled that the United States and China were already cooperating on joint electronic intelligence gathering efforts directed at the USSR on China's western frontier. Still, I reminded myself it was prudent to remember that I was dealing with trained Communist intelligence cadre. My instincts proved correct when I later discovered that during the time of my visit another U.S. Government official, Mr. Larry Woo Tai Chin, was also in Beijing, albeit unauthorized. Chin was later convicted of spying and imprisoned in the U.S., where he eventually hanged himself in a Virginia jail on February 21, 1986.

In interviewing the defectors I was disappointed to learn that the apparent leader of the group was a businessman from southern Vietnam. The man had been jailed for corruption and imprisoned in several detention facilities throughout North Vietnam. The man did provide some information on live Americans held in a facility of the Vietnamese Interior Ministry in the Thanh Tri area on the southern outskirts of Hanoi. The DIA would later correlate this report to Vietnamese commandos from the highly secret wartime 34A operations. This program, initially run by the CIA and then later SOG, parachuted American-trained, paid and equipped indigenous assets into North Vietnam on spying and sabotage missions. Hundreds of these commandos were held in the North after Operation Homecoming was concluded, and it was not unusual for the DIA to discount reports of live Americans by correlating them to South Vietnamese members of Operation 34A. In hindsight, the possibility exists that some live-sightings of American POWs might have been mistakenly correlated to the Operation 34A personnel.

The most important member of the group was the former Senior Captain in the Vietnamese Public Security Bureau. The corrupt businessman was his older brother. The amount of information pertaining to live Americans obtained from the defecting Public Security Officer was unfortunately limited, although once he had successfully tracked down two Americans who escaped from a Hanoi prison during the war. He did, however, contribute a considerable amount of useful information on the Vietnamese penal system. The remainder consisted of the helicopter crew and their wives. The corrupt businessman had fooled the group into believing that he could get them to the States.

With the distinct possibility of future PRC casualty resolution efforts, and not wanting to wear out my welcome, I decided to curtail my interviews of the defectors and leave the other areas of possible exploitation to the CIA station. But the most interesting part was how they managed to escape Vietnam. According to the pilot of the escape aircraft, he had been assigned as the pilot for Lieutenant General Phung Van Thu (cover name Phung The Tai), who at the time of the escape was serving as the Deputy Chief of Staff of the PAVN. During the Lieutenant General's military career, he had also served as the commander of the PAVN Air Defense Forces and as the Director of Civil Aviation. The pilot knew that Thu kept his American-made helicopter parked at the Bach Mai Airfield in Hanoi, and that the only means of securing the aircraft during the nighttime hours was by removal of the battery. The group was able to purchase a battery on the black market and smuggled it onto the airfield just before dawn on the day of their escape. The group had been planning the escape for several months, and as part of their preparations they learned the signal codes for aircraft on unannounced emergency missions flying into the area of the China/Vietnam border. At the time, the sign used by aircraft was a red banner hung from bamboo poles extended out the door on both sides of the helicopter. By using this indicator the group was able to fly from Bach Mai across North Vietnam at a low altitude without challenge until they crossed the border and touched down. Due to fuel constraints the group had decided to escape across northern Vietnam and land inside the border of China, rather than attempt to fly across Laos and land in Thailand. Even with the shortest possible flight route selected, the group still had to carry extra fuel on the aircraft in a 55-gallon drum.

Shortly after my trip to Peking, I began the third leg of my interview routes. The last group of camps I visited was the British colony of Hong Kong, with a one-day side-stop in the Portuguese colony of Macao. In contrast to the previous stops on the interview circuit, Hong Kong was not only clean and free from corruption, but orderly and efficient as well. One fact that became increasingly obvious to me in my travels throughout Asia was that from the standpoint of an inherited government management style, the former British colonies fared far better than those previously under French control. In the regions previously run by Her Majesty's minions, everything seemed on schedule and it would be considered a rare and in fact serious incident if one were to be approached and solicited for a bribe by a civil servant of any previous outpost of the British Empire. Sanitation crews worked late into the night and were out again at daybreak, which made Hong Kong one of the cleanest stops on my regional route. I attributed this entire phenomenon to the well-trained indigenous civil service force left behind by a gradually withdrawing English presence in both Hong Kong and Singapore.

Further, the police in both Hong Kong and Singapore were at the top of the scale. By contrast, the corrupt "white mice" (the South Vietnamese police were known as the "white mice" for the white helmets they wore along with their eternal search for bribes), in the environs of French Indochina left a bad taste in the mouths of most Americans who served there during the war. I considered this a natural development as the French had become involved in Indochina primarily due to economic considerations. Unfortunately for the French, with the noted exception of an approximate ten-year period in the early 1900s, France's operations in Indochina had resulted in financial red ink. There were exceptions, and there had been certain instances where some private enterprises had been able to realize profits from agricultural products harvested from vast plantations scattered throughout Vietnam. But by the time of the Geneva Agreements in 1954 ending the war between the French and the Viet Minh, the French government had no real incentive to shed further blood in defense of its rapidly deteriorating colonial system. The efficiency of the small but nevertheless powerful Portuguese style civil service administration in Macao appeared to fall somewhere between that of the British and the French.

During my trips I worked closely with the Defense Liaison Office of the American Consulate General in Hong Kong. My other main contacts in collecting information on missing Americans were the CIA's "Executive Assistant" Office within the consulate, and its counterpart organization within the Royal Hong Kong Government, the Police "Special Branch." With more emphasis on intelligence than on law enforcement, the Special Branch was little more than a cover for the covert deployment of agents throughout Hong Kong and the adjacent New Territories from Britain's MI-5 and MI-6 Security Services. Key personnel positions were occupied by seasoned expatriates who were veterans of Britain's intelligence services, with the rank and file positions in the murky organization held by the predominantly ethnic Cantonese citizens of Hong Kong.

This arrangement created a formidable organization. The local staff was well versed on the languages and cultures of the area, and they were equally dreadful of the day that Hong Kong would revert to Communist Chinese control under the absolute authority of Beijing. The local staff's capitalistic, free-wheeling spirit and obvious disdain for impending Communist control of Hong Kong heightened their vigilance against penetrations by the intelligence arms of the People's Republic of China, and probably also instilled in them a greater degree of loyalty toward a distant British crown. Unfortunately, while the ethnic Chinese civil servants in Hong Kong involved in the refugee camp system were helpful (as well as the local citizens), they were not the least bit enthusiastic about the large numbers of the traditionally hated Vietnamese pouring into their tiny protectorate. That long-established animosity was held in check, however, by the knowledge that their small colony would eventually be returned to the Communists. A pragmatic people, they realized that in the event of chaos or violence during the return of Hong Kong to China, there was a real chance that they might also be forced to flee by boat. Any prior ill treatment of the Vietnamese refugees would not go unnoticed by the international community.

Due to the complex geographical layout of the facilities used for detention sites of the Vietnamese refugees, Hong Kong was the most difficult travel route for me. Most camps in Hong Kong and the New Territories had previously served as either a prison for illegal entrants from China, or for local residents convicted of crimes and sentenced to jail by the courts. Some of the most inaccessible camps had been modified to serve dual purposes. These camps detained boat refugees, while at the same time doubling as treatment centers for drug addicts from the local population.

Perhaps the most fearsome camp I worked in was Victoria Prison. In my opinion, Victoria Prison was more like a dungeon than a prison. The massive stone and masonry structure had walls over a meter thick surrounding darkened cells reminiscent of Vietnam's infamous Hanoi Hilton. The prison held refugees considered by the local government as being extremely dangerous to both Hong Kong residents and other refugees as well. Some Vietnamese detainees in Victoria Prison also were incarcerated in that locale due to their backgrounds. This category included those refugees who were determined or suspected to be former Communist cadre, and therefore immediately under suspicion by the Hong

Kong authorities as possible spies. The Hong Kong police simply could not take any chances and shipped anyone remotely connected to the Communist cause to Victoria. The Hong Kong police made no exception, since Ho Chi Minh had founded the Indochinese Communist Party in a local soccer stadium during the 1930s. Back then, Communist cadre from Vietnam often used the port as temporary refuge from the vigilant security forces of the French "Surete."

Although I dreaded working in the huge prison, I realized that Communist Vietnamese cadre defecting to the West comprised one of the best possible sources of POW/MIA related information, and I never passed up an opportunity to interview them, regardless of where they were detained. Analysts in the JCRC Hawaiian headquarters were encouraged by the fact that of the number of reports they routinely received from the Hong Kong route, over 60 percent of them were eventually correlated to actual wartime losses. This ratio was by far the best ever achieved from any route during the life of the JCRC, and the accuracy and veracity of reports from camps in other parts of Southeast Asia paled in comparison to those collected in Hong Kong. I attributed this situation to one important factor. The majority of refugees arriving in Hong Kong originated from northern Vietnam. A good many of them had actually served on Hanoi's side during the war and became disillusioned with the situation in the North after the country was reunified under Communist control. A smaller number were normal South Vietnamese civilians who had departed from the beaches of Central Vietnam, generally the area from Danang to Hue. These were people who would have departed in April 1975, but lacked the means to do so. While maintaining a low profile, they had spent the last five to ten years of their lives living in the shadow of Hanoi's dreaded Ministry of Public Security. With financial assistance from relatives in the United States who had been fortunate enough to escape in 1975, this group managed to survive impoverished postwar conditions until the time was right and they were able to flee by boat to Hong Kong.

During my first interview trip to Hong Kong, I was anxious to ask one particular question that had been on my mind for some time. Why were the North Vietnamese people willing to remain there throughout the war, under the threat of constant bombing attacks by American aircraft, and now that the war was over, suddenly decide to flee? The answer was somewhat of a shock, because as it turned out the response I most often received was "we didn't flee because we never thought you Americans would lose." In addition to the unjustified degree of confidence in American military power, another reason cited was the general wartime economic conditions in the North. According to a number of refugees, even with the bombing during the 1960s and 70s, by North Vietnamese standards the tremendous amount of aid from other Communist and socialist countries provided to fight against the Americans created a fairly strong economy. With the cessation of hostilities, the resultant drop in foreign grants caught the people in the North by surprise. Suddenly faced with the requirement to return to rice and vegetable farming in rural communities, but with no seeds, tools or independent financial backing, those who had been gainfully employed in wartime economy jobs were now destitute.

Most interviews that were conducted were simple and straight forward, but occasionally there were instances where the individual providing the information was either a high-ranking Communist official, or the nature of the information itself was so sensitive that it required careful handling. Beginning in 1982, the policy on reports concerning live Americans held prisoner during the war, or on Americans remaining in Indochina after the war ended, were at a minimum given a classification of "Secret." The rationale of U.S. officials working on the issue was that live-sighting reports needed to be treated seriously and investigated in depth, and afterwards the reports could be declassified. Such intelligence, called "live sighting reports" were transmitted electronically to both Hawaii and Washington and analyzed based on the highest possible priority. As soon as the information was examined, a message was sent back to the field for additional questions to be asked of the source.

Given the possible consequences, this so-called "follow-up interview" was actually a more detailed interrogation, with considerable emphasis placed on the reliability and credibility of the Source. This resulted in a lengthy re-interview that at times lasted for several days. With a live sighting report, there were several possible outcomes: the report was judged to be valid and an American actually was being held against his will in Indochina; the information was correlated to someone who had been held prisoner at some point, but had subsequently died or was returned; or the information concerning the live American was deemed to have been fabricated. Additionally, some reports were correlated to Operation 34A personnel, or to Soviet or East Europeans, or were held in a "pending" category awaiting a final determination.

The grueling interview sessions normally included a polygraph examination of the Source by a member of the CIA or one of the DOD's military intelligence components. With Sources providing live-sighting information, DIA almost always asked the refugee to submit to a polygraph. There has been much controversy over the utility of polygraphing Asians. If a Source provided information on live prisoners and then refused to take the test, or took the test and failed, many used it to justify their stance that all Sources who claimed Americans were being held were fabricating. Like most views in the POW/MIA issue, the answer wasn't that clear-cut. Actually, the polygraph situation was quite complex, but trying to explain that to government officials was often impossible. In the case of Hong Kong and Macao, polygraph examinations of refugees needed greatly increased logistical support. Machines used to conduct the exams were normally brought into the country through diplomatic channels arranged by the American Consulate. To facilitate travel by public conveyance, polygraph machines were disguised as ordinary pieces of luggage. To prevent the compromise of a machine or its operator, an escort from the local Police Special Branch would normally travel surreptitiously but in close proximity to the American officials throughout the trip to the camps or interview sites. When the time came for linking up with Special Branch personnel in public places, such as ferry piers or boat docks, we would normally present a prearranged signal, such as carrying a red or yellow shopping bag in one hand and a newspaper in the other. After several trips on the Hong Kong route I was able to easily recognize personnel of the Special Branch, but I was always careful to avoid any form of greeting or recognition while in public so as not to blow their cover. Since the polygraph examiners came and went periodically, depending on the requirements, they seldom knew who their "guardian" angels were.

Since representatives of the United Nations High Commissioner for Refugees were involved in the operations of many of the camps, the police were very wary of their association with the polygraph equipment or the interrogation of refugees becoming known to the UNHCR. The police feared accusations of torturing the refugees and thus creating an international incident. In Thailand we had the same fears and instructed the Sources to tell the UN people that they were going out for a physical. As a result the Special Branch was very creative in arranging for the polygraph examinations. Following their advice, in most cases where the lie-detector machines were utilized as aids to interrogations, I would work out a schedule where I would first take the examiner to an isolated location somewhere in the outer islands of Hong Kong. I would then proceed to the refugee camp where I took physical custody of the refugee for movement to a nearby pier. At the pier I would place the refugee on a public ferry to a second, and in some cases a third pier where I would join the Special Branch personnel. For the next leg of the journey the Special Branch resorted to using a commercial cargo van, complete with painted signs advertising a local convenience store, to transport us to the predesignated interrogation site where the polygraph examiner would be waiting. Normally the site was located in an inconspicuous hotel or government guesthouse located off the tourist vistas. Prior to beginning the interrogations, although the Special Branch assured me that the site had been secured and sanitized, I conducted my own inspection for any possible electronic monitoring devices just to be completely confident.

The polygraph examiners varied in experience and ability. Having previously taught the utilization of the polygraph, I was familiar with the exam routine and quite often directed changes in the manner in which the exams were conducted. For example, at first in order to prove to subjects that they could not escape detection of a falsehood, some examiners used a regular deck of playing cards. This method called for the subject to mentally pick a single card and then shuffle that particular card into a stack of ten randomly selected cards from the same deck. After placing the stack of ten cards face down on the table the examiner would then lift them one at a time for the subject to view. As instructed, the subject would then render a negative response to the question "is this your card?" for all ten cards. Almost invariably, when the subject replied negatively to the card he actually selected, the immediate physiological reaction would expose his intended deception. While it was important to raise the anxiety levels of subjects prior to beginning the exam, I came to the conclusion that in some cases this method of demonstrating the efficiency of the machines, which in the eyes of Asian subjects might be perceived as a simple slight-of-hand carnival trick, caused the anxiety levels of some subjects to actually drop dramatically. I surmised that since Asian Communist methods of interrogation were so draconian and brutal, subjects with any history of prior interrogations would have to be dealt with in a firm, businesslike manner. Any attempt at trickery would most likely backfire, so I halted this practice.

In order to explain to the subjects the importance of relating the facts, rather than just telling me what they thought I wanted to hear, I often used the example of a birthday gift from my mother. I asked the subject how he might react if I had appeared at the interview site wearing a horrible looking purple shirt with yellow polka dots. If I told the subject the shirt had just been given to me by my mother as a gift, and then asked the subject how he liked it, even though the shirt was ugly the subject would most likely say it was pretty. This would be what he thought I wanted to hear, rather than the truth. Most Asians seemed to understand this point very well, and my brief explanation proved to be helpful in convincing them to be straightforward during the interviews. For the most part, however, I personally had little confidence in using the complicated exams on Asian subjects. Due to the cultural barriers and the lack of total control over the environment for an adequate period of time prior to commencing the exams, I believed that the exams were not completely reliable. Not only were genuinely cooperative subjects prone to an unusual degree of naiveté, it was also relatively easy for those subjects merely feigning cooperation to gain access to various types of medications capable of influencing results of the examinations.

The polygraph examinations were entirely voluntary and if the subjects clearly demonstrated reluctance toward participating in the tests, it was cancelled. In some cases the subjects waited until the last possible moment, after the machine and operator were already in place, and then decided to withdraw from the process. This caused both the operators and me considerable frustration due to the planning and logistics involved. At times I was able to schedule the exams in conjunction with my routine "circuit rider" routes, but it was not uncommon to be called upon to undertake trips for specific exams. In cases where the subjects withdrew from the examination process, although technically the DIA considered the results negative, in reality the credibility of the subjects was now deemed to be so low that the information was viewed as worthless. When this type of scenario developed I instead carefully considered the entire situation before reaching any conclusions about a Source's trustworthiness. I believed that consideration should be given to the manner in which the subject was approached by the operator, educational background, along with other mitigating factors such as fear of reprisal against family members remaining in Communist countries should the subject's participation become compromised. Still, DIA had the final word on the subject, and they were not inclined to accept "mitigating factors."

One example of this disconnect was an intriguing report provided by a refugee in Macao alleging a sighting of live Americans. According to this source he observed a number of U.S. pilots in a camp for American POWs called "Thac Ma" (Ma Waterfall or Ma Rapids) in Tuyen Quang province northwest of Hanoi. Although some minor discrepancies in the Source's story were noted, I sensed some element of the truth in the individual's account. However, in a follow-up interview it was pointed out to him that according to American records, there were no POW camps located within Tuyen Quang province. Confronted with this information from the DIA analysts, and after observing the electrical wiring attached to the machine just prior to beginning the polygraph exam, the refugee became frightened and decided to withdraw from the process. DIA immediately labeled him a fabricator. Since the subject had seemed so sure of himself prior to appearing for the exam, I considered the possibility that he had heard the account from someone else and was passing on hearsay as firsthand information. If that were actually the case, the information might still be considered valuable. The DIA, however, didn't believe in spending much time on a subject who declined to take an exam. Unfortunately, however, several years later I interviewed former GVN military members who stated that after being captured in Central Vietnam, they were moved to POW camps in Tuyen Quang province. Although these ex-inmates possessed knowledge of POWs from other countries held in Tuyen Quang, they had no knowledge of any Americans, or a camp called Thac Ma. They did concede, however, that the camps in that area were high security, and that Americans could easily have been held nearby without their knowledge. I was never informed concerning any follow-up efforts by DIA, or for that matter any other intelligence agencies, to obtain information on a camp or specific geographic area in Tuyen Quang province called Thac Ma.

Some other discounted reports that were ultimately deemed fabrications by DIA analysts in the Pentagon continue to plague my conscience. For instance, one refugee from North Vietnam who had worked as a truck driver for the People's Army both during and after the war claimed to have observed two Caucasian Americans in a compound north of Hanoi during 1977.[4] According to the source he was assigned to accompany a crew from Hanoi to the site for the purpose of filming the two Americans. The Source claimed that he held the camera cord during the filming and was able to observe the two Americans at close range. I had a feeling that there was some credence to the man's story but the matter was dropped. I later learned that two Americans captured while smuggling drugs off the coast of southern Vietnam by boat had been transferred to the North and incarcerated during the same time frame reported by the man who was judged to be a fabricator. This discovery led me to place additional credence on other information provided by the same Source pertaining to wartime Vietnamese facilities inside Laos.

Compared to the live sighting interviews, which required a great deal of administrative and logistical support, the debriefings conducted for the collection of information on the crash sites and burial sites of American MIAs were more simplified. In contrast to interview conditions in Thailand, Malaysia, Indonesia and the Philippines, however, conditions in Hong Kong allowed for much greater success. Rather than receiving the information from a Source with a crowd of noisy people gathered round listening in on the conversation, not only distracting the subject but also choking off all fresh air in the sweltering heat of a thatched hut, interviews in Hong Kong were routinely afforded more confidentiality. I attributed this situation in large part to the political clout and professionalism of the experienced military veterans assigned to the CIA station in Hong Kong, and in part to the efficient administrative organization of the Royal Hong Kong Government, which placed considerable emphasis on formality and adherence to proper procedures.

The establishment of the "circuit rider" routes was a critical juncture in the overall intelligence-gathering programs of the JCRC and the DIA. The well-organized, systematic collection effort replaced a totally ineffective "hit-and-miss" effort not worthy of the missing men and their families. The information that was collected provided vast insight into Hanoi's capabilities and intentions regarding the exploitation of the POW/MIA issue. It eventually supported field investigations and excavations throughout former French Indochina. When interviewing official witnesses "introduced" by the Communist officials managing the investigations on the ground, American investigators now had a system of checks and balances in place, plus a degree of quality control. Amazingly, however, in the years to come, just as the field investigation teams would begin to gain momentum on the ground, the refugee interview project would suddenly be abandoned. Ultimately our investigators would have to be content with the orchestrated testimony of witnesses arranged in advance and introduced by the Communist Party of Vietnam. Still, after years of Vietnamese stonewalling, small cracks had begun to appear, offering the slim chance to successfully resolve the issue once and for all.

Chapter Seven

A Faint Glimmer of Hope

THE BLEAK POSTWAR NEGOTIATION record with the Vietnamese and Lao to resolve the POW/MIA issue was a serious concern of the new Reagan government, to say nothing of the JCRC leadership. The administration had come into office grimly determined to raise the issue's priority, and to uncover whether Americans were still held captive. Early in 1981, the Senate voted by joint resolution with the House to make July 17, 1981, POW/MIA Recognition Day, a proclamation signed into law by President Ronald Reagan on June 12, 1981. On November 11, 1982, the Vietnam Veterans Memorial was dedicated in the nation's capital. On January 28, 1983, speaking before the National League of Families, President Reagan formally designated the POW/MIA issue as a matter of "highest national priority." There was also a growing awareness of the issue in mainstream America.

Policy-makers in Washington began privately describing the gamut of potential U.S. reaction to proof that Americans were being held against their will in Indochina as "anything from diplomacy to helicopters in the night." Each report concerning an alleged sighting of a live American was electronically transmitted to various American agencies, including the JCRC, CINCPAC, DIA, State, CIA, and the White House via the National Security Council (NSC). Further, by direct order from the President's primary policy advisor on Southeast Asia, Mr. Richard Childress, who had joined the NSC in September 1981, the NSC command now routed a copy of each report directly to him. An Army veteran with a tour in Vietnam's Mekong Delta region, Childress was deeply committed to work hard on two fronts: bring the families back to a semblance of trust in the government's efforts, and force the Vietnamese to begin addressing the POW/MIA question in a forthright manner. Although often criticized by some radical skeptics for what they perceived as his failure to rapidly achieve progress in resolving this highly emotional question, Childress worked tirelessly, both publicly and behind the scenes, to move the issue forward. I harbored no doubts that the "helicopters in the night" was a thinly veiled reference to the Delta Force at Fort Bragg, North Carolina, and I knew that Childress would not hesitate to recommend that President Reagan deploy the elite force if the JCRC produced a report of live Americans deemed credible by Washington analysts. Based on this sea change in U.S. government attitude, I knew high-level negotiations with the Vietnamese to return to the old battlefields would soon begin, and at some time in the future permission to begin field operations would be granted.

The other Reagan Administration point man on the subject was Deputy Assistant Secretary of Defense Richard Armitage, whom I had meet in 1975 when he helped evacuate the South Vietnamese Navy. Armitage made every effort to publicize the fact that Reagan intended to raise the priority of accounting for America's missing from the Vietnam War, and that he had strongly encouraged such action by the President. As a result, Armitage frequently came to Thailand to evaluate the POW/MIA accounting efforts. With apparent sincerity he pledged the total support of his office in improving and upgrading the overall endeavor.

Like Childress, Armitage also periodically suffered the slings and arrows of the radical crowd. Although smeared with rumors and gossip alleging his involvement in Southeast Asian drug-trafficking by more radical elements of the POW/MIA lobby and leftist critics, despite the slander, Armitage possessed the intestinal fortitude to remain a true friend of the missing men and their families. In listening to the tirades against Armitage and comparing them to the man I knew, it was obvious to me that the more vociferous activists were way off base regarding their accusations. Even more puzzling, I thought that the more radical factions would have appreciated Armitage's straightforward attitude in tackling tough issues head on. But for some reason, this was not the case. I could only conclude that Armitage had rubbed someone the wrong way, and they were now on a vendetta to settle scores. Knowing Armitage, I don't think he lost much sleep over it, and personally I was glad to see a man of his caliber directly involved in the POW/MIA issue, especially at such a high level.

What Childress and Armitage wanted and what they inherited, however, were at polar opposites. They assumed responsibility for a POW/MIA issue that was at a virtual standstill. When governmental relations collapsed over the Vietnamese invasion of Cambodia in December 1978, so concurrently did any movement on the topic. Hanoi was astute enough, however, to realize that the POW/MIA matter was their main means of maintaining our interest in that small country. They wanted economic investment, diplomatic recognition, or some form of reparations for war damage, although they wanted it on their terms. Therefore, despite the current frosty relations, the Vietnamese could not allow this state of affairs to continue indefinitely. But they were neither making concessions on other issues nor wasting the major efforts their intelligence and security services had expended in gathering information and remains of American MIAs. What they probably envisioned was some form of their classic "fighting while talking" strategy, one that they had applied so vigorously during the Paris Peace Talks. They knew, because of our internal political pressures, that we could not turn our back on the POW/MIA question. Therefore, they were free to harangue us at every opportunity and make unreasonable demands, all the while hoping we would eventually reach some accommodation.

Thus, shortly after I arrived in Hawaii, the first postwar meeting between the JCRC and the Vietnamese since the final collapse occurred between October 1 and 4, 1980. It was a low-level meeting, as only Lieutenant Colonel Paul Mather and Jim Tully from the Liaison office participated. The discussions were notably unproductive. The Vietnamese repeatedly lectured them that the "hostile" U.S. attitude was preventing Vietnam from finding more information on missing American servicemen. The Carter Administration's perceived tilt toward China also wasn't well received.

The next JCRC meeting with the Vietnamese, which Harvey participated in, took place between May 27 and 30, 1981, but like its predecessor, it produced mostly banalities. Oddly enough, despite Harvey's admonitions to the higher brass about potential diplomatic flaps without his guiding presence, he promptly created his own incident. During his first meeting with the Vietnamese in Hanoi, he learned that the SRV was repatriating three remains believed to be those of still unaccounted for Americans. When approached by a member of the media and asked for his comments, Harvey stated, "We are pretty damned happy." Harvey quickly regretted having made the comment when it drew strong criticism from several quarters, mainly the families. First, we weren't even sure if the remains were American, second, three remains was considered by some to be a small gesture relative to the twenty-five hundred men who were missing, and third, many thought Harvey should have left the press statements lauding Vietnam to the Washington policy-level bureaucrats.[1]

After the failure of the first two JCRC talks, Armitage traveled to Hanoi on February 24, 1982 to prod the Vietnamese into creating a process whereby American teams could once again begin searching in Vietnam for the remains of missing Americans or conduct investigations for live Americans. This was the highest-level official DOD discussion held with the Communists since 1973. While in Hanoi, Armitage drove home the point that President Reagan was committed to resolving the issue and that the American people fully supported that effort. While the results were again modest, one result of Armitage's visit was that the Vietnamese agreed to hold four more "Technical Talks" with American experts. Unfortunately, the first meeting was delayed until December 1982. However, the Vietnamese also accepted an invitation to send a delegation to visit the JCRC and CILHI in Hawaii. This trip would be the first to the United States by an official POW/MIA commission from Vietnam since July 1978, when a similar group went to Hawaii to meet with an assortment of American officials. This new trip by the Vietnamese was seen by them as a potential political opening, and by us as a possible turning point in the quest to account for our missing men.

In early August 1982, about the same time that the Hong Kong interview project was completely organized, I was informed of an impending three-day visit by five Vietnamese officials assigned to the Vietnamese Office for Seeking Missing Personnel (VNOSMP). This was a special office within the government of Vietnam created solely to assist the Americans account for their war dead. While ostensibly it was the formal counterpart to the JCRC, it was more. The VNOSMP operated under the authority of the Prime Minister, and included representatives from the Ministries of Foreign Affairs, Defense, and Interior, which meant that the VNOSMP cadre came from diplomatic, military and intelligence circles. In preparation for this important meeting, the Liaison Office dispatched Tully to Hawaii in order for him to immediately begin translating into Vietnamese the material planned for presentation to the Communist delegation. My assignment was to escort the mission from Bangkok to Hawaii and back. I knew that any incidents would quickly escalate into a major episode, so I was determined to ensure the trip went smoothly. I had no idea the whole effort would prove to be constant chaos interspersed with moments of pure hilarity.

The American Embassy travel office in Bangkok made the necessary airline reservations for the six-member group based on "invitational" travel orders transmitted by the Pentagon. After the delegation arrived in Bangkok on August 6, I proceeded to the SRV Embassy where I picked up their passports for processing by the American Embassy visa section. While flipping through the pages I immediately recognized two VNOSMP delegates who were former members of the Communist mission to the Four Party Joint Military Team at Camp Davis in Saigon. One was Senior Captain Tran Hao. According to our records, he had been assigned to the PAVN Graves Management Agency. I also remembered that Tran Hao had served as my primary escort when I went to North Vietnam during 1973 to inspect the graves of the POWs who died while being held in prison. In fact, Tran Hao had carried the ledger with the list of American names and the corresponding Vietnamese names placed on the headstones of the graves for security purposes. The second man, Major Tran Trong Khanh, had served as a member of the PAVN Research (Intelligence) Department.[2]

Another individual who had a murky background and had performed duties other than that of "MIA Specialist" was Colonel Vo Dinh Quang, who was currently assigned to the General Political Directorate of the PAVN High Command and had served as a military attaché on foreign assignments, including Indonesia. Unlike most Communist Vietnamese, he seemed very at ease in dealing with foreign officials. Quang continued to work on the POW/MIA issue at the planning level in the General Political Directorate until 1998, when he was reassigned as Vietnam's Defense Attaché in Washington, D.C.[3]

While the first three were military, the only member of the delegation arriving on a diplomatic passport was Mr. Cu Dinh Ba. Ba was a longtime Communist party member and senior intelligence cadre assigned to Communist Military Region 5 (MR-5) in central South Vietnam.[4] His wife was also assigned to the same Region during the war as a doctor at a field hospital. I believe Ba was close friends with Professor Ho An, who had helped run the wartime MR-5 American POW camp. Ho An was instrumental in helping to turn Robert Garwood. Ba was the new head of the VNOSMP, and was concurrently assigned as the North American Officer for the Ministry of Foreign Affairs. Ba was well educated and outwardly possessed a great deal of dignity. After a stint as head of the VNOSMP, Ba would later become Vietnam's ambassador to England. He finally retired in 1992 to a small villa near the old Vietnamese-American Association on the outskirts of Danang.[5]

The final member of the delegation caught my eye and immediately raised my stress level. Ho Xuan Dich had served as a member of the Viet Minh in the Hue area during the Communists' war against the French. While assigned to the Military/Enemy Proselytizing Department of Communist Inter Region 5, (a French era regional designation encompassing some of the same area as MR-5), Dich's duties were oriented toward the exploitation of French military personnel who had either deserted to the Communist side, or who had defected after being captured and successfully "reindoctrinated." Dich concentrated in training French deserters from the non-metropolitan members of the French Foreign Legion, especially those of African descent from Morocco, Algeria and Senegal. Dich was quite effective in employing these colonial French turncoats in terrorist type attacks against government facilities, and assassinations directed at both French and South Vietnamese officials. In other words, Dich had served as a recruiter and trainer of defectors turned killers.

When Vietnam was partitioned at the 17th parallel, Dich was reassigned to Nghe An province above the Demilitarized Zone where he worked as a cadre in an Armed Propaganda Unit. At that time his mission was to prevent local residents in North Vietnam from fleeing the Communists and joining the refugee exodus to the South. He had also probably assisted the savage repression of the peasant rebellions in that area in 1956. We assumed his wartime activities against the U.S. and ARVN forces were similar, but our information was sketchy. We only knew that Dich had worked on the POW/MIA issue as a Security cadre in Hanoi. During the latter stages of the Paris Peace Talks, he was sent to Paris to support the Communist delegations attending the negotiations. Dich continued to labor as a political cadre until after Saigon fell in April 1975. When President Jimmy Carter pardoned Vietnam War era draft evaders on January 21, 1977, Dich received orders for Canada. He continued to work with American deserters in Canada until 1979, when he was declared "Persona Non Grata" by Canadian authorities for "activities incompatible with his diplomatic status." After the Hawaii trip, Dich spent a three-year tour from 1984 to 1987 in the SRV Embassy in Kuala Lumpur, a transit point for many fleeing refugees.

One of Dich's most prized possessions was a floppy camouflage tropical rain hat. He carried it with him everywhere he went. Years later when he and I were working in the field together, Dich casually mentioned that he had received this hat as a memento from an American renegade. Dich made the comment knowing full well that this was an area of great interest to us, and he knew that if I asked whom the deserter was, he would not tell me. I didn't play into his trap. Looking at him closely, I remarked that I found it difficult to believe that after all the efforts the Vietnamese had expended in proselytizing American servicemen to defect, all they had to show for it was Robert Garwood and McKinley Nolan. Dich's mouth dropped open, and he realized that any answer he gave me would be equally damning. He remained sullen for the rest of the trip. To add the final piece to his colorful background, he also had a well-known dislike of Americans.

Once passports, visas and plane tickets were in order, I picked up the group and accompanied them to Don Muang International Airport for departure to Hong Kong. The first technical problem of the trip occurred during flight check-in. I was informed that due to the current heavy exodus of Vietnamese refugees to Hong Kong, any Vietnamese citizens entering the colony were required to be in possession of a valid entry visa. After attempting unsuccessfully to reschedule the flight, I called my contact in the Defense Liaison Office in Hong Kong, Lieutenant Colonel Mike Lombardo, and apprised him of the situation. After Lombardo was informed that the Vietnamese officials were being afforded "Head of State" travel status by the State Department, he pledged to do everything he could to get the visa requirement waived. As we waited, the plane's passenger ramp was taken away and the aircraft had just begun to taxi onto the flight line when the pilot suddenly halted the aircraft. He soon turned around, and we were allowed to board. Upon arrival in Hong Kong, representatives of both the American Consulate General and the Royal Hong Kong Government were on hand to meet us. Thankfully, approval for the one night stay proceeded smoothly.

With six of us, we needed two taxis to reach our downtown hotel. Although several of the Vietnamese had previously been outside their country, they had never encountered anything as fast-paced as Hong Kong. The VNOSMP officials, especially Ba, became paranoid about losing their way and being attacked by refugees from the former RVN. I tried repeatedly to reassure them, but to no avail. Prior to boarding the taxis I was careful to ensure that both taxi drivers were familiar with the hotel's location if we became separated in the heavy traffic. As added insurance, I also gave the hotel address to the group riding in the second taxi. Fortunately, the ride from the airport was incident free, but when checking in at the hotel desk they dutifully informed me that they were not permitted to sleep in individual rooms. After some haggling about whom would sleep where, the members agreed that Ba and Dich would share a room, Quang and Tran Hao would split a second room, and Khanh and I would occupy the third room. Ba also insisted that the three rooms be located in close proximity to each other.

Leading my flock, we all jammed tightly into an elevator car. On the way up to the rooms, the elevator stopped at a floor below ours. As the door opened, Tran Hao suddenly barged out into the hallway just as a throng of people crowded their way inside. The elevator abruptly took off leaving him stranded alone somewhere in the lower part of the building. I got off at the next stop in order to look for him. The remainder of the group reached the floor where the rooms were located, but being concerned about Tran Hao, they took a second elevator back down to the floor where he got off. This happened, of course, while Hao and I were in another elevator riding to the correct floor. Finally I gave up and waited with Tran Hao in the lobby until the group was reassembled. On the second elevator attempt I stood directly in the doorway to prevent any further confusion.

Early the next morning, with an airline-provided breakfast under their belts, the group was ready for some sightseeing. With time to kill before the next day's flight, I arranged a little tour of Hong Kong to show my dedicated Communist counterparts firsthand the evils of capitalism. The first item on the list of modern marvels to visit was the Hong Kong subway system. The VNOSMP representatives were fascinated by the underground maze of trains that seemed to operate with great efficiency. After trying several different lines I guided the group back above ground to the chic Tsim Sha Shui shopping area. Upon entering the huge shopping mall, they were stunned by the quantity and variety of goods displayed. Having waited in long lines to purchase or to be issued rationed staples for years, the sight of so much gold, jade, furs, electric appliances, and fresh fruit, as well as a wide assortment of household items and clothing brought an incredulous look to the faces of the group, most particularly the old Senior Captain, Tran Hao, who stood in the middle of one aisle with his mouth agape, his head swiveling back and forth, looking in disbelief at the merchandise.

Throughout the excursion, Ba tightly clutched a typical brown, leather issue-type briefcase normally reserved for senior cadre. Seeing him struggling at times with the cumbersome case I offered to spell Ba from carrying it, but he only chuckled as if I were joking and politely declined the assistance. I couldn't imagine what Ba might be carrying to a POW/MIA meeting that would warrant such close protection, but in looking at the leather case I noticed that it was exactly the same type as the one with the incendiary device that caused the fire on the C-130 liaison flight from Hanoi to Saigon.

That afternoon we reassembled in the hotel lobby to depart. Naturally, checkout was almost as chaotic as the arrival the previous day. When I completed the group checkout, the desk clerk informed me that several bills remained unsettled. Believing that there was some mistake, I argued that the rooms were provided by the airline as part of the overall ticket cost. Unyielding, the clerk began to leaf through a stack of receipts for room service and minibar expenses. In further checking I learned that Tran Hao had indulged himself long after the others were sound asleep. According to Tran Hao, he had assumed everything on the room menu and in the minibar was provided gratis. He closed the door to any reasonable settlement by adding that he regretted that his government had not provided him with any money for the trip, since it had been assumed that the U.S. side would cover all the costs. I was perturbed but still compassionate concerning Tran Hao's misunderstanding, so I reluctantly shelled out the necessary amount from my own personal funds. My counting was occasionally interrupted by grumbling from Quang to the effect that, prior to dozing off, he had clearly explained to Tran Hao that nothing in the hotel was free.

As the group de-planed in Hawaii, Lieutenant Colonel Harvey appeared on the tarmac with a large entourage to welcome the group. Due to the "Head of State" status bestowed on the delegation by Washington, the U.S. Customs Service waived all the in-processing procedures normally required of foreign visitors, especially those arriving from Communist countries. After having gone through several tense exchanges at Tan Son Nhut during the last few years of the war, I was glad to see the VNOSMP group make the transfer without an incident or confrontation.

All visitors, including me, were billeted in the Hickam Air Base "Distinguished Visitor" quarters, some of the best military digs Hawaii had to offer. As an exception to the normal policy, the rooms came supplied with snacks and minibar. Fortunately for Tran Hao there was no charge for the amenities. I showed the VNOSMP members to their rooms and after giving them some time to unpack, I went back to see if everything was in good order. As I went from room to room I explained to them how to use the American steam irons and other appliances furnished with the rooms. With the exception of Ho Xuan Dich, all members of the group were attentive and appeared to appreciate the help. Dich indicated, however, that he was a seasoned traveler and declined all assistance. Concerned about the unusually warm temperature Hawaii was currently experiencing, I attempted to explain to Dich the correct procedure for adjusting the window air conditioning unit, but again he waved off any aid. Confronted with Dich's arrogant dismissal, I left him alone.

Despite Dich's blithe assurances, when the group assembled the following morning, everyone but Dich seemed well rested. We were all stunned when Dich appeared completely drenched in sweat, looking as if he had just returned from an all night forced march. Dich complained that his air conditioner was not working and that he had suffered continually from the high heat and humidity. All of us then promptly marched over to Dich's room to investigate. When I checked the air conditioner I found that Dich had set the switch to "Exhaust Closed" and "Fan Only." When I flipped the lever over to "High Cool" the compressor immediately cut in. This brought guffaws from the VNOSMP members and left Dich with a sheepish look on his face throughout breakfast.

Just prior to beginning the initial session of the meeting Harvey pulled me aside for a "Honolulu we have a problem" talk. Harvey explained that although Tully had been dispatched to Hawaii a week in advance of the VNOSMP visit in order to translate the material being presented to the Vietnamese delegation, he was far behind in his efforts and practically nothing had been accomplished. Harvey added that a long-time Vietnam hand, Colonel Andre Sauvageot, had just arrived for the meetings as an advisor from the Army staff.[6] According to Sauvageot, Tully's Vietnamese was not adequate for him to serve as translator during the meetings. When Harvey asked if I would be able to "wing it" for the first meeting session and then afterwards translate the material for the later sessions, I told him I was willing to give it my best shot. When I asked Tully for an explanation, the only excuse he could offer was that he had not been able to find the appropriate dictionaries anywhere on the island.

The introductory session went efficiently as very little technical type information was involved. But rather than take a chance on derailing the meeting I decided that since the remaining material was highly technical in nature, I would drop out of the planned social activities and translate every planned presentation. As a result I became a hermit in my room, translating lesson plans, charts and case files each night until dawn the following day. This was a miserable time for me, especially after just having ridden on an airplane for two days. Since everyone else was caught up in the social whirl, I received no help, but fortunately a member of the Hawaiian-based JCRC staff came to my salvation. Marine Master Sergeant Silas Downs, a Vietnam vet and the JCRC Chief of Operations, kept me supplied with enough ice and Jack Daniels sour mash whiskey to get me through the tedious nightlong translations. In my immortal words "it's always embarrassing for a soldier to be rescued by a Marine, but Top Downs did save the day."

The VNOSMP members seemed to feel at ease in the Hickam DV quarters and never expressed any real desire to venture from the base. However, Harvey did arrange some tours around the island and the Vietnamese officials did see some of the local scenery. Toward the end of the visit I managed to find some free time one evening to take the group on a brief tour of a large department store in Pearl City. The VNOSMP members once again seemed excited by the displays of goods, but unfortunately, as was the case in Hong Kong, when Ba observed what appeared to be "boat people" in the store, the tour was curtailed and the group returned to Hickam. Despite Ba's reputation as a smooth operator, he remained paranoid about being attacked.

Back at the base, Ba then requested to make a telephone call from his room to the SRV Ambassador to the UN. As soon as I dialed the connection Major Khanh invited me to another room of the suite where he quickly popped in a music tape by the rock group "Abba." Although the Communist Party in Vietnam had banned music by artists from capitalist countries, music by "Abba" was acceptable due to the fact they were from socialist Sweden. Somewhat embarrassed, Major Khanh proceeded to turn the volume of the music up to a deafening level, apparently to jam any attempts at overhearing Ba's conversation with the Ambassador. Obviously some type of important information was being passed between the two diplomats.

During the meeting sessions the American side presented a detailed outline of how the accounting effort should be developed. We also provided specific examples of each particular type of case and circumstances of loss with recommendations as to how to proceed in resolving each one. As usual, the Vietnamese listened intently throughout the three days of presentations but without much comment. During the final meeting session, the Vietnamese appeared increasingly morose. As the time drew nearer for concluding remarks by Cu Dinh Ba, the delegation's titular head, we began to get suspicious. Our apprehension grew as we carefully watched Dich remove a sealed envelope from the pocket of his suit coat during the last rest break prior to Ba's final presentation. He pulled out a sheath of typewritten "onion skin" documents, the same type I had seen PAVN couriers carrying during the war for quick destruction. After closely examining the contents, he handed one document to Ba and placed the remainder back in his pocket. When Ba sat back down to give his prepared remarks, he began reading from the document given to him by Dich. We became alert, hoping that Ba would deliver some important announcement or at least some gesture aimed at breaking the current logjam over the POW/MIA issue. Our hopes were instantly dashed. Rather than good news of missing Americans being returned soon, as privately hoped, the gist of Ba's remarks was "what has the United States done for Vietnam, why should Vietnam help the United States?" Once again, the Politburo had displayed its true colors.

It may seem confusing as to which Vietnamese official, Ba or Dich, was actually in charge, since Americans traditionally view the highest-ranking government representative as the one in command. In the Communist system, however, the Party is superior to the government. Thus, while Ba was the senior

Vietnamese government representative and head of the VNOSMP, the SRV's official POW/MIA affairs organization, as the chief Communist Party member, Dich was actually in control. Further, since each important matter is compartmentalized, the Party Chapter Secretary dealing with that particular issue is usually the ultimate authority at the scene. Dich's role in selecting the Vietnamese response became clear later when I learned that he was in fact the VNOSMP Party Chapter Secretary. Still, while Dich was the cadre entrusted with overseeing the talks, he was undoubtedly following strict instructions from the highest levels of the Party apparatus on how to react to the range of U.S. actions the Vietnamese had anticipated. Undoubtedly, since our presentation was predictably bland and there was no mention of assistance to Vietnam, humanitarian or otherwise, or any movement forward in the normalization process, Dich selected the appropriate reply commensurate with our presentation, which had been discussed and prepared in advance, and handed it to Ba.

It is almost impossible for Americans to comprehend the degree of preparation Communist cadre make when engaged in diplomatic or political activities of this type. The Vietnamese, quite simply, leave nothing to chance. This is one of the most important lessons Americans need to learn concerning Vietnamese Communist behavior. They spend long hours in meetings discussing every eventuality, all the while smoking non-filter cigarettes and drinking strong tea that would most likely kill weaker constitutions. Based on higher Party instructions, they then determine an appropriate response to all potential scenarios and develop the proper dialogue. Nothing is left to chance, nothing. In this case, Dich had a range of options to choose from based on his assessment of our presentation.

On the evening prior to the departure of the VNOSMP delegation, the senior DOD Representative during the meetings invited all participants to dinner at the Pearl Harbor Officer's Club. At that point a few Americans remained slightly optimistic that the Vietnamese would make some type of additional announcement indicating increased movement in the accounting process, or at least a specific commitment for future consultations. Despite our fervent wishes, that proved not to be the case. Yet, the supper was pleasant and as the meal began to wind down, both sides seemed to drift toward a discourse of "let bygones be bygones." In order to drive home this point I asked the DOD rep's permission to say a few words in Vietnamese. After gaining his consent, I requested that Major Khanh translate my remarks from Vietnamese to English. I decided to plagiarize from a popular Communist poem I had heard many times before from young Vietnamese troops. Filled with enthusiasm and socialist ideology, they had made the hard journey down the Ho Chi Minh trail only to face death or prison or a difficult life in the jungle. The poem began: "If I am a flower I must be a flower that opens to face the sun (sunflower); If I am a bird I must be a dove (bird of peace); If I am a stone I must be a diamond; If I am a person I must have the ability to forget the past and look to the future." According to the original poem the last line should have been "If I am a person I must be a Communist." Not only were the VNOSMP members not offended by the revision, they agreed wholeheartedly with the new rendition. Although the meeting had little substance, at least everyone went home in a good mood.

The following day it was business as usual as I briefed the Vietnamese on the return flight to Vietnam. Prior to boarding the plane, Harvey called me aside to inform me that he had just received notification that I had been selected for attendance at the Army's prestigious Sergeant Major Academy in Texas, and due to class scheduling I would have to immediately accept or decline attendance. Attending would end my JCRC assignment. Faced with losing one of his key staff, Harvey mentioned how he would hate to give up my expertise, but at the same time understood why attendance at the academy was important for my career.

Although saddened about the possibility of leaving the JCRC, I was naturally excited about the promotion and possible advancement in my military career. Having spent twenty-three years away from home, I also relished the thought of an assignment back to Texas where I would at long last have an opportunity to visit relatives still living there. But after the recent technical exchanges between the U.S. and Vietnam, and given the significant amount of valuable casualty resolution information being collected from the refugee camp interview program, I decided that I had to continue my work at this important post. Despite our differences, Harvey seemed pleased to initiate the paperwork in order for me to decline attendance at the academy.

On the return flight the group stopped in Tokyo rather than Hong Kong. Hoping to do some shopping for duty free items, Dich approached me and stated that as the manager for the Vietnamese delegation during the trip, he felt compelled to inquire as to when I intended to disburse the per diem for the VNOSMP members that had been provided to me by the U.S. Government. When I informed Dich that there was no per diem available, the incredulous look on his face left no doubts that he suspected I had kept the money for myself. Caught off guard and embarrassed, I related to Dich how I had already spent a considerable sum out of my own pocket on the Vietnamese delegation, all without any expectation of reimbursement. I expressed my understanding of the inconvenience inherent to travel without funding for meals and other necessities, and as a gesture of kindness I invited the delegation to dinner at my home in Bangkok the following evening. As further indication of goodwill I bought each member a small gift, such as a wallet or calculator from the airport gift shop, as a memento of the trip. Apparently assuaged that I wasn't holding out on them, Dich dropped the matter entirely.

Although the VNOSMP did not get the U.S. currency they had anticipated from a per diem allowance, they were nevertheless still able to do some shopping. As we entered the first store, Major Khanh produced a huge wad of French francs. Although complaining bitterly about the low rate of exchange, Khanh converted the francs to American dollars for use in Tokyo. Despite the previous contention of dire poverty, I wasn't surprised that the delegation had actually come with a stipend. I wasn't angry that I had spent a goodly sum of my own money; I expected the Vietnamese perfidy. As soon as I saw the large amount of French currency, my thoughts turned to the French cemeteries under Communist control in North Vietnam. Each year the French Government had to pay an enormous sum for "maintenance and security" of the graves of French personnel killed during the First Indochina War. I calculated that if the U.S. and Vietnam began cooperative efforts in accounting for missing American servicemen and our side was not extremely careful, it was possible that the next time the VNOSMP delegation changed money at an international airport, it would be dollars rather than francs. The leg of the flight from Tokyo to Bangkok had plenty of empty seats, and the group was able to stretch out for some needed rest. Senior Captain Tran Hao took advantage of the empty seats by moving around the aircraft while requesting two drinks from each flight attendant.

Coming on the heels of the Hawaii trip was the September 1982 arrival of a delegation from the National League of Families to begin a fact-finding mission to Thailand, Vietnam and Laos. Although I was very familiar with the official government personnel and apparatus involved in the national casualty resolution effort, this was the first time I had ever met any members of the POW/MIA family organization. This was the first official League visit to Indochina since the end of the war, and was headed by the Chairman of the League's Board of Directors, Mr. George Brooks. Mr. Brooks' son, Navy Lieutenant Nicholas Brooks, had been missing in Laos since January 2, 1970. Other members of the board included Colonel Earl Hopper, U.S. Army (Ret), and Mrs. Anne Hart, wife of a missing aviator. Hart's husband was missing in southern Laos while Hopper's son was MIA in northern Vietnam near the Lao border. The delegation also included the League's Executive Director, Ms. Ann Mills-Griffiths, whose brother, Navy Lieutenant J.G. James B. Mills, went missing when his F-4B aircraft was lost near the coast of central North Vietnam on September 21, 1966.

Having heard that POW/MIA family members were often distraught, emotional, and highly critical of government efforts to learn the fate of their loved ones, I was initially wary of meeting with the League. But after talking with them about the purpose of their trip and learning of their expectations, I immediately realized that I had been misled concerning the organization's purpose and collective attitude. Not only were the League members supportive of government efforts to resolve the issue, they intended to do everything possible to increase the issue's priority. As we talked, I could sense from all of them their deep love for our country and their respect for the U.S. military. This attitude persisted despite their belief, shared by many other League members, that their own government was deceiving them concerning the fate of their loved ones. In spite of their reputation, the delegation seemed to be practical people who harbored no illusions as to the difficulties and complexities that lay ahead in the overall accounting effort. Rather than expecting miracles, the League members were resigned to the fact that many MIA cases would never be successfully resolved. They understood the impracticality of recovering all bodies, especially those cases where their loved ones were lost in crashes at sea or in incidents where the aircraft were subjected to high speed, sharp angle impacts into mountainous terrain.

Another myth I was able to dispel was the rumor that many MIA family members did not want their loved-ones' case resolved in order for them to continue drawing military benefits. I learned that to the contrary, the benefits of the family members depended on the status of their relative at the time of loss. If the individual qualified for retirement based on years of service, then the surviving spouse and children received the normal federally regulated share, as was the situation with any military member who died while in the service. Some families also received Dependency Indemnity Compensation from the Veterans Administration, but this was only a small amount and payable only after death. Other than that the families only received normal Social Security benefits similar to other families whose head of houschold died after working the period of time required to qualify for Social Security. Further, unless the missing man was officially declared dead, the family could not collect on any life insurance. After meeting them, the most important point I learned about the families was that they simply wanted answers. They wanted to learn the truth about what happened to their son or husband. If the men were proven to be dead, the family members wanted to finally say goodbye, and to lay to rest the nagging fear that their loved ones had somehow survived, only to be held as a forgotten prisoner in some jungle hell-hole. I gained a new appreciation for their sorrows despite my own short experience with a sudden loss. Long after they departed, their purpose in discovering the truth, no matter how long it took, remained deeply imbedded in me.

After visiting Laos first, the delegation traveled to Vietnam. In Hanoi, the League members met with Cu Dinh Ba. During their meetings, Ba denied they were holding any remains or living POWs and wasted little time in parroting the usual Vietnamese line that they had turned over all information they had collected. More importantly, he claimed, while Vietnam had agreed to view this issue as a humanitarian problem, the U.S. persisted in slandering the Vietnamese government. He continued in the same vein that the most significant barrier to resolving the issue was the "hostile" policies of the U.S., which made it difficult for them to motivate the people in remote areas to assist in search and recovery efforts. The Vietnamese had reacted to the American "hostile attitude" by delaying repatriations and rescheduling meetings, or when the U.S. government rebuked the Vietnamese for their intransigence on the issue, they responded by cutting off contact and demanding retractions. It was a difficult and fine line American officials had to tread. By protesting their actions and policies the JCRC had uncovered, the U.S. government risked alienating the hypersensitive Vietnamese. If they didn't, the families accused them of coddling the Communists, or worse, being engaged in a conspiracy to abandon hundreds of possible American POWs.[7] To the League's credit, they remained calm and business-like, and repeatedly pressed Ba for increased Technical Talks and for information on the many cases the U.S. had previously asked about.

Their final and perhaps most important meeting was with now Vice Foreign Minister Vo Dong Giang, the former high-ranking cadre at Camp Davis and the person who had made the trip to visit former ARVN Colonel Duong Hieu Nghia to pump him for information. Giang reiterated what Cu Dinh Ba had claimed: hostile U.S. policies were preventing resolution of the issue, and the Vietnamese were cooperating and had turned over all remains and information. It was typical Vietnamese orchestration—claim to be the victim and that the root of the problem was U.S. policies. In essence, the Vietnamese were dangling the POW/MIA issue as a trade-off for what they wanted: a change in American policies, namely dropping support for China and the Khmer resistance in Cambodia.

Leaving Vietnam and returning to Laos, the families met with senior Laotian Communist officials responsible for the POW/MIA issue in the capital city of Vientiane. The Lao blasted U.S. support for the resistance, which they claimed was using the POW/MIA issue as an excuse to make covert raids into Lao territory. Further, the search for American MIAs was very difficult due to the terrain and lack of Lao resources. The Lao also mentioned the "hostile" American attitude, citing it as the reason they had not accepted the Armitage delegation in February 1982. The Lao stressed that their government was not holding any live American personnel, and the League Delegation received promises for increased efforts on the part of the Lao Government, but as usual, there was a price for that improved support. While the Vietnamese were seeking changes in U.S. policy in the region, the Lao were more practical: they wanted economic aid.

However, unlike in Vietnam, where the delegation was restricted to the capital, the League was able to travel by helicopter to Vieng Xai, the wartime capital of the Pathet Lao and their Vietnamese advisers. At least two U.S. Air Force officers, Charles Shelton and David Hrdlicka, were captured in 1965 and held in the warren of limestone caves that dotted the area. According to the accompanying Lao official in charge of the Vieng Xai visit, Colonel Khamla Keophitoune, the American prisoners had died during captivity, and one grave, located outside the cave entrance, was later destroyed by U.S. air strikes. Allegedly the site belonged to Shelton. Khamla even pointed out the sizable bomb crater that supposedly destroyed the gravesite. The League members viewed this all-to-convenient theory with deep skepticism. Khamla also took them to a local crash site, which he claimed pertained to the "Colonels," referring to the current ranks of the two well-known American POWs, who had both been promoted to Colonel while on the MIA list. Although no remains of the American POWs were found during the visit to Vieng Xai, the delegation felt that the trip was worthwhile.

The group was also allowed to visit the site of an Air Force AC-130 aircraft that crashed in Salavan province in December 1972. The crew of the ill-fated aircraft included the navigator, Captain Thomas T. Hart, the husband of delegation member Mrs. Anne Hart. During the League's visit to the crash site Mrs. Hart discovered and retrieved two pieces of human skull. During a subsequent CILHI identification effort in 1985 for remains recovered from the site by JCRC and CILHI personnel, the Chief CILHI Anthropologist, Dr. Tadao Furue, became visibly shaken when told who had recovered the pieces. Furue then related that not only were the skull fragments recovered by Mrs. Hart specifically correlated to her husband, a positive identification of his remains would not otherwise have been possible without it.

After the delegation departed, my old friend, Air Force Brigadier General (Ret) Harry Aderholt, clandestinely recovered the remains of Lieutenant Nicholas Brooks, son of League Chairman George Brooks. At this time Aderholt headed the Air Commando Association in Fort Walton Beach, Florida and had been the last commander of the U.S. Military Assistance Command Thailand before it was disbanded in 1976. He had also worked in many Special Operations assignments in both Vietnam and Laos during the war, including as the first commander of the Joint Personnel Recovery Center, the Vietnam-era predecessor to the JCRC. His wartime work in Laos made him numerous contacts, and because of these old links, Aderholt was able to task former members of the former Special Guerrilla Units to cross the border from Thailand into Laos in order to recover Brooks' remains. Since Aderholt was well aware that he was subject to U.S. laws regarding violation of the Neutrality Act prohibiting cross-border operations into foreign countries, and also the U.S. policy of non-payment for either information or remains of missing personnel, he never divulged to me the entire details of his private POW/MIA recovery efforts in the Thailand-Laos border region. Concerning the recovery of the remains of Brooks, Aderholt only related that he had provided "a sack of rice" to the resistance forces for their successful recovery efforts.

The League visit, which was accompanied by an ABC news team, did accomplish one other important item. They managed to publicize the issue, and the visit also seemed to move the Vietnamese to some action. Vietnam's Foreign Minister (and Politburo member) Nguyen Co Thach appeared on ABC's "Nightline" program from New York City in September 1982 with two other American guests: the League in Bangkok and Richard Childress from Washington, DC. When queried about the storage of American remains, and despite the irrefutable testimony provided by the defecting mortician, Thach flatly denied that Vietnam was holding any. Childress immediately challenged Thach's statement, and was seen to roll his eyes in exasperation. Shortly thereafter, on September 30, 1982 while the League was visiting the Lao, Thach publicly announced that Technical Talks with the JCRC would resume and would be held quarterly in Hanoi. The first meeting was finally arranged for December 1982.

The Technical Talks appeared to be our best forum, aside from higher-level missions, to move the issue forward, and since this was the first meeting in some time, this was an important event. Now we had to find some method to continue and improve the discussions with a basically antagonistic nation bent on using the issue to further their agenda of normalization and economic assistance. The American delegation would include Harvey, Mather, Johnie Webb from CILHI, and me. Harvey and Webb flew in from Hawaii to link up with Mather and me in Bangkok, where we departed for Hanoi. We arrived on December 6 for a three-day visit.

This would mark the first instance that I had returned to Vietnam since the April 30, 1975 evacuation of the American Embassy in Saigon. As the plane made its final approach into Noi Bai Airport I could see a large number of unfilled bomb craters still remaining in the rice paddies surrounding the former tactical jet fighter airfield. After some thought and observation I came to the conclusion that rather than leaving the craters open for the usual propaganda directed at arriving international visitors, the Vietnamese were simply making practical use of the craters as fish ponds.

Upon arrival in Hanoi I sensed that there had been very little change since my last visit to the capital city on April 25, 1975. I felt uneasy regarding what degree of hostility the people might harbor toward Americans. I sensed that we would not be warmly welcomed in the northern capital, but I hoped that we would at least be tolerated. Since the Sino-Vietnamese war fought during the spring of 1979 had been highly publicized in the media, I also was interested to learn the extent of death and devastation suffered by Vietnam. I would soon stumble on the answer.

I was also curious as to what impact Communism had made on the country after the revolutionaries gained complete control. I could easily recall the arrogant lectures on Capitalism delivered by the fanatical northerners at Camp Davis. Upon landing, I immediately observed that the streets were still crowded with bicycles and everyone remained dirt poor. So poor that the place seemed perfectly clean due to the fact that the people generated almost no trash. Nothing was ever wasted, and if anything was thrown away you could rest assured it was absolutely worthless. I instinctively felt sympathy for the common people who had sacrificed their lives by the thousands, only to be impoverished even further by the Party's economic policies. On the ride into town I studiously examined the environs for other images of everyday life, trying to grasp the reality of existence in the Communist North. Soon I noticed scrape marks on the trees along the streets of Hanoi. Upon checking further I learned that the tree bark had been used for making a strong tea said to be beneficial in curing various ailments. Everywhere I looked the grass was hand-clipped flush with the surface of the ground for use as feed for livestock. People on the streets still wore the old wartime drab military-green or laborer-blue clothing. Perhaps poor didn't begin to describe it.

The Vietnamese who met us at the airport took us to the "Ho Hoan Kiem" (Restored Sword Lake), supposedly a tourist hotel. The meeting was held later that day in a room on the hotel's top floor. When we entered the room, Cu Dinh Ba was there to greet us. Hanging back but attentive were several other Vietnamese officials. One was Doctor Vo Ngoc Thu, the VNOSMP's forensic specialist. The other was introduced as Lieutenant Colonel Nguyen Thanh, a tiny but intense officer of the Ministry of Public Security.

We began our presentation by outlining a number of cases in the Hanoi/Haiphong area. As had been the situation during the talks held in Camp Davis during the life of the FPJMT, and continuing through the post-collapse set of meetings, we passed folders stuffed with information pertaining to the still unresolved cases. The files contained narratives outlining the basic facts of the loss incidents, including the circumstances, the type of aircraft or vehicles involved, the locations where they occurred, as well as the dates and times of the clash. The Vietnamese response was typical. Pledging yet again to study the documents carefully at some unspecified time in the future, the Vietnamese officials stacked them to the side of the meeting table. Ba then asked if we had any further documents, as "we would like to get all the information we can." I could only scream inside at the transparent Vietnamese duplicity, as I had seen a similar pattern of feigned cooperation during the cease-fire, and I was positive it would continue far into the future. It was obvious to me that the Vietnamese wanted to milk the American side for all the information it had in its possession on the important cases before even beginning to cooperate on joint efforts.

The U.S. was factionalized on the issue of providing this information to the Communists. I strongly believed it worked against our interests in providing this much detail, as it could prevent a fair investigation of a case once we were allowed on the ground. I wasn't against handing over basic information, but I was dead-set against including anything other than simple loss data. I tried to point out to my superiors and various analysts that basic Communist doctrine regarding dealing with foreigners dictated that everything had to be arranged in advance, with nothing left to chance. Given that policy, the Indochinese officials were acutely interested in obtaining every possible bit of information from U.S. files. I argued further that one primary reason that the three Communist countries involved continued to prolong the POW/MIA case investigations was simply because they wanted to make sure that they were in command of all the facts on the case. They especially wanted those facts known only to the U.S. side, and when arranging future specific investigations, they would seek to avoid surprises. Others on the U.S. side disagreed, even given the continual lack of a Vietnamese response. Some elements in the State Department believed in a link between the handover of folders and the return of remains, noting that of the 281 folders passed to the Vietnamese side from 1973 until 1979, some of those personnel had been returned. Unfortunately, despite my protestations, the U.S. continued its policy of providing large volumes of dossiers, called "case folders," to the Vietnamese officials in attendance.

But this particular technical meeting was somewhat different from previous discussions. The Vietnamese unexpectedly announced they were taking the Americans on a "field trip" to ostensibly examine the crash site of a downed aircraft. Hoping for significant progress, all the Americans were elated at the possibility. After the first meeting session concluded we were invited to stay overnight at the hotel. Our accommodations turned out to be a miserable, damp, dark place with an active population of rats. The mattresses reeked of mildew and were made from rice straw with a degree of hardness similar to cardboard. Although there were better lodgings available, including the nearby Le Thach Government Guesthouse, apparently the Vietnamese wanted to make a point to the Americans. The poor quarters amply demonstrated that although we would finally be allowed out of the city, as far as governmental relations were concerned, such contacts were still considered a very low priority with the Vietnamese, as obviously, were we.

On December 8, we loaded into several well-worn Russian "Volga" sedans and proceeded east on Route 5 out of Hanoi toward the port city of Haiphong. The road was crowded with every type of transport imaginable, from large cargo trucks to the ubiquitous bicycles. Small mopeds weaved dangerously in and out of the traffic stream, often with several people clinging to each one. The careening drivers zigzagged around the slower moving bicycles and rapidly swerved back and forth to avoid lumbering trucks passing on the opposite side. Even though I was used to the indescribable Bangkok traffic, I watched with amazement and no small amount of envy as the death-defying moped drivers dodged every moving object.

While the mopeds managed to avoid hitting any travelers, occasionally our caravan would encounter farmers moving pigs to market by bicycle. The farmers had a unique method of transporting the large animals. Turning the bulky pigs upside down and lashing them onto the rear luggage rack somehow kept the pigs unbelievably docile, and the farmers seemed to have no problem at all in maneuvering the heavy animals through the crowded traffic. To add to the bizarre scenes on the road, at one point I looked out the window and observed a man preparing a dog to be eaten. The man had the dog's carcass lying on a slant board at the edge of a small pond where he was steadily scraping the hair from the dog with a large knife. The dog's white color brought to mind an old saying from the northern part of the country that went *nhat bach-nhi dom,* meaning that white dog is number one in flavor, spotted dog is second. Not realizing that dog was considered a North Vietnamese delicacy, when Harvey observed the animal he exclaimed "look at that poor dog, he's drowned."

Our destination was an old colonial villa in downtown Haiphong. One member of the American group remarked how the normally white stuccoed walls were covered by a coating of green slime, apparently caused by the constantly humid climate and low hanging clouds. Not sure whether I would be called on to interpret the comment, I prepared to be diplomatic by rolling the Vietnamese word for algae *(Tao)* around in my mind. Even with the layer of gunk, the ornate building used by the Communist cadre to receive foreign guests looked surreal standing amidst the miserable shacks and lean-tos of the regular citizenry. Soon, a gaggle of people gathered to observe the strange looking Americans.

Once inside the villa the Vietnamese began with what would prove to be standard formulations regarding the imposing challenges involved in recovering American casualties. Whereas in other parts of the country the primary obstacles would prove to be changes in the countryside due to the elements and a growing population, in the case of Haiphong the flat, indistinguishable coastal terrain would hamper POW/MIA accounting efforts. The Vietnamese excuses ranged from aging witnesses slowly fading from the scene, cadre long since reassigned to forgotten locales, and the terrible American B-52 bombing. Lieutenant Colonel Thanh, who had ridden in the same car with Harvey and me, gave the impression that he had already been to the area in advance of the Americans' arrival. Thanh didn't seem very interested in the details of casualty resolution, and the local Public Security Police in Haiphong gave him a wide berth, indicating that he most likely held a powerful position in the Ministry of Public Security. When one cadre referred to Thanh as "Sanh," I asked him about the disparity. He subsequently informed Harvey and me that he also went by that name.

Now I knew that like the clandestine Communist operatives during the war, quite a few postwar cadre continued to use cover names, apparently for security reasons. Thanh would work with the POW/MIA team for about two more years before an apparent reassignment, with absolutely no explanation from the Vietnamese concerning his absence. As the senior U.S. field investigator, I would continue to unexpectedly encounter Thanh several times over the next eleven years at various locations throughout the country, including one occasion when I saw him at Noi Bai International Airport taking custody of refugees who had been forcefully repatriated from camps in Hong Kong. However, it wasn't until years later that we learned that Thanh had been the head of North Vietnam's Prison Department during the war. With that kind of background, he could have provided us much information. Yet he remained mostly silent throughout the trip.

After the brief meeting, at which the Vietnamese hammered home the difficulty in locating crash sites, the group moved by car to an expanse of rice fields bordering the ocean on the eastern edge of Haiphong in the direction of the Do Son peninsula. While the Vietnamese officials discussed the particulars of the case with local officials, I studied a map and a geographic printout of cases I had brought along for the trip. Based on a quick analysis, I informed the group of an incident involving an American aircraft that occurred at the same location during the war. This action caused Harvey to immediately become noticeably upset. Apparently Harvey believed that since I had a map and geographic printout for the area, I had been able to prepare myself based on some advance information from the Vietnamese that had not been shared with the other American members of the team. With little success, I explained to him that since a field trip had been a possibility and the group only intended to be in Hanoi for three days, I had assumed that any site visited would fall within a one day driving radius of the city. In order to be ready in the event of field trip, I had brought along maps as well as a printout of the surrounding area. Harvey seemed to understand what I was telling him, but he obviously didn't believe it.

The Vietnamese took us to view a mud filled crater, and after taking photographs, we proceeded to the beach where another "possible" crash site was said to be located on a distant sand bar. We found nothing. After taking more photos of the empty horizon above the mud flats the tired and muddy group began the trip back to Hanoi. Traffic on the return to the capital was even worse than it had been that morning on the way to the coast. Steering a precarious course between the large cargo trucks and the weaving mopeds and bicycles on the narrow road, the drivers of the Volga's kept everyone on the edge of their seats. Rather than cope with the stress, however, Harvey finally slid down into the sagging rear seat and somehow managed to doze off.

Back in Hanoi that evening I decided to take a stroll through the city to calm myself after the day's hectic schedule. Due to a lack of motorized vehicles the streets were ghostly quiet and only waves of bicycles could be seen undulating through the downtown area. After dark a local traffic law required that headlamps on all motorized vehicles be extinguished, with only the running lights illuminated. Unfortunately, some drivers assigned to foreign diplomatic missions were simply too squeamish about driving at night with no headlights in a large, crowded city with very few streetlights. As a result, whenever a vehicle with its headlamps on suddenly turned onto a busy street, those on bicycles temporarily lost their night vision, instantly resulting in a series of loud crashes. While walking along one street I witnessed a vivid example of this. A car suddenly passed by, probably driven by some foreign Embassy personnel, which immediately blinded a large group of Vietnamese cyclists. The ensuing sounds of crashes and people being thrown to the concrete were immediately followed by loud fits of cursing and screaming directed at the foreigners. I discreetly removed myself from the scene before their night vision returned.

The streets of central Hanoi were generally organized into guilds oriented toward a particular profession, or based on the type of goods sold there. For example, a street might be called "Silk Street" and all merchandise on that street would be made from silk. While out for my walk I happened onto a street where grave markers were carved from stone. I was amazed at the huge number of grave markers leaning against buildings and compound walls for several blocks. In some places the headstones were placed several rows deep. Then I noticed the names and dates on the headstones were those of young Vietnamese men who died during the 1979 war with China. I knew from news reports that both sides had suffered heavy casualties during the recent battles, but I really had no idea that the level of Vietnamese casualties had been so great.

The following day our group returned to Bangkok, without having gained any new information that might be useful in the accounting effort. But we all were in agreement that allowing the Americans to travel outside the confines of Hanoi was an important step forward and could reasonably be interpreted as a herald for future field investigation efforts. One positive side effect of the trip for me was that it brought home the importance of interviewing in the refugee camps. Based on these two interactions with the Vietnamese, it further reinforced to me that I had to prepare myself to deal with a clever enemy who not only had almost ten years to plan for their American adversaries, but decades of prior experience with the French. In essence, to succeed I would have to know more and think faster than the Vietnamese security cadre. To accomplish this and to counter Communist claims of not being able to locate witnesses, or to defeat assertions to the effect that the terrain had greatly changed over time, my only hope was to become completely familiar with each geographic area with a high density of loss incidents. I reasoned that by memorizing maps of the vicinity, supplemented by more up-to-date hand drawn sketches provided by refugees who had resided in the region for many years, I would be able to manage interviews conducted with witnesses introduced by the Communists. I understood the inherent danger of completely relying on the testimony of witnesses entirely under Communist control, and I vowed not only to make every conceivable effort to locate independent sources, but to also become as familiar as possible with the countryside of Vietnam. I was determined to strive for a level of expertise exceeding even that of the Hanoi cadre. Otherwise, without an extensive background of all aspects of the issue, from the war to the local terrain, to the units and the cadre who led them, not only for just a particular year but also for almost a decade of war, we were completely at their mercy.

I knew this was a formidable challenge just to absorb such a prodigious amount of information, but even more was required. Alongside learning about the various units, I needed to understand the complete Communist POW organizational structure and polices, a structure hidden from us by a cloak of wartime secrecy and deliberate postwar mystery. I was well aware that Communist doctrine regarding the exploitation of prisoners and remains dictated that nothing was to be overlooked if it could be used to further Party policy. Their wartime policy was to extract useful intelligence from American prisoners, generate propaganda statements designed to influence the anti-war movements in the prisoners' home countries, and also to collect the remains of the dead to be used in future negotiations. Broken down to its basic strategy, live prisoners were to be used for political concessions, remains for economic considerations. For live prisoners, it was also important to "educate" and convert the POWs to Communist beliefs so that upon their return, the POWs could lead a Communist revolution in their homelands. Remains could be doled out over time for money, either directly or in the guise of economic or humanitarian assistance.

We knew the Communist forces had recovered some unknown number of remains. We also knew there existed a wartime Communist policy of purposely concealing remains to keep us guessing as to the missing man's true status. Without knowing if a man is dead or alive, it's difficult to stem any possible intelligence damage, let alone assuage the uncertainty for the man's family. The problem lay in overcoming any Communist deception, while at the same time convincing them our effort wasn't a thinly disguised intelligence-gathering operation, all the while persuading the American families that we were doing an honorable job.

Since the Communists had traditionally used their own postwar teams for intelligence gathering missions, or to install secret caches of arms and ammunition, they assumed we would also seek to take advantage of a similar opportunity. Moreover, in view of the fact that they undoubtedly had something to hide in regards to various missing men who were captured and then probably tortured to death, along with the entire matter of harvesting remains in exchange for economic considerations, the Indochinese leadership was intent on not allowing the U.S. to turn this important agit-prop weapon against them. Undoubtedly deep hatred, mistrust, and ideology also played major roles in their reactions. From their perspective we were still the imperialist giants who had waged a devastating war on their homeland, and they were suspicious to the point of paranoia regarding American intentions in the region. Our methodical approach was designed to calm those fears and edge our countries toward civil relations, as much as bitter ideological enemies a decade removed from fierce combat could enjoy a semblance of normal diplomatic contacts.

After comparing the information collected from interrogations, captured documents and signals intelligence during the war with that obtained from postwar refugee interviews, I began to see another consistent theme emerge. The Vietnamese had placed great emphasis not only on capturing American POWs or their remains, but also on recovering and cataloguing any material possessions. Some refugees reported that after hastily burying the bodies of Americans during periods of intense fighting, cadre often arrived in the area several days and at times even weeks after the bodies had been buried. The purpose of the visits was to inventory and photograph bodies, as well as every item of personal effects associated with the incident.

Remains and personal effects were not the only items to be harvested from the wreckage of American aircraft. Refugees also reported having observed, and in some cases having been actively involved in, the salvage of downed U.S. aircraft. According to the refugees, the recovery operations were organized and sanctioned by Hanoi. With the exception of a few sites reserved for future media visits, most aircraft crash sites were scavenged for metal and any other items of value shortly after the war ended. According to the refugee sources, due to the amount of gold used in engine welds, electronics and other aircraft assemblies a single U.S. aircraft with two engines, an A-6 for example, could yield as much as twelve ounces of precious gold. Although the profit from the sale of the recovered metal was shared by the local administrations at the district and village levels, any skeletal remains, weapons, or personal effects discovered during the course of such operations were routinely turned in to the authorities. My greatest anxiety was that by the time we would finally be allowed into Vietnam or Laos to conduct recovery operations, the Communists would have already cleaned the old battlefields and then deny that they had retrieved anything. This would be followed by exorbitant charges for excavating these sites, leaving us so little to find that we would chase our tails trying to determine the true outcome of our aviators' final missions, to say nothing of the even more difficult ground losses. Sadly, my suspicions came true with the first two excavations.

I was also keenly aware of a detailed study of Communist Vietnamese methods in exploiting the remains issue in the aftermath of the French Indochina War. The report, published by the Rand Corporation for the U.S. government in January 1969, declared:

> *Despite the substantial political and economic concession the French have made to Hanoi since 1954, France has never received a full accounting for its missing and dead. The Vietnamese Communist government has consistently circumvented and violated the terms of the 1954 agreement concerning the accounting for France's missing servicemen. Hanoi's actions clearly demonstrate that its only interest in the French military graves in Vietnam and the requests for remains by the families of the deceased is in the economic and political benefits that the Vietnamese Government can derive from control of these remains. We should keep this in mind in dealing with Hanoi. We can anticipate that Hanoi's objective is to obtain increasingly large economic and political concessions in exchange for piecemeal releases of remains and information about our missing servicemen.*[8]

Based on what I had seen in the field, I considered the Rand Corporation assessment completely accurate. I was also concerned by another appraisal rendered by the government of France in response to a postwar inquiry by the U.S. State

Department in 1976; "The French believe that the U.S. may encounter some of the same basic problems from the Vietnamese: broad political 'payment' to establish a program and then steep financial concessions for each body at each step of the way." The State Department then added this comment:

> *The PAVN has remained the DRV representative for these matters. No deserters or ralliers have been repatriated. No remains of Prisoners of War who died in captivity have been repatriated. Quai officials commented that the operation appeared to be run to provide revenue for the DRV. The French found that they had to pay fairly stiff commercial prices for each body. They thought the U.S. would have to do the same.*[9]

I later learned from discussions with officials in the French Embassy in Hanoi that the French were in the process of completing their own casualty resolution operations in Vietnam. The French Assembly had passed a law that any family could repatriate remains, and the French government would pay for it. When the Vietnamese got wind of this, they immediately began charging large sums of money for each body. Tired of the Vietnamese ripping them off, in 1986, the French decided to repatriate all the graves, some twenty-four thousand remains. Although the French officials would not reveal the specific amount paid to Vietnam's Communist Party to elicit cooperation, they did indicate that the sum was "quite large." Knowing that for the previous thirty years the Vietnamese had heavily relied upon the French payments for cemetery maintenance to finance most of their Party operations, I found it strange that Hanoi would suddenly be willing to kill the "goose that laid the golden egg." Instinctively I feared the closing of the French "revenue source" would have on our efforts. After mulling the matter over, it was obvious that since the same officials previously working with the French were now being transferred to work with American POW/MIA specialists, Hanoi already had a new goose in its sights.

Following up on the September 1982 League delegation visit to Vientiane and Hanoi and the December 1982 Technical Talk, I traveled to both cities for further meetings. Between February 12-14, 1983, the JCRC had its first meeting with the Lao. The U.S. Embassy had pushed hard for serious discussions during this follow-up trip, but the cautious Lao viewed it primarily as a get acquainted meeting. During their visit, the League requested a crash site survey as soon as possible in order to begin an excavation. The Lao, however, did not permit the survey for another eleven months after the League visit because according to them, an investigation would be too difficult during the rainy season. Also, publicity by the *Bangkok Post* of a Bo Gritz attempt to covertly enter Laos using Lao resistance personnel to search for alleged American POWs was a convenient excuse for the Lao to delay our mission. I doubt that the weather had much to do with our visit. It was more likely that they needed some time to prepare the site for our excavation, and to confer with their mentors, the Vietnamese. The Vietnamese were always quietly behind the scenes in Laos, trying to make the Lao policy an adjunct of their own.

Further Technical Talks with the Vietnamese occurred in March and early June 1983. Again we plied the Vietnamese with case folders, but the only notable aspect of either trip was the Vietnamese announcement during the March 9-12 meeting that they were ready to repatriate twelve remains. Increasingly isolated by most of the international community, their economy crumbling, I believe certain factions in the Vietnamese government and Party were now looking for ways to expand their contacts with the American government. Regardless, the Vietnamese remained hypersensitive to any perceived slight or hostile rhetoric emanating from the American side.

The visit to Hawaii by the VNOSMP members, followed by the visit to Hanoi by the JCRC personnel, set in motion what would eventually become a fairly regular exchange between the two sides regarding the issue of casualty resolution. Very few of the meetings, however, would occur on American soil. Due to their military adventures in Cambodia and the resultant conflict with their Chinese neighbor, the Vietnamese were flat broke. Although they strongly desired to break out of their international isolation by sending their cadre abroad to extol the virtues of socialism, and thus gain sympathy in the form of foreign aid for Vietnam, the Vietnamese were in no position to travel or fund trips overseas except for senior officials visiting the UN, a few international meetings, or to fellow Communist states. Instead, due to their huge collective ego, the Vietnamese could only drop subtle hints aimed at prompting American offers of assistance. Fearful of being labeled as beggars, they were extremely reluctant to ask for or suggest that the frequency of trips by Vietnamese officials to the U.S. be increased. They made their needs known, and then waited for us to submit a proposal to meet those needs. Cash-strapped, any Party personnel on official business turned over a significant portion of any currency they received to Party coffers.

The meetings did provide a valuable venue for coordinating efforts and exchanging ideas with the Vietnamese officials involved in the accounting process. The talks were also expanded to include the Lao and Cambodians. But I never lost sight of the fact that at least 85 percent of the Americans missing in Laos, and close to 90 percent of the Americans missing in Cambodia, were lost in areas under the wartime control of Vietnamese Communist forces. Although designed to be a give-and-take exchange regarding the POW/MIA issue, the Vietnamese officials also used the early Technical Talks as a forum to air grievances on many subjects. For two countries with no diplomatic relations at this time, the Vietnamese attempted to initiate dialogue aimed at issues outside the scope of POW/MIA. In such cases the U.S. official on the receiving side would politely decline from becoming engaged in discussing the matter, but at the same time would pledge to pass on the points raised by the originating side. In diplomatic terms such points were called "verbal nonpapers," and any substantive discussion of topics not directly related to POW/MIA would be called "side margins."

More often than not, the American participants would leave the meeting empty handed, which would result in an immediate drop in morale for some team members. To keep the U.S. side dangling, however, the Vietnamese side would strategically release information at preplanned intervals. For me, this gradual issuance of information was not unexpected and generally followed the outline contained in the Rand paper on the French experience at casualty resolution in Vietnam. The piecemeal tactic required a great deal of patience from the Americans, and the American team members stayed on the edges of their seats throughout each meeting, hoping that they would have some degree of progress to report to their superiors at the conclusion. At times, critical remarks by some POW/MIA family member organizations and activists to the effect that the Technical Talks could more appropriately be described as "begging and groveling meetings" were not far off the mark. However, the talks were necessary to further even the slightest hint of progress.

Despite the increased overtures, we began to see the importance of the Vietnamese policy on recovering personal effects as well as remains. In mid-1982, refugees began flooding us with what became known as "dog tag" reports. Some refugees provided actual dog tags while others made copies by rubbing a pencil lead across slips of paper placed on the raised letters and numbers stamped into the tags. Others handed over photocopies. The dog tag reports came from a wide assortment of people—refugees, defectors, smugglers, volunteer aid workers in the camps, civilian and military officials of the host countries where refugee camps were located, tourists and business people traveling to Vietnam, and sometimes even foreign diplomats. The small metal disks or slips of paper were sometimes mailed from Vietnam through the postal service. In some cases, the Sources resorted to ingenious means of surreptitiously sending or carrying the information out of Vietnam. Some were placed inside cakes, toothpaste tubes, beneath photos or inside handicrafts. More cautious Sources went to the trouble of sewing the information into the hems or collars of clothing they were wearing when departing Vietnam to avoid detection during physical searches at the airports. Although we received thousands of dog tag reports, only a very small percentage of them were actually correlated to missing Americans. We nevertheless filed a report on each dog tag or paper copy we received. They were forwarded to the DIA's Special Office for POW/MIA Affairs, which attempted to examine them for trends.

During one trip to Washington I received a DIA briefing that was focused on the dog tag reports we were receiving in the field. Robert Destatte and another long-time Vietnam hand, Sedgwick Tourison, who were assigned to the DIA office at the time, presented this particular briefing. In order to explain their theory concerning the dog tag phenomenon, they arranged charts on a wall in a conference room similar to those used by intelligence and law enforcement agencies while tracking down leads or clues during the investigation of a complex case. As one part of their study, they noted distinguishable marks peculiar to certain copy machines in Ho Chi Minh City. Other cross-referencing related to the number of times particular names or serial numbers appeared. The consensus at the time in the DIA Special Office was that the dog tag reports were a Vietnamese directed misinformation campaign and the primary agency behind it was the Ministry of the Interior, which was alternately designated over the years as the Ministry of Public Security. The presumed purpose of the scheme was twofold: first, tax our collection and analytical abilities to the point that other, more important information regarding the critical live prisoner or remains issues went unnoticed, and thus concurrently create suspicion of all refugee reporting; second, in 1984 Vietnamese officials bluntly told American investigators that the dog tag reporting would make future investigations of cases lengthy, complicated, and expensive, and would require the United States to directly fund Vietnamese efforts for joint investigations, along with cash incentives for finding and confiscating remains supposedly in "private" hands.

After the briefing Harvey asked me for my views on the DIA's theory. After considering all the information provided I believed that the DIA was correct in its assessment of Vietnamese intentions regarding the dog tag reporting. While DIA believed the deluge of reports were designed to tie them up, and they probably wanted us to refrain from sending them in, we had little choice because a small percentage of the dog tags were being correlated to unaccounted for American personnel. Therefore, I felt compelled to advise Harvey to continue our reporting. However, as time went on I began to believe there was another motive to the Vietnamese actions. I considered that the large increase in dog tag reporting within several years of the Vietnamese vehemently denying the accusations regarding remains warehousing was not a coincidence. Once the Mortician told us about the warehousing, along with the other reports we received indicating that Vietnam had cataloged a relatively large number of American remains, given the previous and current angry denials by Hanoi, the Communist officials were now pressed to find a way to exit their dilemma of returning remains without being accused of the inhumane warehousing of bones. They needed to find a scapegoat so that when the previously collected remains were returned with evidence of storage, they had someone else to blame. To that end, the Communists created "remains traders" so that the blame would be placed on private scavengers, not on a callow Vietnamese government. After some back and forth with DIA on the subject, in the end Harvey agreed with my analysis of the situation, and even indicated willingness to request additional personnel to cover the increase in reporting. Harvey also instructed the JCRC analysts to begin compiling a roster of names received through dog tag reports with a numerical reference as to how many times each name had been previously reported.

By the mid-1980s I felt vindicated when the SRV began to unilaterally hand over full skeletons with chemical preservatives and other obvious signs of storage on them that they claimed had been confiscated by the Public Security police from "remains traders." While Childress had negotiated out many of the remains, which were returned in several large groups, as I had anticipated, based on the large number of dog tag reports, the Vietnamese began to explain these sudden discoveries of missing Americans by blaming it on "grave robbers." Reluctant to label fellow North Vietnamese residents with such repugnant titles, the Communist authorities further refined their description of such unscrupulous elements as "decadent remnants of the former regime in the South," which had managed to enter remote areas throughout Vietnam in search of American remains with the express purpose of selling them for monetary gain. As an example, when I investigated the case of Air Force Captains Busch and Apodaca in Quang Binh, the province just above the DMZ in North Vietnam, the VNOSMP cadre explained the absence of remains at the crash site by claiming that although Captain Apodaca stayed inside the aircraft and was killed at the time, his body was removed from the site by remains traders from Hue, which is inside the boundary of the former RVN.

The Communists were also making a strong case for "remains traders" having taken materials from sites to allay suspicions that they had previously cleaned the sites. The blame for a lack of remains could now be placed on local scavengers, which in turn could dampen U.S. pressures on Vietnam about a remains warehouse, especially if the U.S. reached an analytical conclusion, either from intelligence work or by political fiat, that the Vietnamese were no longer warehousing and therefore, were cooperating on this important part of the issue.

Further, if we examined a crash site and managed to find a few remains, and the CILHI was able to identify the small number of bones through DNA, the family might be skeptical of the identification. If the U.S. Government insisted on upholding the identification and dismissed the family's concerns, the family might become alienated and align themselves with more radical activist groups critical of the government's handling of the issue. If the American officials respected the family's concerns and continued the investigation, it would be an expensive and time-consuming endeavor, much to the financial benefit of both the Vietnamese and Lao. Since many aircraft went down in a densely populated area, with military units located nearby, it would seem logical that any crash incident was immediately investigated and any remains, wreckage and personal effects were collected and inventoried by Communist authorities in the usual manner prescribed by policy. Instead of turning over such material to us in the spirit of their oft-stated cooperation, we had to spend a significant amount of money hiring local labor to dig up the crash site, only to find what they had missed in their excavation. Responsibility for the absence of such material was then easily transferred onto the shoulders of "grave robbers" and "remains traders."

While the Communist-orchestrated dog tag reports were designed to create external analytical problems for us and provide a convenient excuse for the Vietnamese to return already harvested remains through private citizens, we also had internal problems with the more important live sighting reports. There was a distinct division of labor between the Bangkok LNO office, the JCRC headquarters, and the DIA POW/MIA Special Office in Washington. At the LNO office, for several reasons our role was strictly that of collectors of information. In the intelligence world there usually exists a doctrinal wall between the collector and the analyst, mainly so that the analysts can objectively perform their duty without becoming emotionally involved with an issue or a Source. DIA did the lion's share of the scrutiny of the Sources and all of the live-sighting reports, while Ray Spock and the analysts in his JCRC headquarters section in Hawaii performed relatively detailed studies of crash sites, grave sites and remains.

DIA rigidly enforced this policy with the caveats that the field people didn't have all the facts, that we were simply seeing the raw information, and if not careful, we could inadvertently raise the hopes of the families or create future analytical problems. DIA had the final say-so on any type of analysis, usually adding a one-page report providing their study of the merits of the live-sighting report. The JCRC headquarters in Hawaii did the reports dealing with gravesites. Additionally, Spock in particular did not want us in the LNO office participating in the analytical process, since it might threaten the positions of his analysts. This was especially true in cases where the information received could be correlated to a specific individual, because this automatically created the requirement that the information not only be placed in the file of the individual associated with the report, the information would also have to be shared with the MIA's family. In many cases a less than timely transmittal of the information to the family would result in a complaint, thus increasing the workload on Spock's section. By prohibiting interviewers in the field from correlating the information at the time of collection on the report, Spock and his analysts were able to adopt a more leisurely approach to their analysis. This time lapse was further increased by not including the date that the reports were received by the Records and Analysis Division on the final analytical results sent out to the families.

In many cases the results of a live-sighting interview would not be returned to the collector for months and in some cases even years. Due to the fact that we had no analytical tracking capability at the Liaison office, we could never be sure that we received analysis of all the reports we submitted since we were in the field so much and not in the office managing the voluminous paperwork. Still, with no local analysts available we did what we could to conduct a "field analysis" of each case in order to facilitate follow-up and comparative analysis as much as possible, but due to turf problems with JCRC headquarters at one point we were instructed to move any comments to a separate report to prevent the information from being associated with the case. This was apparently based on the legal requirement that any information correlated to a specific individual be included in his case file and at some point released to the family of the missing man. Since this would have almost doubled the workload and the administrative burden for the JCRC headquarters personnel to publish these informal reports, we resigned ourselves to making handwritten comments on the file copies of the documents that we retained in the Liaison Office. It eventually became obvious to the collectors like myself that we were programmed only to look for new Sources to maintain the volume of reports, without considering the quality or applicability of the information being collected on a daily basis. If we disagreed with an analytical decision regarding the viability of a Source our only option was to add our own handwritten remarks to the Bangkok file copies. If I disagreed with any of their conclusions, no protest channel was available. My only recourse was to make the notations on my copies of the files and then go out searching for corroborating sources. In the future, these Bangkok files with their handwritten notes would be a major source of contention.

Because of the lack of analytical return, I undertook an additional duty project of sorting all the reports collected by the Liaison Office, and a large number of reports submitted by the headquarters as well as other agencies, into files organized by province. This was similar to the projects I had done during the war such as when I worked on the "VC/NVA Terminology Guide." In the early days we had no computers, so I created manual listings in order to begin cross-checking not only the new information, but old wartime intelligence as well. My personal system included creating rosters by aircraft type, reports by province, and other types of lists. In other words, to make the file functional I placed the live-sighting reports in separate folders based on the location where they occurred. With a secretary's help, by 1986 I had these folders completed and had a good start on the reports dealing with remains and dog tags. My strategy was to organize a collection plan based on the locations of the sightings of live Americans, but after producing two copies I forwarded one to the Records and Analysis Division in the JCRC headquarters and I loaned the second copy to the DIA's Stony Beach[10] team in Bangkok. Unfortunately, that was the last time I ever saw the "by province" live-sighting file, as they claimed both were lost.

Even though Spock prevented us from conducting pertinent analysis regarding the reports, his Records and Analysis Division rarely produced significant analytical comments. In most cases the R&A unit would only include a brief remark to the effect that "JCRC files contain no information indicating that the individual is alive." However, once a Source of live-sighting information was interviewed and a report published, shortly thereafter we normally received a request for follow-up from the DIA's Special Office. The requirements or questions to be used during subsequent interviews were quite detailed and usually asked for the Source's background from the time of his birth until such time as he departed his native country to defect or enter refugee channels. Some of the questions posed included a physical description of the terrain and buildings at home, the names of teachers throughout the period that the Source attended primary, secondary and college level institutions, the names of everyone else who escaped on the same boat, friends, relatives or acquaintances in foreign countries, dates and circumstances of certain events that transpired over the years and other seemingly endless, miniscule details. I was aware that the particulars were being asked in order for the DIA to be in a position to gauge the credibility and reliability of the Sources providing the information. But I also learned to my chagrin that the large amount of information was at times being misused to "debunk" many of the reports due to the inability of the Sources to recall every fact being asked during later, supplementary interview sessions. While it was critical to separate the fabricators from the potentially viable sources, the vast amount of detail was also occasionally used to browbeat Sources that were trying to be helpful but like most people, often couldn't remember precise details clearly or simply were wrong in their recollection of certain events. Sometimes it seemed that the amount of time and resources expended, as well as the inherent emotional cost of actually producing a truthful witness of living Americans, was so potentially great that some analysts subconsciously didn't want it to occur. From this developed what became known as the "mind-set to debunk."

MIA family members and activists coined the term when they gradually became frustrated when reports of live-sightings were consistently deemed fabrications, or at best inconclusive. Those reports that were not easily dismissed as fabrications festered in the files of the DIA while policy makers remained in a quandary as to what action should be taken to resolve them. Since the standards for launching a rescue mission were so rigid—and considering the ramification perhaps justifiably so—there was no easy answer. In the interim, criticism regarding this attitude was temporarily deflected by the prospect that at some point in time Vietnam would allow U.S. investigators access to the areas where the live Americans were reportedly observed, and thorough, unannounced investigations conducted by experts might be allowed. No one involved in the issue knew when this time would come, but eventually it did. As usual, though, even that optimism was unfounded. Nothing about the investigations was thorough or unannounced. However, despite all the setbacks and intransigence shown by the Communists, after continual United States government pressure to resume efforts to account for the missing, the Communists relented. The real operations we had sought for so long now were about to begin.

Chapter Eight

Full Shovels, Empty Caskets

SHORTLY AFTER THE JUNE 1983 Technical Talks, Jim Tully decided to retire from his Civil Service position at the JCRC Liaison Office. When the Personnel Office in Hawaii posted the job, I inquired about the position. Even though I had spent twenty-three years in the Army, Tully's civilian position was essentially the same job but paid twice as much. While I had some misgivings about leaving the Army, since I was already working full time in civilian clothes, subconsciously I believe I had made the mental break. I soon learned that in addition to higher pay than my military salary, the civilian billet allowed for a paid twenty-day home leave back to the U.S. every two years. Since I had not returned to the States to see my mother and stepfather for a long time, this was indeed a welcome perk. As expected, a relatively large number of people responded to the job announcement. The applicants included several members of the Honolulu-based academic community as well as from the local retired military population. One candidate was even a former Ambassador.

I talked to Harvey about applying for the job, but I was surprised to learn that in order to apply, let alone qualify, I would first have to retire from the military and then submit my application after my retirement papers had already been processed. If I didn't get the job I was literally out on the street. Harvey aptly described the tough combination of leaving the military and the consequences of not being selected, along with the high level of competition, as the proverbial "rolling of the dice." Nevertheless, I discussed the situation with Nam-Xuan and we decided that I should apply and accept the risk to the family.

I submitted my military retirement paperwork, and after the family was packed and sent home to Arkansas, I forwarded my application to the Civilian Personnel Office at Pearl Harbor. As the only applicant with language skills in Vietnamese, Lao and Thai I believed I was in a fairly good position. But even with my abilities the competition was still close. After being notified that I had the job, I heard that I beat the next best contender by only a scant two points, probably due to my five-point veteran's preference in hiring and additional five points for my Purple Heart award. My retirement application having been approved, I flew to Hawaii from Bangkok where I said goodbye to the military on July 31, 1983. Harvey had a small party for me and I was awarded the Legion of Merit. I was sworn in for the new position on August 1. One drawback to taking the job was that I had to depart for Thailand the same day, with no opportunity for leave back in America.

This was especially troublesome, as I had wanted to visit my stepfather. He was in poor health due to serious wounds suffered in combat during WWII. Reluctantly, I settled for a telephone call. Unfortunately, I never got home to see him, and during one interview trip to the Cambodian border, my stepfather passed away. Mather tried to contact me through the refugee offices, but since there were no communications from the remote camps, I did not learn of his death until several days after the fact. When I returned to Bangkok, Nam-Xuan met me in the yard with tears in her eyes. The funeral had been held the day prior to my return to Bangkok. It was a terrible blow; he had helped raise me and I didn't get a chance to say goodbye. It was another in a long series of sacrifices my colleagues and I made for the POW/MIA issue.

Fortunately a competent investigator, Army Warrant Officer Thomas R. McKay, quickly filled my vacated military position in the Bangkok Liaison Office. Reassigned from Army Special Forces, McKay was a fluent Vietnamese linguist. I had known McKay since Operation Homecoming when he served as the interpreter for the Reception Team receiving the American POWs released in South Vietnam in February 1973 at Loc Ninh.

Just before I took the new position, however, the issue heated up again. Secretary of State George Schultz traveled to Bangkok at the end of June 1983 to meet the various Foreign Ministers of the Southeast Asian countries. During his remarks, he publicly castigated the Vietnamese for their "cruel actions" in storing remains, a comment that Childress had drafted as part of the Secretary's talking points. In typical fashion, the prickly Vietnamese promptly broke off further Technical Talks. Yet the Vietnamese eventually signaled an increased willingness to engage in more substantive discussions by passing the POW/MIA issue to a more senior interlocutor, Foreign Minister Nguyen Co Thach. Richard Childress and Ann Mills Griffiths moved quickly to patch up the strained relationship and maintain the dialogue. Griffiths met with Thach in New York City on October 3, 1983. At the meeting, Thach at first railed about U.S. policies, but under questioning, Thach made a startling comment: he agreed Americans might be living outside the central government's control, but disclaimed any personal knowledge. After the meeting, they had dinner in a private suite, during which Griffiths continually stressed the importance of resolving the issue on "humanitarian grounds," a position Childress had developed as a face-saving device for the Vietnamese to return remains we knew they had recovered. In addition, Childress developed the code word "Hanoi/Haiphong area" to describe the warehouse. Childress also stated that while resolution of the issue should not be perceived as a precondition to improved relations between the two countries, by rapidly establishing a viable plan for moving forward both sides were in essence making an investment toward better future relations. Eventually, Childress and Griffiths convinced the Vietnamese to host another high-level U.S. delegation. Bridging from those discussions, Richard Armitage, Childress, and Griffiths traveled again to Hanoi in February 1984 and managed to get the stalled Technical Talks started once more. However, the Vietnamese repeatedly postponed the meetings, and it wasn't until August that the talks were held. During this same time, the Vietnamese turned over another eight remains, all showing signs of storage.

Our continued hope was to gain permission to begin examining crash sites and former detention facilities throughout Vietnam, and of course, searching for any men still alive. The U.S. Government had developed a long-range plan to solve the two issues of recovering remains and unraveling the live prisoner question. We envisioned the initial first step to be excavations of aircraft crash sites in the Hanoi-Haiphong corridor, mainly because of the high-density of losses and the proximity to the capital. Once in progress, and after we had built some degree of trust, the type of digs would be expanded to locations where American personnel were either purposefully buried by Communist forces, or simply left behind by either side without having been interred. The incidents included a wide range of situations involving destroyed vehicles, ground incidents in enemy controlled territory, losses at sea, and bunker complexes that collapsed due to enemy fire or exploding ammunition.[1]

After we had finally gained clearance to conduct excavations in the three countries of Indochina, our hoped-for next step would be detailed investigations of the cases associated with the men who were last-known to be alive at the time of their disappearance. Depending on the depth of cooperation from the Communists, these investigations would be patterned after basic "missing persons" searches similar to those undertaken by law enforcement agencies throughout the world.

Believing that excavations would soon be permitted, DIA and JCRC began to search the database for possible crash sites that would not only enable us to recover remains, but would be acceptable to the Communists. When I was asked for my input as to which crash sites might be suitable to the governments involved, I soon realized that the security threat perceived by the Communists in allowing American military and civilian officials to enter their countries was only one important factor. A secondary security consideration was that areas other than where the actual excavations would be conducted would have to be transgressed by Americans during the course of the operations. I also realized that customs and immigration concerns would require the American teams to initially land with their equipment and supplies at an international airport approved for visitors from the West. In the case of Laos this would be Vientiane, and for Vietnam, Noi Bai Airport just north of Hanoi.

Based on my recommendations, we decided to break the icy state of affairs by first proposing to excavate sites in areas that could be easily controlled by the host countries. While we obviously wanted to go after the high-profile cases first, our feelings were that the Vietnamese would not allow trained observers to travel freely throughout the country, especially until they had an opportunity to assess the security implications. If it seems like we were acquiescing to the Communist obsessions, we had little choice but to make the concession and hope for the best. We were essentially looking for a site that fit within their established security concerns—without either of us having to acknowledge that fact—and therefore making it difficult to deny our request. The Vietnamese were not only subtler than their Lao brethren in dealing with foreigners they were also even more paranoid regarding the security aspect. While both governments were obsessed about security, the Lao were more straightforward in indicating this fact. The Vietnamese, however, never made this point directly. Rather than cite security concerns they would simply either ignore our travel requests, or in some cases would claim that the people would be upset by the presence of Americans in their area due to war-time destruction.

Thinking back on the many flights I had taken from Thailand to interview refugees in Hong Kong, Macao and Beijing, I recalled how I had been able to look down from the commercial airline flights and observe the terrain of Salavan province in central Laos. I knew that since both Laos and Vietnam were strapped for cash, in exchange for a fee they had permitted foreign commercial carriers to fly a route that would transverse the middle portion of Laos and Vietnam. The aircraft crossed into Laos near Pakse and traveled east, exiting Vietnam near Danang. The aircraft going west simply reversed the process. The route paralleled the long-established "amber" route used by commercial carriers during the earlier stages of the Vietnam War.

Considering that the approval for commercial aircraft to over fly the area had come from the highest levels of the Communist governments only after years of haggling, I recommended that the JCRC request approval from the Lao government for an excavation directly beneath the commercial flight route. Since it was already considered a "safe" area, the Communists would have less reason to reject our proposal. Consequently, for the preliminary operation in Laos I further reasoned that the Lao government would most likely be inclined to allow U.S. personnel to fly near the Mekong River. Since the area near the broad waterway was currently subject to extensive monitoring from adjacent Thailand, the Lao would assume that the U.S. was already in possession of considerable strategic and tactical data for the region. Thus we were looking for a locale along the commercial air route near the Mekong River. I realized with a start that the Hart case would be a perfect choice, especially since the National League of Families had previously visited the site.

For operations in Vietnam, at first I recommended a site in close proximity to the Noi Bai Airport. I added a caveat by proposing that after the completion of the excavation at the first site, the JCRC should approach the Vietnamese for permission to quickly conduct operations in areas where large-scale building projects were planned that might adversely impact future undertakings. I knew that Vietnam was attempting to develop its infrastructure, and such massive construction projects might disturb or destroy sites where Americans were known to be missing. My concerns were well-founded: I had recently learned during routine monitoring of official Vietnamese radio broadcasts that huge hydroelectric projects were underway in both North and South Vietnam. In recommending future site locations in the potentially affected areas, I cited as an example the Tri An area of the old War Zone "D" in Dong Nai province, formerly Bien Hoa and Long Khanh provinces. According to official accounts, a large portion of the old War Zone "D" would gradually become inundated to establish a water reservoir capable of supporting the generation of electrical power for Ho Chi Minh City. Considering the extent of the project and what was on the drawing board, I realized that once the area was flooded the costs for underwater recovery efforts would be insurmountable.

However, the JCRC analysts in Hawaii disagreed with me and seemed to think that operations in the South were too far into the future to even discuss. Harvey pledged to give my recommendations some serious thought, but ultimately he relied heavily on his Hawaii-based JCRC analysts for guidance. I continued to argue that the Vietnamese officials, while dogmatic, were nonetheless practical, and I believed that by fully explaining the situation to our Vietnamese counterparts we could gain approval for the operation in time to be effective. After broaching the issue again several times with Harvey without success while the dam project continued to progress, I finally resigned myself to concentrating on the original Hanoi area plan. Unfortunately, as I predicted, the Tri An area was inundated prior to our scheduling any operations there.

As we began to plan for future field operations in Vietnam, there was a considerable thirst in U.S. intelligence circles not only for POW/MIA information, but data on the current political, economic, and military situation in the country.

As part of my own research effort, each time I went to Vietnam for technical meetings or field investigations, I tried to purchase Vietnamese publications, primarily PAVN unit histories and those dealing with tactics and strategy. I also obtained a large number of technical publications, including dictionaries with technical terms. Since the publications were often official accounts by PAVN units of engagements with U.S. forces, they were often marked "For Internal Distribution" *(Luu hanh Noi bo)* or "Secret" *(Mat)*.

Obviously, the publications were not available to foreigners, but during trips to Vietnam I learned of a location in downtown Hanoi where street vendors were said to be selling official Communist publications, albeit for a relatively high price. Intrigued, I went to the site and looked at some of it. I was astonished to see that many of the items being sold were marked "Secret." Although somewhat verbose and at times heavily saturated with propaganda, many of the unit histories provided accounts of loss incidents of American personnel during various battles and campaigns. At least some of the information could be correlated to loss incidents that we were investigating, so I began buying like crazy. My pockets stuffed with thin plastic shopping bags from the Bangkok Embassy commissary, each time I set out for the "book store" I set a blistering pace on a circuitous route to shake the security tail. Some of the people I bought material from were quite afraid of being compromised, and their operations were covert to the point that it was almost like a drug buy.

On one occasion when I was unable to find anything new, I worked a deal with some youths for "ordering out." The following day they showed up with books from the personal collections in the private libraries of senior PAVN officers. I received so much material that I was afraid to pack it inside my suitcase for fear it might be searched. Instead, I hid my treasure trove in a large cardboard box. Sure enough, when we departed the hotel for the airport there was a mix-up in luggage and my box was left in the hotel lobby. Since much of the material was classified I thought I was about to encounter serious problems with our hosts. When I told Harvey about the contents of the missing box he was noticeably upset, but luckily the flight was delayed and I was able to recover the fortunately unopened box. This particular incident served as a good lesson for me, and in the future I kept my purchases to a minimum.

Although negotiations in Laos stalled due to security issues stemming from the much-hyped foray of Bo Gritz, the Lao finally consented to allow us to make the site survey, which was conducted on December 21, 1983. I participated as a member of a JCRC/CILHI team that surveyed the crash site of the AC-130 "Spectre" Gunship site where Anne Hart's husband had been lost. Even though the National League of Families delegation had previously examined the site during its visit in September 1982, an initial JCRC site inspection was necessary before we could properly begin to excavate. While I was sure the Lao weren't pleased about Gritz, I believe that they also wanted plenty of time to visit the crash site in advance to ensure that there were no surprises, especially spontaneous witnesses. They were also concerned with the security aspect, and wanted adequate personnel in place in Pakse and at the remote site. This would also give them an opportunity to call a meeting of the Communist party subchapter of the guesthouse where we were to stay in order for all staff to be briefed on contacts with American officials. During an earlier Vientiane meeting with our Lao counterparts we discussed the schedule for the trip, how much time we would be allowed on site, what type of equipment we could bring, who from the American Embassy in Vientiane would accompany us, the fact that no digging would take place during the survey, and that no materials would be taken from the site.

Soon after the meeting in Vientiane, the Survey team was lifted into the area by an aging Soviet-built MI-6 helicopter. As usual, travel to and from anywhere throughout Indochina was an adventure. The appearance of the oil-stained, dinged up Lao helicopter raised more than a few safety concerns, which in the name of diplomacy we decided to overlook. I also took no comfort from the fact that the Lao pilot flew the chopper with a case of locally produced Lao beer wedged between the front seats.

Surviving our teeth-clenching flight, we arrived in Pakse just before dark. Our team spent a miserable night in a hot and humid guesthouse with very little water available for bathing or drinking. The following morning at daybreak we were flown via the same aging helicopter to a natural clearing near the crash site. I considered the initial survey very important, not only for the precedent it was making, since this was the first effort, but in regards to lingering suspicions regarding potential survivors.

The case involving Captain Hart was controversial. The ill-fated Spectre 17 gunship took off on December 21, 1972, when the specially designed, high-tech aircraft was tasked with an infrared sensor mission and interdiction mission in Laos. After engaging a ground target, the aircraft was hit in the left wing by return enemy fire. Fuel soon began seeping into the cargo compartment. Between the fuel leak and wing damage, the pilot declared an emergency and began to return to base. A second Spectre aircraft designated Spectre 07 just departing on a similar mission was diverted to fly escort for the stricken Spectre 17. While en route to Spectre 17's location the second aircraft observed a bright fireball plunging toward the ground. Upon arrival in the crash area the orbiting aircraft made radio contact with two survivors. Both men were rescued that same night but no contact was established with other crewmembers. The two survivors indicated that everyone had been aware of the extremely serious situation prior to the crash, but neither of them observed anyone else exit the aircraft.

The following day a Royal Lao helicopter with U.S. Army Warrant Officer Fred Untalan (who later became the Aviation Officer for the DEA in Thailand) on board from the DAO in Vientiane, reached the crash site and recovered the arm and hand of one man, which was later identified by fingerprints as the partial remains of Captain Joel Birch, who was then declared KIA. Untalan left fairly quickly due to enemy ground action and did not make a complete area survey.

But there was much more to the case. Foremost was the fact that a Pathet Lao officer who was interrogated in Vientiane in October 1973 told American investigators that his unit was ordered to investigate the site the next day after the aircraft went down. He said he found five fully deployed parachutes on the ground near the wreckage. In addition to the possibly life saving parachutes, two small piles of blood soaked bandages were also observed nearby. The dismembered remains of what appeared to be five or six individuals were piled into a mass grave and buried. He found no other indications of survivors and soon departed.

What had also piqued everyone's interest was the May 1973 discovery on imagery of an "evader symbol" on the ground that perhaps correlated to Captain Hart, even though it was some three hundred miles north of the crash. The symbol observed mashed into tall grass consisted of the letters "TH" followed by the number "1973," or possibly "1573." Pentagon analysts interpreted the letters "TH" to mean "Thomas Hart," although the meaning of the number was unclear. DIA later determined that the report probably correlated to the crash of Emmet Kay, an American civilian aviator who was shot down with his crew and held by the Pathet Lao. The photo of the symbol occurred some five miles away and thirteen days after Kay's crash. When Kay was later released, however, that analysis was disputed when Kay stated he did not make the markings and that his crew was captured fairly quickly. To this day, the symbols remain a mystery.

After surveying the site, we confirmed that the crash location matched the information contained in official American files. After our search revealed aircraft debris, and we recovered eight small bone fragments, the team recommended the site be excavated during the dry season when the weather was more suitable. After considerable lobbying with the Lao government, permission was granted to begin the operation and we finally excavated the site in February 1985, over two years later. This was the first excavation of a wartime aircraft loss by an official American team since the end of the war. The team was comprised of members of both the JCRC and CILHI, and was augmented by two Army Explosive Ordnance Disposal personnel and one Special Forces medic. An American Foreign Service Officer from the Embassy in Vientiane also accompanied us. A contingent of Lao People's Army Engineers joined us at the site. I served as the interpreter throughout the operation and as expected, many of the Lao also spoke Vietnamese.

In typical anthropological fashion we made a grid of the area and then conducted a systematic dig. As the first layers of soil were removed we began to encounter unexploded ordnance, primarily 40mm rounds. We placed the unexpended ammo in a safety bunker surrounded by sandbags to await destruction at the closeout phase of the excavation. Another serious health problem encountered was the relatively large amount of fiberglass material removed from the crater. The fine fiberglass dust from the aircraft insulation aggravated the skin, and when breathed in, the particles caused considerable irritation to the eyes and lungs.

The Americans and Lao worked well together, and the job proceeded smoothly throughout the dig. In conversing with the Lao soldiers I learned that many of them had recently been working with PAVN Engineers on the construction of an expansion of strategic Route 9 from Quang Tri province in Vietnam west across Laos to the border of Thailand at Mukdahan. In addition to the Army engineers, the Lao side of the excavation team included several military cadre assigned to the important Military Affairs Committee of the Ministry of National Defense in Vientiane. The military cadre were responsible for the physical security of both sides during the operation. The Lao also included two Communist Party officials from the Ministry of Foreign Affairs who were responsible for interfacing with the Americans and the media who were covering the expedition.

At several times during the dig, the American Chargé de Affairs of the Embassy in Vientiane, Ms. Teresa Tull, arrived to visit the site accompanied by Lao Foreign Ministry personnel. Ms. Tull was the current head of the American mission to the Laotian government. The U.S. government had downgraded the Embassy after the Pathet Lao takeover, and no Ambassador was currently assigned to Vientiane. A career diplomat, Ms. Tull appeared determined to complete her assignment in Vientiane without incident in order to move up another rung on the diplomatic ladder. Though a veteran of the American Consulate in Danang during the last stages of the war, her previous wartime experience apparently had not stiffened her resolve. Ms. Tull seemed overly concerned that the operation would encounter unusual difficulties and possibly create some sort of diplomatic incident, thus staining her opportunity for advancement. Tense to the point that it became readily apparent and annoying even to the laid-back Lao, it didn't take long for the American team members to come up with the nickname "Nervous Nelly" in referring to the rather sizable Ms. Tull. For example, as a Lao gesture of goodwill, during a visit to the site the officials from the Ministry of National Defense brought in some Lao beer and bananas for the excavation team. Approving the bananas without hesitation, Ms. Tull then suggested that consumption of beer by the American team members might lead to an altercation and ordered us to refrain from sharing the beverages. Shaking their heads in amusement, and obviously puzzled that such a decision could be made by a female, the Lao officials took the Lao team members aside to a shade tree where they enjoyed the beer while the envious Americans looked on.

During the course of the investigation we found very few items at or near the surface of the ground. However, we did find numerous charred fragments of human skeletal remains and pieces of wreckage deep inside the hand-dug crater, along with a few personal effects and I.D. tags. Since the Lao had almost two years to prepare since our initial survey, I suspected that they had already examined the site prior to our arrival and gathered any surface materials. My theory was subsequently reinforced when refugees and other Sources on into the 1990s reported information from identification media, mostly dog tags, correlated to crewmembers on the aircraft. We also never found the mass grave, which also raised my suspicions.

This material was quickly transferred to the CILHI laboratory in Hawaii. Despite our limited recovery of the many small unidentifiable fragments and a few personal items, the operation was still considered a success, mainly because it had occurred. Every member of the excavation team received some type of award for the effort. I received the Civilian Meritorious Service Medal from Admiral William J. Crowe, the commander of all American forces in the Pacific. After approximately four months of study, CILHI recommended to the Armed Services Graves Registration Office that the thirteen crewmen be listed as identified. They accepted the CILHI recommendation, and Mrs. Hart was notified on July 1, 1985 that her husband had been identified based on the two bone fragments she had found in 1982 and five others recovered at the crash site.

However, in an unfortunate effort to emphasize CILHI's professional prowess, after the conclusion of the excavation the U.S. government publicly announced that the CILHI had used the tiny bone fragments to positively identify all thirteen men missing in the incident. CILHI made the further mistake of stating that it had found bone fragments corresponding to each crewman. Originally planned as a positive media blitz, the announcement quickly became a public relations disaster. Mrs. Hart became furious when she realized that there had been thirteen identifications. Although CILHI was basing its conclusion that the pieces had been found at the crash site, along with various personal effects, she felt that CILHI did not take into account that five individuals may have been buried in a common grave and their remains not recovered, or that based on the parachutes and bloody bandages found at the scene, that some men might have survived. She also believed that there should have been fourteen identifications, since only Capt. Birch's arm and hand were found initially. Only his I.D. card was recovered in 1985.

Mrs. Hart immediately requested that another expert examine the remains and provide a second opinion. The military refused. In spite of the denial, Mrs. Hart contacted Dr. Michael Charney, a forensic anthropologist at Colorado State University, to determine whether he would be willing to provide a second opinion. Dr. Charney agreed, and Mrs. Hart promptly filed suit in the Northern District of California to prohibit the Government from forwarding the remains to the families before Dr. Charney examined them. The Air Force relented, and Dr. Charney examined the bones purported to belong to Lieutenant Colonel Hart (he was promoted while still on the MIA list), and concluded that it was impossible to tell whether those fragments came from Hart or even from an individual at the crash site.

Based on Dr. Charney's disagreement with the CILHI, the question now was what to do with the disputed fragments; Mrs. Hart declined to accept them, making her the first family member to reject remains. Government counsel told the district judge that the remains would be held in mortuary storage. Based on his confidence in the identification, however, Secretary of the Air Force Verne Orr sent a letter to Mrs. Hart on October 9, 1985 stating that if she did not wish to accept the remains, they would be buried at Arlington National Cemetery with full military honors. December 2, 1985 was set as the interment date.

Meanwhile, the Army decided to commission an independent civilian inquiry into the CILHI identifications. Doctors Ellis R. Kerley, William R. Maples, and Lowell Levine, forensic anthropologists and fellows of the American Academy of Forensic Scientists, were enlisted as the investigating team. Mrs. Hart heard of the investigation and requested that the burial of the remains be delayed. Secretary Orr complied with this request. From December 9 through December 12, 1985, the team conducted an on-site inspection of the CILHI laboratory. The team's report was devastating, and recommended changes in CILHI procedure and personnel. In fact, Dr. William Maples characterized CILHI's failure to exercise proper standards of identification as "blatant." The panel concluded that it could confidently confirm only two of the Pakse identifications. The other identifications did not appear to be justified according to standard forensic methods, and could not withstand scientific scrutiny. Worse, Doctors Kerley and Maples only saw the actual remains after the issuance of their report. After viewing the remains themselves, the two doctors reaffirmed their earlier findings that the remains did not provide sufficient information to make the kinds of identifications CILHI had made.

The Air Force contacted the families of the other crewmembers and explained that if they wished, the identifications of their loved ones would be reconsidered. Mrs. Hart and the family of another crewmember, Captain George McDonald, requested reconsideration. On June 10, 1986, the military rescinded the identifications of Hart and Captain George McDonald. The Government did not, however, return the men to unaccounted-for status.

That action only served to further inflame Mrs. Hart. On October 30, 1986, after exhausting all administrative remedies, Anne Hart, along with her husband's mother, Vera Lee Hart, and his daughter, Gillian Elaine Hart, filed suit in the Northern District of Florida. The Harts sued for the intentional infliction of emotional distress under the Federal Tort Claims Act. The complaint alleged that the Army and Air Force knowingly made a false positive identification of Lieutenant Colonel Hart's remains, that they persisted in this identification in spite of overwhelming evidence to the contrary, and that they improperly issued an "ultimatum" about his burial, and that they refused to return Lieutenant Colonel Hart to unaccounted-for status after rescinding his identification.

The Government filed a motion to dismiss the case on December 29, 1986. They argued, among other things, that the court had no jurisdiction. The district court denied the motion on March 17, 1987. In reviewing the evidence presented, the court ruled that the Government had admitted all of the matters that the Harts had brought forth. The Hart's legal team then moved for partial summary judgment on September 21, 1987. On January 12, 1988, the court granted the motion, finding the Government liable to Anne Hart under Florida law for intentional infliction of emotional distress, calling the government's actions "outrageous." After a trial on October 6, 1988, the district court found the Government liable as well to Vera and Gillian Hart. On October 20, 1988, the court awarded the plaintiffs a total of $632,814.62: $382,814.62 for Anne Hart and $125,000.00 each for Vera and Gillian Hart.

However, the Government appealed the case to the 11th Circuit Court of Appeals. On March 1, 1990, the higher-level Federal appellate judges overruled the Federal District judge in Florida. The main argument of the government lawyers was that "all government efforts to identify and bury dead servicemen are based entirely upon policy judgments…" The judges sided with them, and further stated that:

> *The Government maintains that its actions in this case reflected a longstanding policy of attempting to search for, recover, and identify dead American servicemen. This policy was developed for two reasons. First, the United States military maintains that everyone who dies in service to the United States deserves burial with full military honors. Second, POW/MIA families during the Vietnam era expressed a desire for the Government to attempt to identify individual remains if possible. Thus, the Government argued that the identification procedures used in this case were not merely scientific and forensic, but also were based on issues of public policy…. Government efforts to identify deceased personnel are clearly discretionary functions. Further, ordinary forensic standards are inappropriate in cases such as the Pakse crash, where the remains of a number of persons are commingled, severely burned, and shattered. In such cases, military forensics examiners draw conclusions not only from the remains themselves, but from the fact that the remains were recovered at the crash site, that personal effects were found among the remains, that the remains showed the effects of high temperatures associated with fires and explosions, and that the deceased personnel were listed as crew members on the plane's manifest.*[2]

The Hart's subsequently appealed to the Supreme Court, but the court in late November 1990 refused to take the case, effectively ending the Hart's final effort. Despite the court ruling, in my mind the lawyer's reasoning was a horrible mistake.

While legally correct, for families already deeply suspicious of U.S. government motives, the notion that men could be identified (in their minds, written off) based not on sound forensic science but on a policy decision sent them into spasms of indignation. Due to the astronomical odds against identifying all the men based on bone chips, some family members of the men as well as activist groups began a crusade. Railing against the mass identification, several family members began calling for a thorough investigation of the professional and ethical standards followed by the CILHI during its efforts to recover and identify remains. Congressional anger soon resulted in an investigation into the academic background of the chief forensic scientist at the CILHI. It was discovered that Tadao Furoe, the Japanese born scientist in charge at the laboratory, did not have a Masters Degree from a university in Japan that he claimed to have, and he was not a doctor. Furoe was forced to resign. In the ensuing years the CILHI was moved to a newer, more modern facility in Hawaii and completely reorganized under new leadership. While the upgrade had been planned before the imbroglio over the Hart case, largely as a consequence of the uproar, the planned changes were sped up. Sadly, from my perspective, nowhere in this entire episode was it mentioned that the Lao might have provided answers as to whether any of the men had survived.

The families were not the only ones upset with the CILHI. Perhaps the most frustrating internal matter in investigating the MIA cases was the lack of information we in the field got back from CILHI. Investigators like myself seldom, if ever, received the results of the forensic analysis conducted by the lab on the returned remains, as CILHI always closely guarded all such data. I was never clear as to whether they were more concerned with civil litigation from MIA next-of-kin, or if they were simply trying to conceal the duplicity of the Communist officials in order to perpetuate the periodic doling out of remains. This aspect was quite exasperating, because as in any investigation involving a relatively large number of candidates, comparative analysis is at times the most important tool for the investigator in the field to have. Comparative analysis was extremely critical in cases involving several individuals in one incident. For example, if information in our files indicated that all six members of an aircraft reportedly perished inside the aircraft in a shoot-down, but the remains of at least one crew member later returned by Vietnam indicated no apparent trauma, the entire focus of the investigation into the fate of the five remaining crewmembers should logically shift to the more demanding standards of a missing person type investigation. If, however, investigators were never informed of the condition of the remains, they would continue the investigation as a basic crash site excavation in order to recover bones, rather than a last-known-alive investigation requiring much more detailed field efforts.

In particular, other than personal side comments made to colleagues or myself, the CILHI rarely officially provided any information regarding the time of death of the recovered Americans. The only excuse I ever heard regarding this aspect was that the science was not that accurate, and that the CILHI was reluctant for that reason to make estimates. In reality, however, I gained the impression that the CILHI simply did not want to offend the Vietnamese with evidence that was at best circumstantial. However, in one unusual instance the CILHI Commander, Lieutenant Colonel Johnie Webb, revealed to me that one set of remains returned by Vietnam exhibited signs of "malnutrition deprivation" due to a prolonged period of incarceration, but that according to our records the man was never known to be in the prison system.

Intrigued, I quietly began further research on the case, and I learned that the same remains also exhibited clear evidence of having been wired together, apparently for display. I recalled having debriefed several refugees in Hong Kong who described their observation of American skeletal remains wired together for use as training aids in various medical schools in North Vietnam. One set was being used at a province-level medical school in Quang Ninh province northeast of Hanoi. Although I was pleased that the Communists finally returned the individual's remains to the United States, at the same time I was concerned that we were not illuminating the true circumstances of his death. This is what the families really wanted, the truth about how their loved one died, not hurried excavations that recovered a couple of fragments so that the government could scratch another case off the list. Because the remains had been unilaterally returned, we were not making the extra effort to conduct a detailed investigation, or for that matter to ask any follow-up questions whatsoever. Personally, I felt that unilateral Vietnamese remains returns should warrant even more scrutiny than those recovered jointly by U.S. and Vietnamese teams, mainly because we had no method of determining the true circumstances of his loss or understanding the true chain of custody. However, in order to expand the search for American POW/MIAs, we had to convince the Communists that this was a "humanitarian" mission, not (in their minds) a thinly disguised intelligence gathering operation. Unfortunately, this also tied our hands. Once the remains were identified, there was no longer any need to investigate the circumstances of his loss if this truly was a "humanitarian" venture.

But in the case of the remains used as a training aid in Quang Ninh, several points caused me deep concern. Given Webb's statement to me that these remains showed "malnutrition deprivation," a fancy way of saying starvation, obviously the man had survived for some period of time. However, that he was never identified by the other returnees as being in the prison system—a major point continuously used by certain elements of the U.S. government to defend their position that no one was held back by the Vietnamese—should have raised some eyebrows. Second, when American forces captured a Cuban-built airfield in Grenada they also secured a number of photographs depicting Cuban personnel in military uniforms in Vietnam. In reviewing the photos I concluded that they had been taken in Quang Ninh. I knew that Cubans in Hanoi had directly interrogated and horribly tortured over twenty American POWs during the war in an attempt to extract war-crime confessions from them. While many Cubans served in North Vietnam, some working on the Ho Chi Minh Trail while others were all the way down to the DMZ, it was not outrageous to speculate that perhaps the Cubans had another interrogation program that we were unaware of. Third, after the Communists invaded and occupied South Vietnam, they moved a significant number of intelligence personnel from the GVN's Central Intelligence Office to Quang Ninh province for long-term interrogation and exploitation, and while they didn't see Americans, the fact that the intelligence personnel were held in this area might indicate this facility was used as a strategic interrogation center. I came to the possible conclusion that the pilot whose remains showed "deprivation" but who never appeared in captivity and whose skeleton was used as a display in the same province where former intelligence personnel were held captive might logically have also been imprisoned there separately for some time. In my mind, we should have gone back to the Vietnamese for more information or attempted to further investigate the case, especially to gain insight into their POW policy and intelligence gathering system. But, since we had the remains, for the U.S. government, the case was closed, even though the CILHI believed his remains showed he had survived for some time after his capture. There would be no further investigation of the man's true fate, regardless of the policy and intelligence implications.

If the Lao excavation was a joke from the standpoint of gaining resolution, the first Vietnamese effort made that one seem like a serious endeavor. After the conclusion of the first Lao effort, officials from other nations, especially Indonesia, joined us in lobbying the Vietnamese to move forward on the issue. The recalcitrant Vietnamese were non-committal until April 1985 when they finally agreed to permit a JCRC/CILHI team to travel to Vietnam and excavate the crash site of a B-52 aircraft shot down at Yen Thuong hamlet, just north of the capital during the Christmas 1972 "Linebacker" bombing campaign. During the initial site visit, the accompanying Vietnamese cadre made the point that due to the close proximity of the actual crash point to a local residence, the house would have to be destroyed in order to complete the excavation. According to the officials, an elderly lady who resided in the house, Mrs. Le Thi Dao, was the surviving spouse of a person killed by the exploding bomb load. Realizing the odds against that, I asked to interview Mrs. Dao. I noted that at the beginning of my interview with Mrs. Dao that she seemed well composed, but suddenly became emotional and cried on cue from the VNOSMP cadre. The village chief at the site was also very animated and emotional in relating his account of the crash. Despite the apparent confirmation from Mrs. Dao, I would soon discover my suspicions were correct.

During the preliminary survey, I managed to escape my handlers and spoke briefly with some nearby residents whom the Vietnamese officials had not planned to introduce as witnesses. The spontaneous discussions with the locals uncovered an account of the incident quite different from that of the VNOSMP witnesses. According to their recollection, the people who were killed at the time were actually inside a bunker that collapsed during the bombing. Almost everyone else in the area at the time had been evacuated to regions further outside Hanoi, and only those considered essential to the war effort were left behind, including some railroad workers employed at the nearby Gia Lam railroad yard. More telling, they also indicated that officials had already examined the crash site at the time of the incident. I received one report of a flight suit that was recovered intact and turned in to the Central Military Museum in Hanoi. When the Communist cadre in the area of the crash site learned that I was conversing with villagers, the local inhabitants suddenly vanished and did not reappear during the operation. I also took note of the fact that both the village chief and Mrs. Dao were featured in a film production titled "The 10,000 Day War." In comparing the testimony provided by the witnesses introduced by Communist officials with that of the people I spoke with, and after having watched the film "The 10,000 Day War," it was obvious that the Vietnamese had completely staged the testimony of the witnesses they had presented.

After the initial survey was completed, the U.S. asked for and received permission to airlift a backhoe from Hawaii to aid in the excavation. When the American team arrived at the site in September 1985 to begin the excavation, Mrs. Dao had vacated her house. As part of their plans, the Vietnamese had already arranged several visits to the site by various groups, including Ann Mills Griffiths and Richard Childress, international media reps, and the Indonesian Ambassador to Vietnam. Apparently the Vietnamese wanted as many people as possible to receive the message that they had begun to cooperate on the issue. During the first few days of the operation the house previously occupied by Mrs. Dao began to slowly disappear. In typical Asian fashion, the house tiles and rafters were removed from the roof of the house and carried away. With a per capita income in Vietnam at the time of approximately $200 per year, and with the cost of new construction at least half that amount, efforts to save the building material of even a small, one room house with dirt floor such as Mrs. Dao's was understandable. Since the disassembly of the house occurred during the evening hours while the American team members were away from the site, it was a surprise each morning to see just how much of the house was still remaining. Over the three-week excavation period, as the crater being dug by the backhoe gradually approached the foundation of the house, almost every bit of material used in originally constructing it was gone. Nevertheless, the Vietnamese Government was not the least bit embarrassed in billing us $120,665.00 for the house and the excavation, which to my considerable consternation, we paid.

I suspected the Vietnamese had already spent substantial time surreptitiously working on the site. My reservations were confirmed when after three weeks of digging by backhoe and by hand we found absolutely no remains or personal effects of the crew. Not one item. If any such objects had remained, the gray clay soil, typical of the alluvial Red River delta region, would normally have preserved them. Although we did find some pieces of aircraft wreckage, such as fuel bladders and parts from the engines and landing gear, we did not recover any evidence to link the wreckage to a particular aircraft. In essence, we had spent over one hundred and twenty thousand dollars and expended much time only to find nothing of any real analytical value.

Yet the team did find some non-specific items of American origin. Several "Stars and Stripes" military newspapers were found still in pristine condition. Based on the dates of the newspapers and the location of the crash site the team was able to narrow the aircraft down to two possible candidates, one that had originated from Guam, and a second that had flown its mission from Utapao Air Base in Thailand. We did find one other clue that strongly suggested the airplane's base, although it was not by any means positive proof. Given the large number of unopened prophylactics found at the site, no doubt intended for use in the notorious sex dens dotting Thailand, we were in agreement that the mission had originated from Utapao.

Although the Vietnamese officials claimed that the site was undisturbed prior to the excavation, with the exception of the prophylactics and newspapers, no personal effects, bone fragments, or any other piece of evidence capable of shedding any light on the fate of the crew was found during the entire operation. Although I had anticipated that the Communist officials had already examined the crash, even I was amazed by the Vietnamese audacity. Basically I had expected three things: the excavation would be difficult, well controlled and expensive, but never did I imagine a complete lack of any identifiable physical evidence. I believed that the Communist intelligence and security personnel would leave enough material for us to at least confirm a particular aircraft, and possibly even one or more crewmembers. I would never have predicted that every shred of specific evidence would be collected and removed from the site in advance of our arrival. After the very frustrating experience I could only conclude that the Communists were merely making the point that in order to resolve the issue, the U.S. government was willing to send personnel and equipment to the other side of the globe and also pay them $120,665 to dig up sites containing absolutely nothing of analytical value. Subsequent to this, Childress informed Thach that selection of sites would be a joint US/VN effort, not a unilateral choice by Hanoi.

Despite the failure of this first Vietnamese excavation, we pressed the Vietnamese to increase the number of field operations. Even though the Lao had received much favorable media publicity from the Pakse excavation, they immediately reverted to their demands for economic aid and ordinance removal. They did, however, acquiesce to sending a delegation to visit the JCRC and

CILHI. I did not assist this group, which arrived in September 1985. After a lengthy debate, in mid-December 1985, Congress agreed to remove Laos from the list of countries that could not receive U.S. economic aid. Immediately, the Lao agreed to allow the next site survey, this time of another C-130 crash site near Muong Phine near the town of Tchepone. They also allowed another JCRC team to investigate a third site.

One sign that the Vietnamese were beginning to take the accounting process more seriously was the improvements in our lodgings. When the U.S. team traveled to Hanoi during the mid-1980s, we were now billeted at the Cuban-built "Thang Loi" (Victory) Hotel located on the shore of the West Lake. While far short of meeting western standards for a hotel, (but vastly better than the earlier Restored Sword Lake Hotel), the Thang Loi was a step up from the hotels generally available at the time in downtown Hanoi. Only a ten-minute ride from the site where the Technical Talks were held, the inn had a decent dining hall and a bar with a wide rooftop veranda. While the mattresses had been improved and some of the rats banished, the meals were still served Communist bloc style—an abundance of pork and greasy cabbage. I felt as though I consumed more breaded pork cutlets in Hanoi during the meetings than the dreaded "pork sausage patties" I had choked down from rusting, Korean War era C-ration cans throughout my military career. Most Americans were also unable to withstand the powerful *Lua Moi* (rice whiskey) of North Vietnam, which was always in supply at the hotel bar. Straight it was horrible, so I smuggled in a blender, and by adding a few ice-cubes and fresh bananas to the *Lua Moi* and mixing it together, I taught the bartenders to make frozen daiquiris. This new fad quickly spread throughout the capital. I called it a banana daiquiri but the Vietnamese called it *Lua Moi chuoi,* (rice whisky banana).

Bad hotel food, however, wasn't my only staple. State dinners sponsored by both sides during the meetings provided opportunities for relaxed exchanges between the two blocs. Usually I was strategically seated in order to serve as interpreter for non-Vietnamese speaking Americans and non-English speaking Vietnamese. I was frequently called upon to translate countless jokes and humorous personal anecdotes for the two sides. This required fast thinking, because some of the witticisms simply did not have meaning if translated directly, and in many cases would have had an adverse effect on the atmosphere. To ensure the cordiality of the American-sponsored dinners, I normally purchased fresh Washington State apples from the American Embassy in Bangkok and carried them to Hanoi in my luggage. The huge red apples were always a big hit with the Vietnamese as this was the first time most of the Communist officials had ever tasted them. I normally took enough apples for the Vietnamese to be able to take some home to their children, and this gesture was always genuinely appreciated.

The dinners were usually followed by a long series of toasts. The Vietnamese and Cambodian officials were normally decent about putting aside their animosities, and the toasts were generally accompanied by wishes for good health and happiness, or for success during future talks between the two sides. In contrast, during meetings with the Lao in Vientiane the Communist Party cadre were much more robotic and took advantage of the situation to launch into tirades denouncing America and everything it stood for.

The first time such an incident occurred with me in attendance was during a dinner held at the residence of the American Chargé de Affairs in Vientiane. A Lao cadre, Colonel Khamla Keophithoune, who had led the 1982 League delegation to the caves at Vieng Xai and was ostensibly the head of the Lao POW/MIA organization, delivered a fiery speech denouncing America, and then laughingly raised his glass for a toast to the Lao People's Democratic Republic. I was the only American present to decline the offer. Although at first tempted out of simple courtesy to raise my glass in unison with the other guests, I immediately reconsidered. All those present were sitting in American chairs, around an American table located on U.S. diplomatic property while enjoying food and drink provided at the expense of American taxpayers. Although I realized the gesture would not be appreciated, I refused to ignore the cadre's rudeness or participate in his salute to Laos.

Perceiving a loss of face, Colonel Khamla was livid and he made sure I knew it. He stared at me menacingly the rest of the night. I ignored him. Sympathetic to the diplomatic predicament of the American Chargé and his wife, after Khamla left, I asked them for some Tums or Rolaids. I hoped that my "diplomatic illness" would provide them cover in the event Khamla or his colleagues complained about my actions. Unsure if I would ever be granted another visa to reenter Laos, I could only hope that on future diplomatic dinners someone in the U.S. government would back me up. Surprisingly, my next visa request was immediately approved. Although I could never figure out why, during subsequent trips Colonel Khamla seemed to always find a seat next to me in order to engage me in friendly conversations spoken entirely in Vietnamese.

However, I was not entirely in the dark concerning Khamla's background. I had made it a point to canvass refugee camps holding Lao refugees for anyone with knowledge of the key players in Laos assigned to the POW/MIA issue. I learned from refugee sources that Khamla was an avid hunter who often rode in his military jeep to areas outside the city to shoot small game. This information seemed to fit when I noticed that Khamla had provided two wild turkeys for our team to dine on during a state dinner sponsored by the Lao side. Other refugees described an unidentified Colonel from southern Laos with a scar on the side of his neck that worked in a high security vault located in the "Phone Keng" compound of the Ministry of National Defense (MND) building in downtown Vientiane, not far from the American Embassy. When I recalled having observed a similar scar on the neck of Khamla, I knew I was headed in the right direction.

Additional information indicated that Khamla had received intelligence and security training in the USSR during the war, and that after the war ended he was placed in charge of official Lao government records on American POW/MIAs. Khamla's assistant in the POW/MIA records vault was identified as Lieutenant Colonel Thongkham, a native of Muong Sing who also received intelligence and security training in the Soviet Union. By using photographs during my interviews I was able to establish that Thongkham was depicted as an armed guard in a picture taken of Lieutenant Charles Klusman, an aviator who was shot down and captured in Laos on June 6, 1964. Klusman later managed to escape, one of only two Americans to escape from a Lao prison during the war.

Further information revealed that the high security vault was originally constructed for safeguarding the payroll of Royal Lao Government military forces. During later interviews with refugees who were former officers of the Royal Lao Army recently released from lengthy political thought reform sessions, I learned that some of them had been placed on forced labor details inside the Phone Keng MND complex. I also heard accounts from the former officers that while conducting work inside the vault they had observed documents relating to American POWs where Khamla and Thongkham both worked.

I had conducted enough interviews to realize that I was onto something important. Based on my experience I had a gut feeling that the refugees were being truthful. I believed that, like their brethren in the Vietnamese government, the Lao had steadfastly stonewalled official U.S. requests for records on missing Americans. I decided to test the veracity of the refugees by asking to personally view a sample of the records the refugees claimed to have observed.

Apparently some of the refugees had contacts inside Laos who were still working on the labor details. Soon afterwards, an official Pathet Lao document titled "Biography of a Prisoner" was provided to me in the Na Pho refugee camp. In looking at the document I quickly concluded that not only was it genuine, it pertained to the case of Army Special Forces Captain Walter Hugh Moon. Moon was from Arkansas and was captured on April 22, 1961 by Communist forces near Vang Vieng. The document was actually a photocopy, but the source offered to sell me the original. Restricted by the official U.S. government policy I was compelled to decline the offer. This same document eventually found its way to Bo Gritz.

I immediately began an all out effort to locate additional refugee sources who possessed knowledge of the vault's entire contents. The fact that senior Lao personnel known to be involved in the POW/MIA issue worked in a secure area where records pertaining to missing Americans were stored led me to seriously consider the vault might also contain the remains of American personnel. We had several SIGINT reports of Lao personnel being sent to search for American remains, and in several cases the intercepts indicated the Lao had been successful. Soon thereafter, a refugee who knew of my interest in the vault departed Na Pho and crossed into Laos. He then returned to the camp with partial skeletal remains he alleged were American. A forensic examination of the remains resulted in the positive identification of Air Force First Lieutenant Arthur H. Hardy, who was shot down in Salavan province in Laos on March 14, 1972. My suspicions were raised when the forensic exam scientific evidence indicated that the remains had been in storage for at least several years.

This information immediately made me fear that what had occurred in Vietnam might happen in Laos. Concerned that the Lao Government might become aware of my discovery and decide to move the documents and remains from the vault to a new hiding place, I strongly recommended that the U.S. Government immediately confront the Lao leadership concerning the documents and remains.

Unfortunately, my request was denied at the technical level, although I learned later that Childress had brought it up in his discussions. Diplomatic concerns and ongoing negotiations over other aspects of Lao-U.S. relations, such as narcotics control, apparently took precedent. The subject of the vault, as well as the roles of Colonel Khamla and Lieutenant Colonel Thongkham, was filed away with other reports considered damaging to relations between the countries. Worse, we later received intelligence reports that after the Vietnamese learned we had discovered the vault's existence, they immediately confiscated its contents.[3] Colonel Khamla was later transferred from Vientiane to Salavan province. After completing his tour in southern Laos, Colonel Khamla was reassigned as the Lao Military Attaché in Beijing, China. Several years later a non-Lao speaking interviewer was dispatched to Beijing to interview Khamla, but the interview yielded negative results. To the best of my knowledge, U.S. officials never interviewed Thongkham.

Although the refugee interviews and field operations were gaining momentum, there was still a great deal of suspicion and concern regarding the overall effort by POW/MIA family members and veterans organizations across the United States. While most members of the League were aware of the heightened efforts by the Reagan Administration, and Dick Childress, Richard Armitage, and Paul Wolfowitz in particular, some earlier efforts aimed at restoring their confidence in the official government policy regarding the accounting effort and the overall policy of reestablishing relations with Vietnam were starting to bear fruit. In August 1979, after the Director of DIA moved to reclassify all live-sighting reports, he quickly provided Ann Mills Griffiths a security clearance to enable her to view these reports. Further, in 1980 an Inter-Agency Group (IAG) was formed that included members from the League and U.S. government agencies working on the issue. Although the basic idea of a "working group" was not new, the IAG was unique in that it included not only government bureaucrats, but an MIA family member as well. As the Executive Director of the National League of Families, Ann Mills Griffiths became the first private citizen to join the inner circle as a full-fledged member in addressing the casualty resolution effort. In addition to Griffiths, the IAG included members from State, the Defense Department, the National Security Council, and occasionally CIA.

The most important aspect of the IAG was that it gave the POW/MIA family members a voice in the accounting process, and a forum to present their views on moving the process forward. Plus, when family members became confused due to the complexity of the government system, or simply reached their final level of patience in dealing with the bureaucrats, they felt fortunate to have one of their own on the IAG whom they could turn to for answers and advice. Although members of the organization were considered equals, there was no doubt in anyone's mind that if the issue were to be resolved satisfactorily, it was ultimately the family members who would have to be convinced by the effort. In the interim, U.S. government agencies could only do whatever work was permitted by Vietnam, Laos and Cambodia, and at the same time try to leave as clear a record as possible as proof that honest efforts had been made.

Unfortunately, this situation led to "busy work" at the various DIA offices, where charts and briefings were the order of the day. This might have been acceptable to the Congress, but not to Ann Mills Griffiths. She took her IAG assignment seriously, and she was determined to drive the government not only to work harder, but smarter as well. With her on board, the DIA analysts were often challenged over their conclusions, which did not earn her any kudos, but which did improve the analytical product.

As time went on, there appeared a certain degree of reluctance, and at times even downright enmity, displayed toward her by some career bureaucrats and members of Congress. The fact that a private citizen had been granted a security clearance and was actively involved in an official decision making process, had clout with high-level government officials and was not afraid to use it, created more than a few animosities. Ann is a formidable, strong-willed woman who possesses a tremendous intellect. Combined with her encyclopedic knowledge of the issue and her low tolerance for fools, she created more than the occasional disdain from officialdom. Further, there was also a growing measure of jealousy exhibited by members of other private POW/MIA organizations outside the League of Families, and even among some League members. They grew to see Ann's close involvement with Richard Childress, along with what was perceived as the League's parroting of the government's position, as an unholy alliance and to their minds a growing deterrent to the issue. The fact that Griffiths was the only member of a private organization to be allowed access to classified meeting sessions and files only reinforced that view.

The reality was much different but impossible to convey. When the Reagan administration came to power, Childress was appalled by the Carter Administration's decision to exclude the League and its views from governmental deliberations. He strongly believed that the only way to gain the respect and trust of the families was to work closely with them, that family involvement would dispel the growing myth that the government was engaged in a deliberate cover-up or abandonment of its military. Having instilled a great deal of discipline in the organization, Griffiths constantly stressed to the membership the need for civility, patience and faith in the government. Her basic strategy was to work within the system rather than rail against it publicly. But the glacial pace of the negotiations and the need for secrecy in dealing with a wily and cunning foe created even more frustrations, and the more radical elements turned their anger inward. Fortunately, even under withering criticism both individuals did not cave in to the human temptation to chuck the whole affair, and have continued to this day to work hard on resolving the issue.

Nevertheless, as time passed and even less progress was achieved on the possibility of live prisoners, some MIA family members became increasingly vocal and eventually formed a separate POW/MIA family member organization called the National Alliance of Families. This group is still headed by Mrs. Delores Apodaca Alfond, the sister of Vietnam MIA Air Force Captain Victor J. Apodaca Jr.. The National Alliance was quite critical of government efforts to account for the missing, issuing harsh condemnations of officials and policies. Yet according to members of the organization, regardless of what the U.S. Government had done they still viewed themselves as patriotic Americans. The main problem was that the members of the National Alliance had simply lost all confidence in the government's ability to conduct a fair and honest accounting, one they believed was engaged in a massive cover-up of the abandonment of many American servicemen. While the League enjoyed at least proper working relations with policy makers, government officials were often reluctant to deal with what they perceived to be the more bellicose National Alliance, although in recent years DPMO has provided briefings at the Alliance's annual meeting.

While the Reagan administration was improving relations with the families and pushing the Communists to permit us to conduct in-country field investigations, our workload was dramatically escalating. Even with McKay on board, the increasing flow of refugees put such a strain on the JCRC Liaison Office in Bangkok that all the employees literally found themselves living out of suitcases during seven-day workweeks at remote locations throughout the region. In 1984, just at the point when the situation seemed almost unbearable, as if sent by a divine power, the Chairman of the Joint Chiefs of Staff, General John Vessey, arrived at the American Embassy in Bangkok. General Vessey immediately requested that the Ambassador to Thailand, John Gunther Dean, convene a meeting of key Embassy personnel, including Mather and myself, in the Ambassador's office. Vessey opened the meeting by stating that he was "speaking for the President." He continued his remarks by stressing that there was considerable interest in the White House regarding the accounting for American personnel missing from the Vietnam War, and that the President expected all government agencies to fully support the effort.

Several members of the staff, including the Ambassador, appeared baffled by Vessey's remarks. This was probably due to the fact that the JCRC operation had traditionally been a low-key priority, and the Embassy personnel were simply not aware of the recent increase in the pace and scope of activities, or the raised level of priority afforded the issue by the White House, largely due to the efforts of Childress, Armitage, Wolfowitz, and Griffiths. But no one harbored doubts that General Vessey was serious or expressed any noticeable degree of hesitation at carrying out the President's instructions. During the brief visit to Thailand, Vessey spent most of his valuable time discussing POW/MIA matters with JCRC personnel. Apparently he was concerned about the paucity of resources available to the Liaison Office, and Vessey continually probed for a realistic appraisal of the situation. Realizing Mather's parsimonious nature, I took the lead in outlining my perception of improvements necessary for enhancing mission success.

In discussing the resources aspect with Vessey, I outlined three areas I considered as being critical to improving our process. I mentioned adding clerical support for publishing and disseminating POW/MIA information reports, purchase of a vehicle, and hiring a Lao linguist to assist with interviewing the large influx of Lao refugees. Although not considered mission essential I also mentioned that with the exception of JCRC Liaison personnel, all other personnel assigned to the Embassy, both military and civilian, were in the Embassy's housing pool. I further explained that Thailand was a high cost area and the local real estate market was very competitive due to the fact that international corporations employed a relatively large number of foreigners in Bangkok, including Americans. The large corporations, especially the oil companies, were willing to pay high costs for suitable accommodations, leaving only substandard lodging available to JCRC employees living off the normal military allowance.

Within two weeks of Vessey's visit conditions began to improve. The Embassy procurement section arranged for us to lease a Toyota sedan on a yearly basis. CINCPAC came up with funds for leased housing and the JCRC personnel were incorporated into the Embassy housing pool. Additional funding was made available for local hire employees and Mather finally decided to cry uncle and hire a part-time secretary to help him keep up with the administrative workload. With thirty-nine hours of professional clerical assistance each week the office was able to collect, produce, and disseminate reports much more efficiently. To help me with the interviews in the Lao refugee camps the Air Force assigned a Lao linguist to the office, Master Sergeant William "Bill" Gadoury. Fortunately, he had previously worked in Air Force Intelligence as an analyst and his Lao was excellent. The JCRC Headquarters in Hawaii also hired another civilian employee, James Coyle, to round out the group. Coyle was a PH.D. candidate at Cornell University and a former Army Lieutenant who had served a tour during the war as a Psychological Operations officer in Pleiku, Vietnam. Coyle's Vietnamese was somewhat rusty, but he would soon have plenty of opportunities to regain his fluency by interviewing hundreds, if not thousands of refugees.

Despite the poor results from the initial excavations in Laos and Vietnam respectively, Childress and Griffiths decided to press ahead for more field operations. In January 1986, just prior to Tet, the traditional Vietnamese Lunar New Year, they traveled to Hanoi for more policy level talks with the Communist leadership of Vietnam. The timing was right, because in typical Asian fashion, as the old year came to a close the Vietnamese were ready to evaluate past efforts, draw experience, and plan for the new year. The policy level exchanges began to attract growing media attention, and the subsequent increase also created considerable optimism on the part of the MIA family members, who had waited so long for answers concerning the fate of their loved ones.

The amplified level of awareness soon spurred interest by other governmental agencies, and the JCRC and the CILHI became the subject of congressional inquiries. The investigations were for the most part based on letters and telephone calls from MIA family members to members of Congress. Between the congressional scrutiny and the improved reporting by the international and American media regarding the policy level talks under way in Hanoi and New York City, I soon found myself conducting a number of briefings for U.S government officials arriving in Southeast Asia. If there was such a thing as an issue safe from the hazards of bipartisan politics, in my eyes the POW/MIA issue was it. Republicans and Democrats alike, members of both houses of Congress, and officials in the Reagan/Bush Administration seemed to have a heightened awareness of, and expressed support for, the effort to gain information on the missing men. Congressional requests often demanded case specific information, while appointed officials were more concerned with the overall policy implications of recent progress, and the prognosis for future developments as a result of the increased contacts between the various sides.

The amount of time spent on the issue by government officials, however, quite often depended on the dynamics of the situation at the time. For example, Secretary of Defense Casper Weinberger arrived in Bangkok on April 14, 1986. Members of the JCRC Liaison Office were invited to a working breakfast with the Secretary the following morning. Although seemingly concerned about the plight of the missing men, Weinberger seemed preoccupied throughout the meal. When out of the clear blue sky one staff member asked Weinberger what he intended to do about the recent bombing attacks by Libyan terrorists on U.S. military personnel, the Secretary almost choked on his food. After gaining his composure and exhibiting a wide grin, Weinberger informed the man that plans were currently underway for some type of unspecified retaliation. Shortly thereafter U.S. aircraft launched a surprise bombing attack on Libya.

Members of Congress continued to arrive in the area throughout the year. Representative Steven Solarz from New York traveled to Bangkok during August 1986. At the time of his trip, Rep. Solarz was Chairman of the Subcommittee on Asian and Pacific Affairs of the House Foreign Relations Committee, which had under it the POW/MIA Task Force. Solarz was keenly interested in the issue, due in part no doubt to the constant hounding by a relatively large number of MIA family member constituents in his district. Prior to departing Washington, Solarz had requested the Embassy to schedule a detailed POW/MIA briefing during his visit. Arming myself with a considerable array of facts and statistics, on August 21, 1986 I attended a working lunch with Solarz and members of his staff. During our lunch, Solarz seemed intrigued by the intricacies of recovering wartime casualties from Communist control and the overall complexity of the POW/MIA issue. He asked me to accompany him to the airport in order for him to have more time for questions. I gathered my briefing notes, secretly overjoyed at the unexpected opportunity to discuss the issue in greater detail with someone in an influential position that had expressed such a high degree of interest. Unfortunately, shortly after arrival at Don Muang Airport one of Solarz's aides came running into the departure lounge to inform him that Benito Aquino had just been shot to death moments after stepping from a plane at Manila Airport. Almost immediately a throng of Bangkok-based media descended on Solarz for his comments on the incident. As had happened so many times in the past, the POW/MIA issue was suddenly moved from the front to the back burner of the political stove.

Throughout the time that the operations and refugee interviews continued at the field level, the U.S. government continued to prod the Vietnamese at the policy level. While emphasizing the humanitarian nature of the POW/MIA issue and the political problem of listing it as a precondition to the normalization of relations, both sides were cognizant of the fact that the main obstacle to overall progress was the Vietnamese occupation of Cambodia. In my opinion, the Carter Administration made a terrible blunder when the President instructed the U.S. Ambassador to the United Nations to abstain from voting against membership by Vietnam in the UN. Carter's policy, brought about by a foreign policy viewpoint that believed providing inducements to Vietnam to modify its behavior before the Politburo had actually done so, a program that the Clinton administration would also attempt, proved to be an incredible piece of good fortune for Hanoi. In typical fashion, shortly after gaining the coveted membership, Vietnam launched an all-out invasion of Cambodia. The PAVN presence in Cambodia had been a sore international spot since that time. Although noncommittal in detail, the Americans did occasionally drop hints to the effect that an agreement for the withdrawal of PAVN forces from Cambodia could be realized as part of a framework for a regional settlement.

To get the negotiations back on track, Childress eventually came up with the idea of creating a short-term Presidential envoy to move the issue forward.

After several months of searching, Childress and Griffiths agreed that General John Vessey might be a perfect candidate. General Vessey had recently retired as the nation's top military commander, and was replaced by the former CINCPAC commander, Admiral William J. Crowe. Once President Ronald Reagan made the appointment in February 1987, Vessey firmly took the reigns in an effort to drive the POW/MIA issue forward as rapidly as possible.

I initially greeted this appointment with enthusiasm based on my earlier meeting with Vessey. However, my optimism began to wane after helping the General prepare for negotiations with Foreign Minister Thach. Vessey visited the JCRC Liaison Office in Bangkok, and Mather and I briefed him on the issue. To begin the meeting, Vessey made two points he obviously perceived as being fundamental to the manner in which he planned to tackle the delicate issue. First, in Vessey's opinion the fact that America had sustained casualties in the Vietnam War, several thousand of which still remained unresolved, was to be expected. According to Vessey "when you have a war you have casualties, it's time to move on." Second, Vessey was of the opinion that "some of the people involved in the MIA issue have made it their whole life."

Given his earlier support for the issue, I was a little taken aback by this new attitude. Personally I had the utmost respect for Vessey. As a former enlisted man and Master Sergeant, I felt a certain degree of camaraderie with him. The General had worked his way from Private to Master Sergeant prior to being commissioned as an officer in World War II. But being a former infantryman, I also realized that he was unskilled in Communist psychology and that his current philosophy regarding the accounting for our missing was tempered by his years in the combat arms. If given the mission to resolve the POW/MIA issue, I realized he might plunge forward quickly and decisively, bypassing any perceived pockets of resistance along the way. In particular, I feared the important "last-known-alive" cases might be delayed until so much time had passed they were no longer viable candidates for detailed investigations.

I responded to Vessey's question as to why some family members were unwilling to believe that everyone was dead. I mentioned what I called the "controversial" cases, wherein the men involved were alive at the time of their loss incident, and in some cases in the actual physical custody of Communist forces. I also mentioned cases where the missing men were depicted in photographs taken after they were captured, and the pictures clearly showed that they were alive. I also mentioned other "controversial" cases where the missing men were heard making radio broadcasts, where letters written by them dated after the time they were reportedly killed were found, or news accounts indicated they were captured, but the Vietnamese claimed to have no knowledge. Although Vessey was already aware of these various cases, he pledged to take them under consideration.

During a subsequent visit Vessey told me he had tasked both the JCRC and the DIA Special Office for POW/MIA to review every available file in order to come up with a listing for all such cases. It was Vessey's intent that rather than to expect the Vietnamese to rapidly resolve more than twenty-three hundred MIA cases all at once, with the help of our analysts he would come up with a list of the controversial cases. The JCRC analysts referred to such cases as "Vessey cases." Once such a list had been compiled he would be able to use it as a "yardstick to measure progress" regarding Vietnamese cooperation. Although there was probably a desire on the part of the JCRC and DIA analysts or within the Interagency Group to refer to the cases as the "last-known-alive" list, after conferring with DOD, the DIA, and the JCRC, the term "Discrepancy Case" was formally adopted. Although the initial list contained only several dozen names, a continuing review of the master case files, including Laos and Cambodia, by the DIA and the JCRC, the list grew to 305 cases, with 196 of these cases in Vietnam.

This list was selected as the highest possible priority for accounting efforts in Indochina. According to U. S. government policy at the time, a case could only be considered resolved if one of three conditions was met. Either the missing man or his identifiable remains would have to be returned. If this was not possible, an investigation would have to be conducted, the results of which would provide a clear explanation as to why neither the man nor his remains could be returned, and the explanation would have to be able to withstand public scrutiny.

Vessey then traveled to Hanoi to meet with Foreign Minister Thach in August 1987. This was the most important POW/MIA meeting since the war. Typically, Thach noted that the "hostile" U.S. attitude toward Vietnam was preventing the Vietnamese from finding more information or remains. When he returned, General Vessey told me he felt somewhat intimidated by Thach's verbose statements. When asked for my opinion as to how he should overcome this obstacle, I suggested to him that since the Socialist Republic of Vietnam constantly harangued the U.S. on a daily basis via Radio Hanoi, he should compile a selection of Foreign Broadcast Information Service reports and take them with him to his next meeting with Foreign Minister Thach. Vessey had someone do precisely that. Upon arrival at the meeting site, Vessey later told me he placed the large stack of reports on the table and informed the Vietnamese that they could see for themselves who was maintaining a hostile attitude against whom.

Vessey's August trip resulted in an agreement whereby the U.S. side would be permitted to send in investigators to conduct an investigation on each individual whose name appeared on the discrepancy case list. The American teams would be comprised of JCRC/CILHI personnel including a Team Chief and an analyst from the JCRC, and a CILHI Search and Recovery Specialist. Composition of the Vietnamese teams would be left up to them, but it was expected that their teams would mirror that of the American side. Although the Vietnamese would provide a counterpart team, all other aspects would be furnished by the American contingent.

Since the cases to be investigated were spread out across Vietnam, including many in very remote areas, ground transportation was essential. Due to the extremely poor infrastructure and rough terrain, four-wheel drive vehicles were a must. American military vehicles were out of the question, as the Vietnamese expressed grave concerns about U. S. military personnel traveling throughout Vietnam so soon after the war. The American side was able to overcome this obstacle by flying in four Jeep Cherokee vehicles. Other team equipment consisted of laptops, ground positioning systems, and cameras.

Once the Vessey-Thach agreement had been reached, the JCRC and CILHI experts began to brief the working-level VNOSMP officials on the overall concept. The Vietnamese seemed anxious to begin the field investigations, but no decision was made to put teams on the ground until the summer of 1988. At that time I was informed that I would be participating in the investigations, but my exact duties were not spelled out. Apparently Harvey and Lieutenant Colonel Johnie Webb planned to accompany the investigation teams, but no one had any idea what their role would be. Finally, in August 1988, I was notified that the investigations would begin the following month and that I would be in overall charge of the American contingent, as well as the Team Chief of one investigation team. Jim Coyle would lead the second team.

During the technical meeting in which the Vietnamese were notified of the composition of the American contingent, talking points issued by the Office of the Secretary of Defense were presented to the Director of the VNOSMP at the time, Mr. Nguyen Can. According to the talking points, due to the serious nature of the investigations, the U.S. side did not desire any news media to accompany the teams. Obviously anticipating a propaganda blitz, the Vietnamese were stunned by the request. At first the Vietnamese lobbied to include the media, but after the U.S. side emphasized the need to avoid a "carnival-like atmosphere," they finally relented and dropped the issue for the time being.

While I was elated to have been picked to lead the first team back into Vietnam, I found myself somewhat weary of Vietnam after twenty-three years of involvement with that strange land. Feeling homesick to a degree, I contemplated the difficulties of the impending field investigations to be conducted throughout the country. Recalling just how unforgiving her terrain and climate could be, I understood clearly that any endeavor related to Vietnam would never be simple or easy, and I began to wonder if I really wanted the challenge. I knew that this would be a long and arduous process. But like a powerful narcotic, over the years the mystery surrounding the fate of over two thousand of America's young men had slowly seeped into my blood, and I discovered I couldn't let go. Slowly I admitted to myself that, despite the rigors involved, I wanted to finish what I had started all those years ago, not only for myself, but for all the families who had also lost their son or husband, but unlike me, never got a chance to have a funeral or say goodbye. Yet, as I sat telling my wife and family that I was about to embark on yet another adventure, I had little foresight just how challenging it would be.

Chapter Nine

On the Ground in Vietnam

FINALLY, WHAT WE HAD HOPED FOR, planned for, and in no small amount, prayed for, had arrived. General Vessey and Foreign Minister Thach agreed on an initial increment of MIA cases to be investigated by joint Vietnamese and American teams. These first field investigations, called "iterations," were scheduled to begin in September 1988, and the main focus was placed on examining seventy compelling discrepancy cases. For the first time since World War II, Americans were working directly in the field with Vietnamese Communist counterparts. Beyond all the possible implications for the MIA issue, what potentially also was at stake was the future relations of our two countries. Since everyone on both sides was watching our actions with intense scrutiny, our margin for error was tiny, while the potential for disruptions from cultural misunderstanding, political imbroglios, staged propaganda displays, run-ins with overzealous Public Security officials, or a maze of other landmines, both known and unknown, remained enormous. Each government would have denied this, but I now clearly understood what the phase "under the microscope" meant.

By agreement, the time for each investigation period was limited to ten days. The cases selected for each "iteration" were mutually decided in advance during technical meetings held between the two side's experts. Although restricting the initial number of cases to seventy did facilitate preparation to a degree, given the very poor infrastructure, especially the lack of roads and bridges and considerable distances between many loss sites, in reality the brief time period hampered flexibility. Further, while the original list contained seventy cases, the number slowly grew as U.S. analysts promoted additional ones. Because of the growing number, we were often unable to get back to a case till much later if our initial investigation was delayed by weather or other events. Still, although neither side harbored any doubt that the list would expand, the Vietnamese constantly grumbled about the moving goalposts, since each new case meant the Communists would have to prepare for Americans tramping around asking questions.

Each team included a Team Chief and an Intelligence Analyst from the JCRC, and one Search and Recovery Specialist from the CILHI. This composition served as the basic concept for the first two years of joint efforts. Since we were examining discrepancy cases, no excavations of human remains were planned during our initial probes. However, the CILHI specialists were included to facilitate site surveys, and the examination of physical evidence in order to properly prepare for excavations planned for the near future.

My initial Investigation Team included Army Master Sergeant David Atherton from the JCRC, and Army Sergeant First Class Tommy Baughman from the CILHI. In his youth Atherton had spent several years in remote areas of Southeast Asia as a child of Christian missionaries, making him well accustomed to the impoverished situation in war-torn Vietnam. Atherton had years of experience in Human Intelligence collection and spoke both Vietnamese and Thai. While Baughman didn't have Atherton's worldly experience, he was in excellent physical condition and had a great attitude, which was helpful in the stressful conditions we worked under. Since he was young and had never served in Vietnam, the Vietnamese immediately liked Baughman better than any other American, believing that his lack of participation in the war might make him more sympathetic to their cause.

The second team, led by Jim Coyle, included Air Force Master Sergeant Richard John from the JCRC and Army Sergeant First Class Randall Nash from the CILHI. Randy Nash was a seasoned Vietnam veteran and had participated in numerous personnel recovery operations in both wartime combat situations and during the tense period after the 1973 ceasefire. He was on the unarmed JCRC team that was attacked in December 1973 by Communist forces in South Vietnam, and had been wounded during this well-known ambush. Master Sergeant Richard John was also a Vietnam veteran with many years of experience as an Air Force Intelligence Analyst. He relished the Vietnam field trips, not so much for the language or culture, but simply because he hated a garrison environment. A good, experienced analyst, he felt more at home in the field where less "spit and polish" was required. Coyle was also a Vietnam veteran, having served with a Psychological Operations unit. His recent JCRC tour had rebuilt his foundation in the Vietnamese language and culture, but his investigation and report writing talents were largely undeveloped. Further, like many of the team members, Coyle had worked at a desk in recent years, and since the JCRC did not have a physical training program, he would suffer for his previous inactivity while rebuilding his stamina and endurance. Overall, I considered the wide experience of the team members critically important to ensuring a quality investigation, as I knew the Vietnamese would send cadre even more experienced than ours.

As expected, our counterpart field teams came primarily from the Vietnamese Office for Seeking Missing Personnel, although occasionally fellow cadre from Public Security or the Ministry of Defense augmented them. As I mentioned previously, behind the scenes, the VNOSMP Party Chapter controlled this ad hoc governmental organization. The composition of the Vietnamese teams heavily emphasized expertise in the Political, Intelligence, and Security fields, especially Intelligence. Despite their assigning Intel and Security cadre to their teams, the Communists would occasionally raise their concerns to senior American officials regarding our assignment of personnel with intelligence backgrounds to the investigation teams. According to the Communists, such personnel were a threat to their national security. The difference was that we were assigning men that had experience in collection and analysis regarding Vietnam, while almost every member of the Vietnamese organization had been involved in intelligence and security operations directed against the United States.

There were numerous examples of VNOSMP cadre who were secretly intelligence officers. Prior to beginning the field investigations, the VNOSMP had been headed by Mr. Ngo Minh. A professional staff officer of the Research (Intelligence) Department, Ngo Minh traveled as a POW/MIA Specialist with the Vietnamese delegation that visited Hawaii in July 1978. He was then introduced as the head of the VNOSMP in February 1982. After running a name check I considered the possibility that Ngo Minh was actually Ngo Quang Minh, who had been assigned as the Chief Interrogator in the COSVN Security Camp (code named C-53) during the 1960s. This camp held American POWs, including at least one who was executed.

Ngo Minh was replaced as VNOSMP head by Mr. Tran Hoan, who first appeared in January 1973 as a member of the Four Party Joint Military Commission in Saigon. Overtly an officer with the rank of Lieutenant Colonel detached from the Ministry of Public Security, Tran Hoan was actually a professional case officer of the Research Department. During his tour with the FPJMC, Tran Hoan worked under Senior Colonel Nguyen Don Tu, the head of the North Vietnamese Delegation, who covertly was also the Deputy Chief of the Intelligence Department for the Ministry of Defense. Tran Hoan had a brief stint as VNOSMP head. He was replaced by Cu Dinh Ba, also a case officer of the Intelligence Department, who had previously been assigned as an instructor in the Research Department's Strategic Intelligence Course.

Continuing the trend, at the time the joint investigations began, the man in charge of the VNOSMP was Mr. Nguyen Can, a Political Officer assigned as the Chief of the America's Department in the Ministry of Foreign Affairs. Can's nominal second-in-command was assassin trainer Ho Xuan Dich, the Party Chapter Secretary who participated in the POW/MIA Delegation to Hawaii in 1982. Another key Vietnamese member at the team level was Mr. Ngo Hoang, a former Political Officer and member of the French-era Armed Propaganda Teams first organized during World War II by General Vo Nguyen Giap. A native of Binh Son district in Quang Ngai province, Hoang had served as an Intelligence Case Officer in India and more recently in the Philippines while posing as a member of the MFA.

A man who would eventually spend years in the POW/MIA issue was Colonel Nguyen Ngoc Bich. He controlled the political security and counterintelligence aspects of working with Americans for the Vietnamese side. Bich was detached to the VNOSMP from the Special Propaganda and Enemy Proselytizing Department of the General Political Directorate. The GPD served as the controlling political arm for the Defense and Security Forces in Vietnam. As with other senior personnel detached from the GPD, Bich had considerable power and authority.

While I expected someone like Colonel Bich to carefully monitor us, even I was surprised by his extreme thoroughness. Several years after the field investigations began, I learned that during a previous trip to Hanoi for a technical meeting, when Lieutenant Colonel Mather and I had held a brief conversation with a local resident in a small pub, we were already under Bich's scrutiny. Although the conversation was insignificant and lasted only a few minutes, the unfortunate man was hauled in the following day for questioning by the Public Security. After being repeatedly harassed by the Security forces in attempts to learn what he had discussed with Mather and I, the man finally threw in the towel and escaped from Vietnam by land route to the Thai-Cambodia border. After arriving at the border the man proceeded to write Mather a letter informing him of his ordeal in Hanoi, and mentioned that his main tormentor was Colonel Bich. Had Mather not given the man his business card at the time we had our chance encounter, we would never have known about the incident. This caused me to reflect on the many people I had encountered in Vietnam over the years that might have had similar difficulties after our chance meeting, but I was never made aware of it since I failed to give them my name and address. I also wondered what would have happened to the man if he had been caught trying to escape. I'm sure the paranoid Public Security police would have viewed that as an admission of guilt.

Other members of the Vietnamese teams included personnel from the wartime "Office 22" organization. During the war years Office 22 was, in my estimation, subordinate to the National Intelligence Office, which used the cover name of "Office 2." Office 22 was subdivided into two separate offices; one in the North called "A-22" and one in the South designated "B-22." Office 22 was a strategic intelligence office created to serve the Politburo, the Party Central Committee, and the Central Military Commission in Hanoi. B-22 served COSVN in the South.

The personnel assigned to wartime Office 22 were tasked with planting and training agents. Office 22 worked secretly and independently without being subjected to direct control and leadership by the typical party chapters supervising other organizations. The Office 22 personnel were detached from a number of organs, including the Military Protection Department of the Border Security Forces of the Ministry of National Defense, and the Political Security Department of the Ministry of Public Security.

The first time I became aware of Office 22's direct involvement in postwar POW/MIA accounting efforts was during the March 2, 1988 remains repatriation in Hanoi. I observed that custody of the sealed caskets was noted on the outside of the containers by a small stamp with the word *Phong* (Office) and the numerical designation 2 squared, apparently denoting "Office 22" as a sub-office of Office 2. At that time I also noticed a significant change in not only the manner in which the repatriation was conducted, but also in the personnel involved in the ceremony. For the first time, as a backdrop to the repatriation, the Vietnamese deliberately arranged for a flight of Soviet-supplied MIG jet fighter aircraft belonging to the PAVN Air Force to take off at Noi Bai airport just as the ceremony was beginning. Completely drowning out the proceedings with engine noise, the aircraft continued to take off and land as each casket containing American remains was carried into the waiting U.S. transport. It probably was not a coincidence that several of the Americans were killed in incidents involving aerial combat with Vietnamese Air Force fighter planes, including the crew from an Air Force RC-47 aircraft shot down by MIGs over northwestern Vietnam on July 29, 1966 while on a highly classified electronic eavesdropping mission. Several supposedly new members of the Vietnamese POW/MIA organization were introduced at the time, but I recognized some of them as having worked as interrogators or security personnel in wartime POW camps. One new member, Lieutenant Colonel Pham Cong Khoi, had been involved with American POWs at Hoa Lo Prison, including Lieutenant Commander John S. McCain.

Several other unusual items caught my attention at the time of the repatriation. I saw that the vehicles used to transport the remains to the airfield were covered in a red, powdery dust. Had the remains been transported from other facilities that we were aware of in well-paved Hanoi, the dust would not have been so obvious. Based on the time of the ceremony and the possible distance involved, I surmised that the remains had probably been stored at and moved from a facility called Bat Bat, just west of the airport. Bat Bat had been mentioned in several previous intelligence and refugee reports as being a main storage facility for some six hundred U.S. remains, flight suits and personal effects under the control of one of my old nemeses from the ceasefire days, Pham Teo.

Not surprisingly, Lieutenant Colonel Pham Teo was now another key VNOSMP member. In addition to his participation at Camp Davis with the Four Party Joint Military Team from 1973 to 1975, and his attendance at the technical meetings held in Hawaii, my contacts with Pham Teo had continued, mainly on various diplomatic escort missions while accompanying Communist officials on trips to technical meetings in Hawaii. Teo's name was also familiar to me as a result of interviews I had conducted with refugees and defectors from Vietnam after the war. Based on the various Source reports, then Captain Pham Teo had been a key player in the collection and storage of American remains both during and after the war ended, particularly at Bat Bat. Apparently Teo had done a good job, because he had risen in rank fairly rapidly.

Given the Source reporting on him, I watched Teo closely. Throughout the time that we were preparing for the field investigations, I followed General Vessey's advice when dealing with Communist officials: "Don't get friendly, get familiar." His words had considerable meaning for me because as an intelligence professional I realized that in order for us to succeed in an undertaking where our adversary was in control of the situation, we would need to acquire a thorough understanding of their capabilities, limitations and intentions. In researching the situation I concluded that we were up against some of Communist Vietnam's "best and brightest," and we would have to make an unprecedented effort in overcoming numerous obstacles placed before us. Thus, I subtly cultivated a relationship with the usually quiet and reclusive Teo, and as a result of our numerous contacts, I felt that I had developed a fair degree of rapport with him.

This working relationship finally proved fruitful in September 1987 when I arrived in Hanoi for a remains repatriation ceremony. During the repatriation I noted with interest that according to the VNOSMP identification specialists, one of the caskets contained the remains of Air Force Captain Michael J. Bosiljevac, whose F105G aircraft had been shot down by a surface-to-air missile (SAM) near Noi Bai airport on September 29, 1972. Although other American aircrews had observed two fully deployed parachutes and a beeper signal was heard, only one officer from the two-man crew was released at the time of Operation Homecoming. Despite many requests, no further information was ever received regarding Bosiljevac.

Along with ignoring repeated requests for information on men who had simply disappeared, traditionally the Vietnamese had also not been forthcoming regarding the circumstances of death of American personnel whose remains they did return. Since the U.S. government rarely asked, the circumstances of death for many men were still hazy. But in a departure from the norm, when I approached Pham Teo out on the tarmac at Noi Bai, I decided to give it a shot. Quietly talking to him, I casually asked him about the circumstances surrounding Bosiljevac's death, and unexpectedly, he provided some previously unknown information. According to Teo, Bosiljevac had in fact been captured alive, but by Chinese rather than Vietnamese troops. He then described how the Chinese troops, who were on a temporary assignment to defend the airfield, shot Bosiljevac in the chest shortly after his capture. CILHI forensic experts later confirmed that Bosiljevac's skeletal remains did have evidence of a bullet wound to the chest. Although Pham Teo's account did not provide a great deal of detail, I considered his revelation as a positive sign that the Vietnamese might becoming more candid than in the past. However, given that most Chinese troops had withdrawn from North Vietnam by this time, and given the current enmity between China and Vietnam, I was guarded regarding the veracity of this information. Still, after the repatriation ceremony concluded I reported Teo's account, hoping that we might start asking more of these questions, not only to get to the truth but to dig deeper into Communist procedures and policies. Predictably, however, Harvey was noticeably upset by my initiative. Apparently he was furious that I had received some new information outside the formal setting of a technical meeting. Since the technical meetings were Harvey's primary justification for travel to Southeast Asia, he wanted to restrict the flow of information to that venue.

As we headed into the field investigation phase, Harvey and I continued to occasionally butt heads. However, I took some comfort in knowing that the JCRC was headed by an officer with the rank of Lieutenant Colonel and was considered a technical organization, rather than a regular military unit with a more senior officer in charge, as it was eventually to become. This did much to insulate the organization from politics and the inherent pressure to remove cases from the discrepancy case list based on "new" information provided by witnesses introduced by Communist officials in Vietnam. Although there was occasional friction between Harvey and me, whenever I became aware of efforts to replace him at the JCRC helm with someone more politically astute, I frequently found myself lobbying with Washington-level contacts, both military and civilian, to keep him in the job. I reasoned that Harvey was as far up the ladder as he could go and he knew it. Therefore, he had no motivation for ingratiating himself with his superiors by condoning shoddy investigations to rapidly reduce the MIA list in order to establish commercial and economic ties with Communist Vietnam. To the contrary he would probably be more concerned with the family members perception of him and the JCRC.

As we began heading toward Vietnam for the first investigation, I believed that the Communist cadre were operating on three different levels regarding the POW/MIA issue. I discovered long ago that Communists functioned on three stages: overt, covert, with ultra secret behind the first two. The overt category in the POW/MIA issue included the basic facts known by both sides about the individual cases. This was information reported from various media originating within the Communist bloc, and included basic loss data that the U.S. had provided, or had been publicized in American papers. The covert aspect was applicable to "subsequent information" developed after the incident occurred, which was known by one side or the other, and in some cases both. Behind those two was a category the Vietnamese called Ultra Secret. This level would include unilateral intelligence information on American POW/MIAs produced and disseminated internally only to those organs privy to sensitive intelligence information, such as the Politburo, the Central Military Commission, and the General Political Directorate. The Ultra Secret category might also include any joint Vietnamese-Soviet or Vietnamese-Chinese exploitation efforts, the ultimate disposition of American POW/MIAs who might have cooperated, personal effects and/or human skeletal remains, as well as weapons, aircraft parts, communications-electronics, and other sophisticated equipment the Communists were attempting to reverse engineer or trade.

The Communist intelligence and security organs of all three Indochina countries considered most POW/MIA information a matter of national security, which placed much of this information in either the covert or ultra secret category. POW/MIA information could be used for political, military, or economic advantage, and thus became for them a matter which all intelligence agencies closely guard, the hallowed "sources and methods." Using American POW/MIAs to gain economic concessions or political tradeoffs, or for trading captured military equipment for aid from the Communist bloc, was an intelligence "method." Alerting us to that fact would, from their standpoint, compromise that method. Same as allowing us to know what had happened to a particular man might compromise a Source. When accused of trading in bones or hiding the truth, they claimed they were humanitarian in their sense of the word, and this was simply their policy.

Given this mindset, it was obvious to me that the Communists would operate on their long-standing principle that everything must be arranged in advance, with nothing left to chance. Only the tactical situation would be allowed to develop naturally. Our job would be to "develop the situation" to our advantage and obtain all possible information and evidence on the assigned cases as quickly as possible. However, despite our best efforts, the Vietnamese tightly controlled the situation, and we soon found ourselves struggling to maintain the balance required to conduct objective investigations in a dynamic, ever-changing environment.

As I mentioned earlier, in beginning the first joint field investigations, those of us on the American side knew that we would be setting precedents. We intuitively grasped that the manner in which future investigations were conducted, including the important "live-sighting" investigations, would be directly influenced by our initial efforts. Unfortunately, the only guidance we had from General Vessey was "lay bare the facts and let the facts speak for themselves." Although this might appear profound on the surface, due to the complex nature

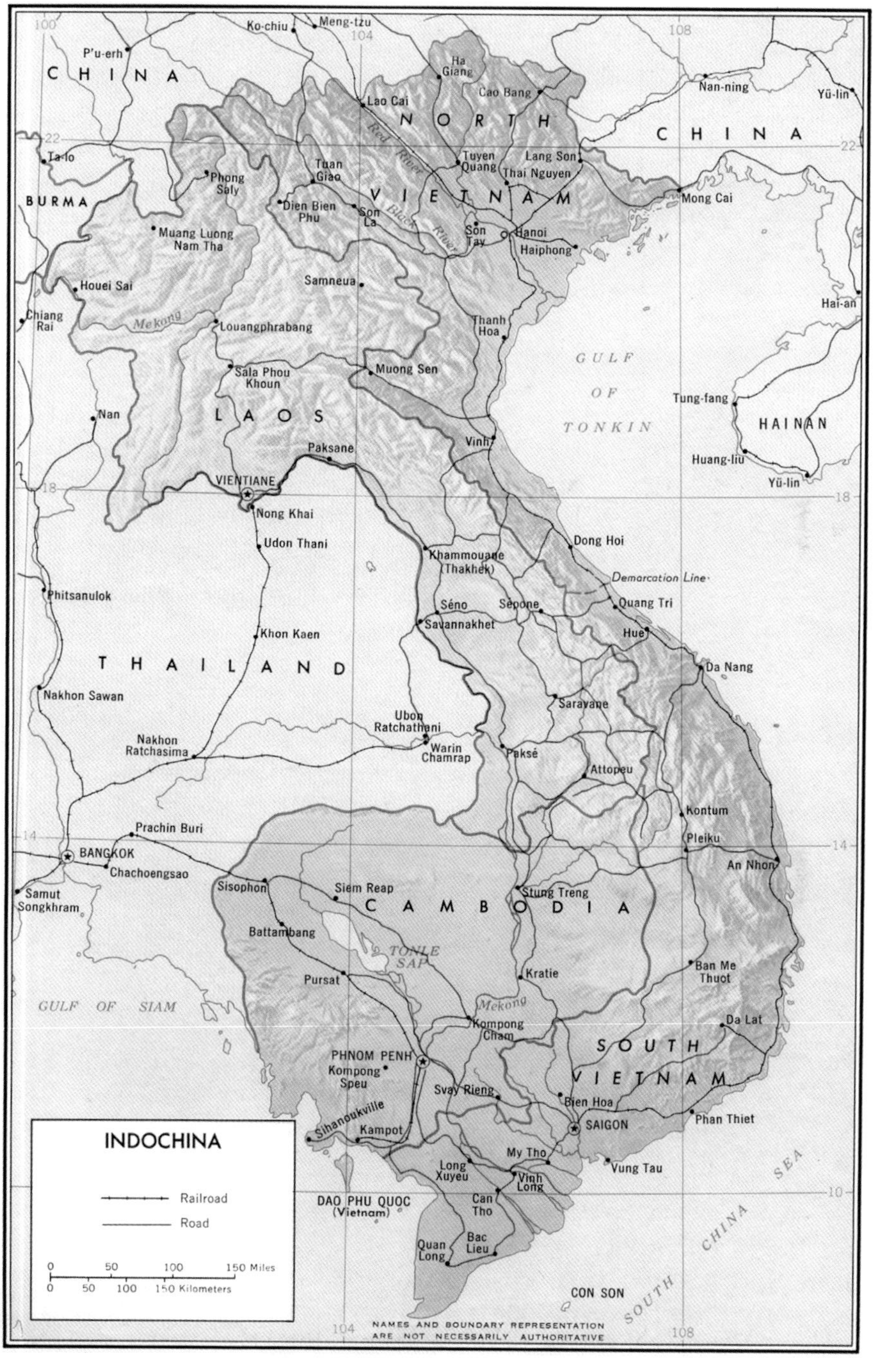

Figure 1. Southeast Asia

Figure 2. Bill Bell in 1953.

Figure 3. Bell at Airborne School, Fort Campbell, Kentucky, 1960.

Figure 4. Bell in Hue in 1968.

Figure 5. Release of U.S. POWs captured in the South but held in Hanoi by the Provisional Revolutionary Government of South Vietnam (Viet Cong) during the implementation of the Paris Peace Agreements, 1973. From Left: Bui Thien Ngo, U/I PRG cadre, Le Van Long, Colonel James R. Dennett, Bill Bell.

Figure 6. The body of slain JCRC officer Captain Richard Rees being evacuated from Saigon to Thailand by helicopter after the ceasefire violation by Communist forces south of Saigon in December 1973.

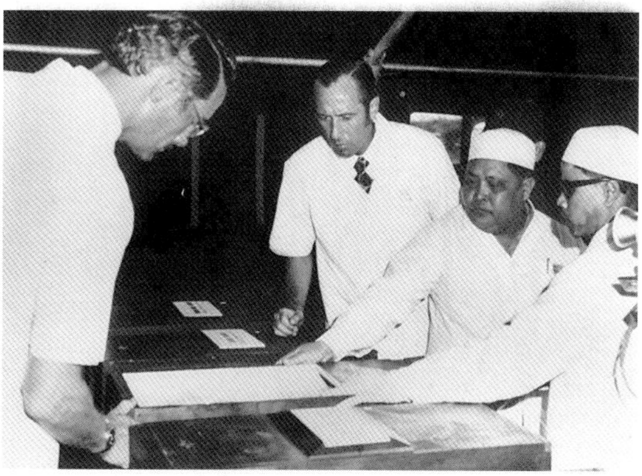

Figure 7. Group Remains Repatriation, Hanoi 1974. Left to right: John Rogers and Thorne Helgensen of CILHI; Vietnamese mortician who defected Tran Vien Loc, U/I.

Figure 8. Nova, Michael, and Andrea Bell in Saigon, March, 1975.

Figure 9. Bill Bell and Pathet Lao troops during the excavation of a U.S. C-130 in Savannakhet province, Laos in 1985.

Figure 10. Bill Bell in 1985 at the Thailand-Cambodia border interviewing a former ARVN officer and "re-education camp" inmate who escaped by the landroute across Cambodia. The man claimed to have personally observed live Americans remaining in North Vietnam after Operation Homecoming.

Figure 11. U.S. humanitarian delegation to Vietnam, 1986. Left to right: Frederick Downs, Paul Mather, Johnie Webb, Colonel Carl Savoy, M.D., U.S. Army, Larry Ward, Bill Bell, and Joe-Bob Harvey.

Figure 12. Bill Bell talking with witnesses at the seacoast in Ha Nam Ninh Province in 1988.

Figure 13. Remains repartiation in Hanoi, 1988.

Figure 14. Bill Bell in 1990 after traveling from Hanoi to a mountain at the border of Laos in Nghe An Province, Vietnam.

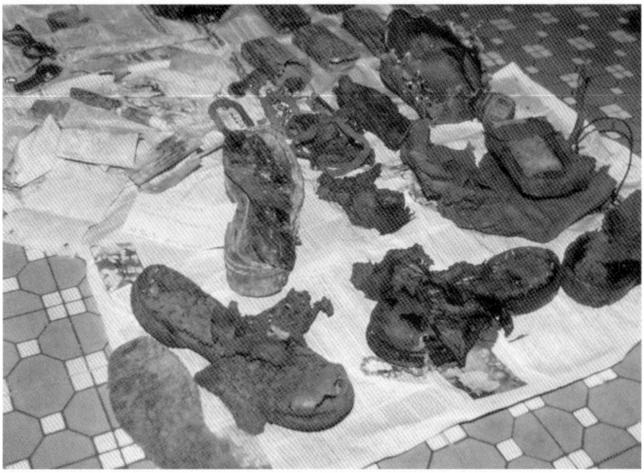

Figure 15. Recovered personal effects from an American MIA investigation.

Figure 16. Vietnam Communist Party POW/MIA Chapter Secretary Ho Xuan Dich with Bill Bell during a break from technical talks. Hanoi, 1991.

Figure 17. Bell and Dave Atherton meeting with the Province Task Team in Hai Phong, 1991. One-time VNOSMP head Pham Van Que is third from left.

Figure 18. Bell with VNOSMP members. From top to bottom: Pham Teo, Ngo Hoang, Ho Xuan Dich, U/I driver. Hanoi, 1991.

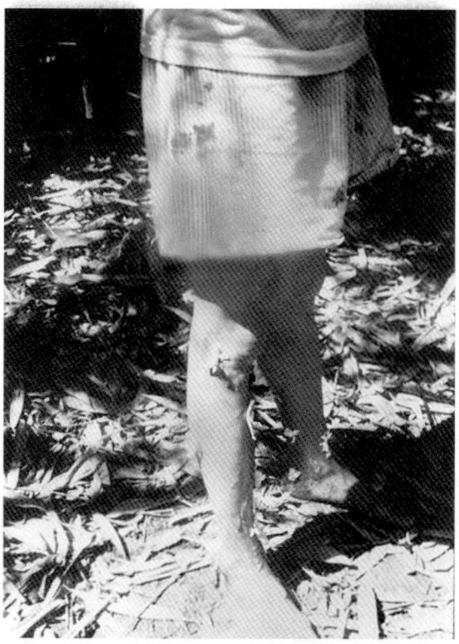

Figure 19. Leeches from the Dak Pri swamp search.

Figure 20. Bill Bell with his family in front of the Restored Sword Lake in Hanoi, 1992. From left to right: Nam-Xuan, Elisabeth, and Scott Bell.

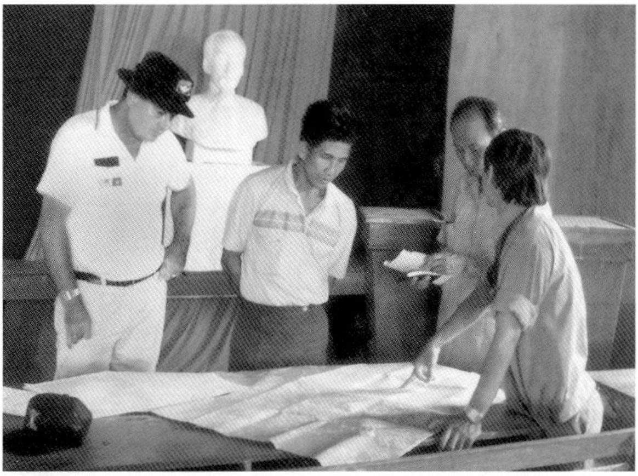

Figure 21. Bill Bell going over maps with provincial officials in Bu Dang, Song Be Province, 1992.

Figure 22. Bill Bell and Vietnam Communist Party Secretary General Do Muoi, Hanoi, 1993.

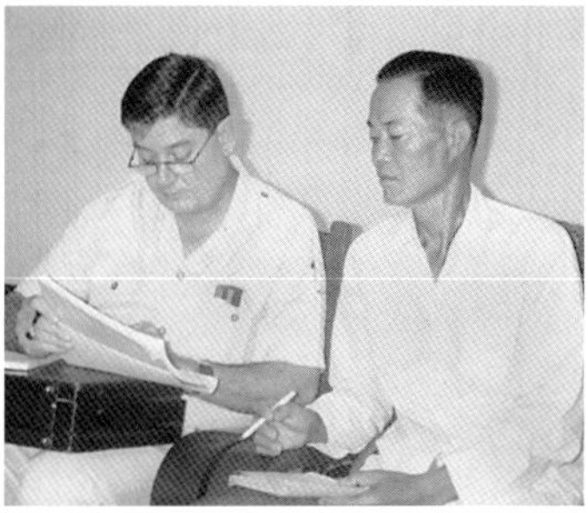

Figure 23. Bill Bell, at Rach Gia, Vietnam, March 1993, interviewing the wartime commander of the Military Region 9 (Mekong Delta) Camp for U.S. POWs. (This is the camp where Nick Rowe and Dan Pitzer were held.)

Figure 24. Bill Bell with Senator Bob Smith (R-N.H.), and Mr. Nguyen Xuan Phong, Director of the MFA's Americas Division and, later Consul General in the SRV Consulate in San Francisco, Hanoi, 1993.

Figure 25. Bill Bell and Muhammed Ali, Hanoi, October 1994.

Figure 26. From left to right: Jay Veith, Mike DePaulo, Artie Muller, and Bill Bell, at the Rolling Thunder 2003 convention. Photo: Patrick Hughes.

of the cases, it wasn't much help. After sitting across various negotiating tables from the procrastinating Vietnamese cadre for so many years, and after having carefully read the Rand Corporation study detailing how the Vietnamese officials had systematically manipulated the French POW/MIA issue, I knew that we would have to set high standards for our investigations from the outset if we were to prevent the same thing from happening to us. Moreover, the overriding moral issue of giving the benefit of the doubt to the missing men remained foremost in our minds. All things considered I was determined to follow all possible leads until they were exhausted, and at that point if there was no compelling evidence of death, to hold the investigations open until such time as Hanoi's leadership at the highest level made the political decision to provide us full cooperation in resolving the case. I also knew that at the lowest level I would meet resistance from Communist cadre assigned to work with our teams. But I believed that due to the high national priority assigned to the issue by the U.S. government, when the time came I would receive the necessary back-up from Washington. Although Vietnam's Communist Party was more interested in developing their own military through improved commercial and economic ties with America than with helping us recover our missing men, I believed that American officials, especially members of Congress, would make every effort to ensure that our POW/MIAs were fully accounted for prior to any movement forward in relations. Only later did I discover how much this U.S. government attitude would change.

In preparing for the field investigations, however, one issue in dealing with the Communists continued to cause considerable debate within the JCRC: the amount and type of information provided to the Communists prior to arriving at the sites. Senior Master Sergeant Ray Spock, the Chief of the Records and Analysis Division, staunchly supported giving them everything in advance. Spock seemed intent on providing as much information to the Communists as possible, regardless of the requirement for objectivity. I remained strongly opposed to providing a complete file to the VNOSMP prior to our arrival at a site. I felt that we should follow their behavior and provide them only the basic facts, which in reality would amount to more than they ever provided to us. I was concerned that not only would they take advantage of the information in order to manipulate the teams, there was the unsettling prospect that in order to resolve the most controversial cases, especially those situations where American personnel were known to have been alive and in their custody, the Communists might simply regurgitate the same information the Americans provided to them, which we would then accept as "new" information on which to gauge Communist cooperation.

After careful deliberation I was convinced that calculated disclosure of information based on the developments during the course of the investigation, rather than complete provenance in advance, was extremely important in cases where the American side was in possession of "subsequent information" which the Vietnamese did not know we had. Such information included reports from escaping refugees who were able to provide their accounts while not under the direct control of Communist authorities, as well as information collected by satellite imagery and signal intelligence intercepts. Other new information came from DIA and CIA sources, such as defecting Communist officials.

Another reason I didn't want to provide the Communists with materials from our files was that the JCRC's records of American eyewitness accounts were unmatched anywhere within the U.S. Government. Whereas the military services were bound by legal stipulations to declare men dead based solely on the passage of time or other factors, this was not the case with the JCRC. We were morally rather than legally bound to categorize cases. Thus the JCRC was not only considered the U.S. Government's conscience in resolving cases, but also served as an important check and balance against political machinations as well. The JCRC had compiled detailed accounts from American personnel directly involved in the combat actions resulting in the losses, as well as accounts provided by personnel participating in rescue operations.

Another major problem was conducting research on a particular case while operating in a totally insecure environment and traveling great distances on foot with only rucksacks to carry our gear. It was virtually impossible for the American team members to be in control at all times of JCRC files brought in during field investigations, so we had to protect ourselves from the efforts of the Communist intelligence services to surreptitiously copy our materials. For instance, during the very first investigation iteration Master Sergeant Atherton left some files pertaining to a Haiphong case in a storage room in Hanoi while we traveled to a different province. During a later investigation of this case, the Vietnamese were able to quote the information contained in his files almost verbatim. As a result of this incident I instructed other members of my team to only carry condensed versions of the files, a problem I solved by transcribing them in miniscule handwriting into a small, three inch by five-inch standard green notebook issued by the Federal Supply Service. Cumbersome at first, with practice I learned that I was able to carry a relatively large amount of data in one small notebook, and due to its size, I was able to keep it on me at all times.

Still, condensing our data did not provide protection if the Vietnamese authorities decided to make some type of search and seizure. Knowing from experience that physical security was not considered an important issue by most U.S. Government officials involved in casualty resolution, I knew that if we were to be afforded any protection, I would need to broach the matter at a higher level. Fortunately, Richard Childress from the National Security Council soon arrived for a visit. Since he was well-versed concerning Vietnamese manipulation of the American POW/MIA issue, Childress acted quickly on my request and ensured that the State Department issued diplomatic passports to both

Coyle and I based on our positions as investigation team chiefs working in a Communist country. Although not absolutely guaranteeing our security, or the sanctity of the files in our possession, the Vietnamese officials obviously had to consider in their calculations the diplomatic immunity afforded by the impressive black and gold passports.

As we prepared our vehicles and equipment for departure from Hanoi on our first mission, there was considerable press interest. Some members of the international media reminded us of the historical significance of our impending mission by comparing our joint US-Vietnamese POW/MIA search effort to the World War II era "Deer Team" missions that were jointly manned by members of the Office of Strategic Services (OSS) and by members of General Vo Nguyen Giap's Armed Propaganda Teams. Ironically, the primary mission of these teams was to rescue American flyers shot down while flying supply missions across North Vietnam into China. Although we Americans did not immediately pick up on this bit of nostalgic déjà vu, the accompanying Vietnamese officials not only mentioned the "Deer Teams," they even invited some former members from the American side back to Vietnam. One high-ranking Communist official related to me that "even former U.S. intelligence personnel can return to Vietnam, if they have changed," a comment I wasn't sure how to interpret. I was soon introduced to one former American team member at the Hanoi guesthouse where our investigation teams were staying. The obvious parallels in our joint efforts didn't sink in until I looked at the first photograph taken of my team and our Vietnamese counterparts working together on our mission standing side by side in the mountains of northern Vietnam.

On day one of the scheduled investigations the American contingent arrived at Noi Bai airport with six people divided into two three-member teams. The first case assigned to my team for investigation was that of Navy Lieutenant Richard C. Clark from the state of Washington. A Radar Intercept Officer launched from the USS *Coral Sea* on October 24, 1967, Clark's aircraft was damaged by a surface-to-air missile approximately fifteen miles west of Hanoi. In accordance with his escape and evasion training, the pilot of the F-4B aircraft, Commander Charles R. Gillespie, attempted to maneuver the crippled aircraft to "Thud Ridge," a huge ridgeline in Vinh Phu province northwest of Hanoi. For bombing missions in the north, the ridge had served as a predesignated pick-up point for fliers downed in the area between Hanoi and the huge Thai Nguyen steel mill located north of the ridge. After the SAM struck the aircraft, a wingman confirmed that both engines were on fire and recommended that both crewmembers eject. Gillespie stayed with the aircraft until he believed it was about to disintegrate and then ejected from the aircraft. Once out of the aircraft, Gillespie did not see Clark again. However, crewmembers from other aircraft in the area did observe two fully deployed parachutes descending in the area. The same crewmembers also reported that they heard at least one beeper signal, and that they observed at least one crewmember on the ground. Due to enemy activity in the area, no rescue attempt was made. Later that same evening Radio Hanoi announced that on the afternoon of October 24, 1967 eight U.S. aircraft had been shot down and a number of American pilots were captured. Commander Gillespie was captured shortly after reaching the ground and was released during "Operation Homecoming."

Prior to departing Hanoi on the investigation, I was informed that Mr. Tran Van Tu, a cadre assigned to the Ministry of Foreign Affairs, would lead my counterpart Vietnamese team. Initially expecting it to be led by either Dich or Hoang, I inquired concerning the reason for the unexpected change, but never received any answer. Since previous to beginning the joint operations the Vietnamese had constantly emphasized the degree of difficulty in searching for MIAs, due to the rough terrain and climate, I was somewhat apprehensive concerning the last minute appearance of the younger and stronger Mr. Tu as a replacement for senior cadre like Dich and Hoang.

During the afternoon of September 29, 1988, the Joint Team departed Hanoi in U.S.-supplied Chrysler Jeep Cherokees. As the teams traveled north from Hanoi through the village of Vinh Yen en route to Thud Ridge, I could see the massive, mist shrouded peaks looming in the background. The Vietnamese name for the ridgeline was Tam Dao (Three Islands). Apparently the name was derived from the fact that the ridgeline connected three relatively high peaks reaching some forty-two hundred feet. As we crossed the Red River we winced from the foul smell of the water caused by run-off from the huge chemical plant complex at nearby Viet Tri. The dangerously polluted water flowed southeastward toward Hanoi and Haiphong and the densely populated Red River Valley. There it would be used by millions of impoverished peasants as potable water for cooking, bathing and drinking, most likely resulting in an unusually high rate of birth defects and other illnesses.

After passing through the village of Vinh Yen the team drove by the entrance to a small road at the base of the ridgeline. According to information I collected during one of my interview trips, the road, which disappeared from view into the thick forest, was the entrance to an interrogation facility of Vietnam's Criminal Science Institute. I surmised that any American personnel captured in the Vinh Phu and surrounding areas during the war would have been taken to the facility for interrogation prior to being evacuated onward to Hanoi. Knowing that the facility was considered "Ultra Secret" by the Vietnamese, rather than raise such a nettlesome issue with them at the very beginning of the joint investigation efforts I decided to wait until a more opportune time.

Despite straining under the weight from the passengers, and loaded with equipment and baggage, the Jeep Cherokees performed well during the ascent of Thud Ridge. The drivers provided by the VNOSMP appeared intent on learning to drive the foreign imports. Due to the chaotic traffic situation we Americans did not do any driving. However, I made sure that members of both teams understood that this would be permitted in the event of an emergency. In negotiating the vehicles on the serpentine logging road leading up the ridge the only problems the drivers encountered were the power brakes and the power steering. Other than that, they appeared to have good driving abilities and considerable experience behind the wheel.

Unlike the U.S. and other western countries, enlisted men did not serve as drivers in Vietnam. According to the Communist system the drivers were considered "specialists," and after graduating from specific training they were awarded officer rank. Their resultant levels of driving experience and proficiency were often overstated, however, since a great deal of the training time was oriented toward Marxist-Leninist theory, with the primary focus on political thought. Unfortunately, I found the same situation in other career fields, including engineers, medical doctors and airplane pilots.

We normally rode in two Jeeps, with at least one Vietnamese cadre riding in each vehicle during each iteration. We did have a few incidents involving traffic accidents, but these were no fault of the drivers. When accidents did occur or where injuries were involved the Communists were unusually fair concerning reparations. This aspect of our relations puzzled me, because they had proved to be so uniformly unfair about charges for everything else. During the time while driving around, the only diplomatic incident we encountered was when an angry resident in the outskirts of Hanoi spat on Master Sergeant Atherton through the window of the Cherokee. Ordinarily Atherton would have been upset, but in this case he was consoled by the fact that the person yelled out "Russian go home!" just prior to spitting on him.

Upon reaching a small rest area at twenty-seven hundred feet we unloaded our equipment and prepared to spend the night in a small barracks type building constructed of wood and asphalt paper resembling a guard shack. The following morning we interviewed witnesses at the village of Tam Dao who claimed to be aware of the capture of Commander Gillespie, but professed to have no knowledge of a second crewmember. Although some of the witnesses claimed to have observed small pieces of aircraft wreckage, they added a caveat to their statements by reporting that Chinese troops present in the area at the time had collected souvenirs from the site, implying that the site might have been completely scavenged. With this comment and Teo's, I began to wonder if the Vietnamese would start blaming the Chinese, still their enemies, for certain aspects of the MIA issue, but they didn't.

The Vietnamese wasted no time in pressing the American contingent for more precise information on the location of the crash site. When we demurred, the Vietnamese didn't seem convinced when we informed them that due to the situation at the time, U.S. files contained only the general location of the crash that we had already provided to the VNOSMP during technical meetings in Hanoi. The

VNOSMP cadre responded by delaying the arrival of witnesses as long as possible to give the American side more time to produce the anticipated information.

During the course of the witness interviews and meetings with local officials, Mr. Nguyen Can, who arrived at Tam Dao from Hanoi in a small Russian "Lada" sedan, visited our joint team. Though in a cheerful mood, Can allowed as how he truly wanted to accompany us into the mountains to locate the crash site but was prevented from doing so by his busy work schedule. Can also cited other unspecified tasks he would perform in conjunction with the team's mission as his reason for not accompanying the team into the jungle.

Prior to bedding down for the second night Mr. Tu took the members of both teams on a hike to a famous waterfall located nearby called "Suoi Bac" (Silver Creek). The side trip to the falls required the team to descend several hundred feet down a series of steps, portions of which were constructed from masonry, with some parts actually carved into the stone face of the steep cliff. During the tiresome trip up and down the steep steps Mr. Tu lagged behind, paying close attention to the climbing ability and physical condition of the American team members. As a result of the "pleasure climb" before the scheduled hike into the jungle the following day, I went to bed that evening tired and sore. Having worked with the Vietnamese Communists for several years I knew that everything they did or failed to do was reasoned. Based on what I had seen up to that point in the trip, I had a gut feeling that we Americans were about to be challenged.

Just prior to daybreak the following morning the joint team met with one of the witnesses who claimed to have been to the crash site. The man, who agreed to act as our guide, was a member of the "Muong" ethnic minority, which represented the original inhabitants of the area, centuries before the arrival of the Vietnamese from southern China. Similar in stature to H'mong or T'ai hill tribesmen, the Muong were at home in the mountains.

After entering the jungle, our witness led us at a blistering pace along an abandoned trail running along the top of the thirty-mile long mountain range. When we halted for a rest break several miles into the trek, we quickly learned why the witness had insisted on maintaining such a fast rate of movement. Shortly after halting we were besieged by leeches. Rather than the jelly-like aquatic leeches normally seen in the marshlands of the south, the leeches encountered on Thud Ridge were the terrestrial variety. Gray in color and initially about the size of a match stem, after feeding on our blood for only a short time the land leeches grew to the size of a man's finger. I had encountered the same variety during the war while in the Central Highlands, and I recalled horror stories about how such leeches had worked their way inside the ears and penises of troops in the field, causing extreme anguish.

The leeches prompted us to begin moving again but the trail gradually disappeared into the edge of the mountain. We then began to move along a narrow rock ledge on the side of the highest peak. As the ledge became even narrower we had to inch along sideways while facing into the cliff, clinging to the side of the mountain by roots and vines growing into crevices. We moved slowly until we finally reached a point where the ledge had crumbled completely away, leaving a gap of about six feet. Although the gap was not so wide that we could not traverse it, the ledge was extremely narrow on both sides and the distance from the ledge to the rocks below was some two thousand feet almost straight down.

Undaunted by the precarious situation, like a cat the Muong guide leaped across the gap and landed on the far side. Sizing up the situation I was tempted to abort the mission and head back to the village. In studying the terrain, however, my mind drifted back to my Ranger training at Camp Merrill in the mountains of Georgia where I had faced a similar problem. At the time I had stood far back in a line of trainees at the base of a high cliff where mountain climbing instructors were teaching "free-climbing" techniques. I had watched as young West Point grads futilely tried to gain holds with their hands and feet that would enable them to climb the sheer cliff. Declaring the effort impossible, one by one the students rotated to the rear of the line. After several students failed to negotiate the initial phase of the climb, a seasoned instructor, perceiving that I was older and more experienced than others in the group, called me to the front. Partly out of fear of being embarrassed, and partly due to determination, I scaled the cliff. Shortly thereafter the other students began to follow and most of them were able to reach the top.

Knowing that the Vietnamese would be elated to see the Americans back out of the planned mission, I removed my rucksack and used one hand to sling it across the divide. Gaining as much momentum as possible by crouching I dived headlong onto the far ledge, and by grasping roots, pulled myself up to a standing position. Turning and holding my outstretched hand for the next team member, the remaining men leapt across the chasm in similar fashion. No one, Vietnamese or American, said a word as the team crossed. After bypassing the mountain's highest point the trail returned to the ridgeline and we again made good time. In hindsight had I aborted the mission I don't believe the Vietnamese would have used this to prevent further investigations because as it turned out, they knew in advance that we would have to come back and go through the entire drill again. They were simply demonstrating how difficult and dangerous the effort was. But we proved that we could take what they had to dish out. When it was over they were tired and sore too, the only difference was that they had the advantage of knowing what to expect in advance while we were always kept in the dark.

That same afternoon we reached a small clearing in otherwise dense jungle near the center of Thud Ridge. After studying the area for only a few minutes the guide, who claimed to have visited the crash site, called Mr. Tu over for consultations. A solemn Mr. Tu then broke the bad news to the rest of us that the guide had become disoriented and was not able to locate the crash site. The rest of the bad news was that the crash site could not be reached from the present location and the team would have to return to Tam Dao village for more specific information and a new guide before attempting another search of the ridgeline.

It was a frustrating experience, and in discussing the situation we were in agreement that it was difficult to comprehend that the Vietnamese had been willing to risk the lives of members of both teams just to drive home their oft stated point: "searching for MIAs is a very difficult and dangerous task." With dusk approaching we had no alternative but to move at a double time back along the route in order to be able to traverse the dangerous chasm before dark. Reaching the break in the ledge at dusk we crossed safely and soon relocated the old trail on top of the ridgeline.

However, several hours of fast movement on the slippery rock-strewn trail in total darkness took a heavy toll on our unconditioned feet. Equally troublesome, the rattan bushes with two-inch long razor sharp spikes and heavy clusters of barbed wire-like bamboo briars shredded our skin and clothing. With no supply or procurement apparatus in place the JCRC had not been able to provide us with any suitable clothing or footgear. Unfortunately, however, even if the JCRC had been successful in obtaining military issue items through normal logistics channels, due to Vietnamese restrictions placed on the import of any military equipment, such equipment would have been useless. As a result, the flimsy athletic shoes purchased individually in Thailand and Honolulu disintegrated on the rocky trail. After returning to the base-camp and peeling away our sweat-soaked clothing and footgear we all left bloody footprints on the cabin floor.[1]

Since I was required to adhere strictly to the prearranged schedule of case investigations, as soon as my team departed Thud Ridge we proceeded to Ha Nam Ninh province, located about 140 miles southeast of Hanoi on Vietnam's seashore. The next case involved Navy Commander Charles L. Putnam, who was shot down on March 9, 1967, after launching from the USS *Kitty Hawk* to fly a photoreconnaissance mission along the coast. Shortly after beginning his photo run, the pilot of an F-4 flying escort radioed Putnam that automatic weapons were firing on his aircraft. The RA5C aircraft immediately became engulfed in flames just before both Putnam and his Navigator ejected from the aircraft. They made it out okay, descending under two fully deployed parachutes. A "may day" call from the escort aircraft resulted in two fixed wing A1H aircraft and one Search and Rescue helicopter arriving on station to keep Communist forces away from the two downed aviators, but the Navigator was immediately captured by a group of Communist troops. Spotting him in the open being marched away, the two A1Hs dived to strafe the area with withering fire, forcing most of the guards to scurry for cover. With only two guards between him and the rescue helicopter, the Navigator decided to take his chances. Pulling a hidden

.22 caliber derringer from his boot, the Navigator shot one guard to death and then attacked the second guard with his bare hands. Escaping from the guard, the man ran to the rescue helicopter, which whisked him to safety. The crew of the F-4 flying escort thought they saw Putnam running along the beach but further attempts to rescue him were unsuccessful.

In investigating the case I felt a certain sense of irony, because I recalled having discussed the same case with the Communist delegations of the Four Party Joint Military Team at Camp Davis in Saigon during December 1973. I also recalled having received information on Putnam's case from two refugees escaping from Vietnam to Thailand in 1983. In each case the Source had indicated that Putnam had been decapitated at the time of the incident. What was incomprehensible was that while Putnam had been killed in a densely populated area with Communist troops on the scene, and despite our repeated requests, during the ensuing twenty-one years the leadership in Hanoi refused to provide any information to relieve the suffering of Putnam's loved ones.

Shortly after beginning the witness interview phase of the investigation in the coastal fishing village of Nghia Phuc, a typhoon suddenly struck Vietnam's coast. Still, by October 3, 1988, my team had interviewed a number of witnesses, all whom recalled the crash of the aircraft and the Navigator's rescue. None of the witnesses, however, remembered having observed Putnam when he was still alive. According to the witnesses, they found his headless body floating in the water and they buried it in a large earthen dike that formed part of a flood control system along the coast. When we went to the area of the reported burial to conduct a gravesite survey, conditions were miserable, with the rain pounding so hard that it was difficult to hear or see. By holding a rain poncho over a camera we did manage to get some photographs and a sketch of the area. It was obvious that excavating the dike would release floodwaters into the village and the operation would be extremely expensive.

After we completed the survey, additional witnesses informed us that when Putnam's body was buried, they also discovered his military identification and Geneva Convention cards. In checking we determined that both cards had been turned over to the U.S. Government in Hanoi on August 14, 1985. The witnesses also informed us that several days after Putnam's headless torso was buried in the dike, his head was found floating in the ocean adjacent to Nghia Lam village. Putnam's cranial remains were then moved to Nghia Lam village where they were buried.

During a meeting later that day with Nghia Lam village officials, we were informed that the villagers had decided to transfer custody of Putnam's skull to our joint team. During a short break, the Chairman of the village People's Committee[2] departed and then reentered the meeting room, whereby he ceremoniously produced a small, bright red, wooden container. Placing the container on a table the Chief proudly announced that the village People's Committee and citizens of Nghia Lam were ready to return the remains of Commander Putnam. With a flourish, the Chief attempted to open the box in order for me and the other Americans present to view the cranium. As he went to raise the lid, he began struggling with it and it refused to open. After several unsuccessful efforts to lift the lid, the Chief stopped and stood nervously holding the box, obviously embarrassed. Mr. Nguyen Can, who had arrived earlier from Hanoi to attend the ceremony, quietly provided verbal instructions to a VNOSMP cadre who quickly stepped forward and opened the box by sliding the lid forward, rather than lifting it up. Rather than having been recently exhumed in the local villages, Commander Putnam's head had most likely been transported from a storage warehouse by Nguyen Can in the trunk of his Russian "Lada" sedan.

After departing Ha Nam Ninh province we turned over the head to the VNOSMP in Hanoi where it was "examined" for one month. The Socialist Republic of Vietnam repatriated the cranial remains to the U.S. on November 3, 1988. The Armed Forces Review Board approved the identification of the cranium as Putnam on February 17, 1989. During a later technical meeting with Communist officials the American side informed them that the U.S. Government was satisfied that Putnam's case was resolved and that excavation of the dike in Ha Nam Ninh to exhume the decapitated body was not desired.

In all, during the first iteration our teams managed to investigate six cases. Upon completion of the first case investigations both teams returned to Hanoi to jointly compile written reports in both English and Vietnamese. I worked with Tran Van Tu to compile our joint report, while Jim Coyle worked with Ngo Hoang. As the senior U.S. official present at the time, I advised Coyle in advance not to sign anything until I had an opportunity to review it. I was not only concerned about Coyle's lack of experience, I knew that Ngo Hoang was a seasoned cadre with long years of experience in dealing with foreigners on the POW/MIA issue. This instruction proved to be prudent, because unchecked, Coyle's first reports written jointly with the Vietnamese would have led to numerous problems. Filled with speculation and subjective comments, in all cases detrimental to the missing men, it would have been virtually impossible to gain approval from the Vietnamese to conduct additional investigations of the cases assigned to Coyle had the original reports been signed and accepted by the two sides. As it was, some of his reports contained no real evidence indicating that the men whose cases he had been assigned to investigate were dead. In helping him edit his reports I noted some good leads warranting further investigation, and successful recoveries were made during subsequent iterations. Although inexperienced in investigating cases Coyle was a mature individual and ultimately he appreciated my guidance. Coyle gradually gained the necessary level of expertise, and within a short period of time his reports were being compiled in a professional and objective manner.

The joint investigations continued on a regular basis with Coyle and me leading teams throughout northern Vietnam. It was certainly not Club Med.

During our travel, in most of the cities and large towns we stayed in, the guesthouses were absolutely filthy. In some cases feces and urine from toilets had backed up in clogged sewers giving the buildings a horrific odor. Another serious problem was the seemingly endless streams of rats that entered our rooms as soon as the lights went out. We considered leaving the lights on at night but there was no electrical power and flashlight batteries were hard to come by in remote areas. I finally learned that by placing a green banana in the corner of the room farthest away from my bed, I could draw the rats away, at least until the fruit was consumed. The rats were even more aggressive than those I had encountered in the refugee camps, and at night they would use their sharp teeth to try and peel the skin from our fingers and lips. Apparently they were after any trace of grease or salt left on our skin. In at least one case, a team member was bitten and as a result he had to take a series of rabies shots. Another team member fashioned a blowgun from a piece of plastic pipe and was able to kill a significant number of rats. By placing the dead rats in conspicuous places around the guesthouses the Vietnamese staff were also made aware of the problem.

One reason for the unsanitary conditions was that only family members of Communist cadre were authorized to be in contact with foreigners. This created a situation where those responsible for cleaning felt that based on their status it was beneath their dignity to perform seemingly menial tasks. On the other hand, in the rural villages, although little more than sheds, the small guesthouses were normally clean and well maintained.

Travel around North Vietnam was extremely difficult. The roads connecting the populated areas were in terrible shape and most bridges appeared to be on the verge of collapse. In areas where bridges had never been constructed, or had been destroyed by bombing attacks, we used ropes or cables to pull ourselves, as well as our vehicles and equipment across streams and rivers on ferry boats and barges. At some major crossings we were transported across swirling muddy rivers by antiquated motorized ferries. It was obvious to us that if the boat operators suddenly lost an engine we would be immediately swept away by the powerful currents with no possibility of being rescued.

During my first few weeks in the countryside of northern Vietnam, I soaked in the environment like a sponge. I noticed that like in America, people in the North lived at a faster pace than in the South. In some of the larger cities, although the people spoke a clear dialect of northern Vietnamese, they tended to speak so rapidly that I, as well as any accompanying Vietnamese cadre from the South, had to listen intently to understand them. The language situation reminded me of my early days in the military when I tried to comprehend other soldiers in my unit who were from large northern cities such as New York, Detroit or Boston. The attitude of the northerners also appeared to be more determined than their southern brethren. I surmised that like in other areas of the world, faced with a cold climate and the real possibility of starvation the northerners simply had to be more aggressive in order to survive.

Another readily apparent aspect was the abject poverty. Despite the overblown predictions of the wartime Vietnamese cadre, the people of North Vietnam were beyond poor. In considering how or why the populace would be willing to live under such harsh conditions without overthrowing their Communist rulers, regarding modern standards of living the people in the North had no basis for comparison. It was a situation reminiscent of the old parable "one cannot miss what one never had." Although not completely content, by 1988 many northerners who had previously lived in mud huts with thatched roofs lighted by candles had upgraded to wooden huts with tin roofs lighted by kerosene lamps; in their perception they were experiencing at least some progress. I gained one indication of just how impoverished the people truly were when we saw several farmers working out in the cold wind while wearing windbreakers made from tree leaves laced with vines and twigs.

The people in the rural areas of the North appeared to have a strong work ethic, and with the exception of Communist party members, who attended countless meeting sessions each day, the peasants were in the fields early and stayed late. It seemed that the women worked even harder than the men, many of them doing strenuous farm work with infant children strapped to their backs. Most farmers working at state collectives maintained private vegetable plots and animal-raising pens on the side; virtually every inch of ground that could be cultivated was yielding some type of edible crop, including the steep slopes of hills and mountains which were planted in cassava. Farmers growing cassava took advantage of the roadways by slicing the tubers and laying them on the pavement to dry. The intense heat from the concrete and asphalt prevented mold from developing, and it provided a free source of energy for the farmers. Once the sliced tubers were dried they were cooked with rice for human consumption or ground into pellets or powder and sold as feed for livestock.

While on the road we stopped at numerous villages, at times to eat our meals and occasionally for stretch breaks. Almost without exception the many villagers would be gathered at small stands that sold noodles, tea or rice whiskey. At each location we observed loudspeakers atop poles scattered through the area. The elevated speaker systems were constantly blasting out Radio Hanoi, the only station the people were permitted to listen to. At first the speakers were extremely irritating, but like the villagers we eventually became accustomed to the shrill voice of the Ministry of Propaganda and Culture. The people didn't seem to be listening intently to the loudspeakers, but rather accepted them as a part of daily life. We weren't sure how the loudspeakers were powered since electric generators were rare. We did observe some overhead power lines, however, and the locals were illegally tapping into the elevated cables by flinging long, thin copper wires with fishhooks attached to the end over the wires. This theft of services appeared to be open and blatant as if no one was overly concerned with getting caught.

Despite the fact that the accompanying cadre from Hanoi constantly reminded us that the people were still angry due to the destruction caused by American bombing during the war, during our stops we never detected any animosity on the part of the people, only curiosity. The people seemed to be keenly interested in American culture. I normally carried an assortment of tapes, and wherever I took my meals I would first inquire if a tape player was available. If it was, I would ask them to play the tape and later leave while "forgetting" the tape. Unfortunately very few citizens possessed tape players and the owners of the small restaurants where I did manage to leave tapes most likely came under the scrutiny of the "Cultural Investigation Team."

Knowing that political security and cultural inspection cadre were always nearby I didn't want to provoke them by openly presenting anyone with American music or other forms of our culture. At locations where no tape player was available I carried a small stereo cassette player with two detachable speakers for listening to music. My selections included the Drifters, the Platters, the Impressions, George Jones, Hank Williams, Sam Cook, Tammy Wynette, Bobby Bland, Merle Haggard, and many other American musicians. At times I also included music by a group of Vietnamese refugees in America called "New Wave." The music by New Wave proved to be so popular that a copy of one particular tape I "left behind" in Hanoi ended up in remote Son La province in the northwestern part of the country a mere two months later.

Although the political security cadre tolerated my propagation of American music, they didn't like it. According to them everything, regardless of its origin, has at least some political connotation. This included music, poetry, art in any form, and especially news broadcasts. After listening to Communist music extolling the people to emulate the hard working, award-winning labor teams consistently leading the way in production, and after viewing dull, colorless paintings depicting rifle-carrying laborers and peasants surrounded by gear wheels and farm implements, I could see why they would hold that opinion.

Another aspect I noted was that the only available source of fuel for warmth or for cooking was wood. This resulted in the forests being stripped at an alarming rate. Since domestic livestock grazed on all available grass, the areas around villages and roads had the well-manicured look of freshly mowed fairways. Looking out over the countryside, the broad expanse of closely cropped grass and cultivated crops spread into the distance to meet constantly receding well-defined walls of jungle and tall rain forest. Like ants, villagers scurried to and from the forest in long, undulating files, returning laden with cumbersome bundles of hand-hewn timbers. Pulled from the ground by water buffalos and then split into small pieces, wood from gnarled tree stumps was stacked along the roads for sale to passers-by. My observation of the rapid deforestation brought to mind one of Ho Chi Minh's most famous slogans "the forests are gold and must be protected." I surmised that Chairman Ho was probably rolling in his grave due to the tragic forest situation.

Given their poverty, the Vietnamese personnel assigned to work with us were ill equipped for our missions. They were especially unprepared for the rough mountainous terrain and relatively cold winter climate in the northern part of the country. After I saw just how miserable they were in the field I decided to provide some relief. At the first opportunity, in conjunction with my refugee interview trips to Hong Kong, I used my daily per diem allowance to purchase jackets, rain parkas, gloves, caps and shoes for all Vietnamese personnel who were assigned to the field investigation teams. This gesture led to an instant improvement in team morale, and the Vietnamese team members worked harder as a result. I also designed and purchased several hundred "Joint US-Vietnam Search Team" pullover shirts with an eagle and a dragon faced off on the reverse side, and U.S. and Vietnamese flags on the front. Some of the Vietnamese team members were hesitant to wear shirts with an American flag, but the shirts did help stave off the cold wind, so they wore them beneath their regular clothing. Eventually most of the shirts were handed out as souvenirs to people we met along our routes. After several months of field operations the Joint Search Team shirts were considered collector items and everybody wanted one, even cadre in Hanoi who were not involved in the effort.

Despite my efforts at building team morale, the Vietnamese who worked with us on a daily basis remained secretive concerning their own unilateral operations, which I expected but had hoped to break by resorting to a small amount of charm coupled with considerable perseverance. In addition to being protective concerning their official records on U.S. casualties, as a carry over from the clandestine nature of their war against the Americans, they appeared reluctant to provide any information concerning their personal lives, including information about their families and in some cases their real names. For example, when we signed our joint reports we Americans always placed our true names and signatures on the official versions of the joint investigation reports. The Vietnamese on the other hand were not so straightforward. I noticed that according to available intelligence, one cadre, who used the name "Pham Van Manh" in signing our joint reports, was actually named Nguyen Hung Manh. In order to let the Vietnamese know that we were following their activities closely, I waited until "Pham Van Manh" was assigned to another team operating in a different province and then sent some packages of warm clothing for each Vietnamese team member by way of a routine supply vehicle. After receiving a package I had labeled "Nguyen Hung Manh" the cadre immediately went to Ngo Hoang to inform him of the apparent compromise in his supposedly secret identity. After Ngo Hoang apologized to me for the incident I informed him that it was not a major issue, but that I wanted to ensure that our joint reports were accurate and credible. I raised the possibility that if we were not honest in some of our reporting the information in all reports might be considered suspect. Indicating that he understood the point, the cadre began to sign his reports using his true name.

I noticed something else regarding the secrecy aspect when we were in Hanoi preparing to go into the field. In order to better prepare for the field operations I would routinely attempt to pry at least some advance information out of my counterparts. Almost without exception they would indicate that we would have to wait until our arrival at the scene for any details. I was not certain, but it appeared to me that my counterparts were also being kept in the dark. I also noticed that when we arrived at the province, district or village level there was also a general lack of knowledge by local officials regarding the cases.

I finally solved this mystery when I unexpectedly walked up on a meeting being held by a just arrived Vietnamese team. As I approached the table where the team was seated for lunch at a small noodle shop, one of the team members was in the process of opening an official-sized envelope that was addressed to that particular team. As I stood silently, unnoticed by the Vietnamese, the team member began to read off instructions for carrying out the investigation of the first scheduled case. The only return address on the envelope was "Vo Nguyen Quang." Since I had never met or even heard about anyone named "Vo Nguyen Quang" assigned to the POW/MIA issue in Vietnam, I immediately considered the possibility that this was a reference to an unidentified individual I had heard about who was reportedly a military officer related to the famous General Vo Nguyen Giap. Based on the written instructions, opened only after the team arrived at the local level, I confirmed that the investigations were being closely controlled from Hanoi. My information was later confirmed a second time via highly reliable intelligence means.

Our Vietnamese counterparts were also extremely cautious concerning the aspect of physical and personnel security. Unless we resorted to ruses, we never went anywhere without surveillance from the Political Security Department. Coverage on me in particular seemed to increase after every confrontation I had with political cadre at the local level. Prior to departing the American Embassy in Bangkok on one iteration I was forewarned by a U.S. Intelligence Agency that the Political Security Department in Hanoi had notified local officials in one particular area in the south that I was a "dangerous element" and subject to undertake political activity at any time. The Political Security Department informed the local authorities that a named cadre from their department would arrive in the area in advance to meet me, and then would follow my activities throughout the duration of the investigation iteration. Since security personnel had routinely followed me to the restroom in Hanoi, this was really no surprise. When the new security agent introduced himself to me by a cover name when I arrived at the airport, this was also no surprise. But when we departed from Vietnam at the close of the investigation iteration, in the process of saying goodbye, I shook the cadre's hand while referring to him by his true name and at the same time praising him for a fine job of protecting me. He immediately became red-faced.

Throughout the course of the investigations the Vietnamese security cadre assigned to monitor our movements remained constantly vigilant, intent on leaving nothing to chance. In some cases cadre were overheard instructing witnesses to inform the Americans that when aircraft were hit by ground fire they had seen fully deployed parachutes descending but not to provide any further details. Such coaching obviously impacted on the objectivity of the investigations. The orchestration of witnesses became so flagrant that both Coyle and I complained to the JCRC and the VNOSMP. Such protests were received reluctantly by both sides and were largely ignored. Apparently the most important facet of our investigations of the discrepancy list cases was the time factor; the issue of witnesses being coached was considered secondary to rapid completion of the initial case list. Not working at the policy level, I did not have a good grasp of the strategy being planned in Washington, but I was determined to make sure that the lack of genuine cooperation was reported. Another hindrance to objectivity, at times the security cadre accompanying the team were so invasive that the witnesses felt intimidated, raising more complaints from us. When things finally deteriorated to the point where the investigations were becoming a charade I decided to risk expulsion from the country and possible loss of my job by trying to rectify the situation.

During the planning phase for the next iteration, which included eight cases, I was informed that I would be assigned to northwestern Vietnam's Son La province. Realizing that I would be working in a remote area where U.S. intelligence agencies had had little or no access since the battle of Dien Bien Phu in 1954, I scanned refugee records to locate clusters of former residents of Son La province, including members of the "Tai" ethnic minority, who had fled Vietnam. I then traveled to northeast Thailand to the Na Pho camp located on the Mekong River separating Thailand from Laos. Located approximately 260 miles south of Son La, the Na Pho camp was the closest possible destination for refugees escaping from Son La.

Quickly reestablishing contact with my net of informants from past years, I located a refugee who had been previously employed by the Provincial Museum in Son La. In addition to loss incidents occurring in the Son La area, I debriefed the former museum staff member concerning records and photographs held at the museum. The refugee also provided information on the activities of wartime Soviet advisers operating in northwest Vietnam, including facilities where they had worked and stayed during their tours. The refugee was also able to draw sketch maps depicting the area for me to carry back into Vietnam.

When our joint team traveled to Son La the first case scheduled for investigation was that of Air Force Major Marvin Lindsey from Louisiana. At the time of his loss incident on June 2, 1965, Lindsey was the pilot of an RF101C aircraft flying as the lead aircraft in a flight of two aircraft on a photoreconnaissance mission. Lindsey's aircraft took a direct hit from 37mm ground fire, and as the aircraft continued forward the wingman called for him to eject. As the powerful RF101C rolled to the left, the left wing broke off from the fuselage. At that same time the wingman saw a cylindrical object, which he believed to be the ejection seat, leave the cockpit area. As the burning wreckage spiraled downward, the wingman flew into a cloudbank and lost site of the crippled aircraft. Search and rescue personnel who arrived in the area were not able to locate Major Lindsey's parachute or beeper signals and recovery efforts were terminated without success.

Meetings with local officials produced no useful information for our team. In order to provide a liaison with the American experts, Province Task Teams, normally consisting of from five to ten Vietnamese "specialists" were formed in provinces throughout the country. The Province Task Teams were comprised of members of the regional and local military commands, the Communist Party External Affairs Department, and the Ministry of the Interior/Public Security. To reinforce to the American contingent the difficulties involved in searching for MIAs, the Son La Province Task Team took us on a grueling trek to the top of the highest mountain in the area. Although Lindsey's aircraft had flown over the mountain while en route to Son La town we found nothing related to the investigation. The Chief of the Province Task Team, Colonel Nguyen Van Tho, apologized for the lack of results and pledged to strive to obtain more information in the future. Tho also told me that he wanted to cooperate and he asked me to inform him should we encounter any difficulties while investigating cases within the province.

During the course of the meetings with the local officials I requested that the joint team be allowed to visit any museum or other facility in the area maintaining records on U.S. losses. We were informed that no museum existed in Son La. With the exception of a two-hour lunch-break, when in the typical fashion of tropical bureaucrats the Vietnamese officials normally ate their noon meal followed by a two-hour siesta, the Son La province Public Security had closely monitored our activities. Noticing that the Public Security personnel also observed the two-hour siesta tradition, I decided to skip the siesta and take the American contingent on a unilateral tour of Son La.

By referring to one of the sketch maps provided by the ethnic T'ai refugee in Thailand, I was able to proceed directly to the Son La Museum, which according to the local Vietnamese officials did not exist. Since the director of the museum was away for lunch I engaged a staff member in a brief conversation that resulted in the American contingent being invited in for a guided tour. Expressing interest in photographs and records, only a few minutes after our arrival we were busy photographing and transcribing records and photos pertaining to American personnel killed or captured during the war. After approximately thirty minutes of unilateral research the Public Security personnel hurriedly arrived at the museum and informed me that we were not authorized to be in the facility and that we would have to leave. Satisfied that I had made my point concerning the lack of cooperation regarding the provenance of records, I took the team back to the guesthouse to gather our gear.

That same afternoon we were escorted to the ruins of a large building that local officials said was the site of a former hospital destroyed by U.S. bombing attacks. The members of the Province Task Team spent considerable effort in describing how much suffering had been caused to the local populace due to the loss of their only hospital. Referring to another sketch map of the area I corrected the officials by informing them that according to my information, the destroyed building was actually an army barracks, which was a legitimate military target. Caught by surprise the local officials sheepishly admitted that the building had housed a PAVN unit and that they had been mistaken in identifying it as a hospital. Considering the misidentification of the building as the second incident of manipulation, I felt compelled to remind Colonel Tho of his offer of assistance should we encounter any problems while working in his province. Tho attempted to pass the incidents off as misunderstandings.

We ultimately debriefed witnesses who reported that an American pilot had been killed by ground fire as he descended into the town of Son La under his fully deployed parachute. The point where the pilot's body touched down was said to be a field medical training facility, raising the possibility that Lindsey's skeletal remains, like the remains of other downed crewmembers in other provinces of Vietnam, had been prepared for use as a training aid at the medical school. According to the witnesses, after removing all personal effects, personnel on duty at the time buried the pilot's body near the medical training facility. A few days later, however, some Intelligence Officers arrived on the scene and issued instructions for exhumation of the body. After the body was examined and photographed it was reburied at the same location. We proceeded to excavate three different burial sites pointed out by the witnesses, but the reported remains of the pilot could not be found. The Son La Museum later produced a photograph of a recently deceased American pilot with the rank of Captain, which was Lindsey's actual rank at the time of his incident, visible on his flight suit. A notation on the back of the photo indicated that the pilot was shot down on June 27, 1965. A CILHI anthropologist examined the photo, but could not positively identify Lindsey. Although pleased to see a glimmer of cooperation from the Vietnamese, I nevertheless took the opportunity to remind them of the importance of locating burial sites and photographs rather than wasting time climbing up and down mountains to sites unrelated to the case.

Although the Vietnamese cadre insisted that the Americans strictly follow the schedule for case investigations, I remained persistent in trying to gain access to Sources not scheduled for interview that could provide information on other cases. For example, while in Thai Nguyen City, Bac Thai province, on the first evening of our arrival in town I took the American contingent on a tour of the city. Less than five minutes after entering a street-side noodle stand I began to receive information from a waitress concerning a loss incident involving two Air Force enlisted men who were assigned as crewmembers on an aircraft during a rescue mission in Nghe An province on March 14, 1966. As soon as I heard the location and circumstances I remembered the unusual case. Amazingly, Nghe An is some three-hundred kilometers southeast of Thai Nguyen, and according to the waitress she had lived near the beach where the two Americans were lost before moving north to Thai Nguyen. When the local Communist cadre found out about me obtaining information from someone they had not scheduled and prepared in advance, they were livid. When I went back to the noodle stand the next day no one there would talk to me.

Concerned by the possibility of retribution from Communist cadre, I realized that I would have to exercise caution in gaining additional information not planned for release by the central authorities. But at the same time I accepted the fact that I had signed on to perform my duties in an objective manner, and I had no other alternative. My attitude, considered "dangerous" and obstinate by the Communist cadre, would cause me further problems in the days to come.

Chapter Ten

Across the DMZ

BY JANUARY 1989, we slowly began working our way southward toward the DMZ and the former Republic of Vietnam. My language ability and knowledge of the country continued to be a source of great worry for our accompanying VNOSMP cadre, as they had a difficult time controlling my attempts to go outside their unwritten parameters regarding no contacts with civilians not unilaterally prearranged for the investigations. This was especially true when our teams went into areas by helicopter, since the unusual sight of a helicopter landing in a field near a remote village routinely drew large crowds of curious residents. In such situations, immediately upon landing, but before the cadre had an opportunity to brief the local Public Security on crowd control, I tried to maneuver my way through the throngs of villagers in search of anyone who appeared to be old enough to have knowledge of the war.

My spontaneous interviewing once again paid dividends when shortly after landing by Soviet-made MI-8 helicopter in the Dong Hoi area in Quang Binh province just above the DMZ, I quickly exited the aircraft and made my way to a Vietnamese man I had spotted from the air sitting atop a bicycle a few hundred yards from the landing site. After only a brief discussion in the Vietnamese language concerning my origin and mission, the man began to relate that the remains of seven Americans had already been recovered from crash sites, specifically from the nearby Le Phu Ninh Pass inside Laos. The strategic pass straddled

Route 20, and was one of the most important infiltration routes from North Vietnam into the South. The man claimed direct knowledge of the recovery, and presented this in a very straightforward, believable manner. He appeared to be genuinely helpful and didn't ask for anything in return. Apparently the Good Samaritan on the bicycle knew what he was talking about because at the time we spoke, JCRC files contained numerous loss incidents near the Le Phu Ninh Pass. He also provided information on the recovery of American remains by PAVN troops from two separate areas of Quang Binh province in Vietnam. While I was pleased that the man had provided the information in such a straightforward manner, once again I felt guilty because I knew he was in serious trouble with Public Security. What the man had intended as a decent act would undoubtedly result in a nightmare for him and his family.

Still, while some remains from Quang Binh had already been repatriated by Vietnam, as of this writing, no remains have ever been returned from the Le Phu Ninh Pass area of Laos. If true, this meant that the Vietnamese were now gathering remains from inside Laos and storing them, which would seriously impact our efforts in that country. In my view, the main reason that the Vietnamese might search for remains from Laos was that they could in the future collaborate with the Lao on cases close to the ill-defined border, sending U.S. teams on expensive, time consuming search and recovery missions into remote areas of Laos, most likely to be followed by even more expensive excavation operations requiring considerable labor, helicopter transport fees and other chargeable resources. Such speculation might seem like paranoia, but consideration of the families, not to mention protecting American interests, required everyone in the casualty resolution business to guard against and prepare for such possibilities.

Based on this important information on the remains recovered from Le Phu Ninh Pass, I decided to begin submitting a new report that eventually became known as the "Additional Information Report." Although I strongly believed in obtaining as much spontaneous POW/MIA information as possible, once again I found myself in a bureaucratic battle with JCRC headquarters. Back in the Records and Analysis Division, Ray Spock fought against the idea because it only created more work for his analytical staff. I also wanted to put a sequence number on the report similar to other refugee reports, but Spock fought against this as well, since placing a sequence number would establish a paper trail, making it easy for family members to determine when the report was received and how long it took to be processed and released to the next-of-kin. Ultimately, it resulted in a bureaucratic draw, and it was left to the Team Chief's discretion if they wanted to submit these reports, but Spock didn't want anyone questioning the length of time it took to analyze a report. The sequence number idea died a quiet death.

Underscoring the importance of gathering information in this manner was proven in my mind when during a future iteration, a Recovery Team learned of a grave location containing the remains of Americans killed in combat on Route 20, just east of Le Phu Ninh Pass. Although these new witnesses claimed that the site had been left undisturbed since the incident, the team that later excavated the site discovered fresh green leaves from nearby trees buried deeply inside the grave. While salting of sites wasn't prevalent, occasionally we would arrive at reported graves and find them recently excavated. Nearby I would find scraps of blue plastic sheeting, which was typical PAVN rain poncho issue, along with wire that appeared to have already been used for tying bundles. When we asked Communist officials about the obvious excavation, they denied any knowledge, leaving us completely stymied.

Fortunately, I knew that Childress did read the field reports, and that he would bring it up during negotiations and use it to measure the true level of Communist cooperation. Eventually, his efforts paid off. The increase in case investigations brought about a parallel boost in remains being repatriated, some as a result of the joint investigation efforts, and some due to Vietnamese unilateral recovery operations. On July 13, 1988, Vietnam repatriated twenty-five boxes of remains, on November 1, twenty-three remains, and on December 15 another thirty-eight were returned. The majority of the remains from the last two were almost complete skeletons with clear scientific evidence of having been preserved and stored for a prolonged period of time. Most were released as a result of Childress's prior negotiations with Foreign Minister Thach, but in my view it was also a subtle signal to President George Bush's incoming administration concerning Vietnam's ability to rapidly account for MIAs, and perhaps even a plea for improved relations by demonstrating their willingness to show "progress" on the all-important MIA issue.

But the increase in the return of remains was certainly no real indication that our efforts on the ground would become easier. For example, in December 1988 in the area of Dong Hoi City in central Quang Binh province I investigated the case of Major Victor J. Apodaca from Colorado and Captain Jon T. Busch from Ohio. On June 8, 1967, Apodaca and Busch were shot down when their F-4 aircraft was hit by enemy fire during an armed reconnaissance mission. Although other aircraft in the area heard weak beeper signals, Apodaca's aircraft was never located and search efforts were terminated due to darkness. According to the Vietnamese, two of the July 1988 remains were Apodaca and Busch. Although the remains labeled as Busch were identified, those labeled as Apodaca were determined to be "non-human," possibly the remains of a pig.

Although Vietnam later admitted that Busch had been captured, but that he had died shortly afterward due to injuries, we decided to investigate the incident when forensic analysis on Busch's remains indicated that he had successfully parachuted from the aircraft. This was one of the few times CILHI ever shared detailed forensic information on remains, not because of the "live prisoner" implications in this instance, but because the Vietnamese had us in a dilemma on this case. Without being obvious, behind the scenes the U.S. government placed considerable emphasis on resolving this case, since Victor Apodaca's sister is Dolores Apodaca Alfond, the head of the National Alliance of Families. The Vietnamese were well aware that Ms. Alfond is quite vocal in her condemnation that the U.S. puts too much priority on remains recovery, while ignoring the live-sighting issue. To some in the U.S. government, if the crash site revealed her brother's remains, one particularly vocal critic might be put to rest. One would think that even the Vietnamese would have been glad to see her removed, but as usual, they were more interested in the money.

When my team arrived at the purported crash site, located in very close proximity to Highway 1, we conducted a site survey but were unable to locate any remains, personal effects, or life support items indicating that anyone was inside the aircraft at the time of impact. Worse, although we were able to recover some aircraft debris, nothing specific could be identified. More ominous, a person residing next to the crater was identified as being a "remains trader" who worked on the state road construction unit. Based on the information concerning the witness' involvement in trading human remains, his position with the road construction unit, and the various types of metal and sundry items inside the crater, I concluded and wrote in my report that the crash site was "probably staged." My opinion was further reinforced when the Vietnamese Team Chief objected to the inclusion of information in our Joint Investigation Report indicating that the witness was employed by the state road construction unit. I believed that the Communists were planning to manipulate the investigation to not only force to the U.S. to fund a new highway section, but to reemphasize the futility of seeking a full accounting due to local citizens trafficking in human remains. Separately reinforcing my written comments, the Search and Recovery Specialist from the CILHI also did not recommend the site for excavation. My Team Analyst was equally certain that nothing indicating an actual crash site was present.

A few months later Vietnam returned more boxes of remains. One was labeled "Apodaca Victor." The small pieces of bone contained in this particular box were reportedly confiscated from "remains traders" in Hue. In all, three more investigation teams and a separate "Joint Technical Assessment Team" visited the same alleged crash site. After my tour was over, the Communists and the U.S. reached an agreement to excavate the site, but only after the Americans promised to provide funding for a section of new road. Although the U.S. requested that the excavation start at the beginning of the dry season, the Communists insisted that the effort be initiated at the onset of the rainy season. Shortly after the excavation team began its complex project the monsoon arrived and the site was totally inundated. Extensive efforts to reinforce and shore up the muddy crater were futile. A request to postpone the excavation was denied, and the project was finally abandoned without any remains or material evidence being found. Eventually the small bone portions reportedly confiscated from "remains traders" were determined through DNA comparison to be those of Apodaca, although his sisters still dispute the findings. With the money made from the overall operation the Communists were able to completely rebuild that section of Highway 1, and no doubt took satisfaction in watching the highly critical National Alliance POW/MIA family group continue to be a thorn in the side of the U.S. government.

Leaving Quang Binh, we crossed the war-torn DMZ to begin investigating cases within the former RVN. The first sign we were in the South could be seen in the quality of the roads. After having our heads pounded into the roofs of the Jeeps for several months while riding on the poorly constructed thoroughfares of the North, crossing the bridge over the Ben Hai River was like entering another, more civilized world. Still, Communist mismanagement had relegated what had been a comparatively prosperous RVN into seemingly hopeless poverty in only fourteen years.

On Highway 1 between the Ben Hai Bridge and Dong Ha town we stopped to watch some former ARVN soldiers in mix-matched fatigue uniforms digging unexpended artillery rounds from the ground. Rusted almost beyond recognition, after removing the fuses the former soldiers placed the rounds on the ground in a circle and ignited the remaining explosive with matches. As the rounds burned and spewed the men sat inside the circle monitoring the fires. In some cases the explosive material was removed from the rounds to be used as charges for stunning fish. From the road we often observed young Vietnamese fisherman floating offshore in small, odd-looking round boats made by stretching rubberized canvas over bamboo frames. With the boats in a line parallel to the beach the boys would light the fuses of fist-sized handmade charges and toss them into the water. Shortly after the charges exploded long nets stretched between the boats gathered stunned fish floating to the surface. Many of the techniques for exploiting unexploded munitions were taught by PAVN Explosive Ordnance Disposal (EOD) troops. Considering the amount and variety of U.S., French, Japanese, Chinese, and Soviet manufactured bombs and munitions deactivated or modified and reused by Communist forces during and after the war, the PAVN are undoubtedly some of the world's most proficient EOD experts.

As we traveled from Dong Ha on into Hue we noticed piles of metal along the roadsides. Now we understood the real reason for the former ARVN digging up the old artillery shells. In addition to artillery rounds, perforated steel platform removed from tactical airstrips and huge chunks of metal from American tanks and Armored Personnel Carriers could also be seen. According to the locals, scrap metal of all types was in demand by Japanese manufacturers for use in making automobiles to sell in America. I doubt many American veterans would have been pleased to learn that the shiny new Japanese cars in their driveways contained metal used by the U.S. military to fight the war in Vietnam.

After arrival in Dong Ha we were also amazed by the amount of American military equipment still in use after so many years. Almost every roadside noodle stand used insulated "Mermite" cans to keep their food warm. Some also had large stainless steel beverage containers, as well as the standard issue knives, forks and spoons always seen in American military mess halls. Perhaps most surprising, I noticed that American military issue clothing, especially the cotton "Field Jacket," were worn throughout the country, including the North. People fortunate enough to own U.S. manufactured clothing described it as being both warm and of lasting quality. I found it ironic that we American team members were not allowed to wear any military items, while Vietnamese all over the country considered American made military gear to be of good quality and suitable for routine attire.

We also encountered several small groups of American war veterans who had arrived as tourists in the DMZ area. Some appeared to be satisfied with their tour arrangements, but many complained bitterly about the relative high cost for dismal facilities. I talked to one former Marine who had shelled out over $2,000.00 to return to his old base at Khe Sanh only to find that everything recognizable had been removed from the area by scavengers. Preparing to return to the United States, the former Marine was somewhat frustrated at having traveled such a great distance to find only one nylon C-ration spoon as a reminder of the past.

Continuing on down to Hue, the first of twelve cases to be investigated by both teams during the third iteration was the loss of Chief Warrant Officer Solomon H. Godwin from Hot Springs, Arkansas, which was assigned to my team. Godwin was a Marine Corps Counterintelligence Officer who had been an advisor to the Hue National Police Special Branch. Similar to the Federal Bureau of Investigation, the Special Branch was a secretive organization heavily involved in counterintelligence and espionage. The close proximity of the ancient imperial city of Hue to the DMZ and North Vietnam forced the local Special Branch to be especially vigilant in defending against espionage and acts of terrorism by northern infiltrators, thus making them high on the list of targets for VC assassins and kidnappers.

At the time of the initial assaults by PAVN forces on the city during the Tet offensive in 1968, Godwin was located in a "safe house" that also served as his living quarters. By February 5, regular Communist troops as well as Special Action squads had infiltrated his area, and Godwin had planned to escape from the house in order to link up with an American unit. The last radio contact with him was at 1400 hours that same day. When American forces finally arrived, Godwin had disappeared without a trace.

While in Hue, our team stayed overnight at several official government guesthouses that had been confiscated by arriving Communist forces in March 1975. One of the guesthouses was the same safe house that Godwin was captured in during the offensive. According to our information, a female noodle vendor located next door to the safe house pointed out Godwin to his captors. During the time that we stayed at the facility we ate noodles served by a female vendor at the same location, but we were unable to ascertain whether she was the same lady who informed on Godwin.

During the case investigation, witnesses indicated that Godwin and another prisoner, Mr. Eugene Weaver, a CIA officer also captured in Hue during the offensive, were both evacuated along Route 12 through the A Shau Valley to A Luoi district on the border with Laos. According to the witnesses, Godwin and Weaver were initially held with other POWs captured in Hue, but were eventually separated from them and moved inside Laos to a POW camp administered by the Ministry of Public Security, rather than a camp under military control. I'm convinced that they were split from the others because they were police and/or intelligence personnel.

Unfortunately, after being subjected to interrogation for a prolonged period of time, Godwin's health began to fail. According to Weaver, he last saw Godwin lying on the ground motionless and he appeared to be dead. Shortly thereafter Weaver signed a death certificate witnessing Godwin's death provided to him by camp cadre. Weaver was then moved to North Vietnam. During 1992, when the Senate Select Committee on POW/MIA Affairs was in operation, it was learned that just before the American POWs were released, Weaver's captors allowed the Soviet KGB to meet with him. The KGB attempted to recruit Weaver, and gave him a telephone number as a point of contact with them after he returned to the United States. While Weaver refused their entreaties, it is my understanding that during his POW debriefing he didn't mention the KGB contact, and the matter only came to light some years later during a routine polygraph examination related to his CIA employment. I don't recall whether the CIA ever informed anyone in DOD about this discovery. This is the only contact between American POWs and Soviets (other than journalists) during the war acknowledged by the Vietnamese, although other meetings have been speculated on for years. Godwin is still unaccounted for.

As we began to investigate cases in the South, I also sadly learned how much of the money we paid the local hires actually ended up in their pockets. During the course of investigating Godwin's case, as well as other cases involving recon personnel lost on missions deep into enemy controlled territory, our joint team hired members of the ethnic minority tribes residing in remote areas near the Lao border. The guides consisted primarily of members of the pro-Communist Ta Oi and Pa Coh tribes. Like the Rhade and Jarai Montagnards I had worked with during my first tour in the Central Highlands, the Ta Oi and Pa Coh tribesmen were honest, hard working people who seldom complained about anything. However, after about one week trekking in the difficult terrain of the A Shau valley and other areas west of Hue and Danang, during the evening hours several of the Montagnards approached me out of earshot of the accompanying cadre from Hanoi. When they asked me what the U.S. Government was paying them for their work, the question caught me off guard and I was unsure how to respond. After some thought I decided to give them the facts because I believed that if they thought they were being treated fairly, they wouldn't have raised the issue, and secondly, since they were doing a good job, I felt I owed them an honest answer. When I revealed that my government was paying the officials in Hanoi $25.00 per day for their services, they moaned in unison.

According to them, while they were working with us and neglecting their normal work at home, especially labor-intensive agricultural production, they were being compensated at the rate of only $1.75 per day. From that amount they were required to purchase their own meals and incidentals. They then requested in a somewhat sheepish manner that I ask the Vietnamese officials to raise their daily per diem rate to compensate for their loss of income. The polite and straightforward manner in which the Montagnards raised the issue touched me deeply. The thought that immediately leaped into my mind was that after so many lives had been lost, and so much national treasure expended, the people who deserved our help more than perhaps anyone else were still no better off. I later talked to the Vietnamese Team Chief about the situation, and he promised to research the compensation issue. However, he pointed out that the Vietnamese cadre assigned to work with the American teams received only $5.00 of the $50.00 daily rate that we were paying Hanoi for them, and that the drivers were also only being paid $5.00 each.[1]

At that point I made up my mind to raise the issue with my superiors, since I knew where the bulk of the money for hiring the guides and cadre would continue to be paid...into the bank account of the Vietnam Communist Party External Affairs Committee. Instead of the U.S. paying for "cemetery maintenance," the Vietnamese were finding other methods to milk the POW/MIA issue for badly needed foreign currency. Labor costs weren't the only items we were charged: "landing fees" from $600.00 to $1,200.00 for each airfield landing, including landings at airfields in the former RVN that were built with U.S. taxpayers' money. At times I was able to negotiate a reduction in landing fees by haggling with airport managers, but we always paid the $600.00 minimum. In postwar Vietnam, this was an enormous sum of money. The U.S. raised the matter of Communist authorities withholding salaries from laborers and cadre, as well as exorbitant fees that charged up to $1,500.00 per province for "organizing" each iteration, in unilateral discussions, but whenever the topic was broached during technical meetings, the Communists ignored our requests for clarification. Confronted with the Communist demands, and despite my misgivings, ultimately the U.S. took no action. Since then, the monetary rewards for minimal Vietnamese efforts have only escalated. For example, a League of Families trip to Vietnam in February 2003 discovered that the Joint Task Force-Full Accounting (JTFFA, the unit that eventually replaced the JCRC) is paying the Vietnamese unilateral teams $1,500 for each source interview, regardless of the outcome. Even the worst businessman can see how that arrangement can be abused.

The Party cadre also continued to play psychological games with us, although with some of them, it was hard to tell which were state approved and which were personal spite. Once we stayed at an impressive French Colonial era villa, located at Number 5 Le Loi Street on the romantic Perfume River in Hue. The French-era Governor of Central Vietnam and native of Hue, Mr. Ha Van Lang, had once occupied the villa. Governor Lang was the brother of the well known senior North Vietnamese diplomat Senior Colonel Ha Van Lau, who had participated as an advisor for both military and POW/MIA affairs in negotiations with the French at Geneva in 1964 and with the Americans in Paris in 1973. In post war years Lau served as a Deputy Foreign Minister and as Vietnam's Ambassador to France. On the first evening of our stay at this particular villa, I was visited in my room by my counterpart team chief, Ho Xuan Dich. With studied casualness, Dich related how he had been a student prior to secretly joining the Communists as a member of the POW exploitation element in the Hue area. After informing me that he was aware that Mr. Ha Van Lang was related to my wife, Nam-Xuan, who is also a native of Hue, Dich went on to describe how his unit had managed to gain the cooperation of some French POWs captured from the Foreign Legion to work with Vietnamese assassination squads.

According to Dich, in order to bypass the tight security placed on Governor Lang's residence, he had instructed one of the Caucasian French POWs to approach the villa dressed in civilian clothing. At the same time two Vietnamese pedicab drivers staged an accident on the street in front of the villa. While the guards were momentarily distracted the French collaborator passed quickly through the gate and entered the residence unchallenged. Once inside the man proceeded to locate Governor Lang and killed him with one shot to the head. The French collaborator then fled the scene and was never captured. Then, with mock astonishment, Dich suddenly remembered that the killing had occurred in this very room, and mentioned if I looked closely, I might still be able to see bloodstains on the floor. Dich then cheerily wished me a good night's sleep and departed the villa. Although I was bone-tired, Dich's rendition of the assassination raised my anxiety level considerably and kept me awake most of the night. Not to be outdone, a few weeks later I bought an electronic Christmas greeting card in Singapore that I mailed to Dich at his office in Hanoi. Having participated in numerous terrorist-type activities I knew Dich would appreciate the red flashing lights and shrill, computerized Jingle Bells music when he opened the card. After receiving the card Dich informed me in a somewhat gruff manner that he had gotten the message.

While in Hue I took the opportunity to visit some of my wife's relatives. This visit was not easily arranged, and I had to provide the address several days in advance to my Vietnamese counterparts for clearance by Public Security. When

I arrived at their home inside the ancient imperial capital in the section known as the "Citadel," my wife's aunt and uncle were quite surprised to learn that their niece was married to an American. They were even more surprised to learn that I spoke Vietnamese, and completely taken aback by the fact that I spoke the unique Hue dialect. The uncle, a former ARVN officer assigned during the war as the Operations Officer for Quang Tri Subsector, had recently been released from more than twelve years of incarceration in a Communist prison camp.

Although I had never met the uncle, I had heard about his opposition and obstinate behavior toward Communist authorities from other ARVN officers who were incarcerated with him in prison. The uncle was particularly well known after he organized a demonstration in a prison camp during 1976, demanding that all former ARVN officers be released. He contended that the officers were only guilty of having served in the military during the war and that they were not criminals. Therefore, they should be either charged or released. For his role in organizing the demonstration the uncle was placed in solitary confinement in a small metal "Conex" shipping container for four years. After visiting the aunt and uncle's home, they came to visit me at the hotel the following day. Pulling me aside from the accompanying officials the uncle revealed to me that Public Security agents had arrived at his home on the day prior to my visit. He said that they had planted listening devices throughout his house, including the sofa I sat with him on during my visit.

Since some 80 percent of all cases involving missing Americans had occurred in four provinces of Central Vietnam (Quang Binh, Quang Tri, Thua Thien and Quang Nam) we began to focus our efforts on that geographic area. By 1990 we were working in the Danang area of Quang Nam province. Moving lower into South Vietnam we were occasionally shocked by developments. While we were there to investigate American losses, except for lower level working meetings with the Province Task Team, most of the province and region-level cadre we met were assigned to duties dealing with the development of the economy, especially tourism. Although the Communists knew that a trade embargo was in place and that Americans were prohibited from engaging in commercial enterprise with Vietnam, they took every opportunity to remind us that their top priority was development of their shaky economy. During state-sponsored dinners the senior cadre constantly mentioned vague but tantalizing business ventures available for American investors, once the embargo was lifted of course. Since politically the embargo would only be lifted in the event of their withdrawal from Cambodia, and real progress on the POW/MIA issue (or so I thought), I used this time to press them on genuine cooperation, which invariably subjected me to long speeches about Ho Chi Minh's humanitarian approach to prisoners of war, and how Vietnam was cooperating, etc. Given their poverty, I could only imagine how U.S. government funding of the POW/MIA issue was being calculated in balancing the national budget.

Given their pronouncements concerning tourism and its potential effects upon their economy, I quickly discovered that local officials were using my team as experimental guests for their fledgling hotel and tourism industry. When my investigation team arrived in Danang we were billeted at a fairly large hotel called the "Bach Dang." No one was positive, but locals in the area believed that the hotel had served as a Bachelor Officers Quarters for Americans during the war. At least one local resident said that the hotel was formerly called the "Liberty," and that Communist Special Action units had bombed it during the 1960s.

Not surprisingly, in talking with some of the hotel employees I learned that all the working staff, including kitchen personnel, room maids, gardeners and repairmen, actually comprised one subchapter *(chi bo)* of the Vietnam Communist Party. The Secretary of the Party subchapter, who served as the hotel's cook, had served in the RVN Air Force for several years during the war and he was able to speak limited English. During the time we stayed at the Hotel I happened upon several meetings held by the Subchapter Secretary with the staff, and on each occasion great emphasis was placed on them being wary of the American visitors. I also learned that although the hotel was touted as a tourist facility, in reality it was owned and operated by the PAVN Military Region 5 Headquarters. The "manager" was actually the wife of a PAVN general officer who served as the Deputy Chief of Staff of the High Command at the time, and who later became the Deputy Minister of Defense. The same lady had also served as the manager of a guesthouse located inside Laos on the Ho Chi Minh Trail during the war years. During that period her clientele had been comprised of senior officers on temporary duty assignments from the northern command center. PAVN personnel were permitted, and in some cases even encouraged, to engage in for-profit commercial enterprise. This somewhat unique financial arrangement had permeated the entire governmental system in Vietnam under the guise of "self sufficiency." Both the general and his wife who managed the hotel were listed as "National Heroes" for fighting against the Americans.

Lodging was one issue, food was another. Since it was often difficult to find suitable food during our trips, we relied on our "Meals-ready-to-eat" as a backup. Strangely, we discovered that just about anywhere we traveled, we could supplement our less than tasty rations with locally made French-fried potatoes. Since freezers and refrigerators were generally not available, when we did stray from the basic menu of bread and French-fries by ordering fresh meat, some of the younger members of our team were alarmed to hear the screams of animals being slaughtered out back of the restaurant only minutes after we placed our orders.

The Vietnamese, of course, invented numerous ways to rip us off. The rooms we rented in Danang fell far short of the $40.00 price charged, as they were dull and drab with very few furnishings. When we first began our case investigations

I noticed that there was a dual track system in place for calculating room rates at various hotels throughout Vietnam, especially in Hanoi where the policy was prominently displaced on walls near the reception desks. According to the signs, guests from socialist countries were charged $10.00 per night, while guests from other countries were charged $40.00 per night. Upon observing the signs I always made it a point to inquire concerning the origin and justification for the pricing policy. Usually I was told that the policy was a "Party decision," and that the reason the policy was established was because socialist countries have very little money. Upon hearing this I couldn't resist the temptation to launch further inquiries as to why the guests from socialist countries were broke and unable to afford to pay the higher rate for rooms, but all I received in response were wide grins.

Most of the rooms in Danang did have air conditioning, which was greatly appreciated. It also became amusing to watch the accompanying Vietnamese cadre from Hanoi insist on rooms with American air conditioners that had been left behind after the war, rather than rely on the newer models imported from the Soviet Union. The first time I stayed in a room with a Soviet air conditioner I discovered why. In addition to emitting a noise similar to a B-52 engine, it stopped running in the middle of the night. To add to the ambiance, not only was the noise from the air conditioners sleep depriving, due to the lack of caulking or sealant the glass in the windows constantly rattled. I usually solved this problem by jamming rubber bands down into the cracks with toothpicks. Packing toilet paper into the windows to block the mosquitoes also helped alleviate the noise from the vibrating appliance and glass.

One newer hotel was the "Peace" Hotel. Actually this hotel was still under construction, and due to its close proximity to the Immigration Department of the Ministry of the Interior/Public Security I suspected that at some point in time we would be "invited" to stay there. At the time of our visit to Danang the requirement was still in place that anyone, Vietnamese or foreigner, staying at a hotel had to be registered each day by four p.m. with the local Public Security.

Another hotel was owned by the local Danang City Party Committee, and was called the "Friendship" Hotel. The cadre from Hanoi who accompanied us during our case investigations normally stayed there. I also accidentally discovered the hotel also served as a base for both foreign and domestic communications intercepts. Once while looking for some VNOSMP cadre who were going on a mission with us, I entered an upstairs room in the hotel that was filled with sophisticated communications gear, including telephone equipment, amplifiers, receivers, and huge tape recorders.

Still, despite the "four-star" accommodations and "friendly" staff, I looked forward to moving into the Danang area, as several cases provided some of the most compelling "last-known-alive" investigations during my involvement in the POW/MIA issue. One of the most important cases was Army Private First Class Donald Sparks from Iowa. In the early morning hours of June 17, 1969, Sparks and another man were walking point for their unit, 1st Platoon/Bravo Company, on a search and destroy mission against enemy forces operating in the area near densely populated Thang Binh District, Quang Nam Province. The unit was moving through the morning haze when suddenly, withering automatic weapons fire trapped the lead elements in a well-planned ambush sprung by battle-hardened troops of the PAVN 2nd Division. Initial bursts of fire quickly felled the two Americans at the point, and in the ensuing firefight casualties mounted steadily on both sides.

Members of the 1st Platoon who survived the initial contact believed both men were dead. Sparks was thought to have suffered a serious chest wound. After trying unsuccessfully to recover the bodies of their fallen comrades, the unit withdrew from the immediate area and called for "tac-air." Soon after, the ambush location erupted in a series of violent explosions as both 500 and 1,000-pound bombs saturated the area. The shrill sound of fighter-bomber aircraft reverberated across the rice fields as the mission changed from HE to napalm. Soon the entire enemy position became engulfed in a sea of fire, and 1st Platoon/Bravo Company retreated.

The following morning battle-weary elements of Bravo Company returned to the bomb-devastated area to recover the two bodies reluctantly abandoned the previous day. Digging through a maze of bomb craters the unit was able to recover one body, but there was no sign of Sparks. Members of the unit subsequently reported that Sparks' body had been completely destroyed by air strikes. In accordance with the established procedure, his family was notified of his death and like thousands of his comrades he became just another statistic in America's Vietnam War.

As the grueling war dragged on Sparks slowly faded from the memory of his comrades. Then, on May 17, 1970, a U.S. patrol ambushed and killed a PAVN Major. Miraculously, they found two handwritten letters in the pocket of the dead officer. The two intriguing letters were in English and dated April 11, 1970. The two letters were forwarded to the Crime Lab of the 8th Military Police Group where experts concluded that Sparks had written both letters, some ten months after his body was reportedly destroyed on the battlefield. In the ensuing years, little new information on Sparks was reported until shortly before the ceasefire. In February 1973, a Communist defector reported that during April 1969, he saw an American POW with wounds caused by gunshots and shrapnel from an air strike being moved into a camp located next to a river west of Chu Lai. Analysts correlated this report to Donald Sparks.

Shortly after his release in March 1973, American POW Major Floyd H. Kushner reported that while being held in the Military Region 5 camp for U.S. prisoners, camp staff told him that an American called "Don" would soon arrive.

Since Kushner was a doctor, he was also informed that Don's arrival would be delayed due to an injured foot. "Don," however, never joined the group. In September of that same year an ARVN prisoner released by the Communists reported to the Defense Attaché Office in Saigon that he had seen an unidentified American POW entering a camp in February 1970. He said the man used a walking stick to support his injured feet and legs. He later heard that the same POW died due to beriberi in June 1971. At the time, this information was also correlated to Sparks, but after careful consideration I concluded that the report might correlate to Case 0835, Lance Corporal Harold R. Reid, a Marine missing since September 13, 1967. Reid was assigned to an observation post of the 3rd Battalion/7th Marines near a bridge over the Thu Bon River. At 0430 hours on the morning of September 13, Reid informed the Marine relieving him that he intended to cross the bridge to visit a friend assigned to the 2nd Battalion/5th Marines. After Reid departed from his unit he was never seen or heard from again. While a Vietnamese Source later reported finding the body of a Marine in the same general area, and the information was judged to possibly correlate to Reid, Reid's body was never recovered and identified.

Since the captured letters written by Sparks indicated he was still alive and in the custody of Communist forces, his name was added to the "last-known-alive" list. Although Childress repeatedly discussed the Sparks case at the highest levels in the mid-1980s, and files on him were passed to Communist officials seven times between August 1987 and December 1992, no response was forthcoming.

Despite Vietnamese intransigence, we slowly gathered more information on Sparks. In April 1989, a JCRC team interviewed a witness in Tien Phuoc District who testified that during 1969, he saw four PAVN soldiers carrying an American who suffered a leg wound during a battle in Thang Binh District. Other witnesses interviewed by JCRC members said a male Caucasian American POW was present in the CK120 Hospital where he was treated for an injury to his right hip from July 1969 to January 1970. After recovering from his wound, the American was last seen during 1970 being escorted by Communist officials along the Tranh River. In January 1993 I interviewed witnesses who also said that during the summer of 1969, a wounded American soldier was admitted to the CK120 Hospital for treatment. The American was then transferred to a POW camp. The witnesses mentioned another seriously wounded American who was being held near the camp in 1969, but a search at the reported burial site did not result in the discovery of any remains.

The information on Sparks was becoming more and more interesting. Intrigued, I found other eyewitnesses who related to me that during a POW camp raid in July 1970 by combined ARVN and American forces, a wounded U.S. POW ran away from the CK120 hospital for several hours but later returned after Allied forces departed from the area. The witnesses claimed that another wounded American soldier, Private First Class Larry D. Aiken from New York, was left in his hospital bed at the time of the raid, although in reality Aiken's guard struck him on his skull with a machete. Although still alive, the steep hillside where Aiken was held prevented the rescue helicopter from landing. An American solder from the 101st Airborne rappelled from the helicopter to recover him, and then carried him several hundred meters down the hill to a spot where the helicopter could land. Unfortunately, Aiken died from his wound ten days later without ever regaining consciousness.

Obviously, Sparks had survived the initial battle, been wounded in the leg and captured, and then taken to the CK120 hospital. Why, then, would he run away during a POW raid? As I continued to seek more information, during another interview session, one former member of the Military Region 5 security force (then assigned as the Chairman of the Tra My District People's Committee), informed me that Sparks could speak Vietnamese, a surprising fact. A former nurse assigned to the hospital also told me that Sparks' blood was used in transfusions for wounded NVA soldiers. Obviously Sparks learned Vietnamese from someone, and since his blood was used for transfusions, perhaps some form of medical records would have been maintained, yet despite repeated requests, the Vietnamese did not turn over any records. The information concerning the blood transfusions made sense because according to our records, Sparks did have universal type "O" blood.

Regardless of the source reports, the two letters written by Sparks after his capture provide the most compelling evidence in his case. One of the letters was addressed to his mother, while the second letter was addressed to a Communist cadre identified by Sparks in the letter only as "DM." In pressing the Communists for answers on Sparks' fate, I read the letter written to his mother out loud to accompanying cadre. The thought of a young serviceman far from home, wounded and lonely, writing to his mother waiting patiently on the family farm back in Iowa stirred my emotions. The cadre had no response and sat impassively. The second letter written to a Vietnamese identified only as "DM" was more of a plea than anything else. According to the letter, whoever "DM" was had apparently promised Sparks that he would be released, but for some reason the deal did not go through. In the letter Sparks wanted to know why this promise had not been kept. The tone of the letter, as well as the other letter written by Sparks' to his mother, indicated to me that Sparks was not a happy camper and he wanted to go home.

Due to variations in the Vietnamese language it is not possible to determine whether the "D" in this case is a hard "D" (e.g. as in delta), or a soft "D" (e.g. "Z" as in zoo). Based on the manner in which the "D" was written in the letter and Sparks' reported Vietnamese language capability, I believe the "D" is most likely a "soft" consonant pronounced as "z" or "y," depending on the dialect. This being the case, one possible candidate is the former commander of the Quang Nam-Danang provincial military forces and concurrently the Commander of the

1st Regiment of the 2nd PAVN Division, Senior Colonel Duy Minh. Although I requested that the VNOSMP cadre arrange for me to interview him, it was never scheduled before I completed my assignment. In reviewing the case file years later I could find no indication that Senior Colonel Duy Minh was ever interviewed by U.S. investigators.

Another possibility was that someone with whom Sparks had become acquainted was named "Diem." If Sparks understood spoken Vietnamese but did not understand the writing system I can see where he might write the Vietnamese name "Diem" for "DM." Still, based on the source reporting, Sparks was held for several years outside the normal POW camps, although apparently, he was being sent to the main MR-5 camp. Most intriguing to me, during the course of the Danang investigations, I received information indicating that Sparks was still alive and in the area in August 1991. I spoke with an American, at that time working for an international organization, who claimed to have seen an American wearing what appeared to be a PAVN military uniform and in the company of PAVN officers at the Military Region 5 guesthouse in Danang. The American official selected a photo of Don Sparks as closely resembling the man he saw in Danang. The Source who provided the information was not only a combat veteran, he had extensive time in Asia and knew the Danang area well. When I asked working-level Communist cadre from Danang if it was possible that Sparks was still in the area, they would only smile, without ever giving a clear answer. To this day, I'm told that JTFFA officials still receive the same enigmatic smile when they inquire if Sparks survived the war. The fate of Donald Sparks remains a complete mystery.[2]

Another intriguing case that generated a large volume of wartime reports concerned two other Americans being held in the mountains west of Danang. This case, despite the accompanying uproar with local cadre, proved to be one of the most satisfying for me. Many of these wartime reports were correlated to two young Caucasian Marines who were captured while off duty and sightseeing on motorcycles rented in Danang. At the time of their loss on June 7, 1964, Private First Class Robert Greer from California and Private First Class Fred Schreckengost from Ohio departed their unit after informing another Marine that they intended to go to the top of a nearby hill overlooking Danang to take pictures. That same afternoon villagers residing in the western outskirts of the city reported the capture of two Americans. According to the local residents, after parading the Americans through several villages the capturing Communist forces intended to put the two men through political training for five months and then release them back to American control. Ominously, however, a June 25, 1964 report indicated that two Americans being held prisoner in the area west of Danang had attacked a guard and attempted to escape on June 8, 1964. According to the report, both of the POWs were shot dead by Communist forces. This report was also correlated to Schreckengost and Greer.

Still, later reports placed the two men at various locations west of Danang. In the case of Schreckengost, numerous Sources who were shown photographs during their debriefings positively identified him as being observed at locations throughout Central Vietnam as late as 1974. At least one such report placed Schreckengost in Laos. Since it was doubtful that all identifications could have been accurate and the photo of Greer was not selected, I finally came to the conclusion that Schreckengost's physical appearance matched the description of what the average Vietnamese believed was a typical American; brown hair, fair complexion, high nose, prominent facial features.

In investigating the Schreckengost and Greer case, our team was first taken to the bank of a river outside Danang where a witness described how local guerrillas captured both men while they were taking photographs. According to the witnesses, the motorcycles were thrown into the river and the two Americans were moved to a temporary detention camp. Shortly after arrival in the camp the two men were killed during an escape attempt. Both men were buried in an unmarked grave in a cemetery outside the village, but the grave was later "robbed" by persons unknown.

When we arrived in the village where the two men were reportedly killed and buried, the authorities had assembled a large crowd of villagers. Prior to our interviewing any witnesses, a cadre from the local Communist Party Chapter began addressing the crowd. First he outlined the course of events leading up to the reported death and burial of the two men. According to the cadre, both men were part of a large contingent of "American aggressors" who had arrived in Danang to occupy the area. At the time of their arrest by members of the "Revolution," both men had invaded the local area to engage in spying. The cadre added that based on Vietnam's traditional humanitarian policy, the government had decided to assist the Americans in resolving the case. Many of the local residents present seemed impressed by the wartime account given by the cadre, and they beamed with obvious pride in listening to the official account of the incident.

When asked if I had anything to add, I thanked the local authorities for allowing our team to come into their area to conduct investigations into the fate of missing Americans. I then stated that although it was common to see discrepancies between accounts of loss incidents contained in both American and Vietnamese files, in the case of Schreckengost and Greer there was a significant disparity. Referring to official U.S. Government files I expressed my opinion that rather than being two "American aggressors" who invaded the area for spying, the two Americans involved in the case were actually two young servicemen who were not even on duty at the time of their capture. Having heard about the beautiful landscape of rural Vietnam, the two men rented motorcycles on the local economy in order to take photographs to send home to their families. I said that the actions of the two men were no different from those of many foreign tourists presently traveling throughout Vietnam during 1990, which had been designated the "Year of Tourism" by the Vietnamese government. To the consternation of the accompanying Communist cadre the villagers appeared to accept my account explaining the presence of the two young Americans.

Apparently the VNOSMP Team Chief did not appreciate my version of the loss incident, because while enroute to the cemetery where the two men had reportedly been buried he cautioned me about becoming engaged in politics. Defying intimidation by the official I told him in no uncertain terms that I did not intend to participate in any propaganda sessions conducted by Communist party officials in conjunction with our investigations. Stressing the importance of genuine cooperation and mutual understanding between the two sides, I also indicated that based on the accounts by the witnesses thus far and the information contained in wartime U.S. files, local officials should have knowledge of the current whereabouts of the two men. He said nothing and left in a furious mood.

Despite my demands to the cadre, the more witnesses I interviewed the more skeptical I became of Communist intentions regarding this case. Some witnesses I interviewed proved to be wartime POWs or defectors who had already been questioned during the war. The problem was that no one in the JCRC headquarters or the DIA Special Office picked up on the names until long after the interviews were conducted. At the time it would have been very helpful to have the previous testimony of these particular witnesses prior to conducting the interviews, or at least to use as a basis for comparison afterward. Concerning the witness objectivity, I observed that some wore military uniforms that did not fit, some had rank insignia that had been rearranged, and some spoke dialects that contradicted their claimed previous places of residence.

I harbored no doubts that some testimony was canned, and in checking out this situation I learned that there were several organizations available for assisting the Communist cadre in "guiding" our investigations. For example, in the Danang telephone directory I noticed that both the "Speaking Company" and the "Acting Company" were listed, and that both were located in close proximity to the local Ministry of Information and Culture (formerly the Ministry of Propaganda) Office in Danang. These two companies were comprised of members of the Propaganda and Indoctrination Department. During the war years the members of these two companies were the same people, at times seemingly innocent little old ladies, who told American troops in hot pursuit of retreating Communist forces "they went that-a-way," thus concealing the true withdrawal route from the gullible young military officer leading the American unit.

After digging up the purported grave, the visit to the cemetery yielded only a few scraps of cloth from a Vietnamese shirt and some rubber from the sole of a locally manufactured shoe. After no remains or personal effects of the two missing men were found I requested to meet separately with the VNOSMP Team Chief. During the terse meeting I reiterated my position that local officials knew where the remains were and if they didn't, then possibly the two men were still alive and being held against their will. I also expressed anger at being led on a wild goose chase, and stated that I didn't intend to dig up the countryside to find the remains of two men who had obviously been in the custody of Communist officials. I made it clear I wanted answers, or my team would pack up and go home, and that whatever happened after that would be up to the policy-level officials of the two countries.

After calling a side meeting with local authorities the VNOSMP official returned to the group to announce that a new "witness" had been located. Shortly thereafter the new witness appeared and informed the joint team that the remains of the two men had been disinterred from the cemetery and moved to another location in a nearby village where they had been reburied. Arriving at the new site we were taken to a recently cultivated sweet potato patch where the remains were reportedly reburied. After haggling for what seemed to be several hours concerning the cost of damages to be paid for excavating the sweet potato patch, we finally received approval from the local authorities to excavate the site. Digging in the soft ground was quite easy, and it didn't take long to recover the remains. Based on the condition of the remains it was our consensus that they had been stored at a different location and only recently moved to the site. I came to the conclusion that the Vietnamese had intended to use delaying tactics in the hope that we would acquiesce to hiring a large pool of local laborers, rent heavy equipment and pay excessive damages to locate the remains over a prolonged period of excavations. After taking temporary custody of the remains the Vietnamese officials eventually repatriated them to the CILHI on November 20, 1990. The Armed Forces Identification Review Board approved the identification of the remains on March 27, 1991 as those of Schreckengost and Greer; after twenty-six years the families of the two men finally reached closure. VNOSMP officials later complained to Harvey concerning my attitude during the operation. Harvey admitted that he had at first considered counseling me, but had decided not to because "you can't argue with success."

During the war, several reports correlated to Schreckengost and Greer were also placed in a special file called the "Salt and Pepper" file. This file contained reports of sightings involving two unknown Americans, one white and one black, who were believed to have defected to the enemy and who were actually fighting on the side of Communist forces. Although both Marines were white, due to the significant number of reports and numerous positive identifications by different Sources of Schreckengost, their association with the "Salt and Pepper" file generated considerable interest in their case among American collectors and analysts.

The entire deserter/defector question was a difficult problem for the JCRC. Further, recovering Schreckengost and Greer raised perplexing questions: Did these reports actually relate to the two Marines we had just recovered, did the reports relate to other American personnel who had crossed over to the enemy and who were still unidentified, or were the reports simply fabrications?

Classification to deserter status normally occurred after an individual was absent without leave for a period of thirty days. At that point he was "Dropped From the Rolls." According to the official Department of Defense policy at the time, although deserters from the armed services remained subject to the Uniform Code of Military Justice, the ultimate disposition of possible criminal charges against deserters could only be made after their return to military control. Since prosecution was a discretionary matter within the authority of the Secretaries of the military departments, in routine cases involving the voluntary, cooperative return of long-term deserters, administrative discharges were as expeditious as possible, especially given the passage of time and the previous clemency programs for Vietnam-era deserters and draft dodgers. DOD considered it appropriate to treat any voluntary, cooperative returnees with compassion. The degree of compassion, however, was considered in light of the circumstances at the time of the desertion and the person's conduct while in absentee status. A person who deserted to avoid facing charges of murdering a fellow soldier or one whose conduct led to the death or injury of other Americans would not merit the same compassionate consideration as a routine deserter.

At the height of the anti-war movement in America in 1971 the average rate of desertions in Vietnam was approximately thirty individuals each month. After 1975, those on the deserter list were gradually re-categorized as they returned to military control: they were either discharged from service, or had their status changed from deserter to deceased. Since at least some deserters who remained in Vietnam after 1975 finally made it home safely, by 1979 the files of the Defense Intelligence Agency carried the names of only two service members, both Marines, who were listed as deserters in Vietnam: Private Earl Clyde Weatherman and Private First Class Wilfredo D. Singson. During the course of the field investigations I learned from Vietnamese witnesses that after deserting from his unit, a Vietnamese female working in a pharmacy befriended Weatherman and then guided him to a location on the outskirts of Danang where he could voluntarily surrender to Communist forces. Weatherman was then moved to the MR-5 POW camp where he was reportedly killed during an escape attempt. I was never able to determine the fate of Singson.

Although the DIA carried only two individuals on their deserter list, JCRC files held some forty-three military personnel as deserters. Although deserter records complied by the various services at the time were haphazard at best, by 1982, as the JCRC continued to refine its database in preparation for the field investigations, the Army Personnel Center at Fort Benjamin Harrison forwarded a list of twenty Army personnel who were still carried in deserter status from the war. Throughout my involvement in the POW/MIA issue, to the best of my knowledge, of the twenty men on the Army's list, live-sighting reports were received on only one individual, Private First Class McKinley Nolan. While being held in the Long Binh jail, Nolan overpowered a guard and escaped. Nolan and his ethnic Cambodian wife then fled to Cambodia where he reportedly joined the VC. The last live-sighting reports concerning Nolan placed him in Cambodia as of 1974/75. Neither Nolan nor his remains have ever been found.

Due to the paucity of information, the issue of deserters and defectors remaining in Vietnam was one of the most confusing aspects of our investigations. Almost everyone involved in the POW/MIA issue found the reports of defecting Americans who cooperated with the enemy repugnant, and there was obvious reluctance on the American side to pursue this aspect of the investigations. Even though deserters were an altogether different matter, this issue was also avoided. I had difficulty understanding whether the military, including the JCRC, simply wanted to steer clear of responsibility in accounting for these men, or if it was simply the fact that the analysts did not have enough data to support an investigation into the fate of soldiers who had, in many cases, simply disappeared. Still, I hated the thought that men might have been given the dishonorable label of deserter who didn't deserve it. In the case of Vietnam, there was always the possibility they were lured to capture due to being in the wrong place at the right time because they were naive to Communist tactics due to a lack of training in subversion, espionage and terrorism prior to their assignments. Another distinct possibility in almost every case was the criminal element that existed in most large towns and in cities throughout Vietnam. Although most cases involving deserters were never scheduled for investigation, I instructed the members of my team to be constantly alert for any leads concerning their fate. As a result of our efforts, during the course of the investigations we learned that not all of the men whose family honor and reputation had been stained actually deserved the loathsome title of "deserter."

The vast majority of Americans, including a considerable number of veterans, don't realize the extent of Communist efforts at luring men into places of ambush or capture. Dozens of men were killed or lost in Vietnam during the war due to incidents that cannot be considered typical military action, especially from the result of Communist terrorist tactics employed by Special Action units. Undoubtedly, the criminal element in some cities also is responsible for several MIAs. I'm not suggesting every American soldier who walked away from his unit fell into some nefarious Mata Hari type trap, as pure chance encounters with local guerrilla units also played a large part. But far too many men disappeared under strange circumstances, especially in the Danang/Chu Lai area.

One such case involved Army Private Wilbert Walton from North Carolina. Walton disappeared from his unit in the Chu Lai area on January 3, 1970, and he was never heard from again. After being absent without leave for thirty days he was dropped from the rolls and classified as a deserter. Although Walton's parents tried repeatedly to obtain information on his case through law enforcement agencies and by requesting assistance from various members of Congress, all their efforts failed.

However, we received a report from an Orderly Departure Program (ODP)[3] applicant concerning Walton. The Source claimed that a friend had found Walton's remains, along with an identification tag. The dog tag information matched data available on Walton. In 1990 we also received a letter from another Source in Vietnam who claimed that he had turned the remains and one of Walton's dog tags over to the Public Security Police in the Chu Lai area on January 5, 1987. This dog tag also matched the known information on Walton.

While conducting investigations in the Danang area I interviewed a witness who reported that Communist guerrillas near Chu Lai had actually captured Walton, and that he had been killed when U.S. helicopters approached the area with searchlights. The witness also reported that the remains of Walton had already been recovered and turned in to Public Security. I was also aware of at least one other report from a refugee in Thailand indicating that an American serviceman, whom I believed to be Walton, had been stabbed to death in Ky Khuong village near Chu Lai during the night while he was asleep. I believe that Walton was most likely lured to the house by a female agent. Vietnam finally returned Walton's remains to the U.S. on November 14, 1991 and they were positively identified on September 24, 1992. As of this writing I am not clear whether Walton's family was ever informed concerning the actual circumstances of his death, especially since I doubt the Vietnamese ever told us, or the U.S. government ever asked.

Another case involving an American erroneously presumed to be a deserter involved Private Dewey A. Midgett, a twenty-year old soldier from Virginia. On November 25, 1967, while serving with the 335th Assault Helicopter Company, 145th Aviation Battalion in Phu Yen province on Central Vietnam's coast, Midgett was allowed to go on pass but was instructed to return to his unit by five p.m. that same afternoon. Midgett departed the unit and was never seen or heard from again. Midgett was declared a deserter and dropped from the roles. On February 4, 1980 Midgett was administratively presumed dead with an official date of death of November 25, 1967. However, while reviewing refugee reports I came across information indicating that while on pass near the airfield where he was stationed Midgett was killed while out walking alone. To prevent discovery, the young men who killed Midgett, most likely criminals bent on robbing the young solder, buried his body in an unmarked grave alongside a railroad track near the Phu Hiep airfield.

In dealing with information on potential deserters, I occasionally encountered difficulties. While attending a National League of Families annual meeting held in Washington, D.C., I met with members of Midgett's family who were naturally concerned about his status. During the course of the conversation I mentioned the reports from refugees in Hong Kong, and I indicated that I was optimistic that a sketch pinpointing the gravesite forwarded with the reports would lead to a successful recovery of his remains. On hearing about the report from me, the family became upset, claiming that they had never received any such information. The family seemed equally as anxious to dispel the troublesome deserter status issue as they were to recover the remains. After the family confronted Ray Spock about the report he promised to investigate the possibility that the report had been inadvertently left out of the case file, but I never learned whether or not he followed through on his pledge.

As was often the case, Spock was noticeably angry with me that I had revealed information on an MIA case to a family member based on my own evaluation, rather than accept the final analysis of his people. Since relations were often contentious between the field personnel like myself and Spock's analysts in Hawaii, I didn't let Spock's attitude bother me. I continued to answer questions posed to me by MIA family members based on my own evaluations of reports I had received. I figured that since Spock had never been trained as an analyst, had never even served in Vietnam, much less ever been in Phu Yen province where Midgett went missing, I could do little harm by revealing what I did know while Spock continued to gloss over what he did not. I held the firm belief that as field level investigators it was imperative that we retain the complete confidence of MIA family members, and that we should be straightforward in answering any questions they posed. Nevertheless, in each case I qualified my answers by reminding family members that I worked at the field level, and any information I passed to them should not be considered a final analytical product.

During the course of our investigations in Central Vietnam, in addition to case specific intelligence I managed to pick up a significant amount of general information that was either previously unknown, or at best suspected but not confirmed about wartime military matters. For example, I debriefed one former member of the Danang Special Action unit who had been involved with bombing incidents at several military buildings and compounds housing American personnel. According to the former PAVN officer, then assigned to the People's Committee in Danang, the entrance to his well-concealed tunnel complex was located a scant few meters from the fence around Danang Airbase. The underground network of tunnels was constructed in 1965 and was used throughout the war. Allied forces never detected the extensive network of tunnels.

The Danang airfield, however, was not the only American facility in close proximity to clandestine Communist units. I learned from Ta Oi tribe members residing in the area of the Lao border west of Danang that during the war some of their personnel had been assigned to a unit operating from a system of caves inside Marble Mountain. This meant that Communist units were located right under the noses of the top-secret SOG Command and Control North (CCN) that was launching missions from the airfield at Marble Mountain. Since the CCN routinely assigned members of the ethnic minorities to their reconnaissance missions, it is likely that at least some of them were cooperating with the Communist ethnic minority personnel working out of Marble Mountain.

The Communist command also employed Montagnards as counter-reconnaissance against allied forces. The Montagnards were skillful trackers with considerable experience handed down through generations of hunting for wild game in the rugged rain forests of Central Vietnam. Many had been moved to North Vietnam for political and military training before being reinfiltrated into the South. I noticed that a small number of what appeared to be key personnel, who were perhaps assigned to political officer duties, spoke Vietnamese with a distinct northern accent. Although poorly paid and equipped with outdated weapons and equipment, the Montagnards proved to be very effective in locating and attacking small American recon teams during the war. The members of the Ta Oi tribe I worked with while searching for missing Americans in the area between Hue and Danang related to me that they had been deployed as soon as the sounds of helicopters were heard. Once they discovered the American tracks, they closed very slowly with the American units. I was surprised to learn that one tactic they had considerable success with was tracking American recon teams until lunch time, and then launching their attack while the Americans were relaxed and eating. They said that this tactic was so successful that it eventually became standard operating procedure. Although the Montagnards were paid little outside of pep talks from political officers, they were motivated by the possibility of being allowed to keep some of the personal effects captured from American personnel. In some cases they were rewarded with goods made in other countries, such as wristwatches from the USSR.

I also learned that the Communists had maintained an extensive hospital system in the MR-5 area, including a secret hospital in the Marble Mountain caves. At least one American POW, Private Robert Garwood, was treated there during the war. Medical personnel assigned to the hospital network also revealed to me that Chinese advisers assigned to PAVN units in MR-5 were likewise treated in these medical facilities. Based on information provided by personnel formerly assigned to Communist medical facilities, my team recovered remains that later proved to be those of a "North Asian" who died while being evacuated from a small field hospital in the environs of Danang to a larger field hospital in Laos. However, since North Korean personnel were also operating with the MR-5 proselytizing element, the CILHI was not able to determine whether the remains sent to the lab were Chinese or Korean.

These same Communist medical personnel disclosed for the first time that during the war wounded U.S. POWs entering the hospital network for medical treatment were used for blood transfusions for wounded PAVN troops. Although I had received reports from Sources assigned to medical facilities in North Vietnam during the war indicating that sections of bone from dead American personnel had been used in hospitals in the Hanoi area, the thought that the Communists in the south would use captured Americans for blood transfusions had never crossed my mind. I actually stumbled across this information when I inquired about the blood types of captured U.S. personnel while trying to ascertain the extent to which Communist hospitals maintained medical records on foreign prisoners. But in considering the fact that Communist forces in the south did not have access to refrigeration for maintaining adequate supplies of blood, I can understand why they would resort to using the blood of American POWs.

While it should come as no surprise that the Communists maintained extensive intelligence networks in MR-5 directed at American forces, the degree of penetration they managed to achieve is a real eye opener. For example, in early 1964 the 525th Military Intelligence Group established a safe house in Danang. The mission of the unit was twofold, with efforts toward both intelligence collection and counterintelligence operations. The safe house containing the unit's operations was rented from a Vietnamese English Language Professor teaching at the Danang University of Foreign Languages. The professor, Ho An, alias Ho Huu An, introduced a Vietnamese female, "Miss Hoa," to work for the 525th MI as a housemaid. After ensuring that the telephone system was in good working order, Professor Ho An withdrew from the villa leaving Miss Hoa to care for the American intelligence personnel.

What the Americans assigned to the unit did not know was that Professor Ho An was actually a "legal" residing in Danang as a legitimate citizen of the RVN, while at the same time secretly working for the Communists. Virtually everything said in the 525th MI safe house in Danang was monitored, as were all telephone calls. At the same time as the 525th personnel were responsible for collecting intelligence, including POW/MIA information, Professor Ho An was a member of the MR 5 Proselytizing Office, ultimately responsible for managing all foreign prisoners, including Americans, throughout the region. One of the few English speakers in the Communist leadership, Professor Ho An periodically traveled from Danang to the MR-5 POW camp. The good professor conducted indoctrination sessions at the MR-5 camp and encouraged the POWs to make tape recorded statements and write leaflets with themes designed to lower the morale of other U.S. and allied troops in the area. Due to the professor's somewhat stoic demeanor, American prisoners in the MR-5 camp gave him the name "Stoneface."

Learning the extent of the Communist intelligence operations, and their covert military infrastructure in the Danang area, help me to put the losses of several men in this area into perspective. In reviewing the cases I noted that although the modus operandi of the Communists in luring men were consistent, the captured men were assigned to different units and different branches of the services as well. In searching for a link between the men, I suddenly realized that the Vietnamese students of Professor Ho An not only learned their English from him at the University in Danang, some were fortunate enough to attend English language classes taught at the Vietnamese American Association *(Hoi Viet My)* in the city of Hoi An near the Rest and Recuperation facility at China Beach. This was the only U.S. military facility in Central Vietnam where personnel from different units and branches of the services were together with Vietnamese civilians. Although this might be a coincidence, I felt that this connection warranted additional study. Like the Vietnamese-American Association managed by the Communists in Hanoi today, the Association in Hoi An, as well as those in other areas of South Vietnam, was ostensibly established to promote friendship and understanding between the peoples of the two countries. Since both Vietnamese and Americans considered "progressive" (those with liberal views and strong feelings against the war) generally staffed the facilities, perhaps a closer look at the organization might reveal a darker side.

In considering the Association, and the various intelligence operations, it suddenly came to me. While it was no secret that tourist jobs after the war were a front for security and intelligence personnel, the extent to which they permeated the tourist industry astounded me. It dawned on me that perhaps this was also true during the war. In investigating both aspects, I learned that the postwar manager of the Vietnamese Government Hotel at China Beach, where the wartime R & R Center was located, was Lieutenant Colonel Nguyen Van Be. While a member of the Intelligence and Security Services, Be interrogated a number of captured Americans, including Robert Garwood. Moreover, in 1991 the various "companies" oriented toward tourism, including those then organizing tours for Vietnam veterans, were headed by and in most cases staffed by former members of the Proselytizing Department responsible for American POWs. While it may seem logical on the surface that the Vietnamese had placed English-speaking personnel in the tourism industry, the real reason was counterintelligence, since all contacts with foreigners were closely monitored.

This is when I found the link that had been eluding me. Amazingly I found that many of the Vietnamese personnel then working in the tourism industry in Central Vietnam learned their English from the Vietnamese-American Association prior to being employed at the China Beach R&R Center during the war. For example, during the time that I investigated cases in the Danang area in 1991, the Team Chief of our counterpart "Province Task Team" was a Public Security Officer in charge of counterintelligence in Danang with the rank of Major. In 1992, after being promoted to Lieutenant Colonel, the officer, Mai Quy Trung, suddenly "retired" and became the Director of the East Asia International Tourism Company in Danang. I also later discovered that one of Professor Ho An's most promising students was one Nguyen Van Hung. Hung was also able to develop his English language skills at the Vietnamese American Association to the extent that he was selected by the MR-5 Proselytizing Committee for an assignment as interpreter in the MR-5 camp. Although Hung underwent considerable training in the English language at Hoi An, the same location where Private First Class Robert Garwood was captured shortly before his planned return to the United States, he nevertheless found it necessary to rely on Garwood for occasional interpreting assistance in the camp.

Communist interest in English language training was based on the need not only to exploit Americans in detention, but also to lure even more Americans into the web. This is not unusual for Communists. Witness the North Koreans, who have been kidnapping Japanese for years to help them train their agents in that language. Thus, all American soldiers, especially those assigned to support roles, even civilians, were at risk. While rumors concerning the use of women and children by the Communists to kill or capture American personnel circulated throughout the country, in many cases there existed a tendency toward disbelief and many troops simply choose to ignore these tales. In the POW camps, many POWs were extensively interrogated about seemingly inconsequential personal data. The reason was that the Communists realized that to create effective propaganda, they needed to understand Americans, at least to some extent. The Communists relied on the American psyche and the reluctance of American troops to kill women and children or to imagine them as agents of their destruction. After learning this from my extensive wartime interviews with captured Communist cadre, I was able to quietly watch and listen while postwar cadre related with no qualms how during the war everyone was considered a resource in carrying out the revolution, even small children.

In a somewhat atypical case that occurred in Danang in June 1965, a merchant seaman, Mr. John Tavares from the USS *Audry J. Luchenback,* disappeared. He was last seen alive at the bar of the "Pacific Hotel" on Bach Dang Street. Although U.S. officials visited the hotel in September 1974, they were unable to obtain any additional information, because according to their report "most personnel now employed at the bar were hired after the incident date." However, when I went to the establishment in 1993, I learned that the name of the hotel had been changed to the "Seafood Products Hotel." The current manager of the bar, in addition to her position as Secretary of the Party District Committee, had been employed there as a bartender prior to Mr. Tavares' disappearance. Although she professed not to have any information concerning Mr. Tavares or any other unaccounted-for Americans, she did admit to me a startling fact: her husband was the former commander of the wartime Danang Special Action Unit, and that he later became the Secretary of the Danang Party Committee. This meant that her husband had held the number one terrorist position in the area.

In early 1993, I interviewed her husband, Mr. Nguyen Thanh Nam, alias Nam Dua, in which he verified his former assignment with the Danang Special Action unit. During the session he did provide some very valuable information concerning Americans lured to capture in the Danang area, although he denied any involvement in the Tavares case. One MIA that Nam had been involved in luring was that of Lance Corporal James R. Moore from New York. On February 28, 1967, while a member of the 1st Marine Division working near Marble

Mountain, Moore was assigned to provide flank security for some engineer equipment operating on Highway 13. Moore left his position and crossed some sand dunes to the west and was never heard from again. On February 28, 1967, various intelligence Sources reported that two Communist females posing as prostitutes enticed an American rifleman away from an engineer project in the same area. On August 31, 1967 another report derived from captured enemy documents indicated that the Communists used a female agent to lure an American to his death. According to the report, a search of the American's body yielded $260 and change, a rifle and five ammunition clips. A team from the JTFFA and CILHI traveled to the area in 1992 and conducted an excavation but nothing was found. When I interviewed Nguyen Thanh Nam in early 1993 he provided me a different location for the burial than that contained in our case files, but I do not know if the new information was pursued.

Being lured to capture by Communist agents was not reserved only for Americans, other nationalities working in the MR-5 region were affected as well. One case involves five West German medical personnel, including three women, who were working for a volunteer hospital funded by the Knights of Malta organization in Danang. Apparently believing that volunteer medical personnel from a country not directly involved in the conflict were immune from capture, the five-member group made the tragic mistake of accepting an invitation from a Vietnamese female nurse, also working at the same hospital, to visit her native village. Shortly after arriving at the village and taking some photographs, the group was captured by Communist agents and led away into the jungle. While being detained in the MR-5 POW camp, two of the women and one man died and were buried there. The remains of the man and one woman have since been returned by Vietnam, but the remains of the other woman, a young dental assistant, have never been recovered. The two surviving members of the group were evacuated through Laos to North Vietnam. When I first saw them in Hanoi during "Operation Homecoming" in 1973, I concluded that they were both very fortunate to have lived, because they were extremely emaciated and in terrible physical condition.

While in Danang, we managed to resolve some complex cases, and I learned a great deal more about the wartime Communist infrastructure, especially their methods of luring Americans. I took considerable pride in the fact that we not only tried to reduce the numbers by recovering remains, we completed some valuable research that could enable us to improve the quality of the investigations of other cases where the fate of the individuals was never determined. I left Danang determined to return again and leave no stone unturned in finding out what really happened to our missing men. As we began to repack for a new iteration in the remote Central Highlands, I wondered just how much things had changed there, and whether the terrain was still as unforgiving as it was when my last tour ended there in 1966. I was about to receive an unwelcome answer to my question.

Chapter Eleven

Back to the Beginning

AFTER INVESTIGATING THE INITIAL CASELOAD in the coastal region, I took my team southwest into the remote Central Highlands, scene of my old infantry days. It had been twenty-three years since I had departed Pleiku in 1966, and I was looking forward to revisiting the sights and scenes of what my body was now reluctantly concluding had been my youth. During the ensuing years, I knew fierce battles had taken place, especially during the 1972 offensive. Due to the enormous tonnage of bombs dropped and shells fired, the 1972 campaign became known in ARVN military history as the "Summer of Fire." Despite the ravages of the war, I hoped the place had still retained its beauty.

When I arrived, and even given the time lapse, I still remembered the place fairly well. The first locale I visited was Bien Ho Lake, but unfortunately, my earlier fears were realized when I saw that the once beautiful lake was now hardly recognizable. The large statue of the Buddhist Goddess of Mercy at a nearby famous shrine had been toppled and lay scattered in fragments. The dense growth of tall trees that had once surrounded the lake had been completely razed. Beggars and homeless people searching for scraps of wood to use for cooking fires now occupied the once serene site. Perhaps the most glaring change was the almost total absence of Montagnards, who during my first tour were the majority population residing throughout the province, including the environs of Pleiku City. A small number of Montagnards still remained, but rather than living in the traditional stilted "long houses" constructed from wooden beams with roofs made from bamboo and thatch, they were now residing in makeshift huts made of scrap lumber and tin. Their poverty was excruciating to observe, especially after all they had done for us.

While the GVN had slowly moved Vietnamese settlers into the region, the Politburo strategists in Hanoi, realizing the strategic importance of the Central Highlands, had accelerated the process. They had plenty of reasons for their major attention to this area. From Pleiku the PAVN High Command could control the military situation in northeast Cambodia and southern Laos, as well as the vast timber and mineral reserves located throughout the region. As I traveled across the region, I noticed that the Vietnamese had heavily manned key Route 19 running from Vietnam's southern central coast across the highlands to the "Tri-border" area where the boundaries of Vietnam, Laos and Cambodia converge. When I visited the former Montagnard Training Center I was not allowed inside the perimeter wire. I was told that personnel of the Border Defense Forces inhabited the facility. The former base camp of the 3rd Brigade, 25th Infantry Division was occupied by squatters from poorer areas of the north, along with a sizeable number of troop dependents from the PAVN 3rd Corps now stationed in what used to be the headquarters of the U.S. 2nd Field Forces. To my perhaps biased viewpoint the PAVN appeared almost as an army of occupation.

As I reviewed the cases in the Central Highlands, I was reminded that this area did not have a large number of Americans lured by civilian agents like the coastal region near Danang and Chu Lai. However, my first discrepancy MIA case did involve two American civilian technicians who disappeared near Pleiku on May 30, 1970. Both men were discharged from the military and re-employed by the Dynalectron Corporation, a Department of Defense contractor. Upon my arrival, I discovered there were few leads to follow.

On June 1, 1970, the two young civilian employees from Texas, Charles R. Duke, Jr. and Kit T. Mark, were reported missing when they failed to report back to Dynalectron in Pleiku. The two men were scheduled to return to work after the Memorial Day weekend holiday. Ordinarily their failure to come back would have gone unnoticed, as it was not unusual for employees to return late from weekend jaunts. But in this case something was noticeably wrong, because like Robert Garwood, one of the men, Charles Duke, was scheduled to board a "freedom bird" and depart Pleiku the following day to return to his home "back in the world," as the old slang went.

Since Garwood was captured shortly before he was to go home, some analysts in the Defense Intelligence Agency had long considered the possibility that Garwood was passing information to the Communists prior to being captured. The analysts debated the prospect that the Communists believed that like their own personnel on foreign assignments, immediately upon his return to the U.S.,

Garwood would be subjected to a security debriefing in which he would be required to report all foreign contacts. Garwood was, therefore, captured in order to prevent him from compromising the identities of the covert Communist agents with whom he had been in contact. I believed this theory was plausible because Garwood had been assigned to the Intelligence Section of the USMC headquarters, making him a good target for exploitation. Although in reality Garwood was merely a jeep driver, his bragging and boasting regarding his actual duty assignment could have caused the Communist agents in the Danang area to overestimate his worth, especially since their own drivers were "specialists." Duke, however, was only a jet aircraft engine technician, and there were no Communist airfields or other facilities involving aircraft in the Central Highlands. If his capture had been planned to coincide with his departure from the area, then it must have been arranged with some other purpose in mind.

Nothing of that nature, however, appeared in his case file, and the circumstances of their disappearance were sketchy at best. Dynalectron employee Mr. Landel Scott was the last American who saw Duke and Kit Mark. On Saturday, May 30, 1970, the two men told Scott they intended to ride motorbikes to an area known as Bald Mountain, about seven miles south of Pleiku. When they didn't return, Mr. Warren L. McKean, the manager for Dynalectron at Pleiku, notified the corporate office in Saigon on June 1, 1970. All U.S. and South Vietnamese military authorities and hospitals in the Pleiku area were checked, but neither man could be found. A search of the Bald Mountain area, the Bien Ho Lake area, and the road network around Pleiku conducted by helicopter on June 1, 1970, yielded no results.

On June 17, an American Embassy Consular Officer visited Pleiku to inquire about the disappearance of the two men. The official was informed that the measures taken to locate them included a June 1 ground sweep, a check of local military facilities, and the helicopter search conducted by elements of the U.S. 4th Infantry Division. Montagnard tribesmen were also hired to make discreet inquiries in the nearby villages. Leaflets advertising a reward for information about the two men were also dropped in the area, and the South Vietnamese sent intelligence agents to nearby villages, but all search efforts were unsuccessful, although there were initial reports that the two men had been killed by Communist guerillas. After 1973, they were declared dead, body not recovered. U.S. negotiators made further requests to Communist officials over the years for all available information and records on the men, but none were ever provided. Several years later, after I had left the government, Charles Duke's mother asked me to examine the case. Her interest had been stimulated by reports of American POWs working as jet aircraft technicians in North Vietnam up until 1979. In reviewing all aspects of the case what I found convinced me that the two men had not simply disappeared, but I was never able to uncover any information on their fate while assigned to the JCRC.[1]

From Pleiku my team proceeded down Route 14 through Ea H'leo and Buon Ho villages toward the rural farming town of Ban Me Thuot, the provincial capital. Along the road I noticed that like the Pleiku area many lowland Vietnamese had been resettled into the area since the war ended. Although some Montagnards were visible from the road, most had been relocated to uncleared areas of the jungle. Dac Lac province, formerly Darlac province during the war, has some twenty different tribes of mountain people, with the Rhade the largest tribe. During the war, the few Vietnamese living in the area were concerned with the lack of security, and had concentrated themselves in Ban Me Thuot and another village closer to Nha Trang on the coast.

When we arrived in Ban Me Thuot I sensed that the security situation was very tense. When my team was introduced to the local Province Task Team whose members would be working with us, it was obvious that most local team members were from the Ministry of Public Security/Interior. We could not walk across the street without security cadre closely following us. They weren't even trying to hide, unlike earlier times when they tried to remain semi-inconspicuous. The cadre accompanying my team from Hanoi also cautioned us about recent operations conducted in the area by the anticommunist Montagnard organization "United Front for the Liberation of the Oppressed Races," called "FULRO" based on the French title of this organization.

When the accompanying cadre warned us to maintain our distance from the Montagnards for our own safety, I laughed out loud. I insisted that we Americans had nothing to fear save a possible incident aimed at propaganda contrived by some individual or organization with ill intent. As usual, the cadre outwardly ignored my response. At first he was outgoing and friendly, then in normal fashion, he noticeably stiffened before presenting that message. After years of watching this sudden behavior shift, I started responding to their statements, knowing they would report my reaction and comments. It was my way of indirectly replying to their policy-makers. Once his mission was complete, he returned to his normal self, as if a switch had been turned on and off.

A region dotted by extinct volcanoes, Dac Lac province contains some of the richest basalt soil in the world. Due to the mild climate and terrain, with cool evenings, moderate annual rainfall, and an average elevation of six hundred meters the area is particularly suited for coffee, tea and pepper. While walking around the town I talked with several Montagnards who arrived with wagons laden with coffee and pepper. They described very difficult times since the withdrawal of the Americans. Although they were allowed to use state owned land for cultivation, they received only a fraction of the actual value of their crops. They claimed that they were only permitted to sell their produce to Communist party farm cooperatives, and therefore, they were unable to obtain a reasonable price for their harvest. In essence, they were forced to take whatever the state offered them. The Montagnards I saw were dressed in rags and appeared to be in very poor health, their eyes whitened by cataracts and their frail frames indicating a lack of proper nutrition. I could barely control my emotions every time I saw them, sickly, barely able to care for themselves, yet still stoic despite the incredible hardships they had endured since the war. The Communist thirst for vengeance on those who fought on our side, and who apparently were still stinging the Vietnamese on occasion, knew no end. No doubt the Communists would secretly rejoice if the Montagnard population, whom they considered an inferior race, disappeared, so that ethnic Vietnamese could be moved into the region to relieve their chronic over-population and secure this vital strategic region.

The primary case scheduled for investigation in Dac Lac involved three American missionaries with the Christian Missionary Alliance (CMA) who had worked at a Leprosarium dedicated to the treatment of minorities suffering the ravages of the dreaded Leprosy disease. The Leprosarium was located south of Ban Me Thuot in the village of Ea Ana. At the Leprosarium the Reverend Archie Mitchell from Nebraska provided spiritual guidance, while Dr. Eleanor Vietti, a young woman from Texas, served as the medical doctor for the patients and their families. Mr. Daniel Gerber, a Mennonite and conscientious objector from Ohio, worked as the maintenance technician for the hospital compound maintaining the electric power generator and a Land Rover vehicle used for transportation. The hospital staff also had several female volunteer nurses who assisted Dr. Vietti, including the fiancée of Mr. Gerber. The Montagnards greatly appreciated the treatment the Leprosarium provided, and the three Americans working there, especially Dr. Vietti, were well known throughout the Central Highlands. In fact, the medical services provided were so effective that the Regional Communist Party Committee became concerned that the CMA was "winning the hearts and minds of the people." To prevent that, the Committee decided to send an Armed Propaganda Team to halt the CMA operation. In contrast to the Special Action Units normally deployed in densely populated areas, in rural areas the Communists continued to depend upon smaller, more lightly equipped Armed Propaganda Teams, first formed by General Vo Nguyen Giap in the 1940s, as the primary means of assassination and intimidation.

According to the accounts provided by survivors of the incident, on the evening of May 30, 1962, the Team arrived at the hospital and separated the occupants into three groups. Referring to them as "oppressors of the people," they took the three missionaries into custody and removed them from the hospital. After delivering a stern lecture, the Communists raided the hospital for food, medicines, cloth and other supplies, and then departed the hospital in the Land Rover normally driven by Mr. Gerber. The three missionaries were never seen or heard from again.

Aside from the five West German medical personnel assigned to the "Knights of Malta" voluntary hospital organization who were captured west of Danang, this was the first case I investigated where civilian volunteers were involved. I was aware, however, that numerous incidents had occurred in the Central Highlands involving foreigners who were killed or captured by the Communists. According to what I had been told during my previous military tours, the Communists were keenly concerned about the degree of influence civilian volunteers might have over the ethnic population in the mountainous regions. The Communists had not forgotten how the French had seized control of Vietnam under the guise of religious proselytizing, and they viewed the Montagnards as a potential source for future problems regarding political and administrative control of the sparsely populated highlands. As a result of this mindset, the Communists sought to restrict the operations of civilian volunteers, especially missionaries.

Prior to the abduction of the three from the Leprosarium, the Communists had halted a vehicle traveling from Saigon to Dalat carrying two American missionary families. The group included Reverend Elwood Jacobson, his wife and daughter, and Reverend Gaspar Makil, his wife and three children. Both men spoke Vietnamese, and they clearly identified themselves as missionaries, but in a brazen and brutal act the Communist force fired into the vehicle with automatic weapons fire killing both Jacobson and Makil, and Makil's infant daughter.

These weren't the only American missionaries killed by the Communists in the Central Highlands during the war. Another group was executed during the 1968 "Tet" general offensive at the Christian Missionary Alliance compound in Ban Me Thuot. In that incident, Reverend Bob Ziemer was killed while holding a white flag of surrender. Others executed at the same time included Mr. Carl Thompson, Mrs. Ruth Thompson, Mr. Leon Griswold and Miss Ruth Wilting. Ironically, this was the same Ms. Wilting who was Daniel Gerber's fiancée. She had escaped the 1962 incident, only to die four years later. Mr. Griswold's daughter, Carolyn Griswold, survived but died a few days later after she had been evacuated to a U.S. Army field hospital.

During the course of the case investigations in Dac Lac I had the opportunity to talk to several Montagnards who previously worked for or with the U.S. They informed me that after the war ended, Communist officials arrived at the CMA compound and removed the remains of most of the people who had been buried there after the "Tet" offensive. The remains removed included those of several young female Montagnard nurses who had been forced to kneel down in the courtyard of the compound before being shot in the backs of their heads at close range by Communist political cadre. I took my team into the compound but we found only two headstones still remaining. We placed flowers and said prayers over the two headstones that had the following inscriptions:

Carl Edward Thompson
Born February 13, 1924–Killed February 1, 1968
That they may rest from their labors and their works do follow them
Revelation 14:13

Ruth Stebbins Thompson
Born July 6, 1923–Killed February 1, 1968
Accept a corn of wheat fallen to the ground and die,
it abidith alone but if it die it bringith forth much fruit.
John 12:24

As part of planning the investigation, I was required to meet with officials from Dac Lac province. The Province Task Team, comprised entirely of Vietnamese, informed me that they had located one witness for interview. According to the Vietnamese, the witness was a Montagnard who was a member of the Armed Propaganda Team that captured the three Americans. The witness stated that in 1961, when he was only seventeen years old, the Communists accepted him into the Armed Propaganda Team. At the time of the interview the witness held the rank of Major in the PAVN and was assigned as a district-level military commander. The witness said that sometime in May or June 1962, his team was assigned the mission to enter the Leprosarium and capture spies. The team was only at the hospital for about forty minutes, and then departed on foot with two American men and one American woman. After traveling about one kilometer the team met with another armed group of Communists at a prearranged point, and there they transferred custody of the three Americans. The witness said that his team did not return to the hospital, and they also did not take any supplies. The witness recalled that a Vietnamese headed the armed group receiving custody of the Americans. He said that several members of the other group were local Montagnards who had been taken to North Vietnam for political training before being returned to the Dac Lac area. The witness heard that the three captured Americans were killed later that same night, but he did not know where the three bodies were buried.

After hearing his testimony I concluded that either he was not involved in the incident as claimed, or he was purposely withholding information. I was somewhat surprised by the physical appearance of the witness, because although he had the facial features of a Montagnard he spoke fluent Vietnamese with a noticeable Hanoi accent. I also observed that the witness was well dressed in the latest Saigon fashion, and sported long, well-manicured fingernails and beauty parlor-styled hair. When speaking he maintained a rapid voice rate, and used gestures and mannerisms similar to a typical Communist political officer or commissar. After the witness departed from the interview site I raised objections regarding his testimony with both the Province Task Team and the accompanying officials from Hanoi. They agreed that the testimony of the witness appeared to be lacking in detail, and pledged to take the matter up with him during a subsequent unilateral session.

At the next interview with the same witness, he altered his testimony and provided additional details concerning the incident. He said that after leading the three missionaries to an area about one kilometer from the hospital he and other Montagnards waited on a trail outside the village where the hospital was located while the Vietnamese who received custody of the three Americans led them forty to fifty meters into the forest. After "completing their mission" the group departed the area. When pressed for a definition of "completing their mission" the witness said that the three Americans were killed and buried that same night. The witness also admitted that the group did use the hospital's Land Rover to carry supplies from the compound back to a Communist base area. When asked how his group was able to drive the vehicle the witness claimed that one Vietnamese who accompanied the armed group that killed the three Americans had previous experience as a driver. Later, my team traveled to the site where the Americans were allegedly killed and dug numerous test pits but no remains, personal effects or other evidence was found.

Although the Vietnamese officials stated that the American side now had ample evidence to consider the investigation completed, I refused. I opined that this would not be possible because all we had was the verbal account by a witness who had changed his testimony. During an off-duty side session with the leader of the Vietnamese contingent in my hotel room later that night, we compared the account provided by the witness with the information contained in official U.S. files. In addition to the Vietnamese Team Chief, Master Sergeant Atherton was also present. In discussing the case I pointed out that the most disturbing aspect was that several live-sighting reports had been received indicating that at least two of the missionaries survived the incident. According to those reports, two of the missionaries, Dr. Vietti and one of the men (believed to be Reverend Mitchell), had remained alive in custody for several years after they were captured. I added that in November 1962, a reconnaissance team recovered Mr. Gerber's passport several kilometers east of the site where the Americans had been reportedly killed. This made no sense since the alleged withdrawal route was toward the west and Cambodia.

Somewhat perturbed by my remarks, the Vietnamese Team Chief informed me that he had received additional information on a unilateral basis from local cadre who were assigned to the area at the time, but not directly involved. According to him, with the exception of the Montagnard already interviewed, no one else directly involved at the time was still living. The Vietnamese Team Chief then provided an account indicating that Communist forces had planned to capture a larger number of missionaries, perhaps nine, who had been present at the hospital for a wedding of two staff members. For some reason, however, rather than remain at the hospital overnight, the group decided to return to Ban Me Thuot by vehicle just before dark. When the raiding party arrived at the hospital Dr. Vietti was in the shower. One of the members of the raiding party knocked on the door and handed her some clothing but no shoes. The raiding party then took Dr. Vietti, Reverend Mitchell and Mr. Gerber to a predesignated site about one kilometer from the hospital where a local resident who was secretly working for the Communists gave them information concerning the position held at the hospital by each American, as well as certain acts they had performed that aroused suspicions that they were spies. I thanked him for his "unilateral" information while stressing that more evidence and information was still needed. I knew, for example, that survivors had stated that Dr. Vietti at the time was suffering from leg ulcers and was having a difficult time walking. Yet the official "witnesses" never recalled this fact.

After the side meeting with the Vietnamese Team Chief, both central and local officials renewed their attempt to locate other witnesses and records. One member of the Vietnamese contingent of the Joint Investigation Team received hearsay information to the effect that the three missionaries were initially taken south in the Land Rover, and that after the three were removed from the vehicle, members of the raiding party returned to gather medicines and supplies from the hospital. The three missionaries were then killed and buried by a stream. Unfortunately the Source of this information could not be found; therefore, we were not able to obtain a more precise location for the alleged gravesites in order to conduct a site survey.

One unexpected source did turn up years later. Perhaps back in 1975 the DAO in Saigon had taken seriously the Santilli family warning, because just prior to the attack on Ban Me Thuot, a young Montagnard Captain working for the DAO, Y Tin H'wing, was choppered into the town. Y Tin H'wing, aka "David Piedro," was a very special young man. H'wing was a member of the Rhade tribe and had been trained during the war by both American Special Forces and its Australian counterpart, the Special Air Services. As a cover for his specialized training, H'wing had actually traveled to Australia as a "college student" at the University of South Wales. After completing his training he returned to the Central Highlands where he participated in cross border raids into Cambodia. H'wing's organization was called the Truong Son Group, a play on the Vietnamese name for the Ho Chi Minh Trail. This group was well known and respected in the U.S. intelligence community due to its numerous live prisoner "snatches" and capture of valuable documents from PAVN camps inside Cambodia during the war.

H'wing had been dispatched to Ban Me Thuot with a two-fold mission: check out the Communist plans and assist in the rescue of any U.S. officials who might became stranded there in the event of a PAVN attack. During the assault on the city, H'wing was able to establish radio contact with the Province Representative from the American Embassy, Mr. Paul Struharik. Despite hiding in his home during the initial attack, Struharik was soon captured. H'wing was still in the area when the PAVN overran the town. We lost contact with him and feared for his life.

However, all his training must have paid off. While interviewing refugees for POW/MIA information at the Thai-Cambodia border in 1987, I encountered a group of some two hundred Montagnards that recently had defected from the Khmer Rouge. The group included several members of both the Rhade and Jarai tribes with whom I had worked during the mid-1960s. Seeing that the group was in dire straits I purchased clothing, food and cooking utensils for them. The Montagnards were extremely happy to know that they still had American friends after so many years. During the ensuing debriefings I received information that H'wing had been arrested shortly after the capture of Ban Me Thuot, but was later released to reside at his native village.

Knowing he was alive was a great relief for me. During the course of MIA investigations in 1991, I searched for and found him living in Ban Me Thuot. H'wing appealed to me for help in getting his exit papers so he could depart Vietnam under the auspices of the Orderly Departure Program, the American refugee resettlement plan. H'wing said he wanted to join his former Montagnard comrades-in-arms from the war years who had recently arrived in North Carolina. The problem was that in order to obtain the necessary permits to enter the program, H'wing would be required to pay substantial "fees" to the Communist authorities. On a salary of approximately $5.00 per month earned growing coffee and pepper he simply did not have the money. H'wing gave me the names of all the American friends he could remember, and I wrote to those whose addresses I could locate, explaining the situation. After receiving no response from H'wing's "friends," I decided to go it alone.

I next met H'wing in Danang during 1992. At that time I obtained permission from my Vietnamese counterpart on the MIA team to give H'wing $1,000 of my own money. After receiving the money H'wing returned to Ban Me Thuot intending to pack his bags, but apparently he felt so obligated by my gift that he changed his mind and decided to remain in Vietnam to help search for MIAs. After returning to Bangkok I received a letter from H'wing passed to me by American missionaries visiting Vietnam. The letter contained information on the three missing Americans.

H'wing's report, in which he interviewed several Montagnards who either witnessed the attack or took part (which cast doubt on the Vietnamese claims that everyone else was dead), indicated that shortly after their capture that night, Mitchell had fallen into a punji stake trap and was seriously wounded. He was killed and buried in the general vicinity of where we first dug. H'wing even marked the grave's location for a future effort. Gerber and Vietti were killed shortly thereafter and buried. His report also contained information on other losses in the Central Highlands.

I was impressed by the amount of detail in the testimonies. In thinking about H'wing's report, I recalled the successful recoveries made by the JCRC with Montagnard assistance during 1973-74. I believed it might be a good idea to research the possibility of again employing the Montagnards who formerly worked for the U.S. to search for MIAs in the Central Highlands. Unfortunately, when I broached it with the JCRC commander, LTC Joe Harvey, he didn't like the idea at all. He remained convinced that the only way to solve the issue was to employ only those witnesses "introduced" by the Communist cadre assigned to the VNOSMP. To him, the U.S. and the Communists had established at least some kind of MIA program, and he felt it best to maintain this status quo. Since then, H'wing has emigrated to North Carolina.

Due to the close proximity of the loss locations I also began case investigations involving two more American missionaries who were captured in Ban Me Thuot, but during the 1968 "Tet" offensive. The two Americans, Mr. Henry F. Blood, a protestant missionary and linguist from Oregon, and Miss Elizabeth "Betty" Olsen, a nurse from Pennsylvania, were captured on February 1, 1968, when the Christian Missionary Alliance Compound was overrun by Communist forces. After capture they were taken to a POW camp located a few days walk from Ban Me Thuot. There Mr. Michael Benge from Oregon, who was assigned to the U.S. Agency for International Development, joined them. Mr. Benge was captured in Ban Me Thuot on January 31, 1968. Both Blood and Olsen died in captivity.

During the course of the investigations into the fate of Blood and Olsen, the officials of the Province Task Team offered the opinion that live-sighting reports on the cases of the three missionaries captured at the Leprosarium in 1962 had somehow become confused with the cases of Henry Blood and Betty Olsen, who were captured in 1968. After conferring with my analyst I conceded this possibility, but also expressed the opinion that obviously none of the reports prior to the February 1, 1968, capture date of Blood and Olsen could be considered.

The Province Task Team then presented new information it had received from a Montagnard witness from Ho Chi Minh City visiting relatives in the Ban Me Thuot area. According to the local officials, the witness had been in a command position during 1962 when the incident occurred. The witness said that the Province Party Secretary had issued the order for the raid to be carried out, and initially the purpose of the raid was to obtain medicine for Communist personnel involved in the war effort. However, the raiding party believed that the three missionaries were spies so they decided to take them prisoner. With the exception of the Montagnard Communist member of the Armed Propaganda Team already interviewed by the Joint Investigation Team, all other witnesses were now deceased. The new witness provided the same account as the Montagnard Communist previously interviewed except that he described the killing of the three missionaries. According to his version, the Montagnard Communist was instructed by the Vietnamese in overall charge of the operation to wait on the trail with Dr. Vietti while he and other members of his group took Reverend Mitchell and Mr. Gerber into the forest. A few minutes later the Montagnard Communist was told to bring Dr. Vietti to the same location. When he reached the site where the others were waiting he saw both Reverend Mitchell and Mr.

Gerber lying dead on the ground next to a hole. The Vietnamese in charge then asked Dr. Vietti "woman, do you have anything to say before we beat you to death and throw you in this hole?" After Dr. Vietti stood silent for a few moments the group beat her to death with wooden clubs. The group then departed the area and the witness did not know the disposition of the three bodies.

After the provincial officials provided the most recent account of the incident the accompanying Vietnamese officials sat smiling, waiting for a reaction from the U.S. side. Apparently they believed that the killing of the three missionaries represented an outstanding achievement. While contemplating the brutal deaths of the three humanitarians, especially Dr. Vietti, I could feel anger welling up inside me. When queried as to whether I had anything I wanted to ask, I could no longer control myself. I sharply queried the members of the Province Task Team as to who replaced the three missionaries at the hospital in order to continue providing medical treatment for their patients. The Chief of the Province Team responded that no one replaced them and the hospital fell into ruin. I then said that I didn't know why Dr. Vietti had declined to make a statement prior to being beaten to death, but if I had been in her shoes I would have made the following statement: "yes man, I do have something to say. I am a lady doctor working here without salary to help the poor unfortunate Montagnard people who suffer from a horrible disease. If you kill me they will have no one to care for them. If you are that ignorant, this probably means that twenty years from now you will still be poor and hungry and begging for medicine from foreign countries."

After I made my statement the conference room in the province headquarters fell completely silent. The only thing audible in the room was the ticking of an ornate, hand-carved clock on the wall. Since everything was being spoken in Vietnamese, Master Sergeant Atherton was the only American aside from me present who could understand what was being said. He stared at me with absolutely no emotion showing on his face. Suddenly a member of the VNOSMP from Hanoi, my old counterpart Pham Teo, broke the deafening silence by blurting out "you cannot say that, you cannot say that!" The room then erupted into activity as small groups of Vietnamese huddled unilaterally to discuss what they should do. After a brief recess the session reconvened. I answered criticism from the Vietnamese side concerning my remarks by saying that my summation had been made entirely in the hypothetical and therefore, there was no basis for any complaint. After some stern looks from the Vietnamese side the discussions eventually continued in the normal manner.

After receiving the new information from the Province Task Team, I then interviewed the former Communist Party Secretary of Dac Lac province, Mr. Nguyen Khac Tinh, concerning the case of the three missionaries. I wanted to compare his version with the story provided by the new witness. The former chief Party official of the province stated that he had first entered the area from North Vietnam to fight against the French in 1945. In 1955 Tinh returned to North Vietnam and then reinfiltrated the South in late 1960 or early 1961. After his arrival in the area he served as a member of the Inter-Region 5 Party Committee, and the Secretary of Darlac province until 1966 when the province was placed under the direct control of Hanoi through the B-3 Front. While assigned to the Central Highlands area, Tinh disguised himself as a Montagnard (which certainly caught my attention since the first witness introduced by the Vietnamese who, although he looked like a Montagnard, spoke and acted like a Vietnamese political officer). He used the cover name of "Ma Ban." In 1966 he moved to the Binh Long-Phuoc Long area where he served as a member of the Region Party Committee of Region 6, which was subordinate to COSVN. He held that position until 1975 when the war ended, and then he retired to Ho Chi Minh City.

Tinh stated that the raid on the Leprosarium had been conducted in order to question the three Americans for information concerning the activities of the Diem regime and U.S. forces operating in the area. The raiding party also captured one vehicle in which they loaded the three Americans and took them South to the K'rong K'no River. After hiding the vehicle the raiding party took the three Americans across the river where they were attacked by ARVN ground troops and U.S. aircraft, killing several Communist personnel and all three of the Americans. After burying the bodies, including the Americans, the raiding party withdrew to the south.

The information from the former Province Party Secretary created a situation where I was faced with two different accounts of the same incident. On the one hand, testimony from the lower ranking party members directly involved in the incident indicated that the three Americans were killed near the hospital shortly after being captured. On the other hand, the highest ranking Party official in the province at the time was telling me that the three Americans were taken away in the hospital's vehicle and killed a considerable distance from their point of capture two or three days later. After checking additional U.S. intelligence files I was able to determine that the ARVN had been able to recover the Land Rover vehicle shortly after the incident. The vehicle was found in the same area as described by Nguyen Khac Tinh. However, Tinh failed to mention that the vehicle had been disassembled, cut up into four separate pieces and then buried, obviously to conceal the actual route of withdrawal of the raiding party. ARVN forces also discovered two large barracks-type structures and a field hospital in the same area. This would seem to indicate that the raiding party had originated from a major headquarters for Communist forces operating nearby. The mention of a field hospital immediately drew my attention due to several live sighting reports of the missionaries after the incident. Some of the reports indicated that the missionaries were being employed providing medical treatment for wounded Communist personnel. According to one of the most recent reports the missionaries were moved back near the Leprosarium just prior to the 1968 "Tet" offensive in order to establish a staging area for wounded PAVN troops participating in the attack. Since Betty Olsen and Mr. Henry Blood were not captured until after the offensive began I concluded that this report could not be correlated to either of the two.

To make matters even more confusing, the Vietnamese Team Chief participating in the joint investigation informed me that based on unilateral information he received, "grave robbers" had stolen the remains from the burial site sometime during 1988. According to him, both Vietnamese and Montagnards were involved in removing the remains of the three Americans from the same area where my team had dug the test pits in April 1989, and they wanted to exchange the remains for ten ounces of gold. He said he had also heard the figure $5,000 mentioned as a possible reward for turning in the remains. Since the Communists in charge of the program already knew the schedule for the case investigations when the graves were reportedly robbed in 1988, I suspected that the "grave robbers" report was just another ploy not only to milk the U.S. Government for more money, but also to conceal the time of death and the manner in which the three Americans were executed. In other words, any postmortem damage or any partial loss of remains would be blamed on the "grave robbers."

I also suspected that Communists were deliberately coaching the witnesses to prevent the true facts of the case from being revealed. They were deeply worried about this case for several reasons. First, they were afraid of any ramifications given the many Non Government Organization (NGO) programs helping people throughout postwar Vietnam. This was a very lucrative source of income for the Communist controlled government. They not only siphoned off donated aid money to finance their operations, they also managed to receive credit for whatever portion of the money eventually trickled down to the people. Second, they didn't want to lose face for having captured and then executed humanitarian workers, especially a lady doctor; and third, they may have forced the missionaries to assist them in the war effort, including treating wounded PAVN personnel. As far as I know the remains of the three missionaries have never been recovered.

After temporarily suspending the investigations into the fate of the missionaries I contemplated the events that had transpired while in Dac Lac. Had it not been for the political climate at the time, the incident involving the unarmed, civilian missionaries would have been investigated as a routine robbery/homicide. In an attempt to understand the motivation of the Communist forces in carrying out their brutal acts, I tried to place myself in their position at the time of the incidents. Was it possible that the missionaries were actually spies? While I knew that the CIA maintained a field station in Ban Me Thuot during the war because I had received information from the office myself, I very much doubted this aspect. Nevertheless I did recall that during my previous tour in the area from 1965 to 1966, our Intelligence Section had attempted to establish some degree of rapport with any foreigners we encountered, especially Americans. While we never planned to recruit such people, we routinely asked some questions regarding the military and political situation in the area that were most likely inappropriate. I believe this was especially true regarding ministers and priests residing in isolated areas with their congregations whom we visited on a routine basis. Obviously we were interested in finding the enemy so we could kill them, and perhaps not surprisingly the missionaries assigned to voluntary and religious organizations in the Central Highlands loathed the Communist presence there. In violating their own moral and ethical codes they probably felt like their indiscretions were made for a good cause. Still, for the paranoid Communists, any foreigner was a spy.

Another aspect also troubled me. During the time that I worked at the national level collecting intelligence on the Communist party organization, names of individuals developed from my information ultimately ended up on "white," "gray," or "black" lists maintained by the "Phoenix" program. In order to eradicate the Communist infrastructure, those on the blacklist were candidates for capture, although killing them was not uncommon. Those on gray lists were also suspect, while those on white lists were considered favorably known. Since the GVN officials who routinely served as the Chairman of the province-level Phoenix Committees could unilaterally choose who would be captured, and who would be killed, the committees were at times used to settle personal vendettas or to eliminate rivals. Since no information can really be considered rock-solid, I had no doubt that our side had needlessly killed some innocent people during the war, especially in cases where vague reports indicated that certain "high-level" Communist officials would be gathered for meetings at predictable times in a war where almost every other aspect was unpredictable.

Unfortunately, however, this was a too often traveled path to impressive combat decorations for bravery by those who sought to avoid the daily, year-long drudgery of an infantry assignment, fighting rifleman to rifleman. I concluded that the Communists were most likely no different. For all I knew, the Armed Propaganda Team and other cadre responsible for the deaths of the missionaries in the Central Highlands were decorated with medals for their "heroic action" in killing foreign spies and accomplishing what the Communists called "resupply by ambush" by taking the vehicle load of medical supplies and equipment from the helpless leprosy patients. It began to dawn on me that any attempt to analyze the war in Vietnam from both sides quickly became an emotional tug-of-war, especially for me, even though I had spent so much time and energy learning the Communist viewpoint. Maybe the cadre with whom I met in Ban Me Thuot had actually earned some perverse right to be proud of their achievements, and maybe the anger I had felt in listening to the accounts of their actions was misplaced. I had to remind myself that nothing was ever easy or simple in Vietnam.

Not surprisingly, this introspection had started shortly after leaving Danang. As I began to contemplate the Communist program of luring Americans, I found it strange to suddenly realize that in some odd way I was fortunate to have been assigned to a combat unit operating in remote areas of the Central Highlands, where the primary concern was PAVN regular troops recently infiltrated from North Vietnam. It took me awhile to appreciate the rather unbelievable thought that I might have been safer in a combat zone than hanging around in Danang. Still, although my unit rarely came in contact with the local populace, I began to recall occasions when civilians approached me. I'm sure I wasn't the only GI taking a bath or washing clothes at Bien Ho Lake who was beckoned by Vietnamese females. I'm equally certain that many other GI's like me were approached by locals who simply wanted to practice their English, or perhaps learn something about people from America, as well as the customs and history of our country. In hindsight I sometimes wonder what would have happened to me had I not attended the training courses taught by ARVN exchange officers before being sent to Vietnam. The training probably saved my life, and I regret the fact that more Americans didn't undergo the same training, rather than rely solely on rumors and scuttlebutt concerning the Communist's employment of civilians against our forces. In such a climate, how does one then differentiate between the genuinely curious soul who only wishes to make an American friend, and the smiling female terrorist secretly trying to lure a lonely eighteen year old into a deadly trap? Between Danang and Ban Me Thuot, from the sea to the mountains, I found myself struggling with many newfound emotions. Worse, I never reached a clear verdict; it was the Vietnam War in miniature.

But I didn't have long to dwell on the subject: as always, another case awaited me. The next MIA discrepancy case I investigated while in Dac Lac province involved Airman 2nd Class Benny L. Dexter from Oregon. On May 8, 1966, without any approval, Dexter departed Pleiku Airbase in a "Jeep" with his rifle and ammunition and headed south on National Highway 14. After a brief stop in Ban Me Thuot, he continued his trip but ran out of gas just south of the town. After obtaining more gas from an unidentified friend, Dexter returned to town where he spent the night. The following day Dexter continued south again on Highway 14, but his vehicle stopped on the road about ten miles south of town.

RVN intelligence agents reported seeing Dexter in Ban Me Thuot on May 9. They also reported seeing his vehicle parked beside Highway 14 about ten miles south of town. Intelligence sources also reported that three armed Communist personnel captured Dexter, and then led him away into the jungle. At the time Dexter left his vehicle he was smiling and made no attempt to resist. The same sources reported that Dexter's captors had planned to nab him when he departed Ban Me Thuot the previous day, but that he had been driving so fast that he passed by them before they were prepared to stop his vehicle. When he turned his vehicle around and started back to Ban Me Thuot to spend the night, he appeared so unexpectedly they were not able to capture him.

Based on this information, I could never determine Dexter's motivation or what his plan was that night. A subsequent report indicated that in late June 1966, an American captured while driving on Highway 14 was being carried in a hammock by three PAVN troops. According to the report the American was unable to walk due to sore feet. After being interrogated the American was moved further south to Phuoc Long province. Another report indicated that an unidentified American being held east of Duc Lap (a town south of Ban Me Thuot in the old GVN Quang Duc province), died due to starvation and was buried there in February 1967. Although this report might possibly correlate to Dexter, it could also result in a possible correlation to other Americans held in the area at the time, including the missionaries.

In Ban Me Thuot I interviewed a witness who was a retired cadre assigned to the Quang Duc province military forces during the war. He claimed that Dexter was taken to a remote prison camp near the border between Darlac and Phuoc Long provinces in what at that time was Communist Military Region 6. The witness said that Dexter showed him and members of his staff a photograph of his family in the United States. In order to prevent Dexter from escaping the cadre removed his boots and eyeglasses. After being held two months, however, Dexter did manage to escape but he was recaptured shortly thereafter. According to the witness, after Dexter's first escape attempt failed he did not try to escape again until one day when an L-19 aircraft flew over the area. At that time Dexter began to run, and after he failed to stop running when ordered to do so he was shot dead on the spot and buried near where he was killed. The cadre also claimed that everyone who knew the precise location of the grave is now deceased. All documents and personal effects were reportedly turned over to unidentified authorities of Communist Quang Duc province.

In reviewing the testimony offered by the witnesses, however, the reported evacuation route was simply not plausible. According to all available information, the policy in effect at the time would have required that Dexter be evacuated to the COSVN POW camp (since he was captured in an area under COSVN control). But in order to ensure that no stone was left unturned I agreed to lead my team on a search and recovery mission in an attempt to locate Dexter's alleged grave and recover his remains, or at least some type of evidence indicating a burial site. The effort took us into the Dak Pri swamps where we navigated through chest deep mud in some of the most difficult terrain I ever encountered, even for Vietnam.

Prohibited from wearing American military clothing, in preparation for the trip, Master Sergeant Atherton had gone shopping at the Base Exchange near the JCRC headquarters. The only items of clothing made from durable material he was able to purchase were Navy "bell-bottom" dungarees with flared trouser legs. Unfortunately, however, the wide trouser legs provided easy access for leeches and during the trek through the swamps Atherton had more than sixty bites from the blood-sucking creatures clinging to his body. The remainder of our group was not spared from the leeches, and the Vietnamese Team Chief, Mr. Ngo Hoang, was second runner-up to Atherton in the total number of leech bites.

Our principle witness and guide for the trek was a seasoned veteran of the Communist war effort who appeared to be genuinely familiar with the seemingly impregnable area. The elderly cadre was in unusually good physical condition for his age, and like the proverbial "Brer' Rabbit" in a briar patch he glided effortlessly through the deep mud and thick "wait-a-minute" vines with sharp thorns. Although we Americans and the accompanying cadre from Hanoi perspired profusely, the sun-leathered skin of the old revolutionary leading the long, serpentine file of investigators through the mire showed no indication of moisture. Cackling with glee at the sight of us pulling and thrashing behind him, occasionally the old cadre would pause to let us catch up while swigging from a one-gallon jug of homemade moonshine pulled over his shoulder by an index finger jammed through a plughole in the neck of the jug.

When we finally arrived at the site where Dexter was reportedly buried we found ourselves surrounded by a marshy area with the appearance of a peat bog. Judging from the deep wallows in the bog and piles of elephant dung scattered throughout the area it appeared that the site was a frequent gathering place for wild elephants. Optimistic at the possibility of finding the remains of Airman Dexter, our hopes were dashed when the smiling guide waved an extended arm across an undefined section of the bog while commenting that according to his recollection, the grave was located "somewhere" in the bog. After digging unproductive test pits for several hours we threw in the towel and decided to locate the former prison cage where Dexter was held or at least some type of structure indicating that a camp was actually located there during the war. Ultimately we were not able to find anything to indicate that the site had ever contained a grave or any type of wartime facility.

We all returned disheveled and frustrated by the lack of positive results. On the route back we shared the clear, powerful rice whiskey carried by the witness. During one rest break, and after a few nips at the jug, the cheerful guide abruptly mentioned hearing about a helicopter that crashed in the same general area. Based on my analysis of the information I concluded that the report most likely correlated to case 1046, a "Dustoff" medical evacuation mission flown on the evening of February 12, 1968 by four Army personnel (First Lieutenant Jerry Roe from Texas, Warrant Officer Alan Gunn from Georgia, Specialist Four Wade Groth from Michigan and Specialist Five Harry Brown from South Carolina) from the 50th Medical Detachment. Flying from Ban Me Thuot to the Special Forces camp at Gia Nghia, the UH1H helicopter simply disappeared that night from the radar screen.

This was an intriguing case, because in April 1969 a Source identified a photo of Brown as being a live POW he personally observed. Again in August 1969 a Source provided a description of two American POWs and identified a photograph of Brown as one of the two men he saw being held in Darlac province. In 1974 two Vietnamese located the wreckage of an unidentified aircraft and turned in data plates to the U.S. Government, but due to the lack of maintenance records no correlation could be made. In addition to these reports, while interviewing refugees in preparation for the field investigations I received reports concerning an "American named Brown" who had survived his incident and was living somewhere in Central Vietnam. Some of the reports indicated that "Brown" was an officer with the rank of "General." During the initial stages of the field investigations I also received a similar report from a Communist cadre in Hanoi. Since the reporting on "Brown" was so sketchy and no precise information was ever obtained, American POW/MIA analysts generally discounted these reports because U.S. files did not contain a general officer named Brown who was missing.

In October and November 1992 a JTFFA team investigated this case and discovered enough wreckage at the site to be able to identify a specific aircraft. Personal items found at the scene indicated that one or more crewmembers had died in the crash, which raises the possibility that as many as three of the crewmembers could have survived the incident. No information was obtained pertaining to the possible survivors. All things considered I believed that the incident was survivable, and the fact that an American named Brown had been identified from photographs after the incident indicated to me that the reports of an American named "Brown" who was seen alive in Vietnam after the crash should have been investigated. I fully realized that there was no officer named "Brown" listed as an MIA who held the rank of "General."

In evaluating information provided by the guide I was reluctant to discount any item he revealed to me, while at the same time pondering whether he had only mentioned the medical evacuation helicopter incident to placate us with the potential for locating an alternate site with multiple crewmembers. I held this out as a distinct possibility because the guide knew we were irritated by his apparent high level of confidence in finding the grave before we began the trek and his sudden loss of memory after we made the miserable trip into the swamps.

Another strange coincidence that has always puzzled me occurred during the two-day fiasco to search for the bamboo tiger cage where Dexter had been confined. On precisely the same day that we reached the area where the tiger cage was said to have been located, Colonel James "Nick" Rowe, a POW who had escaped after five years of captivity in the Mekong Delta, and who now was serving as an advisor to the Philippine Army, was assassinated by Communist forces in Quezon City. Like Dexter, Rowe had been held in a tiger cage, and the timing of Rowe's death seemed almost too coincidental. Perhaps I was becoming overly paranoid after so many years of dealing with the Vietnamese, but subconsciously

I felt they were sending us a message to the effect that everything evened out in the end.

Further arousing my suspicions, at the conclusion of this joint field investigation, the Vietnamese Team Chief, Mr. Ngo Hoang, who had recently completed a tour in the SRV Embassy in Manila, gave me a letter addressed to the former ARVN officer, Mr. Le Van Phap, who owned the car rental business in Quezon City. His car rental business had become quite prosperous due to the business provided by the official American presence in Manila. At the time he gave me the letter for Phap, Hoang informed me that intruders had recently killed Phap's mother and father in their family home in Can Tho in southern Vietnam. Hoang indicated that he was sending the letter to offer his condolences to Phap. When I passed the letter to technical experts in the Bangkok embassy they were able to surreptitiously open the letter and analyze its contents. According to them, the letter could have been perceived to be a genuine letter of condolences, but its wording could also be construed as a warning to the recipient that if he failed to follow the instructions given him regarding a future mission, events even more devastating might occur. I always wondered if anyone ever asked Phap which of the two it was, or whether his parents were killed because he failed to perform a requested favor for the Communists during the Rowe assassination.

Although we were unable to obtain any human remains or material evidence sufficient to resolve Dexter's case, the information we did gather was valuable to the Defense Intelligence Agency. During a technical meeting with the VNOSMP in Hanoi after the trek into the swamps, we presented some follow-up requirements for unilateral research by the Vietnamese that were prepared by the DIA. These requirements resulted from some information contained in several recently declassified American intelligence reports. Since the normal procedure had been to give virtually everything to the Vietnamese in advance, as soon as I learned of the pending transfer of sensitive information, never made available to the American public or to the family members of the missing men, I was deeply concerned. I was nevertheless astounded when I read the details of one particular report that appeared to meet the criteria of the proverbial "smoking gun"indicating that live Americans were left behind after Operation Homecoming.

According to the report we presented to the Vietnamese officials in outlining future leads to follow in investigating the case of Airman Dexter, in September 1974 five Americans were being held in another POW camp which was still subordinate to COSVN but separate from the military run camp. The camp, under the control of Public Security forces, was located in northwestern Tay Ninh province and had been given the designation "C-53." The intelligence information indicated that as of September 1974, five Americans, including one Caucasian named "Benny" were still alive and in this camp. Experts of the Defense Attaché Office in Saigon who collected the information deemed the Source reliable. Not only did the Source volunteer to take a polygraph examination concerning the validity of his personal observations, he also volunteered to lead a rescue party to the site in order to liberate the American POWs. Unfortunately however, before an operation could be planned, the situation on the ground in Vietnam began to deteriorate and neither the polygraph exam nor the rescue operation materialized.

To be fair, however, even if the situation had been more conducive for rescue operations, it is likely that no action would have been taken at the time due to the long-standing requirement for two independent Sources to identify a camp where live Americans were held. In the case of the September 1974 live-sighting report in northeastern Tay Ninh province, although an American with the same name as that of one of the reported prisoners held in the camp was missing in a location that would require his evacuation to this type of camp, there was no separate Source identifying a camp designated as "C-53." I did not realize it at the time, but in the not too distant future I would receive irrefutable evidence that a camp with the same numerical designation did exist at the same time and same location provided by the Source of the September 1974 report. The confirmation of the live-sighting report would ultimately put me on a collision course with not only the U.S. Pacific Command in charge of the field investigations, but with Washington policy makers as well.

Chapter 12

On the Road to Saigon, the "Pearl of the Orient"

AFTER TEMPORARILY SUSPENDING the case investigations in the Central Highlands, I took my team to the coastal region along Vietnam's eastern shore for some quick R&R. We traveled to the slow-paced seaside city of Nha Trang, a favorite wartime resort for American personnel in search of red sun, white sand, blue surf, and some of the best seafood in the world. After a meal of huge, scrumptious "Tiger Prawns" grilled in garlic and butter sauce, we began an aimless stroll along the beach hoping the sea air and salt water would relieve the torment from the leech and insect bites we had suffered in the highlands. Although the setting was absolutely beautiful, we found it difficult to enjoy since our reverie was periodically interrupted by shrill propaganda diatribes emanating from numerous loudspeakers, alongside which flew gaudy red banners embossed with white or gold patriotic slogans extolling the virtues of communism, all thoughtfully placed along the beach by the Ministry of Propaganda and Culture for consumption by the local populace and the occasional bewildered foreigner. In tortuous fashion, each time we began to relax our tired minds in response to the soothing sounds of the surging waves, the loudspeakers would suddenly erupt, spewing rabid political jargon.

However, in typical American fashion, in an attempt to compete with the obnoxious lectures, a CILHI Search and Recovery Specialist assigned to my team, Staff Sergeant Calvin Grant, began to loudly croon an old wartime GI favorite called "My Girl." Using only his talented voice and a portable stereo cassette player as background, the young black soldier quickly drew a large crowd at the beach. As the familiar chords of the more than two decades old song drifted across the beach and through the stately palm groves shading the many indigenous tourists, the crowd suddenly began to grow. It was obvious that Grant was an immediate smash, and that the people were genuinely excited by the familiar sounds from the past. Despite my admiration for Grant's abilities, I grew increasingly concerned by the growing size of the crowd, which might provoke intervention by the zealous "Cultural Police" responsible for such matters. Soon I had to curtail the fun, and we proceeded back to the hotel.

Having been already exposed to a considerable amount of propaganda at previous locations during our trip, I was surprised by the more abundant verbal and visual displays in a sleepy coastal town like Nha Trang. Then I recalled that during the war the U.S. had operated several covert intelligence-gathering operations from this well-secured coastal enclave in Khanh Hoa province. From Nha Trang, the CIA had planned and controlled espionage missions in the Central Highlands, while top-secret SOG special operations teams had launched third-country reconnaissance missions. Then, after the war ended, Nha Trang became the favorite R&R site of the large number of Russian technicians assigned to the Soviet Signals Intelligence Unit, as well as the Soviet naval facility in Cam Ranh Bay just south of Nha Trang. Additionally, the former RVN Naval Academy at Nha Trang was reorganized as the Naval Academy for Communist Vietnam. The previous wartime intelligence efforts alongside the current sensitive military facilities probably caused the Communists considerable political security concerns.

After departing Nha Trang, we moved southward to coordinate meetings with local officials in an area administratively designated Thuan Hai province. This region actually encompassed the former GVN provinces of Binh Tuy, Binh Thuan and Ninh Thuan. With the exception of Ho Chi Minh City, at the time of our arrival in Thuan Hai province, Vietnam's economy was in shambles. People were looking for work, any kind of work. But in Thuan Hai we noticed an unusual degree of optimism about the economy's future course. For one thing, although the Soviet Union had recently collapsed, the Russians were still occupying both the Signals Intelligence Unit base west of Highway 1 and the port facility at Cam Ranh Bay on a long-term, renewable lease. This created some jobs for the local citizenry. Like Danang and Nha Trang, the tea left in the cups of fleeing RVN personnel at Cam Ranh had not even had a chance to cool when the Russians arrived to establish a base. Based on the rapid postwar deployment of Soviet intelligence personnel into these critical coastal areas, it was obvious that bilateral operations between the Soviets and the Vietnamese Communist were already well organized. Although the U.S. intelligence community was never able to gain a clear understanding of wartime Soviet intelligence assistance, each time I heard mention of the "Walker spy case" I thought about the Soviet trawlers constantly operating off the Vietnamese coast. Information gleaned by Walker could have easily been transmitted to PAVN units operating in the mountains to the west, since the trawlers possessed line-of-sight communications with them.

Some Russian technicians from the Cam Ranh Bay base also visited the large ocean-side hotel in Phan Thiet, which featured saunas with boiling hot water. The hotel menu contained several East European dishes, which generally meant an abundance of greasy pork and cabbage. But the real economic impetus of the area seemed to stem from the recent cultivation of grapes. Although much of Thuan Hai consisted of arid, desert-like sandy soil with scattered cactus, the area adjacent to the sea had been blessed with terrain and weather similar to California. In gauging these conditions I concluded that Thuan Hai did have genuine prospects for development of not only a wine industry, but a citrus industry as well. Grapes were scarce in the rest of Vietnam, but we were able to find them easily at almost any small shop or noodle stand along the eastern seaboard. Having researched this in advance, as a goodwill gesture, I presented the local administration a set of videocassette tapes containing three volumes describing in detail the international history of wine making.

For the most part, we had come to Thuan Hai to begin the investigations of two cases: one American and a foreign national, and another American by himself who were abducted while traveling by vehicle along Route 1. These were unusual cases in that the missing people were navigating a well-traveled, main transportation artery running from the Demilitarized Zone in Central Vietnam south to Saigon. During the war years Highway 1 was normally crowded with American, Korean, or ARVN military vehicles. Military installations, ranging from small guard posts located at key bridges to divisional headquarters, dotted this linear communication route running the length of the country. However, due to the vast expanse covered by Route 1, there were certain isolated sites where an enjoyable road trip could suddenly become a nightmare. The famous French writer Bernard Fall called the section of the highway just south of the DMZ "The Street Without Joy."

The first case I investigated in Thuan Hai involved Mr. James E. Simpson from North Dakota, and Mr. Thomas G. Cornwaite, a British citizen. Simpson and Cornwaite were electrical technicians working at various American facilities throughout Vietnam. On November 5, 1968, both men departed Qui Nhon City in central Binh Dinh province in a military "Jeep" traveling south down Route 1 to Tan Son Nhut Airbase near Saigon. They never arrived at their destination.

According to our initial information, a wartime defector reported that he had been assigned to a Communist tax-collection unit of Ninh Thuan province that had the mission of stopping vehicles on Highway 1 in order to raise revenue to support the war effort. The same defector described how his unit captured two male Caucasians wearing civilian clothing while riding in a white "Jeep." The defector was able to provide an accurate physical description for both Simpson and Cornwaite. Another wartime Source stated that while attending a meeting of Communist officials of Ninh Thuan province, he received a report indicating that two men captured in a "Jeep" had managed to escape from captivity in neighboring Binh Thuan province but that they were later recaptured and executed. Another defector guided Air Force personnel to a site where the "Jeep" had been hidden at the time of the incident, but he was not able to provide any further details. Aside from these sketchy reports, during an interview trip to Japan in 1986 I did receive some information from a refugee concerning the capture of two Americans near Phan Rang, the capital of Ninh Thuan province during the war (and the scene of a last ditch battle in April 1975), but analysts evaluated this report as only a "potential correlation."

During the course of the investigation I interviewed other witnesses who described how the two men were arrested in late 1968, and were then turned over to a Communist propaganda unit. According to the witnesses the two men were subsequently transferred to the custody of a female assault platoon, and then were placed in the custody of Communist military intelligence personnel. The two men later escaped, and after being recaptured they were immediately executed. Unfortunately, however, none of the witnesses could locate the alleged burial site. Some four years later, in 1992, a JTFFA team returned to the area to conduct a follow-up investigation, but no new leads were ever developed.

To me this was just another example of poor Communist cooperation. The information I received concerning the female militia unit and the propaganda unit made sense to me, because I had seen this same modus operandi before in other areas. In those instances, regardless of which unit actually captured the American POWs, sometimes they were filmed for propaganda purposes being captured by females. In the macho world of Asian males, this was a message to the troops and masses that the Americans were not so tough after all, that even women were capable of capturing and subduing them. However, I found it difficult to believe that foreign personnel in the custody of Vietnamese Communist intelligence personnel could simply disappear with no record of their burial or other information useful toward resolution of their case. My reasoning was that if the Americans were transferred to the custody of an intelligence unit, personnel trained in both interrogation and the English language were available to facilitate exploitation. Although I was willing to concede that due to the military situation the Americans might well have been executed before exploitation, I had difficulty believing that their bodies and personal effects had simply become misplaced. The Communists had been selling French remains back to France since the 1950s, and they were well aware that foreign skeletal remains were more valuable than gold. The idea that some low-level commander, especially someone in charge of an intelligence unit, might "lose" American remains and personal effects and not forward any record of the final disposition was ridiculous to me.

The Communists often claimed that the wartime situation prevented them from creating such records, or that the fierce fighting had destroyed the records, that the local terrain had changed dramatically in recent years, or my favorite, that the savage B-52 bombings had obliterated any trace of the graves, all of which prevented them from being able to find remains or locate records. I could accept a certain percentage of lost information due to lazy bureaucrats, or the wartime destruction or death of the people involved. But the Communists used these excuses constantly, and it became obvious that they were an orchestrated response. Worse, many American analysts working the issue, even some who should have known better, began to accept the Communist song and dance. What most Americans don't know is that Allied forces captured several million pages of Communist documents during the war, everything from weapons inventories to POW policy documents. The entire collection is now open to the public in the National Archives in College Park, MD. To me, this vast assembly of materials was just a representative sample of what the Communists could produce. Moreover, postwar PAVN publications often contain detailed "After Action" type descriptions of battles, some even from the 1940s. These accounts occasionally include references to the military interrogations of shot down (and ultimately released) American pilots, or mention the capture of U.S. soldiers. Yet when it came to the critical POW/MIA issue, records were scant or non-existent. For instance, other than the Died in Captivity list handed to U.S. officials in 1973, no Communist POW/MIA document concerning American prisoners in South Vietnam has ever been turned over by the Vietnamese, despite our capturing dozens of them during the war.

Uninspired by the lack of results in investigating our initial case in Thuan Hai, we opened an investigation of another American, Mr. Jack Erskine from Oregon, who disappeared on November 13, 1968. Erskine's loss circumstances are very similar to Simpson and Cornwaite; he was abducted a week later and in the same area. At the time, Erskine and his co-worker, a Philippine national, had left their Jeep and were surveying for road construction when they were jumped by armed insurgents near Ca Na, a rocky point jutting out into the South China Sea south of Phan Rang. Erskine's coworker was fortunate to escape, but members of another survey party on a nearby hill saw Erskine being lead away into the underbrush across Highway 1.

In October 1969 a defector reported that Erskine was being held in Ninh Thuan. A captured Communist document dated February 18, 1970, contained three hand-drawn pictures with a caption in Vietnamese indicating that two Communist guerrillas were escorting "Jack" from the area. In January 1975, a Military Assistance Command Vietnam identification card issued to Erskine was found in an abandoned house near Phan Thiet, well south of the site where Erskine was kidnapped some five years earlier.

We interviewed one witness who reported that sometime during November an armed unit from Ninh Thuan province ambushed and captured an American riding in a Jeep. According to the witness, the American was placed in the custody of the Enemy Proselytizing Section of the province, and shortly thereafter the decision was made to further evacuate him west across Vietnam to the main COSVN POW camp. Supposedly, a Captain escorted the American from the area. Unfortunately, however, as the unidentified Captain and his American prisoner approached Route 20 in neighboring Lam Dong province, the American refused to continue on and the Captain shot and killed him. The witness attempted to justify the killing of the POW by claiming that Route 20 was at that time under ARVN control; therefore the Captain was subject to compromise and capture due to the American's obstinacy. The same witness testified that after killing the POW, the Captain buried him by the road and then submitted a report of the incident to the military headquarters of Ninh Thuan province. When we asked for a copy of the report the Vietnamese said that they were unable to locate it due to the time lapse. When we asked to interview the unidentified Captain personally, the Vietnamese said that he was killed during combat after the incident. The local authorities claimed that they were not able to identify any additional witnesses who could assist us in locating Erskine's grave.

In reviewing our investigation results I noted several discrepancies in the account provided by the witness. For one thing, I found it incredulous that the local authorities would evacuate an American POW, especially a civilian who would have been suspected of having been a spy, in the custody of one lone individual. Moreover, as a matter of policy, members of the Enemy Proselytizing sections were specially trained for handling American prisoners, and by the time of Erskine's capture incident a national-level policy document issued by the Communists requiring the safe-guarding of American POWs for future use as bargaining chips in negotiations with the United States (another in the numerous POW handling documents we captured) had been widely distributed throughout Vietnam. Like the case of Simpson and Cornwaite the case of Erskine was too simple, too pat. As far as I know the families of Simpson, Cornwaite and Erskine are still waiting for answers.

Another aspect that troubled me regarding the circumstances of capture of these people on Route 1 was the coincidence of the timing between the arrival of their vehicles at certain locations, and the appearance of the capturing parties. During one visit to Nha Trang I might have stumbled onto the answer to this question. The driver of my vehicle, a native of central Vietnam who regrouped to the north when the country was divided in 1954, recommended a hotel where he believed my team might be comfortable. It turned out that the driver's sister was the hotel manager, and during the war she had worked there as a staff member. I concluded that if she had worked there during the war, it was likely that others either loyal to the Communist cause or who had contacts with the Communist apparatus were employed there as well. Since Nha Trang was the logical place to stay overnight during a trip from Central Vietnam to Saigon, it would be very easy for a staff member of any hotel in Nha Trang to simply pick up a telephone and inform a contact that the Americans were departing at a specific time, describe the vehicle and possibly even supply a tag number.

My team also made a side trip to the mountain resort city of Dalat, although the city and the surrounding area was an area of low American casualties. We wanted to visit the former RVN National Military Academy, but it was under tight security at the time of our visit. I heard from locals that after the Chinese invasion of North Vietnam in January 1979, the Politburo moved the command post of the PAVN High Command from Hoa Binh province in the north to the Academy. While there we stayed at the aging but still beautiful Palace Hotel over looking serene Ho Xuan Huong Lake, the subject of much Vietnamese poetry and literature over the years. Close-by, shabby lean-to shelters made from tarpaper and scraps of tin constructed by economic migrants from the crowded northern cities contrasted sharply with the regal swans paddling gracefully across the deep blue waters of the tranquil lake.

As was the case in the Central Highlands, along the eastern seaboard we worked with several ethnic minorities who joined the Communists during the war. This time, we worked with members of the Roglai tribe who appeared to have some ancestral relation to the dark-skinned Chams that had once ruled central and southern Vietnam. Although possessing small arms and upper bodies, the Roglai had powerfully built, long legs enabling them to traverse the difficult mountainous terrain lying between Saigon and Dalat. The cadre in charge of the local Province Task Team during our visit, a PAVN Colonel, was also a member of the Roglai tribe. When visiting with the Americans in our hotel, he seemed somewhat ill at ease. I tried to relieve his anxiety by inviting him to join us for an American movie we planned to show by hooking up the video player we carried in our vehicle to the community television located in the hotel lobby. For the past several weeks while traveling around Vietnam, we had heard much discussion about the movie "Platoon." It was the only American war movie I was ever aware of that was approved by Communist authorities for viewing by Vietnamese civilian audiences inside Vietnam. "Platoon" was also shown at various official "cultural centers" of the Ministry of Propaganda and Culture throughout the country. In order to be more balanced I had been showing the movie "Hamburger Hill." As we turned on "Hamburger Hill," it quickly drew a large crowd. I was a little concerned that the movie might prove to be too graphic, but the Roglai Colonel stayed on the edge of his seat throughout the show. When it was over he thought it was the most realistic movie he had ever seen.

Although we did not uncover any new leads in Dalat, we did receive one live-sighting report by sheer happenstance. Due to a flat tire on our Jeep Cherokee in the village of Ninh Son on the road from Phan Rang to Dalat, we waited beside the road while our driver changed the tire. During our brief halt a young Vietnamese boy walking on the road stopped to chat. When he asked us where we were from I told him we were from America and that we were searching for Americans missing from the war. When I asked him if he knew anything about Americans remaining in Vietnam after the war ended, much to our astonishment he replied "yes." The lad went on to add that an elderly American man resided in Ninh Son with his wife and children. When I asked our accompanying cadre, Ngo Hoang, about checking out the report he said we would have to do it another time due to time constraints. Relenting, I informed Hoang that I would write up a report on the incident at the conclusion of the current iteration of case investigations and when I did so, I gave him a copy for his files. I also submitted a written report to all of our normal addressees involved in the accounting process when I returned to Bangkok. Unfortunately, I never had another opportunity to follow-up on the report, and I am unaware if any action was ever taken. I believe it is quite likely that the report was relegated to the "rumor file" and never investigated.

By early June 1989 my team was finally headed for Saigon, the "Pearl of the Orient." Although I had traveled to Hanoi on a regular basis since 1982, this would be the first time I had seen Saigon since April 30, 1975, the final day of the Republic of Vietnam. Traveling down Highway 1A we made our way into Dong Nai province, which was called Bien Hoa province in the old days. The former Bien Hoa Economic Development Area was still a hub of activity, but from a maintenance standpoint its facilities appeared to be in very poor condition. Production in the early 1970s had been oriented toward the manufacture of durable goods, including automobiles such as the small "La Dalat" passenger car. Now most enterprises depend on the manufacture of some type of chemicals. Acids for storage batteries, lacquer for handicrafts, plastics, rubber, paper, monosodium glutamate and various types of paints and mineral spirits, all gave the area the appearance of a toxic waste dump. Unfortunately, for the metropolitan Saigonese, the plants are located upriver from the former capital. With the steady flow of deadly pollutants and constant discharge into the rivers and streams of caustic chemicals from postwar factories, the local people now live in constant danger from a host of environmental diseases and potential birth defects. It seems that Saigon is still far from safe, even during peacetime.

On the way from Bien Hoa City to the former capital I reflected back on my first trip to Saigon in 1966. At that time I was returning from Camp Zama Hospital in Japan back to my infantry unit in the Central Highlands. Forced to spend three days waiting for a military cargo plane to Pleiku airfield, I tried to make efficient use of the time by seeing as much of the beautiful city as possible. Unfortunately, I had only scratched the surface when it was time to leave. I had probably looked odd in my wrinkled fatigue uniform and jungle boots drinking French cognac from fancy crystal in the nightclubs where the Vietnamese elite partied away the long, sultry nights in splendor. Back then I vowed that I would find a way to pull at least one tour of duty in the enchanting city, and in 1968 I finally got my wish. As luck would have it, only a few days prior to my arrival a follow-up attack to the 1968 "Tet" Offensive had just occurred and curfew was set at 6:00 p.m. for all American personnel in the city.

Upon entering Saigon it was immediately obvious that the scene here was far different from that in Hanoi. The people on the streets did not have the sordid look of depression on their faces, and the traditionally drab Communist colors reserved for clothing and buildings seen in the north had not been accepted in the south. Although there were few females observed wearing the Vietnamese "long dress," called *ao dai,* there was nevertheless a welcome induction of bright outfits with flowers and pretty colors. It seemed odd that Vietnam's most colorful and risqué city could end up named for one of the country's most frugal and conservative leaders.

Approaching the city a slight, foul, methane-like odor could be detected hanging in the humid air, giving the impression of a colossal landfill. As we neared the Binh Thanh Market, however, the unpleasant odor was gradually overpowered by the smells of countless spices: garlic, ginger, cinnamon, pepper, mint and onions. Buddhists and ancestor worshippers also contributed to the aromatic atmosphere as wisps of frail smoke from incense burning on family altars drifted across cracked and decaying sidewalks onto busy streets. I was saddened by the condition of many buildings and houses that had suffered serious decline under Communist rule. The once brightly-colored French era official office buildings with colonial style ornate facades that had been frequently painted "prosperous yellow" with fresh coats of lime and water were now mildewed and lifeless under the new regime.

I went to my old house located at 49 Cu Xa Tu Do Street. It also looked to be poorly maintained. I heard from neighbors that a high-ranking Communist cadre had taken over the house shortly after the surrender. No one could recall what became of my old Chevy Corvair left in the driveway when I departed during the evacuation. I also went to visit an old friend who lived across the street, Lieutenant Colonel Tran Quoc Binh, but he didn't seem very happy to see me. When I embraced him he cringed in fear. He whispered to me that he was only recently released from a Communist prison camp, and he was fearful of being re-arrested if the Communist authorities suspected him of having any contact with Americans. In driving around the city I passed by the three facilities where I worked during the war, but due to tight security I couldn't stop or get close to two of them. The former Combined Military Interrogation Center off Plantation Road was still utilized for conducting interrogations, now by personnel of the Criminal Investigation Department of the Ministry of National Defense. The old National Interrogation Center was also still used for conducting interrogations. I was able to enter the compound of the former National Defector Center, but except for a few bicycles parked in a rack, it appeared to be almost empty. Predictably, Communist bureaucrats occupied all other former GVN offices.

While traffic was heavy, except for a small number of aging Citroen and Peugeot automobiles, almost everyone rode the popular "Honda" motorbikes. Winding their way through the crowded streets, throngs of Saigonese clung to smoking and sputtering bikes leftover from the war years, although a few motorcycles from the Communist Bloc countries, such as Bulgaria, could now be seen. One thing that always puzzled me was how the Vietnamese students, girls in white long dresses and boys in white shirts, were able to ride in such thick smoke without ever getting their uniforms dirtied. Although difficult to estimate, it appeared that the number of vehicles on the streets of Saigon when I returned there in 1989 was probably somewhat less than when I departed in 1975. Like their predecessors in the "white mice" RVN police units, at various strategic points throughout the city the dreaded Public Security Forces could be seen accepting cash payments for all types of traffic offenses. Those cited for minor infractions were still bold enough to actually attempt bargaining down the price of their citations in much the same manner as they would in haggling with a local shopkeeper over the cost of goods. Perhaps there is merit to the old adage that "some things never change."

During our first visit to Ho Chi Minh City we were billeted at a government compound formerly reserved for members of the wartime International Commission for Control and Supervision (ICCS). Prior to arriving at the former ICCS compound I had been under the impression that the individual villas housing American and other foreign diplomats during the war were the best that the RVN had to offer. But in examining the beautiful French Colonial villas where we stayed it became readily apparent that the ICCS had been skimming the cream. The luxurious villas were nestled in groves of Tamarind trees with well manicured lawns laced with hibiscus, birds of paradise, and jasmine. After unpacking, however, any thoughts we might have had that our Communist counterparts were upgrading our status were quickly dispelled. Our seemingly good fortune in the assignment of living quarters had been predicated on the fact that many former RVN civilian and military personnel were anxious to meet with official Americans to plead their case for resettlement in the U.S. Our Communist counterparts did not want to create a situation wherein crowds in a public hotel in downtown Ho Chi Minh City would mob us, thus the unusual upgrade from one star to five.

Even with the tight security we were nevertheless contacted by a number of former ARVN personnel, most of whom had left their native homes in the provinces in order to be as close as possible to Tan Son Nhut Airport, the final stop for those departing Vietnam by legal means. These persistent gentlemen would wait until we started out the gate of the compound and then descend upon us with small scraps of paper containing messages to wartime American counterparts or relatives residing in the U.S. It seemed as though the unfortunate ARVN personnel held the common belief that if anyone in a foreign country could be made aware of their circumstances and the fact that they desired to leave Vietnam, that person could take some type of unspecified action to "pull them out of Vietnam." My team members generally accepted the notes from the men but acting on instructions from me, they refused to accept any mail or packages. Not only was I concerned with the possibility of drugs or contraband, I knew that it was a crime under Vietnamese law to accept mail destined for a foreign address.

Some of the notes passed by the former ARVN contained information on aircraft crash sites and skeletal remains, and a few did correlate to actual cases of American personnel who were still unaccounted for. The first POW/MIA information I received in Ho Chi Minh City was provided by a disheveled former ARVN who approached me as I exited the gate of the former ICCS compound. I immediately recognized the name on the handwritten copies of a military identification card and "Controlled Restricted Access" badge as that of Air Force Staff Sergeant Gary Pate from Georgia. Pate had been listed as missing after the C-130 aircraft in which he was a crewmember disappeared while flying a night mission in Salavan province in Laos on May 22, 1968. This was unusual, because Salavan province was a considerable distance from Ho Chi Minh City. Pate and his eight fellow crewmembers were eventually classified as "presumed dead" and the documents passed to me by the ARVN soldier comprised the first information received by the U.S. Government after the loss incident.

Prior to going out on the town our counterparts from Hanoi briefed us on city conditions. One thing they were most concerned about was the level of crime in Ho Chi Minh City due to the collapsed economy. We were warned of unscrupulous "pedicab" drivers, and strangers coming to visit us at our quarters selling fake goods. Perhaps the most unnerving element in the city, though, were the pickpockets. Shortly after our first trip to the tourist area on famous Tu Do Street I got my first glimpse of just how serious the pickpocket problem really was. A foreign tourist had just arrived in a taxi from Tan Son Nhut airport and was unloading his bags in front of the Lotus Hotel after paying the taxi driver. As the man gathered his belongings a group of people, mostly children, gathered around him momentarily before he entered the hotel. Shortly after proceeding inside to the reception desk the man staggered erratically back out to the curb and stood motionless, staring out into space as if dazed or stunned. The man's attention was suddenly focused on a former ARVN, legless from his groin down, who used his hands to pull his upper torso toward the foreign tourist on a piece of automobile tire strapped to his buttocks. When the pitiful ARVN extended his upturned hand and begged for money the tourist released a thunderous, gut-wrenching scream "get away from me, you have already taken everything!" Unaware that the tourist had just been robbed the disabled ARVN cringed and stared at the man as if in disbelief. Judging from the man's accent I figured he was not an American and I later heard from hotel staff that he was from Belgium. According to the clerk at the desk, the man had just arrived in Vietnam for the first time, and before he could get inside the hotel he was robbed of all his money and passport. In essence the man was now stranded, alone and penniless in a city with very little support or foreign representation.

There were no banks or ATM machines available at the time, and traveler's checks were worthless. Prior to our arrival in the city I briefed each American team member on the necessity of carrying cash in pouches suspended from their belts inside their trousers. I also instructed them to leave high-value items in the hotel safe in sealed and signed envelopes and I stressed the importance of carrying only enough cash for each particular outing. Despite our precautions, the pickpockets still proved to be very adept at their trade. Normally they worked in pairs or in groups of three or four females, confining their operations to the busy streets frequented by foreign tourists. The primary method called for the deployment of one individual with a bamboo fan or folded newspaper at the front of the formation. Then at just the right moment, the lead person would raise the fan or paper in front of the tourist's face, suddenly blocking his view. I learned that for some reason, when one's view is blocked his concentration is quickly shifted solely to what is directly in front of his eyes. At that precise moment another individual bumps into the victim, while yet another pickpocket slithers his hand inside the victim's pockets to remove his cash, jewelry or other valuables, such as eyeglasses or pens. Like a seasoned quarterback completing a handoff, the pickpocket removing the items quickly passes them to another individual moving in another direction. All those involved quickly discard the typical white shirts they were wearing to expose bright red, yellow or green pullovers worn underneath. While the hapless victim scans the crowd searching in vain for a female of average height and weight with black hair and brown eyes wearing a white shirt, the pickpockets, now wearing different colored attire, quickly blend into the crowd and disappear.

Catching pickpockets became a game for me, and I was successful on several occasions. After apprehending pickpockets red-handed on city streets, I would proceed to give them a lengthy lecture in Vietnamese and hold them until Public Security personnel arrived. Unfortunately, however, the Public Security didn't seem to be very interested, and I had the feeling that the perpetrators would be quickly released with no real action taken. But the stern, Vietnamese folk opera-style lectures given to the exposed pickpockets by a foreigner in the Vietnamese language provided a source of amusement for passers-by, and they seemed to appreciate the fact that at least someone had had enough and was taking action. Foreigners were not the only targets for pickpockets, however, and my counterpart at the time, Mr. Ngo Hoang, also fell victim to this scourge shortly after cautioning me on the subject. By using the fan and bump from the side technique, the pickpockets were able to remove Ngo Hoang's prescription eyeglasses and $75.00 in cash from the pocket of his shirt.

To be honest, I didn't escape unscathed. Once while at a local market purchasing Communist military memorabilia for a friend who is a collector of such items, my attention was drawn to what I thought was a remarkable deal. The vendor at the stall selling military items held up several "hard-to-find" Communist branch insignia, and quoted a price that proved too good to be true. As he eased his outstretched hands slowly to my right side, as my head turned with them I felt only the slightest twinge at my left trousers pocket. By the time I realized what had happened the seemingly innocent young female standing beside me was gone and so was the cash I carried in my pocket. As I reached into my pocket to find my money missing I could sense from the vendor that he knew I would not be able to meet his unbelievably low price.

Concerning the workload, during this initial trip to Ho Chi Minh City I had several complex cases to investigate, including some cases inside the metropolitan area of former Saigon-Gia Dinh, as well as in neighboring Song Be province, which had incorporated the three former provinces of Phuoc Long, Binh Long and Binh Duong. In order to begin coordination with the local officials my team attended a meeting chaired by the Deputy Chairman of the Ho Chi Minh City People's Committee, Mr. Le Quang Chanh.

Although cordial, by dispatching the Deputy Chairman of the People's Committee to meet with us, the Communists made certain that we knew our POW/MIA accounting mission was still not a top priority with them. Nevertheless, we attended a quite enjoyable state-sponsored dinner and the Deputy Chairman proved to be a likeable, easy-going man with a sense of humor. But he didn't seem to know very much about the POW/MIA issue, and he expressed little interest in the matter. As was always the case in attending such meetings I carefully scrutinize all participants on the Communist side to see if I could recognize any faces, but I didn't identify anyone. During the course of a decent meal the Deputy Chairman indicated that the local administration was anxious to cooperate with the American side in order to resolve the issue as quickly as possible. That was all he had to say about POW/MIA.

I initially briefed the members of the People's Committee on two cases, one in Cu Chi district of the city and the second case in easternmost Thu Duc district. The first case involved Private First Class Vernon Z. Johns from Maryland. Johns had been missing in Cu Chi district since February 3, 1968, three days after the 1968 "Tet" offensive began. At the time of his incident Johns was assigned as a machine gunner on a M-113 Armored Personnel Carrier that was attacked by Communist forces with small arms and rocket-propelled grenade fire. The driver and loader on the APC were both wounded but managed to escape. Johns was last seen blazing away with his 50-caliber machine gun. The account of Johns' loss was complicated by a report indicating that he had been evacuated for medical treatment, but the unit medic later denied any knowledge of this. Johns was subsequently classified as "presumed dead." On April 27, 1989, only two months prior to beginning the investigation of Johns' case, Communist authorities returned one set of skeletal remains that they believed were those of Johns. After conducting an examination of the remains, however, the CILHI determined that the remains were of Mongoloid origin. Since Johns' medical and personnel records listed his race as Negroid, the CILHI felt comfortable with its findings.

Prior to going to Cu Chi I had carefully studied a report complete with sketch map that I had collected from a refugee back in 1984. According to the refugee, Communist forces had already recovered the body of an American soldier from an Armored Personnel Carrier at the same location where Johns had gone missing, and the remains had been reburied in a cemetery under the control of a military medical clinic. I had little doubt that this report correlated to Johns. When we arrived in the incident area we were taken to a site in a former rubber plantation where the incident occurred. Local representatives of the Ministry of Social Welfare and War Invalids, an organization similar in function to the U.S. Veterans Administration, informed us that the remains of an American had recently been recovered from the site and turned in to local authorities. After I interviewed several witnesses, who provided information that closely matched Johns' incident, I was at a loss for an explanation. One Ministry representative, a war veteran and amputee, became upset that the U.S. Government had failed to identify the remains that he discovered in 1987 and turned over to Communist authorities in 1988.

Confident that the CILHI was correct in its forensic analysis of the remains, I informed the man that his account was not entirely correct. According to my information the remains had been recovered at least five years previous, and rather than being turned in at the time of discovery, the remains had been "stored" in a local cemetery along with the remains of numerous Communist troops killed-in-action. I then produced a copy of the detailed sketch with explanations written in Vietnamese. The suddenly wide-eyed cadre couldn't argue with the facts, but he still maintained that the remains of Johns had been turned in. Our effort ended on a tense note with the veteran insisting that he had personally turned in the remains of Johns, and with me telling him that further investigation was required because the remains he had turned in were Mongoloid. The CILHI specialists continued to work for two more years on the case from April 27, 1989, when the remains were repatriated, until they discovered that Johns did in fact have some Asian ancestry. Once that fact was established the remains were finally identified as Johns on April 16, 1991. I felt bad about the situation with the Veterans Association in Cu Chi, because even though the accounts provided were not entirely straightforward, I realized that the veterans were merely carrying out the instructions of the Communist leadership. The fact that the remains had been returned, even several years after the fact, did count for something and since the Communists seldom did anything right I felt it was important to give them credit whenever they did. I planned to return to Cu Chi to give the veterans association some positive feedback, but I never was able to make the return trip. One of the Vietnamese Team Chiefs did promise me that he would pass word to the Cu Chi veterans association on my behalf thanking them for their cooperation, and I hope he followed through on his pledge.

Another case I briefed the local officials on involved Staff Sergeant Dallas R. Pridemore from Ohio. On September 8, 1968, Pridemore was abducted from a civilian house in which he was staying in the former French plantation area of Thu Duc on the outskirts of Saigon. At the time Pridemore was living with his Vietnamese girlfriend, who apparently unbeknownst to him was actually a member of the Communist underground. A member of a Military Police unit responsible for security in the Saigon area, Pridemore probably represented a valuable target to Communist Intelligence. One aspect of Pridemore's case was that he had already completed his one-year tour in Vietnam, and then decided to return for a second tour after he traveled back to the U.S. and divorced his wife. According to our information, a team of terrorists in a "Special Action Unit" arrived in Thu Duc during the middle of the night with the mission of capturing a former Communist officer who defected to the RVN. While allegedly searching for the "former" officer the unit encountered Pridemore hiding under his bed in pajamas, and they marched him off under guard. During the course of our investigation we learned that the "former" Communist officer was most likely the father of Pridemore's girlfriend.

One of the witnesses in the Pridemore case was Senior Colonel Nguyen Van Tang, who had used the cover name "Tu Tang" during the war. As soon as I saw Tang he looked familiar to me. He was the type of person not easily forgotten, and I felt sure that I had seen him somewhere in the Saigon or Bien Hoa area during the war years. I also vaguely recalled that he had been wearing the rank of a Senior Noncommissioned Officer or Warrant Officer, but I never did connect the dots. One evening at the guesthouse where our team was staying Tang consumed several beers, and during the course of a conversation with me he revealed that he had worked for COSVN on classified intelligence assignments in the area from Saigon City north to Quang Duc. Tang said that during the war he often disguised himself as an RVN Marine or Airborne troop, and that he carried forged documentation to match his uniforms. I knew that this claim was entirely plausible because I had handled some excellent forged identity documents during "tradecraft" training I received at a compound of the 525th Military Intelligence Group in Saigon during the war. Tang also claimed to have been in charge of some forty abduction missions during the war, including Pridemore. Tang said he had used explosive demolitions in two separate attacks, one on the downtown Victoria Hotel and a second attack on a large barge carrying ammunition up the Dong Nai River to the huge logistics depot at Long Binh in Bien Hoa. After telling me that he knew plenty of attractive females in Saigon, Tang invited me to go out on the town with him for an evening of fun. But considering his background I politely declined his offer, lest I inadvertently increase his impressive abduction statistics to forty-one.

According to witnesses in the Pridemore case, the capturing unit moved the unfortunate military policeman to a swamp in the outskirts of Saigon where he and several members of the Communist unit were killed by bombs during an air strike by U.S. aircraft. I took my team by boat to the site but we were not able to locate any witnesses who could pinpoint Pridemore's burial site. One thing of interest that I did see during the site visit was a "Certificate of Achievement" under the glass table covering in the home of a local citizen. According to the certificate, the owner of the house, a Mrs. Ma Chin, had served as a member of the "Secret Self-Defense Force" during the war. The certificate indicated that the elderly lady was awarded the certificate for killing an American on May 7, 1973. Not knowing it if was real or a deception, I acted like I hadn't noticed, but promptly reported it to DIA/JCRC, hoping it would be quickly analyzed. I reasoned that due to the high priority afforded the issue, after my report was received in Washington, the intelligence community would dedicate special assets to focus on the incident mentioned in the report. However, to the best of my knowledge, I never received the analysis of the information, and I don't know if a live-sighting investigator checked it out. The information was certainly worthy of further investigation, because this placed the death of the unknown American almost five years after Pridemore's abduction, and over two months after American troops were withdrawn in conjunction with the Paris Peace Agreements, although other Americans remained in Saigon after the Paris Accords.

Further complicating the Pridemore case, American files contained a September 1968 report indicating that Pridemore was being held in the same general area where the witnesses said he was killed by bombs. However, another report in January 1969, based on information from a Communist rear service postal clerk, indicated that the clerk had seen the name "Dollas Pridmont," along with the descriptive information "Sergeant, Military Police, U.S. Army" on a roster at a temporary screening and interrogation center for American POWs in Svay Rieng province, Cambodia. The Source reported that Pridemore had been brought to this camp from Gia Dinh province on or about September 25, 1968, and that he was wearing civilian clothing when he arrived.

Thus there was a glaring discrepancy between the version of events contained in our files and that offered by the Communists. Although the Communists have never attempted to clear up this matter, analysts within the intelligence community have offered the opinion that the information indicating that Pridemore was moved from Vietnam to Svay Rieng province Cambodia was fabricated. I agreed with them, but for different reasons. It would seem that if the Communists were actually holding Pridemore in close proximity to Saigon while attempting to deceive American collectors into believing he was held in Svay Rieng, they had some reason for doing so. Moreover, the fact that Pridemore's abduction was carried out by clandestine forces inside an area ostensibly controlled by U.S. and GVN forces, and afterwards fabricated but relatively precise information relating to Pridemore came into the possession of U.S. collectors, the probability of central, high-level involvement must be considered. Given Pridemore's duties as a Military Policeman, it is possible that he was exploited for information on potential targets for terrorist-style bombing attacks, such as those mentioned by Tang, or to help plan other sensitive missions by the Communist intelligence and security services. It is also possible that Pridemore was exploited for information on Military Police escorts for convoys traveling to and from Saigon. There were several such incidents involving American personnel that have still not been resolved. Perhaps this also explains why the certificate awarded to covert cadre Ma Chinh indicated that she killed an American on May 7, 1973, because by that date Pridemore's information would have been obsolete. To my knowledge, U.S. authorities investigated the Pridemore case at least six times in the 1990s, with no resolution. Not surprisingly, the Pridemore case remains active.

On the way back from the marshy site during the Pridemore investigation we stopped for a rest break at a small riverside restaurant oriented toward domestic tourism. The senior cadre accompanying our joint team was a Lieutenant Colonel who was assigned as the command representative from Communist Military Region 7. Over warm "Halida" beer and stale cashew nuts the sharply dressed and spit-shined cadre asked me what kind of feelings I had after having been sent to fight in the war, and then returning to see the country as it was today. Trying to be honest but short of insulting, I told him that as a young soldier I, and my contemporaries, had been led to believe that if we did not make a stand against communism in South Vietnam, Communists from the North would invade and occupy the South. Once occupied the Communists would take complete control of everything, leaving only the most menial tasks to be performed by southerners. Obviously agitated the cadre informed me that he was not referring to this particular aspect. The conversation ended on that note.

We took advantage of our mission to Ho Chi Minh City in order to visit Thu Dau Mot, the provincial capital of neighboring Song Be province, the scene of an all-out attack on a camp manned by South Vietnamese personnel and four American advisers that occurred on February 9, 1965. During the war years the area was called Phuoc Long province, and the fierce attack on the camp in Duc Phong district began sometime around midnight. By morning Communist forces were in control; around 9:30 that same morning an American was observed in the custody of enemy forces. Unfortunately, helicopters were not able to rescue him due to heavy enemy fire. Sometime that same afternoon hard-fighting ARVN

Rangers retook the camp, and the bodies of three Americans were found among the dead. The remaining American adviser, Army Specialist Fourth Class James H. McLean, a twenty year-old medic from California, was listed as captured.

ARVN officers who either escaped, or who were released from captivity, reported observing an unwounded McLean at several POW camps. According to the reports, McLean was in good health throughout 1965. A nighttime parachute raid was planned for October 15, 1965 on the camp where McLean was held, but at the last minute it was cancelled. According to the same reports, sometime during mid-1966 McLean contracted malaria but later recovered. An ARVN intelligence agent reported observing a live American in October 1966, and analysts also correlated this report to McLean. One Source reported that an American medic and an interpreter were brought to another POW camp in April 1966, and that the American medic was scheduled to continue on to Bu Gia Map (a village on the border of Vietnam and Cambodia) to perform surgery. Although the report of an American medic being sent to perform surgery could not positively be correlated to McLean, a captured document dispatched from the Current Affairs Committee of Song Be province to a POW camp designated "T-52" where McLean was held during mid-1966 contained the following instructions:

> *Nguyen Thiet (Vietnamese prisoner) village 3, Duc Bon, Phuoc Binh District-kill in secret and afterwards put his body in a bomb crater. After, if his family wants to know where he is, we will show them. Hang him; do not shoot him because his family will know the round in his body. We will tell his family we put him in prison for three years, but his death was by bombs. Duong Thuc (Vietnamese prisoner) village 2, Duc Bon, Phuoc Binh district-kill here, do not move to his area. American soldier-need to send his documents to Security Area Office to check again.*[1]

This document is a clear indication that Communist officials were aware of the presence of McLean, who due to his advanced Special Forces medical training was capable of providing a valuable medical service for them. Moreover, the mention of the location where the medic was to perform the surgery, Bu Gia Map, is also significant since after the report about the pending surgery, a cross border raid by Army Special Forces personnel into Cambodia yielded a headband from an American made military cap. McLean's name and service number was stenciled inside the headband that was recovered. The fact that McLean's records were being forwarded to the regional security office is unusual since such action was normally reserved for those suspected of having performed duties dealing with intelligence or espionage.

When I traveled to Song Be province in June 1989 to investigate McLean's case I talked with witnesses who claimed that McLean was captured but later died due to dysentery and malaria. None of them, however, could point out a grave location. They speculated that U.S. bombing destroyed the burial site. At least one witness reported that McLean was transferred to central authorities, and that he was in the company of an unidentified light-skinned female whom they speculated was assigned as an interpreter for McLean. At least one witness indicated he heard that at the time of the attack McLean was seen following the camp cook out the back door of the camp's kitchen. The identity of the cook was never established, and it was undetermined as to whether McLean had any long-standing relationship with the cook. I was also not able to determine whether the cook was able to speak English, and if so whether the degree of fluency would permit the cook to act as an interpreter for McLean during interrogations or possible future assignments, such as performing surgery on wounded Communist troops. As far as I know the case of McLean is still being investigated and no new information has been developed.

During the course of the investigations in Song Be we used several types of motorized vehicles to travel the old logging roads to drop-off points where we proceeded on foot. Our primary means of transportation was an old American manufactured "John Deere" tractor. Known as a "Popping Johnny" in my younger days on the farm, the aging metal dinosaur had obviously seen better days, and I was surprised that it could still run after so many years of service. The local farmers in Song Be had patched holes in the badly worn tires by inserting steel bolts from the inside of the tire with nuts and washers on the outside holding the bolts tightly in place. Rather than hindering operations, the protruding bolts actually gave the tires better traction for traversing the muddy clay soil. As darkness descended each day our approach was quite visible due to the long ribbon of blue flame streaming from the vertical exhaust pipe mounted on the hood of the tractor. Knowing the Vietnamese ability for field expediency in maintenance and repairs I'd bet that the old "Johnny" is still in service somewhere in Vietnam today.

While in the Ho Chi Minh City area I also tried to develop some new leads on another interesting case, that of Army Specialist Four Edward D. Reilly Jr. from Pennsylvania. Reilly, a member of the 1/16th Battalion, 1st Infantry Division, was captured when he became separated from his unit on April 26, 1966. Unfortunately for Reilly, while his unit was engaged in searching for Communist units, Reilly accidentally stumbled into the camp for the powerful COSVN Security Section. A Communist interrogation report captured later indicated that Reilly was questioned in an underground facility of the COSVN Security Section on the same day. According to instructions issued by the individual controlling the COSVN Security Section, Cao Dang Chiem, alias Sau Hoang, Reilly was to be "killed immediately after the interrogation." The same document also included the instruction that rather than being left in the secret tunnel with the other prisoners, the English-speaking Vietnamese female interpreter used to interrogate Reilly was to be moved from the camp to COSVN Headquarters after the questioning.

I traveled to Tay Ninh province to investigate Reilly's case, but obtained very little information of analytical value. I received a report from a witness indicating that the female interpreter, Ms. Tran Le Linh, had been assigned to the same camp where Reilly was executed, and I confirmed the wartime location of the COSVN Security Camp. I also received a report that an American named "Het" had been captured in Thu Duc in the outskirts of Saigon, but that after being moved to a camp in Cambodia he had died of malaria. This report correlated to Gustav Hertz, an American Embassy official captured in 1965 who was the subject of many covert efforts to trade him for captured Communist personnel. All efforts fell through when the Cambodian government told U.S. authorities that the Vietnamese had informed them that Hertz had died in September 1967. On April 27, 1989, I participated in a remains repatriation ceremony in Hanoi wherein the SRV government returned twenty-one boxes purported to contain the remains of American personnel. According to the Vietnamese officials, at least three of the remains were confiscated from a "remains trader" from the Saigon area. Some eleven years later in 2001, one of the remains the Vietnamese confiscated was identified as Gustav Hertz. Reilly's remains were returned in the same group but were identified much more quickly. Beyond the questions about the COSVN Security camp, I learned that in June 1966, only two months after he had gone missing in Vietnam and long before the U.S. Government was aware of the fact that he had been executed in the COSVN security camp, two Asian females visited Reilly's wife at their home in Radcliffe, Kentucky. They attempted to recruit her to perform anti-war efforts, but she refused and promptly reported the incident to the local police. I always wondered how many other times similar incidents occurred.

The investigation of the Reilly case did turn up some other significant information. According to the information we received, the camp was designated "C-53" and it had been located at Xom Ba Diet hamlet in the Lo Go village area about forty-five kilometers northwest of "Black Virgin Mountain" in northwestern Tay Ninh province. We traveled to Tan Bien town, the capital of the district where the camp was formerly located, but witnesses were reluctant to provide testimony concerning Americans held in the camp. In looking at photographs of cadre on bulletin boards in government buildings I noticed that the faces of several had been scratched off, apparently to preclude identification. The village office where we held our meeting was nothing more than a bamboo hut with open sides and a thatched roof. The building was identical to the buildings I had worked in while interviewing refugees who fled from Tay Ninh across Cambodia to the border of Thailand. It seemed ironic that after spending several years on the western border of Cambodia, constantly alert to sudden artillery and rocket barrages fired during battles between the various Cambodian resistance factions and the occupying Vietnamese forces, here I was now on the eastern border facing the same situation.

While in Tan Bien I also attempted to obtain more information on the female interpreter who had assisted in the interrogation of Reilly, since I felt that she would be a key witness regarding several discrepancy cases associated with the COSVN Security camp. I particularly wanted to interview her in person. At least one report indicated that the female interpreter had been employed by the U.S. Government until 1965 when she was captured, along with a civilian "security engineer" employed by the Raymond, Morrison and Knudson Company in Saigon, and her younger sister named Tran Bao Linh. According to a report compiled by the Judicial Police Office in Saigon, the trio was boating on the Saigon River near the Ben Loi Bridge one afternoon in February 1965 when their motorized pleasure boat was attacked by Communist forces. All three individuals were taken prisoner and immediately moved northeast to Song Be, formerly Binh Duong province. At that point a decision was made to release the younger sister of Tran Le Linh, but at the same time instructions were issued indicating that the location where she was held and then released from should be kept secret through the use of deception. Upon her release the younger sister stated that she did not know what happened to the Security Engineer after they were taken to the other side of the Saigon River.

The civilian who performed security duties, Mr. William H. Wallis, a British citizen, was suspected of spying and moved to the COSVN Security Camp where he was interrogated over a prolonged period of time, with Tran Le Linh acting as his interpreter. A U.S. unit on patrol in the area of the COSVN Security Camp recovered a bundle of Communist documents in March 1967. Included in the bundle was an identification card of Wallis. A CIA report received in June 1974 indicated that COSVN security personnel had concluded Wallis was a "British Colonel." After refusing to cooperate after one year of interrogation and indoctrination, he received a death sentence from the Camp Committee. According to the same report, Wallis was buried near the camp where he was held. According to witnesses later introduced by Communist authorities, however, Wallis vanished from the camp during a bombing attack by American aircraft. The same witness, a former guard in the C-53 Camp, opined that Wallis's body was disintegrated by the bomb blast and that no remains could be found.

According to the Saigon police reports, Tran Le Linh's mother worked in the Cho Lon area of Saigon as a secretary in a factory that processed duck feathers. During the course of the case investigations in Saigon during the summer of 1989 I received information from witnesses indicating that the owner of a duck feather factory in Saigon was captured during the 1968 "Tet" offensive, and that he had also been held in the area of the Vietnam-Cambodia border. This was Mr. Charles K. Hyland, an Australian citizen and owner of the same duck feather factory. He was captured in Binh Chanh district of Saigon on February 6, 1968. Hyland was released in Phnom Penh on November 25, 1968. The connection between Hyland, Tran Le Linh, and Linh's mother, who worked as a secretary at Hyland's factory, was never explored, although in 1975 Hyland was rumored to have become the Communist hard wood exporter. However, it was obvious that at least two foreigners associated with Tran Le Linh, Wallis and Hyland, were abducted by Communist special action units.

Perhaps the most intriguing aspect of the information confirming the designation and location of the C-53 camp was the fact that another Source had reported in September 1974 to the DAO in Saigon that he had recently observed five live Americans being held in the camp. According to the Source, three of the Americans were Caucasian and two were black. All five men were "deserters" who had been transferred from neighboring Military Region 6 to the C-53 Camp after the implementation of the 1973 Paris Peace Agreement. The Source reported that one of the Caucasians was named "Benny." The Source also reported that a Vietnamese female, who had worked for the Americans until 1965 when she was captured, served as the camp's interpreter. Analysts in the Defense Intelligence Agency correlated the female interpreter to Tran Le Linh. This is the same report that DIA analysts correlated to Airman Benny Dexter during his case investigation conducted in the Central Highlands only two months earlier in April 1989.

To me, the critical question as to whether the Vietnamese had held back live Americans after the conclusion of "Operation Homecoming" was answered by this report. In my mind the issue of the men's status and whether they were POWs or deserters was not a critical point. Having been trained in the art of interrogation, I knew from experience that a prisoner's mental state was a complex issue, and that almost anyone can be manipulated when faced with long-term interrogation, indoctrination and exploitation by trained professionals. In essence, we had a credible report indicating that five Americans were being held at a specific location as of September 1974, and one of those Americans was identified by name.

In analyzing the information confirming the location of the wartime C-53 POW camp located near the Cambodian border, the first thing that came to my mind was: why would the Communists be holding five prisoners in their Military Region 6 after the ceasefire? Was it possible that their communications were so bad that they simply had not had time to affect the release in conjunction with the withdrawal of U.S. troops? Or was this a matter of security for the Communist side due to the fact that the five Americans were being utilized to perform some type of role to further the Communist war effort? I believed it was important that the Source of the C-53 camp report had referred to the five Americans as "deserters," because according to Communist doctrine "deserters" are not normally placed in the same camp system as prisoners captured on the battlefield. Whereas personnel captured on the battlefield were placed in the custody of the Enemy Proselytizing Department which operated under the General Political Directorate, those who "crossed over" to the Communist side, either at the time of their capture or after undergoing indoctrination, were detained under the authority of the Military Proselytizing Department which operated under Party, as opposed to military control.

In looking at available files, I could not find any information indicating that Airman Dexter possessed any critical skills needed by the Communists based on his Air Force training. However, Dexter spoke English, and this could be a valuable asset if the Communists were able to gain his cooperation. A native fluency in English could be especially helpful in translating and interpreting signal communications transmitted by American units, or translating captured documents (something I believed Garwood had done), but by September 1974 most U.S. personnel had been withdrawn. However, the DAO in Saigon was still in business, as were numerous official U.S. offices oriented toward reporting the political, military and economic aspects of the still-ongoing war. Such offices were located at the regional and provincial-levels throughout South Vietnam. This meant that although the American combat presence had been withdrawn, a significant level of important communications still had to be intercepted and translated by Communist collectors.

During the war years deserters had routinely been exploited for information of propaganda value, but by late 1974 there were no American troops fighting in Vietnam against whom to direct the propaganda, so I eliminated that possibility. Yet, the Communists had no way of knowing just how much longer the war would last, and the possibility that the GVN might capture and execute certain key Communist cadre likely remained a concern for the Communist leadership. Moreover, a significant number of high-ranking Communist prisoners, including Nguyen Cong Tai, were not released by the RVN in accordance with the 1973 ceasefire. Therefore, it is also possible that the five live Americans were retained as an insurance policy to prevent the GVN from having the upper hand regarding prisoners captured after the ceasefire.

Historically, there are numerous examples of Vietnamese Communist employment of foreign defectors to further their war effort: either in the form of critical skills needed or for the domestic and international propaganda value of having enemy troops join the Communist cause. During the French War in Vietnam, over one hundred soldiers from the Foreign Legion joined the Communist side. For example, in 1945 the Communists launched a fledgling People's Army of Vietnam Air Force with only two antiquated British and French aircraft and eighty-one students. The only pilot available to fly the aircraft, however, was a German who had served in the Legion prior to being captured and defecting to the Communist side. Two other deserters, one a German and one an Algerian, captured in the Mekong Delta in 1946, soon "crossed over" and fought alongside Communist forces until after the withdrawal of French Forces from North Vietnam in 1954. Both men were eventually allowed to return to their native countries, along with their Vietnamese wives and children.

Another deserter/defector from the French Foreign Legion, a native Pole named Stefan Kubiak, was given the Vietnamese name "Ho Chi Toan." Kubiak crossed over to the Communists in 1947 and was assigned to the Enemy Proselytizing Department where he served as a PAVN officer with the rank of Captain. Kubiak died from illness in 1963.

A citizen of the Ukraine, Platon Aleksandrovich Skrzhinskij, joined the French Foreign Legion shortly after World War II ended, and then deserted to the Communists on August 17, 1947. Working under the name "Nguyen Van Thanh," Skrzhinskij posed as a French soldier on numerous occasions in order to assist Communist forces in capturing small, isolated outposts occupied by French troops. Due to his fluency in the Vietnamese language, after moving to Moscow in 1955, Skrzhinskij worked as a commentator for the Vietnamese language section of Radio Moscow.

A Greek native, Sarantidis Kostas, deserted from the French Foreign Legion and fought as a PAVN soldier from 1946 to 1956. A member of the Greek Communist Party, Kostas attained the rank of First Lieutenant while operating in the Danang-Hoi An area of Communist Inter-region 5. Using the name "Nguyen Van Lap," Kostas served as the Commander of the Quang Ngai province POW camp from 1952 until 1954 when he regrouped to North Vietnam. In 1956 Kostas was transferred to the Ministry of Propaganda and Culture. Kostas returned to Greece in 1965, and in 1987 he wrote his memoirs concerning the Quang Ngai POW camp, some thirty-three years after he served there as Camp Commander.

Perhaps the best-known French era deserter in Vietnam was Erwin Borchers, a native of Strasbourg, Germany who joined the Vietnam Communist Party in 1944. Borchers went to Vietnam as a member of the French Foreign Legion in 1941, but began secretly working for the Communists in Hanoi during 1944. Using the Vietnamese name "Chien Si" (Warrior), Borchers was assigned to the Military Proselytizing Department by senior Communist officials. After becoming a member of the Indochinese Communist Party, Borchers worked as a commentator in the German and French language sections of the Voice of Vietnam Radio in Hanoi. Borchers was also a correspondent for "The Republic" newspaper, which was later changed to "The People" newspaper. In 1947 Borchers became a PAVN officer with the mission of distributing propaganda to convince French and German members of the French Foreign Legion to defect to the Communists. In 1950 Borchers presented a paper on Enemy Proselytizing at the 3rd Conference of the Indochinese Communist Party. During the battle of Dien Bien Phu, Communist officials credited Borchers with causing 123 French troops to desert. In 1955 Borchers was transferred to the Ministry of Propaganda and Culture where he worked for two years before becoming the Hanoi-based press attaché for the German People's Democratic Republic. In 1966 Borchers returned to East Germany.

The Communists also employed Japanese deserters from the World War II era. One man, Koshiro Iwai, deserted from the Japanese Imperial Army to join PAVN forces in 1945. Using the name "Nguyen Van Sau," Iwai served as the commander of a reconnaissance company in the PAVN 174th Regiment; during combat against the French he was awarded several decorations for valor. Iwai was a member of the Communist Party's of both Japan and Vietnam. After returning to Japan in 1955, Iwai and a fellow deserter, "Nakamura," who used the Vietnamese name "Minh Ngoc," established the Japan-Vietnam Friendship Association. In 1990 Iwai returned to Vietnam as the Chairman of the Japan-Vietnam Trade Association.

Since only one of the five American prisoners being held in the C-53 Camp during September 1974 had been identified by name, I found it difficult to compile a list of possible candidates for the remaining four men. In reviewing MIAs lost in the general area with my team's analyst, I considered one case wherein an American soldier disappeared under strange circumstances. This case involved Army Private Jimmy M. Malone from Virginia, who was assigned as a radio operator in the 1st Battalion/503rd Infantry, 173rd Airborne Brigade.

On May 4, 1966, in Tan Uyen district, Song Be province, Communist Military Region 6, Malone was instructed to pick up his platoon's mail but failed to report for a patrol briefing scheduled for that same afternoon. After determining that Malone was missing from his unit a search was launched outside the unit's perimeter, and jungle boot prints believed to be Malone's were observed on the ground. Other prints, similar to those made by sandals worn by Communist forces, appeared to link up with those of Malone. The prints made by both individuals were followed to a fortified enemy position, and then on to an area about fifteen hundred meters from the unit's perimeter. A search party, under periodic sniper fire, continued following the prints but was forced to abandon the search due to darkness. A helicopter equipped with a loudspeaker system was used to broadcast instructions to Malone to assist in his recovery, and an additional ground search was launched the following morning, but Malone was never seen or heard from again. Due to the location and circumstances of Malone's disappearance and his duty position of radio operator, I considered him a possible candidate for one of the five men reportedly held in the C-53 camp in late 1974. After Malone's disappearance, American troops discovered a secret base camp of a Communist signals intelligence unit in Song Be province. The mission of that unit was to monitor and intercept communications transmitted between U.S. units. The unit was equipped with American made PRC-10 and PRC-25 radios, but no American POWs were found with the enemy intelligence unit.

Concerning possible candidates for the two black Americans said to have been transferred from Communist Military Region 6 to the C-53 camp during late 1974, our files also contained a CIA report indicating that as of May 1974 two Americans were being held in a camp located at Mimot, just inside the Cambodian border adjacent to Tay Ninh province Vietnam. The two American prisoners were one black identified as "Buller," and one Caucasian identified as "Chaigar." The Mimot area bordered on Tay Ninh province where the C-53 camp with the five Americans was located. When I reviewed our files to see if I could find a correlation, based on the physical description and other details concerning a Cambodian wife and children I correlated the report of the black American to Private McKinley Nolan, a well-known deserter.

Nolan managed to escape from the stockade by overpowering a guard after his ethnic Cambodian wife arranged for him to desert to the Communist side. Nolan and his wife were then guided to western Tay Ninh province near the border with Cambodia where they resided throughout the war. Rather than being entered into the regular camp system for American POWs, Nolan was placed in a separate camp system reserved for deserters. Nolan reportedly moved inside Cambodia with his wife and children sometime during the early 1970s.

Considering the location, physical description and phonetic spelling of the name "Chaigar," in compiling a list of candidates based on the information pertaining to the Caucasian held in the Mimot camp with Nolan during May 1974, available files contained at least two possibilities; Staff Sergeant Dallas Pridemore and a French Journalist named Gilles Caron. The physical description of the Caucasian prisoner held in the Mimot camp provided in the CIA report more closely matched that of Pridemore, but Caron was captured in Svay Rieng province along with two other Frenchmen on April 5, 1970. According to later reports from the area, Communist forces in the same area held a Caucasian journalist, but the reports did not contain enough information to permit a positive correlation to Caron. Other reports indicated that Caron was eventually moved to a camp in Kratie province, Cambodia, which bordered on Communist Military Region 6 in Vietnam at the time. The Mimot Camp mentioned in the May 1974 report was located just outside the southern boundary of Kratie province and near the wartime COSVN headquarters. In essence, the report indicating that one black and one Caucasian prisoner were held in the Mimot camp as of May 1974, and the report indicating that five prisoners, including both Caucasians and blacks were moved from Military Region 6 to the COSVN Security Camp in September 1974 could hardly be considered a coincidence.

After returning to Saigon I attempted to interview some of the cadre previously assigned to the COSVN Security Section during the war. My counterpart during the trip, Mr. Ngo Hoang, appeared sincere in his efforts to arrange such interviews, but he met with stiff resistance from the national-level bureaucrats responsible for state security. The Communists also ignored my requests to interview other cadre previously assigned to the COSVN Security Camp, apparently because some had not retired and were still engaged in sensitive work with a requirement for protecting their identities from compromise. Perhaps the most important cadre I had scheduled for interview was the former Chief of COSVN Security, Mr. Cao Dang Chiem, the man mentioned as having ordered the execution of Edward Reilly. After conferring with the higher-ups, however, the best that Ngo Hoang could do was elicit a promise of a unilateral interview by Communist officials at some later date. Eventually Cao Dang Chiem became Deputy Minister of Public Security in charge of "Office B" of the Ministry of Public Security, which was responsible for state security from just north of Danang to the southern tip of South Vietnam.

In attempting to arrange the interviews my counterpart did glean some policy-level information concerning those Americans unfortunate enough to be held in sensitive wartime facilities. According to what Ngo Hoang learned from the former cadre, there were several circumstances wherein American prisoners like Reilly might be killed. One circumstance was when the camp holding the Americans was compromised and rescue appeared imminent. Another situation was when due to their confinement they became aware of secret activities or were able to view the faces of their captors serving in sensitive assignments. According to Ngo Hoang, Americans could also be killed in situations where they rebelled or attempted to escape. Lastly, when Communist personnel were executed by the GVN, in some cases the Communists executed Americans in retaliation. To illustrate his final point Ngo Hoang referred to the execution of Nguyen Van Troi, who attempted to assassinate former Secretary of Defense Robert McNamara by exploding a bomb as the Secretary's motorcade passed by on a Saigon street. Hoang recalled that at least two American servicemen had been executed during the war, Sergeant First Class Kenneth Roraback from New York and Captain Humbert "Rocky" Versace from Virginia. Their deaths were broadcast as retaliation for the GVN's execution of captured communist spies, whereas Reilly's was kept secret.

As we prepared to temporarily close out our investigations in the South, I felt a great deal of frustration at not being able to gain access to witnesses involved in the capture, evacuation and exploitation of American personnel, especially those on the discrepancy case list. I learned from VNOSMP cadre that a few years after her "capture," one of the principle witnesses on my list, the interpreter Tran Le Linh, had married a guard assigned to the COSVN Security Section. After the war ended she was transferred to Saigon where she worked as an officer in the Ministry of Public Security under Cao Dang Chiem. I never learned if the former Australian prisoner who owned the duck feather factory in Saigon, Mr. Hyland, had anything to do with it, but sometime during 1983 the government of Australia accepted Ms. Linh for resettlement in that country.

In looking back on the initial arduous trips throughout Vietnam to conduct the first case investigations, I could see that we had achieved mixed results. But perhaps more importantly we had set the standards for thorough, objective case investigations. In those instances where the Communists dragged their feet and were not cooperative, we made sure this was included in our reports and that the cases remained open until such time as genuine investigations could be conducted. By the time we completed our first two years of operations both Jim Coyle and I were quite experienced in conducting the tedious investigations; during the same time we had managed to understudy several other JCRC members in order to prepare them to lead investigation teams for future, expanded operations. As the pace and scope of the field operations increased it was hoped that the expected increase in results would create an environment for further expansion of the effort, to include up to five investigation teams and up to two excavation teams to be deployed during each iteration. The JCRC analysts and linguists and the CILHI search and recovery specialists were, and still are, a source of great pride for me. Primarily Vietnam veterans, the men were completely dedicated to finding out the truth about what happened to their still unaccounted for comrades-in-arms. Under some of the most hazardous conditions imaginable they had risen to meet the challenge, and the Communists gradually came to the realization that our teams also suffered no shortage of perseverance.

The case investigations continued on an intermittent basis until April 8, 1991 when the Bush Administration presented its "roadmap" to senior Communist officials, linking steps towards the normalization of relations to progress in POW/MIA matters and Cambodia. According to the U.S. position at the time, a key step towards solving the POW/MIA issue was the establishment of a U.S. Office for POW/MIA Affairs in Hanoi. This would be the first official American presence in Hanoi since the American Consulate General was closed at the time the country was partitioned in 1954, and the first presence anywhere in Vietnam since the evacuation of the embassy in Saigon in 1975. Content with my role as the Senior Team Chief of the field investigation teams, I focused my efforts toward more detailed research on the important last-known-alive cases. I had no idea what impact a new American presence in Vietnam would have on my job, but I was prepared to stay the course until our mission was completed. Little did I know how much my life was about to change.

Chapter Thirteen

America Returns to Vietnam

IN EARLY APRIL 1991, I learned that I was receiving my first promotion after eight years of Federal Civil Service. On the federal pay scale grades ranged from 1 to 15. I was elevated from level 13 to 14. The advancement meant that my status was changed from "Specialist" to "Supervisor," or in government bureaucratic terms, from "GS" to "GM." Concurrent with my advancement, I was named the Chief of a newly created "U.S. Office for POW/MIA Affairs" in Hanoi, the first official U.S. government presence in Vietnam since April 30, 1975 and in North Vietnam since 1954. The office would be the focal point for efforts to resolve the status of Americans still missing in Vietnam. I was told that the promotion resulted from the high degree of confidence in me by the President's Special Emissary, General John Vessey, the POW/MIA Interagency Group in Washington, and especially, by the POW/MIA family members. Although I appreciated the pay raise, I also suspected that politically, the promotion was convenient. While my attitude may sound suspicious and cynical to the reader, I was all too familiar with the political intricacies of the government's POW/MIA bureaucracies. Plus, I knew that the positions of my DIA and other Defense Department colleagues working the issue had been upgraded several times recently, while those of us assigned to the JCRC had remained stagnant. Moreover, during the past few years, high-ranking DOD and DIA officials had visited our Bangkok office and indicated that since the topic currently held a much higher national priority, "now is the time for the JCRC to also upgrade its positions." Since these and similar suggestions had traditionally been ignored by Harvey, I was a little suspicious about my sudden promotion.

Having already worked in Vietnam on a temporary basis the past three years, I knew the area was considered a "hardship tour." But I had very little information concerning the considerable administrative and logistics aspects in opening a new U.S. government office, and I had no one to turn to for advice. Worse, it was subtly presented to me as a "take it or leave it" arrangement. Still, when both sides reached an agreement on April 8, 1991—but not publicly announced by Hanoi Radio until April 20—whereby the U.S. would open its office at a temporary location in downtown Hanoi, I decided the following month to take the deal. I certainly wasn't looking forward to living in a filthy, impoverished place like Hanoi, but I simply could not resist the challenge of engaging the Communists full-time on the complex POW/MIA issue. I figured that since I had been able to get some limited results from periodic work, dealing with them on a daily basis might enable me to bring about far greater progress. My old friend Bob Destatte initially joined me as the only other person in the new office.

After confirming that I would head the new center, I traveled to Hanoi in conjunction with a regular Technical Meeting scheduled for mid-May 1991. During the talks, I learned the location for our new office, which the U.S. side had accepted at face value as a wonderful sign of improved Vietnamese cooperation. According to the Communists, the only readily available site for our new office was the SRV's official Le Thach guesthouse across from the "Metropole Hotel," near the famous "Restored Sword Lake." I was instantly upset by the news. The Le Thach guesthouse was under very heavy audio and video surveillance by Vietnam's Intelligence and Security Services. I had learned from my interviews with defectors who were formerly assigned to the Hanoi area that the Vietnam Tourism Company (code named Department K-51) had the guesthouse wired with a listening post established at nearby 192 Quan Thanh Street. Undercover security personal posing as bell hops and room maids covertly conducted searches through personal effects looking for politically sensitive materials like cassette tapes of banned Western music, and also gleaned intelligence from documents brought into Vietnam by foreigners. The telephones were monitored by the Leadership Protection Unit (code named K-10), which operated Audio Office 1 of the Ministry of Public Security's Technical Reconnaissance Department. This department also supervised Mail Censorship Office 2, which reviewed any items mailed from the guesthouse or Hanoi's nearby Main Post Office. The Technical Reconnaissance Department also supervised the activities of Surreptitious Entry Unit 3, which was responsible for opening locks on luggage, safes and other containers.

Conveniently located next to the Vietnam Tourism Company was a building occupied by the Vietnam Communist Party's Youth Group, which handily was near the Vietnam-America Friendship Association. The Youth Group was used to closely observe these U.S. citizens, despite the fact that the Association was a meeting place for American individuals and groups considered "progressive," and therefore useful to the Communist Party in furthering its aims. From a building at 192-A Quan Thanh Street, a regiment-sized force of the Youth Group operating on foot, bicycles, and in some cases motorcycles performed surveillance missions on these foreign and even sometimes domestic targets. Since those accepted into the Youth Group comprised the fourth generation of Vietnamese born since the founding of the Vietnam Communist Party, rather than a unit designation implying a connection to the Ministry of Public Security, they were called simply "the fourth generation." Although I was upset about the location, at the same time I knew that there was no other facility readily available, and it was the best the Communists had to offer. We would simply have to live with it.

Shortly after settling into our new workplace, Destatte and I started making POW/MIA related trips throughout northern Vietnam. Most of our first investigations resulted from haphazard leads from our Vietnamese counterparts that eventually proved to be casualties from the French War or cases not involving unaccounted for U.S. personnel. However, within days of opening the office, Communist officials bluntly asked us to leave the country. Their stated reason was the imminent opening of an important Congress of the Vietnam Communist Party scheduled in Hanoi during June 1991. According to the VNOSMP cadre, accommodations for delegates from throughout the country as well as from foreign countries were very scarce. Somewhat perturbed by the interruption of our initial work period, Destatte and I packed our bags and returned to Bangkok. Like so many other trips made to Vietnam in the past, I didn't know whether I would ever be back again.

But, like the Sirens, Hanoi beckoned us back to its loving if somewhat moldy arms. When we returned to the capital a month later, we were advised that a new location for our office had been arranged in a three-storied building called the "Boss Hotel." I was told that the hotel formerly belonged to an organization called the "Oil Services Company of Canada," or "OSCAN" for short, and that the name of the hotel had recently been changed from "OSCAN" to "Boss." After a few days in rooms on the lower floors we were finally moved to the top floor, which had previously been occupied by the Trade Representative of Taiwan. Apparently the SRV made some other arrangement with Taiwan, but I never saw any official Taiwanese Trade Office at any other location in Hanoi.

With the move to the Boss Hotel, my staff increased by the addition of two JCRC Intelligence Analysts/Linguists, and one CILHI Search and Recovery Specialist. The two personnel from the JCRC were Master Sergeant Keith Flanagan and Sergeant William Newell, both Air Force. The CILHI representative was Army Sergeant First Class Randy Nash. All three men had served on my field investigation teams during the previous two years, and I was pleased to have NCOs of such high caliber working for me in the new office.

As we began to establish ourselves in our new digs, we searched for additional space to store supplies and equipment. After discovering a small closet at the end of our floor we decided to use it for storage, but found it was locked. I located a room maid who indicated that the tiny closet held some of the hotel's mops and brooms. She agreed to remove the items from the closet so that we might use it, and after emptying it the maid gave me the key. Filling the cabinet with our supplies, I locked the door and carried the key back to a box in a room that we were in the process of organizing as a Research and Analysis Section. As I went to put the key in the box, I noticed that the words "Boss Hotel" along with a room number were printed over with what was obviously fresh paint. Using my thumbnail I scratched off some of the paint to reveal the words "Ministry of Public Security Guesthouse." I don't know why I was surprised, as I should have realized that any facility the Communists arranged for us would be under tight control. I covertly informed my staff that we had just moved into a building owned by the Ministry of Public Security, and cautioned them to remain vigilant regarding security.

In order to confirm the status of the building and the fact that the "Boss Hotel" was merely a cover name for a facility managed by the Ministry of Public Security, one evening after dinner at a downtown restaurant I hailed a small three-wheeled manually operated vehicle called a "cyclo" or "pedicab." When I climbed on board the chain-driven tricycle the driver asked "Where to." I told him, "Take me to the Ministry of Public Security Guesthouse." Without any further directions the driver proceeded straight to the Boss Hotel. Soon thereafter, a low-ranking member of the hotel staff revealed to us that our rooms were "bugged," which did not come as a newsflash. I also suspected that the hotel was equipped with video surveillance when I learned from members of the diplomatic community that a senior official in the Australian Embassy had recently been sent home after being compromised due to homosexual activity between he and a Vietnamese national that occurred in the hotel.

Knowing we were under constant scrutiny, we exercised great caution in our work and conversations. Although we had been careful not to bring any classified material into the country, I remained deeply concerned about the compromise of the documents we did have with us, which included extensive case files and other correspondence relating to our strategy for future Technical Meetings. I wanted to prevent the Communist experts from gaining access to our files, and then regurgitating the same information back to us in order to close cases. I therefore ordered that all documents be placed in locked containers during the evening hours, and as a further precaution, after we noticed that the room maids seemed very interested in our trash, I immediately made sure all such materials were shredded. Further, to make it as difficult as possible for those attempting to gain intelligence from our discarded documents, anything I perceived as remotely sensitive was not only shredded but also flushed down the toilet as well. I did not have a good grasp of the workings of the Hanoi sewer system, but I certainly didn't envy the people who were assigned the task of recovering our trash.

Despite our "cozy" accommodations and the usual VNOSMP admonitions about the "hatred" of the Vietnamese people, most locals seemed pleased to have us open an office in Hanoi. I believe they perceived us as a glimmer of hope that America was re-engaging Vietnam, and with the collapse of the USSR, they needed as much assistance as they could get. Even the newspapers and Hanoi radio toned down their anti-American rhetoric to a large degree, and although I realized that Americans must constantly be on guard in any Communist country, I felt slightly more relaxed.

I did, however, have one tense moment with the locals. Needing a haircut, I wandered around downtown Hanoi until I spotted what appeared to be a former French owned barbershop from the early 1900s. Upon entering, the atmosphere seemed quite friendly, with a wall facing the street made of French colonial windows rising from the floor to the ceiling, thus affording a nice view of the busy boulevard. Noticing a foreigner in his shop, an apparently friendly barber waved me into his chair.

While he began cutting my hair, I struck up a conversation with the man, who was all too happy to have someone with whom to share the latest gossip. The barber related to me how a huge unexploded bomb dropped by a U.S. aircraft during the war into a tunnel inside the Ministry of National Defense compound had recently exploded as PAVN engineers attempted to remove it. The blast was heard all over the city and numerous windows were broken from the explosion. He noted that several PAVN officers had been killed. The barber also described how a Russian mortician responsible for maintaining the remains of deceased President Ho Chi Minh in a vacuum-tight glass case within the Ho Chi Minh Museum had died under mysterious circumstances. According to my well-informed stylist, the Russian mortician was actually a diplomat assigned to the Russian Embassy in Hanoi. The diplomat was assassinated when some unidentified person doused him with gasoline, and then set him ablaze on a bustling Hanoi street in broad daylight. No one had yet been arrested for this crime.

The barber expressed his belief that since I was assigned to the Russian Embassy, I probably knew more about the incident than he did. When I informed him that I was an American and I had never even been inside the Russian Embassy, the man was curious to know how an American was able to speak Vietnamese so fluently. I explained to him that after studying the language, I served in the south during the war. I managed to relay this stunningly important piece of my past just as he was beginning to edge my sideburns with a straight razor. Upon hearing the news, the barber seemed to freeze momentarily with a strange, contorted look on his face, as if reluctantly recalling events from the war. With tears brimming in his eyes the barber told me in a strained, halting voice how American aircraft struck the Kham Thien area of Hanoi during the war, killing his wife and children. I felt a chill pass through my body and goose bumps spread across my skin as the barber stood silently staring down at the razor for what seemed to be an eternity before finishing the haircut. After paying the man I went outside and walked a few steps before turning around to survey the scene. I had anticipated a possible scenario wherein the barber would be laughing with his friends as he related to them how he had just caused an American tourist to wet his pants by scaring him half to death, after which the other barbers would reply, "You didn't pull the old Kham Thien trick again did you?" But the still scowling barber beckoned to the next customer in line and continued cutting hair. I promptly decided to find another barbershop for future haircuts.

As a part of opening the new office, I was tasked with conducting a survey of available health facilities in Hanoi in the event of a medical emergency for our personnel. After I came up with a list, I notified headquarters and a military doctor was placed on travel orders from Hawaii to make a professional assessment. The doctor who arrived was a Lieutenant Colonel assigned to the military hospital at the 25th Infantry Division's Schofield Barracks in Hawaii.

Together, we personally visited the most important medical facility in Hanoi, Military Hospital 108 (MH-108). When we arrived there, we were informed that, like other facilities in Vietnam, we could not meet with the hospital Director but only with the Chief of the External Affairs Department. In other words, the Secretary of the hospital's Communist Party Chapter. The Chief of the External Affairs swiftly informed us that the hospital was restricted to military patients only. When I told him that most of our personnel were military he found my comment hilarious. Despite his amusement, he was proud of his facility and he invited us to go on a hospital tour, which was unexpected but helpful, since the hospital had treated some American POWs during the war. MH-108 also served as the primary medical treatment point for personnel assigned to the substantial wartime Soviet Military Advisory Group.

After a brisk tour (while I covertly looked for any type of skeletal remains being used as training aids), the Chief invited us into his office. He quickly produced a large photo album with gruesome pictures of cases the hospital had been tasked to handle. One photo that caught my eye was that of a young Vietnamese man lying on his back in obvious pain. I could see that the man's penis had been severed and another photo provided a close up view of the penis displayed on a bedside table. When the military doctor from Hawaii looked at the photo, he cringed, saying, "This must have been caused by some type of industrial accident." When I saw the photo, I knew immediately. Only *danh ghen,* what the Vietnamese call "jealous fighting," could have caused the incident. Laughing again, the hospital cadre confirmed my suspicions about the actual cause of the unfortunate event.

When a wife is cast aside for another lover, most vow some type of vengeance to save face for themselves and their family. Vietnamese women believe that the most drastic form of revenge is cutting off the errant husband's penis. I was aware of several incidents that occurred during the war, the last of which happened in Saigon during late 1973. At that time we medically evacuated a civilian employee of a Department of Defense contractor who had his penis severed by a jealous wife after she was shoved out the front door of her home by the American and his new girlfriend whom he had brought home from a bar. The individual in that case was evacuated from Tan Son Nhut by aircraft with his penis accompanying him in a small ice chest.

To graphically illustrate the ghastly tradition of severing penises, and no doubt to stem the rate of adultery, the SRV occasionally issued postage stamps and cards depicting women holding a meat cleaver aloft while chasing after men, closely followed by flocks of ducks. The nuance was that the ducks were aware that the man's penis was about to be chopped off, and they congregated in order to compete for the tender morsel as soon as it hit the ground. Nonetheless, I was curious as to the results of the reattachment surgery, and when I asked, the Chief indicated that the victim was not doing too well and that he held little hope the operation would be successful. Our tour ended on that not too positive note.

After our examination of Hanoi's medical facilities, the Doctor determined that none in the city were acceptable. In most cases, the Doctor's preferred treatment method for our office personnel was medical evacuation (Medivac). However, after further study we learned that there were only two Medivac possibilities: a commercial organization with the capability to fly to Singapore at an approximate cost of $25,000.00 per incident, or second, U.S. Military Medivac by C-9 "Nightingale" coming from and then returning to either Guam or Okinawa. The only facility in Hanoi judged by the doctor to be up to Western standards for routine medical care was a small clinic operating under the authority of the Swedish Embassy. No dental care was available anywhere in the city, and such treatment would require a flight to Bangkok. In summary, as long as we didn't need any dental care, were extremely careful with our documents and what we said in the office, avoided getting a haircut in certain places, and could drink the water and eat the food without getting sick, Hanoi was a great place to work.

Although I had traveled to Hanoi off and on since February 1973, now that I was living there on a permanent basis, I was curious about a variety of subjects I had heard rumors about over the years. I welcomed the opportunity to see for myself what conditions were really like for both local and foreign residents. One report around since the 1980s was that Vietnamese citizens were being forced to undertake "slave labor" assignments to Communist bloc countries in Eastern Europe. In talking with the residents of Hanoi, I discovered that such overseas jobs were actually highly sought after by the North Vietnamese. Many had to pay bribes in order to be selected for what American officials believed were harsh labor projects. With Vietnam's economy in shambles the overseas labor projects provided a welcome source of income for northerners, who unlike their southern brethren did not have relatives residing in America and other Free World nations who were capable of sending back hard currency and care packages from their new homes. Although so-called "guest workers" departing Vietnam were bound for arduous jobs in unsanitary factories with miserable working conditions, and were required to relinquish upwards of 80 percent of their salaries to the government, their fate was still far better than the slow death by starvation many faced in the corrupt, centrally managed Vietnam.

While we continued organizing our office, the field investigations remained at the usual pace. In addition to my new position as head of the Hanoi office, I also still served as a field Team Chief. This called for a great deal of travel away from Hanoi, where the office's primary focus was on records research in the various museums and archives of the central government. Almost everyone directly involved in the POW/MIA issue saw access to archives as an important, perhaps the most important element, of the casualty resolution process. I also learned that the "room maids" were actually the wives of staff members assigned to the various museums and archives of the military branches. These museums, operating under the authority of the General Political Directorate, were the very same facilities we were in the process of negotiating access to for our research. I felt that we should do everything possible to rapidly begin these efforts. Destatte was heading our archival research, and he had some good ideas how to facilitate additional access to official archives. Once while I was preparing to depart for a two-week trip to Central Vietnam, he broached an idea wherein he would invite all the key players involved in archival research, as well as several members of the local and international news media, to a reception at the Boss Hotel. Seeing merit in his plan, and considering that it was obviously business oriented, I approved his request without hesitation.

Unfortunately, however, when the bill for $492.85 dollars for the reception plus $11.11 for business cards to advertise our office was rendered to Hawaii, someone at CINCPAC didn't like the idea. They construed the expenditure of funds for the function as being "representational," and since representational funds were closely guarded and used exclusively by senior flag officers to wine and dine visiting dignitaries, the uproar was intense. As a result I received a terse facsimile complaining about Destatte's reception. Agitated that some "bean counter" relaxing on the beach in Hawaii was miffed because we had tried to do our jobs, I rendered a somewhat sarcastic response that included a reference to a well-publicized U.S. Government-funded dinner recently hosted by then Secretary of Defense Dick Cheney for the heads of several airlines that had helped ferry troops to the Gulf War. Unfortunately however, despite my protestations Destatte's initiative went down in organizational history under the category of "certain problems have been identified."

Trying to make the best of our situation in the Boss Hotel, we reorganized the physical layout into both offices and living quarters on the same floor. I figured that such an arrangement would limit access to the upper part of the building by the general public, thus increasing the safety and security of our operation. I converted one sleeping room into an office for myself and another larger room into a combination conference room/canteen for both meetings and for relaxation during off duty hours. We organized another room as a Research and Analysis Section while a third room was designated a Logistics Section with a small forensics examination area for the CILHI. The first Forensic Anthropologist to arrive for duty in the new office was Dr. Peter Miller, Ph.D. Dr. Miller was a straightforward, no-nonsense expert with many years of experience in examining and identifying human skeletal remains.

During the Hanoi office's first few months, Destatte and I canvassed several museums in the Hanoi area in search of records pertaining to loss incidents. We also purchased numerous additional Vietnamese language publications, all of which required translation into English. Destatte and I, along with the JCRC analyst/linguists, worked on the books, but due to the heavy workload we supplemented our efforts by hiring a small number of part time translators, paying them by the page to help with the translations. Within a few weeks of beginning our efforts, we made good progress in identifying PAVN units capable of answering many of our questions.

Moreover, within days of opening the new office, people who claimed to have information on unaccounted for American personnel began to arrive. Some brought in data recorded from dog tags and various types of identification cards, and some even presented human skeletal remains. With a computerized database on hand and two Intelligence Analysts working in the office, it didn't take long to determine if the information provided was genuine. More importantly, however, the presence of Dr. Miller made it possible to obtain on the spot field analysis of potential human remains. Whereas in the past we had been obligated to process animal bones and other items not associated with human remains back to Hawaii at great expense, we were now in a position to make a preliminary categorization of such items in order to focus our efforts on items of greater interest. This was the first time in JCRC history that we had the capability to simultaneously analyze both information and remains in the field. Dr. Miller was able to conclude that a number of skeletal remains turned over to us were human, and some of these remains were associated with dog tags or identification cards bearing the names of active MIA cases. But due to "turf problems" and the tendency for micromanagement of the remains identification effort by the CILHI, the on-site laboratory was never fully developed.

As usual, our efforts to collect information and remains were also closely followed by Communist officials. When VNOSMP members began to show up at the office shortly after the departure of Sources who claimed to be "private citizens," I gained the impression that the officials were merely checking to see whether we were keeping them appraised of our activities in their country. The vigilance by Communist officials was at times probably justified in their minds, as some of the people who visited our office only used the provenance of POW/MIA information as a ruse to gain face-to-face contact with American officials. Once inside what they considered to be a secure area, they began to criticize the Communist regime and some actually made requests for arms, ammunition and financial support to help them overthrow the Party. Since I knew that our rooms were wired for audio surveillance, I was careful in my conversations with claimed dissidents and I instructed my staff to do likewise. Furthermore, at that time the Soviet Union and its Communist Party were in a period of upheaval, and the Vietnamese were a tad tense regarding the possible impact events in Russia and Eastern Europe might have on Vietnam. Although angry citizens throughout the former Soviet empire were busy toppling statues of Vladimir Lenin, not one such statue had met a similar fate in Vietnam. However, a few Lenin statues had been vandalized and the Public Security Forces were increasingly vigilant to prevent such occurrences.

With all of us constantly traveling throughout the country, it soon became apparent that additional staff were needed in our office. Since the Communists wanted to hold the official American presence in country to a minimum, and due to the inherent logistics requirements of living in Hanoi, our headquarters agreed to fund the hiring of local national Vietnamese employees. When I informed my Vietnamese counterparts of the desire to hire some locals, I learned that the only way I could hire anyone was by going through the official "Diplomatic Service Corps." Not surprisingly, a senior cadre of the Diplomatic Service Corps was none other than the wife of one of my VNOSMP counterparts, Mr. Ngo Hoang.

Deciding to play the game, I actually interviewed several prospective employees introduced by the government. I learned from the applicants that regardless of the salary they received from the U.S. Government, they would only be allowed to keep 40 percent. I understandably felt uneasy about selecting any of the candidates, but at the same time I wanted to avoid a confrontation with the Communist authorities, especially during the initial stage of opening our new office. Since we were still using the Le Thach guesthouse for technical meetings, several applicants contacted me there. One applicant, using initiative quite rare for a Communist cadre, was the female receptionist at the registration desk who overheard my conversations with the other applicants. She also inquired about the possibility of employment in our office. I was acquainted with the receptionist since I had talked with her on numerous times in the past while checking in and out of the facility during the time that we maintained a temporary office there. The lady not only spoke English well, she appeared to be quite efficient. More impressive, rather than sitting on her backside during slow periods knitting clothes to be sold at the local market, I observed that she was continuously studying some type of written material in order to improve herself. Not only did the lady seem to know her duties, she was not intimidated by the usual throng of Communist cadre who hung around the guesthouse trying to look busy. When I informed her of the requirement of initiating hiring through the Diplomatic Service Corps, she said that although this was the normal procedure, if I decided to hire her it would not be a problem. When I asked why, she politely informed me that her father was Vice Foreign Minister and former Ambassador to Thailand, Mr. Le Mai, and therefore, she felt confident of gaining the requisite approval. Judging from her demeanor and apparent self-confidence, I concluded that hiring the receptionist would not only ensure that I had a qualified employee, it would also solve the problem of going through the Diplomatic Service Corps. As promised, everything went smoothly and I used the same process to hire a driver away from the VNOSMP. Both new members of our office proved to be high quality employees, and as far as I know they are still working for the U.S. Government in Hanoi today.

Apparently, I wasn't the only one facing housing and employee difficulties in the early days of Hanoi's opening to the world. The representatives of Non Government Organizations (NGOs) working in Vietnam encountered many of the same problems I did. Many of them had arrived in Hanoi several years earlier, filled with optimism and eager to help the Vietnamese people. In my discussions with them, they appeared to be inspired by the belief that they, as unofficial civilian volunteers, would be able to rebuild what official military destruction had torn down. As the years passed by, however, the corruption, mismanagement and bureaucratic red tape inherent to the Communist regime in Hanoi began taking its toll. The once enthusiastic aid workers complained bitterly about the difficulty of finding office space and living quarters, as well as the relative high cost associated with any facilities approved for their use by Communist authorities. The NGOs were also required to hire employees through official government channels, and the Communists skimmed salaries paid to local nationals hired by the NGOs for the usual 60 percent. As an omen of future bad tidings for our operation, the NGO volunteers described how vehicles and equipment to be used for humanitarian efforts were not exempted from taxation upon import into the country. The NGO personnel had a difficult time accepting the fact that humanitarian items brought in by non-profit organizations to be used strictly for the benefit of people in need of assistance were being taxed by the central government. Having grown short of patience many of the NGO personnel simply packed up and returned home, shaking their heads in frustration. It was sad for me to see people with so much good in their hearts be short-circuited by egotistical cadre. I could never figure out whether it was more important for the Communists to receive political credit for every bit of humanitarian assistance that reached the people, or if it was more important for them to gain the money for funding the operations of the Communist party. In hindsight I believe it was both.

The presence of an official U.S. office in Vietnam after so many years created considerable interest among the foreign diplomatic corps. Shortly after we opened the office I began to receive invitations to official and private functions from the various foreign diplomatic missions in Hanoi, including Marius Grinius, Charge d'Affaires, Canadian Embassy (they didn't have a full ambassador at that time); Claude Blanchemaison, Ambassador of France; Surapong Jayanama, Ambassador of Thailand; Peter Williams, Ambassador of Great Britain; Hiroyuki Yushita, Ambassador of Japan; and Juwana, Ambassador of Indonesia. I confess I felt a tad strange receiving formal invitations from people at this level, even though I had come a long way from that young grunt studying the bush of the Central Highlands so many years ago. In that strange journey, I had truly gone from being a soldier to a diplomat.

Several other foreign Ambassadors and Attachés also visited my office. During each meeting I stressed to them that we Americans were in the country for the express purpose of accounting for American personnel, and not as political cover for some future embassy. Still, all of them seemed pleased that America had finally decided to establish at least some official presence in Vietnam, and all seemed interested in supporting our effort.

The West German Ambassador in particular was keenly interested in accounting for the German voluntary medical personnel who had been captured west of Danang while sightseeing on April 27, 1969. I explained to the Ambassador that in addition to the two medical personnel who were released in Hanoi during Operation Homecoming, the Vietnamese had returned the remains of two others, one of whom was identified on February 22, 1989. On April 10, 1986, the Communists had returned remains they believed were those of Marine Corps Corporal Edwin R. Grissett, who had been held in the same camp with the five Germans. A forensic examination by the CILHI, however, determined that the remains labeled as Grissett were actually those of Nurse Hindrika Kortman. The identification of her remains was approved on April 10, 1991. Unfortunately, I was not able to provide the Ambassador any new information on the remaining West German, Maria Luise Kerber.

The Japanese also proved extremely helpful, and Ambassador Yushita promised his full support for our efforts. I followed up this pledge and agreed to a request from the Japanese Embassy in Hanoi to conduct a one-on-one briefing with Mr. Ichiro Uchida, the private Secretary to Mr. Michio Watanabe, Japan's Deputy Prime Minister and Minister for Foreign Affairs. Impressed with my assessment of America's POW/MIA situation, Mr. Uchida rendered the following comments in a letter to me after he returned to Japan:

Dear Mr. Bell:

I am writing to thank you for meeting with me during my recent visit to Vietnam, especially since you agreed to see me on such short notice. I appreciated your candid views and insights, which helped me gain a much deeper understanding of the MIA/POW issue.

After meeting you, I saw Mr. Nguyen Xuan Phong, Deputy Director of the Americas Department of the Vietnamese Foreign Ministry. I mentioned some of your concerns about the MIA/POW issue, and stressed that all levels of the Vietnamese government should work harder to resolve this problem. Frankly, my talks with him were not as fruitful as I had hoped. I found there remains a fairly substantial divergence of opinion on the matter.

With this in mind, I would like to express to you that Foreign Minister Watanabe will continue to actively encourage a solution to the MIA/POW problem. It is high on his agenda.

I too will do whatever I can to facilitate a resolution to the problem. If there is any way I can be of assistance to you, please do not hesitate to contact me either through the Japanese Embassy in Hanoi or directly through the Foreign Ministry in Tokyo.

Best regards.

At the time I greatly appreciated the support from Uchida and his comments from Watanabe. The fact that he had personally lobbied for more cooperation with one of our principle interlocutors, Nguyen Xuan Phong, was a major step forward. Vietnam's economy was in shambles and aid from Japan was sorely needed. Politicians such as Watanabe and Uchida were fervently searching for all possible excuses to gain support from the Japanese Diet to approve monetary assistance to Communist Vietnam. I was certain that Phong would not lose anything in the translation when he forwarded Uchida's comments to his superiors. Uchida's personality and demeanor during our lengthy meeting indicated to me that he was a down-to-earth guy who was serious in his support.

Several months later, I was able to take Uchida up on his "please do not hesitate to contact me" offer. My good rapport began to pay off when I learned of some twelve hundred Mitsubishi "Pajero" type vehicles that had arrived in Saudi Arabia right at the end of the Gulf War. The Government of Japan had intended the vehicles to be a humanitarian donation to the Coalition Forces, but due to the late arrival the vehicles were left abandoned in a desert parking lot. According to my contacts at the Japanese Embassy in Hanoi my office could have the entire twelve hundred vehicles if I wanted them, the only catch being that I would have to furnish transportation from Saudi Arabia to Hanoi. I quickly passed this information on to Headquarters, and at the same time I arranged a meeting with my Vietnamese counterparts. Of course, Headquarters thought my idea was crazy, but after some checking on space available ship transport they suddenly began to lobby to use the vehicles in Hawaii. In also discussing the matter with the VNOSMP they felt that we could quicken the pace of our efforts if we furnished some of the vehicles to our counterpart "Province Task Teams" and, of course, to the VNOSMP. In the end JCRC received seventy-six of the brand new vehicles, and my office received twelve of them.

As we settled into our strange existence in Hanoi, our quiet little operation abruptly became front and center to one of the biggest brouhaha's ever to hit the POW/MIA issue. In mid-1991 the question of live Americans remaining in Vietnam suddenly gained world-wide notoriety when a photo collected by private POW/MIA activists from a refugee camp in the area of the Thai-Cambodia border began appearing in the media. The photo, along with identifying data on three Americans who were unaccounted for in Vietnam and Laos, created quite a stir within the POW/MIA family organizations, in particular the National Alliance. According to information obtained with the photo, three American prisoners were being held in a camp west of Danang. The camp was said to be under the control of a Communist cadre with the rank of "General" who was called "Ngo Hau Phuoc." Although the photo was a murky multi-generation copy and difficult to analyze, some family members announced that they were certain the photos depicted their missing loved ones. The provocative picture resulted in calls from some members of Congress for rapid investigations. Due to the concurrent release of a popular movie, in the POW/MIA community the document instantly became known as the "Three Amigos" photo.

About the same time that interest peaked in this and other photos of men supposedly held in Laos, I was leading an investigation team headed for the Lao border area west of Danang. I sensed that something unusual was pending because for the first time the Communists had us billeted at the "Non Nuoc Hotel," a fairly nice place located in the old "China Beach" area in the outskirts of Danang. After checking in at the hotel the telephones suddenly became inoperative, and all contact with the outside world was cut. The Communist police were also tense concerning any type of photography, still or moving picture. In fact only a few days earlier I had an encounter with one surly policeman who arrived on a bicycle and challenged me while I was filming a street scene in downtown Hanoi with my portable video camera. The man insisted that I produce a written permit allowing me to film in Vietnam. Unaccustomed to such treatment I ignored the man, whose appearance was disheveled to the point of being humorous. Believing that the man was a crackpot I quickly forgot the incident and continued filming after I arrived in Danang. After an initial trip by Russian helicopter to Tra My and Giang districts outside Danang, when I returned to my room I noticed that the door of the tape cassette housing on my video camera was cracked, but I assumed that it was broken due to an accidental bump.

Although the Communists attributed the sudden loss of communications at the Non Nuoc Hotel to a problem with the telephone lines, I didn't believe them. I proceeded to the Danang post office where I was able to telephone our office in Hanoi. I learned that members of the media were enroute to Danang, and that Assistant Secretary of State Kenneth Quinn was headed for Hanoi. I decided to return there to meet with him. Quinn knew that there was a great deal of interest in the recent live-sighting reports, and having promised members of Congress that an investigation of the "Three Amigos" photo would be conducted promptly, he traveled from Washington to Hanoi to meet with Vice Foreign Minister Le Mai and other key members of the SRV Government. During the meeting, which was the first and only high-level meeting I ever participated in with the Vietnamese leadership conducted entirely in Vietnamese, Le Mai granted approval for me to conduct a live-sighting investigation of the photo as soon as I could return to Danang. I avoided mentioning hiring his daughter so as not to embarrass him or jeopardize her employment. After all, it wouldn't look good for the college-educated daughter of a senior Communist official to be clerking for the imperialists who had bombed his country.

After briefing Quinn on the situation I returned to Danang only to find that my hotel room had been burglarized during my absence. Apparently the reports in the media containing photographs of alleged live Americans remaining in Vietnam had caused Vietnam's security forces to be on edge. The only two items taken were my portable video recorder and my 35mm still camera. After reporting the incident to the police, who probably already had possession of my camera and video recorder, I met with the press in Danang. Several members of the press had just received permission from local and central government authorities to accompany me during a live-sighting investigation to Tien Lanh prison camp located southwest of Danang.

After visiting the An Diem prison camp west of Danang on August 1, where we thought the reports of Americans being held prisoners might in fact be some Westerners working on a nearby hydro-electric project, I immediately began reviewing all of our files for the follow-up trip to the Tien Lanh camp. I had collected quite a bit of information on it over the years, and as I prepared for the trip, I was somewhat concerned with the presence of the press, but to be fair, for the most part the Communists had refrained from turning our operations into a propaganda event. Still, by inviting members of the media to tag along they had created a carnival-like atmosphere. I could only hope that the Communists would allow us unfettered access to the camp, its records, the inmates, and the prison personnel.

My optimism was soon extinguished. We visited the camp on August 3, 1991. That very same day, Washington time, the U.S. Senate passed legislation (Senate Resolution 82) creating a Senate Select Committee on POW/MIA Affairs. Rather than a spontaneous visit, upon arrival at the prison it was obvious that the camp staff were expecting our arrival. Moreover, we were required to wait outside the site while accompanying VNOSMP officials went inside to coordinate the investigation. When we were finally allowed into the compound we were permitted to walk freely around the camp, but were closely monitored by cadre who followed us throughout our visit. The inmates we observed were either political or criminal prisoners. In our brief conversations with them none mentioned any knowledge of Americans still in Vietnam. We did not observe anyone in the camp who might be an American, and we also did not notice any markings or discarded items associated with the previous detention of an American.

Still, when I meet with the camp cadre, I asked them questions about any present or former American prisoners, or foreign prisoners from any other country having once been held there. I was told that only Vietnamese prisoners had ever been detained in the camp, so our request to examine camp records was denied. Stymied, I reviewed our Source information on the camp. As I looked it over, I concluded that the memory sketches provided by at least some of the Sources detained in the camp were accurate. In checking the names of cadre assigned to the camp, I noticed that the Source accounts were also generally accurate but some recent changes had occurred. For example, the cadre who was introduced to me as the Camp Commander was listed in our files as the Political Officer. When I inquired concerning the apparent discrepancy, the Camp Commander informed me that until recently he had served as the Political Officer, but that due to a promotion he was reassigned as the commander.

After departing Tien Lanh, I concluded that it would be virtually impossible to conduct an objective live-sighting investigation that the families could accept if Communist authorities were informed in advance of the arrival of U.S. investigators. We needed to be able to conduct unannounced investigations; at this point in our relationship, however, the Communists simply would not allow it. Even though our intelligence on the camp was good, Communist officials had been aware on July 27 of our intended target. We had arrived at the camp on August 3, giving them eight days in which to prepare and move any potential American prisoners held in Tien Lanh out of the area. My other fear was that allowing the press to accompany our team might result in a perception of "openness" or "genuine cooperation" of the Communist officials by the media reps. Sure enough, some press articles appearing after the Tien Lanh investigation, including at least one by Reuters complete with photos of us accompanied by Communist officials, gave the false impression of a "major breakthrough." While not true, I was still happy that at least we had begun the process of investigating the important live-sighting reports.

The "Three Amigos" reports associated with the Tien Lanh camp were somewhat vague and at first glance appeared to be implausible. However, one part of the report intrigued me tremendously. The information alleging that Americans were being held in a camp commanded by a cadre with the rank of "General" named "Ngo Hau Phuoc" brought to mind intelligence in our files concerning an actual cadre named "Ho Huu Phuoc," who used an alias of "Ho Nghinh." Ho Huu Phuoc was said to be a brother of Ho Liem, alias Hoang Bich Son, a well-known, key member of Vietnam's Intelligence and Security Services who had served as SRV Ambassador to the United Nations and as Vice Foreign Minister. Other reports indicated that as a high-ranking member of the MR-5 Security Committee, Ho Huu Phuoc had supervised a program during the war wherein American POWs taught female agents the English language in order to lure Americans to capture. When the war ended, a "Ho Nghinh" became the Chairman of the Danang City Military Management Committee, and later the Secretary of the Danang City Party Committee. Brother "Ho Liem" eventually served as Chairman of the National Assembly and as Chairman of the Committee for Overseas Vietnamese. This raised the possibility that the original Source of the "Three Amigos" report was simply misunderstood in his pronunciation of the cadre's name in overall charge of the prisoners, since Ngo Hau Phuoc and Ho Huu Phuoc sound very similar. With the case of Donald Sparks now fresh in my mind (I had just received the report from the American citizen who identified him as a man he saw in the company of Communist military officers in Danang after the war), the "Ngo Hau Phuoc" portion was quite intriguing. At the same time the "Three Amigo's" photo was so ludicrous that I was afraid that it might cast a shadow of doubt over all the information we had managed to collect up to that point. Fortunately, however, I decided not to place a great deal of emphasis on pursuing the photographic leads, and they were subsequently proven fraudulent.

Regardless, the photo and others in Laos sparked a heightened interest from Congress in the POW/MIA issue. While Rep. Steve Solarz and a few others like Rep. Ben Gilman and Rep. Bob Smith had stayed focused, most had dropped the issue. Now that it was on the front cover again, the politicians were scrambling. Then they discovered our new office. When I returned to Hanoi, I received a stack of travel advisories informing me of various Congressional Delegations, called "CODELs," arriving in Hanoi on POW/MIA "fact finding" missions. Most of the visitors were small delegations from the House and Senate, as well as accompanying staff assistants. Other groups included the leaders of Veterans Service Organizations, key members of the American business community, and individuals representing various charitable organizations seeking to initiate projects in Vietnam.

One of my first visitors was Ms. Francis Zwenig, Legislative Staff Assistant for Senator John Kerry, (D, MA). Zwenig appeared quite animated about learning the issue, surprising me by her aggressive demands for my time to teach her the issue. I soon learned that her forceful attitude was most likely predicated on the soon-to-be announced appointment of her boss as Chairman of the new Senate Select Committee on POW/MIA Affairs. Shortly after Zwenig's preparatory visit, in July 1991 Kerry arrived at the Boss Hotel to make his own survey of our office. Kerry seemed fascinated by the evolution of our office, and his questions were oriented primarily toward gauging what contributions he and other members of the Senate Select Committee might make to enhance our success. During a requested one-on-one briefing session on the general POW/MIA situation, Kerry indicated that he was also keenly interested in the historical aspects of the issue. The fundamental part of the accounting process, I stressed to the Senator, was that rather than perceiving the issue as a problem to be solved by the latest American business school management technique, or for that matter seeing it as an obstacle to diplomatic and trade relations, Congress should view the POW/MIA question as a legitimate national concern with a compelling basis for fair and honest resolution. Kerry agreed and pledged to instill such an attitude in the committee. At the same time, he realized that the committee would be under considerable scrutiny by the general public, especially the family members due to their perception of U.S. Government stonewalling of the issue.

Based on his line of questioning, I gradually began to conclude that Kerry was keen to ferret out my views on the issue of live Americans who might have been left behind in Indochina after "Operation Homecoming." But each time he approached the specifics of this controversial question he appeared to intentionally avoid receiving a concrete answer. From my responses Kerry undoubtedly deduced that it was my opinion that at least some men were held back in 1973. But after discussing the issue at length with me, and also visiting with Communist officials responsible for POW/MIA affairs, Kerry seemed satisfied that he had a good grasp of the issue and the situation on the ground in Vietnam. Without being specific Kerry indicated that he and other committee members would be working closely with me in the near future to ensure that our new office received the support necessary to accomplish our mission. To help the Senator in addressing the support factor with his colleagues in Congress, I presented him with a detailed plan outlining the administrative and logistical requirements to initiate and sustain accelerated field operations, including live-sighting investigations, archival research and an Oral History Program (OHP) oriented toward interviewing former cadre involved in the capture, evacuation, treatment and detention of unaccounted-for American personnel.

In addition to initial start-up costs and funding for the first year of operations, I considered the most important part of my plan the procurement of U.S. helicopters for use by our field teams. This was one point that I considered absolutely critical. Not only were they an important safety factor given the horrible condition of the Vietnamese and Lao helicopters, if we were to conduct genuine unannounced live sighting investigations at points throughout Vietnam where reports had indicated Americans were being held, American helicopters flown by American pilots would be the only reliable means of transport by which we could accomplish our work. Moreover, Harvey, CILHI's Johnie Webb, and myself had recently witnessed first-hand how risky it was to fly Air Vietnam. We had gone to Bangkok's Don Muang airport to board a Vietnam Airlines Soviet-built TU-134 aircraft, one of several in the small fleet. Due to a critical shortage of all types of petroleum products in Vietnam, the Air Vietnam aircraft had taken on minimum fuel in Hanoi in order to top off its tanks in Thailand and ferry the excess fuel back to Hanoi. Unfortunately the aircraft ran out of gas and crashed and burned while approaching the airport while we stood waiting in line at the departure gate ready to board. This experience, as well as the obviously poor maintenance condition of the aging Russian-supplied military helicopters, was a huge red flag, and I wanted to avoid flying on Vietnamese aircraft, military or civilian, as much as possible. I also had too many close encounters with death while flying over mountainous Laos. I found it nerve wracking indeed to peer out the windows of lumbering Soviet aircraft while flying through dense rain and cloud formations and see sharp peaks of limestone karsts on both sides of the airplane.

Overall, it was difficult for me to get a good grasp on Kerry. While obviously intelligent, he seemed interested in learning about the issue, but only to confirm conclusions he had already reached. He demurred on funding for U.S. helicopters, not wanting to offend the Vietnamese, but he was obviously enthusiastic in establishing some type of program wherein we might interview former Communist cadre for POW/MIA related information. When I emphasized to the Senator that Oral History interviews could be productive only if transparent and viewed in light of other critical aspects, such as unfettered access to witnesses and unannounced site inspections at locations where live Americans were alleged to have been seen, including wartime prison camps, Kerry unfortunately didn't seem to be interested in how the plan was to be carried out, or for that matter what the results of the effort might be. He was mainly concerned with compiling a list of things that based on my years of experience we needed to do, and then methodically cross them off until we reached the end of the list. In essence, I sadly came to believe that in his view, the process was more important than its results.

Wanting to stay on top of the field situation, I decided to let Destatte and the other office personnel brief members of Congress who continued to arrive in Hanoi, while I maintained my position as Team Chief on a field investigation team. Still, even in the field I couldn't escape the visitors. While conducting case investigations in Central Vietnam, we were visited on the early August 1991 trip to Danang by a delegation that included Representative Pete Peterson, (D, FL), a former Vietnam-era POW, along with Jim Kolbe, (R, AZ) and several others. The members of Peterson's group seemed to be predisposed to the idea that our work was going entirely too slow due to the lack of a strong commitment of personnel and resources by the Defense Department. Although I briefed the CODEL at length, they insisted on a face-to-face meeting with the investigation and recovery team members. Aware that headquarters would frown upon such an exchange, I nevertheless relented and arranged the meeting. As anticipated my men took advantage of the encounter to air their grievances, primarily concerning the need for more and better equipment. While the congressmen stood attentively, pen and paper in hand, the men methodically laid out their justification for cameras, laptop computers, global positioning systems and other equipment. Somehow the spectacle annoyed me, because if the system was working properly, and in if fact this was the highest national priority, we shouldn't have had to essentially act like beggars or children at Christmas.

Apparently the congressmen had done considerable research into our field efforts, because in addition to their interest in our equipment needs they also expressed a desire for reorganization of the JCRC. According to Kolbe, in order to move quickly forward and achieve progress, the JCRC would require an officer with the rank of general, a "one star" as he termed it. At the time I didn't realize it, but their comments about the slowness of our operations, despite my protests that the Vietnamese were the ones stalling us at every turn, and the need for reorganization, were an ominous portent of things to come, especially after I received a high-ranking visitor in September to discuss that very point. Strangely, during this first visit, I saw little of the former POW, Pete Peterson. Instead of talking to us, he spent almost his entire time in Danang talking to the senior leadership of the Quang Nam/Danang party organization.

Not only were the CODELs swamping us, unofficial American visitors were also flooding our Communist counterparts. Representatives from the American Legion, the Veterans of Foreign Wars, the Vietnam Veterans of America and other organizations arrived to assess just what role each organization might be able to play in achieving postwar normalization of relations between the two sides. Although primarily interested in accounting for American servicemen, the veterans also discussed topics such as prosthetic devices for amputees and providing information helpful to the Communists in locating their wartime casualties buried or left on battlefields by American troops. Other discussion points included various charitable projects, such as providing school supplies to children and the construction of medical clinics.

It was a wonderful humanitarian gesture by many former vets, and the Communists took full advantage of it. Although desperate for the assistance, the Party made sure that all aid went to those specifically selected by the Communists, and that the Party received political credit for providing such aid. For instance, school supplies donated by American veterans was distributed to members of the "Ho Chi Minh Young Pioneers" and the "Ho Chi Minh Children's Organization." These were the so-called "red scarf" children of loyal party members who received political thought orientation at an early age. They wore red scarves around their necks as a pledge of future loyalty to the Party. Prosthetic devices were reserved for amputees wounded in combat while fighting on the side of the Communists against American or ARVN units. The Communists maintained firm control in distributing almost all of the humanitarian assistance provided by NGOs to residents of North Vietnam. Although its position on the distribution of foreign aid changed slightly as the war slipped into the past, the Communist Party remained staunchly against the sharing of significant aid with America's former allies, referring to them as "decadent remnants of the Saigon regime."

But the most profound change in Communist behavior came about from the entry of American businessmen into the city. Despite the furor over the "Three Amigos" photo, Communist officials were hinting at further POW/MIA cooperation along with a general reformation of the economy. This reformation had actually begun with what was considered a momentous decision during the Party Congress of 1986, called *doi moi* (new change) by the Vietnamese. There had been tradeoffs, however, and one of them was the need for drastically increased internal security. One concession made by reformers was the acceptance of large numbers of Public Security personnel, up to battalion size units, to be deployed into the provinces throughout the south. Although the powerful Politburo had decided on reform, it was nevertheless reform with limits and restrictions, the utmost being continued tight Party control, regardless of changes in the economic structure. I came to believe that in order to deceive the West regarding the extent of *doi moi* the Communists were willing to accept, the Party relied upon its Proselytizing Department to fashion a cover for its "new change."

In order to closely manage the *doi moi* era, the Proselytizing Department dispatched large numbers of seasoned cadre to work with the various foreign organizations involved in the development of Vietnam's economy. Through partnerships and ventures with Western business representatives, such entities as the Vietnamese Import and Export Commission, Oil and Gas Exploration Commission, and other organizations oriented toward tourism, were designed to lure in American businessmen—once the embargo was lifted and political relations were normalized—with visions of large contracts for upgrading Vietnam's infrastructure. At the same time, Communist strategists maneuvered "retired" proselytizing cadre from the military branches into Vietnamese veteran's organizations, placing them in direct contact with targeted U.S. veteran's groups.

As more and more emphasis was placed on development of the economy, a gradual shift in strategy became detectable. While the Communists continued to place considerable importance on political warfare, psychological operations and propaganda, they gradually moved from shrill jingoism to tactics oriented toward exploitation and the manipulation of character defects, especially greed, since the general perception of Americans by the Communists was that our desire for money is even stronger than patriotism. The idea was to identify, evaluate, and influence enough prominent Americans across a broad spectrum of U.S. society in order to facilitate the normalization of relations with the United State without the Communists ever having made any significant concessions, especially regarding the two prickly issues of democracy and human rights. Whereas during the war the Proselytizing Department had relied upon the manipulation of emotions through propaganda to inflame antiwar sentiments in the American people, in the postwar situation it resorted to the lure of economic opportunity.

Apparently, the Vietnamese had us down cold, as the American business community was particularly keen to get its foot in postwar Vietnam's economic door. Consumed with the heavy workload, at first I didn't notice how many American business personnel were arriving in Vietnam until they started visiting me in droves at the Hanoi office. Perceiving a huge, pent-up demand for goods and services in poverty-stricken Vietnam, they looked upon the country as some sort of "last frontier." Most who came calling were entrepreneurs with impressive but unrealistic business plans on how to make fast profits. Many were young, idealistic Ivy-Leaguers living on shoestring budgets while hoping to strike it rich by acting as "middlemen" for major American corporations seeking business ventures in Vietnam. The common theme was "when the trade embargo is lifted this place will boom." Unfortunately, few had much compassion for or interest in the POW/MIA issue or for the loved ones of the missing, seeing them as a roadblock to opening the trade doors. They were only concerned with beating the Europeans or the Japanese to the proverbial punch. Without ever providing or possessing any sound reasoning or factual basis for their optimism, let alone a modicum of knowledge about the Vietnamese, the American businessmen seemed to think that economic change would make the Communists more reasonable and humane, and by extension, more forthcoming on accounting for our missing.

One typical group of businessmen arriving to check the investment climate was headed by former U.S. Ambassador to Thailand, Morton Abramowitz. In speaking to me, he was curious to know what impact increased commercial contacts between America and Vietnam might have on the POW/MIA issue. I told him that due to Vietnam's collapsed economy and international isolation, we currently had a rare window of opportunity to settle the POW/MIA mystery. If we could wisely use this leverage to set ground rules and gain concessions from the Communists to ensure the objectivity of our case investigations, while at the same time maintaining our policy of strict reciprocity regarding humanitarian issues, I believe we could eventually accomplish our mission. Once the solid standards had been agreed to and implemented I didn't think the economic aspect would have a significant impact on our operations. Personally, I felt that if American businessmen wanted to invest in Vietnam and trust the Communists with their money, it was their call. They should be smart enough to set their own ground rules, as I was trying to do on POW/MIA. Abramowitz seemed to understand my point and he indicated that although he could not speak for the entire business community, he was nevertheless confident that the business activities of his particular group would have no negative impact on our operations.

I told this same story to other arriving businessmen, but it fell on deaf ears. The more contact I had with the business community, the more concerned I became that the Communists might be correct in their perception that for Americans, profits were more powerful than patriotism. In judging the manner in which the business community undertook its efforts, I had difficulty in determining whether it was simple naiveté, or rather that they were all too willing to turn a collective blind eye to the reality of Vietnam, and in particular, what lifting the embargo and normalizing relations without solid concessions would do to the POW/MIA issue. Worse, as the lobbyists began to concentrate on securing financing from the Export-Import Bank, thus gaining protection for their client's investments from the taxpayer funded Overseas Private Investment Corporation (OPIC), I began to realize that they were actually setting a dual standard. The families of the missing men were expected to "trust" the Communists to "act in good faith" at some future unspecified time in resolving the status of their loved ones, while the business community would look to the American taxpayer to carry the burden of securing its investments. "In case something went wrong, you know, we can't carry all the risk ourselves," they would tell me. The obvious question, never answered by these captains of industry, was if the businessmen didn't trust the Communists with their money, how could the families be expected to trust them with the far more sensitive issue of an honest accounting for their loved ones? The business community wanted to move the trade and commerce train forward, and they never really considered the POW/MIA question, except for the attendant bad publicity for moving too fast in normalizing relations.

Unfortunately, many were also willing to ignore the Communist political machinations. To maintain political control, the Party spread into every level of Vietnam's fledgling market economy. While the Party was dead set on developing the economy, at the same time it demanded tight rule of all political and social aspects of daily life. Like a cancer, Party committees were already established in all schools, labor unions, military units, hospitals, farms, factories and mass associations organized for veterans, farmers, women, and youth. All state-managed enterprises had a Party committee in charge of all aspects of their operations. For joint US-Vietnam projects, the Party committees were located inside the Vietnamese partner. In the representative offices of foreign corporations the Party committees were located inside the Diplomatic Service Corps that acted as the local employment agency for foreign entities. Like my initial rude awakening, the American business community would learn that the Party would prohibit the hiring of employees from a free labor market and that all local hire staff members would be subject to a set of political rules that the Americans would know nothing about.

I thought to myself, surely the businessmen could see that the seldom-used Presidential Palace in Hanoi stood noticeably silent, overgrown with weeds, while the nearby Communist Party headquarters buzzed with activity. Businessmen who must rely on not only personal experience and intuition in dealing with potential business partners, must have known that the government of Vietnam had no real power. The Communist Party ran everything, including the economy, the POW/MIA issue, and human rights. They would also learn that publicly disclosed government or economic positions and job titles meant nothing, and that only positions held within the Party hierarchy counted. They could never be sure that the individuals with whom they had sealed deals truly held the clout necessary to move the projects forward. For example, most senior executives who met with Foreign Minister Nguyen Manh Cam assumed that he had the final say regarding foreign policy in the country, when in reality Mr. Song Hao, as Chief of the Party's External Affairs Committee, held the real power.

Holding internal discussions on business strategy with members of the local staff as "trusted employees" was also ludicrous. In order to guarantee that the loyalty of those hired by foreign corporations was to the Party first and to the employer second, the Party maintained personal history dossiers, called *ly lich*, on each employee. The *ly lich* were closely held in political channels and reviewed at each step of the employee's career, whether within the ranks of the party, in a state owned enterprise, military unit or foreign corporation. The *ly lich* was also important regarding foreign travel by the employee, because a passport was not possible without a favorable review. I only understood this situation when I asked one of my counterparts about the seemingly insurmountable red tape encountered by anyone in Vietnam seeking a passport. The cadre related to me that it was much easier for a common citizen to obtain a passport than a government or party official. According to him, the primary concern was the degree of knowledge concerning the operations of the Communist party held by the individual. Anyone with access to information considered sensitive by the Party would only be allowed to travel under special circumstances, and during the period of travel the individual would be under continuous close scrutiny by elements of the internal security apparatus. Cadre selected for assignments of long duration in western countries had to be of proven loyalty, usually demonstrated by previous close combat with significant risk to life, and in many cases wounds received in action against enemies of Vietnam. Throughout the 1960s, 70s and 80s, it was not unusual for the Party to select combat veterans of the 1954 Dien Bien Phu battle to represent Vietnam in western capitals. Younger staff members assigned to overseas missions were carefully scrutinized prior to receiving their orders, and it was common for such positions to be filled by second or third generation Party members who were either married with small children or who had pregnant wives. This was done in the belief that the family situations of the personnel would prevent them from defecting once abroad.

"Human rights" remained another stumbling block for the normalization of relations. Although tight political control had been established in the northern half of the country since 1954, "reactionary elements" in the south still remained a thorn for postwar Vietnam. In order to relieve political tensions over "human rights," whenever the pressure neared the boiling point the Party took measures to facilitate the departure of certain dissident elements from the country under the guises of the "Orderly Departure Program," or through regular refugee channels by movement in leaking boats across the South China Sea. The Party's manipulation of the refugee program operated in much the same manner as a pressure cooker, in that it took a certain amount of steam to build up to bring about a release. Once the pressure subsided the outlet temporarily closed to await a subsequent increase in pressure.

The departures of refugees not only served to assuage Western political demands, once resettled in a western country, the refugees could be expected to provide a much-needed source of hard currency by sending home remittances to family members in the form of cash or consumer goods, such as medicines, clothing and appliances. By returning as tourists, with charges for individual visas ranging from $40.00 to $100.00 or more, the hundreds of thousands of refugees also contributed to Vietnam's economy. They also invested in business ventures planned for overseas Vietnamese, primarily in the south. By 1991 most experts were of the opinion that Vietnam received more hard currency revenue from refugees than from the total export of all its products.

In essence the Communists were trying to have their cake and eat it too. In the development of Vietnam's postwar economy they intended to take advantage of every possible aspect of relations with the West, especially the United States which, correctly or not, they perceived to be a country which was "rich but not strong." They had effectively organized their system in order to exploit both refugees and humanitarian assistance. They didn't like American culture, they didn't like American values, and they certainly didn't like democracy. But they thirsted for power, and they needed money to strengthen and modernize their military forces. Throughout the war years the Communists had spouted rhetoric calling for the people to make every possible sacrifice in the quest for freedom and independence. Once they had seized power in 1975 and then consolidated the nation by "reunifying" it under the Communist banner in 1976, the word *Dan chu* (Democracy) was quickly removed from the letterhead of all official government stationery. All publishing houses were warned against publishing any words in dictionaries that might provoke "reactionaries" into action. Terminology such as "multi-party" and "political plurality" was expressly prohibited.

Despite these ill-omened clouds, by the fall of 1991 we had managed to resolve a number of complex MIA cases, and our Vietnamese counterparts seemed to be increasingly resigned to the fact that our standards for resolving cases would remain firm regardless of any movement forward in the bilateral relationship. The number of our field investigation teams had gradually expanded and the men on each team had gained the degree of experience necessary to permit the breakdown of the basic teams into individual investigation and recovery elements as the situation developed on the ground. This gave me considerable flexibility, because after arrival in remote provinces I was able to not only factor in the experience level of each individual team member relevant to the complexity of the individual cases, but also the physical conditioning of each member in light of the degree of difficulty of the terrain to be navigated during the course of the investigations. This was one valuable lesson I learned from our Communist counterparts, and by moving our team members to correspond with the Communists' team composition, I was able to match brains and brawn. By prioritizing the sites to be visited I was able to avoid many situations organized by the Communists as little more than time killers.

I was determined to keep our operation at an optimum level but with a strong emphasis on quality, not quantity. Rather than the Defense Secretary McNamara type statistical charts indicating spectacular increases in numbers of missions, sorties, or body counts, I concentrated on the careful, methodical investigations of each individual last-known-alive discrepancy case. I believed that in the cases of the men whose fate had not been determined the investigation of their cases was literally a matter of life and death. As for those who were obviously dead but not yet recovered, they were important but not the number one priority. Like refugees and humanitarian assistance, the Communists were obviously intent on exploiting the POW/MIA issue for financial gain, but I worked equally hard to deny them the opportunity, lest we meet with the same fate as our French counterparts who were squeezed and milked for over three decades. One fortunate aspect for France was Vietnam's critical need for flat, unobstructed land for positioning Satellite communications in the 1980s. Since the French cemeteries were the only feasible plots of urban land readily available, the French were able to quickly recover the remains of French nationals, for a sizable sum of money of course, from several large cemeteries in Vietnam's major cities.

Although I had not paid much attention to Rep. Kolbe's remark in August about needing a "one star" to head our operations, in September 1991, an Admiral named Mike McDevitt visited me from the Office of the Assistant Secretary of Defense for International Security Affairs. Prior to his arrival I hadn't received much information regarding his visit, and I really did not understand his involvement in the POW/MIA issue. But after spending some time with him and after analyzing his line of questioning, it became obvious that although I didn't know McDevitt and had never even heard of him, he was a key player in the military pecking order. Ultimately he seemed impressed with my operation and plans for the near future. The Admiral repeatedly mentioned to me that we were going to receive increased funding and priority. However, on the way to the airport for his trip home, he expressed deep concern over how all the different organizations touching the POW/MIA effort could be better organized for command and control purposes. After thinking about it for a few minutes, I suggested that we organize our field operations as a Task Force. I pointed out to him that we already had used the Task Force concept successfully in Laos, and I was confident it could be expanded to include all three countries. My suggestion of a Task Force model seemed to set the flag officer's mental wheels in motion and he pondered the idea as we rode to the airport for his flight back to Washington. I later learned that one of his tasks during his trip was to evaluate my performance and decide whether to replace me as head of the POW/MIA Affairs Office with a military officer. Apparently he was satisfied that I was doing a good job because he recommended that I be left in place. Harvey, as usual, was another matter. After he heard about my idea of a Task Force, he fired off a message informing me that in broaching my idea, I had just eliminated my position.

In the Department of Defense, the official with primary responsibility for the POW/MIA issue was the Admiral's boss, Assistant Secretary of Defense for International Security Affairs, Carl W. Ford, Jr. A former Army Intelligence Officer assigned during the war to the Central Highlands, Ford was able to clearly distinguish the levels of priority for the various responsibilities of our office inside Vietnam, especially in properly addressing the critical live sighting issue. Due to his expertise in the intelligence career field Ford would later become the Assistant Secretary of State for Intelligence and Research in the George W. Bush Administration. In a memo I was given much later, Ford took my suggestion for a task-organized effort and ran with it. Apparently I had impressed the Admiral, as Ford wrote that "the U.S. Office for POW/MIA Affairs in Hanoi [should] be the focus of our efforts." Additionally, at that time CINCPAC was proposing a new field investigation concept that called for the examination of all cases in what it termed a "geographic approach." Basically, cases in one specific area would be investigated all together, regardless of whether they were categorized as a last known alive case or one requiring a time consuming excavation for remains and aircraft parts. In a letter from Ford to the Director of the Joint Staff dated September 19, 1991, he made some recommendations for major changes in our current approach:

> *First, the Hanoi Office should be given lead investigatory responsibility for (1) the Vessey discrepancy cases, (2) the additional 64 "last known alive" cases not included in the Vessey cases, and (3) the 13 cases involving Americans classified by their services as POW but who did not return at Operation Homecoming and who are not included in the Vessey cases. The Hanoi Office should be required to investigate the above cases on a full-time basis. At the same time, all of the other cases should be organized by Province/district and scheduled on a geographic basis, similar to the way cases were organized in the draft plan. These two efforts—the cases worked by the Hanoi Office and the cases addressed by the JCRC in the geographic approach—would proceed in parallel. Naturally, some of the cases over which the office has cognizance may require field assistance that only a JCRC or CILHI team could provide; such supplementary support would be requested and scheduled by the Chief, Hanoi Office.*

After completing his own assessment visit to Hanoi, and realizing the complexity of his concept, Ford called for a revision of the command and control already in place.

Once the Hanoi Office is established as a permanent activity, which we anticipate will be soon, the command structure must accommodate the unique composition of the office which includes personnel from the Joint Casualty Resolution Center, the Army Central Identification laboratory, the DIA Special Office for PW-MIA Affairs and DIA Stony Beach. Since the first common superior of all these organizations is the Deputy Secretary of Defense, a command arrangement that puts CINCPAC in charge is required. We suggest you consider designating the Hanoi Office as JTF Hanoi, reporting to [Secretary of Defense] via CINCPAC and [Chairman of the Joint Chiefs of Staff]. We further recommend designating JCRC, CILHI, DIA Stony Beach, and DIA (POW-MIA) as supporting commands to JTF Hanoi. Implementation of these command and control changes will assure that the Hanoi Office has authority commensurate with responsibility in carrying out the functions of the office and will be the first step in putting in place a command structure that can expand to cover Laos and Cambodia if and when necessary.

Emphasis was also placed on the need for accurate and objective reporting of our investigations, as well as a mechanism by which cases could be thoroughly reviewed for closure.

We strongly urge that each case be the subject of an individual investigative report, forwarded by the lead investigatory activity, which would be either the Hanoi Office or the JCRC field team leader, to OSD/ISA via CINCPAC (JCRC) and DIA (POW-MIA). Each case investigation report should be formally endorsed with comments, recommendations, concurrence/nonconcurrence by USCINCPAC (JCRC) and then by DIA (POW-MIA). [Office of Secretary of Defense/International Security Affairs] will then assume responsibility for the next step in the resolution process—closing the case, returning it for further information/investigation, or other appropriate disposition. It is vitally important that the recommendations of the "on-the-ground" investigator be included, and then be reviewed and commented on at each step of the case review process by those activities that have the analytic and historic background necessary to put the case in proper context.

All of this was unknown to me at the time, and I was more concerned with Harvey's puzzling and unexplained broadside. However, shortly after he gave me the bad news that my job was about to be abolished, I received news indicating otherwise. In October 1991 General Vessey returned to Hanoi on another visit during which he met with senior Vietnamese officials, including the Prime Minister and Foreign Minister. The purpose of his visit was to iron out further details of the POW/MIA office, along with certain actions the Vietnamese were expected to take in order to rapidly increase progress. Our unilateral discussions concerning negotiating strategy for Vessey's meetings with the Vietnamese leadership took place at the Le Thach guesthouse, where Vessey had a special suite reserved for him by the Vietnamese Foreign Ministry's protocol office. After a sweep, a communications security specialist accompanying Vessey located ten "hot spots" where listening devices had been placed in Vessey's room. We resorted to communicating between ourselves with special masks designed to thwart eavesdropping by our hosts. After he was satisfied that he had a solid grasp of the situation, Vessey attended an executive meeting with Foreign Minister Nguyen Manh Cam. I did not attend the meeting, but soon after it adjourned senior Communist cadre lined up to shake my hand while telling me "congratulations, you are still the American representative in Vietnam." Shortly after Vessey returned to Washington the State Department transmitted a joint State/Defense message instructing the American Embassy in Bangkok to inform the Government of Vietnam through the SRV Embassy in Bangkok that the U.S. Office for POW/MIA Affairs was now permanent.

Complete funding for our new office also began to gain momentum. Currently our office was being funded out of the CILHI's budget. On September 26, 1991, Senator Frank Murkowski, (R, AK) spoke on the Senate floor to offer an amendment to H.R. 2521, "Making appropriations for the Department of Defense for the fiscal year ending September 30, 1992, and for other purposes." Murkowski offered the amendment on behalf of himself, Senator Mitchell and Senator McConnell, and joined by Senators John Kerry, Bob Kerry, McCain, Danforth, Leahy, Cranston and Pell. The amendment called for the provision of $5 million for our new office, which Murkowski described as "embarrassingly underequipped." According to Murkowski's wording: "Their needs are simple indeed, a few copy machines, a fax machine, a water purification unit. In addition there is a need for transportation equipment such as vans, motorcycles and a helicopter." Although our office had opened in May on a temporary basis, Murkowski correctly listed the actual day that I returned to Hanoi from temporary exile due to the Party Congress: July 8, 1991. The Senator from Alaska sealed his legislative initiative by stating "Mr. President, I'd like to thank the co-sponsors to this amendment and the bipartisan spirit with which it was received. In addition, I believe we will owe our gratitude to General Vessey and his staff, especially Mr. Bill Bell, the Director of the U.S. POW/MIA office in Hanoi."

I felt honored by Murkowski's remarks and his inclusion of a helicopter in the amendment was a huge relief. I saw the helicopter as a potential lifesaver and the most critical item contained in the amendment. At the same time however, the mention of $5 million for funding our office was an immediate cause for concern. I knew we truly needed the money, but I also knew that funds of this magnitude might catch the attention of the CINCPAC staff in Hawaii. The CINCPAC Headquarters had traditionally ignored anything even remotely connected to POW/MIA, but if our priority was being raised and new money was being appropriated at a time when U.S. forces were winding down in the

Philippines and other parts of the Pacific Theater, the new money might be tempting. Once word was out regarding our new funding, I could envision the CINCPAC staff spending almost the entire amount simply traveling back and forth to Vietnam in order to form their own perception of what we really needed in order to accomplish our mission.

In early November, I was informed that I was being called to testify before the Senate's Select Committee on POW/MIA Affairs. Prior to my departure the Communist cadre with whom I dealt with on a routine basis were unusually cheerful and upbeat. I gained the impression that they perceived the Select Committee's hearings on the POW/MIA issue as some type of important mile marker affecting the budding bilateral relationship between the two countries. As a result, the Communists tried to pump me for some indication as to what the American position might be. I explained that by the nature of the manner in which the hearings would be conducted, the testimony of those appearing would not always be unilateral and spontaneous. I told them that to a certain degree, such testimony largely would be dependent on the questions posed to the individuals testifying by the Committee members. During the course of the field investigations I had been quite candid with my interlocutors. I told them I believed they were not affording us genuine cooperation, especially in resolving the last-known-alive discrepancy cases. My candor caused the Communists to be concerned that I might be just as straightforward with the Committee about these incidents.

On one occasion during Harvey's visit to Hanoi, the Communists even went so far as to corner him in my presence and express their concern about what my testimony might be. Harvey only smiled them off, as he knew that I, as well as the men working for me, had just gone through several agonizing years in Vietnam, and that I wasn't about to provide cover for the Communists because they could have been far more cooperative given the political will to do so. I took their "concern" as a veiled threat about my testimony.

Despite the warning by my counterparts, when I departed Vietnam for Washington, I was prepared to render my own opinions to the Select Committee, regardless of the consequences. In regards to Communist cooperation in carrying out our work, I was determined to give credit where it was due but at the same time make known to the Committee my areas of "concern." I realized that a great deal of skepticism existed on the part of POW/MIA family members, veterans and activists concerning the potential impact of the Committee's efforts on the national casualty resolution process, but I tried to be optimistic, hoping that the Committee members would keep the best interests of the missing men and their families at the forefront of their inquiry. However, I was about to learn a valuable lesson in political correctness and about how governments really work, from both the Senate Select Committee and the Communist Party of Vietnam.

Chapter Fourteen

Bill Bell Crosses Over

WHEN I ARRIVED at the Pentagon in early November 1991, I checked in with my POW/MIA colleagues from DIA. Shortly thereafter Harvey informed me that a meeting had been arranged with the CINCPAC J-3, Major General George Christmas, to coordinate the JCRC testimony. Only two JCRC personnel would be speaking to Congress: Bill Gadoury and myself. Gadoury was still assigned to the JCRC Liaison Office in the Bangkok Embassy, and while I would be testifying primarily on our operations in Vietnam, as the resident specialist on Laos, Gadoury would speak regarding our efforts there.

This was my first meeting with Christmas, and I knew little about the man. When Gadoury and I reported to a small room deep inside the huge Pentagon where Christmas was waiting for us, he informed us that the purpose of our meeting was to conduct a "murder board." I had never heard of a "murder board," but I soon learned that the unusual procedure was actually a training session in which personnel scheduled to testify before legislative committees were coached in advance to ensure that the desired responses were presented to Congressional investigators. Still, when Christmas handed both Gadoury and me folders containing over one hundred potential questions, I was somewhat taken aback. The questions provided to us were titled "POW/MIA Affairs Testimony, 'Murder Board' Questions (J1)."

However, the real shocker occurred when Christmas produced yet another list with prepared answers for each of the possible questions. I had been led to believe that the reason we had traveled from literally the other side of the world was to enlighten members of Congress responsible for oversight concerning the actual situation on the ground in Indochina, particularly regarding the status of the accounting efforts. Although Christmas never actually directed Gadoury or me to respond to questions with only the answers provided, that was the implication as we sat across the table from him while he played the role of Committee members.

Although Christmas seemed to think the rehearsal was amusing, I thought to myself that if the families find out, the "conspiracy" theory would be raised again regarding what might be construed as an effort to purposely mislead Congress. Only one question touched on the sensitive live American issue. Our canned answer was: "We have as yet found no evidence that prove unaccounted for Americans are alive in Southeast Asia. This is why we take reports of Americans alleged to be alive so seriously and attempt to pursue them aggressively."

While some families welcomed the hearings, for a variety of reasons, the National League was opposed, and their Board drafted a resolution against the formation of the committee. Others expressed concern about the paramount presence on the Committee of the Chairman, Senator John Kerry. Having achieved decorated veteran status, Kerry had returned home and made a crucial decision to turn his back on the troops still fighting the war. His public opposition to the Vietnam War, including his membership in the "Veterans Against the War" organization, lead to his disdainful testimony on the war in 1971 in front of a Congressional hearing, and his alleged act of throwing his medals over the White House fence in a symbolic gesture of repudiation of the war, fostered suspicion as to his true motivation in aggressively seeking the Chairmanship.

Kerry frequently kindled the fires of criticism by egotistically asking almost anyone who questioned his subsequent Committee actions by asking: "are you decorated?" The implication being that Kerry considered himself a hero, and he looked down upon anyone who wasn't. To make matters worse, as the Committee drew to a close, and it became apparent that Kerry considered opening ties with Vietnam the most effective way of getting answers to the fate of the missing men, a position vehemently opposed by the majority of the families, his own familial ties with the owners of a large international corporation, Collier Forbes International—a company that would later receive the first foreign owned real estate license from Communist authorities in Hanoi—made family members and activists very concerned by the possibility that Kerry might be sacrificing their desires to realize personal financial gain from a rapid normalization of relations with Vietnam. When after the closing of the Committee his main staffer, Frances Zwenig, became a primary member of the U.S.-Vietnam Trade Council, any doubts held by family members were erased. Ultimately, Zwenig became the President of this organization designed to promote trade between the two countries. The Council heavily pushed for normalization of relations, Export-Import

Bank financing, and the Bi-Lateral Trade Agreement, which was signed in 2001. Not surprisingly, when it came to POW/MIA, they always lauded Vietnamese cooperation, since the issue of the missing men was an obstacle standing in the way of economic ties.

Since Zwenig was Kerry's main Legislative Assistant, she served as the primary coordinator throughout the November hearing. Like a stage director, Zwenig constantly scurried around the hearing chamber rearranging the schedules for witnesses giving testimony and passing out notes to staff assisting Committee members. Although openly friendly to me during her visit to our Hanoi office during the fall of 1991, by the time the hearings began in November she had transformed into a frigid and detached bureaucrat. Her attention was riveted solely on her preplanned script, and she seemed determined that the hearings would unfold exactly as planned.

Perhaps the only member of the Committee who enjoyed the trust and respect of the families, and concurrently the contempt of the government folks, was the Committee's Vice Chairman, Senator Bob Smith, (R, NH). Although until recently most Committee members, excluding Senator Charles Grassley, (R, IA), had ignored the POW/MIA issue altogether, or at best rendered occasional lip service, Smith had for years lent his full support to the families. In addition to being a former Navy Seaman and Vietnam veteran, since becoming a member of the House of Representatives in the mid-1980s, Smith had devoted one full-time staff member to work the POW/MIA issue, always pressing each consecutive administration in upholding the nation's moral obligation to the missing men. Surprisingly, I discovered that in regards to Senator John McCain, most family members were very suspicious of his attitudes toward them. Despite being an ex-POW, or perhaps because of it, McCain had not supported the family's quest over the years.

In addition to Gadoury and myself as JCRC representatives, the Committee was scheduled to hear testimony at this opening hearing from the Commander of U.S. Pacific Forces, Admiral Charles Larson, as well as Major General Christmas, members of the DIA, elected officers from the Veteran Service Organizations, the POW/MIA family organizations, and a small number of individual family members. From the outset of the hearings there was clearly a degree of camaraderie between certain members of the Committee and some of the individuals testifying. For example, Senator McCain had been a roommate of Admiral Larson during the time both men attended the Naval Academy. The obvious bond between McCain and Larson was probably strengthened by the fact that McCain's father had once occupied Larson's position. Committee member and former Marine Colonel Senator Charles Robb had served with Christmas in the Corps, and both had participated in the bloody battle for retaking the ancient imperial capital of Hue during the 1968 "Tet" offensive. Due to the long-standing friendships, when the high-ranking CINCPAC officers took their places at the witness table, the smiles and nods gave the impression of a reunion.

When it came time for me to testify I felt somewhat uncomfortable sitting in the center of a huge chamber before distinguished members of Congress while the public, primarily family members and veterans, packed the seats to my rear. Media people armed with cameras and microphones filled the area between the witness table and the rostrum where the Committee was seated. At the last moment Colonel John Cole, the Chief of the DIA's "Stony Beach" live-sighting report investigation team, joined Gadoury and I at the witness table.

As the hearings began, things proceeded smoothly. Although Christmas had done a fairly thorough job of rehearsing us, some questions posed by the Committee had apparently not been anticipated. One question I was asked was whether anyone had ever restrained my efforts to find unaccounted for personnel, or had diverted or covered up information that I had provided. This particular question hit a sore spot with me because over the years I had argued with Harvey and the JCRC analysts concerning the editing of our field reports by the JCRC headquarters. I felt it was done primarily to isolate information contained in our reports down to the point that it could be correlated to only one individual or loss incident. The concern about listing more than one individual or loss incident in the same report resulted from the requirement that the analysts in the headquarters forward copies of all reports correlated to a specific individual to their next-of-kin. This created a substantial administrative workload for the analysts, and they welcomed any opportunity to reduce the number of reports being disseminated. Although investigators in the field often included their own field analysis as to which individuals the reports might possibly correlate, in many instances all references to specific individuals or case numbers were removed before the reports were published.

For me, the altering of reports was a major concern, as the investigators and the analysts had different goals in using intelligence gained from the information reports. For investigators the main objective in interviewing Sources was to obtain the maximum amount of usable information in the shortest time possible. We were concerned with the amount of time spent with each Source due to the relatively large number available for interview.

Usable meant different things to analysts and investigators given their separate responsibilities. Once the information was collected the analysts were more concerned with correlating the resultant intelligence to an individual. For the investigator, however, there were several other important points of consideration. For example, one of the investigator's primary interests was to be able to use the information in order to actually travel to the area mentioned in the report and locate a camp, gravesite, or crash site on the ground, not only to recover the remains of any one individual mentioned in the basic report, but also to investigate the area in order to determine whether other Americans had been detained or buried in the same area. Another important consideration was whether there were other loss incidents in the same area with personnel who had survived, or who were presumed dead based solely on circumstantial evidence. The altering of reports created a problem for the investigators because there was no way to cross reference camp locations with the men missing in the same areas.

This also impacted on the ability of both investigators and policy makers to monitor Communist policy regarding manipulation of the casualty resolution process. For example, in 1980 I interviewed a refugee in the Philippines who provided a first hand account of his observation of an American aircraft shot down by a missile in the area of the Uong Bi power plant in Quang Ninh province, North Vietnam. Based on the time, location and circumstances I listed a possible correlation of the report to case number 0220 involving Commander Billie J. Cartwright and Lieutenant Edward F. Gold, both Navy and both MIA. When the report reached the JCRC headquarters it was altered and the reference to case number 0220 removed. I was particularly interested in this report because according to the witness, shortly after the crash, Communist officials arrived at the scene and photographed the wreckage of the aircraft as well as the burial of the two American aviators. In 1982, pursuant to an announcement of a pending remains repatriation by Vietnam in conjunction with a visit to Hanoi by members of the Vietnam Veterans of America, on July 1, 1982, the JCRC Liaison Office in Bangkok delivered to the SRV Embassy in Bangkok a narrative concerning case number 0220.[1] On October 14, 1982 the SRV repatriated a set of remains alleged to be Cartwright, but after examining the remains the CILHI concluded that the remains were those of Air Force Captain Robert D. Trier, case 0216. In his debriefing a survivor of the 0216 incident reported that he heard gunfire near his position shortly after he touched down, and Communist officials informed him that Trier had been killed while resisting capture. Although Trier's remains were repatriated, Communist officials provided no information regarding his death. I believed that the information in the report I collected in the Philippines had policy implications. The Communists had confused the remains of Trier with Cartwright in the 0220 incident, even though Communist officials photographed the wreckage of the 0220 aircraft and the burial of the bodies. Yet, neither the bodies nor any information from Cartwright's incident was forthcoming. This was another clear example of manipulation on the part of the Communists, but once the report was changed to "uncorrelated," the policy implications went into a black hole.

During the hearing Kerry also asked me if I had any indication of a "cover-up." I responded that I didn't have any such indication, but in my opinion there were instances where certain information had not been acted on. While I wasn't specific, my response to Kerry's question was based on my knowledge of instances where detailed reports indicating that live Americans were being held had been received but no timely action was taken due to the chaotic situation in Vietnam in the waning months of the war. Information in this category included the reports indicating that live Americans were being held in Tay Ninh province and Cambodia during the fall of 1974. Already acutely aware of the inaction problem, Smith interrupted Kerry to ask me if I was referring to incidents in the past, to which I replied in the affirmative. Smith noted he had heard the same problem addressed by some of my colleagues who had already testified before the Committee in earlier sessions.

Senator Hank Brown, a former OV-1 pilot and Forward Air Controller (FAC) who served in I Corps, then raised the thorny issue of cooperation from the Communist governments in conducting our operations. He asked the three of us whether we had ever been able to gain unfettered access to locations in Vietnam, Laos or Cambodia. After we replied in the negative, Brown quickly summarized his perception of this major problem by stating "So the fact is, we've never had an ability to follow up on reports without the SRV Government going along and having notice?" I appreciated Brown's question because I believed it was fundamental to an honest and objective accounting for our men. I also hoped his question would put Communist officials of all three countries on notice that we would soon be demanding unannounced inspections of reported detention sites and unfettered access to genuine witnesses.

During the exchange with Brown I deliberately raised the critical issue of transportation for our personnel entering the field. In an attempt to gain support for our use of U.S. helicopters, I informed Brown that I had been involved in negotiations with the Communists and that they were currently considering our use of civilian helicopters on a "joint venture" basis.

As I mentioned earlier, it was my belief that with U.S. helicopters, the level of safety would be much higher. Moreover, the DOD and the JCRC had recently been discussing the possibility of sending Vietnamese pilots to the States for training, and the possibility of joint aircrews and joint maintenance had also been debated. I considered the aging Soviet aircraft "accidents waiting to happen." Much to my dismay, my predictions eventually proved correct. In April 2001, a helicopter carrying American and Vietnamese POW/MIA officials crashed, killing all abroad, and consequently halting operations for several months.

In considering the issue of field inspections to sites where Americans were reportedly observed, Brown questioned the value of relying on records provided by the Communists in conjunction with preplanned trips to the field. Although I understood his concern I felt obligated to point out to Brown that approximately one half of the 105 live sighting reports pending investigation at the time pertained to Americans who were said to be living freely among the Vietnamese people. I also reminded Brown that when Representative Sonny Montgomery's Congressional Task Force on POW/MIA visited Vietnam during December 1975, the Communists announced that there were no Americans remaining in Vietnam, even though Private Robert Garwood was residing not far from where the Task Force received the terse reply from Vietnamese Prime Minister Pham

Van Dong. I further explained to Brown that during a meeting between Senator Kerry and senior Vietnamese officials that I attended in August 1991, I had asked the Communists for clarification concerning Garwood during the visit by the Montgomery POW/MIA Task Force. According to the Communists, they failed to reveal the presence of Garwood to Montgomery for two stated reasons: first, Garwood had crossed over to Communist forces, and second, Garwood had requested that they not reveal his presence to the U.S. Government. If that was their policy, then it held much wider implications for other men.

Senator Chuck Grassley, a veteran of the Korean War, then honed in on his apparent perception of possible Communist duplicity in conducting the field investigations. As a comparison Grassley recalled past incidents involving DOD contractors where the DOD had forewarned the contractors in advance of inspections in order for the contractors to conceal fraud, waste and abuse. Grassley's contention was that by giving the Communists any advance notice of our intended investigation targets they would be in a position to stage the scene and orchestrate witnesses. Grassley's suspicion was that they would move prisoners out of the area before we could arrive. I found it difficult to argue with his logic, but I did indicate that in at least some cases I felt we would be able to conduct operations on a one-day notice. My reasoning was that if we could negotiate with the Communists to accept a one-day requirement regarding the general area and not announce the specific target site until we were in route, we had at least some chance of conducting an objective investigation. I felt that it would be difficult, if not impossible for us to gain approval from the Communists for no-notice takeoffs, if for no other reason due to the safety factor and requirements for filing flight plans. I also mentioned the importance of continuing to locate independent Sources in refugee camps, no longer under the control of the Communists, for information to supplement our investigations on the ground inside Vietnam, a program that had recently lapsed. Trying to be straightforward with Grassley, and at the same time feeling somewhat embarrassed after having been coached by Christmas the previous day, I apparently fueled the fires of the Senator's suspicion by openly admitting to him that during our earlier investigations we had detected signs indicating that the Communists had been involved in rehearsing witnesses.

Then came the question everyone dreaded. Senator Hank Reid asked all of us "did any of you have any information or knowledge or belief that there were Americans alive in Vietnam after Operation Homecoming terminated?" As I was asked to respond first, many different issues raced through my mind as I considered my answer. At first I thought to myself, "what's going to happen when I answer yes," but then I thought about the Americans who were last known alive at the time of their loss incidents with absolutely no evidence indicating death, either wartime or current. I also recalled the numerous informal sessions spent with colleagues working on the issue, many of whom believed that men were left behind after 1973. Some of us had even picked out candidates from the POW/MIA photo book for correlation to unidentified individuals remaining in Vietnam after 1973 depicted in composite photos compiled with the help of Sources. I also felt compelled to consider the results of our ongoing case investigations in Vietnam, especially those associated with the COSVN Security Camp. Additionally, I knew from talking with CILHI personnel that the Communists had returned two "fresh" remains in the past few years that according to the experts, neither of the men had died prior to 1975. In fact one of the two bodies still had a considerable amount of flesh attached to the skeleton. Due to its condition the CILHI staff had named the unidentified body "Stinky."

Despite knowing the firestorm it would create both in America and in Vietnam, I felt compelled to answer Reid's question in the affirmative.[2] My response resulted in a momentary silence followed by gasps and murmurs from Committee staff members and spectators. As the brief period of calm gradually became a series of excited conversations among small clusters of people huddled throughout the chamber, members of the media hurriedly worked their way forward blinding us with a flurry of brilliant flashes. Like British regulars assaulting Bunker Hill, the journalists closed on the witness table, kneeling and firing their cameras at me. The following day my photograph appeared on the front page of USA Today. Startled by the response and unsure what the reaction by other members of the Committee might be, I tried to maintain my composure and continue answering their questions. When pressed for more specific details by Reid as to how many Americans were left behind after Operation Homecoming, I quickly came up with the figure "ten or less." Reid was also interested to know if we had any knowledge of any Americans being transferred from Vietnam to another country. Cole and Gadoury (who had made negative replies to Reid's earlier question), and I all indicated that we did not possess such information, but I did add the caveat that based on my understanding of the testimony provided by a defecting mortician, who reported observing at least three Americans alive in Vietnam up until 1979, such a possibility did exist.

Members of the Committee then focused on associated issues such as the question of what constitutes evidence in evaluating a live sighting report. Smith seemed to feel that the evidentiary standards were so high as to preclude confirmation of a live sighting report. Kerry inquired about my knowledge of official U.S. efforts to rescue live Americans after the war. I informed him that I was aware of only one such operation that occurred during 1981 in Laos. Kerry also asked me about the case of Robert Garwood, and I explained to him that after he was captured in 1965, other POWs held in the same area with Garwood were aware of his whereabouts until sometime in 1969. At that point our intelligence became inconclusive, and he did not firmly reappear until after 1975 when he was observed by South Vietnamese prisoners in prison camp in the north, where he worked repairing electrical generators, hanging electrical wire and translating American military technical manuals in order to assist the Communists in assembling captured U.S. military equipment.

Senator John McCain wanted to know whether I had knowledge of anyone other than McKinley Nolan being alive after Operation Homecoming. I told him I did. He also asked me if other than the fact that the U.S. withdrew from Vietnam, were there any other reasons the reports I had mentioned were not acted upon. I told him that in my opinion the reports of live Americans were not acted on due to the inadequacy of the information (the two source rule), and the fact that we no longer had access to the area where the men were held. Still not satisfied McCain asked me specifically if there was any other reason, and I told him no.

Grassley broached the subject of Communist misinformation on the POW/MIA issue. In responding I deferred to the DIA Special Office for POW/MIA Affairs. I had attended DIA briefings where charts and graphs had been prepared regarding Grassley's area of interest, but I felt that I didn't have enough information to go into details on this subject. I knew that the DIA was convinced that the Ministry of Public Security was manipulating the issue, and that most key members of the Special Office for POW/MIA Affairs had carefully studied the extensive Rand Corporation study on Communist manipulation of the French POW/MIA issue. The DIA investigators had also created diagrams clearly showing the connections between those providing information and Vietnam's Intelligence and Security Services, so I decided to leave it to them to enlighten Committee members regarding this aspect. Following up on this at a later time, the Committee's legal counsel, Mr. William Codinha, interviewed DIA personnel on February 12, 1992. Codinha was informed that the DIA experts believed that the "North Vietnam Government" was behind the dissemination of dog tags and human skeletal remains. The DIA experts also told Codinha that they believed the Communists were holding some 450 American remains and that "cooperation on the POW/MIA issue was to bring in revenue."

Senator Grassley asked us what improvements the U.S. Government could make to help us do a better job. Gadoury seemed to think we didn't need any. According to him, all we needed was a "mechanism" for gaining access to the countries where our men were missing. Cole, however, answered differently. Apparently concerned with what was on the horizon, Cole made two emphatic points. First, he stressed the need for experienced personnel. He then focused on a topic of concern for everyone who had been working on the project for the past several years: reorganization. A seasoned officer with many years in uniform, Cole had been wounded in action and awarded the Silver Star for gallantry during a tour in Vietnam's Central Highlands. Having seen the detrimental effects of micromanagement by senior staff during his career, he realized that bigger was not necessarily better. Cole advised the Committee that only yesterday he had learned that the total POW/MIA effort would be reorganized as a CINCPAC Joint Task Force. Cole then put his career on the line by stating: "As one of the operators down at the lowest levels, all I ask is, whatever we've got going now not be disrupted by the coming organization or reorganization. We got the apparatus in place, we're getting the qualified people, let's go with it."

Cole's remarks were probably a source of comfort for MIA family members because during his earlier testimony, Christmas had raised eyebrows with his version of a command-level casualty resolution concept. Exhibiting a strange lack of caution, Christmas shocked both family members and investigators alike when he publicly blurted his intention to quickly resolve the complex POW/MIA cases by organizing a "Desert Storm type roll across Vietnam." Apparently Christmas believed that only remains needed to be recovered from a bunch of well-defined gravesites, and all we needed to do was go in and police them up. Christmas' poorly defined statement later resulted in a strong reaction by the wary Communist regime in Vietnam.

The remarks by both Christmas and Cole caught me off guard. Up to that point I hadn't realized that a rapid "roll across Vietnam" operation was even on the drawing board. When Grassley shifted his attention to me I told the Committee that I agreed with everything Cole had just said, adding that the need for experienced personnel in the analytical section was also critical. I also stressed the importance of the recent DIA live sighting investigations being conducted, with coordination between our refugee interviewers and Cole's team during the process in order to confirm or deny what we were hearing from witnesses introduced to us by Communist officials in the field. In the back of my mind I considered that investigators would not be able to carry any sensitive classified information into the Communist countries where we were working, especially satellite imagery. But I was convinced a small DIA element, such as Cole's "Stony Beach" team, based in close proximity to the target area, could successfully complete the complex task. Since Cole's live sighting investigation team was based at the American embassy in Bangkok, a mere ninety minutes by air from Hanoi, Saigon, Vientiane or Phnom Penh, I felt certain that rapid deployment would be possible once we had a firm commitment from the Communists to do so. At the same time, I felt that my presence in Vietnam as head of the POW/MIA Office would enable me to provide quality control in order to ensure that the investigations were thorough.

Senator Herb Kohl from Wisconsin aimed his questions at the problem of declassifying information on the POW/MIA subject for release to the families of the missing men. Working with the information on a daily basis I had come to the conclusion that much of it was over-classified. I also knew we would have a problem with the security of such information when we carried it into Communist countries during our missions. Having already discussed this particular issue with my colleagues at length I decided to speak my mind and tell the Senator how I felt about it. I told Kohl that with the exception of the 105 live sighting reports currently under investigation, I believed all other files should be declassified and placed in the public domain. Seemingly surprised and relieved at my suggestion, Kohl was obviously ready to move forward in what he termed a release of information that "might help clarify some of the anguish and concern by families that are trying to find out everything they can about the MIAs." I couldn't have agreed with him more, but at the same time I realized that government bureaucrats would not warmly receive my statement, especially those in the intelligence agencies who considered information as power. Once released, people could start poring over the reports, and begin questioning the DIA and JCRC analytical conclusions, something both agencies desperately wanted to avoid.

Senator Nancy Kassenbaum tried to appear interested in the proceedings, but had apparently done little homework. At times she seemed somewhat detached and disoriented, especially during periods of rapid exchanges. Senator Tom Daschle, a former Captain in Air Force Intelligence, drifted in and out of the hearings, seemingly engrossed with other hearings or legislative matters dealing with issues unrelated to POW/MIA. While present in the hearing chamber he mainly sat quietly starring out into space. Senators Jesse Helms and Bob Kerry seemed genuinely concerned about the issue of missing American servicemen, but at the same time appeared to have precious little time available to learn such an intricate subject.

After indicating I was reluctant to provide specific details in a public forum concerning live Americans remaining in Vietnam after Operation Homecoming, I was asked to give additional testimony in a closed session. After I was instructed to report to the Senate Security Room, a military officer from the office of the Assistant Secretary of Defense for International Security Affairs, Major Charles Gittens, offered to accompany me and lend assistance during the questioning. According to senior officers present at the time, Major Gittens was an attorney from the Judge Advocate General and he would be with me in the event that Senate Investigators attempted to "beat up on you." Gittens would later gain some degree of fame by representing the Captain of the submarine USS *Greenville* after it collided with a Japanese fishing trawler off the coast of Hawaii on February 9, 2001. Although I had no problem with a JAG officer sitting in on the closed hearing, I would later learn that by acquiescing to the presence of Gittens I was making a costly mistake.

From the outset, Francis Zwenig managed the closed hearing. Committee Legal Counsel William Codinha assisted Zwenig in asking me a number of questions taken from a prepared list that apparently included interrogatories from all the Senators who had participated in the open session earlier that day. Zwenig appeared to be interested in developing leads directed toward several aspects of the POW/MIA issue. Focusing intently on her tightly held list she went back through previous years asking me about efforts I had been involved in, including classified project Doberman Dawn. Zwenig touched briefly on the 1981 reconnaissance mission in Central Laos conducted by the CIA with the Delta Force on standby in Thailand. I explained to Zwenig that I was sure the Laotian Special Guerrilla Unit personnel recruited from refugee camps by the CIA to undertake the mission were able to reach the target area in the Gnommarath area because of electronic monitoring devices placed in their equipment.

Then Zwenig honed in on the testimony I provided to the committee concerning live Americans left behind in Vietnam after Operation Homecoming. In response to her questioning I told her about the report in the fall of 1974 indicating that five live Americans, including a Caucasian named "Benny" were being held in the C-53 camp in Tay Ninh province. I explained that at the time the reports were received the American intelligence community was not able to confirm their presence due to the deteriorating situation and eventual overthrow of the Saigon Government. I further explained how during the course of our postwar field investigations in Vietnam I was able to confirm the location of the secret camp, and after submitting my investigation report the DIA correlated the report of the American in the camp called "Benny" to Airman Benny Dexter, case 0333. I also brought Zwenig up to date on the reports of two live Americans held in the Mimot area of Kampong Cham province, Cambodia just across the border from Tay Ninh province where the C-53 camp was located. I offered my opinion that while the DIA analysts had been able to identify only one of the two men as McKinley Nolan, based on the physical description and the phonetic pronunciation of the name "Chaigar" used by the second man, I believed that he was actually Dallas Pridemore, who was abducted from his home in the outskirts of Saigon at night after being betrayed by his Vietnamese fiancé, who later resettled in the U.S.

I also related to Zwenig my opinions regarding three Caucasians observed in Hanoi by the Vietnamese Mortician in the area of the Ministry of National Defense Compound in downtown Hanoi during the period 1974 to 1979. I opined that although I had no concrete proof as to the identities of the three men, but based on the circumstances of their disappearance, the type of work they were reportedly engaged in after the war, their physical descriptions and their resemblance to composite artist sketches completed with the help of the Mortician, I had chosen three candidates: Charles Duke, Kit Mark, and Jimmy Malone. I also mentioned the fact that Duke and Mark had been employed as jet aircraft technicians, which matched information in other reports indicating that American personnel were held after the war to work on jet aircraft at a base north of Hanoi. I figured that with enough imagination the DIA analysts might try to explain away the Mortician's sighting of the two aircraft technicians by claiming that they were actually Soviet advisors or technicians from some other Communist bloc country. Yet since we had already raised the issue with the Vietnamese, obviously they could have provided us with the identities of the two men regardless of their nationality or origin, which they have not done. Lastly, I apprised Zwenig that although the Mortician had identified one of the Americans he described in making the composites as Robert Garwood I believed he was mistaken and the person he thought to be Garwood was actually Kit Mark.

The other man I mentioned to the Committee was Navy Lieutenant Clemie McKinney, who was shot down in his F-4J aircraft just below the DMZ on April 14, 1972. According to reports from an American eyewitness at the time, McKinney's aircraft was hit by anti-aircraft fire during a bomb run and exploded on impact. No ejections were observed and no electronic beepers were heard. Based on the account provided by the eyewitness it was believed that there was no chance of survivors. Another aviator, Lieutenant Joseph G. Greenleaf, was also in the aircraft. The Communists repatriated a set of unidentified remains on August 14, 1985, but the CILHI was not able to identify them until much later, announcing on February 8, 1988 that they were McKinney. Part of the problem was that the medical and personnel records held at the CILHI had listed McKinney as being Caucasian when in reality he was black. This snafu caused considerable grief for his family, who ultimately were successful in litigation resulting in a considerable sum of money being awarded to them. Based on the circumstances of the McKinney case and the condition of the remains, which indicated an absence of any physical trauma due to an aircraft crash, I believed that McKinney's remains were one of the two mentioned to me by CILHI staff as having died after 1975.

My opinion on the McKinney case was reinforced by a report I received from a Hong Kong refugee. According to the Source, sometime during April 1980 he had gone to fish at the Ben Hai River on the DMZ when he observed the body of a man who was reportedly an American. The Source heard from villagers that Public Security Forces killed the American during an escape attempt. I recalled the Source telling me the American had been shot in the leg. When McKinney remains were returned, part of a lower leg was missing. Considering all the available information I believed that both McKinney and Greenleaf should have the benefit of the doubt regarding survivability of the crash. We also later found information that we believed correlated to McKinney in that he survived the crash and supposedly died enroute to Hanoi. This also pointed out the fact that many times aircraft are seen to go in with no chutes, only to have the airmen turn up alive. Unfortunately, however, I was not able to develop any new leads on Greenleaf prior to my retirement, and this still weighs heavily on my mind.

As I outlined the information to Zwenig regarding the ten men I believed were left behind after Operation Homecoming, Gittens seemed shaken. I couldn't tell whether he was hearing about the highly classified reports for the first time, or if he already knew about the reports and was shocked that I would dare to share them with Senate staffers. After the closed session in the Senate room ended, Gittens acted coldly toward me as we headed to the Pentagon where members of the media and Pentagon spokesman Pete Williams were waiting to interview me. After the interviews I proceeded to dinner at the home of Air Force General Mike Ryan, where most of the senior personnel involved in the hearings had already gathered. Ryan seemed like a regular guy who was sincerely concerned about the fate of the missing men. I enjoyed a pleasant dinner at his home and throughout the evening no one seemed upset with me regarding my testimony. Later that evening my former commander, General Robert C. Kingston, invited me out for drinks. Although we did touch several times on the POW/MIA subject and my work, he never questioned my reasoning for my responses to the Committee. When I went to bed that night I felt like I had been overly concerned about the reaction to my testimony.

The following morning, however, Gittens ended my barely decent interval when he walked into the office of the Assistant Secretary of Defense for International Security Affairs shouting loudly "Bill Bell crossed over, Bill Bell crossed over!" I heard this from a military officer who was working in the ISA office, and who made it a point to find me and tell me what happened. Gittens description of my testimony to the Senate Select Committee as "crossing over" was in effect an alarm to everyone that I had just gone from being a loyal, obedient civil servant serving at the beck and call of the bureaucracy, to the ranks of disgruntled family members, veterans and activists who were pressing the governments of America and Vietnam for more answers. As I sat dejected in a taxi headed for Washington National Airport I knew that there were some in the military establishment who would see me as a whistle blower, and they would be after my head. I also expected that my Vietnamese counterparts in Hanoi would have access to at least the public sessions of the hearings, and they would not be pleased that I expressed an opinion indicating that they held back American prisoners of war. During the flight back across the Pacific Ocean I had plenty of time to contemplate future field operations, and I steeled myself, making a personal vow to press ahead in demanding an honest accounting for my missing comrades. I could only hope that I would survive and continue to serve effectively through what lay ahead.

When my flight touched down at Bangkok's Don Muang airport, I hoped to simply sneak into the Embassy and drop off my passport for processing a new Vietnam visa, and then spend a few days with my family before returning to Hanoi. However, I'm never that lucky. As soon as I arrived, my stealth visit was interrupted when I was called into Ambassador David Lambertson's office for a meeting. I quickly learned that my return to Hanoi was being delayed indefinitely, as Vietnamese Foreign Ministry officials had just announced their intention to deny me a visa. The Ambassador explained that this situation had resulted in a volley of telephone calls and messages from irate members of Congress who were of the collective opinion that the Communists were out to intimidate me and any other American official who might testify in the future before Congressional committees on the POW/MIA issue. The Ambassador didn't blame me for the tense situation, but at the same time he frankly admitted that it was up to the Government of Vietnam as to who would be allowed into their country. He nevertheless offered to lobby with the Vietnamese for me, and to solve the problem as quickly as possible.

After he met with the Vietnamese Ambassador, Lambertson informed me that the main obstacle to my receiving a visa appeared to be merely a question of "documentation." Apparently the Communist officials in Hanoi had already received at least some advance information regarding my testimony before the Senate Select Committee, but they wanted to receive an official transcript of exactly what was said prior to letting me back in their country. I was told to hang loose for a few days while the Embassy Political Officer got everything sorted out. At that point I was feeling somewhat frustrated, but at the same time I felt it was important that the Communists understand that American hearings were not "for internal distribution only" like their Party Congresses in Hanoi, and as a government servant I had every right to speak my mind in my nation's capital to elected officials with responsibility for oversight. Moreover, I was convinced that America was on a course headed toward increased relations with Vietnam and I wanted to make sure that some concrete ground rules were in place before the politicians in Washington got carried away with signing agreements on everything else but POW/MIA. In that vein, I believed my remarks critical of Hanoi's actual level of cooperation would put Vietnamese officials on notice that token cooperation would not be acceptable to our government.

At this point in time the Communists had responded to some demands for progress in what were considered "bilateral humanitarian issues." Unfortunately, the concessions were easily made since every one of them benefited them more than us. For example, Vietnam was anxious to get rid of what they considered an embarrassing wartime stigma: children fathered during the war by American military and civilian personnel, called "Amerasian" kids. While negotiating with the U.S. the Communists were able to rid themselves of some 60,000 such children, including many that had been turned into the streets to live as vagabonds and petty criminals. While extracting what they clearly saw as a concession by America to Vietnam, the Communists were able to deceive world public opinion into believing that Vietnam was actually making a concession to the United States.

The same situation was applicable to the hundreds of thousands of former South Vietnamese civilian and military officials. The Communists quickly processed a large number of our former allies for resettlement in the States, especially those considered "incorrigible" or as "dangerous elements" by the Communist system. Outsiders also considered this a concession by Vietnam, but the Vietnamese viewed it quite differently. To them, more than 200,000 anti-Communists seeking both jobs and freedom were shipped to America under the State Department's "Orderly Departure Program." The aggressive purge of Vietnam's population not only provided the Communists with a much-needed source of revenue, but also allowed them to redirect internal security forces elsewhere, especially to the smoldering border with China.

Regardless, I was determined to get back to Hanoi to set high standards for case resolutions and be in a good position to negotiate for concessions from the Communists that would ensure the objectivity of our investigations in the field. Not that I didn't think other humanitarian issues were important, it was just that unlike the politicians, I couldn't allow myself to forget about the more than two thousand American servicemen still missing.

After a week I received a reentry visa from the SRV Embassy. Arriving in Hanoi I was met by the VNOSMP Deputy, Mr. Ngo Hoang. In a rather subdued manner Hoang told me that his superiors were upset with me concerning my testimony to the Senate Select Committee. Without being too specific, Hoang said that due to certain comments I had made on the subject of Americans remaining in Vietnam after 1973, he and other cadre working on the POW/MIA issue had been instructed by their superiors to treat me "differently" in the future. Hoang and the VNOSMP head, Ho Xuan Dich, had nevertheless interceded on my behalf in order to get my visa approved. Since up to that point I had never been treated exceptionally well, his news was not very encouraging. I soon learned, however, that I was not the only subject of the Communist leadership's criticism, because Hoang took the opportunity to express strong dissatisfaction on the part of his superiors for the "Desert Storm roll across Vietnam" comment made by Major General Christmas. Hoang said that by comparing America's recent military involvement in the Persian Gulf to upcoming operations to search for MIAs by troops of the Pacific Command, Christmas was sending a threatening message to both the government and people of Vietnam. Hoang went on to say that since the American war in Vietnam had still not faded from the minds of the people, Christmas was only making the situation more difficult.

Although initially somewhat cold toward me, within a matter of days the VNOSMP cadre were ready to go back into the field and continue our joint efforts. During the short break from our fieldwork due to the Senate hearings, the VNOSMP and the JCRC made some personnel changes in the offices of both sides and also on the joint field teams. I understood that on our side we were rotating assignments to allow more of our JCRC and CILHI personnel, as well as periodic specialized attachments, such as Explosive Ordnance Disposal and Medical Technicians, to gain experience. I could only assume that the Communists were doing likewise, but except for political cadre and intelligence and security personnel I was not able to detect any unusual additional specialty areas.

I did note one change when a People's Army of Vietnam Senior Colonel named Tran Van Bien suddenly appeared as a member on a Vietnamese investigation team. Bien differed somewhat from the usual cadre assigned to the VNOSMP in that rather than a political hack, he appeared to be a genuine war veteran with plenty of scars from bullets and shrapnel. Bien was also an expert at making herbal liquor *(thuoc bac)*, which he seasoned with various types of roots, reptiles and mushrooms to make a sort of "witches brew." Convinced that his mixture had magical powers leading to a marked increase in stamina and endurance, he often supplied me with samples, which I diplomatically accepted. Difficult to consume at first, I gradually developed a tolerance to his homemade potions. Somewhat stiff and aloof, in the beginning Bien's persona was difficult to fathom, but as time passed I came to admire him. Like most Communist cadre Bien was murky regarding his background, but he did reveal to me that he had participated in combat against U.S. forces in the DMZ area and I Corps. According to Bien, his final assignment in the war effort against us was in Quang Tri province where he had served as the Director of Reconnaissance for the 702nd Command during the 1972 summer offensive. Like other Communist cadre Bien was typically robotic to some degree, but he also outwardly appeared to be exceptionally straightforward and honest. Ultimately I saw Bien's assignment to the Vietnamese team contingent as a plus, but unfortunately, he was killed in the April 2001 helicopter crash.

On our side Gary Sydow from the DIA replaced Bob Destatte as my Researcher-Analyst in the Hanoi office. Sydow had served in South Vietnam in several key intelligence assignments at the national level during the war, and he proved to be a valuable asset. In addition to being an experienced analyst and researcher, Sydow had a knack for fluently speaking both "Pentagonese and Washingtonese," and this talent helped me immensely in my reporting and responses to queries from all quarters. Sydow had a good, albeit slightly dry, sense of humor and even on the darkest days in desolate Hanoi he could find some rays of light with his pragmatic, Will Rogers approach to life. I had a great deal of admiration and confidence in Sydow, and I felt that I didn't need to be overly concerned with the situation in Hanoi when I was on field team missions and far away from the office in remote areas of the country. To this day, Sydow continues to work on the issue at DPMO.

Once I settled back into our office at the Boss Hotel I began to scout the Hanoi area for a more permanent location for our office. Due to the trade embargo it was a very complicated matter to do any type of business in Vietnam, even for those of us who were there in an official capacity. In order to avoid violating any American laws we had to obtain a license from the Office of Foreign Assets Control of the Department of the Treasury. Finally armed with the proper license, I began seriously discussing rates for long-term rental of new office space in Hanoi. Unfortunately for me, in late 1991 the Communist Party of Vietnam was already in the planning stages for fleecing America, one dollar at a time. It was a strange situation indeed, because the Communist cadre believed that all Americans were not only rich but stupid as well. As I began to scour the Hanoi real estate scene, one thing that immediately became obvious was that, like everything else in the country, the Communist party also had its tentacles in the housing market. Since the "state" owned all real property in Vietnam, residents were merely "using" the property under the management of the Communist party. I encountered several situations where local residents initially indicated a willingness to rent property to the U.S. Government, but later changed their minds after being visited by Communist officials. On these occasions, local residents offered to rent old style French villas and fairly large office buildings at ridiculously low amounts, only to raise their prices to the opposite extreme after receiving official visits by Communist cadre after we departed.

Prices were so unrealistic that one had to wonder how they were able to come up with such weird sums. Although a small number of cadre had been sent abroad to study the housing market and real estate prices, apparently they came home with unrealistic attitudes to the effect that if property rented for $10 per square foot in Singapore and Hong Kong, it could go for no less in Hanoi, regardless of the fact that property in Hanoi had no power, water, sewer system and was in filthy, run down condition. My counterparts guided me to some buildings that they suggested were suitable, but proved to be ludicrous choices. Some examples include buildings next to the Mongolian and North Korean Embassies, the Headquarters of the Japanese Communist Party and the former Headquarters of the French Communist Party.

I spent considerable time looking at possible sites for long-term lease. One such building was a 10-storied masonry eyesore located in the city. When I went there it was already partially occupied by the French-owned oil company "Total." According to members of the "Total" staff, they had poured more than thirty million dollars into petroleum research in North Vietnam without even discovering the scent of oil. They had leased and remodeled the top five floors of the "Total" building and were now looking for a way out, since their board of directors had decided to call it quits and go home. When I sent the results of my survey of the "Total" building back to Hawaii the command, especially Harvey, was excited about the possibility of leasing the structure. However, after CINCPAC spent big bucks sending at least two teams of engineers to further survey the building, Communist officials decided that it wasn't available.

The hunt for a new office site continued for several months to the point that I came to realize that the Communists already had a particular facility in mind, and we would rent that facility or nothing. The site preordained for us proved to be a compound formerly occupied by Chinese military advisers providing military assistance during the war years. Australian personnel had also temporarily occupied the compound during the time that their embassy was under construction. The fenced-in compound with two houses and a storage building was located in Ba Dinh district in the northern part of the city. This facility ultimately became known as "The Ranch."

Looking for a new office site proved to be an excellent cover for learning the ins and outs of Hanoi. Over the years I had received a great deal of information, especially from disillusioned former Communist cadre who had defected to the West. I knew the residential addresses and off-duty hangouts of a large number of key players involved in the war and with US/Vietnam relations. By going to the addresses I was able to see just how the other half lived, or in this case, tiny minority. Despite their claims of a just society, there were two separate worlds in Vietnam, one for the people and one for high-ranking Communist cadre. Many of the cadre and their families occupied what at one time had been splendid French villas, most replete with gardens, ponds, elaborate balconies and wine cellars that had been converted to air raid shelters. The villas did have a certain amount of charm but many had been expanded with makeshift rooms added on to the original structures in order to accommodate grown children who married and started families of their own. During the office survey I banged on doors and made inquiries concerning rental availability at homes owned by some of Vietnam's elite, including the Vietnam Communist Party Secretary General, several PAVN general officers, and even the homes of some of the people on our list of potential Sources for POW/MIA information. I knew better than to directly contact cadre in sensitive positions, as the Communist officials working with our office arranged these interviews in facilities operated and controlled by the Party. But based on the level of interest shown by the Senate Select Committee in having American officials interview selected cadre for POW/MIA information, I also knew that we would soon be starting an Oral History Program. I calculated that it would be much harder for the Communists to deny knowledge of the whereabouts of these cadre if I had already pinpointed the locations of at least some of them.

In response to a question posed by Senator McCain as a follow-up to the Committee hearing, I began working on a list of potential interview subjects. Due to the time limitation I decided to put the interviewing of Sources who brought POW/MIA information, remains and personal effects to the office in the hands of the analysts, and I called upon my DIA Researcher to assist me. In this case it was Bob Destatte who had just returned from the Pentagon to rotate with Sydow. Between the two of us we came up with thirty-eight names of cadre to be interviewed, including thirteen general officers or senior party cadre with rank equivalent to that of a general officer. We selected those individuals who we believed could provide information based either on direct involvement with American POWs, or who had command-level knowledge and thus could provide leads for lower echelon Sources. While compiling the list of potential interviewees for the Oral History Program I also tasked Destatte to begin working on a list of wartime detention sites where a significant number of unidentified Americans had reportedly been held. Together we compiled a list of POW camps in Vietnam and Laos, including the Ho Chi Minh Trail. Although many of the sightings were cold by that time, I believed it important that we go to them and investigate, just in case there were any graves, any signs or markings left by inmates, or any witnesses who had lived in the area of the camps during the time they were being used to detain Americans. I was especially interested in interviewing any Montagnards, who routinely roamed the remote areas while hunting and gathering.

One camp we researched was the Lang Ta Camp, also called "Kou Boi Mountain." I had an idea that this was the main camp for Military Region Tri-Thien-Hue, one of the two Communist military regions in the northern part of South Vietnam. Reports indicated that at least ten American POWs had been held in the Lang Ta Camp, including Captain Floyd Thompson. Although Navy Lieutenant Everett Alvarez, Jr. was the longest held POW captured in North Vietnam, it was actually Thompson who had suffered the longest period of detention. In addition to Thompson, a helicopter crew downed in Quang Tri province was also held at the Lang Ta camp. With the exception of one crewmember who was executed while en route to the camp because he couldn't maintain the pace due to injuries, the other men from the helicopter were released during Operation Homecoming. Although six of at least ten POWs held in the camp were identified, no information was developed concerning the identity or fates of the remaining four.

Another camp of interest was the Nam Dong camp located in dense jungle southwest of Hue. The Nam Dong prison reportedly held four POWs during 1966. None of the reported four was ever identified. I had also researched another camp called Ta Pok, alias A Pok camp, located in the Vietnam-Laos border area also southwest of Hue. According to available information this camp was possibly associated with the case of Chief Warrant Officer Solomon Godwin, mentioned earlier. Camps used for evacuating captured Americans north along the Ho Chi Minh Trail were also a focus of attention. In researching these camps I found cases where live Americans were reportedly observed being moved north, but it was unclear as to whether they had ever reached their destination, believed to be camps in Hanoi, or similar camps already identified by photo analysts.

In addition to the Oral History and the POW camp lists we continued to address the subject of archival research. Although we had been into several lower level province museums, as well as the larger Central Military Museum in Hanoi, we still had not gained access to a significant number of sites believed to contain records that could help us. With these three programs running simultaneously, Oral History, Camps, and Records, I was convinced that we could furnish enough valuable leads to maintain the momentum of our Investigation Teams, which could in turn collect enough new information to keep our Search and Recovery Teams working full pace on excavations. Throughout the course of the planning stage I was unaware of exactly how much information concerning the efforts of our office was being passed by JCRC up the chain, but I wanted to make certain that our superiors at Defense, the Senate Select Committee on POW/MIA, and the MIA families were confident that we were off to a good start, and that we were being thorough in our efforts.

We also planned for eventual research regarding American casualties in Laos. Not that we in Hanoi expected to cover that country, but I did expect to be able to obtain information on Americans who were killed or captured in areas under wartime control of Vietnamese Communist Forces. For example, the Central Military Museum in Hanoi maintained some records and personal effects of our personnel lost in Laos. Although I did not initially place a great deal of emphasis on Cambodia, I was able to gather a sampling of material held by the Southwest Military Region Museum in Saigon, also called the Military Region 7 Museum, and a somewhat rudimentary museum in western Tay Ninh province near the border of Cambodia designed to illuminate the wartime contributions made by COSVN. Unspecific as to individual casualties, the material nevertheless allowed me to gain insight concerning the Vietnamese Communist wartime command and control system in Cambodia and was potentially helpful in developing new leads.

By the beginning of January 1992, the various investigation and collection projects of our office were beginning to take shape and I was optimistic concerning the possibilities of conducting sustained operations throughout Vietnam, as well as the adjacent border areas of both Laos and Cambodia. I realized it would be difficult to hold a steady pace, but now that we were permanently based in Vietnam and the requirement to constantly fly back and forth across the Pacific Ocean to our headquarters in Hawaii no longer existed, we were in a position to concentrate on investigating, rather than traveling. For the first time since the war ended it looked like it was finally "all systems go." With the promise of adequate funding still echoing in my ears, about the only thing I was still tense about was gaining real cooperation from the Communists. Having been directly involved in some manner in Vietnam since 1965, I had yet to see the Communists honor and correctly implement any agreement with any party. But I maintained an open mind and a wait-and-see attitude.

Unfortunately, just as the pace and scope of our operations increased, the JCRC headquarters decided to completely abandon the refugee interview program. As far as I was concerned this was a major mistake, because the refugees were a prime source of independent information. Many of the live-sighting reports scheduled for investigation were very complex, while others simply did not contain enough background information and pertinent details to facilitate a thorough field investigation. I felt it was ironic that as we were gaining access to areas of the country where live Americans were reportedly observed, the headquarters tossed the only source of independent verification we had in order to reassign our personnel to what I considered less important duties, primarily crash site excavations. My view was that since many of the crash sites had already been excavated and inventoried by the Communists, we were for the most part wasting government time and money. The crash site excavations required a relatively large number of American personnel who would have to be transported by aging Russian helicopters, so I constantly worried about the safety factor. Since I was somewhat vocal regarding this point, the CILHI personnel cringed when I offered the opinion that "all the bones in Indochina are not worth the life of one American serviceman or woman." I believed that even more when the helicopter crashed in 2001, killing all those people.

Although the JCRC refugee interview program was abandoned, there was at least some good news because the DIA's small "Stony Beach" contingent of intelligence collectors increased its efforts in canvassing the refugee population for information on the "live American" issue. The Stony Beach Team provided personnel to begin live-sighting investigations inside Vietnam, and in most of the same countries I had been covering throughout the 1980s. Working under my supervision and from a list containing 105 reports alleging that live Americans were remaining in Vietnam, the DIA collectors worked as field investigators. The two primary investigators were William Hutchinson and Thomas McKay. I had a great deal of confidence in both men. I knew that Hutchinson and McKay were not only diligent in their work and fluent Vietnamese speakers, they were both Vietnam veterans and completely dedicated to the resolution of what they saw as the single most important American issue in Vietnam. Both men had also worked with me for several years in the refugee interview program, and as a result had extensive knowledge concerning all areas of Vietnam.

Just as the POW/MIA office began to gain momentum, with sustained operations covering almost every work aspect, the looming reorganization cloud that had been gathering suddenly formed. We had been receiving sparse official news and considerable rumors that a big change was underway for the JCRC and the POW/MIA accounting process. Now we heard that the new organization would be called the Joint Task Force-Full Accounting. The first signs, however, materialized in the form of a message I received from Hawaii indicating that General Vessey would be arriving in Hanoi for a meeting with the Vietnamese, and that afterwards he wanted to see me. According to the same message, my old boss, General Robert C. Kingston, who was serving as Vessey's assistant, would accompany him. Included in the delegation was Major General Christmas, and Army Brigadier General Thomas H. Needham, the new Commander of the recently formed JTFFA that had just absorbed the JCRC. When so many Generals wanted to see me, my instincts sensed bad news. It appeared that the "one star" referred to by the visiting Congressman in Danang last year had been more than just a passing thought.

When the high level meetings concluded, Vessey and his entourage visited our office. Recently, Vessey had expressed a growing sense of optimism that the Communists were resigned to afford us genuine cooperation. After the latest sessions with various members of Vietnam's senior leadership, he seemed more reassured than ever, based I assume, on some intuition that alerted him to a future of guaranteed successes. Having worked on the issue for many years, as tempted as I was to allow this contagion to spread my way, without anything tangible to base these feelings on, I remained skeptical. Frankly, I don't know why Vessey began to change, but my fear was that after five years of working with the Vietnamese, he had developed what the State Department bureaucrats called "clientitis," the unconscious desire to make excuses for the other side. No doubt, he also wanted something to show for five years of work as the President's Special Emissary.

After I briefed them on the local situation, Vessey requested that I accompany him back to his VIP Suite at the Le Thach guesthouse for a private meeting. Walking back to his room with him, I had the impression that Vessey was somewhat nervous about what he planned to relate to me, and my earlier fears returned.

After being seated in a stiff-backed chair directly in front of me, Vessey talked about the new Task Force that had just been formed under Needham. Vessey went on to say that I had done a wonderful job in the years that I had been working the issue, but the new commander intended to make some basic changes in the way our organization was manned. After again reminding me of the good work I had done, Vessey dropped the proverbial bombshell by announcing that I would be replaced as Chief of the U.S. Office for POW/MIA Affairs by a military officer from the JTFFA.

At first I couldn't believe what I was hearing; that there must have been some type of misunderstanding. I had never been fired or replaced at anything in my life. Proper or not for a setting with a four star general, I could feel my emotions churning inside me. Rather than a participant, I felt as though I was an observer watching Vessey and someone else engaged in the conversation. I didn't look at Vessey; I looked through him. The scene before me turned to slow motion like a bad movie, and I saw fleeting but important events from my life flash into my memory.

The first thought that seared my brain was that Nova and Michael had died for nothing. It was simply a waste of their lives for me to have even been involved in the POW/MIA issue in the first place. As thoughts of them came roaring back to me, of how they died in such a terrible manner, I felt tears well up in my eyes. I thought of all the sacrifices my new family had made for me, the time away from home, from my children, the weeks spent on the road in god-forsaken refugee camps. Then another thought penetrated deeply into the inner reaches of my mind...since the room was bugged, those Communist bastards are sitting in the control room listening to me get fired and no doubt feeling thrilled by the prospect of having an inexperienced new office Chief represent America's interests in resolving the complicated issue. I knew intellectually that the position wasn't some birthright of mine, that one day I would have to leave, but I knew deep in my heart that this wasn't the right way or the right time.

Seeing that I hadn't appreciated his news, Vessey sought to console me by telling me that I would still play a key role in the issue, and that I shouldn't look at it as having been relieved, I was simply being "replaced due to the reorganization." Hardly encouraged by Vessey's words, I knew my Asian Communist counterparts would most likely see my situation not only as a serious loss of face for me, but a signal of a change in U.S. policy, most likely to their advantage. As if reading my mind Vessey then informed me that he was personally arranging for me to receive a promotion to the next higher grade. Surprised at this revelation, my next thought was that Vessey had never asked me what my current grade was. With an air of confidence Vessey smilingly told me that the promotion paperwork was already underway. Although Vessey's promotion remarks sounded too easy, I thought it might provide me with an avenue to perhaps retain some degree of face with the Communist cadre. Maybe, I hoped, I could still accomplish some good work without being further undermined.

After considering Vessey's good and bad news, I began to regain my composure. Although I was wary of the bureaucratic red tape that would be associated with a promotion I felt I could take Vessey at his word. After all, Vessey was not only an enlisted man who had worked his way up to four-star-general; like me he was a former Master Sergeant as well. I reasoned that anyone with his background would never promise a verbal promotion unless he was sure he could keep his word. I left the room somewhat ashamed that my counterparts were able to listen in on what I considered to be a personal meeting, but at the same time I felt that I had salvaged something tangible from the new reorganization, at least something I could pass on to my wife, my counterparts, and my colleagues that clearly indicated I wasn't being replaced due to a lack of ability or for any other negative reasons.

Unfortunately, however, in the near future I was destined to learn that not only would Vessey's promise of a promotion prove to be hollow, the accounting effort would quickly be reoriented from quality to quantity. Our fleeting last chance at getting the truth, what actually happened to many men, rather than just the bones, was about to go down the proverbial tube.

Chapter Fifteen

A "Desert Storm Roll Across Vietnam"

SHORTLY AFTER VESSEY DROPPED THE BOMB, Needham told me that my replacement would be an Army Lieutenant Colonel, and that the U.S. Office for POW/MIA Affairs would be converted into a military detachment. He then asked me to stay on in Hanoi and fully support the new commander, although his appeal seemed more like an order than a request or a gauge of my desire to assume a new job. Based on this exchange, it was beginning to feel like I was back in the infantry. I could only assume that Needham was unfamiliar with the Civil Service rules that require a negotiated acceptance of transfers or new assignments.

Despite the later public relations efforts that alleged the office needed a military officer to run it because the effort had become too complex, one of the main reasons Needham had pushed for transforming the office into a military station with a military officer in charge was so that he could give an order and it would be acted on. In working with civilians under the Civil Service, if we disagreed, we had clear channels to deal with grievances. I was soon to discover that Needham, a micro-manager of the first rank, tolerated no dissent. Further excuses offered were that the new, expanded office chiefs would engage in major logistics and planning, along with extensive discussions with the Indochinese countries, although this is exactly what the JCRC, and myself in particular, had been doing for many years.

Although Needham had his own rationale for the sudden change, there were other, more subtle behind-the-scenes initiatives that led to transformation of the office into a military outpost. We had traditionally focused on remaining lean and mean, constantly mindful of the fact that the Communists saw our operations as a revenue source. CINCPAC on the other hand, was now more concerned with manning issues, and saw the new organization as a possible way to save jobs, funding, and influence. Not only was the Pacific command in the process of closing down its massive operations at both Clark Airbase and Subic Bay in the Philippines, the quota for flag officer slots (Generals and Admirals) was under constant pressure for reduction. Those of us in the Hanoi office anticipated some gradual, well-controlled expansion of our duties, but none of us were prepared for the sudden explosion of personnel and resources that occurred in early 1992. With the rapid influx of JTFFA personnel, and the simultaneous opening of administration and logistics offices in Singapore by CINCPAC to support the inflated operations, it quickly became obvious that the military command in Hawaii was scrambling to save everything it could after the recent base closures in the Philippines and elsewhere in the Pacific.

Since I knew the JCRC had enough experience to warn against financially stimulating the Communists, it could only mean that either Harvey was asleep at the wheel, no longer had any influence, or CINCPAC ignored his warnings, because suddenly money was no object, and America began its journey down the same slippery slope as our French comrades had many years earlier. When we heard statements from various DOD officials that we were being expanded because our operation was too small and too slow, we were outraged. Not only was it not true, we suspected that this rhetoric was just the beginning of a smoke and mirrors effort to mislead the public into believing that a bloated, top-heavy organization with a catchy new name would be able to quickly achieve a "Desert Storm-type Roll Across Vietnam," something the supposedly too small JCRC would be unable to accomplish.

Shortly after the brief encounters with Vessey and Needham in Hanoi, the new Deputy JTFFA Commander, Marine Colonel William Frizzell, arrived for a visit. Frizzell, sporting closely cropped hair and spit-shined, military-issue low quarters, looked like a typical Marine field grade officer. Unfortunately, at the time of his arrival I was in severe pain due to an infected sinus and resultant blurred vision. During a recent root canal procedure in Bangkok, the dentist had drilled up through the root of a tooth directly into my sinus cavity. As a result, my face, forehead and eyes were swollen to a grotesque manner reminiscent of the Elephant Man. When Frizzell walked into my office and saw me for the first time he shouted: "good Lord what happened to you!"

After I explained to him the situation and the lack of dental treatment available in Vietnam, Frizzell immediately got down to business. He pulled a notebook from his pocket containing a list of specific axes to grind. His first complaint started with "what do you know about this guy who writes for *Parade* Magazine?" When I claimed ignorance Frizzell didn't buy it. Attempting to use the "we know all" interrogation technique, he said he believed I knew who had been writing articles critical of the Government's handling of the POW/MIA issue. After I assured him I didn't have the slightest inkling of what he was talking about, he dropped the subject. I later learned that Frizzell was referring to Al Santoli, an old friend and fellow veteran from the 25th Infantry Division. Santoli is a noted author and researcher who has written several well-received Oral History books about the Vietnam War. By this time he had become a vocal critic of the U.S. government's handling of the POW/MIA issue. Since we didn't receive any magazines in Hanoi, I was unfamiliar with *Parade*. I was unable to ascertain whether this fact had even dawned on Frizzell.

After further discussion and some small talk, Frizzell lastly informed me that my replacement would be arriving some time in late March or early April 1992. Then he made perhaps the most memorable comment I ever heard in the issue, and one that I will never forget. Looking at me square in the face, he solemnly told me, "POW/MIA work can be fun." According to Frizzell, the JCRC had been taking the issue far too seriously, but things were about to change. He suggested that after the new office chief arrived I stick around and join in on the fun. I waited for a punch line but none was forth coming. I had a strange feeling that the effort to account for our men in Southeast Asia was about to take a very different turn.

The first turn taken was the assignment of a new live-sighting investigator to our office. The new man was Air Force Lieutenant Colonel Charles Robertson, an Arabic language instructor at the Air Force Academy in Colorado. Having served a tour during the war and having completed Vietnamese language training at that time, Robertson was not altogether unfamiliar with Vietnam and its culture. But his language skills had grown rusty from lack of use, and his familiarity with the mission and the specific MIA cases was nonexistent. In discussing the cases Robertson would investigate before he went to the field, it became obvious that although he had been provided all available information contained in the live sighting reports, he knew absolutely nothing about Communist Vietnam's system of capturing, evacuating, detaining and exploiting foreign personnel.

Moreover, Robertson did not have enough grasp of the language to pick up nuances, to be able to detect regional dialects, or to conduct a detailed interview. In fact, his language skills were so bad that on those cases where I accompanied him to interview sites or to meet with Communist officials during the field investigations, I had to act as his interpreter. I figured that when I wasn't there, one of the VNOSMP members must have been translating for him. This obviously slanted the investigations, and I was deeply concerned that they weren't being conducted as objectively as possible. I'm not saying that Robertson was a bad person. To his credit, he realized that he was not up to speed on the investigations and he routinely came to me for advice before traveling to the field. This was especially true regarding remote areas of the country where our intelligence holdings were sparse. In my estimation Robertson was caught in a situation where he was simply doing what he had been ordered to do. He was told to pack and move to Vietnam on extremely short notice, and since there were several individuals on the Stony Beach Team who were more qualified than him, he couldn't imagine how or why he had been selected for the job. Since I was somewhat cynical due to past machinations by those in my chain-of-command, I could only conclude that someone in a powerful position far up the ladder had decided to end the live-sighting efforts as rapidly as possible without appearing to have done so. In my mind Robertson's lack of knowledge concerning the issue and his limited capability in the Vietnamese language were most likely the very reasons for his selection.

To judge how things were going, Needham soon visited our office again. He immediately informed me that he had two items to discuss; he had received word that I had been sending back channel messages from Hanoi to Ann Mills Griffiths, and he wanted that stopped immediately. This was not a positive development, as I not only considered Griffiths a good friend, she was arguably the most knowledgeable and dedicated IAG member. While I had periodically communicated with her, I did so only in those cases where the bureaucratic red tape had been insurmountable, and I believed her assistance was critical to accomplishment of our mission. This was especially true regarding diplomatic efforts with the Vietnamese leadership. Moreover, by keeping Griffiths apprised of the situation on the ground, the IAG was in a better position to do its job, which was overall coordination of our efforts, including policy level issues. Second, Needham surprised me by revealing knowledge of his military moniker given him by those of us in the Hanoi office, which was "Prince Valiant." Needham didn't like back channels, and he didn't like monikers. After talking with him only briefly, I knew it would be a while before I could find anything he did like.

Resigned to being replaced by someone who had absolutely no POW/MIA experience and restricted from informal contact with the important Inter-agency Group, I felt increasingly isolated in a city teeming with millions. However, my being replaced didn't go unnoticed, because on February 28, 1992 both Senator John Kerry and Senator Bob Smith from the Senate Select Committee fired off a letter to Secretary of Defense Dick Cheney:

> *We are writing to express our concern about the reorganization of the U.S. POW/MIA Office in Hanoi. Although you sketched out for the committee the changes you planned at our initial hearings last November, these changes are now perceived by some to be in retaliation against Garnett E. Bell for his testimony November 6.*

Mr. Bell has been an integral part of the search for missing servicemen throughout Southeast Asia since the Paris Peace Accords were signed, and the contacts he has cultivated during the past 20 years are valuable. His appointment as Chief of Office in Hanoi sent a clear signal that America is serious about finding our missing American servicemen.

Changing Mr. Bell's position now may diminish him in the eyes of Vietnamese, Lao and Cambodians and undercut our effectiveness in negotiating for access to prisons and obtaining other cooperation.

We are taking special care to assure that no witness is reluctant to come forward for fear that he or she may be punished for cooperating with the Committee. We appreciate your clear statement of the Defense Department's support of our work, and your personal commitment to making a fresh start toward giving the POW/MIA issue the emphasis that a matter of the highest national priority demands.

We also appreciate Assistant Secretary Duane Andrews' response to our letter to you about the way POW/MIA families are treated. Unfortunately, the job descriptions he included at our request do not include changes planned in the Hanoi office.

To avoid any perception that the change in Mr. Bell's duties was a result of his candid and important testimony, we would appreciate your detailing the changes in the Hanoi office. Any information you can provide us about these changes that predates his November 6 testimony also would be helpful.

Thank you for your attention to these matters and for your continuing assistance in the important mission we both share.

Sincerely,

Bob Smith (signed)

John Kerry (signed)

On March 13, 1992, Admiral Larson replied to Senators Kerry and Smith:

I am writing to address the concern you have expressed about reorganization of the U.S. Office in Hanoi for POW/MIA Affairs. Looking back to last May when the POW/MIA Office was temporarily established in Hanoi, the concept was for a very small staff and an austere facility. Indeed, little more was planned than a resident investigation team. Events proceeded rapidly over the subsequent months, and it was soon evident that a much broader role would be necessary for the office.

Concurrently, USCINCPAC identified command and control problems in its organization for pursuing the POW/MIA mission. In October, after careful consideration, Admiral Larson proposed the establishment of Joint Task Force for POW/MIA to ensure unity of effort in meeting the national objective of fullest possible of our missing Americans in Southeast Asia. From the outset, it was envisioned that the organization would be operational in its approach and have four, forward-deployed detachments, each would be commanded by a Lieutenant Colonel with extensive command and prerequisite operational background. This was decided prior to your initial hearings and was an integral part of the concept which Secretary Cheney and Major General Christmas, the Director for Operations, USCINCPAC, discussed in testimony before your committee. During that same period, General Christmas covered this issue in a briefing, which he presented to the POW/MIA Inter-agency Group. Our reason for these changes is simple; we want to insure unity of command and efficiency of operation.

Mr. Bell's value to this critical effort is well recognized. Our intent is to ensure that he is able to devote his full energies to the part of this effort for which his talents are well suited. The officer who assumes command of the Joint Task Force Full Accounting Detachment in Hanoi will have responsibility for what is daily becoming an ever more complex, dynamic operation. We need a commissioned officer there, because it is a military organization and he must exercise command of our forces, which will be sent to Vietnam as a result of expanded access, to conduct search and recovery operations. He will have overall command and will take charge of the time-consuming interface with the Government of Vietnam. In turn, Mr. Bell, who as a civilian cannot command these military units, will be freed from much of the managerial, administrative aspects of the effort, although he will be the commander's chief advisor. He will be permitted to return more actively to duties as our premier investigator and linguist. It will no longer be necessary to hold him in Hanoi for managerial or representational tasks when his talents are sorely needed in carrying out critical investigations working more closely with his Vietnamese counterparts.

Once again, I assure you that none of our organizational changes in Hanoi had anything to do with testimony before your committee.

It was clear that Kerry and Smith not only wanted to prevent intimidation of future Committee witnesses, they also were concerned about the effects a military organization would have on solving the issue. I considered this desire as not politically based, but rather a genuine wish to conduct quality investigations. There was no need to change the JCRC into a military organization, or to make a "Desert Storm Roll Across Vietnam." The Vietnamese could have solved many of the cases immediately if they wanted. Plus, the reference to "command and control problems" in the CINCPAC message harkened back to the business cards ordered for the new office and Bob Destatte's reception held at the Boss Hotel in Hanoi. Another thing that bothered me, I doubted whether the Vietnamese leadership, or for that matter the foreign diplomatic community in Hanoi, would envisage the same sense of priority and importance to a "detachment" of military personnel as they did to our office.

In doing some checking concerning the ongoing reorganization I learned that my replacement would be Army Lieutenant Colonel John V. Donovan, who was assigned as the commander of Camp Merrill, a remote base in the mountains of Georgia. Having gone through Ranger training in the 1960s I was aware that Camp Merrill was a facility of the Army Infantry School's Ranger Department headquartered at Fort Benning, Georgia. After being sent Donovan's personnel file I learned that he had served as a Private First Class with the Marine Corps in Vietnam during 1969 to 1970. After completing a ROTC program while majoring in Physical Education at the University of Massachusetts Amherst Campus, Donovan was commissioned as a Second Lieutenant in the Army. A qualified Airborne-Ranger, prior to his assignment to the Ranger department at Fort Benning, Donovan had served several tours with the 82nd Airborne Division. One thing that was not included in the personnel file was that Donovan and Needham were best friends. The friendship between the two wasn't really of concern to me, and at first I thought it might even be a positive factor for us.

Donovan arrived to assume his duties on March 29, 1992. I met him at the airport. A personable guy, I liked Donovan initially and I didn't feel any resentment toward him. Donovan's charisma notwithstanding, however, it soon became clear that the manner in which he approached his task was what in my younger days we had called a "yes sir, yes sir three bags full" officer. With absolutely no concept of the POW/MIA issue, and with no Vietnamese language capability, I knew that in addition to being a close friend of Needham's, Donovan must have some other skills or traits considered desirable by Needham and his superiors who looked to him to lead the "roll across Vietnam." I soon learned what that was.

One of the first things Donovan did was to organize the iterations for case investigations based on an extant flow-pattern analysis chart he brought with him from the Ranger Department. Shortly after his arrival he arranged the investigations in the field in fiscal year cycles in much the same manner that the Army Infantry Department organized its training cycles for its various subordinate schools. Rather than expand the scope and pace of operations for each iteration from the Hanoi office, Donovan agreed with the JTFFA Headquarters in Hawaii to transport over one hundred personnel in and out of Southeast Asia on commercial aircraft, mostly on Northwest Airlines, from Hawaii.

When I first learned of this new field operation concept, I had a hard time believing that Harvey would support it. But I soon learned that Harvey was in limbo at the JTFFA Headquarters, and not really in a position to give advice. I recalled a telephone call from Rep. Pete Peterson that I received at my Bangkok home right after I returned from the hearings held in Washington. Harvey was the main topic. Surprised to receive a call from a member of Congress who apparently expected me to join him in arranging the ouster of my boss, I could only listen while the Congressman reached the unilateral conclusion "we have to get that guy Harvey out of there." Shortly thereafter Harvey was "kicked upstairs" and moved from Hawaii to the Pentagon where he ultimately became Chief-of-Staff of the Defense Prisoner of War/Missing Personnel Office. Apparently Vessey did the same thing to Harvey that he had planned for me, but I was considered too valuable for the time being at the technical level to be moved.

In meeting with the new JTFFA team personnel, I was astounded by the lack of knowledge and experience concerning the POW/MIA issue possessed by team leaders and members alike. The officers placed in charge of the field teams were very young, a few having had only a brief exposure to actual combat during Desert Storm. They weren't bad troops, just fish out of water. Linguists assigned to the newly formed teams were for the most part young Signals Intelligence personnel from the Navy and Air Force. Considering their level of security clearances, I wondered just how much professional interest the Vietnamese Intelligence and Security personnel routinely assigned to the joint POW/MIA effort would show in the new recruits. I gained an inkling of their curiosity when not long after the "newbies" arrived in Hanoi, a luxurious, air-conditioned nightclub featuring beautiful Vietnamese hostesses announced its grand opening. The fashionable facility called the "Saigon Pull" was located only a scant few hundred yards from the new compound leased by the CINCPAC to house the Hanoi JTFFA detachment. With beautiful Vietnamese girls dressed in chic cocktail dresses and drinks costing the equivalent of several days' wages on the local economy, the potential for local indigenous customers was slim and the nightclub stuck out like a sore thumb. Naturally, the young JTFFA specialists began to frequent the "Saigon Pull," and some resultant romances even led to marriages between the waitresses and JTFFA personnel. To my knowledge, there were no incidents of rowdy behavior, but no one investigated the counter-intelligence aspects of the bar.

After Donovan's arrival, I began negotiating my future job position with Needham. I also learned that the promotion promised me by General Vessey never got any further than talk. When I raised the issue with Needham he looked at me like he thought I was on drugs. The fact that my promised promotion never materialized, the shift in the focus of our operations from live-sightings to crash site excavations, the large, sudden influx of inexperienced personnel, the removal of Hutchinson and McKay from the live-sighting investigations, the arrival of Donovan, plus the length of time I had been separated from my family all crowded my mind when I sat down with Needham to negotiate another two years of overseas service. Despite the serious problems looming, I still felt compelled to help. In discussing my role in the organization, we finally agreed on a new job description for the position of "Special Assistant for Negotiations" and a shorter job title of "Special Assistant." My duty station would be the American Embassy in Bangkok, but I would frequently travel to Vietnam. I held little doubt that the Communists would be ecstatic to see me leave the country so they could work with someone easier. At the same time, however, I also knew that if I reentered the country on official orders from my superiors in Hawaii, and if the senior U.S. players supported my demands for genuine, unfettered access to witnesses, oral history subjects and archives, with frequent trips back into Vietnam I could still make a solid contribution to the effort.

In early April 1992, when word of my new assignment finally reached the media there were numerous requests for further clarification. Apparently the media representatives following the POW/MIA issue in both Hanoi and Bangkok jumped to the conclusion that I was being moved from Hanoi to Bangkok due to my testimony that I believed some live Americans were left behind in Vietnam. Due to the sudden interest by the press, the CINCPAC Public Affairs Office released the following statement:

> *USCINCPAC Joint Task Force-Full Accounting has announced that Mr. Garnett E. "Bill" Bell has been selected for a new position in Bangkok. In his new position, Mr. Bell will be Special Assistant for Negotiations, and be involved in American POW/MIA activities throughout Southeast Asia, including the three nations of Vietnam, Laos and Cambodia. This new position reflects the central role Mr. Bell has played over the past years in contributing to American efforts to account for American servicemen unaccounted for from the Vietnam conflict.*
>
> *Q1. Why was Bell transferred from his duties in Hanoi?*
>
> *A1. Mr. Bell was not transferred. This position, newly established in Bangkok, is needed to provide overall JTF expertise in a central location near to where operations and negotiations are occurring. Mr. Bell is highly qualified to fill this position. This establishment of Bangkok-based position reflects our need to respond to the increased access that Vietnam, Cambodia, and Laos governments have afforded us. Mr. Bell will be dealing with those three nations, including traveling from Bangkok representing the JTF.*
>
> *Q2. When does Mr. Bell begin his new job?*
>
> *A2. About mid-May 92.*

During April 1992 the Senate Select Committee decided to send a delegation to Vietnam to assess the recent changes and to evaluate the newly formed JTFFA. The delegation arrived on an Air Force Boeing 707 that had been reconfigured to accommodate VIPs. The group included Senators John Kerry, Bob Smith, Chuck Grassley, Chuck Robb, and Hank Brown. One important mission of the Congressional delegation was to measure the level of Communist cooperation provided in resolving the live American question. I linked up with the CODEL at Noi Bai Airport and rode with Senator Kerry into Hanoi. During the ride into town Kerry informed me that he planned to discuss with the Vietnamese the issue of unannounced inspections to prisons and other locations where Americans were reportedly held. During meetings with senior Communist leaders, including the Secretary General of the Vietnam Communist Party, the Prime Minister, the Minister of National Defense and the Deputy Minister of Public Security, both Kerry and Smith brought up the issue of the unannounced inspections. At the time, the Communist officials accepted Kerry's proposal, but rather than a blank check the acceptance only covered his visit.

After Kerry huddled with the other members, they decided to make an unannounced inspection to the Public Security Prison located at Thanh Tri, south of Hanoi. After the meeting concluded I traveled from the meeting site riding in the front of a sedan with Kerry and Smith in the back. Just as we entered the heart of the city I observed a man walking from a grassy area in the median toward our vehicle. The man suddenly produced a large rock, about the size of a bowling ball, and with a double-hand push launched the heavy projectile through the front windshield of the sedan. I caught the rock in my lap and shards of broken glass filled my face and eyes. I wasn't badly hurt and Vietnamese security personnel immediately arrested the man and dragged him away from the scene. On the verge of panic the Vietnamese driver accelerated and sped toward our next destination. Due to the speed of the vehicle small particles of glass continued to blow into my face for several minutes. After we arrived at the site of our next meeting Communist officials offered the opinion that man who tossed the rock was simply deranged. As far as I know we never learned the rock thrower's motivation, or for that matter the government's disposition of the man.

During our meeting Kerry took the opportunity to inform the Communists of the general area that his group desired to visit the following day. Kerry and his colleagues felt reasonably certain that without advance knowledge of the specific facility, the Communists would not be able to orchestrate the visit, and with no preparations in advance the site inspection would be objective and thorough. Unfortunately, the prison that Kerry and his group intended to visit was the only such facility in the Thanh Tri area, also called "Hanoi B." The prison was a main facility of the Ministry of Public Security in North Vietnam, thus the word "Hanoi." The letter "B" indicated that although the facility was located in North Vietnam, it was under the authority of the southern branch of the Public Security apparatus. In other words it was a facility reserved for people who were arrested or captured in South Vietnam and later moved to the north, presumably to be near the central court system for ultimate disposition of cases. Foreigners who were captured and detained in the north would normally be held in facilities designated "A."

The following morning I accompanied Kerry's group to the Thanh Tri prison where I served as Interpreter-Translator. Despite Kerry's plan, upon arrival we learned that the prison officials had been informed in advance of our visit. The camp staff admitted that they had received word of our visit the previous day. We were allowed to enter the detention areas and search for any possible American prisoners or any signs that Americans had been held there in the past. During the inspection most of the members of the group simply walked around, unfamiliar with the physical layout or what action they should take. Bob Smith, however, was a different story. Smith had obviously been briefed in detail concerning the layout of the entire prison. He also knew the designations of the separate areas and the history of expansion and development for the camp. In watching Smith inspect the facility I could see that he took the matter seriously, because he was down on his knees in the dirt looking under beds, climbing up into ceilings, looking over walls and even searching trash bins for any possible carving, writing or sign of debris indicating that Americans had previously been held in the facility. With the exception of Smith, other members of the group strolled through the camp like they were on a field trip to a museum or exhibition. Since Vietnamese officials knew about the visit to the prison in advance I didn't expect to find any evidence that Americans were being detained there. From inspecting the prison I was able to ascertain, however, that this was the same prison where at least some of the Americans captured in the south during the war, especially in the Hue area, had been detained. I also recalled reports indicating that many of the Americans held at "Hanoi B" during the war cooperated with the Communists, including the production of propaganda leaflets and broadcasts.

After the visit to the prison we all returned to Hanoi and boarded the Air Force aircraft for a trip to Ho Chi Minh City, where we all registered at the "Rex Hotel." Kerry, in meetings with Communist officials, worked out a plan where he and Bob Smith would go to an area in the Mekong Delta where Kerry was assigned during the war. Both Kerry and Smith were aware of some recent reports indicating that several live Americans were being held in the Delta, and they wanted to check those out firsthand. Robb decided he had had enough of Vietnam and arranged for an early commercial flight out of the city. Grassley choose to remain in Saigon rather than go into the field. He had various requests from ethnic Vietnamese constituents in the States concerning family reunification, and the resettlement of former South Vietnamese military officers. In talking with Grassley I learned that he was completely in the dark concerning the prison system, the reeducation process and the general history of American involvement in Vietnam. To be helpful I stayed up until 4:00 a.m. writing down everything I could think of that would assist Grassley in his meetings. The following morning I slid a stack of tablet sheets under the door of his hotel room. Since I lost a good night's sleep in the effort I hope he found the information useful. In reality, however, I never received any feedback, and for all I know he threw the material in the trash.

After everyone but Senator Hank Brown was scheduled for activities, I met with the Senator, a member of the Senate Judiciary Committee and a former

Forward Air Controller pilot during the war. Brown told me he was open to suggestions as to what activities he should participate in, but that he wanted to be helpful in resolving the POW/MIA issue. Since everyone else was busy inspecting or investigating I suggested to Brown that I take him up to the Danang area and thank local officials for help in recovering the bodies of Schreckengost and Greer. I told Brown that since they did allow us to "discover" the remains of two Americans in the Danang area, we should recognize their contribution in the hope that more "discoveries" might be forthcoming. I also felt that since Brown had been assigned as a FAC in the Danang area he might like to go back for a visit. Brown was elated in having an opportunity to revisit his old battlefield and fortunately the Defense Attaché Office in Bangkok had a C-12 aircraft available to fly from Bangkok in order to transport Brown and me to Danang and then back to Ho Chi Minh City that same evening.

Kerry, Smith and several Communist officials departed for the Mekong Delta by helicopter, and Brown and I headed for Danang in the C-12. We arrived at Danang Airport and after a meeting with provincial officials we loaded into a van for the trip to Chau Son village west of Danang. As we neared the village where my JCRC team had recovered the remains of the two Marines, we found that several boards had been removed from a bridge over the river, causing us to halt on the road. Rather than wait for the bridge to be repaired we decided to continue on foot. At the time I believed that the boards had been removed to slow us down and give local officials plenty of time to make arrangements to receive us. Sure enough, except for small children, only card-carrying Vietnam Communist Party members were present at the time of our visit. I figured the regular village people were removed soon after the boards were taken from the bridge. In the village Brown thanked "the people" for assisting in the recovery of the two remains, but in their remarks to us, the Communist officials left no doubt that the Party was solely responsible for the recovery of the two Marines and that any further future cooperation would come from the Party.

After visiting Chau Son Village we returned to Danang to meet with former senior PAVN officers who were members of Vietnam's National Veterans Association. Although Brown extended an olive branch and stated his desire that both former adversaries let bygones be bygones, the former generals we met with were sullen and surly to the point that I almost got up and walked away from the table. The veterans obviously intended on blaming all of Vietnam's current problems on America and a war that ended some seventeen years earlier. I didn't win any points with them when I asked how much longer they would blame everything on the war, when there were so many other real causes for the dire situation their country was in. Brown on the other hand, appeared to be sympathetic toward the veterans and made excuses for their bellicose attitude. Perhaps the highlight of our trip to Danang, however, was an invitation from the Russian Consul General in Danang for Brown and me to visit him in his office.

Amazingly, the senior Russian diplomat raised the issue of Americans remaining in the Danang area after the war ended. The Consul General said that although he had no firsthand knowledge, he had heard that at least some Americans had remained in the Phuoc Son area southwest of Danang up into the 1980s. The official also informed us that some Vietnamese residents of Danang had been to the Russian compound and asked for assistance in turning over human skeletal remains, alleged to be American.

We returned to Ho Chi Minh City that same evening and learned that neither Kerry nor Smith had found any evidence of Americans in the Mekong Delta. I later learned, however, that at least one American, Mr. Tom Schooley, had been held in one of the prisons Kerry visited. Schooley was arrested in international waters and charged with violating Vietnam's territory and with smuggling drugs. During the time of Kerry's visit to the prison, he had asked the Camp Commander whether any Americans had been or were being held at the prison. Kerry was told that there were none, and that there never had been any Americans held there. A few months after Kerry's visit the Communists released Schooley. I was never certain about it but I heard from U.S. sources that Schooley's wife was required to pay a large fine, in cash, to Public Security cadre for his release. Most important, during Schooley's debriefing he stated that during the same time as Kerry's visit to the prison where Schooley was held, he was moved out one day prior to Kerry's arrival, and then moved back in after Kerry departed from the area. So much for genuine cooperation.

The timing for the trip made by members of the Senate Select Committee was critical, and I believed we had to obtain as many tangible concessions from the Communists as possible prior to giving up our last remaining leverage, the normalization of relations. Apparently the Communist leadership was confident they would prevail, however, because one of their officials in Hanoi later announced to CBS News anchor, Dan Rather, that they were certain the U.S. President would soon lift the trade embargo, "because you Americans will do anything for money."

The following day I proceeded to Tan Son Nhut to accompany Kerry and others on a trip to Vientiane where I was scheduled to serve as Interpreter-Translator for the group. After my bag had already been loaded on the aircraft Kerry came up to me and informed me that he had volunteered me for an on-camera interview by C-SPAN that morning at 10:00 a.m.

I pulled my bag and went back to the Rex Hotel where Brian Lamb and a crew from C-SPAN were waiting in the hotel's open-air restaurant on the roof. Lamb suggested a one-hour interview and I agreed. He began the interview by saying "when you go to Vietnam everybody says check with Bill Bell." Bridging from this lead-in Lamb began a series of initially innocuous questions, but much to my chagrin he gradually increased the political tempo. When he then asked me what the South Vietnamese people thought about Ho Chi Minh, I was flabbergasted. Touching on this controversial subject was a definite diplomatic taboo, and anyone who worked with the Communists in postwar Vietnam knew better than to approach it. Diverting my gaze toward the three vigilant public security cadre standing only a scant few feet from me, I attempted to give Lamb my opinion that at least some of the citizenry were angry that the government of Vietnam had spent millions of dollars on a huge museum in Ho Chi Minh's honor, when he himself had always set an example of being humble and frugal, living in a small bamboo house behind the grandiose residence reserved for the head of state in Hanoi. I also told Lamb that in my opinion all exposure to Vietnamese residents of the country by representatives of the Western press was tightly controlled by the authorities. When Lamb drifted off into such subjects as lifting the trade embargo against Vietnam, or the development of Vietnam's economy, I told him that I was involved strictly in the POW/MIA issue and that I had no opinions about the economy. Due to the presence of the public security cadre, it turned out to be one of the tensest interviews I ever did on camera. In a way I felt sorry for Lamb and the crew from C-SPAN, because they were there to portray the actual situation in Vietnam for their viewers, and they probably had no idea that everything was monitored from beginning to end.

Aside from the CODEL visits prior to my transfer to Bangkok, I had one other official mission to perform as Chief of the POW/MIA Office. In April I accompanied my counterpart, VNOSMP head Mr. Ho Xuan Dich, by Russian helicopter to Dak To in Kontum province in Vietnam's Central Highlands. Prior to going on the trip Dich had informed me that the Kontum authorities had reported that some villagers in a remote area of the province had discovered some human skeletal remains and personal effects. Based on the location and description of the recovered items I had made a tentative correlation of the information and remains to three Air Force personnel who were crewmembers on a B26B fighter-bomber that crashed near the Vietnam-Laos border on September 2, 1963.

My analysis proved to be correct. However, upon arrival in Dak To, I was surprised to learn that rather than have to trek into the jungle to receive the items mentioned by Dich, everything "recovered" up to that point had been brought into town and placed in the custody of Communist officials. When I saw the items displayed on a table in the courtyard of the province compound I couldn't believe my eyes. Although the Communists had informed me that the skeletal remains and other items had only recently been found and recovered from the jungle, it was readily apparent that this was not true. The weapons I saw looked as if I could pick them up and fire them on the spot. Technical manuals were in pristine condition. Even the leather boots worn by crewmembers at the time of the crash were still in fairly decent condition. After examining the items recovered from the site I concluded that it would be virtually impossible for such material to still be in such unusually good shape if left for thirty years in a location with some of the heaviest annual rainfall on the planet. I came away from this particular visit with the impression that the Communists were once again sending us a signal to the effect that they could quickly resolve a significant number of cases, if and when they had the political will to do so.

In May 1992 I transferred to the American Embassy in Bangkok where I quickly learned that I didn't even have a desk, much less office space. I was in a holding pattern while the embassy support section surveyed available space to find a work area for me. Soon, however, the Ambassador received a State Department message informing him that another delegation of Congressmen and Senators, including some from the Senate Select Committee, were preparing for a visit to Bangkok, and during their stopover they requested to visit with me. Suddenly space became available.

Most of the delegation members who came to my office did a quick walk through and then moved on to other areas of interest. Senator John McCain, however, wanted to go into greater detail regarding the accounting situation in Vietnam. McCain expressed interest in several topics, but his primary focus seemed to be on determining, as precisely as possible, the level of cooperation we were receiving from Vietnam. McCain's visit at that point was somewhat reminiscent of John Kerry's visit with me in Hanoi the previous year. Although he briefly discussed the live-sighting issue, he seemed more interested in counting how many documents from archives and human skeletal remains the Vietnamese had currently turned over to us. He was also interested to know what the likelihood was that such transfers of documents and remains would continue in the near future.

I told McCain that we should never get caught up in statistics unless they could be verified or were useful. I cited as an example the number of remains that Vietnam had returned to us in the past, since many of them were obviously either not human or of Southeast Asian Mongoloid origin. McCain wanted to know what my take was on the warehousing and storage of remains by the Communists. I told him how the CILHI data had shown that over 60 percent of the remains returned and identified had exhibited clear scientific proof that the remains had been preserved and stored for considerable periods of time prior to repatriation. I also explained that although Vietnam had repatriated some 442 remains at that point, only approximately 40 percent had been identified. McCain was also interested in knowing whether or not the Communists had ever owned up to warehousing and storing remains. I reminded McCain that Foreign Minister Thach had first admitted to Childress in 1985 that they had been warehousing remains. I also referred to the Vietnamese mortician who defected to the West during 1979. I told the Senator that during the specialist's testimony before Congress, he had estimated that he had prepared and preserved some 452 remains, and that although he could not be certain all of them were American, based on his professional observations over half were. I added that senior Communist officials had admitted to me, as well as to the leadership of some American Veteran's Service Organizations, that although they were guilty of having stored remains in the past, they were now cooperating and no such activity would occur in the future.

I didn't break everything down for McCain, but he should have been able to deduce from my briefing that what the Communists in essence were saying was that while they had stored remains in the past, since they were now caught, they had made up for this shortcoming by turning over 442 remains in their possession. The only thing wrong with this scenario was that a large portion of the remains returned were not American, so the figures were obviously inflated. I could only hope that our politicians were not so desperate for a normalization of relations between the two former adversaries that they would buy the explanation and provide political cover for the Communists in order to move things forward based on a false perception of significant progress. However, as it turned out, this desire for normalization on the part of some Washington politicians would continue to drive the Communists' strategy, since the embellishment of statistics would later spread to the numerical count of documents provided to us from Vietnam's various archives. For example, one photograph of an already accounted for American along with ten photocopies of the same document would be touted as eleven valuable documents.

Obviously, we were intensely interested in any type of written records or photographs that might help resolve cases. In particular, I was sensitized to photographs as early as April 1990 when a private American citizen, Theodore Schweitzer (who would later be the subject of a book, *Inside Hanoi's Secret Archives: Solving the MIA Mystery*), visited my office with a large selection of photographs, many of them depicting American personnel killed-in-action, and personnel effects such as I.D. cards and dog tags he had obtained from the Central Military Museum in Hanoi. Between the report of my interview with Schweitzer and his own efforts, DIA became extremely interested in Schweitzer's access to the Communist archives at the Central Military Museum.

I was also initially impressed with the amount and quality of his personal holdings, but I soon became concerned when I saw some film of his that I had developed as a part of my report. Besides MIA photos, the reel also contained the images of nude Vietnamese females. In looking at the nude photos it appeared that at least some of them had been taken inside rooms of the Le Thach guesthouse in Hanoi. I reasoned that if Schweitzer had taken the photos, then the SRV Intelligence and Security Services most likely already had compromised him, and any information he collected should be considered suspect. Although counter-intelligence officers later interviewed me about Schweitzer after the mission was over, at the time the DIA officials responsible for the collection effort either disagreed with my opinion, or they simply didn't care whether Schweitzer had been compromised. They only wanted to exploit him for his material. The DIA saw the photographs as having considerable value in resolving several troublesome MIA cases where the individuals were shown dead at the scene, but no remains were ever returned. With the photos DIA could conclude that the men were dead and thus remove them from the last-known-alive list. As a result Schweitzer was hired as a spy and given the mission of procuring additional photographs. The U.S. Government would fund his efforts, so in essence Schweitzer, a well-known entrepreneur in Thailand, was given a blank check, along with a villa, sedan and driver, all rented at taxpayer expense.

Not long after Schweitzer began his collection efforts, Bob Destatte began to take offense. Since Destatte was the official government research specialist assigned to Hanoi with the mission of collecting records and photographs, he perceived Schweitzer as infringing upon his territory. Without being specific Destatte related to me that he had "taken care of Schweitzer," which I took to mean that he had in some manner sabotaged Schweitzer's efforts. I'm not sure whether Destatte was responsible or not, but eventually Schweitzer's cover was blown and the Hanoi officials became aware that he was working for the U.S. I tend to doubt that Destatte was solely responsible because prior to Schweitzer's unmasking, a senior Vietnamese official had queried me as to why Schweitzer had the same casualty database on his private computer that we had on our government computers. At the time the only answer I could give him was "you'll have to ask Schweitzer."

After his cover was blown Schweitzer was ultimately awarded the overt title "Personal Representative of the Secretary of Defense," a designation which he broadly advertised by passing out business cards all over Vietnam. Personally I wasn't concerned about Schweitzer's individual efforts because I saw them as a means for the Communists to demonstrate that they did maintain a POW records keeping system, including photographs. However, Schweitzer's purchase of each photo for $25 dollars or more allowed the Communists to set a cost basis for the U.S. to obtain their other material. They certainly weren't going to give it to us for free or for humanitarian purposes. However, I was not prone to allow the taxpayers to be milked by these ridiculous prices, especially since two correspondents from *Time* magazine had already informed me of the availability of similar photographs for much less from the Vietnam News Agency (VNA) archives. For only approximately $1.00 per photograph, these two journalists obtained even better photos than Schweitzer or the ones from Destatte's Ministry of National Defense counterparts. Some of the VNA photos were extremely helpful to us during investigations and excavations of crash sites where little or no information was available. Although I reported the journalist's information concerning the VNA archives through normal channels in my regular biweekly report from the Hanoi Office, including some sample 8x10 glossies, I never received any response. Apparently, DIA would rather employ Schweitzer on his "Maxwell Smart" type spy mission than pay the $1.00 per photo to the VNA archives.

Once Communist strategists were able to establish a cost basis for the photographs, Schweitzer's sources soon dried up. Eventually he asked for help from the U.S. Government to assist him in bringing his fiancée, one of the nude females depicted in his initial film collection and who had worked in the Central Military Museum, out of Vietnam. After obtaining an exit visa for his fiancée from Vietnamese authorities, Schweitzer moved to Florida.

After I moved to Bangkok in May 1992, I began to make trips not only to Vietnam, but also Laos and Cambodia as well in order to advise Needham during Technical Talks. The talks I attended were a farce, and they accomplished little of substance, other than ironing out administrative details, such as water, rations, and transportation. I did attend two trilateral meetings, one in Phnom Penh with the Cambodians and the Vietnamese, and one in Hanoi with the Vietnamese and the Lao. The trilateral meetings were important, but the talking points I recommended concerning use of the Lao and Cambodian consulates in Vietnam to obtain permission for "hot pursuit" border crossings to follow newly developed leads during the investigations were omitted from the script. In attending the trilateral talks I gained the impression that the Vietnamese closely controlled the discussions, and that both the Lao and the Cambodian POW/MIA experts were looking to the Vietnamese for guidance in dealing with the Americans on the issue.

As part of my new duties I also accompanied groups of Vietnamese officials back to the JTFFA headquarters in Hawaii for briefings. When we arrived at Camp Smith, alert members of the Vietnamese Delegation were quick to note the huge sign on top of the JTFFA building that read "Intelligence Center Pacific." Inside the huge building the Vietnamese attended briefings on everything from case lists to the weather predictions for all areas of Vietnam. In the course of the briefings it soon became obvious that the term the JCRC had used for each scheduled series of field investigations, "iteration," was no longer in vogue. The JTFFA planners had come up with a new term "Joint Field Activity" (JFA). After attending one lengthy briefing conducted by CINCPAC meteorologists who predicted the rainfall for the upcoming JFA, VNOSMP head Ho Xuan Dich became somewhat rebellious when he offered the opinion that "in Vietnam it usually rains during the rainy season and during the dry season it usually doesn't." Dich then suggested that rather than waste so much time on weather studies, each team member traveling to Vietnam carry a rain poncho.

I also began taking trips from Bangkok to Pattaya, Thailand where the teams from the JTFFA stayed while loading their equipment to be transported by military aircraft. My main purpose in going to Pattaya was to educate the teams on all phases of conducting field investigations in Vietnam. I tried to make the briefings as interesting as possible, but the lure of the seaside beach resort took its toll on the attention span of the troops. I was able to go over specific cases with the Team Chiefs, and I stressed safety and security with the team members.

I hoped the briefings were beneficial, but Needham soon directed me to travel to Vietnam and spot check the teams. My inspection revealed that some of the points I failed to include in my pre-JFA briefings—in the belief that such mundane matters were unnecessary—would in fact need to be included in the future. For example, I hadn't advised the troops on what to wear, because this had simply never been a problem with the JCRC. We had worn practical, presentable clothing that had proved to be suitable for our missions. I was astounded, however, to learn that the new JTFFA personnel were conducting witness interviews, including sessions with senior Asian cadre, men immersed in issues of face and rank, while dressed in tank tops, athletic shorts and shower tongs. Apparently the teams were wearing casual clothing 24/7 during the duty week, and some were even sleeping in the same clothing they were wearing for duty the following day. In monitoring the interviews I saw that the Vietnamese witnesses were always very conservatively dressed, especially those with the rank of Colonel and above. Some had worn old clothing, but it was always clean and mended and in most cases long-sleeved white shirts were the order of the day.

I could tell that neither the Communist officials who accompanied the teams from the JTFFA nor the witnesses appreciated the tacky, ill-mannered attire being worn by the Americans. The local officials and witnesses also did not appear to appreciate the fact that senior cadre were being interviewed by young analysts, including some apparent teeny-boppers, who had not done their homework and who exhibited very little knowledge concerning both Vietnam and the POW/MIA issue. I had the feeling that although the local officials were not pleased with the performance of the young troops, the VNOSMP cadre from Hanoi were elated by the situation, probably realizing that many of the fruitless encounters at the local level would have to be repeated, thus bringing in much needed revenue for the country.

Appalled by the way things were being handled, including some critical points concerning the lack of detail being pursued during the witness interviews and inadequate research prior to departing for the field, I planned to raise the clothing issue with Needham at the first opportunity. I went to see Needham in the Imperial Hotel in Bangkok where he was billeted to meet with the troops after the JFA concluded. I found Needham in a glass enclosed, atrium style VIP suite at the top of the hotel. Standing in front of Needham's desk I looked out at the spectacular gardens and pools and recalled our days in the small, barely-able-to-squeeze into room in the Bangkok embassy. I then informed him of the discrepancies I had observed during the just completed JFA, including the casual duty uniforms, which I considered improper. Somewhat sheepishly Needham pledged to take a close look at the problem, but he was not very committal. It was at that point that I noticed that Needham was wearing a tank top, swimming trunks and shower tongs.

I soon traveled back into Vietnam to conduct interviews in conjunction with a new Oral History Interview Program we had established just before I transferred from Hanoi to Bangkok. My plan included interviewing cadre from the list that both Destatte and I had compiled, and one by Kerry. My trip would take me down the length of Vietnam.

Amazingly, on the first trip I made back to Hanoi as a "Special Assistant," the VNOSMP, rather than JTFFA personnel, picked me up at the airport. When the VNOSMP members dropped me off outside the compound gate of Detachment 2, I discovered why when I noticed a large crowd of Westerners gathered inside. I was surprised because although we had received visitors from the various embassies in Hanoi during my tour, this was the first time I had ever seen such a large gathering, especially during the middle of a regular business day. In looking at the logos on perspiration drenched pullover "T" shirts worn by the group, I saw the group was comprised of members of a Hanoi jogging and drinking club called the "Hash House Harriers." Apparently they had just completed a run through the city. As I peered through the fence of the JTFFA compound I saw Destatte and Donovan standing while drinking beer and chatting with members of the group. I also saw a Chief Warrant Officer and analyst from the JTFFA headquarters named Gary Fulton crawling across a cement patio in front of the remains examination laboratory of the CILHI. As Fulton slowly crawled on his hands and knees, obviously exhausted by the run, other members of the group poured beer over him while shouting gleefully.

I was engulfed by feelings of loathsomeness as the scene unfolded. Although I realized that the group's activity would not normally raise any eyebrows in a developed country, somehow it just didn't seem proper for the participants, especially those assigned to the JTFFA, to be acting in such a manner in front of a laboratory where the remains of our fallen comrades were routinely examined. In the JCRC we had traditionally maintained a solemn attitude any time we were around human remains or any site where remains were processed. This "code of conduct" included no smoking, no loud, boisterous behavior and certainly no alcohol.

Glancing sideways down the fence of the compound toward a PAVN logistics unit located adjacent to the JTFFA compound, I noticed a PAVN Colonel in uniform taking in the scene. Judging from his leathery skin, graying hair and faded fatigue uniform the PAVN officer probably had many years of military service. Staring at the loud group, the Colonel at first exhibited a look of incredulity at what he was observing. But as he continued to watch the people inside laughing, yelling and pouring beer over each other, the Colonel's face gradually transformed into a contemptuous sneer. I suddenly felt both shame and anger. As the hair on the back of my neck tingled and tears rose in my eyes, Colonel Frizzell's words rang in my ears: "POW/MIA work can be fun." I was suddenly confronted by the stark realization that we were never going to fully account for our missing comrades.

Regardless of my feeling, I was there to do a job, so I put aside my emotions and entered the gate. I walked through the crowd to meet Donovan. In talking with him, I was dismayed to learn that although I was the one who had "scrounged" the twelve Mitsubishi vehicles for the detachment, none of the vehicles were available for my use during my current trip. Somewhat embarrassed I had to rely on the VNOSMP for rental of a Toyota van.

Departing Hanoi I traveled down Highway 1 to Quang Binh province where members of the JTFFA and CILHI were excavating a crash site. Burning under the horribly intense sun, the unfortunate group had been tasked with digging up seemingly endless sand dunes in 110-degree heat. The leader of the team woefully reported that after more than two weeks of digging the group had managed to find only a small shard of Plexiglas that "might possibly" have come from a U.S. aircraft. I wondered who had ordered this excavation, how much it cost, and on what information the site had been picked. I'm sure the VNOSMP was delighted to be able to provide some much-needed revenue to the local Party Chapter of the area.

I continued on to Hue where I conducted several interviews with former cadre involved with POWs during the war. I managed to satisfy some of the requirements regarding Communist POW/MIA policy matters that were high on my list. From Hue I traveled to Ho Chi Minh City where I met with representatives of Vietnam's National Veterans Association. In the course of working with the Communist veterans I learned that they were geared up for tourism and that they expected to make the lion's share of their profits from American veterans arriving as tourists in Vietnam. I also took note of the fact that former Colonel Ha Van Lau, who had also served as Vice Foreign Minister and Vietnam's Ambassador to France, had been appointed as the Chairman of the Veteran's Tourism Authority. Colonel Lau had also served as a Political Commissar in charge of French POWs being repatriated to France in conjunction with the Geneva Accords at the close of the French War in Indochina.

I also began to receive information concerning wartime "swaps" of Communist prisoners for American POWs. Analysts in the headquarters were completely unfamiliar with prisoner swaps that occurred during the war, although they did happen. Based on the usual requirements for follow-up questions after oral history interviews were conducted, I expected at least some interest from both the JTFFA and DPMO/DIA analysts concerning the issue of prisoner swaps. Yet surprisingly there was never any indication that any of the agencies receiving the results of the initial oral history interviews were the least bit interested. In this situation I found the silence deafening. In essence, I gained the impression that although the Communists were willing to step forward and discuss the murky issue of closely held clandestine wartime prisoner swaps, analysts on our side were verbally being instructed not to open this particular Pandora's box.

From Saigon I proceeded to Rach Gia, which was located in the Mekong Delta on the Gulf of Thailand and bordered on Cambodia. In Rach Gia I met with Major Nguyen Chi Cong, a retired Public Security Officer and the former commander of the Military Region 9 camp for American POWs. I had looked forward to meeting Cong because a few years earlier my office had received a handwritten personal letter from him discussing POW/MIA matters. After reading the letter I couldn't figure out if Cong was attempting to speed up the accounting process by going outside official channels, or if he was simply looking for some type of reward from the U.S. for information he considered valuable. Fascinated by his unexpected letter I wrote Cong a handwritten response and mailed it back. After I met with him in Rach Gia I gained the impression that Cong had not been acting on his own, because he acknowledged our exchange of letters in the presence of Communist officials. Although elderly and in poor health, Cong was helpful in providing information concerning the location of several Americans who died in captivity. Expressing his condolences for the death of Colonel Nick Rowe, who at one time had been held in his camp, Cong recalled how Rowe had convinced him that Rowe had been assigned as an "engineer," which had been Rowe's cover story for several years until his true status as a Special Forces officer was revealed to the Communists by anti-war elements in the States. I often wondered why the U.S. government never attempted to track down and prosecute those responsible for this travesty.

In December 1992 I was placed on orders for travel back to Washington to again testify before the Senate Select Committee on POW/MIA Affairs. Apparently concerned that I might provide too much information to Committee members, on this occasion Frances Zwenig made sure that I was seated near an official whom she believed would be providing testimony favorable to those who thought we should move rapidly toward normalization of relations with Vietnam, Bob Destatte. Although Destatte and I were old friends and we both had personally seen plenty of positive proof indicating Communist manipulation of the POW/MIA issue, more recently Destatte had changed his view. Not long after he departed Hanoi for DIA, he began to embrace the unproven theory supported by politicians in favor of normalization to the effect that although the Communists were being difficult for the time being, eventually an improvement in Vietnam's economy would bring about much needed change... change both in the way the Communists dealt with the joint effort to account for our missing comrades, as well as the collective manner in which the Party treated the Vietnamese people. The descriptive term used by politicians to describe this phenomenon was "cooperating in good faith." This in essence meant that by making concessions to the Communists in advance, rather than be realized as a preexisting condition, our goal of genuine cooperation would materialize as a hoped-for byproduct of our government's progressive policy. Ultimately Destatte and I sharply disagreed on the level of actual cooperation we were receiving from the Communists, and that disagreement still exists today.

I also shared the same table with five other witnesses, which meant that time allowed for each individual to testify would be greatly restricted. Shortly after the hearing began there was some commotion when the Commander-in-Chief of the Pacific, Admiral Charles Larson and Major General George Christmas, began testifying to the effect that Communist Vietnam was affording good cooperation to the U.S. Before the Committee members even had time to mentally evaluate this information, Senator McCain read from a message transmitted from a JTFFA team leader to the effect that Vietnam was not only giving poor cooperation, it was manipulating the issue. Although not mentioned by name during the meeting, James Coyle of the former JCRC authored the message read to the Committee by McCain. Unfortunately Coyle was not called to testify at the hearing, since with his nearly five years of conducting investigations while dealing on an almost daily basis with Communist duplicity, he could have provided some very valuable insight. By this time, however, many members wanted the hearings over, and little was done about Coyle's and several other former JCRC Team Leaders reports about the true level of Vietnamese cooperation. Instead, Larson and Christmas were making every effort to give the impression of outstanding Vietnamese cooperation.

Another subject addressed during the hearing had to do with possible secret underground facilities in Hanoi that could have been used to detain POWs or for the storage of American remains. I was aware of reports to that effect in circulation at the time, but I had not been involved in investigating any of them. I listened to Kerry and Destatte discount the possibility of underground facilities in Hanoi, which according to them were not likely given the high water table. Although I had no reason to believe that Americans or their remains were being held underground in Hanoi, to keep everyone honest, at the first opportunity I testified concerning my own personal knowledge of such facilities. Without going into considerable detail I made the point that such facilities did exist. I might add that I never did find out the details of the reports associated with the underground facilities, including some huge bunker complexes in the area of Ho Chi Minh's Tomb and the nearby Ba Dinh conference hall of the Vietnam Communist Party.

The December 1992 hearings were much less intense than those held in late 1991. It was fairly obvious that the Committee members were growing weary of the POW/MIA tar baby, and they sought a return to normalcy in their daily lives. When the Committee adjourned in January 1993, most people harbored the belief that the Committee results would serve little purpose other than political cover to permit the U.S. to move quickly forward in normalizing relations with Communist Vietnam.

Although the final December hearings were somewhat bland there is one incident that I will always remember. As was the case with all those testifying, they were asked the question "do you have any evidence indicating that Americans are still alive in Vietnam?" This time the person sitting at my table next to me was Air Force Master Sergeant William Deeter. Although Deeter joined others seated at the table in rendering a negative reply, he later confided in me that he felt like he was guilty of being untruthful with the Committee. According to Deeter, during the time that he had worked as a voice intercept specialist and Vietnamese linguist for the National Security Agency, he had received traffic from the Dak To area of Kontum province referring to an American present there just prior to the arrival of a JCRC team. Based on a message from higher headquarters informing the Kontum authorities that an American team was en route to the area, Deeter learned that the American's name was either "Johnson or Jackson," he couldn't recall. After the hearing concluded Deeter was in a quandary. While he felt guilty for not revealing the information to the Committee, he also was afraid of retaliation from his agency that could end his career just short of retirement. After contemplating the possible impact of his being candid with the Committee, Deeter decided to remain silent.

When the hearings concluded I returned to Vietnam and continued with the Oral History interviews, but the personnel in the Hanoi-based detachment of the JTFFA had grown envious of my situation wherein I was enjoying the creature comforts of Bangkok while visiting Vietnam for only brief two week periods. This was not unusual, and I interpreted the situation as a common "turf" problem. Soon, however, as the pace of the interviews began to gain momentum, the JTFFA detachment in Hanoi was reinforced with analysts from Hawaii and they gradually took over the Oral History Program. By March 1993 my duties with the Oral History Program were gradually reduced. Just as I was becoming bored and looking for some kind of new work to keep me busy, Needham decided that I should begin to record on paper everything I could remember concerning the discrepancy cases. In other words, a detailed assessment of each specific case on the discrepancy case list. Since my previous boss, Paul Mather, had been put out to pasture to record his direct involvement and observations during his lengthy tour working on the issue, I began to wonder if I was about to meet the same fate. But I put my worries aside and began evaluating each discrepancy case in great detail. For research purposes I relied primarily on the extensive file system located in the former JCRC Liaison Office, American Embassy Bangkok, which had been redesignated as Detachment 1 of the JTFFA. Our office in Bangkok was fortunate to have files dating back to 1973 when the JCRC was formed, including refugee reports from 1975 when personnel from the JCRC first began to interview those fleeing from Vietnam soon after the Communist takeover in April 1975. Our Bangkok files were unique in that they contained handwritten entries that included data not normally allowed in our refugee reports published and transmitted through the CINCPAC in Hawaii.

Due to the complexity of the loss incidents most of the discrepancy case assessments I worked on during 1993 required a great deal of data in order to complete them. I was fortunate that the former JCRC Liaison Office files had been left intact when the office was reorganized as a JTFFA detachment. Although the JCRC Headquarters closely edited all field reports, the Bangkok office collectors continuously added personal comments in the margins of the reports retained in the historical files of the office. Since such comments were not subject to editing and were, therefore, quite candid, they proved to be at times very enlightening. The former JCRC Liaison Office Chief, Lieutenant Colonel Paul Mather, was also very diligent in cross-referencing the reports with pertinent messages from various agencies that were not involved in the acquisition of the original report. Such agencies were interested in obtaining additional details from specific Sources due to their areas of knowledge. Moreover, as evidence mounted of Communist manipulation of the accounting process, the source reports from inside Vietnam became more helpful in understanding various aspects of the manipulation, especially those with policy implications.

In reviewing the Bangkok files I noted that the majority of refugee reports obtained during the earlier years of the collection program were lacking in detail, especially those associated with the critical live-sighting issue, and in some cases were completely inaccurate. I found that certain place names and geographic locations were never located on maps by the interviewers, and those in the headquarters responsible for editing the reports prior to publication were equally unfamiliar with the areas associated with the reported incidents. Further compounding this problem, during later analysis there were often instances where no correlation to a specific individual was reached due to the lack of a specific location on available maps. This resulted in comments in the final JCRC Headquarters analytical product such as: "Does not correlate to anything in U.S. files." As a side-job I took on the mission of reviewing every report in the files of the Bangkok office.

To assist me in this endeavor I contacted the Veterans of Foreign Wars (VFW) Post in Paris, France to request assistance in obtaining French Indochina era maps containing toponyms used by the Communists, most of which were still in use during the time that we were collecting POW/MIA related information from refugees. Officers of the Paris VFW Post were kind enough to send me a complete set of French maps of Indochina. By using these maps, as well as maps of the former Republic of Vietnam obtained from the DIA, I was able to make pen and ink corrections to a significant number of the previously uncorrelated reports. Such notations were designed to bring to the attention of future field investigators the actual locations of terrain features, geographical locations and administrative boundaries incompletely or inaccurately described in the old reports. I believed that this aspect would become even more critical as seasoned Investigation Team Chiefs began to be replaced by young military officers lacking the technical skills to properly supervise the complex investigations. I also felt that the unique method of filing the reports used by the Bangkok office, wherein reports were filed in numerical sequence by year of acquisition and country of origin, would greatly enhance the ability of the new Investigation Team Chiefs to prepare for upcoming JFAs. Although the original reports were forwarded to Hawaii, the filing system there was so user-unfriendly and cumbersome that the headquarters routinely tasked the Bangkok office with locating and retransmitting reports that could not be located in the headquarters files.

Ominously, sometime during early 1993 the commander of the Bangkok detachment, Air Force Lieutenant Colonel David Geraldson, began to query the JTFFA Headquarters concerning the necessity of maintaining extensive files in his office. I later learned from office staff that during the course of the discussions Geraldson made it quite clear to Headquarters that since the JCRC Liaison Office had been reorganized as a military detachment responsible solely for logistical support to field teams traveling from Hawaii and transiting Thailand en route to Vietnam, Laos and Cambodia, there was no need for any POW/MIA case files or reference material to be locally maintained. Geraldson also cited the classified information storage factor, expressing his opinion that the accountability requirements associated with unneeded classified information only increased the administrative burden of his already taxed office.

After I learned of the discussions concerning the files I pointed out to Geraldson that due to the findings and conclusions reached thus far by the Senate Select Committee, most, if not all of the files would soon be declassified, thus the storage of classified material would no longer be a problem. I also told Geraldson that I considered the files essential to my work since I used them on a daily basis in completing the discrepancy case assessments. I also made it known that I wanted to retain at least some of the files in my own work area, but was unable to do so due to the lack of space in my small office. I did offer to take as many files as possible if I was able to obtain larger office space. Strangely, in his deliberations Geraldson failed to mention the fact that four members of the Bangkok detachment, who had previously served as JCRC Investigation Team Chiefs, were also currently using the files in preparation for Joint Field Activities. The most experienced JTFFA field investigators at the time, the four team chiefs normally traveled from Bangkok to Uttapao Airbase where they drew equipment and deployed with their teams that had just arrived by air from Hawaii. As the focus by Geraldson and personnel from the JTFFA J-2 narrowed on the file system, it gradually became apparent why neither my needs, nor the needs of the four team chiefs were being considered, because unknown to me and the team chiefs, the files were about to be shredded.

The actual shredding of the file system did not begin until March 25, 1993. At that time Needham suddenly appeared at Detachment 1 to personally supervise destruction of the files. I took the opportunity of Needham's arrival to inform him of my need for the files. According to Needham, he had been informed by the J-2 that the files were all "duplicates," and I could obtain whatever records I needed by requesting them from Headquarters. Prior to Needham's arrival Geraldson had detailed Mr. Michael Janich to prepare the files to be shredded. Janich was a former JCRC Team Chief, and prior to that he had worked as a Voice Traffic Intercept Specialist and Analyst for the National Security Agency. With many years of experience, top physical condition, and fluency in Vietnamese, Janich was an excellent employee. He was also smart enough to know that destroying the files was a big mistake, and he undertook the task reluctantly. Assisting Janich at the time was a career employee of the Central Intelligence Agency who had been assigned to Detachment 1 on a temporary duty assignment.

In order to handle the large mass of documents, Geraldson borrowed a large, refrigerator-sized emergency evacuation shredder from the embassy. After three days of stuffing files into the giant machine, on March 27 the final cabinet was in the process of being emptied when I left the office and headed home. When I arrived home a houseguest, Steven Mills, the son of Ann Mills Griffiths, was on the phone to his mother in Washington, D.C. Toward the end of his conversation young Mills handed me the phone to say hello to his mom. During the brief conversation that ensued, I discussed my work and I mentioned the shredding of the JCRC historical files. Apparently misunderstanding the information I provided to her, she asked me when the shredding was scheduled to start. When I told her the destruction of the files had been going on for several days the phone went silent. Griffiths then said that she had to make some calls and broke the connection. When I went into the office the following morning there was an air of gloom. I heard from staff members that the previous evening, the American Ambassador, David Lambertson, had arrived at Detachment 1 and queried Needham concerning the shredding of the files. They described Lambertson as "madder than hell." I immediately came to the conclusion that Needham had most likely never obtained approval from higher authorities prior to the shredding, thus the loss of composure by the usually calm Lambertson.

Unfortunately, it was too late, and the destruction of the files was a tremendous loss. In addition to reports from refugees, defectors, foreign diplomats, aid workers, smugglers, business people, religious clergy, and official government agencies, the office files also included the important historical records from the JCRC offices formerly located in Saigon and Vientiane during the war. The files also included extensive information on the penal system in Vietnam, Laos and Cambodia and very detailed sketches of known prison and reeducation camps throughout former Indochina. The files on the prison system contained hand drawn sketches of prisons and detention sites that could be compared with satellite imagery. The files on prisons were periodically used by State Department personnel of the American Embassy who were responsible for verification of refugee claims of political persecution and human rights violations prior to processing them for resettlement. Other records held in the office were associated with boats and ships seized off the coast of Vietnam and Cambodia, as well as files concerning the efforts of the former American Embassy in Phnom Penh, Cambodia to account for POW/MIAs in that country. Files from Operation Homecoming, Inter-agency memos concerning non-refugee Sources of POW/MIA information, and personality files pertaining to private citizens engaged in recovery efforts, including such notables as H. Ross Perot and "Bo" Gritz, rounded out the collection.

The shredding of the files resulted in an uproar throughout the POW/MIA community. While many families immediately jumped to the conclusion that the U.S. Government was involved in a cover-up, others were simply mystified. Those in the POW/MIA business for many years who accepted Needham's version that the files were all "duplicates" were nonetheless incensed that Needham could be stupid enough to shred files associated with the sensitive issue, regardless of whether they were duplicated elsewhere. Had it not been for Janich's dedication and attention to detail, no one would have had any idea as to what files were actually shredded, because no one but Janich came up with the "cover-your-ass" idea to make a master list of file topics prior to destruction of the records. Working hectically and with strict time constraints, Janich had barely been able to list the major file topics, which he made to create a record of effort, prior to commencement of the shredding. During an ensuing "in-house" investigation by the CINCPAC Inspector General, it was determined that some 119 shredded reports could not be located in the POW/MIA files maintained by the JTFFA headquarters. Even given the loss of the important margin information and historical files, however, Needham ultimately was cleared of any wrongdoing and the subject was dropped.

While resigned to the fact that I would be spending more time in Bangkok, I began to receive reports indicating that things were still not going well in Vietnam. Although a military officer in Hanoi had replaced me ostensibly because "certain problems had been identified," the assignment of a military officer was apparently no guarantee that such problems would not occur. For example, I received one report that two members of Detachment 2 in Hanoi had been arrested by the Public Security Police in the company of two Vietnamese prostitutes at the Song Nhue Hotel in Ha Dong City south of Hanoi. After the Ha Dong incident two JTFFA personnel were arrested at China Beach near Danang after they exposed themselves to undercover public security personnel. Several JTFFA personnel were also subjected to court martial proceedings after they were discovered smuggling drugs from Thailand back to Hawaii in conjunction with their official travel. The drug problem increased to the point that at least two JTFFA personnel died after they overdosed on drugs in Vietnam during field operations. In Phnom Penh, the Detachment Commander was relieved due to adultery and the Deputy Commander was fired due to sexual harassment. At the same time JTFFA personnel in Cambodia and Laos were injured in both automobile and motorcycle incidents requiring extensive treatment and hospitalization. Another incident became the source of a complaint by former Secretary of the Navy James Webb. Webb was visiting Danang when he encountered a drunk and disorderly JTFFA team wandering aimlessly late at night on the streets of the city. Webb was so incensed by the incident that he filed a formal complaint with the CINCPAC.

In addition to the disciplinary problems, Needham instituted what he called his "80 percent rule," which allowed for the completion of cases after meeting an 80 percent standard of success. To the former JCRC members, Needham's new rule was an insult to the sacrifices made in the past in conducting thorough, objective investigations. Not long after he arrived, Needham had begun to look for ways to rapidly increase the case closure statistics. Stats were always his measure of success, and his obsession with them was reminiscent of former Secretary of Defense Robert McNamara. I felt that statistics were the only thing on Needham's mind, and he paid scant attention to anything else around him. This was most likely why after serving two tours in Vietnam, including one tour as an adviser to the South Vietnamese Army, Needham still could not ask for the time in the Vietnamese language. Due to Needham's 80 percent rule a number of cases were not investigated properly. For example, during a Cambodia investigation the JTFFA team could not communicate due to the absence of a Cambodian linguist. After the team was satisfied that they had made an honest effort, based on the 80 percent rule, the team departed to Thailand. However, a journalist continued to investigate on his own and shortly after the JTFFA team checked into a hotel in Thailand, they had to return to Cambodia and take custody of the remains of an MIA, a civilian named Wels Hangen, that were recovered by the journalist.

Besides being a huge micro-manager, Needham always seemed hyper. The first thing he did when he awoke each morning was toss down a can of Pepsi followed by a handful of Oreo cookies. Charged by the sudden influx of sugar he would run several miles before work, and he remained spastic all day. He was proud of his unlimited drive, and he once described to me how he had taken over command of a parachute-rigging unit and how he had increased the efficiency of his personnel who were assigned as parachute riggers. By requiring them to work faster for longer hours they almost doubled the total output of parachutes available for use by airborne units in Europe. According to Needham the sharp increase in the number of available parachutes resulted in only a slight increase in casualties due to malfunctions. Needham was proud of his "80 percent" rule, but I knew that the real reason it was instituted was because Needham felt compelled to carry out the instructions of his superiors in conducting a "Desert Storm-type Roll Across Vietnam."

Needham made other changes that distracted from the true job of finding our missing soldiers. After the JTFFA personnel began to man the field investigation teams, the headquarters began to implement new policies regarding the investigation methods and the equipment used during operations. A cumbersome process ensued whereby each Team had to submit daily reports describing its activities. Some of the reports I read were ridiculous. For example, teams even reported when they were digging slit trenches to be used as latrines or when they were erecting antennas required to maintain communication. When we first went to the field, all we asked for were CB radios for use in maintaining contact between vehicles on the road. With the JTFFA, however, daily reports on all activities were required, yet the extremely expensive communications equipment proved to be difficult to secure and equally difficult to maintain. The JTFFA insisted on sophisticated communications systems, and one team member narrowly escaped death when he fell through the roof of a hotel building while trying to install an antenna on top. With the new emphasis on equipment and reporting in minute detail, the situation finally deteriorated to the point that the teams were spending more time on administrative matters than the investigations.

Eventually, young, inexperienced military officers replaced most of the seasoned civil service personnel of the JCRC, ostensibly due to the requirements for top physical condition and stamina. However, some of the JTFFA teams began to conduct site surveys by helicopter from several hundred feet above the ground without ever landing, especially during surveys of remote sites where personnel were lost while on long-range reconnaissance patrols. When I first heard that the new team leaders had justified their actions by claiming that the sites were inaccessible, my response was "how did the men who are missing get into the area in the first place?"

Compared to conditions that we had been under in Vietnam during the life of the JCRC, the JTFFA personnel had a far better working environment. In addition to periodic "Rest and Recuperation" (R&R) trips both in and outside the country, paid for by the U.S. Government, the new personnel also received allowances for the purchase of civilian clothing. Active duty military personnel also received combat pay and income tax exclusions. Aside from that, the JTFFA logistics division coordinated with the CINCPAC to divert high-quality furniture that had been declared surplus from Clark Airbase in the Philippines to "The Ranch." The furnishings included queen-sized beds. In essence Hanoi wasn't such a hardship tour anymore. As of June 4, 1992, the JTFFA headquarters office was budgeted for $1,860,000.00, while the Hanoi office was budgeted for $336,000.00. Travel for personnel of the Hawaii-based JTFFA was budgeted at $1,900,000.00. Helicopter rental for the dilapidated, aging Russian helicopters from the People's Army of Vietnam Air Force was budgeted at $2,844,000.00.

By March 1993 Needham seemed relieved that I was spending most of my time compiling the complex assessments of cases on the last-known-alive discrepancy case list. Although he never told me outright, I sensed that he didn't want me going back to Vietnam, Laos or Cambodia unless I was on a trip accompanying him. Although I never asked for any trips back into Vietnam, I did make several unexpected visits after members of Congress communicated with Secretary of Defense Les Aspin requesting that I be assigned to accompany congressional delegations as both interpreter and technical adviser.

During one excursion to Hanoi in May 1993, I attended meeting sessions wherein Senator John Kerry and Representative Pete Peterson were permitted by the Communists to interview cadre responsible for POWs during the war. Although Kerry sought my advice and even asked questions from a list I had prepared prior to the interview, Peterson was adamantly opposed to any "outside" involvement. During one interview by Peterson with Senior Colonel Doan Hanh, an officer of the Proselytizing Department and the former commander of the Bo Duong POW camp (called "Dogpatch" by the American POWs), I handed Peterson a list of questions to assist him in his interview. Since POWs had been moved from other camps in Hanoi to Bo Duong near the border of China during 1972, one question I included was "what was the reason for moving U.S. POWs from Hanoi to the Bo Duong Camp?" Another question was "were Chinese officials involved in interrogating U.S. POWs after they were moved to the Bo Duong Camp?" Although I felt my questions were legitimate Peterson refused to use them in his interview. He handed the questions in to a member of the Hanoi JTFFA Detachment who in turn handed them in to Needham. I was later counseled by Needham for not passing the questions to Peterson through the proper channels.[1]

During this same trip both McCain and Peterson met with the Communist leadership to reach an agreement between the two sides whereby the Communists would not divulge any unilaterally held information concerning American POWs who were released during Operation Homecoming. Although there was a genuine thirst for such information on the part of family members, veterans and scholars, Peterson's idea was "I don't want to see some guy make a bundle of money from writing about someone else's misfortune." Very few people know about Peterson's efforts in arranging to withhold information on former American POWs held by Vietnam, and while it was probably a genuine effort to prevent sensationalism (although a wonderful book on the American POW experience was later written by DOD historians entitled *Honor Bound: American Prisoners of War in Southeast Asia, 1961–1973*), several of us were stunned at the agreement, since the Vietnamese could use it as an excuse not to turn over other pertinent information.

Another trip I made to Vietnam was with Senator Bob Smith, who remained intent on investigating the live-sighting question. Smith arranged for Robert Garwood to accompany him in order for Garwood to guide Smith and other members of his group to sites where Garwood claimed he had observed live Americans during the time that he remained behind in Vietnam. When we traveled to the remote areas of Garwood's alleged observations, we found nothing indicating that any Americans had ever been held there. I also accompanied Smith and interpreted for him during a one-on-one meeting with Secretary General of the Vietnam Communist Party Do Muoi, where Smith produced aerial photographs depicting Caucasians in Vietnamese controlled areas deep inside Laos at sites not previously investigated by U.S. officials. The Secretary General pledged to have his staff examine the photographs for a later response, but I never learned the outcome.

Despite the requests for me by the Congressmen, each time I made a trip back to Vietnam with a Congressional delegation Needham quickly jumped to the conclusion that I had used a back channel to solicit my participation on the trip. It seemed as though he simply could not believe that I was being requested by name due to my experience level and ability to communicate in the Vietnamese language. Even though I was committed to staying within my chain-of-command, Needham's paranoia steadily increased to the point that he had the commander of the Bangkok JTFFA detachment forward to him a Memorandum of Record (MFR) detailing my every move. For example, on May 7, 1993 the Detachment commander submitted an MFR that read: "At approximately 0830 on 7 May Ambassador Lambertson's secretary delivered a large brown sealed envelope to the Det One office for Mr. Bell. MSGT Cole informed her that Mr. Bell was TDY and would not be back until Monday. She said O.K. and left the package and Mrs. Janich received it for Mr. Bell. MSGT Cole states there was no return address on the package and that it was addressed to Bill Bell – Eyes Only."

Another time, when Senator Kerry visited the Embassy during my absence, he informed the Bangkok JTFFA detachment commander that he wanted to meet with me when he came back through Thailand a few weeks later. The Detachment Commander immediately typed up an MFR describing the conversation and transmitted it to Needham. When Kerry returned to Bangkok on June 3, 1993 an MFR was also submitted detailing my conversations with Kerry, as well as other members of his group.

To avoid another MFR during Kerry's visit I accepted his invitation for drinks at the famed Oriental Hotel. Sitting on the hotel veranda overlooking the muddy Chao Phraya River, I discussed the POW/MIA issue at length with both Kerry and Senator Tom Daschle. After going over how we had ended up where we were, I told Kerry that in my opinion we had not yet and would most likely never conduct a genuine unannounced live-sighting investigation in any Communist country, especially Vietnam. I also stated that most of the crash sites and gravesites in Vietnam, as well as areas of Laos and Cambodia under Vietnamese wartime control, that had at one time contained American remains, had already been excavated by the Communists. By looking at the French experience we could see that history was on the verge of repeating itself, and the Communists were looking for another capitalist sugar daddy to pay them large sums of cash in exchange for permission to conduct expensive operations to recover remains, while at the same time they tried to pull heart strings by claiming to be "humanitarian." My educated guess was that the Communists would continue to dole out remains and personal effects on a "piecemeal" basis, while claiming that "private citizens" only recently discovered such items.

When I further said that for future JFAs, I expected the Communists to pick up the young JTFFA officers at the airport in Hanoi, and drive them around in circles for thirty days before dumping them out for the trip home, Daschle became upset. After letting me know that he was a former Captain previously assigned to duties with Air Force Intelligence, Daschle wondered aloud as to whether I held any disdain toward the military. Quickly informing him that I was a combat vet with twenty-three years of service I continued on with my assessment of what was likely to happen in the future. My outlook regarding Communists cooperation was bleak, and what I had to say obviously wasn't what either Kerry or Daschle wanted to hear. In listening to them talk I gained the distinct impression that they both had already decided on moving forward as rapidly as possible on normalization with Communist Vietnam. While they discussed possible progress in the bilateral relationship between America and Vietnam, I couldn't help but wonder to myself just how many companies seeking to do business in Vietnam as soon as the trade embargo was lifted had already donated to the two Senators' campaigns. I didn't realize it at the time but Kerry's legislative Chief of Staff, Francis Zwenig, was already working with the President of the US/Vietnam Trade Council, Virginia Foote, who worked closely with the Vietnam-America Friendship Association, to facilitate trade and commerce between major American corporations and state owned firms in Vietnam. Virginia Foote, having previously worked hard with the progressive Indochina Reconciliation Project and in the anti-war movement during the war, saw little merit to the POW/MIA issue and did everything possible to remove it as an obstacle to normalizing relations. In fact, Foote went so far as to provide the Vietnamese with declassified POW/MIA cable traffic.

Due to my assignment as Chief of the POW/MIA office in Vietnam in May 1991, I missed my regular cycle for family leave back to the States. In the summer of 1993 my wife, Nam-Xuan, asked me to reschedule the biannual twenty day "home leave" in order for us to visit with our families and also to attend her brother's wedding. My request was denied, however, ostensibly because I had voluntarily broken the regular cycle for home leave, which according to the bureaucrats, I had forfeited. This meant that we had to shell out over $10,000.00 and two weeks of regular annual leave in order for my family to take the trip to the U.S. After we had purchased tickets and were preparing to depart I was notified of the trip to Vietnam with Senator Bob Smith. Since the trip to Vietnam with Smith lasted a week my family departed for the U.S. without me. I ended up flying from Vietnam through Bangkok and then on to the annual meetings of the National League and National Alliance of Families in Washington, D.C. Already hyperventilated due to my trip to Vietnam with Smith, Needham was even more perturbed when I appeared at the annual POW/MIA family gathering. I sat in the audience while Needham fielded sharply posed questions about perceived JTFFA shortcomings interspersed with queries about my replacement in the Hanoi office, and when the families could expect my return to the field in Vietnam. Since I was on leave and had borne the cost of the trip there was little Needham could do about my presence, but he certainly didn't appreciate it.

Afterwards, in late August 1993 Needham returned to Bangkok and met privately with the Bangkok Detachment Commander, Geraldson. The following day Needham called the four Investigation Team Chiefs and me into Geraldson's office to pass on some important information. None of us had any idea what the subject of the meeting was, but we could all sense an air of haughtiness and downright arrogance in both officers. Needham opened the meeting by informing us that the Bangkok detachment was being "realigned." Next he laid bare the reason for his and Geraldson's swollen attitudes by telling us that four of us were being transferred to Hawaii. The remaining Team Chief, Air Force Master Sergeant Gene Cole, was transferred to duties dealing with administration and logistics. His announcement was followed by silence and there was really no discussion as to why, only when. All four Investigation Team Chiefs had difficulty in comprehending why they were being moved thousands of miles from the area where they were expected to conduct complex investigations. I had the same problem in understanding why my being moved all the way to Hawaii would benefit my mission of conducting assessments on the discrepancy cases. It didn't take long for us to reach the inevitable conclusion that Needham wanted to remove anyone with experience from the immediate area. At the same time the reason behind the shredding of the Bangkok office files became clear: without files the investigators, as well as the Special Assistant, would have to rely on the files maintained in the headquarters. We all received a reporting date in Hawaii of October 1, 1993.[2]

Chapter Sixteen

Salute and Go Home

AFTER CONSIDERING THE PROS AND CONS of accepting the transfer or resigning, all four experienced Team Chiefs opted for the new positions. Unfortunately, due to the manner in which their skills were utilized, ultimately three of them resigned after only a short time at headquarters.

Taking stock of my own situation I remained convinced that regardless of the number of concessions already made or pending to the Communists, Hanoi's strategists would continue to manipulate the POW/MIA issue for both political and economic gain. After all my years in Vietnam, I still strongly believed that the two most important factors to be considered by official Americans and private citizens alike were the accounting for our missing men, and democracy for the Vietnamese people, who had suffered under communism for four decades in the North and two in the South.

As for the possibility of success in accomplishing our stated goal of "the fullest possible accounting," everything hinged on America's ability to put in place a viable system of conducting thorough, objective investigations of the last-known-alive discrepancy cases, while at the same time gaining genuine cooperation from the Communists to recover the dead. In my view, both requirements would have to be met, along with high standards for closure of cases, before we gave up our last remaining leverage, the trade embargo against Vietnam. However, the Vietnamese were loudly calling for the removal of the embargo as a prerequisite for improved relations, without of course, making those concessions. Although the United States had maintained the embargo for many years, they remained patient. Their general perception of us, as one cadre once told me, was one of "greedy people." This view was emphasized to CBS News anchor Dan Rather when a Communist official in Hanoi told him point blank that they were sure the President would soon lift the trade embargo, because "you Americans will do anything for money."

Whether accurate or not, their opinion of us drove their behavior. What was laughable to me, though, was that corruption in Communist Vietnam made the old Republic look honest to a fault. During the last years of the war, North Vietnamese media constantly printed articles condemning the rampant pilfering and black-marketeering of materials by their own people, something the international news media, always ready to condemn the South Vietnamese for, never picked up on, despite the presence of numerous English-translations of this material by the U.S. government. In post-war Vietnam, the Communist corruption reached scales unimagined in the RVN, and it continues to this day.

As I contemplated my new assignment, however, the more I became convinced it was becoming hopeless to achieve these requirements. Major problems existed in the POW/MIA accounting effort, not the least of which were the green, naïve American personnel pouring into key positions on our side, while the Vietnamese continued to maintain its group of seasoned experts. For politicians inexperienced with crafty Communist strategists (or who didn't care), it was even worse. For example, the SRV was making what were perceived and trumpeted as concessions on human rights. In reality, they were using a tactic called "catch and release," where the Communists arrest important personalities associated with democracy and human rights, including members of the clergy. They then wait for U.S. officials to demand their release. Such releases are generally forthcoming and are most likely appreciated by embarrassed U.S. officials who had previously touted Vietnam's opening to the world. In some cases the releases are timed to coincide with visits to Vietnam by certain American officials in order to give them credit for their "valiant fight" to bring democracy to the Vietnamese people. Such staged events like the catch and release program serve the same purpose as the release in earlier years of human skeletal remains in conjunction with visiting U.S. government officials.

More disturbing to me, the American business community was exerting heavy pressure on the Clinton administration to open the doors to Vietnam. While the Communists were doling out POW/MIA information piecemeal, they dangled "lucrative contracts" for trade and commerce with a "last frontier" nation in Southeast Asia to the American business community, which soon became completely uninterested in accounting for our missing men, let alone on a thorny issue like basic human rights for the poor Montagnards. Senator Kerry had stated during the Select Committee that with more Americans on the ground, i.e., business people, more eyes would be looking for live POWs. It was a ludicrous statement, and to the contrary, the business community saw the POW/MIAs as an obstacle to their business ventures.

The issue of democracy for the Vietnamese people was equally important to me, but not, it seemed, to the American businessmen. They were in no hurry to promote democracy or even capitalism, since under the Communist system the Party tightly controlled labor unions and strikes. In Vietnam wages were capped at $30.00 per month, and the work week was normally Monday thru Saturday, ten hours per day. In other words it was a businessman's paradise, and the American businessmen were not about to rock the boat, not for Old Glory, Apple Pie, Mom, or the POW/MIAs. Further, campaign contributions from corporations cultivating business in Vietnam poured into the coffers of American politicians, both incumbents and challengers, on both sides of the aisle. The tentacles of huge foreign conglomerates seeking investments in Vietnam, such as the Lippo Group, stretched from Southeast Asia all the way to President Clinton in the White House, and Ron Brown and John Huang in the Department of Commerce. To convince the American people this opening was done for important policy reasons, and not just for business opportunity, many American politicians began making glib statements, such as "Vietnam is not a war, it's a country."

Even some American Veterans Service Organizations sought to exploit the opening to Vietnam. They solicited donations from corporate America to establish permanent, salaried positions for a select few in Vietnam veterans "foundations." In exchange for these donations, corporations would receive tacit approval for doing business with communist Vietnam prior to achieving a full accounting. The solicitation of funds to create "foundations" caused a backlash by the membership of the Vietnam Veterans of America (VVA) organization, and as a result some National Officers, including the President, found themselves being recalled.

Upper levels of the military also appeared to acquiesce to the new way of thinking regarding the Vietnamese. In January 1994 the Commander in Chief of the Pacific, Admiral Charles Larson, traveled to Vietnam. After visiting JTFFA operations in the field, and without any possible justification for doing so, Admiral Larson announced to the press that cooperation in POW/MIA accounting efforts by Vietnam was "excellent across all fronts." In my opinion, Larson's announcement was designed to provide political cover for the Clinton Administration to move forward in normalizing relations with Vietnam, because without gaining any concessions, in February 1994, President Clinton lifted the trade embargo. Although programmed for retirement, Larson was suddenly granted a reprieve when the normal "two star" slot for Commandant at the U.S. Naval Academy in Annapolis was upgraded to "four stars," thus accommodating him for an unprecedented additional five years of active duty.

In contemplating my new position, I knew that Needham resented and distrusted me, and I didn't look forward to working with him on a daily basis while sitting next to his large office at Camp Smith. I realized that the organization had drastically changed, especially the new organizational attitude of "POW/MIA work can be fun" and Needham's 80 percent rule. There was also the possibility that the discrepancy case investigations might be de-emphasized and the priority shifted to the recovery of remains only.

Looking back on the POW/MIA issue and the war in general, it would be easy to rationalize staying longer, but even after all the personal tragedy that had befallen me, I didn't feel like a loser or for that matter a victim. I had served in some damn good units and I had served with some damned good men. All things considered, I felt like I could hold my head high no matter what happened to the issue. I had done my duty to my country, to my fellow soldiers, and to the missing men to the best of my abilities. It appeared increasingly obvious that the entire POW/MIA issue was about to be moved to the back burner of the political cook stove. It was time to face reality: there was nothing I could do to stop it.

Therefore, I decided it was time to salute and go home. On August 31, 1993 I turned in what I considered to be a practical letter of resignation that read:

> *There are currently 2,248 Americans unaccounted-for in Southeast Asia as a result of the Vietnam War. My function is being transferred from Southeast Asia to Hawaii. There are no POWs or MIAs in Hawaii. The most important part of my function (60%) is the review of cases for preparation of specific recommendations for closure or resolution, and these recommendations must be able to withstand the intense scrutiny of a formal review process. The transfer of my function from the area where U.S. personnel were lost negates the possibility of routine access to important sources and research material, thereby rendering my position ineffective.*

Only days after submitting my resignation, it was approved. I followed-up the letter with a request to remain at my current location until the end of December in order for my children to be able to transfer to new schools in the U.S. during the mid term break. According to the normally secretive Geraldson, Needham sensed that my delayed departure would lessen chances of my contact with unfriendly POW/MIA family organizations in the States. He therefore gladly approved my request for a 90-day delay in travel back to America. My family and I returned to the U.S. in late December. Greatly impressed with Fort Chaffee during my tour there, my wife and I decided on Fort Smith, Arkansas as our permanent home.

After returning to Arkansas I continued to work on the POW/MIA issue as a private citizen. Several colleagues and I incorporated an organization called the "National Veterans Research Center." Our planned mission for the non-profit organization was detailed research into the POW/MIA issue in order to support the efforts of veterans service organizations undertaking POW/MIA related projects with the Vietnamese. Unfortunately, rather than come together in a unified approach to resolving the issue, inter-organizational rivalry and petty jealousy splintered the veterans groups into several ill conceived projects, none of which were very successful.

I also accepted an appointment to the Arkansas Governor's POW/MIA Verification Task Force. This state-level commission was initially formed by then Governor William J. Clinton. I also served as the POW/MIA Chairman of the state-level committees of the Veterans of Foreign Wars and the Vietnam Veterans of America, and at the same time I also served as a member of the national-level POW/MIA Committees of both organizations. When a national-level "Ad Hoc Committee on POW/MIA" was formed by the American Legion in Washington, D.C. and chaired by Mr. John Sommer, I initially served as the Committee's technical adviser. Since the Committee included most of the major Veterans Service Organizations and POW/MIA family member organizations, I thought it would be very productive. However, this Committee was also plagued by turf problems between the various member organizations, so I gradually reduced my participation.

Returning to Vietnam in 1994 I acted as interpreter and technical adviser while accompanying former World Heavyweight Champion and Vietnam War resister, Muhammad Ali, and a small group of POW/MIA family members for a series of meetings with Vietnam's leadership. Exhibiting a great deal of character the ever-charismatic "Champ" used his wartime credibility with the Communists to drive home the point that the war was over, and that it was exceedingly cruel for them to delay answers concerning unaccounted for Americans. This particular trip included stops in Hanoi, Hue, Danang and Ho Chi Minh City. I began the trip with a certain degree of disdain for Ali, but by the end, even though I didn't agree with his stance against the war, I had a better appreciation for him as a true humanitarian and a good person.

I also traveled to Vietnam during 1995 when I accompanied a crew from Fox TV to film a documentary oriented toward Vietnam Veterans. That trip included stops in Hanoi, Danang, Quang Ngai/Chu Lai and Ho Chi Minh City. Although I returned unscathed from the 1994 Vietnam trip, my attendance at congressional hearings in 1995, during which time I provided candid testimony concerning my perception of the actual level of Communist cooperation in resolving the POW/MIA issue, resulted in additional Vietnamese scrutiny during my next visit there. Perhaps emboldened by my lack of official status, representatives from the Intelligence and Security Services took the opportunity to visit my hotel room in Danang. Quoting verbatim from my recent Congressional testimony, they criticized me for slandering Vietnam. Sickened but not surprised by this display of arrogance, I deflected the criticism by comparing our primarily open system of public hearings with their closed-door sessions "for internal distribution only." After they left, I decided that it simply wasn't worth the effort to travel to Vietnam again. A positive aspect to the 1995 trip was that after twenty years of anguish, I had an opportunity to visit the crash site of the C-5A aircraft where my wife and son had died on April 4, 1975. I was pleased to note that in the typical Vietnamese Buddhist/Ancestor Worship fashion, a well-maintained shrine affording a place for worship and remembrance of the dead had been erected near the crash site of the ill-fated plane.

Throughout the 1990s I continued traveling across the country attending conventions of the various veterans service organizations, as well as meetings held by POW/MIA family member organizations. In each instance I continued my attempts to enlighten the public concerning what I considered to be the highly exaggerated level of cooperation our government was receiving from the Vietnam Communist Party, and the futility of making concessions in advance.

Regardless of my beliefs, the political winds had changed. I was especially frustrated at the 1996 VFW National Convention in Phoenix, Arizona when several members of the National POW/MIA Committee, including me, tried to amend a motion concerning the organization's Veterans Initiative. VFW officials were periodically traveling to Bangkok and then on to Vietnam for meetings with Communist veterans. The meetings provided opportunities for the VFW officials to hand over photographs and material collected from PAVN dead by U.S. veterans who had acquired such items as "trophies." If adopted, our proposed amendment would have required that VFW officials request that their Communist counterparts allow them to meet with personnel of the former Republic of Vietnam Armed Forces. Moreover, the amendment required that VFW officials also demand that our former allies be granted status as Vietnamese veterans of the War, with all the rights and benefits routinely received by their Communist colleagues. However, senior VFW officials present at the convention, including Kenneth Steadman, Larry Rivers, Gunner Kent, and Billy Ray Cameron, collaborated to derail the amendment, citing as their reason the fact that the "hands of the VFW Commander-in-Chief would be tied," since it was he who ultimately was responsible for the project. They succeeded. The VFW leadership had become a supporter of normalization and routinely praised Vietnam's cooperation. They later worked closely with Virginia Foote of the US/VN Trade Council. A life member of the VFW, it broke my heart to see this fine organization co-opted. It became easy to understand why the organization's membership began to wane, even though the standards and criteria for membership were lowered due to successful lobbying with Congress on the requirement for wartime service in Korea and elsewhere.

Watching the statements that the Vietnamese were "superbly cooperating" gradually materializing into an accepted belief, I considered abandoning the effort altogether. Not only was it a constant drain on the family budget, my wife and children were developing compassion fatigue regarding the issue. I began to hear such suggestions as "honey you've done all you can do," or "honey we have kids in school, we can't afford it anymore."

But just as my resolve was wavering, the "Rolling Thunder" organization contacted me. The National President of "Rolling Thunder," Artie Muller, a former Sergeant in the U.S. Army's 4th Infantry Division, who like me had served during the war in Pleiku, eventually became a good friend. This organization is primarily comprised of Vietnam Vets and motorcycle enthusiasts from across the fifty states that are activists for the POW/MIA cause as well as other veterans issues. They hold an annual ride to D.C. on Memorial Day, and they invited me to speak before the assembled crowd. The first time I stepped up to the microphone to speak to "Rolling Thunder," I looked out across a throng of some 200,000 to 250,000 people, and the number has steadily increased since. Perhaps because the membership has a relatively high number of combat veterans, the Rolling Thunder group appears to have an unusual degree of determination, and I have the feeling that our missing men will truly not be forgotten.

I always feel a great sense of pride in addressing my fellow Americans in order to increase public awareness concerning the plight of almost 2,000 unreturned veterans who are still missing or otherwise unaccounted for on Communist soil. I believe we all have a solemn obligation to bring our comrades home. On 13 February 2004 I took the oath of office as a staff member for Representative Mac Collins, U.S. House of Representatives, a member of the Permanent Select Committee on Intelligence. Shortly thereafter I accompanied him to Vietnam in an effort to revitalize the POW/MIA accounting process. Those efforts are still ongoing. No one ever knows how much longer one has in this world, but I will still be working hard on the important POW/MIA issue until the inevitable echo of taps reverberates to my family and friends from the cold headstones of a national cemetery, and the flag I love so much is folded and gently placed in the trembling arms of my ever-faithful wife. At that moment six of my fellow veterans will finally bring me home from a faraway place called Vietnam.

Notes

Chapter 1

1. My teacher's name was Mrs. Jill Miller. She was the second Vietnamese immigrant to Hawaii, and for years she helped the growing Vietnamese community with everything from taking them to the doctor to arranging for funerals. She came to see me once in Bangkok, a visit I greatly enjoyed. Unfortunately, she passed away on July 5, 2001, at the age of 80. See Bob Knauss, "Jill Nhu-Huong Miller, Vietnamese community leader, dead at 80," *Honolulu Advertiser,* July 7, 2001.
2. For a more complete description of this famous case, see Jeff Stein, *A Murder in Wartime: The Untold Spy Story that Changed the Course of the Vietnam War* (New York: St. Martin's, 1992).

Chapter 2

1. Bach Dang Street has now been renamed Ton Duc Thang Street, and the NIC has been redesignated as the "A-24 Investigation and Interrogation Center."
2. The General Political Directorate is the oldest of the People's Army staff organizations. It is responsible for political education within the Army. Political officers are assigned down to company level. The PAVN has three main staff

organizations: the General Political Directorate, the Command Staff, and the Rear Services Directorate.

3. A PAVN Senior Colonel is equivalent in rank to an American Brigadier General.

Chapter 3

1. For more details on Colonel Dai and the Central Military Museum, see Malcolm McConnell's book, *Inside Hanoi's Secret Archives: Solving the MIA Mystery* (New York: Simon and Schuster, 1995).
2. During the French colonial period the street was Rue Catinat; under the South Vietnamese government it was Tu Do Street (Freedom Street). Today it is Dong Khoi Street (Simultaneous Uprising Street).
3. In his book *Decent Interval,* author Frank Snepp indicates that Tai was deliberately drowned off the coast of Vietnam just before the Communist takeover in April 1975. When I began field investigations in North Vietnam in 1988 I learned that Tai had in fact survived, and after reunification of the country he was appointed as the Deputy Director General of the SRV's Customs Department, a usual front for human intelligence collection activities in Communist Vietnam. Tai has recently written a book about his experiences, entitled *Face to Face with the American CIA: A Memoir [Doi Mat voi CIA My: Hoi Ky]* (Hanoi: The Writers Association Publishing House, 1999).
4. The Capital Police were responsible for securing Saigon, while the Special Branch Police were a combination of intelligence gathering and counter-intelligence. The Special Branch reported to the CIO.
5. After the withdrawal of U.S. forces in March 1973, Gembara was given the responsibility for recruiting spies from the ICCS personnel. Gembara ran the female agents who attempted to co-opt the East Bloc members of the Commission. I never learned how successful he was, but rumors were that they had turned some of the Hungarians. Gembara would continue his mission until the final days of the war.
6. Collette Emberger was involved in at least two MIA cases. In late 1964 Collette escorted family members of First Lieutenant Daniel G. Dawson to the area of his reported crash site. Although Collette introduced the family members to representatives of the National Liberation Front, they were not successful in recovering Dawson's remains. In fact, both Emberger and Dawson were subsequently held prisoner but were later released by the Viet Cong. Collette was also involved with an American salesman for the Ford Motor Company in Saigon, Mr. Daniel L. Niehouse. Communist forces abducted Mr. Niehouse on November 25, 1966 while driving from Saigon to Dalat by car. Three other

prisoners who were released saw Niehouse in apparent good health when they departed a POW camp in late December 1966. However, according to information provided by the Communists, Mr. Niehouse died in captivity on April 12, 1967. Neither the Niehouse nor Dawson's remains have been recovered.

6. The Son Tay operation was a raid by American Special Forces soldiers on a POW camp in North Vietnam in November 1970. The raid was unsuccessful.

Chapter 4

1. Ultimately Lieutenant Colonel Huy and his family were able to escape by boat and reach a refugee camp in the U.S., where we met again. When I recounted the missed opportunity in the DAO, Huy also recalled the encounter. He explained that although he was afraid of missing the evacuation and he was tempted to approach me in the DAO, his relationship with Bergner and the Liaison Division was confidential and he simply could not divulge that to a stranger.
2. Units 101 and 701 were intelligence collection units funded by the U.S. government and advised by the 500th MI Group from Bangkok. We received the intelligence product without having to commit large numbers of American intelligence personnel into the field, which would be an obvious violation of the cease-fire. The MSS was the South Vietnamese counter-intelligence service and was modeled on the French Surete.
3. After the air raid there was considerable speculation that the attack was part of a coup d'état attempt by former Vice President Nguyen Cao Ky. It was later learned, however, that Communist forces had captured the A-37 aircraft in Danang. Normally a short-range aircraft, these particular A-37s had been modified with auxiliary fuel tanks enabling them to fly with heavy bomb loads from the airbase at Phan Rang to Tan Son Nhut and back again. The Communists designated the five A-37s as the "Determined to Win" flight. PAVN Air Force Major Nguyen Van Luc, a MIG pilot from the North, commanded the flight. This was the only air mission flown by Communist forces in support of the final "Ho Chi Minh" offensive. Only four of the aircraft were armed. The South Vietnamese defector, First Lieutenant Nguyen Thanh Trung, the same officer who bombed the Presidential Palace on April 8, piloted the fifth aircraft, which guided the flight into Tan Son Nhut.
4. Around 1530, the F-4 pilots fired a Shrike and several CBU pods that silenced an enemy 57mm anti-aircraft battery. In probably the last American military action of the war, Jolly Green pilot John "Joe" Guilmartin suppressed two 12.7mm sites with machinegun fire between the Keystone Bridge and the DAO Compound about 2130.

5. Valdez was the senior Marine NCO during the evacuation, and would eventually be the last Marine to board the final helicopter.

Chapter 5

1. In 1988, I interviewed a Khmer Rouge soldier who had fought on the island. He described the capture and subsequent execution of one American about a week after the battle. See JCRC Report T88-060.
2. See Thomson/West's Federal Reporter case *McDonald vs. McLucas, et al.*, 371 F. Supp. 837.
3. *Crone vs. the United States,* 538 F.2d 875
4. *Hopper et al., vs. Carter et al.,* 572 F.2d 87
5. The Vietnamese returned, in sequence, in March 1974 the twenty-three American POWs who died while in prison in North Vietnam; to the Montgomery Committee visiting in 1976 the remains of the two Marine guards who were killed at Tan Son Nhut plus the bodies of three pilots; another eleven remains twice: once in March 1977 to the Woodcock Commission, and again in July 1978 after the first Vietnamese visit to CILHI in Hawaii. The last release was another twenty-two after the admission of Vietnam into the UN in September 1977. The Lao returned four sets during this time frame, but only two proved to be Americans. The total remains returned during the 1970s by the Vietnamese was seventy-two. There would be no other repatriation of remains until May 1981.
6. See JCRC Report RP81-013. DIA's position was that many others from the same area were interviewed and none reported seeing any Americans. Thus, if only one person but not many report an incident, it probably isn't true. Readers can decide for themselves the utility of this attitude and analytic method.

Chapter 6

1. For an excellent but general overview of the JCRC and the postwar accounting process, see Paul Mather's book, *M.I.A.: Accounting for the Missing* (Washington, D.C.: National Defense University, 1994).
2. "Refugee Report, Comments from Former Viet Cong Major," JCRC report I79-025, 27 December 1979, p. 3.
3. "Letter and Interrogation Report," Combined Document Exploitation Center, Bulletin 3144, Log 03-2651-67, Records of the Military Assistance Command, Vietnam, RG 472, National Archives II, College Park, MD. This document stated the cadre "must interrogate the soldier as soon as possible and he must

be killed immediately after the interrogation." (Underlining in the original.) Attached were the results of the interrogation, which were miniscule at best. Tran Le Linh was to be used as the interpreter. The remains of Riley—who was originally from Philadelphia, Pa—were returned in late April 1989 and positively identified in August 1989. Hertz's remains, which were recovered at the same time, were only recently identified.

4. See JCRC report H84-048.

Chapter 7

1. The three remains were Lieutenant Ronald Dodge, LTJG Stephen Musselman, and First Lieutenant Richard Van Dyke. Dodge's case had been widely discussed, as a picture of him in captivity shortly after his shoot down in May 1967 was published in *Life* magazine. The same photo also was the cover of the League of Family's brochure. Both covers were done with the concurrence of the Dodge family. His return sparked an outcry from the League, since it was obvious that the Vietnamese had known of his status since his loss. When the U.S. Government sent a message to the Vietnamese asking for an explanation, they decried the "hostile" American reaction and progress once again ground to halt.
2. The PAVN Research Department corresponds to our Military Intelligence. As of April 2001, Tran Trong Khanh is serving in the SRV Embassy in Washington, DC.
3. In April 1999, Quang attended the tri-annual "Vietnam Symposium" at the Vietnam Center, Texas Tech University in Lubbock, Texas. Bell believes that Quang is a relative, possibly a son, of former Minister of National Defense General Vo Nguyen Giap.
4. Military Region 5, aka the B-1 Front, controlled the area from Danang down to the Central Highlands. While most Regions had separate Military and Enemy Proselytizing Departments, MR-5's was combined. Given the large numbers of American ground forces in the Region, they also created an "American Proselytizing" section.
5. Both Professor Ho An and the Association are discussed in Chapter 10.
6. Sauvageot is a fluent Vietnamese speaker who translated for the Mortician when he testified in front of Congress. He also accompanied many delegations to Hanoi as an official translator. After the economic embargo was lifted, Sauvageot became the Country Representative in Vietnam for General Electric.
7. This sort of reaction happened in December 1978 with the Vietnamese invasion of Cambodia, the June 1980 televised hearing with the Mortician by Congressman Lester Wolff, and in mid-1981 when the U.S. demanded an

answer to the Dodge case. In all cases, citing America's "hostile" attitude, the Vietnamese temporarily broke contact or delayed repatriating remains.

8. Rand report RM-5729-1-ARPA, "Prisoners of War in Indochina," dated January 1969, p. 6.
9. State Department cable 3032, From AmEmbassy Paris To SecState: Subject: Repatriation of French Remains from North Vietnam, dated 041725Z Mar 76.
10. Stony Beach is a separate DIA element established to pursue the live prisoner issue and discrepancy cases.

Chapter 8

1. The same general philosophy is currently being used with the North Koreans to account for American personnel from the Korean War, unfortunately with less success.
2. For the Federal District case in Florida, see 681 F.Supp. 1518. For the appellate case that reversed the judgment, see 894 F.2d 1539.
3. See DOD Intelligence Information Report 040928Z Sept.87 and 181635Z Sept.87 entitled "Vietnamese seize Lao POW records."

Chapter 9

1. In December 1990 another joint team led by Jim Coyle returned to Thud Ridge and interviewed four more witnesses not present during the visit by Bell's team in September 1988. According to the new witnesses, at the time of the incident they had observed scattered fragments of flesh at the scene. Coyle's team was guided to a crash site where small pieces of wreckage collected by the team were determined to be consistent with an F-4 aircraft. No data plates, serial numbers or other parts that would permit identification of a specific aircraft were found. The team did find one piece of bone at the site that was placed in the custody of the VNOSMP. On January 16, 1991, Vietnam repatriated the bone fragment and an evaluation by the CILHI indicated that the bone "may or may not be human."
2. Under Communist organization, the "People's Committees" are the highest form of local authority in the villages, cities, districts and provinces. The People's Committees work under the leadership of the similar "Party Committees" of the Vietnam Communist Party at each level.

Chapter 10

1. The daily rate was $25 for laborers, $45 for drivers and $50 for cadre.
2. In mid-2003, JTFFA officials informed the author that they had recently

interviewed a Vietnamese cadre who was escorting Sparks to a POW camp, and that Sparks died enroute. If true, that still doesn't explain why the Vietnamese have refused to provide this information for many years.

3. The ODP was a program designed to assist those qualifying for resettlement in the States to leave Vietnam in a normal fashion, rather than try to escape by boat or overland across Cambodia. Those departing from Vietnam under the auspices of the ODP were temporarily held at the Thai Immigration Jail in the Suan Phlu area of Bangkok. Once medical checks and interviews were conducted the people being resettled were then moved directly to the States, or to a refugee camp under the control of the United Nations located in the Philippines.

Chapter 11

1. For a more detailed examination of the Duke/Mark case, please see Bill Bell's article, "Mysterious Disappearance in the Central Highlands," in the April 2002 issue of *Vietnam* magazine.

Chapter 12

1. CDEC Bulletin 3129, Log 03-2603-67.

Chapter 14

1. The Reagan Administration halted Vietnamese efforts to repatriate remains through private channels, and forced them to return them officially to CILHI.
2. While Bell was the first U.S. government official to acknowledge their belief that the Communists had held men back, in later hearings both Armitage and Childress also expressed the same conviction.

Chapter 15

1. In April 1996, Veith and Bell were scheduled to present a research paper entitled "POWs and Politics: How Much Does Hanoi Really Know," at the Texas Tech University symposium on Vietnam. Also scheduled to speak on the same panel was Mr. Peterson, who had recently become the first U.S. Ambassador to Vietnam. When he discovered he was on the same panel as Bell, Peterson's staff called the symposium's Director, Dr. James Reckner, and insisted that we be removed from the panel, or the Ambassador would cancel his appearance. Since the Ambassador was a far bigger draw for the fledging Vietnam Center than us, Dr. Reckner felt he had no choice but to acquiesce.

2. The moves to Hawaii did not stop here. DIA's Stony Beach was also later moved to the islands. Stony Beach's reports contradicted the glowing JTFFA evaluations, and were clearly interfering with Needham's efforts to put the best possible spin on Vietnamese cooperation.

Glossary of Acronyms, Abbreviations, and Foreign Terms

ARVN	Army of the Republic of Vietnam (South Vietnam)
BOQ	Bachelor Officer Quarters
CCN	Command and Control North (Special Forces Command at Danang).
CDEC	Combined Documents Exploitation Center
CI	Counterintelligence (US)
CIA	Central Intelligence Agency
CILHI	Central Identification Laboratory Hawaii
CINCPAC	Commander-in-Chief Pacific
CIO	Central Intelligence Organization (South Vietnamese intelligence agency, comparable to the CIA)
CJCS	Chairman of the Joint Chiefs of Staff
CMA	Christian Missionary Alliance
CMIC	Combined Military Interrogation Center
CODEL	Congressional delegation
COSVN	Central Office for South Vietnam (highest communist echelon in the South)

CRA	Combined Recreation Association
DAO	Defense Attaché Office
DCM	Deputy Chief of Mission (number 2 position in an American Embassy)
DEA	Drug Enforcement Administration
DIA	Defense Intelligence Agency
DMZ	Demilitarized Zone dividing North and South Vietnam
DOD	Department of Defense
DPMO	Defense Prisoner-of-War and Missing Personnel Office
DRV	Democratic Republic of Vietnam (North Vietnam)
EOD	Explosive Ordnance Disposal
FAC	Forward Air Controller
FBI	Federal Bureau of Investigation
FPJMT	Four Party Joint Military Team
G-2	Intelligence office at division level.
GPD	General Political Directorate (highest echelon of Communist Party control in the People's Army of Vietnam)
GVN	Government of Vietnam (South Vietnam)
Ho Chi Minh Trail	Main supply corridor along the Annamite Mountain chain from North to South Vietnam, named for President Ho Chi Minh.
HUMINT	Human Intelligence (as opposed to technical intelligence)
IAG	Interagency Group working on the POW/MIA issue at the policy level
ICCS	International Commission for Control and Supervision
JCRC	Joint Casualty Resolution Center
JCS	Joint Chiefs of Staff
JFA	Joint Field Activity (One round of scheduled JTF-FA field operations)
JPRC	Joint Personnel Recovery Center
JTF-FA	Joint Task Force-Full Accounting (also JTFFA)
JVA	Joint Volunteer Agency

Khmer Rouge	Cambodian Communist Forces
KIA	Killed-in-Action
LNO	Liaison Office
LPDR	The Lao People's Democratic Republic
MACV	Military Assistance Command, Vietnam
MACTHAI	Military Assistance Command, Thailand
MI	Military Intelligence
MND	Ministry of National Defense (North Vietnam)
MOI	Ministry of Interior (North Vietnam)
MR	Military Region
MPS	Ministry of Public Security (North Vietnam)
NVA	North Vietnamese Army
OB	Order of Battle (strength, composition, disposition of enemy forces)
MIA	Missing-in-Action
MID	Military Intelligence Detachment
NGO	Non-government organization
NIC	National Interrogation Center
NCO	Noncommissioned Officer (Corporal, Sergeant and higher enlisted grades)
NSA	National Security Agency
NSC	National Security Council
ODP	Orderly Departure Program (US State Department refugee program)
OSD/ISA	Office of the Secretary of Defense, International Security Affairs
Pathet Lao	Lao communist forces
PAVN	People's Army of Vietnam
POW	Prisoner of War
PRG	Provisional Revolutionary Government
Rallier	Person who defected from the communist side to the GVN
Recon	Reconnaissance
Reeducation	A communist concentration camp for thought reform for former South Vietnamese military and political officials

RIO	Radio Intercept Officer (Back-seater in aircraft)
RVN	Republic of Vietnam (South Vietnam)
RVNAF	Republic of Vietnam Armed Forces (South Vietnam)
SAM	Surface to air missile
SECDEF	Secretary of Defense
SIGINT	Signals intelligence (radio intercept)
SOG	Studies and Observation Group (Strategic-level Special Operations Unit)
SRV	Socialist Republic of Vietnam
U.N.	United Nations
UNHCR	United Nations High Commissioner for Refugees
USSR	Union of Socialist Soviet Republics
VFW	Veterans of Foreign Wars (U.S. veterans service organization)
VNA	Vietnam News Agency
VNAF	Vietnamese Air Force (South Vietnam)
VNOSMP	Vietnamese Office for Seeking Missing Personnel (counterpart organization to the JCRC/JTF-FA)

Background of Various Vietnamese and Laotian Communist Cadre

Cu Dinh Ba A native of Quang Nam-Danang, Ba served as Director of the VNOSMP and head of the America's Department in the MFA until 1986, when he was assigned to Bonn as the SRV Ambassador. In 1992 Ba returned to retire in Hoi An on the outskirts of Danang.

Ho Xuan Dich A native of Thua Thien-Hue, during the French Indochina War Dich was a member of the Military Proselytizing Department responsible for the exploitation of French deserters and stay-behinds. During the Paris Peace Talks, Dich worked as a forensic linguist for the communist delegations. Assigned to the SRV Embassy in Kuala Lumpur from 1984 to 1987 when he returned to Hanoi to serve as Party Chapter Secretary for the Communist Party in the Vietnamese Office for Seeking Missing Personnel (VNOSMP) during postwar joint US-Vietnam search and recovery operations. Dich was extremely loyal to the Communist Party and his credentials were impeccable.

Khamla Keophithoun A Lao People's Army officer with the rank of Colonel. Bilingual in Vietnamese and Laotian, after training in the USSR Khamla was assigned to Enemy/Military Proselytizing duties. In postwar years he served as Chief of the Political Security Unit of the LPA. During the mid to late 1980's Khamla worked on the POW/MIA issue in Vientiane where he maintained an office in a former Royal Lao Army finance vault used to store records on U.S. POWs. Khamla frequently met with U.S. officials working on the POW/MIA issue. After being elected as a member of the Central Committee representing his native province of Savannakhet, Khamla was reassigned to Beijing, China as the LPDR Defense Attache.

Ngo Minh A professional staff officer of the Research Department, Ngo Minh traveled with a communist delegation as a POW/MIA specialist to Hawaii in July 1978. He was introduced as head of the Vietnamese Office for Seeking Missing Persons in February 1982 but disappeared from the POW/MIA scene shortly thereafter when replaced as VNOSMP head by Tran Hoan. Ngo Minh is possibly "Ngo Quang Minh," who was assigned as the Chief Interrogator for the COSVN Security Camp where some American POWs were executed.

Ngo Hoang During the French Indochina War a member of the Armed Propaganda Teams formed by General Vo Nguyen Giap. A PAVN Political Officer during the French War in Vietnam, Hoang was assigned to intelligence duties just above the Demilitarized Zone in Quang Binh province after the country was divided at the 17th parallel in 1954. During American war he performed intelligence duties at foreign embassies, including the SRV Embassy in India. After serving as personal secretary for SRV Foreign Minister Nguyen Co Thach, Hoang was assigned to intelligence duties in the SRV Embassy in Manila. He joined postwar joint US-Vietnam search and recovery efforts as an Investigation Team Chief and Deputy Director of the VNOSMP. Hoang retired in Hanoi during 1992.

Nguyen Can A native of Nghe An province, he was the former head of the America's Department in the SRV Ministry of Foreign Affairs and concurrently the head of the Vietnamese Office for Seeking Missing Personnel. Now deceased.

Nguyen Khac Tinh Although a northerner, Tinh successfully disguised himself as a Montagnard. Tinh served as the Secretary for the Dac Lac Province Party Committee, a member of the Inter-region 5 Party Committee and the Military Region 6 Party Committee.

Nguyen Ngoc Bich A PAVN officer with the rank of Senior Colonel, Bich served as head of the Department of Enemy Proselytizing and Special Propaganda of the General Political Directorate in Hanoi. Bich's POW/MIA related duties fell into the category of personnel security and counterintelligence. Bich continuously maintained a close eye on all contacts with Vietnamese citizens made by American personnel working on the POW/MIA issue in Vietnam.

Nguyen Thanh Nam He served as head of Special Action Forces in the Danang area during the war. In postwar years he was the Secretary of the Quang Nam-Da Nang province Communist Party Committee. Although arrested by the National Police on at least one occasion, Nam was able to bribe his captors into releasing him.

Nguyen Xuan Phong A native of Quang Tri, during the Vietnam War Phong was assigned to a forward Communist Party political headquarters in the South. Phong also served in the MFA office of the Provisional Revolutionary Government/National Liberation Front in Cuba. In 1973 he accompanied Fidel Castro as Spanish language interpreter during a trip to Quang Tri province in early 1973. Phong was a former acting director of the America's Department, MFA, and at one point he headed the VNOSMP. After working on the POW/MIA issue for several years, Phong was assigned to the U.S. where he served as the SRV's General Consul in San Francisco.

Pham Teo A Lieutenant Colonel in the People's Army of Vietnam assigned to the General Political Directorate, he was primarily responsible for the collection and storage of American remains recovered from wartime battlefields and detention sites. At the time of the cease fire Teo served as a member of the Four Party Joint Military Team. Teo later served as a staff member of the VNOSMP. In the mid 1990s he suffered a severe stroke and withdrew from participation in POW/MIA accounting.

Thongkham An ethnic minority member from Muang Sing, after training in the USSR Thongkham was assigned to Enemy/Military Proselytizing duties. Thongkham is known to have been depicted in a wartime captured enemy photograph of U.S. POW, Navy Lieutenant Charles Klusman, who managed to escape from captivity and make his way back to U.S. control. In postwar years Thongkham worked in POW/MIA Affairs in the same office with Colonel Khamla Keophitoun.

Tran Bien A PAVN officer with the rank of Senior Colonel and veteran of the Dien Bien Phu battle against the French in 1954. During the war against the Americans served in PAVN combat units and assigned as Director of Reconnaissance for a major PAVN command in the DMZ area during the 1972 offensive. During postwar joint US-Vietnam search and recovery operations he served as Ministry of Defense Representative for the VNOSMP. Bien was killed in a helicopter crash in Quang Binh province in 2001, along with American and Vietnamese POW/MIA specialists.

Tran Hao During the war years assigned to the Graves Management Agency of the Military Justice Department. At the time of the cease fire Hao served as a member of the FPJMT. In postwar years Hao was a member of the VNOSMP tasked with remains recovery and repatriation duties. He disappeared after a trip to Hawaii in 1982 and was never seen again by U.S. officials involved in the POW/MIA issue.

Tran Hoan A veteran of the 1954 Dien Bien Phu battle, he served in Laos from 1953 to 1954. A professional intelligence officer, he was overtly a member of the Four Party Joint Military Team with the rank of LTC during 1973. While assigned to the FPJMT Hoan worked directly for the head of the North Vietnamese Delegation, Senior Colonel Nguyen Don Tu, who was covertly the Deputy Head of the Intelligence Department in Hanoi. Hoan also served as Director of both the Americas Department and the VNOSMP. After serving a tour as SRV Ambassador to London, in 1985 he was reassigned as an Ambassador to various United Nations organizations.

Tran Le Linh A female resident of Saigon who either was captured with an American while pleasure boating on the Saigon River, or who led an unsuspecting American to capture and subsequent death. After being interrogated at the COSVN Security Camp Ms. Linh either was forced or voluntary married an Interrogator assigned to the camp. Linh served as the interpreter during the interrogation of several Americans, who were later executed based on orders issued by communist officials. After the war ended Linh served as an officer for the Ministry of Public Security in Ho Chi Minh City. She was ultimately accepted for resettlement in Australia.

Tran Van Tu, aka Tran Dinh Tu He was assigned to the SRV mission to the United Nations in New York during the time that Ho Dang, alias Dinh Ba Thi, was declared persona non grata due to spying. First appeared to work with U.S. officials during a remains repatriation ceremony held at Noi Bai Airport, Hanoi on September 24, 1987. On October 28, 1987 he began attending technical meetings on a regular basis. In September 1988 he became Team Chief of the Vietnamese contingent of a joint US/VN Investigation Team.

Tran Trong Khanh A member of the FPJMT during 1973. A professional intelligence officer of the Research Department with the rank of Lieutenant Colonel. During postwar years he worked as an English Language Instructor at the Foreign Service Academy in Hanoi. He attended meetings with U.S. officials in Hawaii during 1982.

Vo Dinh Quang A native of Nghe An Quang who served as the MND representative in the VNOSMP before being reassigned to the SRV Embassy in Jakarta, Indonesia. Quang attended at least one annual "Vietnam Symposium" at the Vietnam Center, Texas Tech University in Lubbock, Texas. He also served as the SRV Defense Attache in Washington, D.C. Quang is suspected by Bill Bell of possibly being a relative of PAVN General Vo Nguyen Giap

Index